AN EYEWITNESS HISTORY

THE 1950s

Richard A. Schwartz

☑®
Facts On File, Inc.

To my parents, Evelyn and Bob Schwartz,
who brought me into being in 1951.

The 1950s

Copyright © 2003 by Richard A. Schwartz

Maps on pages 463–466 Copyright © 2003 by Facts On File.

Facts On File, Inc.
132 West 31st Street
New York NY 10001

Library of Congress Cataloging-in-Publication Data
Schwartz, Richard Alan, 1951–
      The 1950s / by Richard A. Schwartz.
          p.   cm.—(Eyewitness history)
      Includes bibliographical references and index.
      Contents: Introduction—Postwar prelude: 1945–1949—America becomes the world's policeman:
      1950—The Cold War settles in: 1951—"I like Ike": 1952—New leadership in Washington and
      Moscow: 1953—Separate is not equal: 1954—Disneyland and cold war angst: 1955—Ike and
      Elvis, Budapest and the Suez: 1956—Sputnik and Little Rock: 1957—America enters outer
      space: 1958—America expands into the Pacific: 1959.
      ISBN 0-8160-4597-6 (alk. paper)
      1. United States—Civilization—1945—Juvenile literature. 2. United States—History—
      1945–1953—Juvenile literature. 3. United States—History—1953–1961—Juvenile literature.
      4. Nineteen fifties—Juvenile literature. [1. United States—Civilization—1945–. 2. United States—
      History—1945–1953. 3. United States—History—1953–1961. 4. Nineteen fifties.]
      I. Title. II. Series.
      E169.12 .S385 2003
      973.921—dc21   2002001149

Text design by Joan M. Toro
Jacket design by Cathy Rincon
Maps on pages 463–466 by Jeremy Eagle

Printed in the United States of America

VB JT 10 9 8 7 6 5 4 3 2 1

This book is printed on acid-free paper.

CONTENTS

NOTE ON PHOTOS

Many of the illustrations and photographs used in this book are old, historical images. The quality of the prints is not always up to modern standards, as in some cases the originals are damaged. The content of the illustrations, however, made their inclusion important despite problems in reproduction.

INTRODUCTION

In 1957, when Jack Kerouac published his account of his travels with friend Neal Cassady across the country in the late 1940s, he described an America that was already in the throes of extinction. Kerouac's *On the Road* portrays a racially segregated nation more closely linked to the era of the Great Depression than the space age. At the end of 1949, America had not yet experienced suburban sprawl, nationwide chain stores were rare, and multinational corporations were rarer still; television was a novelty; the manipulation of mass media for political and economic gain was comparatively unsophisticated; space exploration was still the stuff of science fiction; the interstate highway system had yet to be imagined. The atom bomb had ended World War II in 1945, and the cold war became a stark reality, but the threat of immediate, worldwide apocalypse did not exist. If, by the end of the 1940s, America's coastal regions experienced some minimal danger from long-range enemy bombers based across the oceans, its interior heartland had no nuclear fears. The Soviet Union had only just developed its own A-bomb, and the more potent H-bomb was still a scientific fantasy.

In the late 1940s, the postwar baby boom was just making its impact felt; open exploration of human psychology, sexuality, and "deviant" behavior was routinely suppressed; modern jazz was in its infancy; and rock 'n' roll and other types of electronically amplified music were literally unheard of. Also unimaginable at the half-century mark were other libidinal outlets that emerged during the 1950s, including *Playboy* magazine, oral contraception, and works of fiction and art that normally would have been censored before federal free-speech rulings of the 1950s.

By contrast, in 1957, the year *On the Road* was published, the U.S. Congress passed the Civil Rights Act, striking down Reconstruction-era barriers to voting; federal troops in Little Rock, Arkansas, enforced compliance with a 1954 Supreme Court decision ordering integration of public schools; and black tennis champion Althea Gibson received a tickertape homecoming in New York after winning the championship at Wimbledon. When Kerouac was on the road, no black athletes had ever competed in the U.S. Open or at Wimbledon.

Suburban living in 1957 was the lifestyle choice for millions of commuters, who availed themselves of the newly manufactured automobiles that were rolling off postwar assembly lines. The interstate highway system, which President Dwight D. Eisenhower authorized in 1956, was beginning to make it feasible for commuters to live in new, suburban housing developments located farther and farther from the city centers where they worked, and it permitted chains of retail stores to expand throughout the land. Multinational corporations began to exert significant impact on both economic and social norms, as did the growing defense industry. Baby boomers were pushing the nation's elementary school capacities to their limits, and Elvis Presley dominated the music charts as "the King" of rock 'n' roll. Many young mothers opted to stay at home to raise their children, but as the decade progressed, an increasing number of them joined the workforce, typically in lower-paying fields traditionally assigned to women, such as teaching, nursing, and clerical work. Between 1950 and 1955, the number of women employees in the workforce grew by some 40 percent.[1]

In 1950, only some 3.1 million American families possessed televisions, but by 1957 more than 10 times as many sets were in U.S. homes, and well over half of all American families owned at least one "boob tube"—so named because of frivolous programming that supposedly dulled the mind.[2] Yet, by the end of the decade, television had superseded newspapers, radio, and magazines as the public's major source of news.

These developments all made the United States a more secular nation, whose citizens were concerned increasingly with aspirations and notions of success rooted in acquisition of power and material affluence. Although these developments created economic, social, and political conditions that inevitably provoked challenges to traditional attitudes, values, and accepted modes of behavior, Americans nevertheless identified themselves more and more closely with traditional religions during the 1950s. The number of people affiliated with an established church or synagogue rose from 49 percent of the population in 1940 to 55 percent in 1950 and 62 percent in 1956. It peaked at 69 percent at the end of the decade, before declining back to 63 percent in 1970. Moreover, a survey in 1954 showed that 90 percent of Americans believed in the divinity of Jesus Christ, and nearly two-thirds of them accepted the existence of the devil.[3] According to historian Stephen J. Whitfield and others, churches were the most trusted institutions in the nation, more so than the government, schools, or the media.[4] The appeal of religion during the period is supported by the enormous sales of the Revised Standard Version of the Bible, the number one nonfiction best-seller from 1952, the year of its release, through 1954, and by the popularity of such prime-time religious television programming as the *Billy Graham Crusades* (1951–54) and Bishop Fulton J. Sheen's *Life Is Worth Living* (1952–57), which unseated "Mr. Television," Milton Berle, to become the top-rated show in its time slot.

A 1957 survey indicated that 62 percent of Americans identified themselves as Protestants, almost 26 percent as Catholics, and about 3 percent as Jews,[5] and the government was not shy about identifying the United States as a primarily Christian nation. In 1954, in an effort to underscore the notion that America's religious foundation distinguished it from and protected it against atheistic communism, Congress approved and President Eisenhower signed an alteration to the Pledge of Allegiance that changed "one nation indivisible . . ." to "one nation, under God, indivisible. . . ." In 1955, the Senate rejected a motion to amend the Constitution to include explicit recognition of the authority of Jesus Christ, but in 1956, Congress made "In God We Trust," a phrase that had been used on American coins since the Civil War, the nation's official motto.

In 1957, the Soviet Union took the cold war to new levels when it launched the first artificial satellite and developed the first intercontinental ballistic missiles (ICBMs) that suddenly made every American city the potential target of nuclear destruction. Not coincidentally, 1958 saw the beginning of the second Berlin Crisis (the first was the Berlin Airlift in 1949), which along with the 1962 Cuban Missile Crisis became the most dangerous point of the cold war. To many during this four-year span of on-again, off-again crises, worldwide nuclear war seemed not only possible but probable, even inevitable. At the end of the decade, even "Middle America" lived under a shadow of sudden apocalypse unknown to Kerouac and Cassady when they went on the road. It is surely no mere coincidence that 10 years later, when the children who grew up under these circumstances were in their late teens and early twenties, so many of them were attracted to the attitudes of immediate gratification so vocally proclaimed in the late 1960s, when "sex, drugs, and rock 'n' roll" became a rallying cry for a significant portion of that generation.

As dramatic as the alterations to American society during the 1950s were, many portions of the rest of the world experienced even more radical change during the decade, as the European nations, the Soviet Union, Japan, China, and other affected countries struggled to rebound from the devastating effects of World War II. The process often involved instituting new governments, drafting new constitutions, and forming new political alliances. In addition, in such places as Korea, civil war drew in the cold war superpowers. In Asia, Africa, the Middle East, and even the Caribbean, European imperialism crumbled as nationalist movements in former colonies, territories, and protectorates won independence or autonomy.

The 1950s chronicles America's transformation during this pivotal period in U.S. history. Although the focus is on the United States, America did not exist in a vacuum, and significant international events are also treated. Following an introductory chapter covering the late 1940s, 10 subsequent chapters describe each year in the decade. Each chapter contains a narrative discussion, a chronology, and a selection of eyewitness accounts drawn from political documents, literary accounts, memoirs of private and public figures, and other sources. The cold war and the struggle for civil rights stand out as the dominant events of the period, so most chapters include subsections on those topics. In addition, each chapter features major political events, as well as developments in science and technology, business and society, sports, entertainment, and the arts.

1

Postwar Prelude
1945–1949

World War II ended in the European theater on May 8, 1945, when Germany surrendered unconditionally after Soviet troops entered Berlin from the east and then U.S. and British armies penetrated from the west. Franklin D. Roosevelt, America's wartime president, had died less than a month before, on April 12. The war ended in the Pacific theater on August 14, when Japan surrendered unconditionally following devastating atomic attacks that the new president, Harry S. Truman, had ordered the previous week against the cities of Hiroshima and Nagasaki.

The conclusion of the war produced a sense of euphoria, triumph, and profound relief throughout North America. The forces of fascism, which many Americans regarded as forces of evil, had been defeated, and the strength and vitality of free, democratic society had been demonstrated in its most challenging test to date. Whereas the European nations, winners and losers alike, had suffered enormous damage to their cities and infrastructures and had endured massive losses among their civilian populations as well as within their military ranks, Americans and Canadians finished the war with their homelands intact, their industries at peak production capacities, and their labor markets strong.

The United States demobilized quickly, and the large number of veterans returning to a peacetime society quickly changed the nation's demographics, interests, and values. Victory over fascism and the end of the Great Depression infused the period with optimism, and products and services that had been suspended during the war became available once more. Civilians could again purchase new automobiles, and they did so in large numbers, to the benefit of automakers and their workers. Television broadcasts resumed after being suspended during the industry's infancy, and the new communications medium took the first baby steps in its meteoric climb. Soldiers back from the war and the women they had left behind started new families, and the resulting postwar baby and housing booms literally created a sense of new beginnings that persisted throughout the 1950s.

The optimism of the period was evident in such upbeat hit songs as "Chiquita Banana," "Come Rain or Come Shine," "Doin' What Comes Natur'lly," "Chi-Baba Chi Baba," "I'll Dance at Your Wedding," "I'm Looking

1

Over a Four-Leaf Clover," and "Zip-a-Dee-Do-Dah," whose lyrics proclaim that there is plenty of sunshine and everything is "goin' my way." Women's fashions became both more casual and more feminine, especially after French designer Christian Dior introduced the "New Look" that, along with padded bras, boned girdles, and bikini bathing suits accentuated female sexuality. As top athletes returned from military service, football, baseball, basketball, boxing, and other spectator sports enjoyed a resurgence and offered opportunities for men and women to relax and take their minds off their everyday concerns. Comedy prevailed on the radio, as Jack Benny, Fred Allen, George Burns and Gracie Allen, and "Fibber McGee and Molly" regaled listeners. Movies like *Life with Father, The Egg and I,* and *It's a Wonderful Life* presented upbeat visions of the American family, while film musicals like *Easter Parade* and *On the Town* and theatrical musicals like *Brigadoon, Finian's Rainbow, Annie Get Your Gun,* and *Kiss Me, Kate*—Cole Porter's adaptation of William Shakespeare's *The Taming of the Shrew*—expressed a joie de vivre. And whereas in Europe existentialism, a philosophy that posited a meaningless, atheistic universe, was gaining currency, in the United States religious affiliation was approaching its highest levels in history.

At the same time, however, postwar politics in the new age of atomic weapons and superpower confrontation spawned a cold war that caused the United States to redefine its notions of national self-interest and contributed a profound sense of frustration to the spirit of the times. Many had expected that victory in World War II would eliminate political oppression and totalitarian rule. Within just a few years, however, they returned, as strong as ever, but with

President Truman (left) performs with comedian Jack Benny.
(Photofest)

a new face—that of Joseph Stalin, leader of the Union of Soviet Socialist Republics (USSR). Furthermore, fear of communist subversion within the United States sparked the Red Scare that came to a head in the early 1950s with the ascension of Republican senator Joseph McCarthy of Wisconsin.

The uncertain political situation in the late 1940s, the climate of suspicion spawned by the Red Scare, and the new threats posed by atomic weaponry thus tempered postwar optimism with a foreboding feeling that at some deeper, unseen level, all was not well. This sentiment was voiced in such novels as Robert Penn Warren's *All the King's Men,* Saul Bellow's *The Victim,* and Nelson Algren's *The Man with the Golden Arm,* and in such plays as Eugene O'Neill's *The Iceman Cometh,* Tennessee Williams's *A Streetcar Named Desire,* and Arthur Miller's *All My Sons* and *Death of a Salesman.* In the movies, the postwar anxiety that beneath the prosperous surface lurked corruption, betrayal, and doom found expression in gangster movies and such film noir dramas as *The Postman Always Rings Twice, The Big Sleep,* and *The Naked City.*

THE COLD WAR AND INTERNATIONAL POLITICS

The Cold War Abroad

The big losers of World War II were, of course, the Axis powers: Germany, Italy, and Japan, whose economies and infrastructures were devastated and leaders had either killed themselves (Adolf Hitler), been killed by their countrymen (Benito Mussolini), or were tried and executed for war crimes (Japan's general Hideki Tojo and top German leaders convicted in the Nuremberg Trials). But Great Britain and France, which had been dominant European powers before the war, also emerged greatly diminished in their power and influence. Like the rest of Europe, their cities, industries, and infrastructures had been badly damaged; they suffered large numbers of casualties, and their economies and social institutions were impaired. By contrast, even though the Soviet Union had also suffered enormous casualties and had been the scene of some of the fiercest fighting, the postwar USSR emerged as one of the world's two superpowers. Its armies occupied much of eastern Europe, and its wartime industry was working at high capacity to produce a steady stream of armaments. Moreover, the 1945 Yalta agreement among Great Britain, the United States, and the Soviet Union, aimed at establishing a postwar political order, implicitly recognized that the USSR would preside over a sphere of influence that included most of eastern Europe.

The other superpower was the United States, then the world's only atomic power, whose wartime industry was also working near peak capacity. By contrast to the Soviet Union and the European nations, the U.S. mainland had escaped battle on its soil. Its factories had not been bombed; its cities had not been destroyed; its civilian population had not been killed or displaced; nor had the country undergone occupation by a hostile power. Consequently, the U.S. economy was not only intact but strengthened by the war: demand for industrial products and heavy government spending created new jobs and lifted the nation from the Great Depression. Thus, for both military and economic reasons, the United States emerged from World War II as the dominant power on the globe.

The United States has always been insulated from Europe and Asia by the two oceans that bound it, and in the immediate aftermath of the war, public opinion was mixed as to whether America should actively assume its role as superpower or turn inward and resist becoming enmeshed once more in the world's turmoil. It had, after all, paid a large price in human lives, diverted resources, and disrupted plans to help resolve a major European conflict for the second time in the half century. The isolationist sentiments were most vocally expressed by a faction of the Republican party led by Senator Robert Taft of Ohio and other figures from the Midwest. Other Republicans and many Democrats took a more international view and believed that, given its new power and stature, the United States needed to act as a leader in shaping world politics. They supported U.S. participation in the United Nations (UN) in the hope that such an organization might resolve disputes before they erupted into wars that could draw in other nations such as the United States.

The postwar period saw the eventual triumph of the internationalists over the isolationists. Even Senator Taft finally supported the United Nations, which first convened in 1946, with full U.S. participation. The United States asserted its leadership role in world politics in other ways too. Two months after the German surrender, the United States, Great Britain, and the Soviet Union established the terms of the postwar occupation of Germany at the Potsdam Conference. Both superpowers recognized that Germany was central to the reconstruction of Europe and to the shape of postwar European politics. The United States wanted Germany to be a robust, democratic, capitalist society with a strong economy and ties to the West, while the Soviet Union, which had suffered two catastrophic invasions by Germany within a quarter century, wanted the nation to be weak and dependent on the USSR, with a communist economy and a government responsive to Moscow. The Potsdam agreement partitioned Germany into one zone under Soviet administration and three smaller zones administered by Great Britain, France, and the United States. These three zones were later consolidated into a single Western zone. The partitions were intended to be temporary, but Germany remained a divided country until the cold war ended in 1990. In fact, the reunification of Germany under a pro-Western government was one of the primary cold war objectives of the United States, and the superpowers' conflicting interests in Germany account for why that country was later the focal point for two major cold war crises.

Within three years after World War II concluded, the Soviet Union consolidated its rule in eastern Europe, where directly or indirectly it installed communist regimes in Czechoslovakia, Poland, Hungary, Romania, Bulgaria, Yugoslavia, Albania, Latvia, Lithuania, Estonia, and various central Asian republics. All of these countries became de facto Soviet satellites behind what British leader Winston Churchill warned in 1947 had become an "iron curtain." Moreover, in the years immediately after the war, local communist parties, bolstered by support from the USSR and its allies, threatened to prevail in Greece, Italy, and France.

In response, Truman accepted the advice of George Kennan, one of his top experts on the Soviet Union, and adopted a policy of "containment" to thwart communist expansion. The containment policy sought to avoid direct military confrontation with the Soviets, as that could develop into an unwanted, protracted war, possibly even a third world war. The policy thus conceded to the

Soviets the gains they had already made in eastern Europe. But Truman was committed to resisting subsequent growth of the Soviet sphere of influence.

The steps Truman took to contain communism during the postwar period were largely economic. After the withdrawal of British troops from the region, the royalist Greek government fought a civil war against communist insurgents, and Truman authorized military advisers and economic aid in early 1947 to prevent a communist victory. Shortly thereafter, the president issued the Truman Doctrine, aimed specifically at containing the spread of communism. The doctrine included the Marshall Plan for European economic recovery (1947), which was one of the great successes of the postwar era; the Four-Point Plan to provide technical assistance to underdeveloped countries in Asia, Africa, and Latin America (1948); and the creation in 1949 of the North Atlantic Treaty Organization (NATO), a Western military alliance intended to present a unified front against the Soviet Union, which that September, exploded its first atomic bomb, thereby ending the U.S. nuclear monopoly.

The first major test of American will to resist the Soviets came in 1948 and 1949, when the United States refused the Soviet demand for a single, Soviet-controlled currency for all of Berlin. Although located fully within Soviet-controlled East Germany, Berlin remained divided into a Soviet-administered eastern sector and a western sector governed by the Allies. The Soviets believed that by controlling the currency in both sectors they would be able to exert both economic and political control throughout the city. Hoping to compel compliance, they blockaded the land and river access routes to West Berlin in June 1948. Wanting neither to back down nor force a military confrontation, Truman initiated the Berlin airlift, a massive shipment of vital supplies to the 2 million citizens of West Berlin. By spring 1949, the round-the-clock flights were averaging 8,000 tons of fuel and food daily. Finally, on May 12, 1949, the Soviets lifted the blockade and dropped their objections to the formation of a separate West German state. Eleven days later, the pro-West Federal Republic of Germany was proclaimed, with its capital in Bonn. On October 7, 1949, the pro-Soviet German Democratic Republic was formed in East Germany, with East Berlin as its capital. As the United States still sought the eventual reunification of Germany under a government friendly to the West, it refused to recognize East Germany until 1974.

Postwar Asia was also in turmoil. After the Japanese defeat in 1945, a civil war in China resumed between an agrarian, communist faction led by Mao Zedong and the pro-West Nationalist faction led by Chiang Kaishek. At the end of the year, Truman sent newly retired five-star general George Marshall to China as his special emissary. A hero of World War II and one of the most respected men of his time, Marshall was charged with forming a coalition government in which both parties would be represented but which the Nationalists would dominate. In addition to achieving a viable political settlement in China, Truman hoped that Marshall's stature would dampen criticism at home by the right-wing "China lobby" that his administration was willing to "sell out" Chiang to the communists. Despite deep, mutual mistrust between the communists and Nationalists and seemingly irreconcilable demands by each side, Marshall, who had served in China for three years between the world wars, succeeded in negotiating a truce and an agreement to create a national assembly to draft a national constitution. Moreover, both sides agreed to integrate their forces into a single, national army.

In March 1946, however, while Marshall was in Washington, D.C., to consult with Truman, the fragile truce fell apart, and his mission officially ended in January 1947. In his reports, Marshall cautioned that the United States would essentially have to take over the Chinese government in order to preserve Chiang's rule, and that this would involve a continuing U.S. commitment from which it would be difficult to withdraw. Truman heeded the warning and gradually reduced aid to Chiang down to token amounts that would appease the China lobby and other right-wing critics. Subsequently, after the communists prevailed and drove the Nationalists from the mainland, the China lobby accused the Truman administration of "losing China." Mao declared the People's Republic of China on October 1, 1949, and Chiang and his followers established Nationalist China on the island of Taiwan (then called Formosa). Despite Soviet objections, the United Nations recognized Nationalist China and refused to seat a delegation from Mao's mainland China.

In addition, following World War II, Korea was partitioned at the 38th parallel into a U.S.-backed southern sector and a Soviet-backed northern sector. The country, which had been occupied by Japan since the beginning of the century, had been promised independence, but the Soviets thwarted UN efforts to hold elections. Therefore, in 1948, two separate republics were declared. Despite a vow by Kim Il Sung, the leader of North Korea, to unite the two Koreas, the United States and the Soviet Union withdrew their occupying forces, thereby making possible the 1950 invasion of South Korea by North Korea, which marked the beginning of the Korean War.

In Southeast Asia, communist nationalist leader Ho Chi Minh inaugurated a war for Vietnamese independence from French colonial rule and, in 1946, established a communist government in Hanoi, in northern Vietnam. In 1949, France recognized instead the pro-Western government of Bao Dai in Saigon, in southern Vietnam. The struggle to determine which regime should govern the land persisted for almost 30 years and led to U.S. participation in the Vietnam War in the 1960s and 1970s.

Other International Developments

The postwar era also saw the beginning of the disintegration of the European colonial empires. Great Britain lost its colonial rule of Burma (Myanmar) and India in 1947. Afterward, India was partitioned into a predominantly Hindu nation—India—and a predominantly Muslim nation—Pakistan. War broke out among the rival factions soon afterward, and more than a million people were displaced as Hindus in Pakistan fled to India and Muslims in India relocated to Pakistan. Great Britain also withdrew from the region of the Middle East then known as Palestine, and in May 1948, the United Nations authorized the formation in part of Palestine of the state of Israel as a Jewish homeland. This action was bitterly opposed by Arabs in the region, and the first Arab-Israeli war broke out immediately. In January 1949, a peace treaty was signed in which Israel acquired about 50 percent more territory, but Jordan retained control of Old Jerusalem. Jordan and Egypt also occupied or annexed territory that the United Nations had designated for a separate Palestinian state.

The Cold War at Home

Although the term *McCarthyism* is often used to refer to the aggressively anti-communist governmental activities of the early cold war, these practices preceded the senator's rise to power. In fact, they date back at least to the so-called Palmer Raids of 1919 and 1920, when the future director of the Federal Bureau of Investigation (FBI) J. Edgar Hoover, then assistant to Attorney General Mitchell Palmer, oversaw the interrogation and often subsequent deportation, of thousands of alleged anarchist and communist immigrants. In the post–World War II era, the first major anticommunist governmental action was the investigation conducted by the House Un-American Activities Committee (HUAC) into the alleged presence of communist propaganda in Hollywood films. And in fact, some members of the film industry, primarily writers, were communists and communist sympathizers.

In October 1947, HUAC opened hearings to investigate whether procommunist messages were being surreptitiously inserted into Hollywood films. Because the witnesses included many celebrities, the hearings attracted considerable national publicity. Although the hearings did not produce any significant evidence of communist influence on movie content, they did establish a crucial legal precedent when 10 witnesses refused to testify. Initially supported by such liberal members of the Hollywood community as actors Humphrey Bogart and Lauren Bacall, they claimed that the First Amendment of the Constitution protected them from having to discuss their political beliefs or activities with the government. After the committee cited them for contempt of Congress, the witnesses, known as the Hollywood Ten, appealed to the Supreme Court, which in 1950 ruled against them. They subsequently served prison sentences. Thereafter, witnesses appearing before congressional committees could not invoke the First Amendment to refuse to testify. Thus, when committee members asked them to identify other people who were, or might have been, involved with communist organizations, many witnesses, most of them liberals, were placed in a no-win situation. They could cooperate by naming names and thereby avoid legal repercussions for themselves at the cost of condemning current and/or former friends and associates; they could refuse to cooperate and go to jail; or they could cite their Fifth Amendment protections against self-incrimination and refuse to testify without risking jail. But the Supreme Court later ruled that witnesses could not invoke the Fifth Amendment selectively, by answering some questions and not others. Consequently, such witnesses lost the opportunity to defend or explain their own actions without being compelled to identify other people who may have had communist associations. Such "Fifth-Amendment communists," as Senator Joseph McCarthy labeled them, were inevitably blacklisted throughout the television and film industries and were unable to work under their own names. Some writers continued to work for much lower pay by submitting their scripts under the name of someone else, known as a "front," but most were forced out of the industry.

Some historians believe that by calling "unfriendly" (uncooperative) witnesses, refusing to admit their introductory statements, and reading the allegations against them into the record, HUAC was deliberately attempting to create an official list of names that could become the basis for blacklisting. Whether this was the intention, the HUAC listings functioned as a blacklist, as did Attorney General Tom Clark's letters released in 1947 and 1948 to the

Loyalty Review Board, which identified subversive and communist-front organizations, reports from the 1938 Massachusetts House Committee on Un-American Activities, and 1947 and 1948 reports from the California Committee on Un-American Activities, chaired by Senator Jack Tenney. The congressional hearings into the film industry and the practice of blacklisting continued through the 1950s. They finally ended in 1960, when Kirk Douglas openly hired Hollywood Ten member Dalton Trumbo to write the screenplays for *Exodus* and *Spartacus,* and President-elect John F. Kennedy crossed American Legion picket lines to see the latter.

In 1948, former communist Whittaker Chambers made the first serious charge that communists had infiltrated high levels of the government. He accused Alger Hiss, a former ranking member of the State Department under Roosevelt, of having spied for the Soviets in the 1930s. Hiss had participated in the Yalta Conference and played an instrumental role in the founding of the United Nations. Many on the political right believed that Roosevelt had sold out Eastern Europe in Yalta, when the United States and Great Britain acknowledged Soviet influence over territories then occupied by the Soviet army. Likewise, many on the far right opposed the formation of the United Nations, which they suspected of being an instrument of the Soviets.

Hiss vehemently denied Chambers's accusation and sued him for libel. In return, Chambers escalated his charges. He asserted that Hiss had committed treason by passing government documents to the Soviet Union. Chambers theatrically retrieved his proof before news cameras: five rolls of microfilm hidden for safekeeping in hollowed-out pumpkins. Based on this evidence, popularly known as the "pumpkin papers," Hiss was tried for perjury, as the statute of limitations for treason had expired. The first trial took place in early 1949 but ended in a hung jury. The retrial began in late 1949, and Hiss was found guilty of perjury on January 21, 1950. The Hiss case first brought to national prominence future president Richard M. Nixon, then a Republican congressman and a member of HUAC, who pursued Chambers's charges when no one else would.

Other notable domestic cold war developments included the passage of the 1947 Taft-Hartley Act, over Truman's veto, which forbade unions from having communists among their leadership. That year, the Truman administration barred communists and communist sympathizers from employment within the federal government, and in the so-called Foley Square trial of 1949, 11 top leaders of the U.S. Communist Party were convicted and jailed under the 1940 Smith Act on charges that, by virtue of being Communists, they had conspired to overthrow the U.S. government by force and violence. Eventually, 93 people were thus convicted, although in 1957, the Supreme Court declared parts of the act unconstitutional and overturned some of the convictions. In the late 1940s, several state legislatures ordered the firing of public school employees who were communists.

Given that communist doctrine rejects God and religion, the opposition to communism by religious figures of all persuasions is not surprising, and much of the early cold war ideology pictured the United States and the West as a bulwark of Christian morality against the spread of immoral communism. Catholics were especially concerned by communist gains in predominantly Catholic eastern Europe, and among those who sought to galvanize Americans against communism was Bishop Fulton J. Sheen, whose best-selling books *Peace of Soul* (1947) and *Communism and the Conscience of the West* (1948) depicted communism as a threat to Catholicism. Reverend Billy Graham, a popular Protestant evangelical minister who became famous in 1949 with the support of newspaper publisher William Randolph Hearst and *Time* magazine publisher Henry Luce, went so far as to maintain that communism was motivated by Satan. In 1949, Graham received additional support from such political figures as South Carolina governor Strom Thurmond and former secretary of state James Byrnes. He remained in close contact with anticommunist politicians throughout the duration of the cold war and was a religious adviser to President Nixon. Throughout the 1950s, both Sheen and Graham hosted popular television shows that attacked communism.

GOVERNMENT AND SOCIETY

Truman ran for election in 1948, pledging to continue Roosevelt's liberal New Deal agenda. Following his election, he dubbed his package of progressive social programs the Fair Deal. But his prospects for victory in the election had seemed tenuous at best. The Democratic Party had splintered into three factions. Aside from Truman's camp, there were Henry Wallace, who had preceded Truman as Roosevelt's vice president and ran against Truman as leader of the left-wing Progressive Party, and South Carolina's Democratic governor Strom Thurmond, who entered the race as leader of the conservative "Dixiecrats." The latter group opposed Truman's efforts to end racial segregation and insisted upon preserving "states' rights" against federal government intrusion. The Republican candidate, New York's governor Thomas Dewey, had run unsuccessfully against Roosevelt in 1944 but was now the heavy favorite in most of the public opinion polls. Like Truman, Dewey supported such efforts to contain communism as the Berlin airlift and the Marshall Plan, and he favored further progress in civil rights and recognition of the state of Israel. He attacked Truman for being soft on domestic communism, but he did not go so far as to advocate outlawing the Communist Party. In the face of multilateral opposition, Truman took his message to the people in a famous "whistlestop campaign" that consisted of traveling by train throughout the country, stopping along the way to give speeches at selected stations. Throngs gathered to hear the president and shouted, "Give 'em hell, Harry" and other words of encouragement. Despite an infamous banner headline in the *Chicago Daily Tribune* that announced the morning after the election, "Dewey Defeats Truman," Truman pulled off an upset victory and won by more than 100 electoral votes and 2 million popular votes, out of about 48 million cast.

CIVIL RIGHTS

The most significant developments in civil rights in the immediate postwar era came in 1947, when Jackie Robinson broke the color barrier in major league baseball by playing for the Brooklyn Dodgers, and in 1948, when Truman, by executive action, desegregated the armed forces.

Robinson, who served in the army during the war and was discharged as a lieutenant, first integrated professional baseball in 1945, when owner Branch Rickey signed him to a contract with the Montreal Royals, a farm club of the

Brooklyn Dodgers. In 1946, despite vicious harassment on and off the field, Robinson led the league in hitting and was called up to the Brooklyn major league team the following spring. Again, he excelled, despite cruel harassment from fans and other players, and in 1949, he won the National League's Most Valuable Player award after setting records for fielding and batting and establishing himself as a premier base stealer. Robinson's major league career lasted through 1956, and like other black and Hispanic players of the time, when playing in the South, he typically was denied entrance to the restaurants, hotels, and other facilities enjoyed by the rest of his team. Nonetheless, his success on the field made it possible for other talented African-American players to join the major leagues, and baseball stadiums, too, were soon integrated, as black fans no longer had to sit apart, in inferior seats, from whites. Moreover, as the centerpiece of a Brooklyn team that dominated its league in the late 1940s and much of the 1950s, Robinson helped bring respect to Brooklyn, which was often overshadowed by Manhattan in the public mind. Thus, in addition to becoming the focal point for civil rights issues, he also helped forge a new sense of unity and pride in his new community.

In 1948, President Truman delivered his State of the Union address before a largely unresponsive Congress filled with conservative Republicans and Dixiecrats. The president asserted that "our first goal is to secure the essential human rights of our citizens." A month later, he was appalled by what he read in *To Secure These Rights,* the report of his Civil Rights Commission, which documented unwarranted beatings, lynchings, and other atrocities in the South. Truman called on Congress to pass legislation to ensure voting rights, terminate the poll tax that discouraged black voters, end racial discrimination by employers and labor unions, and eliminate discrimination in interstate travel. In addition, Truman asked for a federal law against "the crime of lynching, against which I cannot speak too strongly," and he ordered the secretary of defense to end racial discrimination in the military services. He also asked Congress to act on claims by Japanese Americans who had been forced from their homes and into confinement during World War II "solely because of their racial origin."[1]

Most of Truman's legislative agenda fell on deaf ears in Congress, but he had the authority to desegregate the military by executive action, and on July 26, 1948, he did so. Black Americans who had been serving in separate units, often under the command of white officers, were now fully integrated into previously all-white units. As a result, white and black men worked together as equals, in many instances for the first time in their lives. As a result, they came to know one another more as individuals than as racial abstractions. This change within the military facilitated later changes within the society at large. The Korean War was the first significant military action in which integrated units fought. At the same time that Truman desegregated the armed forces, he issued a separate executive order calling for a fair employment policy in the civil service, declaring that merit and fitness should be the only criteria for employment with the U.S. government.

BUSINESS

Fears that the nation would fall back into an economic depression without stimulation from the war effort proved unfounded. The quick demobilization sparked an immediate need for housing, automobiles, television and radio sets, higher education, and other goods and services, and the business climate immediately following the war was generally good. The G.I. Bill fueled the housing boom, which in turn fueled the economy by financing many of the houses the returning veterans purchased. Low-interest federal loans required no down payment; furthermore, they were guaranteed, so lenders incurred minimal risk. The G.I. Bill also financed college tuition, thereby making a college education widely available to the working class for the first time. The increased enrollments ultimately resulted in a great influx of college-educated workers to the workforce and facilitated a new spurt of upward mobility for workers, while significantly upgrading the labor pool from which companies could hire. At the same time, the expanded enrollments made higher education a growth industry, as the number of universities dramatically increased, creating a new demand both for physical facilities and for faculty, administrators, and support staff.

As the cold war intensified, another industry grew along with it—national defense. Throughout the postwar era, consumer-oriented companies such as General Electric, Chrysler, General Motors, Goodyear, and Westinghouse derived a growing portion of their income directly from defense contracts. The large contractors, in turn, purchased large quantities of raw materials from other major corporations, such as U.S. Steel; they also subcontracted work out to smaller companies. California, in particular, benefited from the defense contracts, which underwrote much of the state's enormous growth during the period. In southern California, more than half of the economic growth between 1947 and 1957 derived from defense contracts, and slightly less than 60 percent of all jobs in greater Los Angeles were directly or indirectly dependent on military spending; in San Diego, the figure was closer to 70 percent.[2] But California was not the only beneficiary; across the nation throughout the late 1940s and the 1950s, defense played an increasingly prominent role in the nation's economy, so much so that in his farewell address on January 17, 1961, President Eisenhower warned the nation to "guard against the acquisition of unwarranted influence, whether sought or unsought, by the military-industrial complex. The potential for the disastrous rise of misplaced power exists and will persist."[3]

After a slow start in 1946, when the gross national product (GNP) declined by 2 percent, in 1947 and 1948, the GNP grew by 11 percent per year, before failing to grow at all in 1949. The unemployment rate rose from about 3.9 percent from 1946 to 1948 to 5.9 percent in 1949. Inflation grew from 4.6 percent in 1946 to 8.4 percent in 1947, then declined to 5.2 percent in 1948 and 0.7 percent in 1949.[4]

In 1947, the average American annual salary was $2,589; for example, a teacher earned $2,261, a factory worker $2,793, and a physician $10,700. Rooms at New York City's San Moritz Hotel started at $4.50 a night, and Broadway theater tickets ranged between $1.20 and $4.30. In 1948, a DeSoto convertible cost about $2,500, a Buick Roadmaster $2,900, a Packard $4,300, and a Rolls-Royce convertible $18,500. In 1949, a one-pound can of red salmon cost 59¢, and rib veal chops cost 69¢ per pound. An Arnold Constable Persian lamb coat could be purchased for $350, and a boy's storm coat for $16.[5]

SCIENCE AND TECHNOLOGY

It was commonly recognized that, in addition to the skill, valor, intelligence, ingenuity, and capacity for sheer endurance displayed by their combat troops, the Allies had prevailed in World War II because they had produced more airplanes, ships, tanks, and other heavy weapons than their enemies. Moreover, they had been more successful in employing cutting-edge science to develop new technologies for the war effort. Among the decisive technologies that had helped secure victory were radar, which had given British pilots early warning of German air raids during the Battle of Britain; sonar, which had enabled Allied ships to counter the pernicious and potentially devastating threat from enemy submarines; and the atomic bomb, which had brought the Pacific war to an abrupt close. Less well known was the way in which advances in cryptology had enabled the Allies to break their enemies' codes and learn their secret plans. Although science and technology had also been important in winning World War I, never before World War II had they been so clearly recognized by so many people as critical to national security, even national survival. As a result, science gained elevated respect—and funding—during the postwar period and throughout the 1950s. This respect not only translated into greater funding, which permitted even more scientific breakthroughs in many fields, but also contributed to a growing set of business, government, and personal values that increasingly prized scientific methodology and denigrated conclusions that could not be supported empirically or quantitatively. Most institutions came to regard a scientific approach to all problems, from production to personnel and policy formation, as the best possible way to function rationally and thereby exert maximum control over the various aspects of private and public life alike. Although resisted by many writers and artists and some social scientists, the rise of "scientism" in the aftermath of World War II was one of the great influences on 1950s America and on modern culture.

One discipline that greatly benefited from this new mindset was computer science. The first information-processing digital computer was the Automated Sequence Controlled Calculator, or Mark 1, developed by American engineer Howard Aiken in 1944. It was superseded in 1946 by the second modern-day computer, the Electronic Numerical Integrator and Computer (ENIAC). Developed at Harvard University, ENIAC could perform calculations 1,000 times faster than the average human brain. Three years later, in 1949, a new computer, BINAC, performed calculations twelve times faster than ENIAC. Without the development of BINAC, the hydrogen bomb would have been impossible, as the computer enabled physicists to perform the complicated calculations necessary for the project. Over the next half century, computer technology also made numerous other things possible and transformed not only the economy but also virtually every aspect of business and society.

Advances in computer technology depend largely on advances in the technology used for computers' circuitry. The development in 1948 of the compact, low-energy-consuming transistor by John Bardeen, Walter H. Brattain, and William Shockley of Bell Labs enabled computer designers to replace large, power-consuming vacuum tubes that were prone to overheating and failure. (Early computers with vacuum tubes occupied entire rooms.) The introduction of the transistor made computers more reliable, less expensive to run, and smaller. Bardeen, Brattain, and Shockley won the Nobel Prize in physics for their invention.

Postwar advances in atomic energy included the development in 1946 of the first synchrocyclotron, a particle accelerator. Built under the auspices of Ernest O. Lawrence at the University of California at Berkeley, the "atom smasher," as it was popularly called, could produce 300 million volts of electricity by inducing collisions between subatomic particles moving at very high speeds. In 1949, the breeder reactor was developed and marked the first time an atomic reactor produced more energy than it consumed, thereby offering the possibility of inexpensive and abundant nuclear energy for peaceful purposes. This prospect had been anticipated in 1946, when the Atomic Energy Commission (AEC) established an atomic pile for peaceful purposes at Oak Ridge, Tennessee, where heavy uranium had been produced during World War II to build the first atomic bomb.

Medical uses of atomic energy also expanded during the postwar era. In 1946, researchers at the University of Pennsylvania experimented with carbon 14, the first human-made radioactive substance to be used in medical research. Two years later, radiocobalt treatment of cancer had its first successes, and in 1949, betatron was first used to treat the disease.

By the end of World War II, the Germans had successfully developed long-range V1 and V2 rockets, which they launched against England from the European mainland. After the war, the United States and the Soviet Union employed many of the German rocket scientists in their missile programs. Postwar advances by the superpowers in the new field of rocketry eventually led to both the invention of long-range intercontinental ballistic missiles (ICBMs), which shaped cold war politics by making any spot on Earth vulnerable to nuclear attack, and the development of rockets that made space exploration possible. Wernher von Braun, one of the German scientists who developed the liquid fuel for the V2, was recruited to the United States, where he served first as technical adviser and later as project director at Fort Bliss, Texas, from 1945 to 1950. He went on to serve as chief of guided missile development in the early 1950s—and then director of development operations for the Army Ballistic Missile Agency, where he developed rockets for the Apollo project that took astronauts to the moon.

Other developments in rocketry and space technology included the development of a new liquid-hydrogen fuel in 1948, the same year in which Captain Charles "Chuck" Yeager first broke the sound barrier in a rocket-powered aircraft. Also in that year, the Mt. Palomar Observatory in California dedicated its new 200-inch reflecting telescope, the largest in the world. In 1949, Gérard Kuiper, of the University of Chicago, offered his condensation theory of the universe, postulating that the solar system was formed some 3 billion years ago from gas and cosmic dust rotating around the Sun. Willard Libby, also of the University of Chicago, first employed carbon 14 that year to determine the age of ancient objects, a process later used to revise estimates of the age of the Earth and other applications. And the de Havilland Comet, the world's first jetliner, made its maiden flight in Great Britain in 1949.

Medical advances included the discovery in 1946 that streptomycin can retard the spread of tuberculosis, and Harry Stack Sullivan published *Conceptions of Modern Psychiatry,* in which he developed a theory of interpersonal relations. Also in 1946, the antihistamine drug Benadryl (diphenhydramine) was first made available to relieve symptoms of hay fever. In 1947, prefrontal lobotomy was found to cure schizophrenia; the discovery of the anticoagulant heparin was announced; and Carl F. and Gerty Cori won the Nobel Prize in physiology or medicine for discovering the catalytic metabolism of glycogen. The following year, the human polio virus was isolated in concentrated form at the University of Minnesota; a cure for anemia, vitamin B_{12}, was isolated; the antibiotics aureomycin and chloromycetin were developed; and Rh hapten was developed to save Rh babies. In 1949, scientists produced neomycin, a drug to combat tuberculosis; ACTH, a protein hormone that stimulates the body to produce cortisone, was first commercially manufactured; the eight amino acids essential for human life were identified; and future Nobel Prize winner Linus Pauling announced the discovery of the molecular flaw responsible for sickle-cell anemia, a disease that mostly affects African Americans.

Other notable scientific achievements from the late 1940s included naval expeditions to Antarctica led by Admiral Richard Byrd and Commander Finn Rone (1947), and Rone's announcement the following year that Antarctica is a single continent, not two islands as previously believed. A more low-tech explorer, Thor Heyerdahl, tested his theory that ancient humans migrated across vast oceans by traveling on his raft, *Kon Tiki,* from Peru to Tahiti (1947–48). RCA produced a sturdy vinyl disc for musical recordings (1946), and Edward Land invented a camera that could develop and print one picture each minute (1947). Al Gross pioneered wireless communications in the late 1940s and 1950s. Gross had invented the walkie-talkie in 1937 and developed a machine for secure air-to-ground communication during World War II. In 1949, he invented the first wireless pager; in 1951, he produced the first wireless telephone; and in 1958, he created the first battery-operated calculator, which he made for the military.

A commercial airline pilot reported "flying discs" over Idaho in 1947, but a U.S. Air Force investigation was unable to verify the citing. Its report, released in 1949, denied the existence of unidentified flying objects (UFOs).

SPORTS, ENTERTAINMENT, AND THE ARTS

Sports

After the war, Americans once again embraced sports enthusiastically—especially baseball, boxing, and football. Many of America's finest athletes served during World War II and therefore did not compete in their sports during the war years. Of those who survived, a number returned to resume their careers; for instance, the "Splendid Splinter," Ted Williams, the gangly star outfielder for the Boston Red Sox, served as a combat pilot and then came back to win the American League's Most Valuable Player award and lead his team to the pennant in 1946. The Red Sox lost the World Series in seven games to the St. Louis Cardinals, who were led by their own slugger, Stan "the Man" Musial. New York Yankee outfielder Joe DiMaggio rivaled Williams and Musial as one of the game's all-time best hitters, and the New York Yankees won "subway series" against the Brooklyn Dodgers in 1947 and 1949. In 1948, the Cleveland Indians, led by Lou Boudreau, defeated the Red Sox in the American League's first pennant playoff game following a season-ending tie, and then went on to defeat Boston's National League team, the Braves, in the World Series.

Some of the other dominating baseball players from the postwar era were Jackie Robinson (Dodgers), Hank Greenberg (Detroit Tigers), Ralph Kiner (Pittsburgh Pirates), Yogi Berra (Yankees), Johnny Mize (New York Giants), Mickey Vernon (Washington Senators), and pitchers Bob Feller (Indians) and Warren Spahn, who led the Braves to the 1948 championship, despite an otherwise depleted pitching staff. That problematic situation occasioned the popular slogan in Boston: "Spahn and Sain and pray for rain."

Professional football began to assert itself as a force in American sports during the late 1940s, although it did not begin to rival baseball in stature until the 1960s. The All-America Conference (AAC) was created to compete with the National Football League (NFL) in 1946, and the leagues merged in 1949, with three AAC teams, Baltimore, Cleveland, and San Francisco, joining the 10 NFL teams to create a newly structured National Football League. The Chicago Bears defeated the New York Giants for the NFL championship in 1946; the Chicago Cardinals defeated the Philadelphia Eagles in 1947, but lost to that team in 1948. Philadelphia prevailed again in 1949, this time against the Los Angeles Rams. Dominant players from the period included Bill Dudley (Chicago Bears), Jim Benton (Rams), Steve Van Buren (Eagles), Tom Fears (Rams), Jim Keane (Bears), and quarterbacks Sammy Baugh (Washington Redskins), Bob Waterfield (Rams), and Tommy Thompson (Eagles). College football saw such outstanding players as Glenn Davis (Army), John Lujack (Notre Dame), Doak Walker (Southern Methodist University), Charlie Justice (North Carolina), and Leon Hart (Notre Dame).

The Olympic Games resumed in London in 1948, after being suspended during the war. The Winter Games were held later that year in St. Moritz, Switzerland. These competitions contributed to the general spirit of renewal, as the nations of Europe continued to rebuild. (The Soviet Union did not compete until 1952.) The United States dominated the games, winning 38 medals and making an unprecedented sweep of the swimming events. Seventeen-year-old Robert Mathias from California won the decathlon. The 1948 Olympics were also notable for the large number of athletes who defected from Eastern European communist countries after the games concluded.

The formation in 1946 of the National Basketball League, which in 1949 merged with the Basketball Association of America to form the National Basketball Association (NBA), offered another example of the blossoming of professional sports after the war. Other sports produced media sensations, including Joe Louis, Rocky Graziano, "Sugar" Ray Robinson, Jake La Motta, and "Jersey" Joe Walcott in boxing; Pancho Gonzales, Jack Kramer, Bobby Riggs, Louise Brough, and Margaret Osborne DuPont in tennis; and Ben Hogan in golf. Hogan was seriously injured in a 1949 automobile accident, but he returned successfully in 1950 and won the U.S. Open.

Television

Although the first television broadcasts occurred in 1927, for all practical purposes the medium was pioneered during the years immediately following

World War II, as first the Great Depression and then the war greatly restricted both technological advances in broadcasting and ownership of television sets by the public. Thus the 1950s was the first decade in which television had a major presence in society, and its impact proved enormous.

Certainly, one of the most potent of television's influences was its ability to shape the public's picture of political reality. At almost any other time in the country's history, Americans would have learned about people and events outside of their firsthand experience primarily through words, such as in conversations with colleagues and neighbors, speeches from local officials, newspaper articles, magazine stories, books, and eventually radio broadcasts. After the advent of television, however, Americans increasingly learned about their world through visual images. Thus, in a very literal way, television transformed how Americans apprehended and viewed reality. By 1959, television had become the most relied-upon source of news in the country.

Moreover, in an era that was becoming increasingly fast paced, television gave immediacy to everything. As journalist Edward R. Murrow said in his first episode of *See It Now* in 1951, "We are impressed by a medium through which a man sitting in his living room has been able for the first time to look at two oceans at once." This capacity for immediate, global information transfer facilitated the fads that swept the nation throughout the 1950s; thus an innovation that previously would have had only local interest, such as the hula hoop, could now reach a national audience. Children and teenagers, especially, became enamored of the new medium, which helped promote the rise of rock 'n' roll with such shows as *American Bandstand* and the performances of singers such as Elvis Presley. Like the movies before it, TV helped establish familiar personalities who became common points of reference for all Americans, regardless of their environment, race, or social class. In that respect, it helped unify the nation. At the same time, by encouraging families to stay at home to watch their favorite shows, it diminished the popularity of more communal activities. And although it literally brought families together in a common living room, it discouraged meaningful communication and interaction among them by focusing their attention on the screen, instead of on one another. Increasingly, television served as a baby-sitter for baby boomers in need of distraction, and it quickly proved itself a powerful tool for commercial advertising that could be targeted at precisely defined demographic targets.

CBS resumed live studio broadcasts, which it had suspended because of the war, in May 1944 with the presentation of the *CBS Television News*, hosted by Ned Calmer. And in August 1945, NBC broadcast the first network-produced, regularly scheduled show, a 15-minute Saturday-night roundup entitled *NBC Television Newsreel*. In 1946, NBC introduced *Radio City Matinee*, an hour-long variety show that appeared on Monday, Wednesday, and Friday afternoons. It was the first live daytime series since the war had begun. Also in 1946, CBS and the DuMont network introduced broadcasts of college and professional football. The three networks pooled their personnel and equipment in 1947 to televise, for the first time, the World Series contest between the New York Yankees and the Brooklyn Dodgers. Children's programming also began in 1947, as DuMont broadcast *The Small Fry Club*, and in late December, NBC produced *Puppet Television Theater* starring "Buffalo" Bob Smith and his marionette,

Howdy Doody. The popular show, soon retitled *Howdy Doody,* ran throughout the 1950s.

Postwar television programming shifted into high gear in 1948, as CBS and DuMont substantially increased their number of broadcasts, and ABC returned to the air after a 15-month hiatus. Ted Mack's *Original Amateur Hour, The Texaco Star Theater* starring Milton Berle ("Mr. Television"), and Ed Sullivan's *Toast of the Town* all debuted that year. Also in 1948, DuMont introduced daytime programming between 10 A.M. and 3:30 P.M. Bud Collyer hosted the first television game show, *Winner Take All;* CBS introduced a dramatic anthology, *Studio One; Arthur Godfrey's Talent Scouts,* a showcase of amateur performances, emerged as a top-rated program; and ABC first televised an NFL championship game. One of the first important political events to be nationally televised was the signing of the NATO pact in 1949. Between 1948 and 1952, when the last major American city was connected to a coaxial cable hookup, television ownership and television programming mushroomed. By 1950, there were some 3.1 million television sets in the United States, a figure that would increase even more dramatically by the end of the 1950s.

"Buffalo" Bob Smith and Clarabell, the clown, appear with marionette Howdy Dowdy on the popular *Howdy Doody* television show. *(Photofest)*

Movies

The conflicting feelings of optimism and anxiety that characterized the mood of the country are evident in the films of the postwar era. On the one hand, many important Hollywood films were affirmative and generally uplifting, such as Frank Capra's *It's a Wonderful Life* (1946), starring James Stewart and Donna Reed; Walt Disney's animated *Song of the South* (1946); George Seaton's *Miracle on 34th Street* (1947), starring Maureen O'Hara, John Payne, Edmund Gwenn, and Natalie Wood; Michael Curtiz's *Life With Father* (1947), based on the novel by Clarence Day and starring William Powell and Irene Dunne; Irving Reis's *The Bachelor and the Bobbysoxer* (1947), starring Cary Grant, Myrna Loy, and Shirley Temple; George Stevens's *I Remember Mama* (1948), starring Irene Dunne; Charles Walters's *Easter Parade* (1948), starring Fred Astaire, Ann Miller, and Judy Garland; Mervyn LeRoy's *Little Women* (1949), starring June Allyson, Elizabeth Taylor, Janet Leigh, and Margaret O'Brien; and Gene Kelly and Stanley Donen's musical *On the Town* (1949), starring Kelly, Frank Sinatra, and Betty Garrett. These films typically endorsed conventional family and social values, demonstrated respect for social authority, and provided a generally positive picture of society that encouraged Americans to feel good about themselves, their neighbors, and their country.

Among the few films that exposed disturbing aspects of American behavior and promoted social change were Elia Kazan's *Gentleman's Agreement* (1948), which starred Gregory Peck, Dorothy McGuire, Celeste Holm, Anne Revere, and John Garfield and exposed the injustices of anti-Semitism, and Kazan's *Pinky* (1949), which featured Jeanne Crain, Ethel Barrymore, and Ethel Waters and attacked racism. *Gentleman's Agreement* won the Academy Award for best picture, Kazan won best director, Holm won best supporting actress, and Peck, McGuire, and Revere received nominations. Similarly, Crain, Barrymore, and Waters were nominated for their performances in *Pinky*. Although critical of discrimination within the society, both films concluded on an upbeat note, suggesting that in the end good Americans will do the right thing.

War movies such as Henry King's *Twelve O'Clock High* (1949), starring Peck, and Allan Dwan's *Sands of Iwo Jima* (1949), starring John Wayne, promoted respect for hard work and authority, self-sacrifice, and uncompromising personal integrity, while William Wyler's *The Best Years of Our Lives* (1946), starring Frederic March, Loy, Dana Andrews, and Harold Russell, honored returning war veterans coping with the problems of readjusting to civilian life.

While these movies showed the triumph of what Americans liked to regard as traditional Christian and American values, another genre of film depicted a society driven by power, lust, and greed. These showed life, itself, to be a fierce, no-holds-barred struggle for survival and domination. Outward appearances in these stories were typically deceiving; motivations, obscure; and the proper course of action, often difficult to determine for both the characters and the audience. Moral choices and consequences were rarely clear-cut.

This vision of an amoral universe of competing self-interests found its strongest expression in film noir, a term coined by French film critics after the war to describe the darkly lit gangster movies of the early 1940s, such as John Huston's adaptation of Dashiell Hammett's *The Maltese Falcon* (1941), starring Humphrey Bogart and Mary Astor; Frank Tuttle's *This Gun for Hire* (1942), starring Alan Ladd and Veronica Lake; and Billy Wilder's *Double Indemnity*

(1944), starring Fred MacMurray and Barbara Stanwyck. Although film noir persisted into the late 1950s and has been revived periodically ever since, many of its finest examples were made in the late 1940s. These include Howard Hawks's *The Big Sleep* (1946), featuring Bogart and Lauren Bacall, who also star together in Delmer Daves's *Dark Passage* (1947) and Huston's *Key Largo* (1948); Tay Garnett's *The Postman Always Rings Twice* (1946), starring John Garfield and Lana Turner; Henry Hathaway's *Kiss of Death* (1947); Robert Rossen's *Body and Soul* (1947), starring Garfield, Lilli Palmer, Hazel Brooks, and Anne Revere and written by Abraham Polonsky; Jules Dassin's *Brute Force* (1947), starring Burt Lancaster, and *The Naked City* (1948); Robert Siodmak's *The Killers* (1946) and *Cry of the City* (1948); Polonsky's *Force of Evil* (1948); and Raoul Walsh's *White Heat* (1949), starring James Cagney. Although not usually labeled film noir, *The Third Man,* Carol Reed's 1949 adaptation of Graham Greene's novel, centers on an innocent American novelist who discovers his best friend is a cynical black marketer in occupied Vienna who profits from the suffering of others.

Many, but not all, of these were sparsely funded B movies whose budgetary constraints may also have contributed to the starkness of their vision. In addition, many of the actors, writers, and directors associated with film noir were politically left of center, although they were not necessarily communists, with the exception of Polonsky, who was a Party member. The corrupt, morally empty societies depicted in these films are consistent with the left's critique of capitalist society.

Major stars from the postwar period typically exuded strength of character, moral righteousness, a clear sense of who they were and what they stood for, and a well-defined sense of masculinity or femininity. Although they project sensitivity and vulnerability, none is weak or frail. These included Bogart, Bacall, Lancaster, Peck, Clark Gable, Claudette Colbert, Cary Grant, Spencer Tracy, Katharine Hepburn, Wayne, Ingrid Bergman, Gary Cooper, and Roy Rogers, who billed himself as the "King of the Cowboys" and later went on to become a television star. Also popular were Betty Grable, Bing Crosby, and comedian Bob Hope.

Literature

The literature of the postwar period was wide-ranging in its topics and purposes. Some books looked introspectively at personal experience and relationships, including Carson McCullers's *The Member of the Wedding* (1946), Eudora Welty's *Delta Wedding* (1946), Gertrude Stein's *Brewsie and Willie* (1946), Truman Capote's *Other Voices, Other Rooms* (1948), and William Faulkner's *Intruder in the Dust* (1948).

Others address social and political matters. For instance, Robert Penn Warren's Pulitzer Prize–winning *All the King's Men* (1946) is based on the assassination of Louisiana's powerful, populist governor, Huey Long. Chester H. Himes's *Lonely Crusade* (1947) describes wartime Los Angeles, where Southern blacks work beside white women on the assembly lines for the defense industry. Himes addresses not only the sexual attraction between blacks and whites but also the anti-Semitism of blacks and their betrayal by communist union organizers who sell out their members for political expediency. Lionel Trilling's *The Middle of the Journey* (1947) describes the author's evolving disillusion with communism and contains a character based on Whittaker Chambers, who later accused Alger Hiss of treason. Saul Bellow's *The Victim* (1947) presents an almost surreal account of a Jewish man who finds difficulty coming to terms with a life dominated by anti-Semitic harassment and familial obligations. Poet Delmore Schwartz's *The World Is a Wedding* (1948) provides a satirical critique of intellectuals, and John Steinbeck's best-selling *The Wayward Bus* (1947) continues the author's concern with the underclass. Nelson Algren's *The Man with the Golden Arm* (1949) addresses the world of heroin addiction. The novel was adapted for film in 1955, with Otto Preminger directing and Frank Sinatra starring in what some consider his finest cinematic role.

World War II was the topic of several important books, including Norman Mailer's first novel, *The Naked and the Dead* (1948), which pitted liberals against conservatives and enlisted men against officers, as well as Americans against Japanese; James Gould Cozzens's *Guard of Honor* (1948); Irwin Shaw's *Young Lions* (1948); Thomas Heggen's *Mister Roberts* (1946), about life on a navy cargo ship in the South Pacific; and James Michener's *Tales of the South Pacific* (1947), which won the Pulitzer Prize in 1948 and became the basis for the 1950 Pulitzer Prize–winning Broadway musical *South Pacific*. *Mr. Roberts* was also successfully adapted to stage and screen. John Hawkes's *The Cannibal* (1949) presented a surreal view of occupied Germany, and Toshio Mori's story collection *Yokohama, California* (1949), described the life of Japanese Americans who were removed to internment camps during the war.

Best-selling novelists in the postwar era included Daphne du Maurier (*The King's General,* 1946); Taylor Caldwell (*This Side of Innocence,* 1946); Frances Parkinson Keyes (*The River Road,* 1946, and *Dinner at Antoine's,* 1948); Frank Yerby (*The Foxes of Harrow,* 1946; *The Vixens,* 1947; *The Golden Hawk,* 1948; and *Pride's Castle,* 1949); German author Erich Maria Remarque, who in 1929 published the World War I best-seller *All Quiet on the Western Front* (*Arch of Triumph,* 1946); Laura Z. Hobson (*Gentleman's Agreement,* 1947); Sinclair Lewis (*Kingsblood Royal,* 1947); Lloyd C. Douglas (*The Big Fisherman,* 1948); John O'Hara (*A Rage to Live,* 1949); and Edward Streeter (*Father of the Bride,* 1949).

Several poets who were well known for their work prior to the war continued to publish new, and sometimes important, work. These included T. S. Eliot; Ezra Pound; Wallace Stevens; e.e. cummings; Robert Frost; John Crowe Ransom; Allen Tate; Mark Van Doren; Archibald MacLeish; H.D. (Hilda Doolittle); Langston Hughes; Robert Lowell, who won the 1946 Pulitzer Prize for *Lord Weary's Castle;* and William Carlos Williams, who published the first three books of his major work *Patterson* between 1946 and 1948, the fourth book in 1951, and the fifth in 1958. Many of these poets continued to write in the highly cerebral, politically conservative, formalist tradition championed by the literary modernists of the 1920s and 1930s; however, several poets who first published during the postwar era challenged the rigidity of formalism and sought to write a more emotional, more spontaneous, less cerebral poetry that spoke to a broader, less culturally elite audience. Among the poets to begin their careers immediately after the war were Howard Nemerov; Randall Jarrell; Richard Wilbur; Elizabeth Bishop; Theodore Roethke; Gwendolyn Brooks, an African-American poet who won the 1949 Pulitzer Prize for *Annie Allen;* and Charles Olson, who, with several other creative intellectuals went on to form the Black Mountain school of poetry, named after the experimental Black Mountain College, in the early 1950s. Among the faculty were poets Denise Levertov, Robert Duncan, and Robert Creeley.

Best-selling nonfiction included Soviet defector Victor Kravchenko's *I Chose Freedom* (1946); Arnold J. Toynbee's *A Study of History* (1947); former secretary of state James F. Byrnes's *Speaking Frankly* (1947); Dale Carnegie's *How to Stop Worrying and Start Living* (1948); General Dwight D. Eisenhower's account of World War II, *Crusade in Europe* (1948); former British prime minister Winston Churchill's book about the origins of World War II, *The Gathering Storm* (1948); Norman Vincent Peale's *A Guide to Confident Living* (1948); Frank B. Gilbreth and Ernestine G. Cary's *Cheaper by the Dozen* (1949); and Betty MacDonald's *The Egg and I* (1946). Also appearing during this time was Dr. Alfred C. Kinsey's *Sexual Behavior in the Human Male* (1948), which together with its 1953 companion, *Sexual Behavior in the Human Female,* revolutionized the way Americans thought about their sexual practices, by showing them to be more diverse and unconventional than previously believed. Important religious books from the period included *The Seven Storey Mountain* (1949) by Trappist monk Thomas Merton; Frank Oursler's *The Greatest Story Ever Told* (1949), a life of Jesus that became the basis for the 1965 film extravaganza of the same name; and Father Fulton J. Sheen's *Peace of Soul* (1947) and *Communism and the Conscience of the West* (1948). Sheen, a fervent anticommunist, became a bishop in 1951 and later hosted a top-rated television show, *Life Is Worth Living* (1952–57).

Other notable nonfiction from the period included *The God That Failed* (1949), edited and introduced by Richard Crossman, which presented accounts by prominent intellectuals who had tried and rejected communism. It contains personal narratives from ex–Communist Party members Arthur Koestler, Richard Wright, and Louis Fisher, and three "fellow-travelers," Ignazio Silone, André Gide, and Stephen Spender. It was cited by anticommunists as firsthand evidence of communism's failings and hypocrisies. However Crossman warned against regarding these repudiations as a facile endorsement of capitalism and Western democracy; instead, he encouraged readers to consider how the moral and political failures of the West provoked such extraordinary people to embrace communism, at least temporarily.

Dr. Benjamin Spock's *The Common Sense Book of Baby and Child Care,* published in 1946, repudiated traditional notions that children should be strictly disciplined according to a rigid set of rules. Spock instead instructed parents to pay attention to concerns that their children expressed and to respond to each child as a unique individual, with distinct needs. Although critics argued that Spock's approach was too permissive, it was widely embraced by the American public, and it greatly influenced the way the baby boom generation was raised during the 1950s.

Hiroshima (1946), John Hersey's account of the atomic bombing of Japan, includes firsthand accounts by survivors, and Theodore White's best-selling *Thunder Out of China* (1946) criticizes Chinese Nationalist leader Chiang Kai-shek in its description of the then-ongoing Chinese revolution. In 1953, Senator McCarthy's aides Roy Cohn and David Schine burned it when they went through the State Department libraries in Europe and removed books they believed to be sympathetic to communism. In *The Cold War* (1947), journalist

Walter Lippmann gives an early account of postwar superpower politics. *The Well-Wrought Urn* (1947), by Cleanth Brooks, became the most influential work of the New Criticism school of literary theory, which favored close attention to the formal characteristics of imaginative writing and tried to detach the literary work from external historical, social, and biographical contexts. Other important nonfiction included William Shirer's *End of a Berlin Diary* (1947), about the final days of World War II; Richard Hofstadter's *The American Political Tradition* (1948); Daniel Lang's *The Early Tales of the Atomic Age* (1948); *This I Remember* (1949), the memoirs of the much-loved, much-reviled former first lady Eleanor Roosevelt; *Modern Arms and Free Men* (1949) by Vannevar Bush, president of the Carnegie Institution who also directed the Manhattan Project that developed the atomic bomb; and *Faith and History* (1949) by theologian Reinhold Niebuhr, who, along with Lionel Trilling, Richard Chase, and such intellectual figures as Arthur Schlesinger, Jr., helped establish the New Liberalism in the late 1940s and early 1950s. This political position rejected the inherently optimistic assumptions of Progressivism, an earlier form of liberalism that maintained that enlightened social policies can create a better world. Disillusioned by the experiences of World War II and the cold war, the New Liberals presented a more pessimistic outlook that recognized how the irrational, gratification-seeking id within the human psyche can and often does dominate human behavior.

Influential literature by foreign writers was also frequently pessimistic in its description of a harsh, sometimes brutal world. French existentialist authors Albert Camus (*The Stranger,* 1946, and *The Plague,* 1948) and Jean-Paul Sartre (*Existentialism,* 1947) sought to find meaning in a hostile, atheistic, and inherently meaningless universe; Alan Paton's *Cry, the Beloved Country* (1948), described and decried racism in South Africa; in *1984* (1949) British novelist George Orwell imagined a future in which an all-powerful, Stalinist totalitarian state arises in the aftermath of an atomic war; and the newly discovered *Diary of Anne Frank* (1947) described the life of a doomed Jewish family in Amsterdam hiding from the Nazis during World War II. British poet W. H. Auden won the Pulitzer Prize for *Age of Anxiety* (1947), a collection of poems that addresses feelings of uncertainty, disconnectedness, and other troubling emotional features of modern existence.

Theater, Music, and the Visual Arts

As in literature and film, postwar theater ranged from lighthearted comedy to serious drama. In the former category were Garson Kanin's *Born Yesterday* (1946), starring Judy Holliday, who won an Academy Award in 1950 for her cinematic reprise of the dumb blond who prevails; Noël Coward's witty and urbane *Present Laughter* (1946); Howard Lindsay and Russel Crouse's *Life with Mother* (1948), based on the 1936 domestic novel by Clarence Day; and a 1949 revival of Mae West's *Diamond Lil,* starring West. More serious drama from the period often looked closely and critically at relationships within American families, social and personal values, and sexual dynamics. Among this trend were Eugene O'Neill's *The Iceman Cometh* (1946); Arthur Miller's *All My Sons* (1947); Tennessee Williams's Pulitzer Prize–winning *A Streetcar Named Desire* (1947), starring Marlon Brando, Jessica Tandy, Kim Hunter, and Karl Malden, and his *Summer and Smoke* (1948); and Miller's Pulitzer Prize–winning *Death of a Salesman* (1949), originally starring Lee J. Cobb as traveling salesman Willie Lowman. More socially and historically oriented Broadway openings included Maxwell Anderson's *Anne of a Thousand Days* (1948); Clifford Odets's *The Big Knife* (1949), starring John Garfield; and Jean-Paul Sartre's *No Exit* (1946), *The Respectful Prostitute* (1948), and *Red Gloves* (1948).

Musical theater from the period included Duke Ellington and John Latouche's *Beggar's Holiday* (1946), starring Zero Mostel and Alfred Drake; Irving Berlin's *Annie Get Your Gun* (1946), about legendary cowgirl Annie Oakley; Cole Porter's *Around the World in 80 Days* (1946), starring Orson Welles; Kurt Weill and Langston Hughes's *Street Scene* (1947); Richard Rodgers and Oscar Hammerstein II's *Allegro* (1947); Alan Jay Lerner and Frederick Loewe's *Brigadoon* (1947); Burton Lane and E. Y. Harburg's *Finian's Rainbow* (1947); *Kiss Me, Kate* (1948), Porter's adaptation of Shakespeare's *Taming of the Shrew;* Weill and Lerner's *Love Life* (1948); Rodgers and Hammerstein's *South Pacific* (1949), which starred Mary Martin and opera star Ezio Pinza and won the 1950 Pulitzer Prize; Jule Styne and Leo Robin's *Gentlemen Prefer Blondes* (1949), starring Carol Channing; Weill and Anderson's *Lost in the Stars* (1949); Berlin's *Miss Liberty* (1949), starring Eddie Albert; and Robert Dolan and Johnny Mercer's *Texas Li'l Darlin'* (1949).

The big swing bands that had flourished during the war remained popular throughout the 1940s. These included groups led by Duke Ellington, Benny Goodman, Woody Herman, and Louis Armstrong, although Armstrong broke up his band in 1947 to begin a smaller sextet. Lead vocalists included Frank Sinatra, Bing Crosby, Perry Como, Frankie Lane, Vic Damone, Doris Day, Eddy Arnold, Ella Fitzgerald, Billie Holiday, Nat "King" Cole, Sarah Vaughn, and country singer Hank Williams. Popular hits of the period included "Chiquita Banana," "Come Rain or Come Shine," "On a Slow Boat to China," and "Mona Lisa."

Jazz, which traces its origins to the music of plantation slaves and evolved earlier in the century from the blues, flourished during and after the war. It manifested itself in a variety of forms that included big-band swing, boogie-woogie blues, and be-bop, which saxophonist Charlie "Bird" Parker first introduced in 1941. Classical composers such as Igor Stravinsky and Leonard Bernstein also wrote for the form; Woody Herman's First Herd premiered Stravinsky's *Ebony Concerto,* a "jazz concerto grosso" at Carnegie Hall in 1946. In the postwar era, bop intensified into hard bop, which employed a spoken music called "scat." Embraced by those who wanted to project an image of being up-to-date and on-the-go, the fast-paced hard bop was later offset by a more mellow, "cool" jazz that Miles Davis and Gil Evans pioneered, and by Afro-Latin and Afro-Cuban jazz that Dizzy Gillespie

"America's Number One Balladeer," Eddy Arnold, hosted CBS radio's rural revue, "Hometown Reunion," in 1948. *(Photofest)*

originated. Among the leading figures in jazz from the postwar period were Parker, Gillespie, Armstrong, Herman, Davis, Thelonious Monk, Stan Getz, and Sidney Bichet. Although jazz originated as a uniquely American art form, it quickly became popular in France, where the first jazz festival was held in 1949. Lively, highly percussive Cuban music was also popular in the United States during the late 1940s, especially as performed by Tito Puente and Celia Cruz.

At the same time that jazz was celebrating the dynamic, new lifestyle of the postwar era, a growing interest in traditional classical music suggested the public's desire to retain the best of the past as well. Jazz, which emanated from impoverished black culture and was often performed in smoky, out-of-the-way "joints" was condemned by some Americans, mostly from the middle and upper classes, as immoral—largely because of its raw sensuality. Although also capable of transmitting deeply felt passion, classical music was typically identified with high culture and performed in lavish symphony halls where the rich and famous gathered to listen and to be seen. It therefore embodied respectability as much as jazz seemed to repudiate it. The major U.S. orchestras grew in popularity in the late 1940s, as they hosted a growing number of music festivals and toured throughout the country and the world. Leonard Bernstein, who composed both jazz and classical music, became director of symphony programs at the New York City Center in 1946, and he conducted the New York City Symphony Orchestra without pay from 1946 to 1948.

The works most frequently performed by North American symphony orchestras were by European masters from the 18th and 19th centuries: Ludwig van Beethoven, Pyotr Ilich Tchaikovsky, Richard Wagner, Wolfgang Amadeus Mozart, Johann Sebastian Bach, and Felix Mendelssohn. Among contemporary composers, Richard Strauss and Aaron Copland received the greatest play. This reflected the audiences' preference for more traditional, tonal, melodic music over the experimental music of modern composers who were still active after the war, including Arnold Schoenberg, who composed his last chamber work in 1946 following a debilitating heart attack; and Charles Ives, who won the 1947 Pulitzer Prize for his Symphony no. 3. Influential Soviet composers of the period included Igor Stravinsky, Dimitri Shostakovich, and Sergei Prokofiev. Other active modern composers included Béla Bartók, Roger Sessions, Paul Hindemith, Walter Piston, Pierre Boulez, Howard Hanson, Virgil Thomson, Samuel Barber, and Benjamin Britten. John Cage was an especially bold experimenter who was one of the first American composers to employ tape recorders and other electracoustic devices to provide a new "palate" of sound for musicians.

In dance, George Balanchine and Lincoln Kirstein organized the Ballet Society in 1946 to showcase new works. In 1948, it took up residence at New York City Center and became the New York City Ballet. Balanchine choreographed Stravinsky's *The Firebird* in 1949. Elsewhere, the Martha Graham Dance Company, which featured soloist Merce Cunningham, continued to pioneer modern dance, as it had before and during the war. Like the modern composers and modern artists, the modern dancers and choreographers appealed to some with their innovation but alienated many others because they challenged conventional definitions of their art form. Audiences expecting traditional forms of dancing were often puzzled, frustrated, or bored by movements they did not recognize or understand.

Prior to World War II, much of the world's art scene moved to the United States, especially to New York, as many artists fled persecution by the Nazis. This was especially true of surrealists and expressionists who had nonrepresentational styles and experimental content, based on such things as dreams and the unconscious, and antifascist attitudes. After the war, Europe was unable to support the arts economically or in other ways, and American collectors were able to purchase artworks and otherwise promote new artists, so expatriate European artists stayed, contributing directly to American arts and greatly influencing American artists. Whereas before the war most American painting, such as that of Edward Hopper and Winslow Homer, was representational, after the war abstract expressionism and other nonrepresentational forms dominated at the art schools and museums of modern art, if not popular tastes. Indeed, the postwar era saw the emergence of a deep schism between the public at large, which often failed to understand the point of abstraction, and the art dealers, collectors, and other influential institutions that financed and defined success within the art world.

Martha Graham pioneered a freer, more expressive form of modern dance. *(Photofest)*

That schism grew deeper through the 1950s. Norman Rockwell and Andrew Wyeth still made popular representational paintings in the postwar era, such as Rockwell's covers for the *Saturday Evening Post* and Wyeth's *Christina's World* (1948), which was widely reproduced as a popular print for home decoration. But abstract artists flourished in the more elite galleries and private collections, especially in New York.

During the war, Jackson Pollock developed his style of "action painting," which, influenced by Native American sand drawings, involved dripping paint onto large canvases spread out on the floor. After the war, Pollock continued to experiment in ways that emphasized color and motion more than line or subject and that sought to communicate pure emotion rather than ideas. Willem de Kooning emigrated from the Netherlands in 1926 and gave his first one-man show in 1948. He worked somewhat more conventionally with paintbrushes, but he was another pioneer of abstract expressionism whose work reflected violence and passion. His paintings drew attention to the texture and other qualities of the medium, not to the subject. Mark Rothko's abstract paintings produced calmer effects but also elevated form over content. Los Angeles–born Isamu Noguchi, who did stage settings for Martha Graham's modern dance company, is best known for the abstract sculptures he designed to accompany architectural structures.

Almost all of the artists of influence in the postwar era were men: Stuart Davis, David Smith, Hans Hofmann, Arshile Gorky, and Alexander Calder, who earlier in the century had begun developing abstract mobiles to make his artwork dynamic, changing over time, and subject to external influences, instead of fixed and static as in traditional Western art. In this respect, he inherited the concerns of Marcel Duchamp, an influential French Dadaist who, before World War I, repudiated the Western artistic tradition and, largely for political and philosophical reasons, rejected the efficacy of language, image, and rational thought. Duchamp moved to the United States at the start of World War II and continued to make "anti-art" throughout the 1940s, 1950s, and 1960s.

Ludwig Mies van der Rohe; Walter Gropius, who chaired Harvard University's department of architecture; and Philip Johnson, who headed the Museum of Modern Art's architecture department from 1946 to 1954, incorporated the stark, cerebral, modernist principles of the prewar German Bauhaus movement within American architecture in such postmodern buildings as Johnson's Glass House (1949) in New Canaan, Connecticut, and later to the Seagram Building in New York City, which Johnson and Mies designed together (1958). Frank Lloyd Wright, who began designing buildings in the 1920s and 1930s, also flourished in the late 1940s and 1950s and sought to integrate architecture more fully with its surrounding environment and make "form follow function." He designed Florida Southern College in Lakeland and New York's Guggenheim Museum in the 1940s, although the Guggenheim was not completed until 1959, the year of his death.

CHRONICLE OF EVENTS

1945

February 4–11: The leaders of the so-called Big Three—the United States, Britain, and the Soviet Union—meet at Yalta in the USSR to map out a new world order in expectation of the defeat of the Axis powers. Among other things, the Yalta agreements establish "spheres of influence" in which particular powers are recognized as dominating particular regions of the world.

April 12: President Franklin D. Roosevelt dies in office and is succeeded by Harry S. Truman.

April 28: Italy's fascist dictator, Benito Mussolini, his mistress, and 11 companions are executed by antifascist Italian partisans.

April 30: Germany's Nazi dictator, Adolf Hitler, and his mistress, Eva Braun, commit suicide in their Berlin bunker.

May 8: World War II ends in Europe with the unconditional surrender of Germany to the Allied powers: Britain, France, the Soviet Union, and the United States.

June 26: Delegates from 50 nations meet in San Francisco to approve the United Nations (UN) charter.

July 15: The first atomic bomb is successfully tested in the desert outside Los Alamos, New Mexico.

July 17–August 2: Truman, Winston Churchill (Great Britain), and Joseph Stalin (Soviet Union) meet at Potsdam, near Berlin, to establish the terms of the postwar occupation of Germany. The Potsdam agreement divides the country into U.S., British, French, and Soviet military zones and establishes a four-power Allied Control Council for settling matters concerning the whole country. It outlaws the Nazi (National Socialism) Party and seeks to abolish Nazi ideology, disarm Germany, and prevent it from ever becoming a military power again. The agreement also calls for fostering democratic ideals and introducing representative and elective principles of government in Europe.

At Potsdam, the Big Three warn Japan that it risks total destruction unless it surrenders unconditionally. While at the conference, Truman learns of America's successful atomic bomb test but does not inform Stalin.

July 26: Britain's wartime prime minister, Winston Churchill, and his Conservative Party are defeated in a landslide victory for the Labour Party. Labour's Clement Atlee replaces Churchill as prime minister and takes his seat at the Potsdam Conference.

August 6: The United States drops an atomic bomb on the Japanese city of Hiroshima.

August 9: The United States drops an atomic bomb on the Japanese city of Nagasaki.

August 14: Japan announces its surrender.

September 2: General Douglas MacArthur, commander of U.S. armed forces in the Pacific, formally accepts the Japanese surrender aboard the battleship U.S.S. *Missouri.* MacArthur then becomes chief administrator of the Allied occupation of Japan, which lasts until April 28, 1952.

1946

January 10: In London, the UN General Assembly meets for the first time. On January 17, the Security Council has its inaugural meeting, and on January 29, Norwegian Trygve Lie is elected the first secretary general.

January 10: The U.S. Army Signal Corps makes radar contact with the Moon, a necessary first step for lunar exploration.

January 21: The United Nations establishes its Atomic Energy Commission in London.

February 8: American scholars complete the Revised Standard Version of the Holy Bible.

February 14: The Electronic Numerical Integrator and Computer (ENIAC), the second modern computer, goes into operation at the University of Pennsylvania.

February 14: Syngman Rhee forms the Democratic Representative Council in Seoul, South Korea. On February 19, Kim Il Sung becomes chairman of the Korean people's government in Pyongyang, North Korea. In fall 1948, they declare themselves independent sovereign nations, U.S.-supported South Korea and Soviet-controlled North Korea, provisionally divided at the 38th parallel; however, North Korea's Kim vows to achieve the ultimate reunification of the country.

March 2: Ho Chi Minh is elected president of the Hanoi-based Democratic Republic of Vietnam (later known as North Vietnam). On March 6, he signs an agreement with France in which France recognizes Vietnam as a free state within the French Union and Ho permits the presence of 25,000 French troops in the country for five years.

March 5: Speaking in Fulton, Missouri, Churchill warns of an implacable threat to freedom that lies behind a communist "iron curtain" in Eastern Europe and the Soviet Union.

March 24: Truman threatens to send battleships to the Mediterranean if the Soviets do not remove their troops from Iran, in accordance with the Potsdam agreements. The Soviet Union withdraws its troops in May, after Iran consents to give it 51 percent of Iranian oil for the next 25 years.

April 18: The United States recognizes the government of Yugoslavia under the leadership of Marshal Tito, following assurances from the communist leader that Yugoslavia will observe existing treaties and adhere to the principles of the Declaration of the United Nations.

April 23: Stalin, a novel by the late Leon Trotsky, is published in the United States. Trotsky, one of the leaders of the 1917 Russian Revolution that brought the communists to power, was assassinated by an agent of Stalin in 1940.

May 5: A civil war in China breaks out between the U.S.-backed Chinese Nationalists led by Chiang Kai-shek and communist Chinese forces led by Mao Zedong. On August 19, Mao formally declares war on the Nationalists.

June 16: The United States presents to the United Nations U.S. statesman Bernard Baruch's plan for international control of atomic energy. The plan is defeated after Soviet objections.

July 1: The United States explodes "Bikini Helen," the world's fourth atomic bomb, in a subsurface test off the Bikini Atoll in the Pacific Ocean. As part of the experiment, 11 obsolete navy ships are sunk and six more are damaged. Bikini Atoll, after which the skimpy women's bathing suit is named, becomes the site of numerous atomic tests during the 1940s and 1950s.

An atomic bomb is tested on Bikini Atoll on July 25, 1946. *(Photofest)*

July 27: Influential American author Gertrude Stein dies in France.

August 18: Physicist Albert Einstein, a pacifist and one of the founders of atomic theory, expresses his regret that the atomic bomb was used against Japan and states his belief that, had President Roosevelt lived, he would not have ordered the attack.

September 1: A referendum in Greece calls for the monarchy to be restored. Subsequently, civil war breaks out between royalists and communists. Under the Truman Doctrine, the United States sends military advisers and some $400 million in military and economic assistance. The anticommunist forces prevail by 1949.

September 15: William Green, president of the American Federation of Labor, cautions American blacks against affiliation with the Communist Party, which, he warns, will use them as pawns in a communist revolution.

September 20: The first Cannes Film Festival, which had originally been planned for September 1939—the month that World War II began—opens in France.

October 2: Scientists at a medical symposium in Buffalo, New York, suggest a link between cigarette smoking and lung cancer.

October 15: The St. Louis Cardinals win the World Series, defeating the Boston Red Sox in seven games.

October 16: Nine top-level Nazis are hanged after being convicted of war crimes at the Nuremberg Trials. Shortly before his scheduled execution, Hermann Göring, Hitler's second in command who was condemned for his role in planning and overseeing the execution of millions of Jews, commits suicide by swallowing cyanide.

November 22: Invented by Lazlo Biró, an expatriate Hungarian, the first ballpoint pen goes on sale in the United States.

December 15: The Chicago Bears defeat the New York Giants to win the National Football League (NFL) championship.

December 27: Led by tennis stars Jack Kramer and Ted Schroeder, the United States regains the Davis Cup.

December 31: Truman declares that World War II is officially over.

1947

January 7: Truman appoints George Marshall as secretary of state to replace the ailing James Byrnes. Marshall, a retired five-star general and World War II hero, reluctantly accepts the appointment out of a sense of civic duty. In a show of the great esteem it holds for him, the Senate takes the unprecedented step of unanimously confirming Marshall without first conducting hearings.

January 19: Truman declares that Polish elections producing communist victories were neither free nor fair and thus are in violation of the Yalta agreements. Thereafter, the Polish government begins to "sovietize" the country.

January 25: Gangster Al Capone dies of apoplexy.

February 3: Baruch claims that Soviet spies have infiltrated American atomic plants in Canada and gained access to secrets about the atomic bomb. Canadian officials deny the charge, claiming that their security measures are as good as those in the United States.

March 12: The Truman Doctrine formalizes the U.S. "containment" policy to halt communist expansion and restrict the Soviet Union to its existing spheres of influence.

March 21: Truman requires loyalty investigations of all federal employees and bans government employment to communists and communist sympathizers.

April 7: Automotive and business pioneer Henry Ford and novelist Willa Cather die.

May 26: General Anastasio Somoza of Nicaragua overthrows President Leonardo Arguella and establishes himself as dictator.

June 3: In Paris, fashion designer Christian Dior introduces the "New Look," an ultrafeminine full-skirted fashion that contrasts the more severe wartime styles.

June 21: Truman accuses the communist minority in Hungary of seizing power in a coup, with assistance from the Soviet military. The United States accuses the USSR of violating the Yalta agreement and suspends a $15 million credit that had been pledged to the Hungarian government.

June 23: The Taft-Hartley Act becomes law over Truman's veto. It denies the facilities of the National Labor Relations Board to unions that fail to file affidavits swearing that their officers are not communists. It also allows the president to temporarily suspend labor strikes against industries that are deemed critical to national security and well-being. Both Truman and Eisenhower will later invoke the act for that reason.

June 28: New York City retires its last trolley car.

July 13: The first dinosaur fossils discovered in North America are found in New Mexico.

July 18: British officials intercept the *Exodus,* a ship carrying 4,530 Jewish refugees attempting to settle in Palestine. The British threaten to send the Jews back to Germany. On September 7, the refugees debark in Hamburg rather than enter France and are escorted to an internment camp near Lubeck. Their experience becomes the basis for *Exodus,* an influential, best-selling novel by Leon Uris (1958) and film by Otto Preminger (1960).

August 15: India and Pakistan achieve independence from Great Britain. India is created as a sovereign, Hindu-dominated, secular state, and Pakistan as an Islamic state. More than 500,000 people are killed in the violence that erupts as minority populations in each country relocate.

August 23: The Edinburgh (Scotland) International Festival of Music and Drama is inaugurated.

September 1: Amid accusations of voting irregularities, communists win the general elections in Hungary.

September 8: The National Security Act, signed by Truman on July 26, takes effect. The act replaces the wartime Office of Strategic Services (OSS) with the Central Intelligence Agency (CIA) and creates the National Security Council (NSC) to advise on and coordinate defense and foreign policies.

September 13: NBC-TV decides not to air crime shows before 9:30 P.M.

September 22: Partly in response to the Marshall Plan, the Communist Parties of the Soviet Union, Bulgaria, Czechoslovakia, France, Hungary, Italy, Poland, Romania, and Yugoslavia introduce the Communist Information Bureau (Cominform), which replaces the Communist International (Comintern).

September 23: The head of the Bulgarian opposition party is executed and Bulgaria becomes a one-party Communist state aligned with the USSR. It nationalizes industry and collectivizes farms.

October 6: The New York Yankees defeat the Brooklyn Dodgers in the final game of the World Series.

October 14: Test pilot Charles "Chuck" Yeager becomes the first aviator to break the sound barrier. Launched from a B-29 bomber, Yeager's experimental, rocket-powered X-1 aircraft, the *Glamorous Glennis,* reaches an altitude of 40,000 feet and a speed of 662 miles per hour, which is greater than the speed of sound at that altitude. Until Yeager's flight, scientists were unsure whether the shock waves produced by such speeds would render a craft uncontrollable.

October 20: The House Un-American Activities Committee (HUAC), under the chairmanship of Republican congressman J. Parnell Thomas of New Jersey, conducts its first full cold war hearings into alleged communist influence in the Hollywood film industry. These hearings center on allegations that communist values and propaganda are being surreptitiously introduced into American films. The investigation features "friendly" and "unfriendly" witnesses. Among the former are Ronald Reagan, president of the Screen Actors Guild, who assures the committee that the guild is not controlled by leftists; actors Robert Taylor, Gary Cooper, George Murphy, Adolphe Menjou, and Robert Montgomery; writer Ayn Rand; animator and studio owner Walt Disney; director Leo McCarey; Louis B. Mayer of MGM studios; and influential union leader Roy Brewer. The unfriendly witnesses include playwright Bertolt Brecht and the "Hollywood Ten": screenwriters Alvah Bessie, Lester Cole, Ring Lardner, Jr., John Howard Lawson, Albert Maltz, Sam Ornitz, and Dalton Trumbo; film directors Herbert Biberman and Edward Dmytryk; and writer-producer Robert Adrian Scott. Eight other unfriendly witnesses are subpoenaed but not called before the committee.

December 1: Tennessee Williams's play *A Streetcar Named Desire* opens on Broadway.

December 5: Boxer Joe Louis, "the Brown Bomber," defeats "Jersey" Joe Walcott to retain the heavyweight championship.

Members of the Hollywood Ten pose with their families. *(Photofest)*

December 27: Initially entitled *Puppet Playhouse,* the children's show *Howdy Doody* premieres on network television. Set in Doodyville, a circus town inhabited by puppets and people, it is hosted by "Buffalo" Bob Smith, his marionette Howdy Doody, and the clown Clarabell. The program, which runs through 1960, features a live, noisy audience of children who sit in the "Peanut Gallery."

December 28: The Chicago Cardinals defeat the Philadelphia Eagles for the NFL championship.

December 29: Former Democratic vice president Henry Wallace declares his candidacy for president as the Progressive Party nominee. Although Wallace never explicitly supports them, he receives the endorsements of the Soviet Union and the American Communist Party. Wallace receives more than a million votes from a total of some 48 million cast in November 1948. Support for Wallace's candidacy is later cited in Federal Bureau of Investigation (FBI) files and such blacklisting publications as *Red Channels* as an indication of possible communist sympathies.

December 30: Romania declares itself a Communist people's republic. Romanian industry and resources are nationalized; agriculture is collectivized.

1948

January 12: In a unanimous decision, the U.S. Supreme Court orders the state of Oklahoma to admit a black American to the University of Oklahoma Law School.

January 30: Mohandas Gandhi is assassinated in New Delhi, India, by a radical Hindu. His practice of nonviolent civil disobedience, which later influences Dr. Martin Luther King, Jr., and other early leaders of the American civil rights movement, played a major role in winning India's independence from Great Britain in 1947.

January 31: Orville Wright dies. Orville and his brother Wilbur invented the airplane in 1900.

February 2: Truman asks Congress to enact antilynching legislation and establish a federal commission on civil rights.

February 11: Russian film director Sergei Eisenstein dies. A pioneer of early cinema, Eisenstein, who directed such pro-Soviet works as *Battleship Potemkin* (1925), *October* (1928), and *Alexander Nevsky* (1938), is known for his use of close-ups and dramatic cross-cutting.

February 16: North Korea declares itself a people's republic. It is immediately recognized by the Soviet Union.

February 25–27: Communists seize power in Czechoslovakia through a coup by police and paramilitary "action committees" that force the resignation of center and right-wing members of the government. This is followed by the assassination of Jan Masaryk, the Czech foreign minister who resisted Soviet demands that Czechoslovakia refuse U.S. aid.

May 14: The United Nations recognizes the state of Israel, and British rule officially ends in Palestine. Israel's Arab neighbors—Jordan, Lebanon, Syria, and Egypt—invade that same day but are repelled, except in the Old City of Jerusalem. The original UN agreement had called for the formation of a separate Palestinian state, in addition to the formation of Israel, and for international administration of Jerusalem; however, a peace treaty signed in January 1949, after the fighting has concluded, expands Israeli territory by about 50 percent and leaves Jordan in control of Old Jerusalem. Jordan and Egypt also annex or occupy territory that had been designated for the Palestinian state.

June 7: World War II hero Dwight D. Eisenhower resigns his position as chief of staff of the U.S. Army to become president of Columbia University in New York City.

June 24: The Soviets blockade West Berlin in an effort to gain economic control over the city. The United States responds with the Berlin airlift. By spring 1949, the round-the-clock flights average 8,000 tons of fuel and food supplies daily.

June 24: Truman signs a draft act into law. The act requires men between the ages of 19 and 25 to register for the draft. In the first year, more than 200,000 men are called up for 21-month tours of duty.

June 25: The Republican Party nominates New York governor Thomas E. Dewey as its presidential candidate and California governor Earl Warren as his vice presidential running mate.

June 25: Joe Louis wins a rematch with "Jersey" Joe Walcott to retain boxing's heavyweight title.

June 28: Cominform calls on the Yugoslavian Communist Party either to remove Marshal Tito or to face expulsion from the alliance of communist parties. Tito earlier purged Stalinists from the Yugoslav Communist Party and army. When Yugoslavia rejects Cominform's ultimatum, the Soviets withdraw military aid and expel the country from the alliance. Although it does not join any Western alliance, Yugoslavia establishes closer relations with the West.

July 7: Legendary pitcher Leroy Robert "Satchel" Paige of the Negro leagues signs a contract with the Cleveland Indians.

July 15: The Democratic Party nominates incumbent Truman as its presidential candidate. Senator Alben W. Barkley is his running mate.

July 20: Leaders of the American Communist Party are arrested under the Smith Act for conspiring to overthrow the U.S. government. They are convicted during the Foley Square trial of 1949.

July 26: By executive order Truman desegregates the armed services. Truman also issues a separate executive order calling for a fair employment policy in federal government civil service.

July 29: Finland forms an all-socialist cabinet that excludes communists.

July 30: Through their control of the ministry of the interior, Hungarian Communists arrest leading politicians, force the resignation of the president, and gain full control of the state. In 1949, Hungary is proclaimed a people's republic, nationalizes industry and resources, and collectivizes farms.

August 3: Whittaker Chambers accuses Alger Hiss of being a Soviet agent. Hiss is indicted for perjury on December 15 and convicted on January 25, 1950.

August 15: The first postwar Olympic Games end in London; the United States wins 38 medals.

August 16: Baseball star Babe Ruth dies of cancer.

August 19: Soviet troops fire on East Berlin demonstrators protesting Soviet occupation.

October 11: The Cleveland Indians defeat the Boston Braves to win the World Series in six games.

November 2: Truman upsets Republican presidential candidate Thomas Dewey.

November 12: Hideki Tojo, Japan's wartime leader, and seven of his accomplices are sentenced to death by an international tribunal.

November 30: German communists establish an independent government in Berlin's Soviet sector.

December 1: Madam Chiang Kai-shek arrives in Washington, D.C., to solicit additional U.S. support for the Chinese Nationalists.

December 6: Chambers reveals rolls of microfilm hidden inside pumpkins on his Maryland farm. According to Chambers and Republican California congressman Richard M. Nixon, the so-called Pump-kin Papers contain evidence that Hiss had been part of a communist spy ring in the 1930s.

December 10: The UN General Assembly adopts a declaration of human rights by a vote of 48-0, with the Soviet bloc, South Africa, and Saudi Arabia abstaining. The assembly gives former first lady Eleanor Roosevelt a standing ovation for her work in drafting the document.

December 10: Poet T. S. Eliot wins the Nobel Prize in literature.

December 19: The Philadelphia Eagles defeat the Chicago Bears for the NFL championship.

1949

January 1: The United States recognizes the Republic of South Korea.

January 5: Wilhelm Furtwängler is dismissed as conductor of the Berlin Symphony Orchestra due to his past Nazi sympathies.

January 10: RCA introduces a 45-rotations-per-minute (rpm) phonograph record. The 45 competes with Columbia Records's newly developed 7-inch microgroove record. Both supplant the older 78-rpm records.

February 8: A six-engine XB-47 jet bomber, averaging 607.2 miles per hour, sets a new transcontinental speed record of three hours and 46 minutes.

February 19: Despite being confined to a mental hospital and indicted for treason for his profascist radio broadcasts during World War II, Ezra Pound wins the first Bollinger Prize for poetry.

February 24: Israel and Egypt sign an armistice ending hostilities that began after the declaration of Israel's statehood in 1948, but Egypt refuses to recognize Israel's existence.

March 1: Heavyweight boxing champion Joe Louis retires with a 25-1 record after 11 years in the ring.

March 2: An American B-52 bomber completes the first nonstop flight around the world.

March 4: Stalin replaces Foreign Minister Vyacheslav Molotov with Andrei Vishinsky, who presided over the notorious purges of the 1930s.

March 8: France recognizes Bao Dai as the head of a noncommunist Vietnamese government in Saigon, in what was formerly French Indochina. In doing so, the French repudiate the Hanoi-based Vietminh's claim to be the legitimate government of

Vietnam. In 1954, the Vietminh drive the French from Vietnam after winning the battle of Dienbienphu.

April 4: The North Atlantic Treaty Organization (NATO), a Western military alliance, is formed to contain communist expansion in Europe.

May 12: The Soviet Union ends its blockade of West Berlin; the Berlin airlift is terminated.

May 23: The Federal Republic of Germany (West Germany) proclaims its existence and designates Bonn as its capital. On August 14, West Germans elect 73-year-old Konrad Adenauer as their first chancellor. He holds the post through 1963.

July 1: Celebrated chemist Linus Pauling reports that he has discovered the molecular flaw responsible for sickle-cell anemia.

August 16: Southern novelist Margaret Mitchell, author of *Gone With the Wind,* is struck and killed by a speeding automobile.

September 23: Truman announces that the Soviet Union has exploded an atomic bomb.

September 28–October 1: The USSR, Poland, Hungary, Romania, and Bulgaria renounce their friendship and mutual assistance pacts with Yugoslavia.

October 1: Mao Zedong declares the People's Republic of China (PRC). Zhou Enlai is elected premier and foreign minister. The Communists immediately introduce a major program of land reform, police control, and nationalization of resources and industry. By April 1950, all of mainland China is securely under Communist control. Although Great Britain recognizes the PRC on October 26, 1949, the Nationalists retain China's seat in the United Nations. The United States refuses to recognize the PRC and does not establish full diplomatic relations with the nation until 1979.

October 7: The German Democratic Republic (East Germany) proclaims its existence. The United States does not recognize it until 1974.

October 10: The New York Yankees defeat the Brooklyn Dodgers to win the World Series in five games. Dodger Jackie Robinson is named Most Valuable Player.

October 16: The three-year Greek civil war ends when communist insurgents agree to surrender their weapons.

December 8: Chiang Kai-shek establishes a Chinese Nationalist government on Taiwan (Formosa).

December 9: Thomas, chairman of HUAC, is sentenced to six to 18 months in federal prison for padding his congressional payroll. Among his fellow inmates at the federal correctional institution in Danbury, Connecticut, in 1950 are Hollywood Ten members Ring Lardner, Jr., and Lester Cole, who are serving their terms for contempt of Congress because they refused to testify before Thomas's committee in 1947.

December 15: Jazz club Birdland opens on Broadway. It is named after saxophonist Charlie "Bird" Parker.

December 18: The Philadelphia Eagles defeat the Los Angeles Rams for the NFL championship.

December 25: Parker performs at New York's Carnegie Hall on Christmas Day.

December 26: Albert Einstein offers a new "generalized theory of gravitation" that attempts to unite the major forces of nature under one unified theory.

EYEWITNESS TESTIMONY

1945

As a result of A's [an unidentified source] chat with Ales the following has been ascertained: 1. Ales has been working with the Neighbors [KGB jargon for the Soviet military intelligence, a.k.a. GRU] since 1935. . . .

2. For some year past he has been the leader of a small group of the Neighbors' probationers [KGB jargon for agents], for the most part consisting of his relations. . . .

3. The group and Ales himself work on obtaining military information only. Materials on the Bank [KGB jargon for the U.S. State Department] allegedly interest the Neighbors very little and he does not produce them regularly. . . .

5. Recently Ales and his whole group were awarded Soviet decorations. . . .

6. After the Yalta Conference, when he had gone on to Moscow, a Soviet personage in a very responsible position allegedly got in touch with Ales and at the behest of the Military Neighbors passed on to him their gratitude and so on.

> *From a cable from the Soviet intelligence (KGB) office in Washington to the KGB office in Moscow, dated March 30, 1945, that was decoded by the National Security Agency's Venona Project and used to identify Alger Hiss as a Soviet agent (the NSA/FBI footnote to the message indicates that Ales "is probably Alger Hiss"), in John Earl Haynes, and Harvey Klehr,* Venona: Decoding Soviet Espionage in America *(1999), pp. 171–72.*

At exactly fifteen minutes past eight in the morning, on August 6, 1945, Japanese time, at the moment when the atomic bomb flashed above Hiroshima, Miss Toshiko Sasaki, a clerk in the personnel department of the East Asia Tin Works, had just sat down at her place in the plant office and was turning her head to speak to the girl at the next desk. At that same moment, Dr. Masakazu Fujii was settling down cross-legged to read the Osaka *Asahi* on the porch of his private hospital, overhanging one of the seven deltaic rivers which divide Hiroshima; Mrs. Hatsyo Nakamura, a tailor's widow, stood by the window of her kitchen, watching a neighbor tearing down his house because it lay in the path of an air-raid-defense fire lane; Father Wilhelm Kleinsorge, a German priest of the Society of Jesus, reclined in his underwear on a cot on the top floor of his order's three-story mission house, reading a Jesuit magazine; . . . Dr. Terufumi Sasaki, a young member of the surgical staff of the city's large, modern Red Cross Hospital, walked along one of the hospital corridors with a blood specimen; . . . and the Reverend Mr. Kiyoshi Tanimoto, pastor of the Hiroshima Methodist Church, paused at the door of a rich man's house in Koi, the city's western suburb, and prepared to unload a handcart full of things he had evacuated from town in fear of the massive B-29 raid which everyone expected Hiroshima to suffer. A hundred thousand people were killed by the atomic bomb, and these six were among the survivors. They still wonder why they lived when so many others died.

> *John Hersey's account of the atomic bombing of Hiroshima on August 5, 1945, in Hersey,* Hiroshima *(1946), pp. 1–2.*

"There she goes!" someone said.

Out of the belly of *The Great Artiste* what looked like a black object went downward. . . .

A bluish-green light . . . illuminated the sky all around. A tremendous blast wave struck our ship and made it tremble from nose to tail. . . .

Observers in the tail of our ship saw a giant ball of fire as though from the bowels of the earth, belching forth enormous white smoke rings. Next they saw a giant pillar of purple fire, 10,000 feet high, shooting skyward with enormous speed. . . .

Awestruck, we watched it shoot upward like a meteor coming from the earth instead of from outer space, becoming ever more alive as it climbed skyward through the white clouds. It was no longer smoke, or dust, or even a cloud of fire. It was a living thing, a new species of being born before our incredulous eyes.

At one stage of its evolution, covering millions of years in terms of seconds, the entity assumed the form of a giant square totem pole. . . . But it was a living totem pole, carved with many grotesque masks grimacing at the earth. . . . The mushroom top was even more alive than the pillar, seething and boiling in a white fury of creamy foam, sizzling upward and then descending earthward, a thousand Old Faithful geysers rolled into one.

It kept struggling in an elemental fury, like a creature in the act of breaking the bonds that held it down. In a few seconds it had freed itself from its gigantic stem and floated upward with tremendous speed. . . .

But no sooner did this happen than another mushroom, smaller in size than the first one, began emerging out of the pillar. It was as though the decapitated monster were growing a new head.

Journalist William E. Lawrence reporting the atomic bombing of Nagasaki on August 9, 1945, in Lawrence, "Atomic Bombing of Nagasaki Told by Flight Member," New York Times *(September 9, 1945), pp. 1, 35.*

The reason that we did this job [build the atomic bomb] is because it was an organic necessity. If you are a scientist, you believe that it is good to find out how the world works, that it is good to find out what the realities are, that it is good to turn over to mankind at large the greatest possible power to control the world and to deal with it according to its lights and values.

There has been a lot of talk about the evil of secrecy, of concealment, of control, of security. . . . I think that it comes from the fact that secrecy strikes at the very root of what science is, and what it is for. It is not possible to be a scientist unless you believe that it is good to learn. It is not good to be a scientist, and it is not possible, unless you think that it is of the highest value to share your knowledge, to share it with anyone who is interested. It is not possible to be a scientist unless you believe that the knowledge of the world, and the power which this gives, is a thing which is of intrinsic value to humanity, and that you are using it to help in the spread of knowledge, and are willing to take the consequences. And, therefore, I think that this resistance which we feel and see all around us to anything which is an attempt to treat science of the future as though it were rather a dangerous thing, a thing that must be watched and managed, is resisted not because of its inconvenience . . . but resisted because it is based on a philosophy incompatible with that by which we live, and learned to live in the past.

Physicist Robert Oppenheimer, scientific head of the atomic bomb project, addressing his team of scientists at Los Alamos, New Mexico, on November 2, 1945, in Robert Torricelli and Andrew Carroll, eds., In Our Own Words *(1999), pp. 151–52.*

1946

We were shot out into the awaiting half-century, a sea of sperm ejaculated into an indifferent womb. Soldiers home from the war and the women who hungered for them were hot to regenerate the species after the carnage of Normandy, Anzio, Saipan and Iwo Jima. I've seen it in nature following hurricanes. Within days plants that never bloom till April or June push out flowers and fill the air with pollen. Just like those post-storm Easter lilies, our parents were driven to repopulate, repopulate, repopulate. Never mind the atomic bomb. Never mind the Holocaust. Never mind the Red Menace. Forget whether it's immoral to bring a child into such a world. Just put that DNA out there and keep the species going. They were driven by a force greater than themselves.

Richard Alan Schwartz's fictional reconstruction of the origins of the postwar Baby Boom, which began around 1946, in Schwartz, "The Best Minds of My Generation," Journal of Evolutionary Psychology *(August 1997), p. 178.*

It will be interesting, now that women are smoking, to see if the much higher ratio of the malignancy of the lung in men is decreased by an increase in the incidence in women.

Dr. William Rienkoff suggesting a connection between cigarette smoking and lung cancer at a medical symposium at the University of Buffalo, on October 2, 1946, in Clifton Daniel, ed., 20th Century Day by Day *(2000), p. 617.*

1947

Experience is the best teacher . . . in choosing a cigarette. Your T-zone will tell you why. More doctors smoke Camel than any other cigarette.

A 1947 advertisement for Camel cigarettes, in Lois Gordon and Alan Gordon, American Chronicle *(1999), p. 446.*

"[A woman must] accept herself fully as a woman [and] know she is dependent on a man. There is no fantasy in her mind about being an independent woman, a contradiction in terms.

An excerpt from psychoanalyst Marynia Farnham and sociologist Ferdinand Lundberg's 1947 book The Modern Woman, *in Lois Gordon and Alan Gordon,* American Chronicle *(1999), p. 446.*

When I say all Americans, I mean all Americans.

Many of our people still suffer the indignity of insult, the narrowing fear of intimidation, and, I regret to say, the threat of physical and mob violence. Prejudice and intolerance in which these evils are rooted still exist. The conscience of our nation, and the legal machinery which enforces it, have not yet secured to each citizen full freedom of [sic] fear.

We cannot wait another decade or another generation to remedy these evils. We must work, as never before, to cure them now.

President Harry S. Truman's address to the National Association for the Advancement of Colored People (NAACP) on June 29, 1947, in David McCullough, Truman *(1992), p. 570.*

The article appeared in the July [1947] issue of *Foreign Affairs,* under the title: "The Sources of Soviet Conduct." . . . Others began to write about it, to connect it with the Truman Doctrine and Marshall Plan, to speculate on its significance. It soon became the center of a veritable whirlpool of publicity. *Life* and *Reader's Digest* reprinted long excerpts from it. The term "containment" was picked up and elevated, by common agreement of the press, to the status of a "doctrine," which was then identified with the foreign policy of the administration. In this way there was established . . one of those indestructible myths that are the bane of the historian.

Feeling like one who has inadvertently loosened a large boulder from the top of a cliff and now helplessly witnesses its path of destruction in the valley below, shuddering and wincing at each successive glimpse of disaster, I absorbed the bombardment of press comment that now set in . . .

A . . . serious deficiency of the X-Article—perhaps the most serious of all—was the failure to make clear that what I was talking about when I mentioned the containment of Soviet power was not the containment by military means of a military threat, but the political containment of a political threat. . . .

I distinguished clearly in my own mind between areas that I thought vital to our security and ones that did not seem to me to fall into this category. My objection to the Truman Doctrine message revolved largely around its failure to make that distinction . . . [T]here were only five regions of the world—the United States, the United Kingdom, the Rhine valley with adjacent industrial areas, the Soviet Union, and Japan—where the sinews of modern military strength could be produced in quantity. . . .

George Kennan commenting in 1967, during the Vietnam War, on the so-called containment doctrine that grew from his article in Foreign Affairs *(July 1947) and became the basis of U.S. cold war policy, in Kennan,* Memoirs: 1925–1950 *(1967), pp. 354–60.*

First of all, I would like to define what we mean by propaganda. We have all been talking about it, but nobody has stated just what they mean by propaganda. Now, I use the term to mean that Communist propaganda is anything which gives a good impression of Communism as a way of life. Anything that sells people the idea that life in Russia is good and that people are free and happy would be Communist propaganda. Am I not correct? Now, here is what the picture *Song of Russia* [1943] contains. It starts with an American conductor . . giving a concert in America for Russian war relief. He starts playing the American national anthem and the national anthem dissolves into a Russian mob, with the sickle and hammer on a red flag very prominent above their heads. I am sorry, but that made me sick. That is something which I do not see how native Americans permit, and I am only a naturalized American. . . . It suggests literally and technically that it is quite all right for the American national anthem to dissolve into the Soviet. . . . It really was symbolically intended, and it worked out that way.

Russian émigré writer Ayn Rand testifying before the House Un-American Activities Committee on October 20, 1947, about communist propaganda in Hollywood films, in Eric Bentley, ed., Thirty Years of Treason *(1971), p. 112.*

Well, sir, ninety-nine percent of us are pretty well aware of what is going on, and I think, within the bounds of our democratic rights . . . we have done a pretty good job in our business of keeping those people's [communists] activities curtailed. After all, we must recognize them at present as a political party. On that basis we have exposed their lies when we came across them, we have opposed their propaganda, and I can certainly testify that in the case of the Screen Actors Guild we have been eminently successful in preventing them from, with their usual tactics, trying to run a majority of an organization from a well-organized minority. In opposing those people, the best thing to do is make democracy work.

Ronald Reagan, then president of the Screen Actors Guild, testifying before the House Un-American Activities Committee on October 23, 1947, in Eric Bentley, ed., Thirty Years of Treason *(1971), p. 146.*

Let us at least be as brave as the people we write about.

Screenwriter Sam Ornitz in conversation with other members of the Hollywood Ten before appearing before the House Un-American Activities Committee in late October 1947, in Victor Navasky, Naming Names *(1980), p. 81.*

MR. LAWSON: Mr. Chairman, I have a statement here which I wish to make—

THE CHAIRMAN: Well, all right, let me see your statement.

(*Statement handed to the Chairman.*)

THE CHAIRMAN: I don't care to read any more of the statement. The statement will not be read. I read the first line.

MR. LAWSON: You have spent one week vilifying me before the American public—

THE CHAIRMAN: Just a minute—

MR. LAWSON: —and you refuse to allow me to make a statement on my rights as an American citizen.

THE CHAIRMAN: I refuse to let you make the statement because of the first sentence. That statement is not pertinent to the inquiry. Now, this is a Congressional Committee set up by law. We must have orderly procedure, and we are going to have orderly procedure. Mr. Stripling, identify the witness.

MR. LAWSON: The rights of American citizens are important in this room here, and I intend to stand up for those rights, Congressman Thomas.

MR. STRIPLING: Mr. Lawson, will you state your full name, please?

MR. LAWSON: I wish to protest against the unwillingness of this Committee to read a statement, when you permitted Mr. Warner, Mr. Mayer, and others to read statements in this room.

Exchange between Chairman J. Parnell Thomas of the House Un-American Activities Committee and Hollywood Ten member John Howard Lawson on October 27, 1947, in Eric Bentley, ed., Thirty Years of Treason *(1971), pp. 153–54.*

I could answer exactly the way you want, Mr. Chairman . . . but if I did, I would hate myself in the morning.

Testimony of Hollywood Ten member Ring Lardner, Jr., before the House Un-American Activities Committee on October 30, 1947, in Eric Bentley, ed., Thirty Years of Treason *(1971), p. 189.*

I felt the Committee acted with absolute banality, the producers acted cowardly, but the Ten acted stupidly—they were trying by their hysterical acting to get the Committee to admit error. They should have quietly but firmly refused to cooperate with the Committee and then held a dignified press conference where they said eight of us are communists, but all of us are Americans and patriots, and the public and the press would have backed them one hundred percent.

Observations by RKO executive Dore Schary, who on November 26, 1947, was tasked with informing the Screen Writers Guild of the decision by the Motion Picture Association of America to refuse employment within the industry to all communists and other subversives, in Victor Navasky, Naming Names *(1980), pp. 83–84.*

On a fifty-five acre tract overlooking the site of the World's Fair of 1939, the country's largest veterans' cooperative apartment community will soon begin to take form, it became known last night.

The new Queens housing center . . . will be for occupancy exclusively by veterans and their families on a tenant-landlord basis. . . . Each building will have its own garage facilities, to be rented separately, for tenants' automobiles.

In furtherance of the plan to create a self-contained community, builders will erect shopping centers at the edges of the property. . . .

Lee E. Cooper, "Vast GI Housing to Rise Near Site of World's Fair," Article describing housing projects for World War II veterans, in New York Times *(November 30, 1947), p. 1.*

I am sure that you must have reservations about the script. I will try to clarify my intentions in this play. I think its best quality is its authenticity or its fidelity to life. There are no "good" or "bad" people. Some are a little better or a little worse, but all are activated more by misunderstanding than malice. A blindness to what is going on in each other's hearts. Stanley sees Blanche not as a desperate, driven creature backed into a corner to make a last desperate stand—but as a calculating bitch with round heels. . . . Nobody sees anybody truly but all through the flaws of their own egos. That is the way we all see each other in life. Vanity, fear, desire, competition . . condition our vision of those in relation to us. Add to those distortions in our *own* egos . . . and you see how cloudy the glass must become through which we look at each other. That's how it is in all living relationships except when there is that rare case of two people who love intensely enough to burn through all those layers of opacity and see each other's naked hearts.

Playwright Tennessee Williams in a letter to Elia Kazan trying to convince Kazan to direct A Streetcar Named Desire *in fall 1947, in* Elia Kazan, A Life *(1988), p. 329.*

When Marlon Brando threw open the door and came into the office, the whole staff went mad. Actually he was younger than the script called for, but one could tell very early on that he had a special dynamism. He didn't come in to read, just to talk; Kazan much preferred having conversations with actors. After, he sent Brando up to Provincetown to read for Tennessee [Williams], but en route Marlon disappeared for two days before he finally showed up. Nobody ever found out where he had been.

Irving Schneider, production manager of A Streetcar Named Desire, *describing the first time he met Marlon Brando, in fall 1947, in Myrna Katz Frommer and Harvey Frommer,* It Happened on Broadway *(1998), p. 68.*

Hollywood rallies to support the Hollywood Ten. *In the front row, from left to right:* Richard Conte, June Havoc, Humphrey Bogart, Lauren Bacall, Evelyn Keyes, Danny Kaye, and Jane Wyatt. *(Photofest)*

There was an electrical charge and almost an animal scent he projected over the footlights that made it impossible for the audience to think or watch the other performers on stage. All you could do was feel, the sexual arousal was so complete. I don't believe this quality can be learned it's just there, primitive and compelling. The only other time I experienced it was when I saw Elvis Presley perform live in Las Vegas.

Actress Shelley Winters describing Marlon Brando in an early performance of A Streetcar Named Desire, *which opened on Broadway on December 1, 1947, in David Downing,* Marlon Brando *(1984), p. 22.*

My recent trip to Washington, where I appeared with a group of motion-picture people, has become the subject of such confused and erroneous interpretations that I feel the situation should be clarified.

I am not a Communist.

I am not a Communist sympathizer.

I detest Communism just as any other decent American does....

I went to Washington because I thought fellow Americans were being deprived of their constitutional rights, and for that reason alone.

That trip was ill-advised, even foolish, I am very ready to admit. At the time it seemed like the thing to do....

I am an American.

And very likely, like a good many of the rest of you, sometimes a foolish and impetuous American.

Film star Humphrey Bogart in an open letter to newspaper columnist George Sokolsky apologizing for his support for the Hollywood Ten in October 1947 (Sokolsky published the letter in the New York Daily Mirror *on December 6, 1947, along with his own sentiment that Bogart's apology did not go far enough, as Bogart did not identify the organizers of the trip to Washington in support of the Ten), in Victor Navasky,* Naming Names *(1980), p. 153.*

1948

Air Power is Peace Power—Lockheed

A 1948 advertisement for Lockheed aircraft, in Lois Gordon and Alan Gordon, American Chronicle *(1999), p. 455.*

Those who do not believe in the ideology of the United States shall not be allowed to stay in the United States.

Attorney General Tom Clark declaring in 1948 his position on admission of aliens to the United States, in Stephen J. Whitfield, The Culture of the Cold War *(1996), p. 53.*

"Have you ever wondered, Robert, why we're fighting this war [World War II]?"...

"With all the contradictions, I suppose there's an objective right on our side. That is, in Europe. Over here . . it's an imperialist tossup. Either we louse up Asia or Japan does. I imagine our methods will be a little less drastic.... There's an osmosis in war, call it what you will, but the victors always tend to assume the ... trappings of the loser. We might easily go Fascist after we win...."

Cummings sat back, enjoying himself.... "I like to call it a process of historical energy. There are countries which have latent powers, latent resources, they are full of potential energy, so to speak. And there are great concepts which can unlock that, express it. As kinetic energy a country is organization, co-ordinated effort, your epithet, fascism.... Historically, the purpose of this war is to translate America's potential into kinetic energy. . . . As you put it, Robert, not too badly, there's a process of osmosis. America is going to absorb that dream, it's in the business of doing it now. When you've created materials, armies, they don't wither of their own accord. Our vacuum as a nation is filled with released power, and I can tell you that we're out of the backwaters of history now.... For the past century the entire historical process has been working toward greater consolidation of power.... Your men of power in America . . . are becoming conscious of their real aims for the first time in our history. Watch. After the war our foreign policy is going to be far more naked, far less hypocritical than it has ever been. We're no longer going to cover our eyes with our left hand while our right is extending an imperialist paw."

Conversation between the conservative General Cummings and his liberal aide, Lieutenant Hearn in Norman Mailer's first novel, The Naked and the Dead, *(1948), pp. 321–22.*

We moved into our first house on Memorial Day weekend, 1948. Our daughter wasn't even a year old.

Norman Mailer published his first novel, *The Naked and the Dead,* in 1948. *(Photofest)*

The two-bedroom, one-bath house was located just outside the city of West Miami, near the corner of S.W. 62 Avenue and 25th Street. Now West Miami lies smack in the middle of Greater Miami, but then it was, indeed, the western boundary. We were literally at the edge of the Everglades, as there was virtually no housing development beyond us. It wasn't uncommon to see egrets, herons, red-winged blackbirds, and other creatures from the Glades.

Four miles south of us, North Kendall Drive was in the process of being built, and it led to nowhere but the swamp. Today, western Miami-Dade County is one of the most densely populated parts of the region, and Kendall Drive is a multi-lane highway that crawls with rush-hour traffic as far west as Krome Avenue, which is more than ten miles west of our old house.

Comparing the life style we lived then with today's frantic pace, especially for the women, it was a relatively easy life, although it didn't always seem so at the time. We had no soccer matches to schlepp the kids to, no tennis tournaments. No football or base-

ball leagues, although towards the end of the decade I coached my son's little league baseball team at the neighborhood recreational park. Maybe once or twice a week we would go downtown to the Olympia Theater to see a movie. Occasionally we would take the kids to a restaurant for supper. Looking back, the '50s were a remarkably pleasant time.

> *Advertising executive Robert I. Schwartz recalling his first house in Greater Miami, which he occupied in May 1948, in private correspondence with the author, September 30, 2001.*

For a number of years I had myself served in the [Communist Party] underground, chiefly in Washington, D.C. . . . I knew it at its top level, a group of seven or so men, from among whom in later years certain members of Miss [Elizabeth] Bentley's organization were apparently recruited. The head of the underground group at the time I knew it was Nathan Witt, an attorney for the National Labor Relations Board. . . . Lee Pressman was also a member of this group, as was Alger Hiss, who as a member of the State Department, later organized the conference at Dumbarton Oaks, San Francisco [that established the United Nations], and the United States side of the Yalta Conference.

> *Whittaker Chambers's first accusation of Alger Hiss being a communist, made in testimony before the House Un-American Activities Committee on August 3, 1948, in Allen Weinstein,* Perjury: The Hiss-Chambers Case *(1978), p. 5.*

The main difficulty with the South is that they are living eighty years behind the times and the sooner they come out of it the better it will be for the country and themselves. I am not asking for social equality, because no such things exist, but I am asking for equality of opportunity for all human beings, and, as long as I stay here, I am going to continue that fight. When the mob gangs can take four people out and shoot them in the back, and everybody in the [surrounding] country is acquainted with who did the shooting and nothing is done about it, that country is in a pretty bad fix from the law enforcement standpoint.

When a mayor and a City Marshal can take a negro Sergeant off a bus in South Carolina, beat him up and put out one of his eyes, and nothing is done about it by the State Authorities, something is radically wrong with the system.

On the Louisiana and Arkansas Railway when coal burning locomotives were used, the Negro firemen were the thing because it was a back-breaking job and a dirty one. As soon as they turned to oil as a fuel it became customary for people to take shots at Negro firemen and a number were murdered because it was thought that this was now a white collar job and should go to a white man. I can't approve of such goings on and I shall never approve of it, as long as I am here. . . . I am going to try to remedy it and if that ends up in my failure to be reelected, that failure will be in a good cause. . . .

President Harry S. Truman in a letter written on August 18, 1948, to his friend Ernest W. Roberts, in David McCullough, Truman *(1992), p. 589.*

I didn't like whites walking into the club where we were playing just to see Bird [Charlie Parker] act a fool, thinking that he might do something stupid, anything for a laugh. . . . It was embarrassing.

Jazz performer Miles Davis commenting in late 1948 on his performances with Charlie "Bird" Parker, in Mervyn Cooke, The Chronicle of Jazz *(1997), p. 137.*

1949

I dreamed I went shopping in my Maidenform bra.

A 1949 advertisement for Maidenform bras, in Lois Gordon and Alan Gordon, American Chronicle *(1999), p. 464.*

Psychologists observe increasing difficulties of sexual abstinence for those who have not trained themselves in self-control and filled their lives with absorbing purposes and activities to the exclusion of sexual experience. . . . Marriage is better late than never. But early marriage gives more opportunity for happy comradeship, mutual development and physical adjustment, for having and training children, building a home, promoting family life as a community asset, and observing one's grandchildren start their careers.

Excerpt from William F. Snow's article "Marriage and Parenthood" (1949), in Lary May, ed., Recasting America: Culture and Politics in the Age of the Cold War *(1989), p. 158.*

The essential act of war is destruction, not necessarily of human lives, but of the products of human labor. War is a way of shattering to pieces, of pouring into the stratosphere, or sinking in the depths of the sea, materials which might otherwise be used to make the masses too comfortable, and hence, in the long run, too intelligent. Even when weapons of war are not actually destroyed, their manufacture is still a convenient way of expending labor power without producing anything that can be consumed.

From George Orwell's anticommunist novel 1984, *in Orwell,* 1984 *(1949), p. 157.*

The Party seeks power entirely for its own sake. We are not interested in the good of others; we are interested solely in power. Not wealth or luxury or long life or happiness, only power, pure power. . . . We are different from all the oligarchies of the past in that we know what we are doing. All the others, even those who resembled ourselves, were cowards and hypocrites. The German Nazis and the Russian Communists came very close to us in their methods, but they never had the courage to recognize their own motives. They pretended, perhaps they even believed, that they had seized power unwillingly and for a limited time, and that just round the corner there lay a paradise where human beings would be free and equal. We are not like that. We know that no one ever seizes power with the intention of relinquishing it. Power is not a means; it is an end.

Opposition leader Goldstein's views on power in George Orwell, 1984 *(1949), p. 217.*

In some crude sense, which no vulgarity, no humor, no overstatement can quite extinguish, the physicists have known sin, and this is a knowledge which they cannot lose.

Robert Oppenheimer, "Father of the Atomic Bomb," discussing the atom bomb in 1949, in Lois Gordon and Alan Gordon, American Chronicle *(1999), p. 464.*

But here was somebody named Nelson Algren writing about Division Street and Milwaukee Avenue, and the dope heads and boozers and card hustlers. The kind of broken people Algren liked to describe as responding to the city's brawny slogan of "I Will" with a painful: "But What If I Can't?"

Newspaper columnist Mike Royko describing in 1981 Nelson Algren's The Man with the Golden Arm, *which was first published in 1949, in William J. Savage and Daniel Simon, eds.,* The Man with the Golden Arm/Nelson Algren: 50th Anniversary Critical Edition *(1999), p. 363.*

The only link . . . between these six very different personalities [Arthur Koestler, Richard Wright, Louis Fisher, Ignazio Silone, Andre Gide, and Stephen Spender] is that all of them—after tortured struggles of conscience—chose Communism because they had lost faith in democracy and were willing to sacrifice "bourgeois liberties" in order to defeat Fascism. Their conversion, in fact, was rooted in despair—a despair of Western values. . . . That Communism, as a way of life, should . . . have captured the profoundly Christian personality of Silone and attracted individualists such as Gide and Koestler, reveals a dreadful deficiency in European democracy. That Richard Wright, as a struggling Negro writer in Chicago, moved almost as a matter of course into the Communist Party, is in itself an indictment of the American way of life. . . .

The intellectual attraction of Marxism was that it exploded liberal fallacies—which really were fallacies. It taught the bitter truth that progress is not automatic, that boom and slump are inherent in capitalism, that social injustice and racial discrimination are not cured merely by the passage of time, and that power politics cannot be "abolished," but only used for good or bad ends. . . . The choice seemed to lie between an extreme Right, determined to use power in order to crush human freedom, and a Left which seemed eager to use it in order to free humanity. . . .

The strength of the Catholic Church has always been that it demands the sacrifice of [spiritual] freedom uncompromisingly, and condemns spiritual pride as a deadly sin. The Communist novice . . felt something of the release which Catholicism also brings to the intellectual. . . . To deny the truth is an act of service. . . . Any genuine intellectual contact which you have with [a communist] involves a challenge to his fundamental faith, a struggle for his soul.

Richard Crossman in the introduction to his collection of essays by former communists, in Crossman, ed., The God That Failed *(1949), pp. 1–5.*

Arthur Miller tapped into something so true about American culture, about the ruthlessness of capitalism, about how people delude themselves into thinking they're part of the American dream. There are lines in the play that give me the chills even today. Like when the owner of the firm tells Willy he has a tape recorder at home, and when he and his family go out on Sunday nights and can't listen to Jack Benny, they just turn the tape recorder on, and when they get home, they listen to him and have a good laugh. And Willy is kissing his ass. . . . Or later, when Willy tells his neighbor Charlie, "Your son, he didn't even say he was going to the Supreme Court to argue a case." And Charlie says, "He didn't have to."

Producer Paul Libin describing Arthur Miller's Death of a Salesman, *which opened on February 10, 1949, in Myrna Katz Frommer and Harvey Frommer,* It Happened on Broadway *(1998), p. 76.*

Arthur Miller has written a superb drama. From every point of view, *Death of a Salesman* . . . is rich and memorable drama. . . . For Mr. Miller has looked with compassion into the hearts of some ordinary Americans and quietly transferred their hope and anguish into theatre. Under Elia Kazan's direction, Lee J. Cobb gives a heroic performance, and every member of the cast plays like a person inspired.

Critic Brooks Atkinson reviewing Arthur Miller's play Death of a Salesman, *in Atkinson, "Death of a Salesman,"* New York Times, *February 11, 1949, p. 27.*

Among modern intellectuals—especially in the universities—the subject of religion seems to have gone into hiding. Is it because the educated portion of mankind is learning to live with less finality and is coming to distrust embracing formulae of all types? Or is it because in their zeal to liquidate pseudo-knowledge and to discover truth in a piecemeal fashion the universities have found it necessary quietly to adopt a thoroughgoing secularism? Whatever the reason may be, the persistence of religion in the modern world appears as an embarrassment to the scholars of today. . . .

During the past fifty years religion and sex seem to have reversed their positions. Writing in the Victorian age William James could bring himself to devote barely two pages to the role of sex in human life which he labeled euphemistically the "instinct of love." Yet no taboos held him back from directing the torrent of his genius into the *Varieties of Religious Experience.* On religion he spoke freely and with unexcelled brilliance. Today, by contrast, psychologists write with the frankness of Freud or Kinsey on the sexual passions of mankind, but blush and grow silent when the religious passions come into view. Scarcely any modern textbook writers in psychology devote as much as two shamefaced pages to the subject—even though religion, like sex, is an almost universal interest of the human race. . . .

The argument of this chapter is that the subjective (personal) religious sentiments of mankind—whatever the fate of institutional religion may be—are very much alive and will perhaps always remain alive, for their roots are many and deep.

Gordon W. Allport, professor of psychology at Harvard University, in his Merrick Lectures at Ohio Wesleyan University in spring 1949, in Allport, The Individual and His Religion *(1950), pp. 1–3.*

[The reduced rate of child bearing by "talented" American women] undoubtedly has to do with the so-called "emancipation" of women. Every field is open to women today, and every year thousands of women leave our colleges and universities determined to make careers for themselves. They often marry, but find reasons to postpone having children. . . . Women who lead very active lives, under conditions of nervous stress and strain, often do not conceive, and when they do, they miscarry. These women are violating their own biological natures; and for this they pay a heavy price. . . . The feminist movement was an attempt to break into a "man's world"—and in the process, through envy, accepted to an alarming extent the values of men.

Dorothy Thompson voicing her objections to women's liberation, in Thompson, "Race Suicide of the Intelligent," Ladies Home Journal *(May 1949), p. 11.*

My last weeks abroad were spent in these countries to the east, Czechoslovakia, Poland, and finally the Soviet Union. Here thousands of people—men, women, children—cried to me to thank progressive America for sending one of its representatives, begged me so to take back their love, their heartfelt understanding of the suffering of their Negro brothers and sisters, that I wept time and time again. . . .

They want peace and an abundant life. Freedom is already theirs. . . .

I love this Soviet people more than any other nation, because of their suffering and sacrifices for us, the Negro people, the progressive people, the people of the future in this world.

At the Paris Peace Conference, I said it was unthinkable that the Negro people of America or elsewhere in the world could be drawn into war with the Soviet Union. I repeat it with a hundredfold emphasis. They will not. . . .

Now these peoples of the Soviet Union, of the new eastern democracies, of progressive western Europe, and the representatives of the Chinese people whom I met in Prague and Moscow, were in great part communists. They were the first to die for our freedom and for the freedom of all mankind [during World War II]. So I'm not afraid of communists. No, far from that. I will defend them as they defended us, the Negro people. . . .

But to fulfill our responsibilities as Americans, we must unite, especially we Negro people. We must know our strength. We are the decisive force. That's why they terrorize us. That's why they fear us. And if we unite in all our might, this world can fast be changed. Let us create that unity now. . . .

If we unite, we'll get our law against lynching, our right to vote and to labor. Let us march on Washington, representing 14 million strong. Let us push aside the sycophants who tell us to be quiet. . . .

Let this be a final answer to the warmongers. Let them know that we will not help to enslave our brothers and sisters and eventually ourselves. Rather, we will help to insure peace in our time, the freedom and liberation of the Negro and other struggling peoples, and the building of a world where we can all walk in full equality and full human dignity.

Actor, singer, and athlete Paul Robeson speaking at a welcome-home rally in New York City on June 19, 1949, in Robert Torricelli and Andrew Carroll, eds., In Our Own Words *(1999), pp. 166–69.*

I've been asked to express my views on Paul Robeson's statement in Paris to the effect that American Negroes would refuse to fight in any war against Russia because we love Russia so much. I haven't any comment to make except that the statement, if Mr. Robeson actually made it, sounds very silly to me. But he has a right to his personal views, and if he wants to sound silly when he expresses them in public, that's his business and not mine. He's still a famous ex-athlete and a great singer and actor.

I understand that there are some few Negroes who are members of the Communist Party, and in event of war with Russia, they would probably act just as any other Communists would. So would members of other minority and majority groups. There are some colored pacifists, and they'd act just like pacifists of any color. And most Negroes—and Italians and Irish and Jews and Swedes and Slavs and other Americans—would act just as all these groups did in the last war: They'd do their best to help their country stay out of war. If unsuccessful, they'd do their best to help their country win the war—against Russia or any other enemy that threatened us.

This isn't said as any defense of the Negro's loyalty, because any loyalty that needs defense can't amount to much in the long run. And no one has ever questioned my race's loyalty except a few people who don't amount to very much.

What I'm trying to get across is that the American public is off on the wrong foot when it begins to think of radicalism in terms of any special minority group.

Baseball star Jackie Robinson testifying before the House Un-American Activities Committee on June 19, 1949, in Robert Torricelli and Andrew Carroll, eds., In Our Own Words (1999), pp. 169–70.

I am not going to permit the issue to boil down to a personal feud between myself and Jackie. To do that would be to do exactly what the other group wants us to do. . . . The committee's efforts to make the loyalty of the Negro people an issue is an insult. How do they dare question our loyalty? I challenge the loyalty of the Un-American Activities Committee.

Paul Robeson at a news conference on July 20, 1949, in Robert Torricelli and Andrew Carroll, eds., In Our Own Words (1999), p. 170.

I believe the American people to the fullest extent consistent with the national security are entitled to be informed of all developments in the field of atomic energy. That is my reason for making public the following information.

We have evidence that within recent weeks an atomic explosion occurred in the U.S.S.R.

Ever since atomic energy was first released by man, the eventual development of this new force by other nations was to be expected. This probability has always been taken into account by us.

Nearly four years ago I pointed out that "scientific opinion appears to be practically unanimous that the essential theoretical knowledge upon which the discovery is based is already widely known. There is also substantial agreement that foreign research can come abreast of our present theoretical knowledge in time." And, in the three-nation declaration of the President of the United States and the Prime Ministers of the United Kingdom and of Canada, dated November 15, 1945, it was emphasized that no single nation could, in fact, have a monopoly of atomic weapons.

This recent development emphasizes once again, if indeed such emphasis were needed, the necessity for that truly effective and enforceable international control of atomic energy which this Government and the large majority of the members of the United Nations support.

President Harry S. Truman announcing on September 23, 1949, that the Soviet Union exploded an atomic bomb, in "Truman Statement on Atom," New York Times (September 24, 1949), p. 1.

God is giving us a desperate choice, a choice of either revival or judgment. There is no alternative! . . . The world is divided into two camps! On the one side we see Communism . . . [which] has declared war against God, against Christ, against the Bible. . . . Unless the Western world has an old-fashioned revival, we cannot last.

Evangelical minister Billy Graham in a Protestant revival meeting in Los Angeles on September 25, 1949, in Stephen J. Whitfield, The Culture of the Cold War (1996), p. 77.

2

America Becomes the World's Policeman
1950

Of the people who towered over the American landscape at the beginning of the decade, perhaps physicist Albert Einstein reflected the social, political, and intellectual currents of the time most fully. Although he had completed his monumental work on special relativity 45 years earlier, along with other work critical to the development of quantum theory, Einstein captured the public imagination in 1950 in part because he embodied many of the key conflicts, hopes, and paradoxes then present in American society. A pacifist, he signed the 1939 letter that convinced President Franklin D. Roosevelt to develop the atomic bomb, yet he was excluded from the Manhattan Project to develop the A-bomb because FBI director J. Edgar Hoover regarded him a security risk for political reasons. At a time when Americans were embracing Christianity as a bulwark against communism and were increasingly distrustful of liberal intellectuals (labeled "eggheads" during the 1952 presidential campaign), this left-leaning Jew who had rejected invitations to reside in the Soviet Union was adored by millions, even while the FBI secretly investigated flimsy and unsubstantiated accusations of past communist activity. For many Americans in the 1950s, science promised a brighter future filled not only with hitherto unimaginable opportunities for better, easier lives but also with prospects for greater national security. After all, radar, sonar, cryptography, and, of course, the atomic bomb had played crucial roles in defeating the Axis powers, and Einstein stood out to the public as the quintessential scientist. At the same time, President Harry S. Truman's Fair Deal carried forth the broad agenda of Roosevelt's New Deal, and Einstein's outspokenness in favor of human rights, world government, and racial equality appealed to those who supported these liberal sentiments.

In an era of growing demagoguery and fractious partisan politics, Einstein appeared as a kindly, grandfatherly figure who spoke in the measured voice of wisdom and reason. The film industry solidified this image as they tapped into the country's developing interest in outer space. Clearly based on Einstein, the benevolent, child-loving Professor Barnhardt in *The Day the Earth Stood Still* (1951) saves the Earth by assembling an international committee of scientists who steer humanity to peace and nuclear disarmament

Albert Einstein was one of the most popular and least understood figures of the decade. *(Photofest)*

after the world's bickering political leaders are unable to agree even on a meeting place where they may listen to the advanced being from another planet.

One of the first of several 1950s films to play out cold war anxieties through science fiction—and one of the few to do so from an overtly pacifist point of view—*The Day the Earth Stood Still* offered an element of wish fulfillment to audiences who were becoming increasingly fearful that only divine intervention or some extraordinary intrusion by well-intended extraterrestrials could break the superpower stalemate and halt their seemingly inexorable progress toward nuclear war. Indeed, just mid-year through 1950, U.S. soldiers had already been dispatched to fight communists on the other side of the world, and Wisconsin senator Joseph McCarthy began raising the specter of communist subversion at home. Bad news from the war front, fears of the "red menace" and/or right-wing demagoguery at home, and an economy hobbled by the demands of a new war effort converged to cast a pall over the beginning of the second half of the century.

THE COLD WAR AND INTERNATIONAL POLITICS

The Korean War

The dominant event of 1950 was the beginning of the Korean War, which was the only cold war military action in which American troops ever faced a major communist power—China. In fact, the Korean and Vietnam Wars were the only prolonged cold war conflicts in which the United States, Canada, and their European allies fought directly against communist combat forces.

Japan had occupied Korea since 1905, and at the Cairo Conference during World War II, the United States, Great Britain, and China promised Korean independence. After the war, the country was provisionally partitioned at the 38th parallel into a U.S.-controlled southern zone and a Soviet-controlled northern zone, with the understanding that national elections would eventually unify the country; however, the Soviets thwarted UN efforts to hold elections, and in 1948, two separate republics were established. North Korea's leader, Kim Il Sung, pledged to unite them again under communist rule.

On June 25, 1950, North Korea launched a sneak attack against South Korea. Within three days, the Soviet-equipped North Korean army had captured Seoul, South Korea's capital. The Soviets were at the time boycotting the UN Security Council due to its refusal to seat the newly formed, communist People's Republic of China, and in the Soviets' absence the international organization voted to intervene militarily on behalf of South Korea. The "police action," as Truman labeled it, in part to avoid asking Congress to declare war, was led by the United States, which furnished most of the soldiers. The UN force also included limited troops from 15 other countries, among them Canada, Britain, Greece, Turkey, and many other NATO nations.

The first U.S. troops arrived on July 1, 1950, although U.S. air strikes had occurred as early as June 28. On July 8, Douglas MacArthur, a highly respected five-star army general and World War II hero, assumed command of the UN forces. Fighting in inhospitable, mountainous terrain, underequipped, lacking tanks and armor, and routinely outnumbered by three to one (and often as much as 10 to one or even 20 to one), the UN allies suffered a string of demoralizing defeats in the intense summer heat and monsoons. American troops were further frustrated by their inability to easily distinguish North Koreans from South Koreans or even soldiers from civilians, as North Korean troops would sometimes change into peasant clothing and infiltrate bands of retreating refugees heading south, behind allied lines. This confusion produced numerous civilian casualties, and in recent years evidence has surfaced indicating that some U.S. troops committed atrocities against civilians in isolated instances during the war, notably near the hamlet of No Gun Ri, where a U.S. investigation in 2000 found that retreating U.S. soldiers were responsible for killing an unknown number of refugees, perhaps as many as 400. Moreover, the brutality against civilians by both the North Korean army and South Korean police force was notorious.

By the beginning of August, the allies had fallen back behind the Naktong River and established a final line of defense in the Pusan region at the southeast tip of the peninsula. Throughout the summer, there was genuine concern that the UN forces might be driven from the peninsula. But on September 15, with Truman's explicit approval, MacArthur launched a dangerous, surprise U.S. landing at Inchon on the west coast. At the same time, the Eighth Army broke out from its defensive position in Pusan, on the east, and caught the North Korean forces in a pincer movement that forced a dramatic North Korean retreat and completely reversed the fortunes of the war.

There was some initial debate over whether the UN forces should cross the 38th parallel into North Korea and attempt to destroy the enemy army and depose the communist regime, as such action was not authorized by the UN mandate to protect South Korea. Moreover, expanding the fighting into North

Korea would create a new objective for the war and increase the risk of direct Chinese or Soviet intervention. Truman was especially concerned that the Korean conflict might erupt into a major war encompassing all of Asia, or even into a third world war, so he strove to contain the fighting within Korea. But upon receiving reassurances from his advisers that the Soviets and Chinese would not intervene if the UN forces crossed into the north, Truman discounted a warning from Chinese premier Zhou Enlai and, on September 27, authorized MacArthur to invade North Korea with the new objective of destroying its armed forces. His decision became official policy on October 7, when the UN General Assembly overwhelmingly approved the course of action. Two days later, MacArthur announced that his troops had crossed the border.

On October 15, Truman flew to Wake Island to confer personally with MacArthur, who foresaw a very optimistic outcome. The general predicted that North Korea's capital, Pyongyang, would fall within a week, formal resistance would end by Thanksgiving, the Eighth Army would be able to return to Japan by Christmas, the United Nations would conduct elections in Korea shortly after the new year, and a full American troop withdrawal would follow soon thereafter. Both men agreed that a military occupation was undesirable. Truman expressed his conviction that the war must not expand beyond Korea, but MacArthur assured him that neither the Chinese nor the Soviets would intervene, and that if the Chinese did join the war, U.S. air superiority would render them ineffective.

Within two and a half weeks after they crossed into North Korea, the allies captured Pyongyang and reached the Chinese frontier at the Yalu River. On October 21, even as the UN forces approached the border, the Chinese invaded Tibet. Then, in late November, after Truman granted MacArthur's request to bomb the Korean side of the bridges spanning the Yalu but expressly forbade the general to widen the war or attack Chinese territory, a Chinese army of some 260,000 soldiers crossed the river and entered the war. Within three days, it drove the allies from the region and compelled the United States and its UN allies once more to reformulate their wartime objectives. No longer committed to deposing Kim Il Sung and reuniting Korea under a noncommunist regime, they returned to their more modest initial goal of protecting South Korea's sovereignty and keeping the communist forces behind the 38th parallel.

Faced with an entirely new set of battle conditions, MacArthur requested large numbers of reinforcements. The general also requested that Nationalist China, a source of controversy between Truman and MacArthur, be allowed to enter the war. MacArthur further called for a naval blockade of China and authority to bomb the Chinese mainland. He warned that unless he was permitted to expand the war into China, the allies faced a disaster in Korea. But on November 28, while the allied forces were being routed, the National Security Council reiterated its position that the war must not expand beyond Korea—a position that Truman still maintained. Fearing Soviet intervention if the United States attacked China, and the subsequent possibility of a major military confrontation between the superpowers, Truman ordered MacArthur not to expand the war. The conflict between the president and his general would escalate into a full-blown crisis in April 1951, but at the time Truman did not want to humiliate the front-line commander who had performed so brilliantly at Inchon. For that reason and despite MacArthur's public statements undermining Truman's policy of limited war, lack of success on the battlefield, and apparent unwillingness to obey orders that displeased him, Truman resisted calls by some of his top advisers to relieve the general of his command.

On November 30, however, while answering questions at a press conference, Truman did threaten to use the atomic bomb in Korea, if it was deemed necessary to stop the Chinese from achieving victory. Although the president did not mention it to the press, MacArthur wanted authorization to drop 30 to 50 atomic bombs in Manchuria and other cities in mainland China, but Truman, committed to restricting the war to Korea, denied him. Regardless of the nuclear threat, Chinese troops crossed into South Korea the day before Christmas, and in early January 1951, the communists recaptured Seoul.

The Korean War was America's first major military adventure as a world superpower, and unlike World Wars I and II, it was fought primarily for geopolitical and strategic reasons, not as a matter of imminent national security or as a compelling moral crusade. As such, it was highly unpopular among large segments of the American public, which in 1950 had little familiarity with Korea, felt no special allegiance to South Korea, and found no reason to intervene in another country's civil war. In this respect, the Korean conflict anticipated the divisive Vietnam War.

Furthermore, the adverse fortunes of the allies opened the new half century on a pessimistic note for many Americans. After almost three months of continuous defeat, MacArthur's September landing at Inchon raised the nation's spirits, but the military reversals following the Chinese intervention sent them plummeting again. Also, although such vocal anticommunists as Senator McCarthy reluctantly supported the war against communism, they vilified the State Department and Secretary of State Dean Acheson for policies that made the country vulnerable to the communist aggression. They also attacked the Truman administration for the military's inadequate preparation and supply of weapons. McCarthy's insistence that American combat troops were suffering because of the machinations of communist infiltrators within the U.S. government contributed to the malaise that concluded the year, as did the prospect of a prolonged war with limited objectives and no end in sight.

Other Cold War Developments Abroad

Although the Korean War dominated international cold war politics, other significant developments also occurred in 1950. Perhaps the most important came on January 31, when Truman authorized development of the hydrogen bomb, a weapon that would be a thousand times more powerful than the atomic bomb used to destroy Hiroshima at the end of World War II. That month, despite Republican calls for military assistance and greater economic aid, Truman refused to increase the level of U.S. support to the Chinese Nationalists in their ongoing battle against Mao Zedong's communists. Yet the administration also criticized Britain for recognizing the People's Republic of China, which Mao had declared on October 1, 1949, after driving the Nationalists from the mainland to the island of Taiwan. Secretary of State Acheson subsequently removed U.S. official personnel from mainland China following the seizure of the U.S. consulate by Chinese communists in mid-January. In February, Mao and Stalin signed a 30-year mutual-aid-and-friendship pact between China and the Soviet Union.

The roots of the Vietnam War also predate 1950, and the struggle between the governments of North and South Vietnam began in earnest that year, too. Ho Chi Minh, a communist nationalist who led an anti-French insurgent group called the Vietminh, had established the Democratic Republic of Vietnam (North Vietnam) in Hanoi in 1946 and that same year signed an agreement in which France recognized Vietnam as a free state within the French Union and in which Ho permitted the presence of 25,000 French troops in the country for five years. Final confirmation of the agreement was never made, however, and in 1949, France established a rival government in South Vietnam under the leadership of Bao Dai, a pro-French leader based in Saigon. Under the agreement, Vietnam was to become an associate state within the French Union, but France would retain control of the country's defense and finances. (In 1950, France also recognized the independence of Laos and Cambodia.) In January 1950, Ho Chi Minh declared that his government was the sole legitimate government of Vietnam. The United States and Great Britain recognized the regime of Bao Dai, but the Soviets and Chinese recognized Ho's government. A civil war ensued in which the Chinese- and Soviet-backed Vietminh sought to drive out the French and unify the country under the rule of Ho. In July, the United States appropriated $15 million in military assistance for the French effort to defeat the communists. The dispute over which government properly represented the Vietnamese people and North Vietnam's commitment to uniting the territory under a single, communist government remained at the core of the conflict until North Vietnam prevailed in 1975.

In the Middle East, Jordan annexed the West Bank in Arab Palestine territory, thereby removing a significant portion of the Palestinian homeland designated by the 1948 UN agreement that created the state of Israel. This action contributed significantly to the ongoing conflict between Palestinians and Israelis.

In Europe, General Eisenhower became supreme commander of NATO forces. As the Marshall Plan continued to spur the economic recovery of America's allies, communist rule tightened behind the Iron Curtain. The United States broke off diplomatic relations with Bulgaria; Hungary confiscated the Catholic Church's property and lands and closed the theology departments in the universities; and the Polish government also decided to confiscate assets of the Church but later reached a compromise agreement. On the other hand, seeking to exploit the breach between Stalin and Yugoslavia's Marshal Tito, Congress passed the Yugoslav Emergency Relief Assistance Act and authorized $50 million in emergency funds.

The Cold War at Home

The conviction of Alger Hiss for lying about his past communist affiliation, the arrests of people suspected of being atomic spies in the United States and England, and the sudden national prominence of Senator Joseph McCarthy interjected deep fears of communist subversion from within into virtually all levels of American politics and society.

ALGER HISS

In 1948, Whittaker Chambers, a former communist, accused Alger Hiss, a top official in Roosevelt's State Department, of having been a Communist Party operative in the 1930s. Hiss vehemently denied the charges, but after Chambers dramatically produced microfilm documents to support his claim, Hiss stood trial for perjury. The first trial took place in early 1949 but ended in a hung jury. The retrial began in late 1949, and Hiss was found guilty of perjury on January 21, 1950.

The conviction of Hiss, who had been an adviser to Roosevelt at the Yalta conference and one of the founders of the United Nations, appeared to vindicate the right-wing charges that Yalta had been a sellout and that the United Nations was a Soviet tool. Even more important, the guilty verdict appeared to give credence to their larger claim that communist agents had infiltrated the government, occupied key positions within the Truman administration, especially within the State Department, and were setting and implementing policies designed to aid the Soviet Union and undermine the United States. Throughout the duration of the cold war, conservatives and liberals continued to argue whether Hiss was guilty of treason, or at least perjury, or if he was the victim of right-wing collusion. They also continued to debate whether the Yalta agreement was a fundamentally pragmatic treaty that served U.S. interests while acknowledging the reality that Soviet armies already occupied Eastern Europe or whether, under the influence of Alger Hiss, the Yalta agreement essentially condemned the Eastern European nations to communist rule by legitimizing the notion of a Soviet sphere of influence. Similarly, the Left and Right continued to disagree on whether the United Nations served Soviet interests more than those of the United States.

The conviction of Alger Hiss (shown here in a 1956 photo) fueled the Red Scare. *(Photofest)*

Because Hiss was a self-assured, highly educated, well-spoken, and well-groomed lawyer from a wealthy eastern family and Chambers was an inelegant, poorly spoken, ill-groomed magazine editor from a working-class family, the case acquired elements of class conflict as well. As both the popular and judicial judgments depended on each man's ability to appear more credible and trustworthy than the other, the controversy further enacted the ongoing battle for respect, authority, and power between the liberal, aristocratic East Coast establishment and the more conservative, less urbane middle class. The significance of the case, then, exceeded the particular misdeeds of which Hiss was accused. Instead, to some extent the jury's verdict and the popular judgment of Hiss also represented a referendum over which group of Americans was the most reliable for leading the nation in the fight against domestic and international communism.

Hiss, who served about three years of his five-year sentence, maintained his innocence until his death; however, historians are now firmly convinced that he had been a Soviet agent in the 1930s. The extent, if any, to which his official actions in the 1940s were designed primarily to aid the Soviet Union is still a matter of debate, although recently released evidence from secret, coded Soviet telegrams that were deciphered by the National Security Agency's Venona Project shows that Hiss was an active agent as late as 1945, when he participated in the Yalta talks.[1]

JOSEPH MCCARTHY

Less than two weeks after Hiss was convicted, more evidence of internal communist subversion surfaced, as police in England, assisted by the FBI, arrested physicist Klaus Fuchs for passing secrets about the atomic bomb to Soviet agents. Fuchs, who confessed his guilt, had worked on the Manhattan Project that developed the atomic bomb for the United States during World War II. His arrest came within five months after the Soviet Union exploded its first atomic bomb; therefore, despite the fact that U.S. officials had privately estimated that the Soviets would be able to develop their own bomb by around 1949 or 1950, the widespread popular perception was that communist spies in sensitive positions had robbed the United States of its nuclear monopoly. This perception was further intensified just four months later, when, in June, a spy ring linked to Fuchs was also arrested for passing atomic secrets to the Soviets. This spy ring included Julius and Ethel Rosenberg, who were later tried and executed as spies. Then nine days after that, communist North Korea launched a surprise invasion against South Korea, and the United States was drawn into its first anticommunist military action.

It was within this context that McCarthy, a Republican senator from Wisconsin, rose to power. On February 9, less than three weeks after the Hiss conviction and one week after the arrest of Fuchs, McCarthy, in a speech before a Republican women's group in Wheeling, West Virginia, held up a letter that he claimed listed 205 members of the Communist Party who worked for the State Department and helped shape national policy. He further maintained that the State Department knew of their affiliation and tolerated it.

McCarthy's charges created an immediate furor. When journalists and Democrats demanded to see his proof, McCarthy declined, saying that it would be improper for him to identify anyone until the appropriate Senate committee convened. He further obfuscated the issue by revising again and again the number of alleged Communists on his list. In one case it was 57, in another 207. Despite these inconsistencies and denials by the State Department, McCarthy's accusations were taken seriously, both by the public and by Congress. The Senate appointed a foreign relations subcommittee to investigate.

Chaired by Democrat Millard Tydings, the committee failed to discredit McCarthy, partly because the Truman administration initially refused to surrender its loyalty files on government employees. Testifying before the committee, McCarthy named 10 people from his list, including Ambassador at Large Philip Jessup and China scholar Owen Lattimore, who was then a professor at Johns Hopkins University. McCarthy charged that Jessup had an unusual affinity for communist causes and that Lattimore was the Soviet Union's top espionage agent in the United States. Former top-ranking American communists Louis Bundenz and Freda Utley supported McCarthy's claims. All of the accused protested their innocence, and the committee ultimately exonerated them. None was ever found guilty of treason or other related charges.

Although the committee officially labeled McCarthy a fraud and a hoax, the senator repeated his charges on radio and television and won a significant public following. When called upon to produce his evidence, he refused, citing new unsubstantiated accusations instead. McCarthy thus emerged from the hearing as a powerful force within the Republican Party and the chief spokesman for a rapidly growing contingent of Americans who believed domestic communists were successfully implementing a treacherous conspiracy to undermine the nation from within.

The Tydings committee reported its findings in June 1950. That same month, the Korean War began. McCarthy reluctantly supported the U.S. intervention on South Korea's behalf but blamed the war on earlier policies made by the State Department, which he maintained, was full of communists, communist sympathizers (called "fellow travelers"), and communist dupes.

THE JULIUS AND ETHEL ROSENBERG CASE

McCarthy's charge of internal subterfuge was dramatically reinforced on June 16, when the FBI arrested two American Communists, Julius and Ethel Rosenberg, for espionage. The couple was accused of passing to the Soviets secrets from the Manhattan Project, on which Ethel's brother, David Greenglass, had worked as a technician at the end of World War II.

Nine days before the outbreak of the Korean War, FBI agents charged the Rosenbergs with heading a Soviet spy ring involving Greenglass, Fuchs, Harry Gold, and Morton Sobell. Their greatest alleged crime was the theft between 1944 and 1945 of technical information about the atomic bomb, which was then under development in Los Alamos, New Mexico. Upon their arrest Fuchs, Gold, and Greenglass confessed their involvement in the spy ring, but Sobell and the Rosenbergs steadfastly proclaimed their innocence.

Their trial began in 1950. The defendants invoked the Fifth Amendment, which protects against self-incrimination, when they were asked about their communist ties; nonetheless, the prosecution succeeded in establishing their communist background, and a former ranking Communist official, Elizabeth Bentley, testified that the Soviet Union controlled the American Communist Party. Greenglass, the prosecution's chief witness, testified that Julius had recruited him into the ring and received from him sketches and diagrams of the lens used for detonating the bomb. Max Elitcher, a college classmate of Julius, also maintained that Julius had tried to recruit him to spy during World War II. Other witnesses corroborated parts of Greenglass's story.

The defense tried to undermine Greenglass and to show that his accusations were actually part of a family feud. Greenglass, the attorneys suggested, had turned against his sister, and his wife, Ruth, had devised the plan to blame Julius and Ethel in order to gain reduced sentences for themselves. Testifying on their own behalf, the Rosenbergs maintained their complete innocence. Gold admitted having received documents from Greenglass but denied ever having met the Rosenbergs.

On March 29, 1951, a federal jury convicted the couple. Judge Irving Kaufman sentenced Sobell to 30 years in federal prison and Greenglass to 15.

He sentenced Julius and Ethel to death, because he believed they had headed the spy ring.

The Rosenbergs appealed the conviction, their attorney, Emanuel Bloch, arguing that the espionage statute was vague and that Kaufman had been prejudiced in favor of the prosecution. In particular, Bloch objected to the judge's admitting evidence that the Rosenbergs were Communists, as this prejudiced the jury against them. In 1952, the Federal Court of Appeals rejected the Rosenbergs' appeal, stating that their communist ties were relevant because they helped establish a motive for the crime and that Kaufman had repeatedly warned jurors not to come to a verdict on the basis of their communism. Later that year, the Supreme Court unanimously turned down a further appeal. After the Supreme Court overturned a last-minute stay of execution that Justice William O. Douglas had granted, the Rosenbergs were executed at Sing Sing prison in Ossining, New York, on June 19, 1953.

The Rosenberg case was highly controversial and able to provoke strong passions while it was ongoing. It remained controversial throughout the cold war. On the one hand were those who, like Kaufman, believed in their guilt and believed their acts of espionage had seriously endangered the United States. To such individuals, the death sentence was well merited. On the other hand, many believed that the Rosenbergs were innocent, their trial had been severely biased against them, and/or the death penalty was excessively severe and unwarranted, especially as the nation was not at war. The Rosenbergs' defenders maintained that they were victims of the domestic Red Scare, their conviction and sentencing were tainted by anti-Semitism, and their execution stemmed from a national need to punish a scapegoat for recent communist military successes in Korea and political victories elsewhere. Other defenders have argued that the stolen information was not crucial to the Soviets' development of the atomic bomb and that Kaufman was inaccurate when he stated that the Russians developed the bomb years before our best scientists had predicted they would. Thus, guilty or innocent, the Rosenbergs were not responsible for the Russian A-bomb. Among those who pleaded for a more lenient sentence were Einstein and Pope Pius XII. Neither Truman nor Eisenhower, who took office five months before their execution, responded to the requests for leniency, despite mass rallies and petitions shortly before the couple's execution.

No consensus has yet been reached on the fairness of the trial, the appropriateness of the Rosenbergs' sentence, the motivations of the judge and prosecutors, or the importance of the stolen information to the Soviet atomic research program. Telegraph cables that were decoded in the 1940s by the Venona Project but not released until 1995, however, indicate that the Rosenbergs, operating on behalf of the Soviet Union, were indeed part of a spy ring that stole secrets about the workings of the atomic bomb.[2]

RED CHANNELS AND OTHER ANTICOMMUNIST ACTIONS

McCarthy's harangues were not the only official expression of fervent anticommunism. During the late 1940s and early 1950s, Senator Patrick A. McCarran of Nevada, a Democrat, led a coalition of conservative Democrats and Republicans that passed a number of anticommunist and anti-immigration bills, including 1947 legislation that permitted the State Department to fire employees whose behavior it deemed harmful to national interests. The 1950 McCarran Internal Security Act required the registration of communist and communist-front groups, even those that were legally established. It also extended the statute of limitations and intensified the penalties for espionage and sedition, and it enabled the Justice Department to deport or detain aliens believed to be subversive and to bar them from immigration. Concerned that McCarran's bill would require cumbersome regulations and restrict constitutional freedoms, a group of liberal senators tried to undermine the legislation with a substitute bill that would establish concentration camps for communists in the event of a national emergency. But conservatives maneuvered to incorporate the substitute within the original bill, and the amended McCarran Internal Security Act easily passed through both houses of Congress. According to the *New York Times* several opponents voted for the legislation because they feared to oppose any anticommunist legislation in an election year. Truman defiantly vetoed the bill, but Congress overrode his veto. Subsequently, communist and communist-dominated organizations were required to provide the government with the names of all of their members and contributors. Moreover, concentration camps for communists were established in Pennsylvania, Florida, Oklahoma, Arizona, and California, although they were never used.[3]

The investigations of the entertainment industry by HUAC had been suspended pending the ultimately unsuccessful appeal by the Hollywood Ten of their 1947 contempt of Congress citations. But in 1950, the publishers of *Counterattack: Facts to Combat Communism,* created by three former FBI agents, released *Red Channels,* a booklet that purported to identify communists and communist sympathizers in the entertainment industry. This book became one of the first unofficial sources for blacklisting in the movie and television industries. It listed 151 men and women whom the editors maintained were either currently linked to communist causes or had been in the past.

Because *Red Channels* began with a disclaimer stating that the listed activities or associations may have been free of subversive intentions, and because the booklet purported only to report factual information from other sources, it avoided legal liability for damages suffered by people whom it listed. For example, when actress Irene Wicker was able to demonstrate that her listing had inaccurately accused her of signing a petition on behalf of a Communist Party candidate, *Counterattack* published her disclaimer but took the position that it had simply reported what the Communist Party publication *The Daily Worker* had published. The editors reiterated their position that *Red Channels* did not call Wicker a communist or communist sympathizer; nonetheless, Wicker remained banned from the television industry for three years. According to her agent, industry officials told him they would not "touch her with a ten foot pole" due to the *Red Channels* listing.[4]

In practice, most individuals listed in *Red Channels* either had to clear their name by demonstrating that they had not, in fact, been affiliated with the named organizations or had to prove that their affiliations had been free of communist influences. Otherwise, they faced blacklisting within the entertainment industry. Among those who lost work because of *Red Channels* were television actors Philip Loeb and Jean Muir, singer Hazel Scott, dancer Gypsy Rose Lee, and folk singer Pete Seeger. News commentators Howard K. Smith and William Shirer were also listed. Smith stated that the listing did not affect him, but Shirer believed that his career was impeded by his three listings, none of which even accused him of being either a communist or a fellow traveler. On the other hand, Ed Sullivan, an early champion of *Red Channels* and industry blacklisting, welcomed the publication enthusiastically in his syndicated newspaper column. Sullivan believed the publication gave producers the background information they needed to make informed choices in their effort to keep communists off the airwaves.

Another publication that contributed to public belief in widespread, well-coordinated communist underground was a widely read three-part article by FBI informant Matt Cvetic that appeared in the *Saturday Evening Post*. In "I Posed as a Communist for the FBI," Cvetic described how he infiltrated a communist cell and over a period of nine years attended some 2,000 meetings of Communist Party and communist-front organizations. Director Gordon Douglas made the account into a film in 1951, entitled *I Was a Communist for the FBI*. In 1952, the story was retold as a radio spy show starring Dana Andrews.

GOVERNMENT AND SOCIETY

The 1950 census counted more than 150 million Americans at the beginning of the decade. Ten years later, there were 178 million an increase of almost 20 percent. Although some of the increase was attributable to immigration, much of it came from the baby boomers, the children born in the aftermath of World War II. The rapid growth of the number of young families sparked demands for new homes in which to raise the children and schools for them to attend. The result was the suburbanization of a great portion of America.

Very little new housing had been constructed during the Great Depression and World War II, but in the late 1940s the same assembly-line methods that had been developed for the war effort were redirected to filling the enormous demand for new homes for the returning soldiers. Most of the new houses were situated in housing developments on hitherto undeveloped properties outside the cities, where land was less expensive. The renewed availability of automobiles, gasoline, tires, and other automotive necessities after the war made it practical for the first time for Americans to commute to work, and it facilitated a dramatic demographic shift of middle-class Americans from the inner cities to the suburbs that persisted through the 1950s. The G.I. Bill of Rights played a major role in financing this development by granting veterans low-interest, federally guaranteed home mortgages that required no down payment. California enjoyed the greatest suburban growth, and in 1950, at the height of the housing boom, one development outside Los Angeles sold 100 homes in a single hour.

Apart from its beneficial impact on the economy, the growth of the suburbs profoundly changed how Americans interacted with one another, what they valued, what their daily concerns were, and how they conducted their lives. In many cases, adult children living with or near their parents in the inner cities moved to the suburbs with their spouse and their own children, while the parents remained behind in the city neighborhoods. As a result of this migration, the concept of the nuclear family, consisting of a mother, father, and children, began to replace the extended family as the model American familial arrangement. The breakdown of the family into smaller units was also evident in the increase in divorces during the decade, although divorce was still generally disapproved of and often regarded as sign of personal failure.

Because families in the suburbs had more private space, they were also more insulated from their neighbors; for instance, they drove instead of walking, so people met less frequently on the street. Moreover, suburban living favored backyards and patios, which unlike the urban porches that looked out onto public streets, directed the occupants to an enclosed, private yard. In addition, because the suburban houses were more spacious than urban apartments, family members could more easily withdraw from one another. The isolation felt by some suburban dwellers is reflected in such novels as Sloan Wilson's *The Man in the Gray Flannel Suit* (1955) and short stories of the period, especially in fiction published in the *New Yorker* magazine.

At the same time, many suburban communities exerted pressures for conformity, not only in the appearance of the homes but also in people's dress, choice of car, social mores, and other matters of personal expression, and, certainly, sexual orientation. Shared interests in children created bonds among suburban dwellers, and Little League baseball and other organized sports for children also helped create communities among parents, as did school parent-teacher associations (PTAs), homeowners' associations, and other groups that represented the new communal interests of the suburbs, which for the most part were not racially integrated and from which religious and ethnic minorities were sometimes overtly excluded.

In 1950, New York remained the most populous state, and New York City was the most densely inhabited urban region. But California, with its growing suburbs, climbed from fifth in 1940 to second, as the population continued to shift away from the industrial Northeast toward the West Coast. Consequently, the influence of the socially looser West Coast upon the rest of the country grew significantly, and a rivalry emerged over which part of the nation would be the locus of power, wealth, and national influence. Many Americans from the East and Midwest found this challenge unsettling. Some lost jobs and suffered financially as their companies relocated out west; others became embittered when the sports teams they had supported since they were children moved away; still others felt that the change reflected a shift in the country's moral character from the values of thrifty, prudent, morally righteous behavior associated with the East Coast and its Puritan heritage, to a spendthrift, licentious, morally lax West Coast associated with the glamour, tinsel, and fast, self-indulgent lifestyles in Hollywood. Their counterparts on the West Coast, on the other hand, regarded the industrial eastern states as old, dirty, and trapped in an outmoded past. They saw the West as the most promising place for young, energetic people with optimism, new ideas, and a passion for the good life.

These bi-coastal tensions sometimes surfaced in cold war rhetoric, as the cold war was cast in the 1940s and 1950s as a moral crusade on behalf of the American way of life and was centered around Christian values. Communism, which is inherently atheistic, was viewed by many Americans as blasphemous. The cold war was thus for some a struggle for humanity's soul. For such people, California's reputation as more relaxed, more sensuous, and more self-indulgent played into suspicions that communists were corrupting American morals. It is not surprising, then, that the Hollywood-based film industry was seen as a communist haven.

Apart from responding to the communist threat at home and abroad, the government took some other significant actions during this year of off-term elections. Among the most dramatic political events were the highly publicized Senate investigation into organized crime, led by Tennessee senator and Democrat Estes Kefauver, and a deadly but unsuccessful attempt by Puerto Rican nationalists to assassinate Truman.

Kefauver Committee

Senator Kefauver's Special Committee to Investigate Organized Crime was created in response to the murder in April 1950 of two gangsters in a Democratic clubhouse in Kansas City, Missouri, Truman's home state. The hearings, which began in Miami on May 26, were aimed, in part, at diffusing Republican accusations of scandal about the Kansas City murders. The committee traveled to six U.S. cities in 1950 and 1951, listening to testimony from judges, police, district attorneys, convicted criminals, and admittedly corrupt government officials. The first congressional investigation to be televised by the major networks, the hearings captured the public interest by featuring such colorful figures as a convicted bookie; a corrupt police commissioner; Joe Adonis, an ex-bootlegger and top gangland official; Anthony Anastasia, the brother of the chief assassin for Murder Incorporated, a murder-for-hire syndicate; former New York City mayor William O'Dwyer, accused of corruption and of having connections to the Mafia; and organized crime leader Frank Costello, who insisted that only his hands be shown on television because he did not "care to submit himself as a spectacle"—a request that the committee honored. The person who attracted the greatest attention was Virginia Hill Hauser, the dramatic, voluptuous former girlfriend of mobster Ben "Bugsy" Siegel. She told reporters upon her exit from the hearing that she hoped an atom bomb would fall on them.

The Kefauver committee concluded that two major syndicates, one in New York and one in Chicago, dominated organized crime in the United States. Although the syndicates also were involved in prostitution, labor racketeering, and illegal drugs, they derived most of their income from illegal gambling and were facilitated by corrupt policemen, judges, and prosecutors who protected them from legal intrusion. The committee further tried to show that both syndicates were controlled by Mafia "capo" Charles "Lucky" Luciano.

In addition to heightened awareness of the problems of organized crime and official corruption, the hearings made Kefauver, a freshman senator, a national figure. He wrote a series of popular articles about the syndicates for the *Saturday Evening Post* and in 1951 published *Crime in America,* a best-seller. This exposure propelled him to a run for president in 1952, but he lost the Democratic Party nomination to Adlai Stevenson, governor of Illinois. In 1954, he was reelected to the Senate; two years later, he challenged Stevenson again and lost again, but accepted the nomination for vice president. After their ticket lost to Republican incumbents Dwight Eisenhower and Richard Nixon, Kefauver returned to the Senate, where he emerged as one of the South's most liberal Democrats and one of its few staunch Senate supporters of the growing movement for civil rights.

Assassination Attempt

The White House was undergoing major repairs in 1950, and during the renovations, the Trumans occupied Blair House at 1651 Pennsylvania Avenue. On November 1, two Puerto Rican nationalists from New York, Griselio Torresola and Oscar Collaza, attempted to shoot their way past the guards at Blair House in an unsuccessful attempt to assassinate the president. The two-minute gunfight took place outside the house, and Truman was never in any immediate danger. But when the smoke cleared, one of his guards, Leslie Coffelt, was dead and two others were seriously wounded. As he bled to death, Coffelt killed Torresola with a single shot to the head. The wounded Collazo was captured, tried, convicted, and condemned to death, a sentence that Truman commuted to life in prison in 1952, as a gesture of goodwill to the people of Puerto Rico. In 1979, President Jimmy Carter augmented that gesture, when he pardoned Collazo, who had by then served 29 years in Leavenworth prison. Ironically, Truman had been more conciliatory toward Puerto Rico than any previous U.S. president. He publically endorsed Puerto Rican self-determination, appointed the first Puerto Rican–born territorial governor, and extended Social Security to the people of the island. But, as Collazo explained upon being pardoned, he and Torresola were attacking the system, not the man.

In other significant governmental action, Congress amended the 1948 Displaced Person's Act to admit a larger number of World War II refugees into the country. In addition, the United States and Canada signed a 50-year treaty to protect the beauty of Niagara Falls while also increasing the power output of the Niagara River. In a separate agreement, the countries pledged to foster economic cooperation and to strengthen continental defenses, which they did throughout the decade.

CIVIL RIGHTS

The early 1950s did not see a large amount of progress in the arena of civil rights; however, in 1950, Hazel Scott became the first black performer to host her own network musical variety show, the 15-minute *Hazel Scott Show* on the DuMont network for two months during the summer. The only other network shows hosted by African Americans during the 1950s were the short-lived *Billy Daniels Show*, which ran on ABC from October to December 1952, and *The Nat King Cole Show*, which ran on NBC from November 1956 to December 1957. The next black performer to host a network variety series was Sammy Davis, Jr., in 1966.

Professional tennis and bowling were integrated in 1950, and American Ralph Bunche became the first black person to win a Nobel Prize. Bunche, who paid for his studies at the University of California and Harvard University by working as a janitor, received the Nobel Peace Prize for his role as the UN mediator in the Arab-Israeli conflict. The integration of military units, which Truman had ordered in 1948, went into full and fast effect once the Korean War began, because as a matter of necessity the process of segregating draftees, training them separately, and establishing segregated units was too inefficient for the war effort. By the end of the year, virtually all the units in Korea were integrated. Later in the 1950s, the decade would also become notable for the landmark Supreme Court decisions that declared unconstitutional an array of laws and policies that had, since the post–Civil War Reconstruction, fostered the practice of racial segregation throughout the country, especially in the South. This was already in motion by 1950.

In the 1930s, the National Association for the Advancement of Colored People (NAACP) adopted a strategy of launching legal challenges to institutional segregation, as it believed that the legislative and executive branches of government were unlikely to promote actively integration in the political climate spawned by the Great Depression. The organization further decided to make equal access to education a main priority—a strategy that culminated in the 1954 *Brown v. Board of Education of Topeka, Kansas* Supreme Court ruling that declared racial segregation of public schools unconstitutional. A series of precedent-setting cases had paved the way for *Brown v. Board of Education*. In the late 1930s, NAACP attorneys Charles H. Houston and Thurgood Marshall won two important Supreme Court verdicts in *Murray v. Maryland* (1936) and *Missouri ex rel. Gaines v. Canada* (1938). In a separate case in 1948, the Supreme Court ruled that the constitutional right to equal protection under the law required Oklahoma to admit a black applicant to its state law school. These rulings granted black Americans access to public law schools that had hitherto been fully segregated.

Thurgood Marshall took over the NAACP Legal Defense and Educational Fund in 1940, and in 1950 his team of lawyers prevailed in two critical cases that helped make possible the 1954 ruling that integrated the public schools. In *Sweatt v. Painter,* the Court ruled that Texas had violated the equal protection clause of the Fourteenth Amendment when it established a separate black law school to avoid integrating its all-white school. And *McLaurin v. Oklahoma State Regents for Higher Education* established that the state of Oklahoma had acted unconstitutionally when it admitted George McLaurin, a 70-year-old African American, into one of its doctorate programs but required him to sit in the hallway rather than in the classroom and denied him full access to the library and dining hall. These two cases made important inroads against the 1896 *Plessy v. Ferguson* ruling that "separate but equal" educational facilities for blacks and whites were constitutionally acceptable, but the Court limited the impact of its rulings by restricting them to the particular facts of these specific cases. In a separate case, the Court overturned the conviction of a black defendant because African Americans had been excluded from the grand jury that indicted him.

Also in 1950, the NAACP filed suit against the school board in Clarendon County, South Carolina, arguing that racial segregation caused irreparable psychological damage to black children. Dr. Kenneth Clark, an African-American psychologist, presented results from experiments he had conducted in which 16 black children between the ages of six and nine were shown black and white dolls. The majority indicated that the black dolls looked "bad" and the white dolls "nice." In addition, the children identified most closely with the white dolls. To further undermine the claim that racially segregated educational facilities were equal, the NAACP showed that the student-teacher ratios in black schools in Clarendon County were nearly double what they were in the white schools. A federal district court ruled two to one against the NAACP, although the dissenting judge wrote forcefully against segregated education, and the court mandated that the disparities in facilities be rectified. The NAACP appealed the verdict to the Supreme Court, and *Briggs v. Elliot,* as the case became known, eventually became absorbed into the landmark 1954 *Brown v. Board of Education of Topeka* ruling that struck down the separation doctrine.

In addition to these court cases, integration continued in the realm of sports. Althea Gibson became the first black American to compete in a U.S. tennis championship sponsored by the United States Lawn Tennis Association, and in response to legal challenges from four states, the American Bowling Congress terminated a rule restricting its membership to white males.

BUSINESS

The economy got off to a strong start in 1950, as the nation was in the middle of a huge postwar building boom that was especially strong in the suburbs. Suburban living created a new lifestyle and unique culture that, in turn, created new demands for goods and services. Suburban shopping centers with large parking lots served the former city dwellers, who were now no longer able to walk to the corner shop. The comparatively spacious suburban backyards generated a demand for products associated with gardening and lawn maintenance, backyard grilling, and home recreation. The new schools that were built to accommodate the children of the young parents—the baby boomers—required not only more teachers and administrators but also new and better educational materials to satisfy the demands of the large number of new parents. Commuter railroads were expanded and improved, and highways were constructed to facilitate the commutes to work.

During the 1950s the American workforce became better educated than ever before, as the G.I. Bill subsidized college education for veterans. As a result, university enrollments swelled during the 1950s, creating an unprecedented demand for college professors, administrators, and support staff and an unprecedented number of college graduates, many with substantial military experience. Most of these graduates thus entered the workforce with both a comparatively high level of skill and education and a maturity gained through wartime service.

When Frank X. McNamara, Alfred Bloomingdale, and Ralph Snyder started Diner's Club, the first credit card, they changed the way Americans handle their finances, while simultaneously stimulating business by encouraging greater spending. The initial 200 members received plastic cards that gave them credit at 27 upscale New York restaurants. Diner's Club then repaid the restaurants after deducting a transaction fee, and it charged customers interest on the loan. By the end of 1951, it was collecting more than $1 million a year.

The explosive expansion of the television industry in the late 1940s and early 1950s spurred a corresponding growth in corporate advertising, which underwrote most of the programming for the new medium. The success of TV advertising stems from the simple fact that manufacturers can demonstrate their products in action. Some demonstrations in the 1950s were simple and

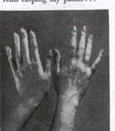 

An advertisement for hand lotion plays on popular cowboys-and-Indians films and star power (in this case, Maureen O'Hara). *(Photofest)*

straightforward; others tried more dramatically to emphasize the virtues of their products, such as adhesive bandages that were strong enough to lift an egg or electric razors capable of shaving fuzz from a peach. Initially, most of the performers on television ads were radio actors, many of whom were not comfortable in a visual medium. But soon, Hollywood actors at the end of their careers found sales on television to be a lucrative way to sustain themselves, and in many cases the pitchmen and -women became popular national celebrities. One of the first of these was Betty Furness, who started working for Westinghouse in 1949 and rose to national prominence in 1952, when she filled the airtime on commercial breaks during the presidential nominating conventions and made the phrase, "You can be sure, if it's Westinghouse" an identifiable part of the shared national lingo. Arthur Godfrey, another pitchman, merged the roles of promoter and entertainer in his highly rated television shows that aired from 1949 to 1959. And Ronald Reagan, who hosted *General Electric Theater* from 1954 to 1962, also worked as a spokesman for the company. The national recognition he acquired in those capacities later made possible his political career.

The meteoric rise of television advertising in the early 1950s is evident in the growth of the television sales department at New York's BBD&O advertising agency, which by 1950, grew from 12 employees to 150. Overall, the total sales for television advertising along Manhattan's Madison Avenue, the heart of America's advertising industry, went from $12.3 million in 1949 to $40.8 million in 1950 and $128 million in 1952.[5] As a rising national phenomenon, advertising soon attracted its critics, some of whom expressed themselves in such fiction as Frederic Wakeman's *The Hucksters* (1946, made into a film in 1947), Sloan Wilson's best-selling *The Man in the Gray Flannel Suit* (1955, made into a film in 1956), and Frederik Pohl and C. M. Kornbluth's science fiction novel *The Space Merchants* (1952), which imagines an America in which advertising corporations are the most powerful entities in the country.

General Motors reported profits for 1949 of more than $656 million, the largest ever recorded by a U.S. corporation to that date, and in 1950 it earned $834 million—a sign of the growing popularity of automobiles and the growth of the suburbs that necessitated them. The automaker then guaranteed a stable labor market by signing a five-year pact with the United Auto Workers that granted pensions and wage increases to workers. In February, Truman invoked the Taft-Hartley Act, which he had unsuccessfully vetoed in 1947, to compel striking coal miners to return to work during an 80-day "cooling off" period; in March, the soft coal operators and United Mine Workers concluded their eight-month dispute with a new contract. The oil industry, however, faced problems at home and abroad: The U.S. Justice Department instituted antitrust proceedings against seven companies in May, and in early 1951, the Arabian American Oil Company was compelled to agree to share profits with Saudi Arabia. But in 1950, the company completed the world's longest pipeline, which ran 1,066 miles, from U.S.-leased oil fields close to the Persian Gulf to the town of Sidon on the Mediterranean. The pipeline cost $250 million to construct. In Louisiana, the Bureau of Mines announced that oil had been produced from coal in practical amounts for the first time.

The Korean War abruptly ended the good times, however, and put the economy on an austerity program again, although the housing industry continued to flourish. On July 19, Truman asked Congress for $10 million for the war and authority to impose internal economic controls. And in September, Congress authorized the Defense Production Act, which established a system of priorities for materials, provided for wage and price controls, and restricted installment purchases. Truman subsequently placed Charles E. Wilson, head of General Electric, in charge of the Office of Defense Mobilization. Congress also created the National Production Authority to manage the economy with regard to war needs. By the end of the year, defense spending had increased by more than four times its prewar levels, to some $50 billion, and on December

16, following communist China's entry into the war, Truman declared a national state of emergency that enabled him to intercede even more forcefully in industry and commerce, where these impinged upon the war effort. His first act was to have the Economic Stabilization Agency roll back prices and institute a price freeze on automobiles.

Even before declaring a state of emergency, Truman ordered the U.S. Army to take over railroads to prevent a strike that would debilitate the nation's ability to deliver the steel necessary to fight the war. Faced with an impending strike by the Brotherhood of Railroad Trainmen and the Fraternal Order of Railway Conductors, Truman issued an executive order that provided for the seizure and operation of the nation's railroads by the secretary of the army in the name of the United States government. Assistant Secretary of the Army Karl Bendetsen was charged with running the rail lines for the next 21 months. Invoking Truman's authority, Bendetsen called several civilian railroad specialists to active duty. Bendetsen organized regional control centers, and in some cases the regional control officers were railroad presidents who held reserve commissions in the army. In one case, the army appointed a control officer directly to the rank of colonel. When union members staged sick-outs (absenteeism on the pretext of sickness) that threatened to undermine the war effort, Bendetsen issued an order that anyone who did not report for duty at his assigned shift without a certificate of illness from an independent, qualified doctor would immediately be fired, losing his seniority and his pension under the Railway Retirement Act. Bendetsen's edict had its desired effect, and the sick-outs ended. In the event of an illegal strike, the government had contingency plans to draft the strikers and then order them to run the trains, but this never proved necessary. The labor dispute was resolved in May 1952, and the railroads were returned to their owners two days later.

In the largest armed robbery to that date, Brink's security company lost over $2.7 million when seven armed men wearing Halloween masks held up its headquarters in Boston. In 1956, the FBI identified 11 perpetrators, six of whom were arrested just two days before the statute of limitations ended for the sensational crime. Two others were already in jail, one had died, and the other two remained at large. Only $50,000 was recovered; the rest remains unaccounted for. The daring robbery captured the public imagination and was later the subject of William Friedkin's 1978 film *The Brink's Job,* starring Peter Falk, Gena Rowlands, and Peter Boyle.

Charles Shulz introduced the "Peanuts" comic strip in 1950 and continued to publish it in the funny pages of newspapers throughout the country for nearly 50 years. Assorted new products of the year included Sony tape recorders, Kraft Minute Rice, CorningWare ovenware, Miss Clairol hair products, Sugar Pops cereal, the Nielsen television rating service, and Smokey the Bear, a cartoon mascot who warned visitors to national parks and forests, "Only YOU can prevent forest fires." Popular fads included cowboy outfits for children, black molasses, square dancing, and the mambo.

SCIENCE AND TECHNOLOGY

The fields of medicine, astronomy, chemistry, biology, and physics evolved considerably during the 1950s, and computer technology moved from its infancy to adolescence. Philip S. Hench and Edward C. Kendall won the Nobel Prize in physiology or medicine for their discoveries about the hormones of the adrenal cortex. The year also saw significant developments in cardiac care. The first successful heart massage was performed at St. John's Hospital in Brooklyn; the first aorta transplant was performed at Ford Hospital in Detroit; and tromexan, an anticoagulant, was reported as a potential heart attack inhibitor.

Other medical advances included the first kidney transplant, performed by Dr. Richard Lawler of Chicago. B. J. Ludwig and E. C. Pich, of Wallace Labs, synthesized meprobamate, a tranquilizer. Antihistamines were introduced to treat colds and allergies, and reserpine, used in India in the form of snakeroot, was introduced as a blood pressure medication.

The element tritium, a hydrogen isotope essential for the production of the hydrogen bomb, whose development Truman had authorized at the beginning of the year, was discovered in ordinary water. Astronomer J. H. Oort proposed that comets were fragments from a distant cloud of matter orbiting the Sun, and studies of radio waves produced new calculations for the speed of light, which Einstein's theory of relativity had established in 1905 as the only constant in the universe. Scientists at the University of California at Berkeley discovered the 97th element, which they named berkelium, and G. T. Seaborg of the University of California discovered the 98th element, californium.

European scientist Alfred Kastler developed optical pumping, a technological predecessor of the laser, and magnetic tape was used as computer memory storage for the first time. John von Neumann, who was one of the dominating figures of early computer technology, produced the first computer-generated 24-hour weather forecast—a notable achievement because of the large number of variables that must be accounted for in a scientifically based weather prediction. In Chicago, scientists John L. Kurantz and Robert J. Moon developed the first practical method for converting atomic energy into electricity with the use of boilers, or dynamos.

SPORTS, ENTERTAINMENT, AND THE ARTS

Sports

The growing romance between television and professional sports moved closer to marriage as Major League Baseball sold the TV broadcasting rights to the World Series for $6 million and assigned some of the profits to the players' pension fund. Players' salaries also benefited from the new contract: Ted Williams signed a record-setting contract for $125,000 per year. The last person to hit over .400 (.406 in 1941), Williams is still regarded by many as the best pure hitter ever to play baseball. But Williams was unable to win the pennant for the Boston Red Sox; the New York Yankees, led by league MVP shortstop Phil "Scooter" Rizzuto, clinched the American League championship and went on to sweep "the Hitless Wonders," the Philadelphia Phillies, for their second consecutive World Series championship and third in four years.

In football, the Cleveland Browns defeated the Los Angeles Rams to win the first NFL championship of the newly merged leagues. The University of

Oklahoma was the top-ranked college team, and quarterback Vic Janowicz, of Ohio State University, won the Heisman Trophy.

Led by star center George Mikan, the Minneapolis Lakers claimed the first-ever NBA championship by defeating the Syracuse Nationals in six games, and City College of New York won the NCAA and NIT basketball championships. Villanova's Paul Arizin was named College Player of the Year. The Detroit Red Wings won the Stanley Cup in hockey; Arthur Larsen and Margaret Osborne DuPont won the singles events at the U.S. Open in tennis, and Ben Hogan recovered from a near-fatal car accident to win the U.S. Open golf championship. Florence Chadwick set a new record by swimming across the English Channel in 13 hours and 20 minutes.

Television

In 1950, two years after television programming had significantly resumed since its suspension during World War II, there were some 3.1 million television sets and four networks in the United States; the first color television sets were sold, and the first color broadcasts were pioneered. All broadcasts were shown live, as videotape had not yet been invented. The logistics of live broadcasting favored variety shows, quiz shows, comedy revues, and live sporting events such as boxing, roller derby, baseball, and football.

Prime-time favorites included Ed Sullivan's variety show, *Toast of the Town; Kukla, Fran & Ollie,* a puppet act; the *Arthur Murray Party,* a dance show that promoted the host's dance studios; *The Goldbergs,* a comedy about a middle-class Jewish family; *Captain Video and His Video Rangers,* a children's science-fiction adventure drama; *What's My Line?* a quiz show; *The Frank Sinatra Show; Your Hit Parade,* featuring performances of popular songs; the *Burns and Allen Show,* starring George Burns as the straight man and Gracie Allen as his comical, irrational wife; *You Bet Your Life,* a quiz show hosted by comedian Groucho Marx and straight man George Fenneman; and *Your Show of Shows,* a revue of comedy skits written by Mel Brooks, Neil Simon, Larry Gelbart, and others, and starring Sid Caesar, Imogene Coca, and Carl Reiner. Now regarded as one of the classics of early television, *Your Show of Shows* mixed clownish physical humor with clever dialogue between well-drawn characters and incongruous, exaggerated plots. The revue also featured parodies of literature, film, and other television shows.

The most popular show of all was the *Texaco Star Theater,* which premiered in 1948. Patterned after old-time vaudeville, it featured guest performers and a regular supporting cast, but the comedy centered around its host and star, Milton Berle, affectionately

Milton Berle, also known as "Uncle Milty" and "Mr. Television," was famous for portraying zany characters of both genders. *(Photofest)*

known throughout the country as "Uncle Milty." The jokes were directed to a middle America audience of children and adults who were generally high school educated. The humor was broad, inoffensive, sometimes ridiculous, always nonpolitical, more visual than verbal, and highly imaginative. By contrast to Caesar's routines, Berle's were less dependent on the writing and verbal interplay and more on the acting and visual humor. Berle would typically deliver his quips dressed in outlandish costumes, for instance, as a joke-telling caveman or as a modern-day taxpayer, naked but for a hollowed-out wheelbarrow to protect his modesty. The show was so successful that it was said to have sold more television sets than any advertising campaign ever achieved, and for many years Berle, himself, was known as "Mr. Television." In 1948, his show sometimes attracted 80 percent of the viewing audience, and stores routinely closed early on Tuesday nights to allow employees to watch Berle.[6]

Movies

The love affair between Americans and their automobiles blossomed during the 1950s, as cars became more readily available in the postwar, post–Great Depression economy. Drive-in movie theaters allowed audiences to combine their love of film and their obsession with cars. Drive-ins were also especially convenient for the growing number of suburban families, as they cut entertainment costs by offering less expensive admissions and eliminating the expense of a baby-sitter, and parents did not have to spend as much time and effort to prepare their children for going out in public. Throughout the 1950s, it was common for children to attend the drive-in movies in their pajamas, ready for bed when they returned home. The first drive-in opened in Camden, New Jersey, in 1933, but they did not become popular until after World War II. In 1950, the number of drive-in movie theaters doubled from the previous year to 2,200. That number increased again by 50 percent by 1952.[7]

Besides coupling Americans' passions for automobiles and film, drive-ins enabled young adult couples to express their passion for each other, as the nighttime theaters offered them a private space where they could engage in sexual activity of varying degrees, with relatively little danger of discovery. Prior to the 1950s, there were few places where teenagers and young adults could be alone without adult supervision. Thus, the postwar availability of cars, in general, and drive-in theaters, in particular, created a new environment that facilitated the liberation of sexual behavior that quietly began during the 1950s and emerged more emphatically in the 1960s as the so-called sexual revolution.

A franker acknowledgment of the role of sexuality in human society, politics, and behavior also emerged in the films of the decade, subtly at first, then later move openly. Several of the movies from 1950 that received notable acclaim deal with sexual manipulation and otherwise speak to the turbulent undercurrents that lurk beneath the placid surfaces of society. In this respect, they are influenced by the sensibility, if not always the style, of the brooding film noir genre that carried over from the 1940s. Billy Wilder's *Sunset Boulevard* presents a cynical critique of the Hollywood mystique, as Gloria Swanson portrays on over-the-hill movie star who draws a young screenwriter, played by William Holden, into her sordid life. The film received Academy Award nominations for best picture, best actor, best actress, and best supporting actor and actress, and it won for best screenplay. Nicholas Ray's *In a Lonely Place* stars Humphrey Bogart as a heavy-drinking, hot-tempered screenwriter who is falsely suspected of murdering a young woman who had accompanied him back to his home. Jules Dassin's *Night and the City,* starring Richard Widmark, shows how a hustling entertainment promoter becomes entangled in his own machinations; and John Huston's *The Asphalt Jungle,* about a carefully planned jewel theft, benefited from the notoriety of the Kefauver crime investigations. Marlon Brando made his movie debut in Stanley Kramer's *The Men,* about a bitter veteran who was paralyzed during World War II, and Cecil B. DeMille directed a new biblical epic, *Samson and Delilah,* which starred Hedy Lamarr and Victor Mature.

Films on the lighter side included Vincente Minnelli's *Father of the Bride,* a comedy about a harassed father who must cope with the logistics of his daughter's wedding. Starring Spencer Tracey and Elizabeth Taylor, it received Academy Award nominations for best picture, best actor, and best original screenplay. Tracy also paired with Katharine Hepburn in *Adam's Rib,* a comedy directed by George Cukor. Judy Holliday was awarded best actress for her portrayal of a "dumb blond" whom William Holden has been hired to tutor in Cukor's *Born Yesterday.* Cukor received a nomination for best director for *Born Yesterday,* and the movie for best film, but those awards went to *All About Eve,* which also received two nominations for best actress. Directed by Joseph L. Mankiewicz, *All About Eve* revolves around female vanity, sexuality, and ambition. It stars Bette Davis as a narcissistic, aging star and Anne Baxter as a seemingly innocent but secretly ambitious fan who tries to take over Davis's life. Marilyn Monroe appears briefly as a cynical starlet. Although Mankiewicz and Davis maintained that the aging prima donna was based on Australian actress Elisabeth Bergner, Davis's portrayal was commonly viewed as a swipe at her rival, Tallulah Bankhead.

The top box office stars of the year were Tracy, John Wayne, Bob Hope, Bing Crosby, Betty Grable, James Stewart, the comedy team of Bud Abbott and Lou Costello, Clifton Webb, swimmer Esther Williams, and Randolph Scott.

Notable foreign films included Federico Fellini's first film, *Variety Lights,* which he codirected with Alberto Lattuada; *Orpheus,* Jean Cocteau's expressionistic retelling of the Greek myth; and *Rashomon,* by Japanese director Akira Kurosawa. *Rashomon* projects a modernist view that shows reality to be fundamentally subjective. It tells the story of a murder and rape from multiple points of view. Although none of the characters appears to be overtly lying, each account differs significantly from the others and is self-serving. The film offers no authoritative perspective that clearly favors any account of the crime over the others, and each viewer is compelled to reconstruct his or her own version of the truth.

Literature

William Faulkner, who released his *Collected Stories* in 1950, won the Nobel Prize for literature that year, too. Faulkner warned in his acceptance speech that fear of nuclear annihilation threatened to obscure "the problems of the human heart in conflict with itself," which, he believed, was the basis of mean-

ingful literature. But despite Faulkner's preoccupation with the potential apocalypse, surprisingly very little literature of the decade directly addresses the
nuclear threat. Most such literature appeared later in the decade.

Judith Merril's *Shadow on the Hearth* is one novel from 1950 that treats the
prospect of an atomic attack directly. Centering on Gladys, a suburban housewife who is woefully uninformed about radiation and survival techniques, the
novel regards postnuclear survival from a female perspective that is rare in early
works about nuclear war. When New York City is struck by a surprise atomic
attack, Gladys's husband is trapped on the other side of town, unable to communicate with her. Fortunately, her daughter has learned in school the technical information necessary for survival. But in the aftermath of the bombing,
Gladys must also deal with the social hazards in her newly transformed society:
looters, marshal law, unwelcome sexual advances from men who have suddenly
acquired power, and vigilantes who want to round up suspected communists.
And she must cope with these hitherto unimaginable pressures while also
attending to her moody teenage daughter and frightened young son.

Existing on the periphery of mainstream fiction, science fiction was the
major outlet for literary responses to the possibility of nuclear war. In 1950,
Ray Bradbury published "There Will Come Soft Rains," a short story about an
empty house whose machines and gadgets live on after all the people and animals have died from radiation. It was reprinted throughout the cold war. Bradbury also published *The Martian Chronicles,* a collection of stories that describes
the human colonization of Mars. Released as independence movements were
springing up throughout Africa and Asia, it raised then-relevant questions
about the problems and inequities created by the practice of colonization.

A 1950 University of Michigan study indicated that half of all Americans
did not read books, but the publishing industry still turned out best-sellers. The
best-selling novels at the beginning of the decade were often violent, sordid,
and tinged with sex, including Mickey Spillane's detective novel *My Gun Is
Quick* and Ross MacDonald's *The Drowning Pool.* Frank Yerby's historical novel
Floodtide brings these qualities to the antebellum South, and Erskine Caldwell
offers a look at the more contemporary South in *A Swell Looking Girl.*

But American tastes were never uniform, and individual readers are often
attracted to literature of conflicting sensibilities. In contrast to the cynicism
projected in the gritty writing of Caldwell and Spillane, other authors provided
a more reassuring view. The popular women's romances, for instance, typically
reached happy, nonviolent conclusions that did not upset the dominant social
order, although they might briefly challenge it. For instance, Frances Parkinson
Keyes's best-selling *Joy Street* centers on the successful quest for an ideal husband. Given that mixed-religion marriages, always rare in popular American
fiction, remained something of a social taboo in 1950, *Joy Street* takes a liberal
stand by making one of the serious contenders for the heroine's hand a chival-
rous Jewish lawyer who goes off to war to seek revenge against the Nazis. The
story ends happily when the lawyer is paired with another woman, and the
protagonist tempers her passion with emotional balance and marries someone
of her own faith.

The best-selling novel of 1950, Henry Morton Robinson's *The Cardinal,*
affirmed not only traditional values but also the belief that virtue and proper
action will ultimately triumph. The book, which sold more than a half million

copies, tells the story of a lower-class Boston-Irish boy who ascends the Catholic Church's hierarchy by learning humility and faith as a consequence of his personal struggles. Its popularity attests to the seriousness with which many Americans took religion and to the inspiration it offered in times of adversity, such as the Korean War era.

Compared with the fiction of the 1930s and 1940s, much of the best literature of the decade addresses personal conflicts dealing with family dynamics rather than with political or social concerns. This depoliticization of American literature resulted in part from the "chilling effect" of the Red Scare; anything that might be construed as procommunist was suspect, and writers expressed such sentiments—and publishers published them—at their own peril. A sense that world politics, in general, and the possibility of nuclear apocalypse, in particular, were spinning out of control may also have led writers to shrink away from those seemingly unmanageable topics. But the changes in U.S. society and family dynamics in the postwar era were profound; interest in psychology was growing, and these subjects would have attracted the attention of writers, regardless of the political climate. Of course, some of the best literature combined personal crises with social awareness.

Fiction published in 1950 by acclaimed literary figures included Ernest Hemingway's *Across the River and into the Trees,* Jack Kerouac's autobiographical *The Town and the City,* Robert Penn Warren's *World Enough and Time,* Sinclair Lewis's *World So Wide,* Brendan Gill's *The Trouble of One House,* Budd Shulberg's *The Disenchanted,* Isaac Bashevis Singer's *The Family Moskat,* and Gore Vidal's *Dark Green, Bright Red* and *A Search for the King.*

The themes of alienation and the pressures to conform in America's postwar corporate-dominated society were developed even more systematically in David Riesman and Nathan Glazer's nonfiction study *The Lonely Crowd,* which argued that the more tradition-based American "social character" of the early 19th century and inner-directed social character of the early 20th century were gradually being replaced by a new, other-directed social character shaped largely by capitalism, industrialization, and urbanization. Lionel Trilling articulated a more pragmatic form of liberalism that attempted to take into account the fundamentally irrational nature of human behavior in his influential *The Liberal Imagination.* This premise reflected Trilling's growing disaffection for communism, which was rooted in a mid-19th-century ideology that assumes people are inherently rational.

Charles Olson, a professor at Black Mountain College in North Carolina at the time, issued "Projective Verse," his influential manifesto insisting that poetry is fundamentally about the transfer of energy from the poet to the audience. In contrast to T. S. Eliot and other early-20th-century poets who were preoccupied with tradition and formal innovation, Olson maintained that form is always an extension of content. Olson became rector of the college in 1951 and subsequently assembled a group of innovative poets, artists, dancers, and musicians in what became known as the Black Mountain school. Among the group he brought together were poets Denise Levertov, Robert Duncan, Robert Creeley, Edward Dorn, and John Wieners, composer John Cage, and dancer and choreographer Merce Cunningham. Others influenced by the Black Mountain school included such Beat writers as Jack Kerouac and Allen Ginsberg.

Notable foreign literature from the year included the absurdist masterpiece by French playwright Eugene Ionesco, *La Cantatrice chauve,* which was later translated into English as *The Bald Soprano* (1965), and the first novel by British author Doris Lessing, *The Grass Is Singing,* about the dissolution of a poor Rhodesian farming couple's marriage and the wife's obsession with a black houseboy who finally kills her. Poet Edna St. Vincent Millay, novelist George Orwell, and playwright George Bernard Shaw died in 1950.

Theater, Music, and Visual Arts

Based on James Michener's tales of World War II, the musical *South Pacific,* which opened in late 1949, won a Tony Award for best musical and the Pulitzer Prize for theater in 1950. *Guys and Dolls,* Frank Loesser's enduring musical about gamblers, missionaries, and showgirls, also opened on Broadway, along with two other notable musicals, Irving Berlin's *Call Me Madam* and Leonard Bernstein's *Peter Pan.* Dramas that premiered on Broadway included Tennessee Williams's *The Rose Tattoo,* Carson McCuller's *The Member of the Wedding,* Clifford Odets's *The Country Girl,* John Van Druten's *Bell, Book, and Candle,* and director Edmond Rostand's 1897 play *Cyrano de Bergerac,* starring Jose Ferrer.

Rock 'n' roll had not yet been developed, and popular music was still dominated by 1940s big-band swing and love songs. The top hit of the year was "Goodnight Irene" by Pete Seeger and the Weavers, who were later blacklisted from television due to their political associations. Other chart toppers were "It Isn't Fair" by Sammy Kaye, "Mule Train" and "That Lucky Old Sun" by Frankie Lane, "Mona Lisa" by Nat "King" Cole, "I Wanna Be Loved" and "I Can Dream, Can't I?" by the Andrews Sisters, and the theme from Carol Reed's 1949 movie, *The Third Man,* which is played on a zither.

Erroll Garner composed the jazz classic "Misty," which he did not record until 1954, and Nat "King" Cole introduced the piano trio, a new jazz medium comprised of piano, guitar, and brass. In New York, Miles Davis, Charlie "Bird" Parker, Dizzy Gillespie, John Coltrane, and Thelonious Monk continued to develop their fast-paced, energetic form of jazz, bebop, which they had started in the late 1940s.

Benny Goodman and the NBC Symphony Orchestra bridged the gap between popular and classical music when Goodman gave the first performance of Aaron Copland's Clarinet Concerto in New York. In 1950, Copland also composed a piano and strings quartet, as well as a song cycle for voice and piano entitled *Twelve Poems of Emily Dickinson.* Arnold Schoenberg, who pioneered the controversial, poorly appreciated or understood, and generally unpopular 12-tone harmonic system in the 1920s, composed "De profundis" (Psalm 130) for unaccompanied choir. Walter Piston premiered his fourth symphony, and John Cage debuted his experimental piece, "Cartridge Music." Leonard Bernstein, Serge Koussevitsky, and Eleanor de Carvalho all led the Israeli Symphony during its 40-city tour of the United States.

The New York City Ballet premiered Bernstein and Jerome Robbins's *The Age of Anxiety,* which is based on the poem by W. H. Auden; choreographer George Balanchine made his first public appearance as a dancer in 22 years; and Merce Cunningham, who had pioneered modern dance as a soloist in the

In 1950, choreographer George Balanchine danced his *Mazurka* with Vida Brown in his first public performance since 1928. *(Photofest)*

Martha Graham Dance Company, started his own company, although he also continued to dance with Graham through 1955. Cunningham's highly experimental collaborations with his partner Cage are especially noteworthy for challenging the very definitions of dance and music.

Composer Kurt Weill, who had collaborated with Bertolt Brecht on the popular *Three-Penny Opera* (1928) and later with poet Langston Hughes, Jay Lerner, and Maxwell Anderson, died on April 3. Russian ballet dancer Vaslav Nijinsky also died that month. Prior to World War I, Nijinsky pioneered modern ballet in such works as *The Afternoon of a Faun* (1912), with music from Claude Debussy's *Prelude to the Afternoon of a Faun,* and *The Rite of Spring* (1913), the score composed by Igor Stravinsky.

A performance of operatic arias sung by Margaret Truman, daughter of the president, occasioned considerable controversy after *Washington Post* music reviewer Paul Hume panned the recital. His review came out during the bleak-est moment of the war, less than two weeks after the Chinese intervention in Korea. Moreover, on the day of the December performance, one of Truman's closest aids, Charlie Ross, died suddenly of heart failure during a press briefing. Truman took out his frustration on Hume, to whom he wrote a blistering let-ter calling the critic a "frustrated old man who wishes he could have been suc-cessful" (Hume was only 39) and promising that if they ever met, Hume would "need a new nose, a lot of beefsteak for black eyes, and perhaps a supporter below!"[8] Hume and the *Washington Post* tactfully elected not to publish the president's outburst, but a copy found its way to the *Washington News,* which printed it on the front page. Although Hume genuinely regretted that the letter had been published and stated that Truman's anguish over Korea and the death of his friend entitled him to an occasional outburst of temper, the president's critics used the occasion to question Truman's mental competence and emo-tional stability. Others berated him for becoming emotional over a trivial per-sonal matter while soldiers were dying in Korea.

While commercial art emphasized realism and conventional values throughout the 1950s, often with religious and patriotic themes, the fine arts were increasingly dominated by abstract expressionism and other forms of nonrepresentational expression. Developed in the 1940s by Jackson Pollock, "action painting" attracted growing popularity. Instead of applying paint with brushes, Pollock and his followers would hurl it against or drip it on the can-vas. The resulting images often expressed a powerful sense of movement, color, and emotion, which was, in fact, the purpose and meaning of the work. In this way, Pollock and the action painters rejected the notion that art should deal with ideas or make a social or political statement. They sought, instead, to make art a visceral, felt experience that bypasses the cognitive process. In 1950, Pol-lock produced *Autumn Rhythm, One,* and *Lavender Mist.* Pollock's work, and that of fellow Americans John Marin and Willem de Kooning were on display at the Venice art festival, which honored 81-year-old Henri Matisse with its grand prize. Elsewhere, in 1950, Marc Chagall painted his *King David,* and, in architecture, the sleek-looking United Nations building opened in New York City.

CHRONICLE OF EVENTS

1950

January 2: In football, Ohio State University defeats the University of California by a score of 17-14 to win the Rose Bowl.

January 5: In defiance of calls by Republican senator Robert Taft and former president Herbert Hoover to provide military protection for Taiwan, Truman denies U.S. military aid to the anticommunist Chinese Nationals on the island and limits assistance to current levels.

January 6: Great Britain recognizes Mao Zedong's communist People's Republic of China (PRC). This action creates a rift with the United States, which continues to recognize Chiang Kai-shek's Nationalists. The British Foreign Office justifies its decision by pointing out that Mao has the support of the Chinese people, and his government maintains military control of the land.

January 10: Soviet ambassador Jacob Malik walks out of the UN Security Council in response to its refusal to replace the Nationalist delegation from China with one from the People's Republic of China. The Soviet boycott of the Security Council lasts throughout most of the year, and after North Korea invades South Korea in June, the absence of the Soviet delegation makes it possible for the United States to obtain UN endorsement of its proposal to defend South Korea, a decision that the Soviets undoubtedly would have vetoed.

January 13: *The Third Man* opens in the United States. Based on Graham Greene's novel, the 1949 British film is set in occupied Vienna after World War II. It stars Orson Welles as a cynical criminal and Joseph Cotton as his childhood friend, an idealistic American who naively becomes caught up in the politics of organized crime and cold war competition in a city divided among the Soviets and Western allies. The film's zither music becomes one of the top hits of 1950.

January 14: Ho Chi Minh, a communist nationalist, declares that his Hanoi-based Democratic Republic of Vietnam is the only legitimate government of Vietnam. China and the Soviet Union recognize it, but the United States (on February 7), France, and Britain recognize instead emperor Bao Dai's Saigon-based government, which was created in 1949 to head

up an associate state within the French Union, with France retaining control of the country's defenses and finances.

January 17: The Brink's security company loses a record $2.7 million when seven armed men wearing Halloween masks rob its headquarters.

January 21: Following a previous trial that concluded with a divided jury, Alger Hiss, a former ranking State Department official, is convicted of lying about past communist affiliations. Four days later Judge Henry W. Goddard sentences Hiss to five years in federal prison.

January 21: T. S. Eliot's play, *The Cocktail Party,* opens on Broadway to great critical acclaim. It goes on to win a Tony Award for best play.

January 21: British writer George Orwell dies. He is best known to Americans as the author of the anticommunist satire *Animal Farm* (1946) and *1984* (1949), a bleak projection of a future under a high-tech, all-controlling Stalin-like regime.

January 25: The Senate adopts the Equal Rights Amendment for women by a vote of 63-19.

January 26: The movie *Twelve O'Clock High* has its world premiere. It stars Gregory Peck as an air force general during World War II, and the opening is planned to commemorate the eighth birthday of the U.S. 8th Air Force and the seventh anniversary of the first daylight precision bombing raid on Germany.

January 31: Truman authorizes development of the hydrogen bomb, which is successfully tested on October 31, 1952.

February 3: Scientist Klaus Fuchs is arrested in Great Britain for supplying information about the atomic bomb to the Soviet Union. Fuchs confesses and is imprisoned until 1959, when he immigrates to East Germany and becomes director of its Institute for Nuclear Physics until his retirement in 1979.

February 5: A month-old strike by soft-coal miners spreads to six states and idles some 400,000 workers. A settlement is not reached until March 5.

February 9: Senator Joseph McCarthy of Wisconsin gains national prominence after charging that more than 200 communists are currently working at the U.S. Department of State. Made before a Republican women's group in Wheeling, West Virginia, McCarthy's unsubstantiated claims of communist infiltration of the government spark his rise to power

Senator Joseph McCarthy's fervent but often unsubstantiated attacks on domestic communists made his name synonymous with the Red Scare. *(Photofest)*

as the nation's foremost communist hunter. The speech begins the fervent anticommunist "witch hunts" soon to become known as "McCarthyism."

February 11: John L. Lewis, president of United Mine Workers (UMW), orders striking miners back to work, but some 370,000 workers remain off the job.

February 15: China and the Soviet Union sign a mutual-defense treaty. The Soviets also agree to return the Manchurian railroad, Port Arthur, and Dairen to China and provide $300 million worth of credit. In return, China agrees to loan hundreds of thousands of workers to the Soviet Union and to install Soviet officers in key positions in the Chinese army, police, and Communist Party.

February 28: Cadillac introduces the first one-piece automobile windshield.

March 1: Chiang Kai-shek officially becomes president of Nationalist China on Taiwan.

March 5: Striking coal miners return to work after receiving a 70¢-per-hour pay raise and other benefits, but the United Mine Workers union suffers heavy fines.

March 5: A survey shows that children spend 27 hours a week watching television, compared to 27 hours and 55 minutes attending school. The children admit that television interferes with their homework, and they express their preferences for Milton Berle, Ed Sullivan, *Six-Gun Playhouse,* and wrestling.

March 12: In the deadliest airplane crash to date, 80 people are killed when a chartered British plane goes down over Wales.

March 13: General Motors Corporation reports its 1949 earnings to be in excess of $650 million, the highest ever recorded by an American corporation.

March 16: Secretary of State Acheson presents his seven-point program to permit peaceful coexistence, "in reasonable security," with the Soviet Union.

March 26: McCarthy charges that former State Department adviser Owen Lattimore spied for the Soviets.

March 29: RCA releases the first color television set.

April 3: Composer Kurt Weill dies in New York at age 50.

April 6: When he arrives in New York, the premier of Ireland is greeted by mass protests against the partition of his country.

April 6: Truman appoints John Foster Dulles as foreign policy adviser to Acheson. Dulles goes on to become secretary of state under Eisenhower from 1953 to 1959.

April 10: The Supreme Court upholds the conviction of two of the Hollywood Ten for contempt of Congress. The Ten had refused to testify before the House Un-American Activities Committee (HUAC), citing their First Amendment protections. The ruling both eliminates the First Amendment as an avenue for witnesses to avoid testifying about their political beliefs and activities and enables HUAC to resume investigations in 1951.

April 12: The United States announces a plan to use penicillin to eliminate venereal disease in Haiti.

April 18: The British-made Avro, the first turbo-jet transport plane, flies from Toronto, Canada, to New York City in one hour.

April 19: Truman authorizes an economic plan for improving conditions for Navajo and Hopi Indian tribes.

April 23: Communist control of mainland China is completed after Chiang Kai-shek orders the evacuation of his Nationalists from Hainan.

April 24: The Supreme Court overturns the conviction of a black defendant because African Americans were excluded from the grand jury that indicted him.

April 27: Great Britain officially recognizes the state of Israel. The United States, Soviet Union, and United Nations had recognized it shortly after its declaration of statehood in May 1948.

May 1: On May Day, a major Soviet holiday, the American Legion of Mosinee, Wisconsin, stages a communist takeover of the city to demonstrate the potential consequences of the communist threat to the American way of life. The event is widely covered by the national print and broadcast media.

May 4: A 100-day auto strike at the Chrysler plant in Detroit ends.

May 6: Truman calls for Hawaii and Alaska to be granted statehood on the grounds that their admission into the United States will strengthen national security.

May 12: The American Bowling Congress rescinds a 34-year-old rule limiting its membership to white men.

May 23: General Motors signs a five-year contract with the United Auto Workers. The deal provides pay raises, pensions, and job security.

May 25: The Brooklyn–Battery Tunnel opens as the longest tunnel in the United States.

May 26: In Miami, Democratic senator Estes Kefauver of Tennessee opens the first hearings by the Special Committee to Investigate Organized Crime. In addition to raising public awareness about the Mafia and other organized-crime syndicates, the committee's investigation is notable as the first congressional hearing to be televised nationally by the major networks.

May 26: The first whooping crane is hatched in captivity in the Arkansas National Game Refuge.

May 27: The United States orders the communist government of Czechoslovakia to close its consulate in New York.

June 4: A record 3.5 million students are reported to have enrolled in Catholic schools for the upcoming fall.

June 5: The Supreme Court rules against segregation in public universities in *Sweatt v. Painter* and *McLaurin v. Oklahoma State Regents.*

June 7: At Truman's behest, the first nationwide conference on aging begins.

Estes Kefauver led the Senate investigation into organized crime. *(Photofest)*

June 8: The Allies grant the Federal Republic of Germany (West Germany) the right to establish its own foreign policy.

June 11: Having recovered from a near-fatal car crash that left doctors doubting he could ever play golf again, Ben Hogan wins the U.S. Open.

June 16: The FBI arrests Julius and Ethel Rosenberg, charging that in 1944 and 1945 they received and passed on to Soviet agents classified information about the atomic bomb, which was then under development during World War II.

June 17: In Chicago, Dr. Richard G. Laoler performs the first human kidney transplant.

June 23: The University of California's Board of Regents unanimously votes to fire 157 employees who have failed to swear that they are not communists.

June 25: In a surprise attack, communist North Korea invades South Korea, thereby inaugurating the Korean War. Later in the day, the UN Security Council meets in an emergency session and authorizes military assistance to South Korea by a 9-0 vote. The Soviet Union is absent because it is boycotting the Security Council for its refusal to seat a communist delegation from mainland China.

June 26: The stock market experiences a dramatic drop.

June 27: Truman orders U.S. air and sea forces to support South Korea.

June 30: An act of Congress extends the military draft and authorizes the president to call the reserves into service.

July 7: Attributing his success to having quit smoking cigarettes, Budge Patty of California defeats Frank Sedgman to win the Wimbledon men's singles tennis tournament.

July 8: General Douglas MacArthur, a World War II hero and military governor of Japan, is named commander in chief of UN forces in Korea.

July 11: Playing in Chicago, the National League wins baseball's All-Star game.

July 26: Truman signs legislation authorizing $15 million in military aid to assist the French effort in their war against communist North Vietnam.

July 26–27: Britain and France agree to send troops to Korea.

July 26–28: An unknown number of South Korean civilian refugees, possibly as many as 400, are killed near the hamlet of No Gun Ri by U.S. troops. Although rumored for many years despite army denials, the killings are not officially acknowledged until a 1999–2001 investigation. Investigators find no conclusive evidence to demonstrate that the killing of refugees was ordered by officers in charge, although some veterans believe that instructions to "stop civilians" meant that they were to use deadly force to prevent unarmed civilians from passing near the hamlet as American troops were withdrawing from the vicinity under pressure. Upon learning the findings of the investigation, President Bill Clinton expresses regret on the part of the United States.

July 31: King Leopold III of Belgium abdicates the throne in favor of his 19-year-old son, Baudouin.

August 3: The Security Council denies communist China entry into the United Nations.

August 6: A B-29 bomber carrying an atomic bomb crashes into a trailer park in California. The bomb does not detonate, but 17 people are killed by the crash.

August 8: Florence Chadwick of California swims across the English Channel in 13 hours and 20 minutes to break a 24-year-old record.

August 12: The Defense Department and Atomic Energy Commission release a 438-page guide on civilian defense against an atomic attack.

August 25: To avert a scheduled strike that could cripple the war industry, Truman orders the army to seize the nation's Class 1 railroads. Threatening to fire or draft union workers who refuse to report to work, the army operates the railways for 21 months, until May 1952, when they are returned to their owners.

August 28: Actress Jean Muir is dropped from the cast of television's *The Aldridge Family* after allegations of communist affiliations surface.

August 29: Althea Gibson becomes the first African-American woman to compete in a national tennis tournament when she enters the U.S. Tennis Open at Forest Hills in Queens, New York.

September 8: The Defense Production Act establishes a wartime system of priorities for materials, provides for wage and price controls, and curbs installment purchases.

September 10: The National Production Authority is established to handle the U.S. wartime economy.

September 15: General MacArthur launches a surprise counterattack at Inchon, the port city for Seoul on Korea's west coast. The landing is quite risky due to the extremely high tides in the region, but the successful assault, which is still regarded among the greatest military maneuvers in history, reverses the tide of the combat in favor of the U.S.-led UN forces.

September 19: British, French, and U.S. foreign ministers announce the official termination of the state of war with Germany and pledge to defend West Germany against attack.

September 19: The UN General Assembly rejects an Indian-Soviet proposal to seat the delegation from communist China.

September 20: Former secretary of state and World War II hero George Marshall becomes secretary of defense.

September 23: Congress overrides Truman's veto of the McCarran Internal Security Act, which establishes concentration camps for communists in Pennsylvania, Florida, Oklahoma, Arizona, and California. The act also requires all communist and communist-dominated organizations to furnish to the federal government the names of all of their members and contributors.

September 23: The Revenue Act increases personal income and corporate taxes.

September 26: UN forces recapture Seoul from the North Koreans.

September 27: Scientists develop the first practical method for converting atomic energy into electricity.

September 28: Premier Zhou Enlai threatens that China will intervene if UN forces invade North Korea. U.S. decision makers believe the threat is a bluff.

September 30: The State Department bans visas to visitors from totalitarian nations.

October 7: After receiving authorization from the General Assembly, UN forces cross the 38th parallel into North Korea. South Korean troops had penetrated into the north about a week earlier.

October 7: The New York Yankees complete a four-game sweep of the Philadelphia Phillies to win baseball's World Series. Philadelphia's Jim Konstanty receives the National League's MVP award; the St. Louis Cardinals's Stan Musial (.346) wins its batting title, and Pittsburgh's Ralph Kiner leads the majors with 47 home runs. The New York Giants's Sal Maglie (18-4) and the Yankee's Vic Raschi (21-8) are the top pitchers in the National and American League, respectively, and Boston's William Goodman wins the American League batting title (.354). Yankee shortstop Phil "Scooter" Rizzuto is named the league's MVP.

October 11: The Federal Communications Commission (FCC) authorizes the Columbia Broadcasting System (CBS) to begin commercial television broadcasts in color.

October 19: The State Department announces an economic plan to assist Iran in the areas of health, agriculture, and education.

October 21: Communist China invades Tibet.

October 24: UN troops reach the Chinese border with North Korea, at the Yalu River.

October 26: UN forces capture Pyongyang, the North Korean capital.

November 1: Two Puerto Rican nationalists attempt to assassinate Truman at his residence, Blair House, in Washington, D.C. Truman and his family are unharmed, but one of his guards is killed and two others are seriously wounded in a shoot-out that also kills one of the assailants. The other is captured and condemned to death, a sentence that Truman later commutes to life in prison.

November 1: Soviet MIG fighter planes enter combat on the side of North Korea.

November 2: Irish playwright George Bernard Shaw dies at age 94.

November 15: Responding to a complaint from National Broadcasting Company (NBC), the FCC rescinds authorization for CBS to begin commercial television broadcasts.

November 17: The United Nations agrees on independence for Libya.

November 18: Roman Catholic priests arrive in Washington, D.C., to protest sex education in public schools.

November 24: Guys and Dolls, a popular hit musical with lyrics by Frank Loesser, opens on Broadway.

November 24–27: Chinese troops enter the Korean War and drive UN forces from Manchuria.

November 30: Truman warns that the United States will use atomic bombs in Korea, if necessary.

November 30: Ending its boycott of the UN Security Council, the Soviet Union vetoes a resolution ordering China to withdraw its troops from Korea.

December 3: In Cleveland, Dr. Charles Bailly reports the invention of a heart-lung machine that can revive the clinically dead.

December 5: Chinese and North Korean troops drive UN forces from Pyongyang.

December 9: Harry Gold is sentenced to 30 years in federal prison for his role in the atomic spy ring that included Klaus Fuchs and the Rosenbergs.

December 10: William Faulkner receives the Nobel Prize in literature, and Ralph Bunche, who mediated the UN settlement that ended hostilities between Israel and the Arab states, receives the Nobel Peace Prize. Bunche is the first black person to win a Nobel Prize.

December 16: Truman declares a national state of emergency after the Chinese offensive in Korea.

December 18: The Brussels Conference convenes. Two notable outcomes are the decision to rearm all the nations of Western Europe and the appointment of World War II hero General Dwight Eisenhower as supreme commander of all NATO forces.

December 24: Chinese troops cross the 38th parallel into South Korea.

December 24: The Cleveland Browns, of the old All-America Conference, defeat the Los Angeles Rams by a score of 30-28 to win the first NFL championship of the newly merged leagues. Ram quarterback Norm Van Brocklin and Ram receiver Tom Fears lead the league in passing and receiving, while Cleveland's Marion Motley is the top running back.

December 25: Middleweight boxer "Sugar" Ray Robinson wins his fifth match in a month while on a boxing tour in Europe. These victories set the stage for a championship fight in 1951 against Jake LaMotta.

December 29: The Yugoslav Emergency Relief Assistance Act provides $50 million of emergency assistance for Yugoslavia, which had earlier broken its affiliation with the Soviet Union.

December 30: In his year-end statement Secretary of State Acheson reiterates U.S. determination to contain communism.

EYEWITNESS TESTIMONY

We know that several eras have gone by since 1932, a year that stood in the recession phase of the depression era, marked the end of the prohibition era, and preceded, by a matter of months, the advent of the Hitler era. We find it hard to recall days and months and years, as we did in the old clock and calendar period, but we remember eras sharply since we have lived through so many of them. We know that the old-fashioned decade, with its gradual changes, has gone forever, leaving us stuck with a new and terrible calculation of time.

Humorist James Thurber recalling the past in his "Author's Memoir" introduction to the re-release of the 1950 updated edition of The Seal in the Bedroom and Other Predicaments, *which he first published in 1932, in Thurber,* Seal in the Bedroom *(1950).*

We must accelerate obsolescence. . . . Basic utility cannot be the foundation of a prosperous apparel industry.

Businessman B. E. Puckett speaking in 1950, in Lois Gordon and Alan Gordon, American Chronicle *(1999), p. 477.*

Modern art to me is nothing more than the expression of contemporary aims of the age that we're living in. . . . My opinion is that new needs need new techniques. And the modern artists have found new ways and new means of making their statements. It seems to me that the modern painter cannot express this age, the airplane, the atom bomb, the radio, in the old forms of the Renaissance or of any other past culture. Each age finds its own technique.

Action painter Jackson Pollock describing the objectives of modern art in an unused tape interview with William Wright from 1950, in Lary May, ed., Recasting America: Culture and Politics in the Age of the Cold War *(1989), p. 214.*

Those who engage in overt acts of perversion lack the emotional stability of normal persons. . . . One homosexual can pollute a Government office.

From a 1950 U.S. Senate report entitled "Employment of Homosexuals and Other Sex Perverts in Government," in Stephen J. Whitfield, The Culture of the Cold War *(1996), p. 44.*

You can't . . . separate homosexuals from subversives. . . . I don't say every homosexual is a subversive, and I don't say every subversive is a homosexual. But a man of low morality is a menace in the government, whatever he is, and they are tied up together.

Nebraskan senator Kenneth Wherry's remarks to a reporter in 1950, in Stephen J. Whitfield, The Culture of the Cold War *(1996), p. 43.*

[This book] is about the way in which one kind of social character, which dominated America in the nineteenth century, is gradually being replaced by a social character of quite a different sort. . . .

In societies in which tradition-direction is the dominant mode of insuring conformity, attention is focused on securing strict conformity in . . . behavior. By contrast, societies in which inner-direction becomes important . . . cannot be satisfied with behavioral conformity alone. Too many novel situations are presented which a code cannot encompass in advance. Consequently the problem of personal choice, solved in the earlier period . . . by channeling choice through rigid social organization, in the period of transitional growth is solved by channeling choice through a rigid though highly individualized character. . . .

The tradition-directed person . . . [hardly thinks] that he might shape his own . . . personal, lifelong goals or that the destiny of his children might be separate from that of the family group. . . . In the phase of transitional growth, however, people of inner-directed character do gain a feeling of control over their own lives and see their children also as individuals with careers to make. . . .

The type of character I shall describe as other-directed seems to be emerging in very recent years in the upper middle class of our larger cities. . . .

What is common to all the other-directed people is that their contemporaries are the source of direction for the individual—either those known to him or those with whom he is indirectly acquainted through friends and through the mass media. This source is of course "internalized" in the sense that dependence on it for guidance in life is implanted early. The goals toward which the other-directed person strives shift with that guidance: it is only the process of striving itself and the process of paying close attention to the signals from others that remain unaltered throughout life. [Italics Riesman]

David Riesman, Nathan Glazer, and Reuel Denney, describing emerging personality types in the postwar era, in Riesman, The Lonely Crowd *(1950), pp. 3–21.*

At first all they saw was a darkening of the sun, a funny color in the sky. They went over to the window, and there it was, blossoming out in the sky away downtown, so beautiful you forgot to be scared.

[An atom bomb has exploded in downtown Manhattan, and Gladys, a suburban housewife, is home with her children.]

Gladys heard the last words [of the governor's radio address] with a sinking sensation of bewilderment. The man had said nothing, nothing at all. Nothing about the city, about the people trapped there . . . nothing but words. . . .

[However, the Emergency Headquarters seems on top of things.] The knowledge, new to Gladys, that the national government had broken down, seemed credible and bearable; as long as something was being done.

[According to the radio,] "Fires are still burning in many parts of the city, but most of the larger buildings are still standing, and many of these are fireproof. Outside the areas of direct hit, many survivors are expected. . . . Local governments are functioning. Trains are running in most sectors. Local wire and telephone services are in operation. Emergency Headquarters are operating in the vicinity of every bombed area. Amateur radio operators are already filling in nationwide gaps in communication. . . ."

[A ranking security force official tells Gladys that preparations for dealing with an attack are secret because] "any time the government let out any information about what we were doing some scientist would start yelling about warmongers, or some reds would have a demonstration. . . ."

"Why he [the official] likes this!" Gladys thought suddenly. "He's having fun."

Judith Merril's description of a fictional atomic attack on New York City in 1950, in Merril, Shadow on the Hearth *(1950), pp. 27–29, 46, 53–55.*

There were no hills or valleys or fields or cities or state lines beneath them. In an uncanny vacuum of darkness they roared eastward. For these few hours they were freed from the land mass that claimed them. The combination of words and wind is an ancient and delicious one. Between them time folds into itself accordion-wise. . . . Halliday's mind, reeling from topic to topic, had fixed on the point of departure between the writer who succeeds only in catching the moment and the artist who relates the

particular moment to the universal, like [T. S.] Eliot. Maybe you'd call him a capitalist lackey, a clerical apologist, a bootlicking Anglophile or worse. But a hundred years from now will people remember that he was a monarchist and that the *New Masses* sneered at him or that he wrote lines like

> April is the cruellest month, breeding
> Lilacs out of the dead land, mixing
> Memory and desire, stirring
> Dull roots with spring rain.

Budd Schulberg challenging Marxist literary theory, in Schulberg, The Disenchanted *(1950), p. 108.*

I am sorry if some people were offended by the appearance of a performer whose political beliefs are a matter of public controversy.

Television host Ed Sullivan apologizing after receiving more than 400 phone calls and telegraphs in January 1950 in objection to the performance on his show of tap dancer and accused communist Paul Draper, in Merle Miller, The Judges and the Judged *(1952), p. 174.*

The flying-saucer yarn was much too good to die young. . . . Latest rumor, presented as truth by the current issue of *True* magazine: "For the past 175 years the planet Earth has been under systematic close-range examination by living, intelligent observers from another planet."

. . . Hundreds of newspapers repeated this fascinating *True*ism; Frank Edwards, Walter Winchell, Lowell Thomas and other radio commentators trumpeted it over the air. Denials from Washington had little effect. . . .

Unearthly tongue. Some time ago, according to one version, a large space ship crashed in flames in New Mexico. Its 15 crew members were burned to a crisp but luckily some of its instruments remained intact. One was a radio receiver, over which at short intervals came cryptic messages in an unearthly tongue.

While U.S. observers were studying the wreck, the story went, a second space craft crashed near by. Both of its two occupants were killed, but one of their bodies, thrown free, was found in good condition. The interplanetary visitor was about three feet tall and a bit primitive, even monkeylike in appearance. His body was rushed to the Rosenwald Foundation in Chicago for expert examination.

Pressurized Prisoners. This fanciful tale was hardly in circulation when a bigger & better version caught up with it. The space ship's space men were not dead at all. Fifteen of them had been captured alive. They would not, or could not talk . . . but one of them obligingly drew a map of the solar system and pointed to the second planet from the sun. Thereupon, at the suggestion of a smart Earthling, all the prisoners were hastily placed in a pressurized chamber filled with carbon dioxide to simulate the atmosphere of Venus.

"Flying Saucer" rumors in "Visitors from Venus," Time *(January 9, 1950), p. 49.*

Amazing Asbestos!
Ancient Romans believed that "magic asbestos" could be found in the desert sands where it got used to fierce heat!

Today, you know that asbestos mines yield the "magic mineral"—with its rock-like resistance to heat and cold . . to any weather.

Years of tough weather doesn't hurt K & M asbestos corrugated walls and roofs on factories, store and other buildings. Maintenance cost stays down!

Advertisement for Keasbey & Mattison Company, purveyor of asbestos, which was widely used in 1950s and later shown to cause cancer in Time *(January 9, 1950), p. 82.*

The Communists' bad behavior [in seizing the U.S. consulate in Beijing] did settle one debate—or rather make it irrelevant. Why should the U.S. worry about whether or not to recognize Communist China, when the Communist themselves didn't seem to wish it, or to care what the U.S. thought?

Editorial reflecting strained U.S.-PRC relations, in Time *(January 23, 1950), p. 2.*

I should like to make it clear to you that whatever the outcome of any appeal which Mr. Hiss or his lawyer may take, I do not intend to turn my back on Alger Hiss. I think every person who has known Alger Hiss or has served with him at any time has upon his conscience the very serious task of deciding what his attitude is and what his conduct should be. This must be done by each person in light of his own standards and his own principles. For me, there is very little doubt about these standards or principles. They were stated for us a very long time ago . . . on the Mount of Olives and if you are interested in seeing them you will find them in the 25th

Chapter of the Gospel according to St. Matthew beginning with verse 34.

Have you any other questions?

Secretary of State Dean Acheson's remarks at a press conference on January 25, 1950, following the conviction of Alger Hiss, in Acheson, Present at the Creation *(1969), p. 360.*

I am very unhappy to conclude that the hydrogen bomb should be developed and built. I do not think we should intentionally lose the armaments race; to do this will be to lose our liberties, and with Patrick Henry, I value my liberties more than I do my life.

[If the United States does not develop the hydrogen bomb, the Soviets will be in a position to say] "We will build these bombs and issue ultimata to the Western countries, and the millennium of Communism will be with us immediately. . . ."

I personally hope very much that the bombs will not explode. . . . However, nature does not behave in the way I should like at times, and so there is no use in engaging in wishful thinking. I think we should assume that the bomb can be built. . . .

Due to some curious prejudice which I think I understand, the advisers to the U.S. Government have not wished to follow certain lines of development in regard to this problem. No such prejudice exists among the Canadians, British, French, and presumably the U.S.S.R. . . . The result of this situation is highly dangerous to the United States; in fact we may have already lost the armaments race.

Nobel laureate Harold Urey speaking before the Roosevelt Day dinner of Americans for Democratic Action at New York's Waldorf-Astoria Hotel in early February 1950, in "The Atom," Time *(February 6, 1950), p. 1.*

Today we are engaged in a final, all-out battle between communistic atheism and Christianity. The modern champions of communism have selected this as the time. And, ladies and gentlemen, the chips are down. They are truly down. . . .

Ladies and gentlemen, can there be anyone here tonight who is so blind as to say that the war is not on? Can there be anyone who fails to realize that the communist world has said, "The time is now," that this is the time for the showdown between the democratic Christian world and the communistic atheistic world? . . .

I have here in my hand a list of 205—a list of names that were made known to the secretary of state as being members of the Communist Party and who nevertheless are still working and shaping policy in the State Department.

One thing to remember in discussing the communists in our government is that we are not dealing with spies who get thirty pieces of silver to steal the blueprints of a new weapon. We are dealing with a far more sinister type of activity because it permits the enemy to guide and shape our policy. . . .

Senator Joseph McCarthy speaking before a Republican women's group in Wheeling, West Virginia, on February 9, 1950, when he first charged that communists occupied high positions in the government, in Robert Torricelli and Andrew Carroll, eds., In Our Own Words *(1999), pp. 174–76.*

[Senator McCarthy] should keep talking and if one case doesn't work out, he should proceed with another.

Senator Robert Taft of Ohio in March 1950, as recalled by Secretary of State Dean Acheson, in Acheson, Present at the Creation *(1969), p. 363.*

With all these charges flying around I want to tell you about the meeting which was being broken up by communists, so the chairman had to send for the police. When they entered the hall, they started wielding their clubs pretty vigorously. The unfortunate chairman got a crack over the head and, when he protested, the cop shouted, "You're under arrest!"

"I can't be," pleaded the chairman, "I'm an anti-communist."

"I don't give a damn," hollered the cop, "whether you're a communist, or an anti-communist, or what kind of communist you are. You're under arrest!"

Secretary of State Dean Acheson in a press conference on March 8, 1950, the day the Tydings committee convened to investigate Senator Joseph McCarthy's charges, in Acheson, Present at the Creation *(1969), p. 363.*

Organize a letter-writing group of six to ten relatives and friends to make the sentiments of Americans heard on the important issues of the day. Phone, telegraph, or write to radio and television sponsors employing entertainers with known front records. There are an estimated two to three fully qualified and thoroughly loyal Americans at present unemployed ready to step into every job vacated by a Stal-

inist writer, actor, or entertainer. Give Americans a break just for a change by giving pro-Communists the bum's rush off the air. . . .

[Readers may obtain names of objectionable performers from] this summary, *Counterattack, Alert, The Sign, National Republic, New Leader,* and other dependable sources. . . .

In writing or phoning radio sponsors and others MAKE NO CHARGES OR CLAIMS.

Merely state that you buy their products or services and enjoy their radio or TV shows but that you DISAPPROVE OR OBJECT TO SO-AND-SO ON THEIR PROGRAMS AND DESIRE THAT THEY BE REMOVED. NOTHING ELSE. . . . DON'T LET THE SPONSORS PASS THE BUCK BACK TO YOU BY DEMANDING "PROOF" OF COMMUNIST FRONTING BY SOME CHARACTER ABOUT WHOM YOU HAVE COMPLAINED. YOU DON'T HAVE TO PROVE ANYTHING. . . . YOU SIMPLY DO NOT LIKE SO-AND-SO ON THEIR PROGRAMS.

Karl Baarslag, editor of the American Legion newsletter, Summary of Trends and Developments Exposing the Communist Conspiracy, *urging readers of the April 1950 issue to pressure sponsors to fire suspected communists or communist sympathizers, in Merle Miller,* The Judges and the Judged *(1952), pp. 159–60.*

Mr. President, I speak as a Republican. I speak as a woman. I speak as a United States senator. I speak as an American.

The United States Senate has long enjoyed worldwide respect as the greatest deliberative body in the world. But recently that deliberative character has too often been debased to the level of a forum of hate and character assassination sheltered by the shield of congressional immunity. . . .

The nation sorely needs a Republican victory. But I do not want to see the Republican Party ride to political victory on the Four Horsemen of Calumny—Fear, Ignorance, Bigotry and Smear. . . . I do not want to see the Republican Party win that way. While it might be a fleeting victory for the Republican Party; it would be a more lasting defeat for the American people.

Senator Margaret Chase Smith of Maine responding on June 1, 1950, to her colleagues' conduct during hearings investigating McCarthy's accusations, in Robert Torricelli and Andrew Carroll, eds., In Our Own Words *(1999), pp. 176–78.*

Ever since W. R. Burnett's *Little Caesar* muscled into films with a quality of arrogance and toughness such as the screen had not previously known, this writer and this type of story—about criminals in the higher realm of crime—have been popular and often imitated, but *Little Caesar* has yet to be surpassed. However, we've got to say one thing: a lot of pictures have come close—and one of them is *The Asphalt Jungle* also from a novel by Mr. Burnett.

> *Critic Bosley Crowther reviewing* The Asphalt
> Jungle, *in Crowther, "The Asphalt Jungle,"*
> New York Times, *June 9, 1950,*
> *p. 29.*

Back in the 1950s, not only was smoking a normal thing to do, it was more, it was a sign of sophistication, of being grown up. Everyone did it. Mother smoked two or three packs of Parliaments a day. Daddy smoked cigars. . . .

My friends and I tried very hard to be grown up by emulating our parents and their friends, starting when we were children by lighting matches, then graduating to cigarettes. By the time we were at Chadwick [a private school] we were surreptitiously smoking, against the rules of course. Unfortunately, I got caught. . . . My timing couldn't have been worse. I had to remain at school the weekend after the end of the semester . . . [on] my sixteenth birthday—the day I was to get my first car.

> *Joan Benny, daughter of comedian Jack Benny,*
> *recalling being disciplined for cigarette smoking*
> *on her 16th birthday, June 17, 1950,*
> *in Jack Benny and Joan Benny,*
> Sunday Nights at Seven
> *(1990), p. 194.*

With television going into its third big year . . . the entire industry is becoming increasingly aware of the necessity to plug all Commie propaganda loopholes. Networks and station heads, with a tremendous financial stake, want no part of Commies or pinkos. Sponsors, sensitive in the extreme to blacklisting, want no part of Commies or their sympathizers. Advertising agencies held responsible by sponsors for correct exercise of discretion in programming, want no controversy of any kind. For that reason, [the] *Red Channels* listing of performers who, innocently or maliciously, are affiliated with Commie-front organizations will be a reference book in preparing any program.

> *Television host Ed Sullivan endorsing the publication*
> Red Channels: The Report of Communist
> Influence in Radio and Television *in his syndicated*
> *newspaper column on June 21, 1950, in John Cogley,*
> Report on Blacklisting, *vol. 2*
> *(1956), p. 50.*

North Korean forces, consisting of seven divisions and five brigades, with an air force of 100–150 Soviet-made planes crossed the 38th Parallel at 4 A.M. Korean time, June 25. The main attack was down the Pochon-Uijongbu-Seoul corridor. Other attacks were launched in the Ongjin Peninsula in the west, against Ch'unch'on in the eastern mountains, and down the east coast road. The ROK [South Korean army] forces initially available for defense numbered only five divisions with no air force or armor.

> *The U.S. State Department's initial report of North*
> *Korea's invasion of South Korea on June 24, 1950, in*
> *Donald Knox,* The Korean War: Pusan to Chosin
> *(1985), p. 5.*

For nine years, ending last February, I worked as an undercover man for the Federal Bureau of Investigation. I was one of a number of ordinary citizens picked to infiltrate the Communist Party of the United States and to all outward appearances act as if I were a convinced communist. For the last seven years of my nine-year service, I was a member of the party itself, and quite active in it.

It was a tough assignment and I'm glad now that it's over. I'm on speaking terms again with my brothers and sisters, who naturally looked upon me as a black sheep. I wish that my mother could have lived to see me cleared, but she didn't. Last year she died thinking I was a traitor to my country, and I couldn't run the risk of telling her I wasn't. . . .

My acting must have been satisfactory. At one time I belonged to twenty-three communist-front organizations. During the whole period of my undercover work the total must have run to seventy-five. I attended about 2,000 communist-front and Communist Party Meetings.

> *Matt Cvetic describing his nine years as an FBI*
> *infiltrator, in Cvetic, "I Posed as a Communist for the*
> *FBI,"* Saturday Evening Post *(July 15, 1950)*
> *(Part 1 of 3), p. 17.*

Everyone must know by now that something has gone wrong, very wrong, in the capital of the United States. And it is deeply important to try to understand what has gone wrong in Washington, and why.

What has happened is really very simple. For the first time in American history, the United States is now faced with the threatened failure of American leadership in a time of great danger. And as a direct consequence of this threatened failure of leadership, a miasma of neurotic fear and internal suspicion is seeping in over the nation's capital, like some noxious effluvium from the marshy Potomac.

> *Joseph Alsop and Stewart Alsop, discussing the effects of the nascent Red Scare, in Alsop and Alsop, "Why Has Washington Gone Crazy?"* Saturday Evening Post *(July 29, 1950), p. 20.*

I thought that to be the policy of the United Nations and of our government.

> *Songwriter Vern Partlow commenting on his "talking blues" song "Old Man Atom," which warns that we must have either "peace in the world or the world in pieces" and was a popular hit in August 1950 before being withdrawn from circulation after protests from the Joint Committee Against Communism, in Merle Miller,* The Judges and the Judged *(1952), p. 178.*

Col. Sidney H. Bingham, chairman of New York City's Board of Transportation, is obsessed with the idea that it is possible to have a city without having a traffic jam. The colonel goes even further. If we don't free our cities from traffic strangulation pretty soon, he says, we won't have any cities; they'll become ghost towns.

On both these points the colonel has been anticipated by impressive numbers of thinkers and planners and ordinary gas-burning worriers like you and me. One school wouldn't even try to save the big towns; write 'em off, it says, and reassemble them in decentralized units. . . . The familiar complaint of the metropolitan cabdriver puts it less elegantly, but no less feelingly, "Let's give it all back to the Indians."

> *Jerome Ellison discussing the effect of the postwar boom in auto sales, in Ellison, "Is Traffic Strangling Our Cities?"* Saturday Evening Post *(August 5, 1950), pp. 34–35.*

On August 13, the Northeastern Military District held a meeting of its commanders at and above the division-level in Shenyang. . . . [T]he PLA's [Peoples's Liberation Army] 13th Army Corps had moved into the Chinese-Korean border area by early August. . . .

The meeting focused on these questions: how to ensure our national security, and how to defend the northeastern borders? Through a most lively discussion, all attending officers believed that, if the U.S. imperialists were allowed to occupy all of Korea, it would retrace imperialist Japan's old path to invade the Northeast and North China. Therefore, the question became: was it actually acceptable for us to allow the Americans to occupy Korea and, then, to invade China? Or would it be better for us to take the initiative now, assisting the Korean People's Army and eliminating the enemy in Korea? . . .

Eventually, the discussion led to a heightened sense of confidence among most of the comrades regarding a fight with American troops. A main reason behind this positive result was that the meeting particularly analyzed the conditions favoring us by which we could win the war.

Our forces, first of all, were superior in numbers. . . . We . . . could continue the relatively easy transfer of our forces to Korea from our more than four million troops in China.

Second, our forces were superior in quality. The American forces were being sent to Korea without a clear mission. Their morale was low. . . . [T]he Chinese army was imbued with an indomitable spirit to crush all enemies.

Third, the logistics service was to our advantage. . . . The enemy's supplies heavily depended on their overseas shipments from America. . . .

Fourth, justice was on our side. Sympathies all over the world were on our side. The enemy was in an unfavorable international position.

> *Du Ping Du Ping, China's director of the Political Affairs Department of the Northeast Border Defense Army, describing a key meeting on August 13, 1950, that led to China's entry into the Korean War, in Du Ping,* My Experience at the Headquarters of the Chinese People's Volunteers *(1989), pp. 17–22.*

One of the worst penalties of crime is loneliness. Every criminal I ever knew was a desperately lonely character. A thief . . . is behind bars so much or so busy running and hiding that he has little time or opportunity for normal romance. Usually his love life consists mostly of furtive episodes with gold diggers and women little or no better than streetwalkers.

He's afraid to get married, because he suspects any woman who'd have him of being after his loot, and because a wife is a hostage to fortune which he can't afford as a hunted man. But even a professional thief longs for real love and companionship.

James "Big Jim" Morton describing how crime does not pay, in Morton, "I Was King of the Thieves," Saturday Evening Post *(August 19, 1950), p. 30.*

I was designated Director General of the United States Railroads [after the army seized control of the railroads]. . . . I organized a small but highly effective staff at the Department level. In addition, I ordered to active duty, by authority of the President, Secretary of Defense, and Secretary of the Army, a number of officers from civilian life who were railroad specialists. I organized regional (divisional) control centers, and in some cases the regional control officers were railroad presidents who held Reserve commissions in the United States Army. In one case, we appointed one control officer directly to the rank of Colonel, Army of the United States, which there was authority to do. . . .

One of the most difficult experiences in this unwelcome job involved the so-called "sick strikes." The employees of the two unions began to feign sickness and fail to report for work. They could not strike against the Government. This was a subterfuge. These practices began to spread rather widely and were seriously disrupting the operation of the entire Class I railroad system. They were reaching the point when they could have very seriously impaired the support of our Korean conflict effort. . . . The idea was this: That I would issue an order that anyone who did not report for duty at his assigned shift without a certificate of illness from an independent qualified doctor would immediately be separated from railroad service, in other words fired; that he would lose his seniority, and that would mean his seniority and his pension under the Railway Retirement Act. . . .

And so I called the President on my White House phone from the office late one evening and I said, "Mr. President, the situation is serious. We are headed for a crisis. I have sought advice; there is no unanimity. I see no place else to go but to have recourse to this drastic action," which I outlined briefly. And his words were, "Well, God bless you and good luck; if you are going to do it, I hope it works. I leave it to you."

It worked.

Karl R. Bendetsen, assistant secretary of the U.S. Army, 1950–52, describing his responsibilities after Truman had the army seize the railroads on August 25, 1950, in Jerry N. Hess, "Oral History Interview with Karl R. Bendetsen" (November 21, 1972), available online.

No Name Ridge is a barren, useless place with a few scrub bushes and a patch of reddish soil in the center, the result of a landslide in some forgotten rainy season. To the right, a dark gully scars its side. It is called No Name Ridge for the quite straightforward reason that it has no name. But No Name Ridge will not be forgotten by the U.S. Marine Corps.

Early one morning last week, a U.S. Marine assault force prepared to storm No Name Ridge. . . . As the Marines advanced down the valley toward the ridge they were met with a hail of fire. From the left rear came the angry eruption of a machine gun. Then another machine gun opened from the valley floor to the right rear as the marines started up No Name Ridge. From the top of the hill came more machine-gun fire, interlaced with blasts from other automatic weapons.

Hell burst around the leathernecks as they moved up the barren face of the ridge. Everywhere along the assault line, men dropped. To continue looked impossible. But, all glory forever to the bravest men I ever saw, the line did not break. The casualties were unthinkable, but the assault force never turned back. It moved, fell down, got up and moved again.

"I never saw men with so much guts," said Marine Brigadier General Edward Craig as he watched through his glasses.

Correspondent James Bell with the U.S. Marines on the Naktong front in Korea, in Bell, "Battle of No Name Ridge," Time *(August 28, 1950), p. 22.*

It was no secret along radio and TV row today that the sponsor and the advertising agency were considerably perturbed about what was believed would be certain public resentment. . . . Amazing, isn't it, that so many of these pink teas seem to "just happen" to the Columbia Broadcasting System?

Jack O'Brian, columnist for the New York Journal-American, *complaining in September 1950 about the appearance on Ed Sullivan's* Toast of the Town *TV show of singer Lena Horne, who was listed in* Red Channels, *in Merle Miller,* The Judges and the Judged *(1952), pp. 185–86.*

The Columbia Broadcasting System wishes to point out that Miss Lena Horne has appeared recently . . . on the NBC *Show of Shows* . . . and has appeared on many other radio and TV programs without comment from the press. Ed Sullivan's record . . as a vigorous fighter of Communism, subversives, and all un-American activities is too well known to require further elaboration by CBS.

CBS vice president Hubbel Robinson, Jr., responding to newspaper columnist Jack O'Brian's charge in September 1950 that CBS coddled communists, in Merle Miller, The Judges and the Judged *(1952), p. 186.*

At the foot of Hill 117 we stopped and waited for an artillery barrage to soften up the enemy. Down the road from the north rolled four or five American tanks. Here comes help, I thought. We were sure going to need their firepower. All of a sudden a machine gun stitched a stream of fire across the company's rear. I rolled over on one elbow and looked behind me. Someone yelled, "God, they're shooting at us." . . . I saw a puff of smoke. Just that quick a shell landed near me. It rolled me over into a little gully. I lay dazed. . . . Down the road, some Marines, waving their arms wildly, raced toward the tanks. It's a miracle they weren't fired on. . . .

Obviously, a lot of men had been hit. . . .

This incident just took the starch out of the company. It was devastating to be shot up by our own tanks. Men moved around but the movement lacked purpose.

Private, First Class, Doug Koch describing "friendly fire" in Korea on September 3, 1950, in Donald Knox, The Korean War: Pusan to Chosin *(1985), p. 178.*

From coast to coast, indignant citizens took after Communists, their party-line friends, and some they just suspected of being party-liners. Distinctions were not always finely drawn, and so the actions they took ranged from sound to silly to unjust. Items:

NBC postponed the fall premiere of the TV version of *The Aldrich Family*, because it had received a lot of protests against one member of the cast, actress Jean Muir. She was identified as a leftie in a directory [*Red Channels*] published by *Counterattack*. Rejoined Actress Muir: "It's strange . . especially since I consider Communism one of the most vicious things in the country today." The sponsor, General Foods, said it

was making no judgment on the charges, but fired her as "a controversial personality."

Members of Joe Ryan's A.F.L. [American Federation of Labor] longshoremen, who a week earlier had balked at unloading inbound cargoes of Russian furs and crab meat, refused to touch 2,000 cases of Polish hams aboard two American freighters at New York docks.

The Peace Information Center, a Manhattan outfit which has been a wholesale distributor of the Red-sponsored Stockholm "Peace" Petition, was directed by the Department of Justice to register as agent of a foreign power.

New Hampshire's Wentworth by the Sea Hotel canceled a scheduled Sunday evening talk by Owen Lattimore [whom Senator McCarthy had accused of being a communist agent] after the management polled the guests, found that more than half who voted did not want to hear him.

An overview of responses to the Red Scare, in "The Heat's On," Time *(September 4, 1950), p. 13.*

Is Korea a preliminary to an all-out struggle with Russia? Or will we have to keep putting out little fires, one by one, as the Kremlin lights them?

Demaree Bess questioning Truman's policy of containing international communism, in Bess, "How Long Will This War Last?" Saturday Evening Post *(September 9, 1950), pp. 22–23.*

The history of war proves that nine times out of ten an army has been destroyed because its supply lines have been cut off. . . . We shall land at Inchon, and I shall crush them.

General Douglas MacArthur, commander of UN forces in Korea, describing his plan to land at Inchon, which he carried out on September 15, 1950, in Donald Knox, The Korean War: Pusan to Chosin *(1985), p. 197.*

Two things scared me to death. One, we were not landing on a beach; we were landing against a seawall. . . . Two, the landing was scheduled for 5:30 P.M. This would give us only about two hours of daylight. . . .

Lieutenant Colonel Harold S. Rose describing his concerns about the Inchon landing of September 15, 1950, in Donald Knox, The Korean War: Pusan to Chosin *(1985), p. 214.*

Five-star general Douglas MacArthur assumed command of UN forces shortly after the outbreak of the Korean War. *(Photofest)*

A poem is energy transferred from where the poet got it (he will have some several causations), by way of the poem itself to, all the way over to, the reader. Okay. Then the poem itself must, at all points, be a high-energy-construct and, at all points, an energy-discharge. . . . [T]he *principle,* the law which presides conspicuously over such composition . . . is this: FORM IS NEVER MORE THAN AN EXTENSION OF CONTENT. . . . [T]he *process* can be boiled down to one statement . . .: ONE PERCEPTION MUST IMMEDIATELY AND DIRECTLY LEAD TO A FURTHER PERCEPTION.

From Charles Olson's 1950 manifesto on poetry, "Projective Verse," which first appeared in Poetry New York in October 1950, in James E. Miller, Jr., ed., Heritage of American Literature, *vol. 2,* Civil War to the Present (1991), pp. 1, 445–46.

Had they [the Chinese] interfered in the first or second months [of the Korean War], it would have been decisive. We are no longer fearful of their interven-

tion. . . . The Chinese have 300,000 men in Manchuria. Of these probably not more than 100,000 to 125,000 are distributed along the Yalu River. They have no air force. Now that we have bases for our air force in Korea, if the Chinese tried to get down to Pyongyang there would be the greatest slaughter.

Transcript of General Douglas MacArthur's statement to President Truman during their meeting at Wake Island in the North Pacific on October 15, 1950, in David McCullough, Truman, (1992), p. 804.

The past week has witnessed the effective elimination of the organized Communist military forces in all of Korea, and the at least temporary disappearance of the Kim Il Sung regime. The question of the future of Korea is therefore upon us. The short period immediately preceding the crossing of the Parallel witnessed frantic efforts by the Communist bloc, and corollary attempts by India and other friendly states, to safeguard North Korea from invasion. The operations of the former were based on the awareness that annihilation of the Kim Il Sung regime would weaken the Communist drive in both Asia and in Europe. The [Jawaharlal] Nehru [prime minister of India] viewpoint, on the other hand, appeared to rest on the conviction that the North Korean state must be saved from extinction, lest too complete a defeat bring about direct Chinese or Russian participation.

Premier Nehru's request for an American promise to remain south of the artificial border ran counter to the logic of the military situation. The granting of this extraordinary sanctuary would have given the aggressors space and time to regroup and to be rearmed by their Communist friends. . . .

Military logic was fortified . . . by other considerations, emotional and pragmatic. The end of the Southern campaign left thousands of American prisoners of war unaccounted for. At the same time, it presents the picture of vast numbers of Korean kidnapees . . . carried away with the retreating armies, in the reborn tradition of a millennium ago. The habitual Communist murder of prisoners (presaged by the mass slaughter of Polish officers eleven years before) had roused reasonable demands for punishment, which would go unheeded if peace were to leave the Northern regime intact. Moreover, the Parallel as a *political* boundary had no economic, ethnic or geographic basis, and had never been recognized by either group as possessing political validity.

> *Leonard M. Bertsch, discussing the problems inherent in a political solution to the Korean War, in Bertsch, "The Problems of Victory in Korea,"* America: National Catholic Weekly Review *(November 4, 1950), p. 129.*

Because two crackpots or crazy men tried to shoot me a few days ago my good and efficient guards are nervous. So I'm trying to be as helpful as I can. Would like very much to take a walk this morning but the S[ecret] S[ervice] . . . and the "Boss" [his wife, Bess] and Margie [his daughter] are worried about me—so I won't take my usual walk.

It's hell to be President.

> *President Truman's diary entry for November 5, 1950, in David McCullough,* Truman *(1992), p. 813.*

(1) Your campaign plan of 07:00 today is perfect. Please carry it out firmly. (2) Please devote your full attention to the enemy parachute troops' landing in your rear area. You should have the control of necessary armed forces and some vehicles in the hands of your Headquarters and the Rear-services Department, being prepared at any time to eliminate the enemy parachute landing forces. The enemy has already had a group of intelligence agents land in the area east of Unsan. They are reportedly moving toward the Yalu River. Please give due attention to taking care of them. (3) Please give your full attention to the security of your command headquarters. You must under no circumstances take this lightly. (4) The enemy may possibly use napalm in this campaign. Please find out methods to deal with it. (5) Your release of the American war prisoners has received a great response from the international community. Please prepare another release of a large group [of the POWs], for instance, about 300 to 400 men, after this campaign.

> *China's leader Mao Zedong in a telegram to General Peng Dehuai and others, November 24, 1950, at the beginning of China's full entry into the Korean War, in Mao, "Mao's Telegrams during the Korean War, October–December 1950," available online.*

It is a great opportunity for our army to destroy the enemy forces on a large-scale, and to fundamentally solve the Korean problem. Forces on your western front should strive for the annihilation of five American and British divisions, and four South Korean divisions. The eastern front forces should try to eliminate two American divisions and one South Korean division. It is certainly possible to do so. The entire campaign may be planned for a period of 20 days. The campaign can be divided into many battles on different scales. The period can include several short breaks, and quick reorganizations between the battles. Allow one or two days at least for each break, and three or four days at most. You can redeploy your battle formation and continue on to the next battle. Thus, in regard to the campaign as a whole, that [continuous fighting] may lessen our casualties and lower the cost. It is hoped you will enhance our army's morale, and strive for a big victory.

> *Premier Mao Zedong in a telegram to General Peng Dehuai and others, November 28, 1950, at the beginning of China's full entry into the Korean War, in Mao, "Mao's Telegrams during the Korean War, October–December 1950," available online.*

To do this [expand the Korean War into China] would be to fall into a carefully laid Russian trap. We should use all available political, economic and psychological action to limit the war.

> *Defense secretary George Marshall in an emergency National Security Council meeting on November 28, 1950, in David McCullough,* Truman *(1992), p. 817.*

It looks very bad. [Italics Truman.]

> *President Harry S. Truman describing the situation in Korea in his diary entry for December 2, 1951, in David McCullough,* Truman *(1992), p. 825.*

Miss Truman is a unique American phenomenon with a pleasant voice of little size and fair quality. She is extremely attractive on stage.

. . . Yet Miss Truman cannot sing very well. She is flat a good deal of the time—more last night than at any time we have heard her in past years. There are few moments during her recital when one can relax and feel confident that she will make her goal, which is the end of the song.

. . . It is an extremely unpleasant duty to record such unhappy facts about so honestly appealing a person. But as long as Miss Truman sings as she has for three years, and does today, we seem to have no

From left to right: Secretary of State Dean Acheson; President Harry S. Truman; his daughter, Margaret; and his wife, Bess, pose for the press. *(Photofest)*

recourse unless it is omit comment on her programs altogether.

Paul Hume, music critic for the Washington Post, *reviewing a December 6, 1950, performance of opera arias at Constitution Hall by President Truman's daughter, Margaret, in David McCullough,* Truman *(1992), pp. 827–28.*

Mr. Hume: I've just read your lousy review of Margaret's concert. I've come to the conclusion that you are an "eight ulcer man on four ulcer pay."

It seems to me that you are a frustrated old man who wishes he could have been successful. When you write such poppy-cock . . it shows conclusively that you're off the beam and at least four of your ulcers are at work.

Some day I hope to meet you. When that happens you'll need a new nose, a lot of beefsteak for black eyes, and perhaps a supporter below!

[Columnist Westbrook] Pegler, a gutter snipe, is a gentleman alongside you. I hope you'll accept that statement as a worse insult than a reflection on your ancestry.

President Truman's letter of December 6, 1950 to Washington Post *music critic Paul Hume, in David McCullough,* Truman *(1992), p. 829.*

HOW CAN YOU PUT YOUR TRIVIAL PERSONAL AFFAIRS BEFORE THOSE OF ONE HUNDRED AND SIXTY MILLION PEOPLE. OUR BOYS DIED WHILE YOUR INFANTILE MIND WAS ON YOUR DAUGHTER'S REVIEW. INADVERTENTLY YOU SHOWED THE WHOLE WORLD WHAT YOU ARE. NOTHING BUT A LITTLE SELFISH PIPSQUEAK.

Anonymous telegram to President Truman from December 1950, written in response to Truman's letter to music critic Paul Hume, in David McCullough, Truman *(1992), p. 830.*

Our tragedy today is a general and universal fear so long sustained by now that we can even bear it. There are no longer problems of the spirit. There is only the question: When will I be blown up? Because of this, the young man or woman writing today has forgotten the problems of the human heart in conflict with itself which alone can make good writing because only that is worth writing about, worth the agony and the sweat. . . .

It is easy enough to say that man is immortal simply because he will endure, that when the last ding-dong of doom has clanged and faded from the last worthless rock hanging tideless in the last red and dying evening, that even then there will still be one more sound: that of his puny, inexhaustible voice still talking. I refuse to accept this. I believe that man will not merely endure: He will prevail. He is immortal, not because he alone among creatures has an inexhaustible voice, but because he has a soul, a spirit capable of compassion and sacrifice and endurance. The poet's and writer's duty is to write about these things. It is his privilege to help man endure by lifting his heart, by reminding him of the courage and honor and hope and pride and compassion and pity and sacrifice which have been the glory of his past. The poet's voice need not merely be the record of man. It can be one of the props, the pillars to help him endure and prevail.

From William Faulkner's Nobel Prize acceptance speech, delivered on December 10, 1950, in Robert Torricelli and Andrew Carroll, eds., In Our Own Words *(1999), pp. 179–80.*

3

The Cold War Settles In
1951

When J. D. Salinger published *The Catcher in the Rye* on July 15, 1951, he tapped into several anxieties then prevalent, both consciously and unconsciously, in American society. Anticipating such later movies as *Rebel Without a Cause* (1955), *Blackboard Jungle* (1955), and *West Side Story* (1961, adapted from the 1957 play), Salinger's novel explores the world of troubled teenagers in the postwar era, a world in which teens have more financial independence, sexual freedom, greater access to automobiles and weapons, and less direct adult supervision than at any other prior time in history. Like Truman Capote's *The Grass Harp,* also published in 1951, *The Catcher in the Rye* is told from the viewpoint of a child who although not ready to grow up, must come to terms with the world of adult sexuality and behavior. Along with such plays as Arthur Miller's *Death of a Salesman* (1948) and Tennessee Williams's *Cat on a Hot Tin Roof* (1955), *The Catcher in the Rye* also points to problems of lovelessness, emotional repression, individual isolation, and stifled communication within the American family. Like the Kinsey reports (1948 and 1953), the story takes a more or less frank look at sexual behavior. Protagonist Holden Caulfield's derogatory opinion of California as a land of sellouts reflected the sentiments of many easterners, whose Puritan ethic was challenged by the promise of an easy, sensuous life on the West Coast. His distrust of an adult world run by posturing phonies resonated in the hyperbole and self-aggrandizement of television showmanship and advertisements, products of a blossoming advertising industry that was quickly learning how to exploit the new medium. Caulfield's feeling of being besieged by phoniness is exacerbated by the self-serving, sanctimonious public pronouncements of religious, business, and political leaders who dominated the news, not the least of whom was the bombastic Senator McCarthy, then still ascending to his greatest power.

The interplay of all these tensions produces confusion and anxiety in Caulfield, whose dream is to be able to guarantee safety to innocents like his little sister and, presumably, himself. Like those children who required protection and comfort in their bewildering postwar society, Korean War–era readers found themselves functioning in a confusing, uncertain, duplicitous world, and they similarly yearned for an adult authority figure to protect them from and reassure them about the unsettling international and domestic threats from the growing cold war.

THE COLD WAR AND INTERNATIONAL POLITICS

The Cold War Abroad

In 1951, the cold war dominated the political landscape. Truman fired General MacArthur for insubordination in April, and by the end of the year, the topsy-turvy Korean War began to grind down to a stalemate, as ultimately inconclusive peace talks began. Although there was a growing rapprochement between Yugoslavia and the West, Hungary and Czechoslovakia became more repressive, and at the end of the year Truman established a program to assist refugees from communist persecution. The level of distrust continued to grow between the United States and the Soviet Union, which exploded its second atomic bomb in the fall, as American scientists were reporting progress on development of the hydrogen bomb. Those reports included not only advances in the technology but also findings that radioactive fallout from the atomic testing in Nevada had traveled as far east as Cincinnati, Ohio, and Rochester, New York. In response to the growing nuclear threat, Congress passed a civil defense act authorizing $3.1 billion for bomb shelters and related needs.

THE KOREAN WAR

Following the communist success at the beginning of the year, the allies counterattacked and liberated Seoul in mid-March and subsequently reentered North Korea. In January, Truman had promised not to bomb China directly unless Congress first declared war and the United Nations authorized such action. On April 11, Truman dismissed MacArthur for insubordination after Representative Joseph Martin read on the House floor a letter from the popular general criticizing Truman's policy of limiting the war to Korea and declaring that "there is no substitute for victory." The firing of the general, who had challenged the president's authority on previous occasions as well, was very controversial, and MacArthur was greeted like a conquering hero when he returned from Korea. He was cheered in Congress after giving a moving speech before a joint session of the House and Senate (in which he stated, "Old soldiers never die, they just fade away"), and he received a ticker tape parade in New York City. Truman's decision to fire the five-star general was investigated by a Senate subcommittee, but the investigators found no impropriety in Truman's action. MacArthur was briefly a candidate for the Republican 1952 presidential nomination, but he was beaten by Dwight D. Eisenhower, another World War II hero.

General Matthew Ridgway replaced MacArthur as commander of UN troops in Korea and recaptured Pyongyang in June. Shortly thereafter, the North Koreans and Chinese proposed peace talks, which began in late July. The first of several truces, reached on November 28, established the 38th parallel as a line of demarcation for a truce agreement. But in December, the communist command gave the UN command a list of 3,100 prisoners of war (POWs), a figure considerably smaller than the United Nations had anticipated. A UN delegation accused the communists of failing to account for approximately

50,000 POWs, and the peace talks subsequently broke down over this issue. A 30-day "trial" cease-fire ended on December 27.

Other International Developments

China dramatically expanded its influence in Asia in May, when it compelled Tibet to become a "national autonomous region" of China. Although Tibet officially remained under the traditional religious rule of the Dalai Lama and Tibetans were allowed to retain religious freedom in exchange for severing ties with the West, China soon introduced extensive land reform and greatly reduced the power of the Dalai Lama's monastic order.

Elsewhere in Asia and the Pacific, the United States concluded mutual defense pacts with the Philippines, Australia, and New Zealand. Shortly afterward, on September 8, 49 nations signed a peace treaty that formally concluded the war with Japan. Opposed by the Soviet Union and communist-bloc countries, the agreement made Japan a sovereign nation again but forbade it to rearm. One long-term consequence of this provision was that very little of the Japanese budget was diverted to military spending during the cold war; consequently, Japan was able to build up its industrial base. The treaty further allowed the United States to station troops in Japan. The United States also signed an additional security treaty guaranteeing it would defend Japan in the event of attack.

In June, the United States formally ratified the charter of the Organization of American States (OAS), which included almost all of the independent nations in the Western Hemisphere. In May, Iceland had agreed to base NATO troops on its soil, and Greece and Turkey were invited into the alliance in August. Elsewhere in Europe, the United States and Yugoslavia developed closer ties, as America first agreed to provide Tito's regime with $38 million in food supplies, then $29 million in raw materials, and then military assistance. The Soviet Union squelched an agreement between East and West Germany to send delegates to the United Nations to discuss free unified elections. On May 1, Radio Free Europe inaugurated broadcasts to the Eastern bloc.

In October, Winston Churchill became prime minister of Great Britain again, and his Conservative Party regained power after a six-year hiatus during which the liberal Labour Party had ruled. In France, the Communist Party garnered the largest number of votes in the general election, and it headed the ruling coalition, but its numbers had declined significantly since the previous election, a development that forecast a decline in their power. Charles de Gaulle's anticommunist Gaullist Party commanded the second-largest number of votes.

An international oil crisis developed after Iran's pro-West premier, General Ali Razmara, was assassinated in March by a fervent nationalist. Razmara had expelled Soviet agents from northern Iran and signed agreements with the British-owned Anglo-Iran Oil Company to develop the nation's oil resources. He was succeeded by Mohammed Mossadegh, a nationalist who provoked the crisis when he voided the agreement with the Anglo-Iran Oil Company and nationalized Iran's oil fields. Mossadegh was elected president of Iran on April 28, 1951, following strikes and riots that forced the closing of the refinery. On June 21, Iran seized British oil installations in Abadan. Despite efforts by the

United Nations to resolve the matter, Great Britain and Iran eventually broke off diplomatic relations over the dispute, which was not resolved until after Mossadegh was deposed in September 1953 by Iranian troops loyal to the shah who were assisted by the CIA.

Elsewhere in the Middle East, the United States signed a friendship treaty with Israel, and Egypt unsuccessfully tried to take control of the Suez Canal from Great Britain by political means and of the Sudan. Ongoing disputes over the Suez culminated in 1956, when a combined British, French, and Israeli force briefly seized the canal. King Abdullah of Jordan was assassinated on July 20, 1951, by members of his own security team as he entered the Mosque of Omar in Jerusalem. He was succeeded by his son, Prince Talial, who was in Switzerland undergoing treatment for a nervous breakdown at the time of the assassination. Talial served for only about a year, after which he was removed due to mental illness and replaced by his 17-year-old son, Hussein, on August 11, 1952. Also assassinated in 1951 was Pakistan's premier, Ali Khan, killed by a Muslim extremist in New Delhi, India, in October.

The Cold War at Home

In 1951, the domestic cold war was dominated by the conviction and sentencing of the atomic spy couple the Rosenbergs, Senator McCarthy's increasingly vicious attacks on the Truman administration, and the resumption of the HUAC investigation of communist influences within the Hollywood film industry. In addition, the Supreme Court upheld the perjury conviction of former State Department official Alger Hiss, who began serving his five-year jail sentence. Dashiell Hammett, a member of the Communist Party and author of *The Maltese Falcon* and the Sam Spade detective stories, was jailed for six months for refusing to identify contributors to the bail bond fund of the Civil Rights Congress, which had been identified as a communist-front organization.

The most dramatic moment in the domestic cold war in 1951 was the conviction of Julius and Ethel Rosenberg for stealing secrets about the atomic bomb and passing them on to the Soviet Union. The death sentence the couple received was met with both jubilation and outrage. Many Americans agreed with Judge Irving Kaufman that the couple had committed a crime worse than murder by endangering the lives of hundreds of millions of Americans. Others believed the couple were primarily victims of the anticommunist frenzy sweeping the country, a frenzy tinged with anti-Semitism. The appeals and protests continued until the couple's execution in 1953.

Since the beginning of the Korean War, Senator McCarthy had intensified his vilification of the Truman administration, which he described as incompetent and/or compliant with a Soviet-led, international communist conspiracy. These unsubstantiated attacks culminated in mid-June, when on the Senate floor McCarthy charged that the "mysterious, powerful" secretary of defense, George Marshall, and the secretary of state, Dean Acheson, were part of an immense communist conspiracy, that Truman's policies were the result of a larger conspiracy controlled by the Soviet Union, and that Marshall, who, according to McCarthy, as secretary of state had enabled the communists to take control of China, was now following a policy of limited warfare that reduced the Korean War to pointless slaughter. Both Acheson and Marshall had a month earlier defended Truman's firing of MacArthur because the general had openly campaigned for expanding the war. By the time McCarthy finished his three-hour speech, all but three senators had walked out of the chamber. The press condemned the demagoguery of McCarthy, who, despite waving papers he cited as "documentation," never produced any substantive evidence for his charges or ever exposed a single communist working in the U.S. government. Nonetheless, McCarthy found receptive audiences as he subsequently traveled through the nation, repeating his accusations of treason.

Believing it would be degrading for the president to "get down in the gutter with a guttersnipe,"[1] Truman refused to respond to McCarthy's harangues, even when he became aware of a secret dossier that had been compiled on the senator, revealing among other things McCarthy's sexual affairs. Instead, Truman tersely responded, "No comment," to questions from the press about McCarthy's claims. Nor would Marshall confront McCarthy directly. He told his friends that if, at this point in his career, he had to explain that he was not a traitor, then it was not worth the effort. In September, due to health reasons and perhaps partly in response to McCarthy's attacks, Marshall resigned from office.

HUAC reopened hearings into communist influence on the Hollywood film industry on March 21. The hearings had been suspended until after the Hollywood Ten's legal appeals were finally denied in 1950 by a Supreme Court decision that established that witnesses could not invoke their First Amendment constitutional protections to refuse to testify before Congress about their political beliefs and associations. Thereafter, witnesses who did not want to implicate former colleagues and associates were compelled either to refuse outright to testify—and go to jail and face blacklisting—or to invoke their Fifth Amendment protections against self-incrimination—and face blacklisting. Another Supreme Court ruling, however, stated that witnesses could not invoke the Fifth Amendment selectively; if they refused to testify about others, they could not then choose to testify about themselves. Consequently, witnesses were unable to explain their own positions before the committee unless they were willing to name names or go to jail. Such "Fifth Amendment communists," as McCarthy labeled them, were also subject to blacklisting.

Among those who testified in 1950 were actors Larry Parks, José Ferrer, and Sterling Hayden; writers Richard Collins and Budd Schulberg; and director Edward Dmytryk, all of whom named names of former associates they believed had communist affiliations. Dmytryk, who had been one of the Hollywood Ten, had served a six-month prison term and was being blacklisted at the time of his testimony. He later maintained that he had already been drifting apart from the other nine for ideological reasons in 1947 but waited until after he was released from prison to break from them, so his action would not appear to be self-serving opportunism. He told the committee that the Korean War, the Alger Hiss conviction, and other cold war events that had transpired since 1947 had convinced him of the appropriateness of changing his position and speaking out against communism. Parks had been one of the original unfriendly witnesses but not one of the Ten because he was not called upon to testify in 1947. He was thus spared from prison but not from blacklisting. The first witness to testify after the hearings resumed, Parks cooperated with

HUAC after begging the committee not to make him "crawl through the mud like an informer."[2] Despite his cooperation, Parks was not removed from the blacklist because those in charge felt his testimony was not given freely enough or with sufficient contrition.

Some scholars, such as John Cogley, who published a well-documented *Report on Blacklisting* in 1956, argue that the goal of the HUAC investigation was to create a blacklist, as the testimony of witnesses became a public record that could be used as the basis for a list. Certainly the hearings had that effect, as everyone who was an unfriendly witness and virtually everyone named as a communist or communist sympathizer by friendly witnesses was blacklisted.

Another source for blacklisting that was introduced in 1951 was an article that J. B. Matthews wrote for *American Legion Magazine,* "Did the Movies Really Clean House." The article named 66 movie personalities whom Matthews identified as having communist sympathies. (Seventeen were listed solely because they had signed an amicus curiae brief in support of the Hollywood Ten, and several others appeared only because they had signed an advertisement criticizing HUAC.) One outcome of the article was a meeting between the American Legion and the movie studio heads, who feared widespread boycotting and demonstrations against films featuring alleged communists listed in American Legion publications. With the understanding that access would be limited to top studio executives and the named individuals, the Legion presented the studios with a list of some 300 people, with the proviso that they check for any factual errors.

According to the Legion, the list was almost immediately abused. It quickly became a de facto blacklist. Those listed and under contract were encouraged to write a letter explaining the charges against them. If they refused, they were fired. The letters from those who cooperated were submitted to the American Legion, which passed judgment on their acceptability. Less clear-cut cases were sent to George Sokolsky, a Hearst newspaper columnist with anticommunist credentials and an apparently sincere desire to assist those who truly repented their earlier political "errors." Sokolsky either rendered a decision or consulted union leader Roy Brewer and/or actor Ward Bond, the first and second presidents of the anticommunist Motion Picture Alliance for the Preservation of American Ideals. Of those who wrote letters, only 30 failed to produce satisfactory explanations; however, individuals who were not currently under contract were never asked to write a letter and were thus not informed of their presence on the American Legion's list or given an opportunity to clear themselves, if they so chose.[3]

GOVERNMENT AND SOCIETY

In addition to the growing perception that the government was being infiltrated by communists intent on doing the nation harm, the public was further demoralized by revelations by the Kefauver committee of rampant corruption of public officials in conjunction with organized crime. And while the Kefauver commission, which concluded its investigations in 1951, primarily addressed corruption at the level of local government, in February a Senate subcommittee chaired by Senator William J. Fulbright, a Democrat from Arkansas, detailed accusations of influence peddling, favoritism, and other abuses that extended to the upper echelons of the Truman administration and involved some of the president's friends and associates. These charges centered on the management of the Reconstruction Finance Corporation (RFC), a government-subsidized agency that made low-interest loans to business. The committee report did not issue any charges of criminal wrongdoing, but it did find numerous instances of unethical conduct. Although Truman initially dismissed the accusations, he subsequently became convinced that the RFC was mismanaged, and he placed former secretary of the air force Stuart Symington in charge, with the mandate to restore its integrity. In addition to the charges against the RFC, the Internal Revenue Service (IRS) became the target of accusations of bribes, shakedowns, and gross negligence. Subsequent investigations by a House subcommittee led to the firing or resignation of several leading IRS administrators. By December, 113 IRS employees, including six regional collectors, had been removed.[4] The embarrassment to the Democrats was somewhat offset by the revelation that Guy George Gabrielson, head of the Republican National Committee, had received $25,000 for "looking after" the loans of a Texas corporation.[5]

The charges of rampant corruption produced a feeling among many that the nation's moral values were crumbling. This sensibility was only intensified that summer when 90 West Point cadets, including its all-American quarterback and eight others from the Army football team, were expelled for cheating. West Point had always made character-building one of its top priorities, so the revelation was especially shocking. The public became further frustrated when several of the expelled students expressed no sense of guilt and instead claimed that they were the honest ones, because they had admitted doing something that everyone did, while many of the remaining cadets had lied about their involvement. Even West Point's football coach, Colonel Earl H. Blake, appeared to miss the basic distinction between right and wrong when he defended the dismissed athletes, including his son, as "men of character."[6]

In the civil rights arena, the NAACP filed a lawsuit that ultimately overturned the doctrine of separate-but-equal and mandated the desegregation of America's public schools. In *Brown v. Board of Education of Topeka,* a racially integrated team of NAACP lawyers sued for the right of a black child, Linda Brown, to attend the all-white elementary school closest to her home, instead of having to travel across town to an all-black school. The federal district court that heard the case ruled against the NAACP, asserting that the Topeka school board had maintained essentially equal facilities. But the ruling also acknowledged that segregation had an adverse effect on black children, and this provided the basis for the appeal that eventually prevailed before the Supreme Court in 1954.

BUSINESS

The government-managed wartime economy limited the availability of consumer goods for purchase. In January, to slow credit expansion, the Federal Reserve Board increased margin requirements for stock purchases by 50 percent to 75 percent. In February, the Office of Price Stabilization imposed profit ceilings on some 200,000 consumer goods. Nonetheless, inflation continued to be a wartime worry, and in late July, the Truman administration imposed wage and price freezes to curb inflation, as the 1939 dollar was now worth 59.3¢ and a 5¢ call from a pay telephone increased to 10¢ in major cities.

In February, a five-day strike by railroad switchmen was broken after the army, which had seized the rails in 1950 by a presidential order, issued an ultimatum threatening to fire the workers. But labor problems persisted, and in August, Truman once more invoked the national emergency provisions of the Taft-Hartley Act, this time to terminate a five-day copper strike. The government, however, did not intervene in a longshoremen's strike in New York harbor that lasted 25 days. In December, Truman expanded his efforts to reduce racial discrimination in the workplace by establishing the Committee on Government Contract Compliance to enforce the antidiscrimination clauses in federal employment contracts.

Despite the difficult circumstances, the housing boom continued to create jobs and fuel the economy, which prospered in 1951. Overall, the gross national product (GNP) rose 15 percent during the year. Unemployment was low—3.3 percent—and inflation was just 0.7 percent. Private incomes also generally rose.[7] The median yearly income for Americans with incomes was $2,422 ($2,952 for men and $1,045 for women.)[8] Federal, state, and local taxes averaged $360.[9]

The suburbs continued to absorb most of the new housing starts, as evidenced by Levittown, a large, popular suburb on Long Island, New York, that was started after the war and reached full capacity in 1951. AT&T became the first publicly owned company to list 1 million stockholders, and Chase and Manhattan banks set in motion the largest bank merger in history to that time.

Among the products and services that first appeared on the market in 1951 was Remington Rand's UNIVAC, the first computer to store data on magnetic tape. Al Gross developed the first wireless telephone, and Deutsche Grammophon marketed the first 33-rpm long-playing (LP) record. Other new products included sugarless chewing gum, Dacron suits, television courses for college credit, power steering in automobiles, vibrating mattresses, the "Dennis the Menace" cartoon strip, the "poodle" hairdo, direct dialing for long-distance telephone service, polarized glasses for watching movies in three dimensions, and Tropicana orange juice.

SCIENCE AND TECHNOLOGY

The year saw many advances in the field of medicine. French obstetrician Fernand Lamaze developed his Lamaze method of childbirth, which emphasized relaxation, breathing techniques, and support from the father during delivery. Dutch researcher Nikolaas Tinbergen published his influential book on animal behavior, *The Study of Instinct*. Canadian researchers developed the first electrical pacemakers to regulate the heartbeat. American chemist Robert Woodward synthesized cortisone and cholesterol; methotexate was first used to treat cancer of the uterus; Antabuse was introduced to combat alcoholism; German-born American biochemist Fritz Lipmann discovered acetyl coenzyme A, which the body uses to break down fats and carbohydrates to produce energy for the cells; and the U.S. Public Health Service reported that fluoridation of water greatly reduced tooth decay. This report subsequently led to the near-uniform fluoridation of the water supply for public consumption, a policy that some suspected was a communist plot to impair Americans by poisoning their "precious bodily fluids," as General Jack D. Ripper charged in Stanley Kubrick's satirical movie *Dr. Strangelove* (1964).

Atomic and subatomic research also proceeded during the year. A U.S. team of scientists led by Edward Teller induced the first thermonuclear reaction, a necessary step for developing the hydrogen bomb. An experimental fast-breeder nuclear reactor, designed by Canadian-American Walter Zinn, was built in Idaho Falls, Indiana, and on December 29, at a plant in Arcon, Idaho, the Atomic Energy Commission produced the world's first nuclear-generated electricity. Earlier in the year, it completed an "atomic apothecary" facility at Oak Ridge, Tennessee, for processing radioisotopes for medical research. A joint Dutch-Norwegian establishment for atomic research opened in Norway, and Robert Leighton of the California Institute of Technology discovered the negative proton, a fundamental subatomic particle.

Interest in outer space intensified throughout the decade, both within the scientific community and among the public at large. In 1951, German researcher Walter Baade identified the first visible objects in space related to a known radio source; Dutch astronomers Jan Oort, C. A. Muller, and Hendrik van de Hulst plotted a map of the Milky Way; Shin Hirayama postulated that asteroids exist in family groups; and Dutch-American Dirk Brouwer first used a computer to predict planetary orbits up to the year 2060 and to track them back to 1653.

SPORTS, ENTERTAINMENT, AND THE ARTS

Sports

Baseball's New York Giants, managed by Leo Durocher, overcame a 13½-game deficit in the final two months of the season to tie the Brooklyn Dodgers in the last game of the regular season. The Giants's Bobby Thomson won the pennant play-off game with a dramatic ninth-inning home run, which was immediately dubbed "the shot heard 'round the world." However, the New York Yankees prevailed in the crosstown World Series, winning in six games.

In football, the Los Angeles Rams defeated the Cleveland Browns 24–17 to avenge their two-point loss to the Browns the previous year and win the NFL championship. The University of Tennessee was named the top college team, despite being defeated by Maryland in the Sugar Bowl. Princeton's running back Dick Kazmaier won the Heisman trophy.

In basketball, Rochester defeated New York in seven games for the NBA championship, and the University of Kentucky took the college championship. However, in a year already tainted by the West Point football scandal, allegations of point-shaving involving Kentucky, the City College of New York, which had won in 1950, and Long Island University shrouded the college basketball season in scandal.

The Toronto Maple Leafs won professional hockey's Stanley Cup, Ben Hogan won the USGA golf tournament, and Frank Sedgman and 16-year-old Maureen Connolly won the U.S. Open tennis singles events. Connolly, known affectionately as "Little Mo," was the youngest player ever to win the women's title. In boxing, British fighter Randy Turpin took the middleweight boxing crown from American "Sugar" Ray Robinson, defeating the long-reigning champion on points in 15 rounds. The loss was only Robinson's second in 133 bouts over 11 years. Robinson, the welterweight champion whom many considered the best boxer in history, earlier became a double titleholder when he defeated Jake LaMotta in 13 rounds for the middleweight crown. Robinson reclaimed that crown on September 12, when he knocked out Turpin in the 10th. "Jersey" Joe Walcott knocked out Ezzard Charles to win the heavyweight title, and challenger Rocky Marciano knocked out Joe Louis to end Louis's bid to retake the heavyweight title. The 1951 Boston Marathon was won by Shige-ki Tanaha, a 19-year-old survivor of the atomic bombing of Hiroshima, Japan.

Television

Television saw important advances in 1951, both in programming and technology, the two converging on November 18, with the premiere of Edward R. Murrow's *See It Now,* a CBS news broadcast. The opening telecast showed the Brooklyn and Golden Gate Bridges side-by-side, live, on a split-screen—the first time ever that America's eastern and western boundaries had been shown together simultaneously in real time. This was made possible by a considerable technological feat: the completion of a coast-to-coast coaxial cable network. The first coast-to-coast broadcast actually took place on September 4, when Truman addressed the Japanese Peace Treaty Conference in San Francisco. Although experimental color broadcasts had first taken place in 1950, the first commercial color broadcast was by CBS in 1951. However, the CBS signal required a special television set, and RCA, which was owned by rival NBC, was also developing a color set with a larger screen. In October the FCC postponed authorization of full implementation of color broadcasts due to war needs.

Murrow, who had earned a reputation as an outstanding radio correspondent during World War II, gave credibility to the fledgling television news medium, initially with his stature and subsequently by demonstrating the high-quality work the medium was capable of producing. During *See It Now*'s seven-year span, Murrow reported on and interviewed such figures as Truman, Eisenhower, Acheson, atomic physicist Robert Oppenheimer, Yugoslavia's Marshal Tito, and China's foreign minister, Zhou Enlai. He made a widely viewed Christmas-day visit to GIs on the front lines in Korea and aired shows on nuclear testing, nuclear weapons and radiation, relations among the Western powers, and problems in Berlin, among other matters of national and international importance. The most memorable and influential episodes of *See It Now* came in 1954, when Murrow ran a well-documented exposé that accused McCarthy of reckless demagoguery. The following month, McCarthy responded on the show by heaping personal attacks on Murrow.

The other important television show to premiere in 1951 was *I Love Lucy,* which became the single most-popular TV program in America during the 1950s. It debuted on October 15 and starred Lucille Ball and her husband, Cuban bandleader Desi Arnaz. The half-hour comedy was one of the few shows to tap into the interest in Cuban band music that was popular throughout the country during the 1940s and 1950s. A more central appeal, however, was the humorous interplay among Lucy Ricardo, a loving but independent-minded housewife; Ricky, her Cuban bandleader husband with very traditional notions about the appropriate roles for men and women; and their friends and neighbors Fred and Ethel Mertz (played by William Frawley and Vivian Vance). The stories, which usually centered around Lucy's schemes to frustrate Ricky's will, typically reaffirmed Ricky's more sober values. However, Lucy comes across as loving, lively, imaginative, and intelligent, if somewhat frivolous and conniving. Her spirit is never broken.

I Love Lucy received enthusiastic reviews from the start and quickly became a major hit. It aired on CBS and was sponsored by the Philip Morris tobacco company. It was filmed, instead of broadcast live, so viewers on both coasts would see the same high-quality resolution. By the end of the 1951–52 season, the American Research Bureau estimated that *I Love Lucy* had been viewed in some 10 million homes. In May 1952, it was featured on the cover of *Time* magazine, and it closed its first season as the third most popular show, according

Lucy Ricardo (Lucille Ball) and her husband, Ricky (Desi Arnaz), argue on *I Love Lucy,* as neighbor Fred Mertz (William Frawley) looks on. *(Photofest)*

to the new Nielsen ratings. It was the top-rated show from the 1952–53 season to the 1954–55 season. It retained its initial half-hour format through June 1957, when it adopted a new hour-long format and a new name, *The Lucy-Desi Comedy Hour*. The television collaboration ended after the 1959–60 season, when the real-life couple decided to divorce. However, spinoff shows starring Lucille Ball remained popular throughout the 1960s and 1970s; one appeared briefly as late as 1986. During the early 1950s, *I Love Lucy* was so popular that president-elect Eisenhower jokingly complained that interest in Ball's real-life pregnancy scripted into the television show was distracting everyone from his inauguration in 1953, which coincided with the childbirth.

Other shows to make their first appearance were *The Chevy Show Starring Dinah Shore* (variety); *The Red Skelton Show* (comedy); *The Sam Levenson Show* (comedy); *The Schlitz Playhouse of Stars*, a beer-sponsored dramatic anthology featuring such famous screen actors as Helen Hayes and David Niven (drama); *The Roy Rogers Show*, starring Roy Rogers—the "King of the Cowboys"—Dale Evans—the "Queen of the West"—horses Trigger and Buttermilk, and dog Bullet (western); *Wild Bill Hickok*, starring Guy Madison and his sidekick Andy Devine (western); *The Cisco Kid*, starring Duncan Renaldo (western); *Superman*, starring George Reeves and based on the popular comic book superhero (action/adventure); and *The Jack LaLanne Show* (exercise).

Perhaps owing to the public's desire to escape from the Korean War, public scandals, and growing fears of domestic and international communism, seven of the top 10 shows were comedies. In addition to *I Love Lucy* and *The Red Skelton Show*, these included five ongoing shows: Milton Berle's *Texaco Star Theater*, *The Colgate Comedy Hour*, *The Jack Benny Program*, Sid Caesar's *Your Show of Shows*, and Groucho Marx's *You Bet Your Life*. Other top-rated shows included *Arthur Godfrey's Talent Scouts*, an amateur variety show that was the most widely viewed show of the year, and *Arthur Godfrey and His Friends*, a variety show. *Fireside Theater*, a dramatic anthology, was another of viewers' most favorite programs. Between 1951 and 1954, evangelical minister Billy Graham hosted *Hour of Decision*, a series of regular Sunday night talks.

Movies

In addition to the already established comedies, tragedies, love stories, adventure stories, crime stories, westerns, and musicals, three new cinematic genres came into their own in 1951: the Korean War film, the space-invader film, and the mutant-monster film. Each of these appealed both consciously and unconsciously to the current events of the time. The Korean War was a direct subject of numerous films during and immediately after the conflict; the space-invader motif was inspired by scientific interest in outer space that became pronounced after World War II; and the mutant monsters were typically products of nuclear radiation, bringing life to unconscious fears about atomic energy.

Although the bulk of Korean War films celebrated the bravery and self-sacrifice of American military personnel, some took a more critical view of the U.S. involvement in the unpopular conflict. This is especially true of films made during the war. Barely six months after North Korea invaded South Korea in June 1950, Sam Fuller released *The Steel Helmet*, starring Gene Evans and Robert Hutton. Written in a week and filmed in 10 days, *The Steel Helmet* does not glamorize warfare; instead, the Korean War experience appears grim, confusing, and dehumanizing.

The protagonists are survivors of massacred squads who join together to capture a Buddhist temple and a North Korean major who is occupying it, and the film centers on the soldiers' struggle for survival in a brutal situation. They are accompanied by a South Korean orphan boy who tags along in search of chocolate. Becoming desensitized proves to be key to survival, because compassion can literally lead to death. The inability of the characters and the audience to distinguish friendly Koreans from hostile ones, which was a genuine problem for American soldiers in the war, reflects the confusion over the purpose of the war. The effect of the film is to render the war as an exercise in ongoing madness. The final credit reads, "There is no end to this story." Later in the year, Fuller also released another grittily realistic film about the war, *Fixed Bayonets* (1951), starring Richard Basehart, Gene Evans, and James Dean. It tells the story of a sensitive corporal who must assume command in a rear-guard action after his superiors are killed. The movie was one of Dean's first significant appearances on screen.

Other, later standouts in the genre include Mark Robson's *The Bridges at Toko-Ri* (1954), which stars William Holden, Grace Kelley, and Frederic March and is based on James Michener's 1953 novel, and Lewis Milestone's *Pork Chop Hill* (1959). *Toko-Ri* expresses initial misgivings about the war but ultimately shows the value of the sacrifices made by the soldiers, seamen, and pilots. Similarly, *Pork Chop Hill* portrays a valiant but absurd struggle over a meaningless hill hours before the armistice is signed. The soldiers perceive only the futility of dying to gain control of an apparently worthless mound, but the film ultimately vindicates their sacrifice when the audience sees how the hard-fought victory convinces the communist negotiators that America and its allies will always stand up to aggression.

Robson's *I Want You* (1951) stars Dana Andrews and Dorothy McGuire in a somber but patriotic view of the war that highlights the impact of the conflict on an average American family. John Farrow's *Submarine Command,* starring William Holden, Nancy Olson, and William Bendix, and Robson's *Bright Victory,* starring Arthur Kennedy, Peggy Dow, Julie Adams, Will Geer, and Rock Hudson, also appeared in 1951 and promoted more traditionally patriotic values. In *Submarine Command,* a guilt-ridden captain tries to atone for the deaths of his comrades in World War II through his actions in the Korean War. *Bright Victory* focuses on a blinded soldier trying to adjust to civilian life.

Many other films made during the decade take an uncritical, patriotic stand, including *Mission Over Korea* (1953), *Sabre Jet* (1953), *Take the High Ground* (1953), *Hold Back the Night* (1956), *Men in War* (1957), and *The Hunters* (1958). Several postwar films from the middle and late 1950s center on patriotic biographies of Korean War heroes. These included Sterling Hayden's portrayal of a one-legged admiral in *The Eternal Sea* (1955), Alan Ladd's depiction of a jet fighter pilot in *The McConnell Story* (1955), and Rock Hudson's enactment in *Battle Hymn* (1957) of a preacher who is also an air force pilot.

A number of Korean War films bring romance to the combat zone. Sometimes the women are damsels in distress, caught in the wrong place at the wrong time, but in other films they have chosen or been assigned to dangerous situations. Part of the drama in *One Minute to Zero* (1952) centers around a U.S.

colonel forcing his romantic interest, a UN official, to evacuate. The same colonel is ultimately forced to bomb the fleeing refugees. *Japanese War Bride* (1952) and *Sayonara* (1954) both address the post–World War II phenomenon of romances and marriages between Japanese women and U.S. servicemen assigned to Japan during the Korean War. Official U.S. military policy forbade such unions. *Love Is a Many-Splendored Thing* (1955) deals with a mixed-race romance between a U.S. war correspondent and a female Eurasian doctor.

Other Korean War films focus on POWs, as did the peace talks between the real-life antagonists. Although prohibited by the Geneva Convention, executions of POWs apparently took place on both sides during the Korean conflict. Moreover, for the first time in history, U.S. POWs were accused of widespread collaboration with their captors, and no U.S. POW ever escaped from a permanent internment camp in North Korea. Nonetheless, *Prisoner of War* (1954), made the year following the cease-fire and starring future president Ronald Reagan, paints a patriotic picture of U.S. soldiers in captivity. Most of them sarcastically defy their captors, and the only soldier who cooperates proves to be planting misinformation to fool the enemy. *The Bamboo Prison* (1955) employs a similar theme, and in *Time Limit* (1957) Richard Basehart's collaboration is also vindicated. Only in *The Rack* (1956) is a career officer, played by Paul Newman, found guilty. The film concludes as he acknowledges the error of his ways.

Other Korean War films made during the war included *Battle Circus* (1952), *Battle Zone* (1952), *Retreat, Hell!* (1952), *Flight Nurse* (1953), and *The Glory Brigade* (1953). The Korean War inspired two other notable films: John Frankenheimer's *The Manchurian Candidate* (1962) and Robert Altman's *M★A★S★H* (1970). Based on the 1959 novel by Richard Condon, *The Manchurian Candidate* stars Frank Sinatra, Laurence Harvey, and Angela Lansbury. It treats accusations that the communists "brainwashed" American prisoners and ultimately attacks McCarthy and the far right. *M★A★S★H* stars Donald Sutherland and Elliott Gould and was written by Hollywood Ten member Ring Lardner, Jr., a decade after the blacklist was lifted. Although set during the Korean War, *M★A★S★H* was released during the Vietnam War and is generally regarded as an anti–Vietnam War film.

Although conflicts between humans and space creatures go back to the earliest days of cinema in such films as Georges Méliès's *A Trip to the Moon* (1902), outer space did not figure significantly in the medium until the post–World War II science of rocketry made space exploration truly conceivable. Tests of rocket-powered aircraft during the late 1940s and early 1950s brought humans closer to outer space than ever before, and it is probably not coincidental that the first sighting of a "flying saucer" was reported in 1947. Despite an official U.S. Air Force investigation that concluded in 1949 that there was no evidence of their existence, the possibility of extraterrestrial visitations quickly caught the public imagination. It is within this context that the space invasion movies of the 1950s arose.

Irving Pichel's *Destination Moon* (1950), whose screenplay was cowritten by science-fiction author Robert Heinlein, and Kurt Neumann's *Rocket Ship XM,* starring Lloyd Bridges (1950), pioneered this new wave of space movies. But in 1951, the subgenre of low-budget "creature features" came into its own. Sometimes shot for 3-D projection, plots centered around invasions from outer space or attacks by terrestrial monsters whose super powers result from mutations due to radioactive fallout from atomic testing. Christian Nyby's 1951 *The Thing,* produced by Howard Hawks and starring James Arness as the "thing from outer space," makes direct, mocking reference to the government report that denies the existence of extraterrestrial spacecraft. Other space-invasion films from the year included Robert Wise's *The Day the Earth Stood Still,* Lesley Selander's *Flight to Mars,* and Rudolph Mate's *When Worlds Collide,* which won an Academy Award for special effects.

In a related 1950s subgenre, planetary survival is also threatened by monsters who have mutated as a result of nuclear tests. Mutant creatures appear in Gordon Douglas's *Them!* (1954, giant ants), Roger Corman's *The Day the World Ended* (1955, three-eyed cannibals), Corman's *Attack of the Crab Monsters* (1956), Jack Arnold's *The Incredible Shrinking Man* (1957), Nathan Juran's *The Attack of the 50-Foot Woman* (1958), Bernard Kowalski's *Attack of the Giant Leeches* (1959), and Kurt Neumann's *The Fly* (1958) and its sequels. The Japanese Godzilla series (starting in 1954) and the film *Rodan* (1957) also feature radiation-spawned monsters and became popular in America. As these Japanese series progress, the monsters evolve from destroying the island nation to protecting it, just as American nuclear weapons destroyed Hiroshima but protected Japan during the Korean War and throughout the cold war.

Although little was made of this at the time of the movies' release, more recent scholarship has demonstrated how the 1950s outer-space-invasion and mutant-creature films frequently play out cold war anxieties. In these readings, the alien creature is typically linked to communism, and the films become metaphors, if not allegories, for the threat posed by the red menace. Given that they were made by writers, directors, and producers of different political backgrounds, they frequently take different positions on how to address concerns about attack from without and subterfuge from within.

For instance, *The Day the Earth Stood Still,* which is the most liberal of Hollywood's space-invasion movies, presents the left-wing argument that the greatest threat to planetary survival comes from those who want to kill the alien/communist without first talking with it and seeking peace. In that film, the external invader proves to be well intended and helpful, and level-headed pacifists are the characters who are most admired.

In centrist films such as *The Thing* and William Cameron Menzies's *Invaders from Mars* (1953) the alien/communist indeed poses a genuine threat, but the trustworthy forces of government actively and competently work to defeat it. On the far right of the political spectrum, Don Siegel's *Invasion of the Body Snatchers* (1956) enacts McCarthy's vision of America in which the sinister pod people/communists have already infiltrated and taken over. Like the stereotypical communist cadre, the pod people work in cells, exhibit no emotions, and are single minded in their devotion to their cause. Furthermore, parallel to McCarthy's claims that communist infiltrators had seized control first of the State Department and then the military, the first order of business for the pod people is to replace the public and police officials with their own replicants. And just as McCarthyites resented accusations that they were paranoid, the protagonist of *Invasion of the Body Snatchers* must combat both the alien creatures and the skepticism of his fellow citizens, who think he is crazy for pointing out a real and present danger. The slimy, sluglike movements of the creature in Irvin Yeaworth's *The Blob* (1958) project an objective correlative for the right-wing warnings of "creeping communism."

Embedded within space-invasion and atomic mutant films lies a question of authority: Whom can Americans trust to best handle the alien threat—scientist and intellectuals or the military? In many respects this conflict mirrored an internal power struggle within postwar America over who could best guide the United States through the cold war. An emerging liberal technocracy that valued science and theory, believed in progress, and sought to improve the human condition through the scientific application of reason and higher education was challenging a conservative establishment that was leery of the motivations of those seeking social change and that trusted practical, straightforward approaches to crisis management over solutions that relied on theory, complicated logic, or obscure knowledge. Even in actual politics these divisions were apparent in the 1952 and 1956 presidential elections between General Dwight Eisenhower, who, although intelligent, projected a more down-to-earth, practical-minded persona, and his unsuccessful Democratic challenger, the liberal Adlai Stevenson, who came across as an intellectual. In fact, Eisenhower's supporters introduced the term *egghead* into the popular vocabulary when they used it to deride Stevenson's highbrow manner.

In the movies, this rift between the liberal intellectual and the conservative pragmatist often found expression in the conflict between scientists, whose thirst for knowledge at times is a source of human salvation and at times is Faustian in its potential for self-destruction, and government bureaucrats and/or military leaders, whose proclivity for recognizing threats and eliminating them in a no-nonsense fashion likewise sometimes saves the planet and sometimes almost dooms it. In *The Day the Earth Stood Still,* for instance, unimaginative politicians and military leaders try to destroy the spaceman who has come to give humanity a final chance before Earth is destroyed because of the danger human aggression now poses to the rest of the galaxy. Fortunately, the community of scientists, led by Professor Barnhardt, a wise and friendly Einstein-like figure, achieves international cooperation where the politicians cannot, and they save the planet. The centrist film *Them!* also finds salvation in science instead of the military, as the rampage of giant mutant ants ends only when the socially inept scientist figures out a solution and is empowered to give orders that enact it. By contrast, in *The Thing* the scientist, who is dressed in a Russian-style fur hat and wears a sinister-looking goatee, endangers the entire planet when he tries to sabotage the military's effort to destroy a dangerous creature that has landed in the Arctic Circle. The scientist wants to save the space alien for its potential value to science. The military officer wants to destroy it, correctly in this case, before it kills everyone.[10]

Space invasion and creature films were usually low-budget, or B, films from the Hollywood studios' second tier. The first-tier A films from 1951 tended to stress intense personal relations. These included Elia Kazan's cinematic adaptation of Tennessee Williams's *A Streetcar Named Desire,* which Kazan earlier directed to acclaim on Broadway. The screen version starred Broadway cast members Marlon Brando, Kim Hunter, and Karl Malden but featured Vivien Leigh instead of Jessica Tandy as Blanche DuBois. Leigh, Malden, and Hunter received Academy Awards and Brando was nominated for his performance.

Streetcar was also nominated for best film, director, screenplay (Williams), cinematography, score, costume design, and sound.

Humphrey Bogart won the best actor award for his performance in John Huston's *The African Queen;* Katharine Hepburn was nominated for best actress and Huston for best director in the World War I story about the growing love between an alcoholic riverboat pilot and a well-bred missionary lady fleeing the Germans in Africa. *A Place in the Sun,* George Stevens's adaptation of Theodore Dreiser's *An American Tragedy,* also received Academy nominations in the major categories, and Stevens won for best director. Alfred Hitchcock's *Strangers on a Train* presents a scheme to commit the perfect murder as two men with family problems discuss exchanging victims, so they cannot be traced. One man is facetious, but the other takes him seriously. Kirk Douglas stands out as a tough police detective with a secret in William Wyler's *Detective Story.*

The year also produced two important film musicals, George Sidney's *Show Boat,* starring Kathryn Grayson, Howard Keel, and Ava Gardner, and Vincente Minnelli's *An American in Paris,* starring Gene Kelly, Leslie Caron, and Oscar Levant. *An American in Paris* received the Academy Award for best picture among others and was nominated in most of the other major categories.

Two important epic films were Mervyn LeRoy's *Quo Vadis,* starring Robert Taylor and Deborah Kerr, and Henry King's *David and Bathsheba,* starring Gregory Peck and Susan Hayward. Like the science fiction movies, "sword and sandal" film epics also had cold war subtexts. Their size and scale showcased the opulence of Western capitalism, and their biblical subject matter reinforced the traditional Judeo-Christian values that were undergoing attack from atheistic communism. For instance, in describing the individual as being at the mercy of the state, the opening narration from *Quo Vadis* depicts Nero's Rome in language often used to describe life behind the iron curtain.

Whereas the top stars of the late 1940s were primarily upright and serious, comedians were among the most popular figures in 1951—perhaps reflecting a national desire to escape the gloom of the war and the Red Scare. The top box office draws of 1951 were John Wayne, the comedy team of Dean Martin and Jerry Lewis, Betty Grable, the comedic duo Bud Abbott and Lou Costello, singer Bing Crosby and his pal comedian Bob Hope, Randolph Scott, Gary Cooper, Doris Day, and Spencer Tracy.

Notable foreign movies that reached American audiences included Zoltan Korda's British-made adaptation of Alan Patton's novel about apartheid in South Africa, *Cry, the Beloved Country,* starring Canada Lee and Sidney Poitier; and David Lean's *Oliver Twist,* starring Alec Guinness and John Howard Davis. Made in England in 1948, *Oliver Twist* was not released in the United States until 1951, after some seven minutes were excised in response to complaints of anti-Semitism by Jewish groups.

Literature

The fact that several novels by notable writers, in addition to *The Catcher in the Rye,* also addressed the themes of sexual identity, personal identity, and alienation and isolation suggests an undercurrent of spiritual longing and incompleteness among some of the more creative members of society. Whether they can be said to speak for the public at large, however, is more problematic. William Faulkner, who also published *Notes on a Horse Thief* in 1951, released his *Requiem for a Nun,* which advances the story of Temple Drake, the sexually tormented, all-Mississippi debutante he introduced in *Sanctuary* (1931). William Styron's *Lie Down in Darkness* explores the psyche of the daughter of a powerful southerner who must come to terms with taboo sexual desire and other aspects of her identity. Carson McCullers's *The Ballad of the Sad Café* is a third southern novel that deals with personal and spiritual crises and twisted love.

Norman Mailer's second novel, *Barbary Shore,* depicts the collapse of the rational worldview. The amnesiac narrator can distinguish neither fact from fiction nor memory from imagination. He rents a room in a boardinghouse where the fellow boarders prove to be spies, double agents, and former communists. The communist power struggle between Trotsky, a Jew, and Stalin, an anti-Semite, provides a backdrop for the political and sexual liaisons that drive the story. Communism proves bankrupt in the book, but so does American culture, and the protagonist must find meaning beyond the failed institutions of politics and religion. Mailer, who claimed to be attempting to bridge Marx and Freud, insists that sex and other psychological and political impulses are interconnected and maintains that history must be shown in personal terms. He addresses similar themes in his next novel, *The Deer Park* (1955).

War stories dealing with conflicts over personal power and authority were among the top best-sellers, and Herman Wouk's *The Caine Mutiny,* a psychologically driven naval story won the Pulitzer Prize for its treatment of military power and authority. In 1954, Edward Dmytryk made *The Caine Mutiny* into an Academy Award–nominated film starring Humphrey Bogart, José Ferrer, Van Johnson, and Fred MacMurray. Other best-sellers included James Jones's military story *From Here to Eternity,* Nicholas Monsarrat's *The Cruel Sea,* Frank Yerby's *A Woman Called Fancy,* and James Michener's *Return to Paradise.* Henry Morton Robinson's *The Cardinal,* a best-seller from 1950, stayed at the top of the lists in 1951.

Nonfiction of note included Wallace Stevens's *The Necessary Angel;* George F. Kennan's *American Diplomacy, 1900–1950;* William F. Buckley, Jr.'s attack on the liberal faculty at Yale University, *God and Man at Yale;* Hannah Arendt's influential study *The Origins of Totalitarianism;* and Oscar Handlin's Pulitzer Prize–winning historical study, *The Uprooted. Kon Tiki,* Thor Heyerdahl's account of his raft voyage from Peru to Tahiti in 1947–48, was a nonfiction best-seller, as were *Washington Confidential* by Jack Lait and Lee Mortimer, *The Sea Around Us* by Rachael L. Carson, *Betty Crocker's Picture Cook Book, The New Yorker Twenty-Fifth Anniversary Album,* and *Pogo,* Walt Kelly's book of satirical cartoons based on his popular syndicated comic strip.

Several poets issued important volumes, including Robert Lowell (*The Mills of the Kavanaughs*), Adrienne Rich (*A Change of World*), James Merrill (*First Poems*), William Carlos Williams (*Patterson, Book Four*), Randall Jarrell (*The Seven-League Crutches*), and Theodore Roethke (*Praise of the End*). Langston Hughes published "Dream Boogie," "Harlem," and other poems that showed the influence of jazz and bebop on African-American literature, and Marianne Moore won the Pulitzer Prize for her *Collected Poems.*

Theater, Music, and the Visual Arts

Broadway ran the full gamut, from the serious to the absurd, in 1951. No Pulitzer Prize was awarded for theater, but two plays that opened in late 1950 received Tony Awards: Tennessee Williams's drama *The Rose Tattoo* and Frank Loesser's musical comedy about gamblers and missionaries, *Guys and Dolls.* Among the Broadway openings in 1951 were Paul Osborne's *Point of No Return,* starring Henry Fonda and Leora Dana; Maxwell Anderson's *Barefoot in Athens;* Anita Loos's *Gigi,* starring Audrey Hepburn; Lillian Hellman's *The Autumn Garden,* starring Florence Eldridge and Fredric March; Donald Bevin and Edmund Trzcinski's story of a World War II POW camp, *Stalag 17;* an adaptation of Herman Melville's story *Billy Budd* by Louis Coxe and Robert Chapman; and Sidney Kingsley's adaptation of Arthur Koestler's anti-Stalinist novel, *Darkness at Noon,* starring Claude Rains and Kim Hunter. Musical openings included Richard Rodgers and Oscar Hammerstein II's *The King and I,* starring Gertrude Lawrence and Yul Brynner; Johnny Mercer's *Top Banana,* starring Phil Silvers; Arthur Schwartz and Dorothy Fields's *A Tree Grows in Brooklyn,* starring Shirley Booth; and Alan Jay Lerner and Frederick Loewe's *Paint Your Wagon.*

The New York City Ballet premiered *Cakewalk,* a modern dance choreographed by Ruthanna Boris; Igor Stravinsky's *The Cage,* choreographed by Jerome Robbins; Béla Bartók's *The Miraculous Mandarin,* choreographed by Todd Bolender; and George Balanchine's choreographies of Maurice Ravel's *La Valse* and Tchaikovsky's *Swan Lake.*

Most "serious" composers explored musical correlatives of abstract expressionism in works that repudiated traditional notions of harmony and tonality. John Cage, for instance, who sometimes worked in conjunction with the Merce Cunningham Dance Company, was one of the most radical experimenters in terms of pushing the limits of what music can be. Composed in 1951, his *Imaginary Landscape No. 4* employs radio receivers to produce noise. In *Music of Changes,* the sounds produced are determined by tossing a coin, presumably to incorporate within the work of art the fundamental randomness of human existence. In England, Benjamin Britten conducted the first performance of his opera *Billy Budd.* Arnold Schoenberg, another experimenter who expanded the boundaries of what is considered music, died at age 78. In the 1920s, Schoenberg pioneered the 12-tone system that challenged traditional notions of tonality and orchestral sound, and he continued to compose until the year of his death.

Jazz continued to flourish in 1951 and to reach new levels of acceptability within so-called high culture and with the public at large. In January, Duke Ellington's *Harlem Suite* was performed at New York's Metropolitan Opera House. Alex North composed a

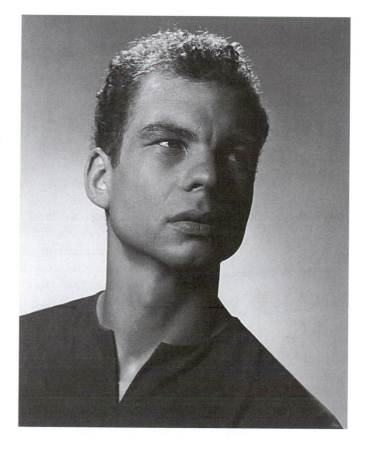

Dancer and choreographer Merce Cunningham (shown here) collaborated with experimental musician John Cage to create radical pieces of modern dance. *(Photofest)*

jazz score for Kazan's film treatment of *A Streetcar Named Desire,* Dave Brubeck formed an influential quartet with Paul Desmond, and Count Basie reorganized his band. Other top jazz performers that year were Charlie Parker, George Shearing, Stan Getz, and singer Sarah Vaughan. Clarinetist Sidney Bechet immigrated to France, and singer and band leader Cab Calloway published an article in *Ebony* magazine pointing out the growing drug problem in the world of jazz. Notable among the performers falling victim to heroin in 1951 was legendary saxophonist Parker, who lost his cabaret card due to his involvement with narcotics and was therefore unable to perform in New York nightclubs.

Other popular performers of the year included Pete Seeger's folk group, the Weavers ("On Top of Old Smokey"), Tony Bennett ("Because of You"), Perry Como ("If"), Nat "King" Cole ("Too Young"), Doris Day ("A Guy Is a Guy"), Rosemary Clooney ("Come On-a My House"), Debbie Reynolds ("Aba Daba Honeymoon"), and country singer Tennessee Ernie Ford ("Shotgun Boogie").

In 1951, Leo Fender introduced the Fender Precision Bass, a four-string electric bass guitar that opened up dynamic new possibilities for music making that were soon exploited in both jazz and rock 'n' roll, which was then in its infancy. The term *rock 'n' roll* originated in 1951, when Cincinnati radio disk jockey Alan Freed used it to describe the black rhythm and blues he played on an experimental late-night show targeted to white teenagers. The show was an instant hit, and Freed went on to promote the music at concerts and dances in New York and elsewhere. By the late 1950s, Freed was one of the nation's most popular radio personalities, but in 1962, as part of a wider scandal involving disk jockeys who accepted payola, or payoffs, he admitted accepting bribes from six record companies that wanted him to promote their new releases.

One of the most significant, enduring, and ever-evolving developments in contemporary music, the rock phenomenon soon spread throughout the country, despite apprehensions by some adults who felt it expressed too much sexuality and by others who feared the influence of a black medium on white children. The music, then usually described as rhythm and blues, or R & B, was initially performed by black musicians, then picked up and adapted by white singers. In 1952, Pennsylvania disc jockey Bill Haley became the first white performer to release a major rock hit when his energetic song "Rock the Joint" sold 75,000 records, and in 1956, Elvis Presley emerged as the first white artist to successfully combine white and black sounds. Known for his hip gyrations as he performed, Presley emerged as the "King" of rock 'n' roll, a form that remained vibrant and continued to evolve through the succeeding half century despite initial predictions that it would be just another passing teenage fad.

Rock was made possible by the development of the electric guitar and other forms of electrically amplified music. Its loud, driving rhythms often exuded sexuality that led it to be condemned as morally degenerate by communist regimes, which prohibited it, and by some right-wing American adults who agreed with that assessment of the music but maintained that rock was part of a communist conspiracy to undermine American society. Most early rock 'n' roll exhibited little direct social awareness, although in the early 1950s Haley performed "Thirteen Women" about the sole survivors of an atomic attack: one male and 13 women.

Much of the artwork that received critical acclaim was by abstract expressionists. Since most Americans had little feel for the genre, the schism between the art world and the general public continued to grow. Jackson Pollock produced several important abstract works; Ellsworth Kelly painted *Colors for a Large Wall;* Clyfford Still produced *Painting, 1951 Yellow* and *1951-N,* and Adolph Gottlieb made *The Frozen Sounds, No. 1.* Other active painters included John Marin and Franz Kline, as well as Stuart Davis, whose *Owh! In San Pão* combines sharp-edged geometric shapes with dots and cylinders and nonsensical, handwritten words and numbers. Expatriate Spanish artists Pablo Picasso and Salvador Dalí spoke more forcefully to the larger public in *Massacre in Korea* and *Crucifixion,* respectively.

Abstraction was also represented in sculpture in such pieces as José de Rivera's *Construction Blue and Black* and Marcel Duchamp's *Wedge of Chastity.* Duchamp had pioneered certain forms of expressionism early in the century, first with his contributions to the World War I–era Dada movement, which rejected language, logic, and reason as corrupted forms of expression and turned instead to pure sensation, and later with his ready-made sculptures that highlighted items from everyday life. Duchamp's objective in making "anti-art" was, in part, to attack the notion that art is reserved for exclusive drawing rooms and museums and to suggest, instead, that it can be found anywhere if we alter the way we perceive everyday reality.

CHRONICLE OF EVENTS

1951

The last of more than 17,000 nearly identical homes is sold in Levittown, a racially segregated Long Island, New York, suburban housing development that began in 1947. Levittown is integrated in 1957.

January 1: Chinese and North Korean forces launch an offensive near the 38th parallel and break through UN defensive positions north and northeast of Seoul.

January 2: The Arabian American Oil Company agrees to share profits with the government of Saudi Arabia.

January 4: For the second time in the war, Seoul falls to communist forces; nonetheless, President Truman announces in a press conference that the United States will not bomb China unless authorized to do so by a congressional declaration of war and a United Nations resolution. This stand places him at increased odds with General MacArthur, who favors expanding the war beyond Korea by attacking targets in China and unleashing Chiang Kai-chek's Nationalist army based in Taiwan.

January 6: The United States agrees to provide $38 million in food supplies to Yugoslavia.

January 8: West Germany's chancellor Konrad Adenauer accepts an East German proposal for talks on reunification.

January 10: Sinclair Lewis, America's first Nobel Prize winner for literature, dies at age 65.

January 12: Congress passes a civil defense act that allocates $3.1 billion for bomb shelters and related needs.

The vast Levittown housing development on Long Island, New York, sold its last new house in 1951. *(Photofest)*

January 15: Truman submits a record "peacetime" budget of $71.6 billion. Much of the increase derives from the "police action" in Korea.

January 15: The U.S. Supreme Court restricts First Amendment guarantees of freedom of speech by ruling that a "clear and present danger" of incitement to riot is cause for arrest.

January 21: Following a 12-hour attack, Chinese and North Korean troops drive UN forces from Inchon, on Korea's west coast.

January 23: Truman creates the Commission on Internal Security and Individual Rights to monitor the campaign against domestic communists.

January 26: The Truman administration imposes wage and price freezes to curb inflation.

January 27–28: The Atomic Energy Commission (AEC) detonates two atomic bombs in its test grounds in the Nevada desert. A five-second flash of light from the second test is visible 45 miles away in Las Vegas, where inhabitants feel a wind blowing through the city streets as a result of the blast. In Boulder City, more than 100 miles away, the explosion illuminates interior rooms in buildings. People report seeing the flash as far away as Utah and California. The AEC grounds all local airplane fights within a 150-mile radius of the test site to allow the radioactivity to disperse, but officials maintain that there is no indication of any radiological hazards.

February 1: The United Nations General Assembly votes 44 to 7 to condemn the Chinese intervention in Korea. Among those opposed is India, whose prime minister, Jawaharlal Nehru, condemns the vote.

February 1: In response to a legislative proposal to limit U.S. troop strength, General Dwight Eisenhower, supreme commander of NATO forces in Europe, tells a joint session of Congress that limiting the number of American troops or the amount of military supplies would compromise the security of Western Europe and gravely imperil the United States.

February 2: Measurements show that levels of radiation in the eastern United States are higher than normal due to the atomic testing in Nevada, 2,300 miles away. Radioactive snow falls throughout the week in Rochester, New York, and Cincinnati, Ohio, but officials from the AEC maintain that there is no evidence that the higher amounts of radiation can harm humans, animals, or the water supply.

February 9: Actress Greta Garbo receives U.S. citizenship.

February 15: The United States sends four military divisions to assist in the defense of Europe.

February 17: UN forces recapture Inchon after inflicting heavy casualties on the communist forces, which withdraw to positions in the mountains of central Korea. In central Korea, communist troops march on Chechon through a blizzard in an effort to drive down the center of South Korea and cut off the UN forces along the west coast.

On the east coast, South Korean troops recross the 38th parallel back into North Korea for the first time since UN forces were driven back by Chinese troops in late December.

February 17: Packard releases its first convertible automobile.

February 25: The Czech government accuses Foreign Minister Vladimir Clementis of conspiring to align Czechoslovakia with the West.

February 26: The Twenty-Second Amendment to the U.S. Constitution is ratified after Nevada approves it. The amendment limits U.S. presidents to two terms in office.

March 1: The television industry passes a morality code to address congressional concerns that television is undermining the nation's moral values.

March 2: The U.S. Navy launches the first K-1 submarine, which is designed to hunt enemy submarines.

March 5: General Motors reports a record $834 million profit for 1950.

March 7: A fervent nationalist assassinates General Ali Razmara, the Iranian premier. He is succeeded by Mohammed Mossadegh, a nationalist.

March 10: Archbishop Josef Beran of Czechoslovakia is arrested. In response, the pope excommunicates everyone involved.

March 12: The U.S. Supreme Court upholds the perjury conviction of Alger Hiss, who begins his five-year jail term 10 days later. He is released in 1954, after serving two-thirds of his sentence.

March 14: UN forces recapture Seoul without a battle.

March 15: French general Jean de Lattre de Tassigny demands more troops for resisting communist Vietminh insurgents in Vietnam.

March 15: Iranian premier Mossadegh sets off an international crisis when he nullifies Razmara's agreement with the Anglo-Iran Oil Company and nationalizes the Iranian oil fields.

March 17: The underground Ukrainian Insurgent Army appeals to the United States for assistance in its fight against the Soviet government.

March 21: Secretary of Defense George Marshall reports that the U.S. military has doubled in size to 2.9 million since the start of the Korean War.

March 22: Herman Wouk publishes *The Caine Mutiny.*

March 24: General MacArthur makes a truce offer and threatens to extend the war to China if it is not accepted. The Chinese reject the offer on March 29.

March 29: Julius and Ethel Rosenberg are convicted of conspiracy to transmit classified military information to the Soviet Union and receive the death sentence on April 5.

March 29: Richard Rodgers and Oscar Hammerstein II's hit musical *The King and I* opens on Broadway.

March 30: Despite reservations by Great Britain and by Truman, U.S. forces under the command of General MacArthur recross the 38th parallel into North Korea, just north of Seoul. Intelligence reports indicate that some 200,000 Chinese troops are massed north of the border to oppose the 160,000 UN troops, most of whom are Americans.

March 31: Draft deferments for college students are introduced, based on performance on national scholastic aptitude tests.

April 2: Military restrictions imposed after World War II are lifted for West Germany.

April 5: Joseph Martin, the Republican minority leader, reads on the floor of the House of Representatives a letter from MacArthur that criticizes Truman's policy of limiting the war to Korea and that declares there is no substitute for victory.

April 11: In reaction to the public reading on April 5 of MacArthur's opposition to his policies, Truman relieves MacArthur of all of his commands in the Far East. Lieutenant General Matthew Ridgway, who had been in charge of the U.S. Eighth Army in Korea, assumes command.

April 16: Truman authorizes $29 million in raw materials for Yugoslavia.

April 17: MacArthur returns to a hero's welcome in San Francisco.

April 18: Senator Arthur H. Vandenberg of Michigan dies at home. An isolationist before World War II, Vandenberg was one of the chief architects of American foreign policy and a key player in winning Senate ratification of the United Nations.

April 19: A record 30 million viewers watch on television as MacArthur addresses a joint session of Congress, during which he defends his actions as military commander and reasserts his position that the war should be expanded into China. Concluding with the lines of a military ballad, "Old soldiers never die, they just fade away," the tearful MacArthur gains an enthusiastic reception. The following day, he receives a ticker tape parade in New York City.

April 21: Hungary releases Robert Vogeler, who had been convicted of spying for the United States.

April 21: Five U.S. soldiers stationed in the Philippines are killed in an ambush by communist Huk insurgents.

April 29: China seizes assets of the British Asiatic Petroleum Company.

April 29: Philosopher Ludwig Wittgenstein dies. Wittgenstein inspired the influential, empirically based school of logical positivism and was known for saying, "The world is all that is the case."

May 1: The United States begins Radio Free Europe broadcasts into Eastern Europe.

May 2: RCA begins broadcasting color television programs from the Empire State Building. Unlike broadcasts from competitor CBS, which require special converters, RCA's telecasts are capable of being received on ordinary black-and-white sets in the New York area.

May 11: According to the United Nations, UN forces have, to date, suffered 248,000 casualties and the communist forces 890,000.

May 12: The U.S. government announces that it is making significant progress in developing the hydrogen bomb. In particular, tests of atomic weapons in the Pacific Ocean are providing important information about the thermonuclear reactions necessary for detonating a hydrogen bomb.

May 15: AT&T announces that it has 1 million shareholders, a first in U.S. history. AT&T, which at the time has a monopoly on local and long-distance telephone operations throughout the nation, represents a safe, dependable stock for many middle-class Americans, and it remains a popular investment through the 1950s.

May 18: UN troops fall back behind the 38th parallel in response to a communist offensive along a 100-mile front.

May 19: General Omar Bradley, a World War II hero and current chairman of the Joint Chiefs of Staff, begins five days of testimony before a Senate subcommittee investigating Truman's firing of MacArthur. Bradley defends Truman's decision to relieve MacArthur, also a World War II hero, of his command and maintains that MacArthur's strategy of expanding the war would have been dangerous. He also criticizes MacArthur for failing to learn in advance that the Chinese intended to attack his forces after they approached the Manchurian border. Secretary of Defense George Marshall, another World War II hero, also supports Truman during the committee hearings.

May 20: Captain James Jabara, a World War II ace, becomes the first jet ace after shooting down his fifth and sixth Soviet MIG fighter planes over Korea. On the ground, a communist attack forces South Korean troops on the east coast back across the 38th parallel. UN troops repulse an assault on the northwest front near Seoul.

May 24: UN troops counterattack and push the communist forces behind the 38th parallel.

May 24: Twenty-year-old outfielder Willie Mays joins baseball's New York Giants.

May 25: Donald Maclean and Guy Burgess, two high-ranking British foreign service officers, disappear and are subsequently believed to have been Soviet agents. Maclean had access to sensitive communications between the governments of Great Britain and the United States regarding such matters as NATO, the Korean War, and the Japanese peace treaty.

May 27: Austria elects a socialist president.

May 28: The Supreme Court reverses an FCC ruling and endorses CBS's method of color television transmission, which is incompatible with that of NBC.

May 29: Captain Charles Blair makes the first solo flight over the North Pole in a single-engine plane.

June 1: Philosopher and educator John Dewey dies at age 92.

June 3: NBC announces that it will make its tricolor TV tube available to CBS.

June 4: The U.S. Supreme Court upholds the rights of states to require job applicants to sign affidavits affirming that they are not communists.

June 10: UN forces break into the communist "iron triangle" in Korea.

June 12: The Ford Foundation initiates a study intended to elevate the cultural level of television content.

June 13: UN troops recapture Pyongyang, North Korea's capital.

June 14: In New Jersey, a human birth is broadcast on television for the first time.

June 15: Heavyweight boxer Joe Louis knocks out Lee Savold in a comeback fight.

June 16: The United States formally ratifies the charter of the Organization of American States (OAS).

June 19: Truman extends the draft to 1955, lengthens the time of service to two years, and lowers the draft age to 18 1/2 years of age.

June 19: United Airlines becomes the target of the first airline pilots's strike.

June 20: Following a Supreme Court decision two weeks earlier that upheld the constitutionality of the Smith Act, under which 11 top leaders of the American Communist Party were convicted in the 1949 Foley Square trial, a New York federal grand jury indicts 21 more party leaders for conspiring to forcefully overthrow the U.S. government.

June 23: In a surprise move, the UN delegate from the Soviet Union calls for a cease-fire in the Korean War. Secretary of State Acheson responds positively but cautiously and asserts that although the eventual unification of Korea under a democratic government is the United States's ultimate objective, a communist withdrawal behind the 38th parallel and accompanying guarantees against renewed aggression would be sufficient to conclude the military conflict.

June 26: For the first time in its 31 years, the NAACP holds its annual meeting in the South. The legal-strategy board promises an all-out attack on discrimination of all forms, with top priority on segregation in education.

June 28: In Budapest, Hungary, Archbishop Josef Groesz is sentenced to 15 years for plotting against the government. Two days later, the pope excommunicates the Hungarian officials involved in the arrest.

July 1: Cleveland pitcher Bob Feller sets a Major League Baseball record by pitching his third no-hitter.

July 1: The Columbo Plan for cooperation and economic development begins in Southeast Asia.

July 5: The International Court in the Hague, the Netherlands, rules in favor of Great Britain in its dispute over Iran's seizure of its oil refineries.

July 8: Representatives from North Korea, China, and the United Nations meet in Kaesong to discuss the scope and conditions for peace talks.

July 9: Mystery and detective writer Dashiell Hammett, author of *The Thin Man* and *The Maltese Falcon,* is sentenced to six months in prison for refusing to name individuals who contributed to a bail bond fund for four communist leaders who subsequently jumped bail.

July 10: In a major upset, British fighter Randy Turpin takes the middleweight boxing crown from American "Sugar" Ray Robinson.

July 13: Arnold Schoenberg dies. The 76-year-old American composer developed a 12-tone system that revolutionized classical music in the early 20th century.

July 14: A state of emergency is declared in Missouri, where floods leave some 500,000 people homeless.

July 15: J. D. Salinger publishes *The Catcher in the Rye.*

July 19: "Jersey" Joe Walcott knocks out Ezzard Charles to claim the heavyweight boxing championship.

July 20: Spain's fascist dictator, Generalissimo Francisco Franco, announces that his two greatest priorities are rearming Spain and seeking friendly relations with the nations of the Americas. Many UN nations severed diplomatic ties with Spain in 1946, in response to Franco's despotic rule. But since then, Franco's strong anticommunist stance has made him more acceptable to the West. The United States resumed diplomatic relations in 1950 and began issuing loans that had been denied under the Marshall Plan.

July 20: Jordan's king, Abdullah, is assassinated by members of his own security team.

July 26: North Korea and China withdraw their insistence that all foreign troops leave Korea before peace talks can begin.

July 28: In a speech in Detroit, Truman warns against opportunistic Soviet aggression.

August 1: The United States ends tariff privileges for all communist-dominated countries.

August 5: General Matthew Ridgway suspends peace talks in Korea due to violations of the neutral zone.

August 7: The U.S. Viking rocket climbs to a record 135 miles above Earth and attains a speed of 1,400 miles per hour.

August 14: Newspaper publisher William Randolph Hearst dies at age 88. The newspaper magnate, who was the basis for Charles Foster Kane, the principal figure in Orson Welles's *Citizen Kane* (1940), was reputed to have provoked American involvement in the Spanish-American War of 1898 with his highly inflammatory journalism.

August 20: Chase and Manhattan banks begin talks that initiate the largest merger in banking history.

August 23: In a major scandal, 90 West Point cadets are expelled or told to withdraw for cheating on their examinations. Army's successful football team is involved in the violations of the honor code—the aspect of the scandal that so many military personnel and civilians find especially upsetting.

August 29: Angered that local officials in Sioux City, Iowa, have refused to allow the burial in an all-white cemetery of a Winnebago Indian who had died in Korea, Truman personally arranges for Sergeant, First Class John R. Rice to be buried with full military honors in Arlington National Cemetery.

August 30: The Philippines and the United States sign a mutual defense treaty.

August 30: The U.S. Navy announces that its rocket-powered Douglas Skyrocket airplane has set new records for altitude and speed. The navy declines to furnish specifics but claims that the Skyrocket exceeded the 13.7 altitude record set by a balloonist in 1935.

August 30: Citing provisions for a national emergency, Truman invokes the Taft-Hartley Act to end a five-day strike against the Kennecott Copper Corporation.

September 1: In response to their concerns about Russian and Chinese expansionism and the revival of Japan as a sovereign nation, Australia and New Zealand sign a mutual defense pact with the United States. The treaty provides for common defense and asserts that an attack on one of the signatory nations will be regarded as a threat against the security of all. The treaty is considered necessary in order for Australia and New Zealand to support the upcoming U.S.-backed treaty of reconciliation with Japan.

September 4: Truman opens peace treaty talks with Japan via the first transcontinental television hookup.

September 6: Portugal grants U.S. rights in the Azores.

September 8: Forty-nine nations sign a peace treaty formally ending the war with Japan. The United States and Japan also sign a security agreement assuring U.S. defense of Japan in case of external attack.

September 10: Czech engineer Frazek Jarda drives his train with 111 passengers past its last stop in Czechoslovakia and continues into West Germany. Among the passengers are Jarda's wife and two children and 21 others seeking political asylum.

September 11: Composer Igor Stravinsky conducts the premiere of his opera, *The Rake's Progress,* in Venice.

September 11: The UN command admits to an accidental plane attack that violated the neutrality of Kaesong.

September 12: George Marshall retires as secretary of defense.

September 12: "Sugar" Ray Robinson reclaims the middleweight crown.

September 13: French general de Lattre de Tassigny visits the United States to garner support for the French war in Vietnam.

September 18: Pianist Jimmy Yancey dies. Yancey pioneered the boogie-woogie.

September 19: Elia Kazan's cinematic adaptation of Tennessee Williams's *A Streetcar Named Desire* opens.

September 20: At a meeting in Ottawa, Canada, the North Atlantic Council agrees to admit Greece and Turkey into NATO.

September 20: Ford Frick is elected to a seven-year term as commissioner of baseball.

September 24: Peace talks break down in Korea.

September 26: William Faulkner publishes *A Requiem for a Nun.*

September 27: The West German parliament unanimously votes to pay reparations to the Jewish people for atrocities committed during World War II. An Israeli spokesman acknowledges the West German gesture but notes that East Germany, which also bears responsibility for the crimes, has not similarly expressed responsibility. The amount of the restitution, based on Germany's ability to pay, is set in 1952, when German and Israeli negotiators fix the figure at $822 million. Most of the money is used to defray Israel's expenses for absorbing Jews displaced by the war. The remainder is distributed to other displaced Jews throughout the world.

September 29: General Nicholas Plastiras is named premier of Greece.

October 3: The White House announces that the Soviets have tested a second atomic bomb.

October 3: The Vietminh launch a new offensive in northwest Vietnam.

October 3: The New York Giants, who had trailed by 13 1/2 games two months earlier, defeat the Brooklyn Dodgers in a National League playoff when Bobby Thompson hits a game-winning home run in the bottom of the ninth inning. The Giants go on to lose the World Series in six games to the New York Yankees. Brooklyn's catcher, Roy Campanella, wins the National League's Most Valuable Player (MVP) award; the Yankees's catcher, Yogi Berra, wins in the American League. Playing for the Giants, Willie Mays is the National League's Rookie of the Year. Pittsburgh's Ralph Kiner leads the major leagues with 42 home runs; St. Louis Cardinal Stan Musial wins the National League batting title with a 355 average, and Philadelphia's Ferris Fain hits .344 to win in the American League. Brooklyn's Preacher Roe and Cleveland's Bob Feller are the top pitchers in the National League and American League, respectively.

October 6: Communist insurgents in Singapore assassinate Sir Henry Gurney, the British high commissioner for Malaya.

October 6: UN troops in Korea retake the bitterly contested "Heartbreak Ridge."

October 6: Breakfast cereal entrepreneur Will K. Kellogg dies at age 91. Famous for his Kellogg's Corn Flakes, the philanthropist developed the first wheat flake in 1894 in Battle Creek, Michigan.

October 8: Egypt announces a decree to eject Great Britain from the Suez region and to take control of the Sudan.

October 10: Truman signs the Mutual Security Bill, which allocates a total of $7.5 billion in foreign aid.

October 14: The UN command admits raiding Panmunjom, the new site for rescheduled peace talks.

October 15: CBS-TV airs the first broadcast of *I Love Lucy,* which runs through June 1957 and becomes the most popular television show of the 1950s.

October 16: Pakistan's premier Leaquat Ali Khan is assassinated by a radical Muslim.

October 16: RCA demonstrates its large-screen color television, but on October 19, the government shelves plans for color operations because of the war effort.

October 20: Truman nominates General Mark Clark to become the first U.S. ambassador to the

Vatican in an effort to resume relations that ended in 1868. Clark withdraws his name from consideration in January 1952.

October 22: The U.S. Air Force tests the first air-to-ground tactical nuclear weapon.

October 26: At age 77, Winston Churchill is once again elected Britain's prime minister after his Conservative Party was swept from power in a surprise loss in July 1945, following the surrender of Germany.

October 27: Twenty-seven-year-old heavyweight boxer Rocky Marciano knocks out former champion Joe Louis in the eighth round.

November 1: While testing another atomic bomb in Nevada, the United States conducts its first atomic warfare maneuver involving troops.

November 8: The Soviets reject a U.S. plan for UN control of atomic power.

November 9: The United States, Great Britain, France, and Turkey announce plans to form a Mideast defense organization.

November 11: Following a coup attempt in September, Argentina's Juan Perón is elected president for a sixth term.

November 11: Truman indicates that he would like to sponsor General Eisenhower as the Democratic presidential candidate in the 1952 election. Eisenhower replies that he is flattered, but most observers do not expect him to accept the offer that would virtually guarantee his nomination.

November 13: Truman announces an economic development plan for the Near East.

November 14: The United States agrees to supply Yugoslavia with military assistance.

November 17: The world's first nuclear heating system is developed in Great Britain.

November 18: CBS broadcasts the first installment of *See It Now,* the influential TV news documentary hosted by journalist Edward R. Murrow. In this first live, commercial, coast-to-coast broadcast, Murrow impresses his audience by showing simultaneously, on a split screen, San Francisco's Golden Gate Bridge and New York's Brooklyn Bridge.

November 27: The FCC predicts that there will be between 1,200 and 1,500 television stations in the United States within five years.

November 28: Negotiators agree to establish the 38th parallel as a line of demarcation for a truce agreement.

December 3: Truman forms the Committee on Government Contract Compliance to enforce the antidiscrimination clauses in federal employment contracts.

December 6: Harold Ross, founder of the *New Yorker* magazine, dies.

December 11: New York Yankee outfielder Joe DiMaggio, the "Yankee Clipper," announces his retirement.

December 13: After meeting with FBI director J. Edgar Hoover, Truman announces he will make new efforts to purge the government of disloyal workers.

December 18: North Korea gives the UN command a list of 3,100 prisoners of war.

December 23: The Los Angeles Rams defeat the Cleveland Browns 24-17 for the NFL championship. Rams quarterback Bob Waterfield leads the league in passing at the end of the season, and Ram Elroy Hirsh in receiving. New York's Eddie Price is the top rusher.

December 24: Libya, a former Italian colony, gains its independence. It becomes the first nation organized under UN auspices. Its mostly Arab inhabitants have the lowest per capita income in the world.

December 27: A 30-day "trial" cease-fire ends in Korea.

December 28: The United States pays $120,000 to free four fliers who were convicted in Hungary of espionage.

December 29: In Idaho Falls, Indiana, for the first time electricity is generated from an atomic reactor.

December 31: The Marshall Plan ends after spending close to $12.5 billion to revive the economies of the democratic countries of Europe. It is replaced by the Mutual Security Agency.

EYEWITNESS TESTIMONY

In 1951 we played a date in Chicago, and, then, found ourselves with some free time before the next date in a nearby city. Bird told us to send our luggage on . . . and come home with him. He wanted us to meet his Ma. We spent two wonderful days there. We woke up every morning to big meals. His mother was very kind. Bird looked a lot like her. A friend of Charlie's owned a small plane and offered to take Bird to the next job. So Max, Duke, and I took the train, and Charlie and Red Rodney went by plane. Red told me that Bird asked if he could take the controls; his friends said yes. Now, Charlie never flew a plane before, but there he was, blithely flying the ship, a broad smile on his face. Suddenly, Bird leans left, and the plane banks to the right. The guy grabs the controls real fast. Red was shaking with fright. Bird said

Saxophonist Charlie "Bird" Parker was one of the major jazz innovators of the 1940s and early 1950s. (Photofest)

he just wanted to hear the motor when he banked the plane.

Musician Tommy Potter remembering jazz saxophonist Charlie "Bird" Parker in 1951, in Robert George Reisner, Bird: The Legend of Charlie Parker *(1975), p. 183.*

After witnessing it once, the exasperated parent is likely to head for the cellar or roof to escape the darned thing. . . . [T]he program is conducted at a noise level roughly five times that of [Milton] Berle, or twenty times that of Lou Costello.

New York Herald Tribune columnist John Crosby complaining in 1951 about the noise on the children's television show Howdy Doody, *in Jane Stern and Michael Stern,* Encyclopedia of Pop Culture *(1992), pp. 233–34.*

Grade school went from kindergarten to seventh grade. After lunch we were allowed to have free play on the playground. (Now there are too many children in school for that.) It was an honor to be in sixth grade and be on the safety patrol. We had patrols to help kids across the street and to mind them on the playground—they don't have those any more because of the legal complications. We climbed on jungle gyms, played hopscotch, dodge ball, jacks, pickup sticks, marbles, and, when we weren't in school, we played with paper dolls. Betsy Wetsy was the first doll I had where you feed her a bottle of water, and she actually wet her diapers. We girls wore dresses with sashes tied into big bows in the back. We all believed that the stork brought babies to families and Santa delivered presents at Christmas. Fairy tales were wonderful to read; boys played cowboys and Indians, and cap pistols were the toys of choice.

Families traveled together. There were no car seats for small children, but the cars did have running boards and vent windows—because there was no air conditioning. On trips, we would watch anxiously for the next set of Burma Shave signs spread across the country. Truman was President, and we all made fun of his daughter's singing. He was considered a hick, even in Missouri, where he was from. The big cities were run by bosses, some good at it, some not.

During the Korean War, all of the boys had to answer the draft. Those in trouble with the law were often given a choice between jail time and military service, where it was hoped they would straighten out and become men. Many women who had never voted before voted for Ike in '52, because they thought he'd end the Korean War.

Telephone numbers were like Grand 6414; you only dialed the first two letters (i.e.: GR-6414). Our first phone was a party line. Someone was always eavesdropping. There was no touch tone. We actually put our finger into the hole on the rotor and dialed.

Maezel Brown, who was in sixth grade in 1951, recalling her impressions of the times, in private correspondence with the author, September 9, 2001.

Only where great masses are superfluous or can be spared without disastrous results of depopulation is totalitarian rule, as distinguished from totalitarian movements, at all possible.

Totalitarian movements are possible wherever there are masses who for one reason or another have acquired the appetite for political organization....

In this atmosphere of the breakdown of class society [during the first part of the 20th century] the psychology of the European mass man developed. The fact that with monotonous but abstract uniformity the same fate had befallen a mass of individuals did not prevent their judging themselves in terms of individual failure or the world in terms of specific injustice. This self-centered bitterness . . . was not a common bond . . . because it was based on no common interest, economic or social or political. Self-centeredness, therefore, went hand in hand with a decisive weakening of the instinct for self-preservation. Selflessness in the sense that oneself does not matter, the feeling of being expendable, was no longer the expression of individual idealism but a mass phenomenon.... Himmler, who knew so well the mentality of those whom he organized, described [those whom he recruited] . . . when he said they were not interested in "everyday problems" but only "in ideological questions of importance for decades and centuries, so that the man . . . knows he is working for a great task which occurs but once in 2,000 years." The gigantic massing of individuals produced a mentality which, like Cecil Rhodes some forty years before, thought in continents and felt in centuries....

It soon became apparent that highly cultured people were particularly attracted to mass movements and that, generally, highly differentiated individualism and sophistication did not prevent, indeed sometimes encouraged, the self-abandonment into the mass for which mass movements provided....

The chief characteristic of the mass man is not brutality and backwardness, but his isolation and lack of normal social relationships.

Philosopher Hannah Arendt discussing the roots of totalitarianism in Totalitarianism, *which was first published in 1951, in Arendt,* Totalitarianism *(1968), pp. 9–15.*

Following an atom bomb explosion, families would become separated and lost from each other in confusion. Supports of normal family and community life would be broken down. . . . [T]here would develop among many people, especially youths . . . the reckless psychological state often seen following great disasters. . . . Under such conditions, moral standards would relax and promiscuity would increase. . . . [There would be a] 1,000 percent increase [in venereal disease].

Dr. Charles Walter Clarke, executive director of the American Social Hygiene Association, discussing likely implications for hygiene in the event of a nuclear war, in Clarke, "Social Hygene and Civil Defense," Journal of Social Hygiene *(January 1951), pp. 3–7.*

A few weeks ago the Chinese Communist radio in Peiping [Beijing] announced that American motion pictures were being kicked out of Red China. The Associated Press story quoted the announcer as stating that the action was taken "to put an end to American propaganda."

When the news appeared in the American press, film-company executives evinced little surprise. They expected it. The surprise, if any, was that the ban wasn't imposed sooner. Ringing the curtain down on American movies has become standard procedure in countries that take their orders from the Kremlin. Movie fans in the satellite countries must be spared, say the Communists, the "degradation" that comes from a "corrupt and materialistic" America....

The policy-makers in the Kremlin, recognizing that motion pictures constitute one of the most powerful weapons in today's psychological warfare, detest our films. They fear them. Why?

Because they know only too well that American motion pictures reflect life in a democracy; that pictures from America, wherever they are shown, eclipse in popularity the films of any other country.

Selling the virtues of communism becomes much more difficult when people see movies that mirror the way of life in a free society. It isn't healthy for "liberated" people to be reminded that there are still countries in the world where the dignity of the individual is respected, where people can speak without fear, and worship as they please. They might become restless. They might get ideas. So the state clamps down.

It is difficult to reconcile Moscow's fear of American films with articles occasionally published in this country charging that Hollywood presents such a dishonest picture of America that our movies are playing right into the hands of Communists.

John G. McCarthy responding to "Hollywood Over Asia," an article by Richard L. G. Deverall, published December 9, 1950, in America, *charging that Hollywood films play into the hands of communist propagandists, in McCarthy, Hollywood Over Asia,* America: National Catholic Weekly Review *(January 13, 1951), p. 432.*

For Arthur Koestler's haunting terror, Sidney Kingsley has substituted a complicated melodrama in *Darkness at Noon.* . . . By and large, this is the same story of a party leader who is arrested, thrown into jail and made to confess to crimes he never committed; and Claude Rains gives a fine, perceptive performance in the part.

But somewhere between the novel and the theatre the intellectual distinction has gone out of the work. For Mr. Kingsley is less a writer than a showman in this theatre piece, and his melodrama comes with elements of the glib propaganda play that we find so distasteful when it is on the other side.

Brooks Atkinson reviewing Sidney Kingsley's theatrical adaptation of the Arthur Koestler novel Darkness at Noon, *in Atkinson, "Darkness at Noon," New York* Times, *January 15, 1951, p. 3.*

If he's running with you, he's a South Korean. If he's running after you, he's a North Korean.

A G.I. distinguishing friend from foe in Samuel Fuller's movie The Steel Helmet, *which opened in New York movie theaters on January 24, 1951.*

The finest specimens [of influence peddlers] claim Missouri as their habitat, have at least a nodding acquaintance with Harry Truman, a much chummier relationship with his aides and advisers, and can buzz in and out of the White House at will. They also have a great fondness for crisp currency.

From a description in Time *of the report of a Senate subcommittee, released in February 1951, about influence peddling associated with the Reconstruction Finance Corporation, in David McCullough,* Truman *(1992), p. 863.*

My argument [in an earlier address about Catholic educational policies] was twofold. The "revolution" had to do with the growing hostility towards religious education, and specifically Catholic education, in this country. I argued that the policy of the National Education Association [NEA] . . . was to regard only public schools as "American" and that the public schools could not teach religion. "If you eliminate religion from the state schools, and then force all the children to attend state schools," the argument ran, "you have gone a long way towards eliminating religion from society." . . .

These "submerged issues" in the Federal-aid controversy, I said, had been brought to light and had "set serious non-Catholics thinking." . . . [Gordon C. Lee, in a January 1951 article in the NEA *Journal*] has . . . tried to "answer" my contentions so as to isolate the Catholic opposition to NEA's politics and to picture us in such guise as to frighten away non-Catholics who might consider supporting us.

Mr. Lee begins by "loading" his definition of the issue. . . . Is the United States to continue to put its faith, its energies and its financial resources into an ever-expanding public educational system or is it to abandon that system to those who would subvert education to partisan and parochial ends?"

Did I say we had to make such a choice? . . . I argued *against* a complete monopoly of education by the state. Mr. Lee twists this into meaning that I argued *for* a complete monopoly of education by parochial schools. . . .

So let me ask Mr. Lee point blank: "Do you, or do you not, regard American Catholic parochial elementary schools as 'integral parts of the American educational endeavor'?" . . . Their "legal right" to exist is something the NEA can't do anything about. . . . [But Lee] regards our parochial schools . . . as schools which "subvert education to partisan and parochial ends," "none of them representing the public interest," as giving an "education whose ends and aims are essentially private or parochial."

> Robert C. Hartnett, S.J., discussing the National Educa-
> tion Association's opposition to federal funding for
> parochial schools in Hartnett, "Mr. Lee 'Examines'
> Catholic School Policy," America: National Catholic
> Weekly Review (February 17, 1951), p. 581.

As one hears over and again that Roger Sessions is the high-minded, serious, cerebral, and granitic American composer, one wonders exactly what compliments and derogations all these terms can imply. First, perhaps, that he is the one American with the strength and integrity to see clearly the musical challenge of the time, and to cope with it uncompromisingly. . . . But the further implication is that his work is recondite, cold, and unconcerned with the expressive functions of music, this does indeed criticize, inconsistently, and I think absurdly.

> Joseph Kerman reviewing the work of composer Roger
> Sessions in Kerman, "Roger Sessions,"
> Hudson Review (Spring 1951), p. 126.

I cannot possibly sign the oath of allegiance you sent me, and I'm sorry I was not told in your first letter that this would be required of me, for a good deal of time and trouble would have been spared both of us.

This is the first time I've encountered this dangerous nonsense, but I have known from the beginning what my answer must be. My memory goes back easily thirty years to the time this law was passed in Colorado, in a time of war, fright, and public hysteria being whipped up by the same kind of people who are doing this work now. Only now we're worse for thirty years of world disaster.

I believed then, and still do believe, that this requirement of an oath of allegiance was more of a device for embarrassing and humiliating honest persons than an effective trap for traitors and subversive people. . . . [I]t is the mere truth that an oath binds only those persons who meant to keep their promises anyway, with or without an oath. The others cannot be touched or controlled in any such way. We all know this so why assist at such a cynical fraud?

I'm entirely hostile to the principle of Communism and to every form of totalitarian society, whether it calls itself Communism, Fascism, or whatever. I feel indeed that Communism and Fascism are two names for the same thing, that the present strug-

gle is really a civil war between two factions of totalitarianism. For Fascism is older, more insidious, harder to identify, easier to disguise. . . .

My family are old stock. They helped to found colonies, to break new trails, to survey the wilderness. . . . They have fought in all the wars, they have been governors of states. . . . We're not suspect, nor liable to the questionings of the kind of people we would never have invited to our tables. . . .

So please destroy the contract we have made, as it is no longer valid. . . . I am not in the least a martyr. I have no time for heroics and indeed distrust them deeply. I am an artist who wishes to be left in peace to do my work.

> Author Katherine Anne Porter refusing to sign an oath of
> allegiance required for publication of her book in a letter
> of March 4, 1951, to Dr. William Ross, in Porter,
> Letters of Katherine Anne Porter
> (1990), pp. 394–95.

With staggering impact, the telecasts of the Kefauver investigation have brought a shocked awakening to millions of Americans.

Across their television tubes have paraded the honest and dishonest, the frank and the furtive, the public servant and the public thief. Out of many pictures has come a broader picture of the sordid intermingling of crime and politics, of dishonor in public life.

And suddenly millions of Americans are asking: What's happened to our ideal of right and wrong?

What's happened to our principles of honesty in government?

What's happened to public and private standards of morality?

Then they ask the most important question of all: how can we stop what's going on? *Is there anything we can do about it?* [Original italics.]

> A full-page newspaper advertisement placed in late
> March 1951, by the advertising firm of Young and Rubi-
> cam, in response to crime and corruption uncovered by the
> Kefauver committee, in Eric F. Goldman, The Crucial
> Decade—and After: America, 1945–1960
> (1960), p. 198.

I believe your conduct in putting into the hands of the Russians the A-bomb years before our best scientists predicted Russia would perfect the bomb has already caused, in my opinion, the Communist aggression in Korea, with the resultant casualties exceeding 50,000 and who knows but that millions more of innocent people may pay the price of your treason.

Judge Irving Kaufman, upon sentencing Julius and Ethel Rosenberg to death after their conviction on March 29, 1951, for espionage, in Stephen J. Whitfield, The Culture of the Cold War (1996), p. 31.

[W]e [in Korea] fight Europe's war with arms while the diplomats there still fight it with words. . . . [I]f we lose the war to Communism in Asia the fall of Europe is inevitable, win it and Europe most probably would avoid war and yet preserve freedom. . . . There is no substitute for victory.

General Douglas MacArthur's statement in a letter to Representative Joseph Martin of Massachusetts, which Martin read on the floor of Congress on April 5, 1951 (this letter was the immediate provocation for President Truman's decision to fire MacArthur six days later), in David McCullough, Truman (1992), p. 838.

General Marshall was concerned about the reaction of certain Congressmen, and he wanted to think over what he felt the reaction of the troops would be. So . . . I said, "General, you go over there and you read all the correspondence that's passed between MacArthur and me for the last two years. Then be in my office at nine in the morning, and if you still feel I shouldn't fire him, I won't."

And the next morning at eight fifteen when I got to my office, he was out there waiting for me. . . . [H]e says, "I spent most of the night on that file, Mr. President, and you should have fired the son of a bitch two years ago."

And so we went right ahead and did it. . . .

General Bradley came over to Blair House and told me . . . if MacArthur hears he's going to be fired before he is officially fired, before he's notified, he'd probably up and resign on me.

And I told Bradley, "The son of a bitch isn't going to resign on me, I want him fired!"

Truman describing his decision to fire General MacArthur on April 11, 1951, in Merle Miller, Plain Speaking: An Oral Biography of Harry S. Truman (1974), pp. 304–5.

I want to talk to you tonight about what we are doing in Korea and about our policy in the Far East. In the simplest terms what we are doing in Korea is this: We are trying to prevent a third world war. . . .

The communists in the Kremlin are engaged in a monstrous conspiracy to stamp out freedom all over the world. If they were to succeed, the United States would be numbered among their principal victims. . . .

The aggression against Korea is the boldest and most dangerous move the communists have yet made. The attack on Korea was part of a greater plan for conquering all of Asia. . . .

We do not want to see the conflict in Korea extended. We are trying to prevent a world war, not to start one. . . . But you may ask why can't we take other steps to punish the aggressor. Why don't we bomb Manchuria and China itself. Why don't we assist the Chinese nationalist troops to land on the mainland of China.

If we were to do those things, we would be running a very grave risk of starting a general war. If that were to happen, we would have brought about the exact situation we are trying to prevent. . . . What would suit the ambitions of the Kremlin better than for our military forces to be committed to a full-scale war with Red China? . . .

A number of events have made it evident that General MacArthur did not agree with that policy. I have therefore considered it essential to relieve General MacArthur so there would be no doubt or confusion as to the real purpose and aim of our policy. It was with the deepest personal regret that I found myself compelled to take this action. General MacArthur is one of our greatest military commanders. But the cause of world peace is greater than any individual.

President Truman's address to the nation announcing his firing of General Douglas MacArthur on April 11, 1951, in Robert Torricelli and Andrew Carroll, eds., In Our Own Words (1999), pp. 181–85.

You cannot appease or otherwise surrender to Communism in Asia without simultaneously undermining our efforts to halt its advance in Europe. . . . [Confining the war to Korea is a path of] prolonged indecision. . . . "Why," my soldiers asked of me, "surrender military advantages to an enemy in the field?" I could not answer. . . .

The hopes and dreams have long since vanished. But I still remember the refrain of one of the most popular barracks ballads of that day which proclaims most proudly that, "Old soldiers never die. They just fade away. And like the old soldier of the ballad, I now close my military career and just fade away—an old soldier who tried to do his duty as God gave him the light to see that duty.

Goodbye.

General Douglas MacArthur's farewell address before a joint session of Congress on April 19, 1951, in David McCullough, Truman *(1992), p. 851.*

We heard God speak here today, God in the flesh, the voice of God!

Representative Dewey Short of Missouri in response to General Douglas MacArthur's farewell speech before a joint session of Congress on April 19, 1951, quoted in David McCullough, Truman *(1992), p. 852.*

[MacArthur's farewell address is] a bunch of damn bullshit.

President Truman's private response to General MacArthur's farewell speech on April 19, 1951, in David McCullough, Truman *(1992), p. 852.*

With me it was [that] defending the Communist Party was something worse than naming names. I did not want to remain a martyr to something that I absolutely believed was immoral and wrong. It's as simple as that.

Director Edward Dmytryk commenting in a 1973 television interview about his testimony before the House Un-American Activities Committee on April 25, 1951, in Victor Navasky, Naming Names *(1980), p. 238.*

In Spring 1951, our troops in Korea waged the fifth offensive campaign. At the end of the campaign, it became clear that it was difficult for us to eliminate large numbers of enemy troops on the battlefield. Facing the situation that we were not in a position to achieve a quick solution of the Korean question by military means, our Party's Central Committee decided to adopt new political and military strategies to end the war.

In May 1951, Comrade Xie Fang returned to Beijing to report to Chairman Mao about the war situation in Korea. Among other ideas, Chairman Mao suggested that we should fully recognize the protracted nature of the Korean War and fully prepare for its difficulties. During his report, Xie Fang told Chairman Mao that our annihilation campaigns were not aimed at eliminating a large number of enemy troops all at once. We were crushing the enemy forces one by one through continuous attacks. Chairman Mao was very happy to know that. He made a vivid metaphor of our tactics as "eating a stinky candy bit by bit."

From then on, this piecemeal approach became a major principle for our armies eliminating enemy troops during the strategic defense period.

Chinese general Hong Xuezhi describing Mao Zedong's Korean War strategy in May 1951, in Hong, Kangmei Yuanchao Zhanzheng Huiyi *(1990), pp. 191–93.*

Twelve years ago, Warner Brothers let loose a hot and lurid blast at Nazi agents in this country with their *Confessions of a Nazi Spy.* Now they are blasting Communist agents with equal fervor and alarm in a hissing and horrendous spy film called *I Was a Communist for the FBI.* Based on the memoirs of Matt Cvetic, a Pittsburgh steel worker who actually did some sleuthing for the Federal bureau as a "plant" in a Communist cell, this film is an erratic amalgam of exciting journalistic report, conventional "chase" melodrama, patriotic chest-thumping and reckless "red" smears. Riding a wave of public interest, it opened . . . yesterday.

In many respects this heated item bears comparison to the hearings before the House Un-American Activities Committee—which, incidentally, it extols. For in telling its story of a valiant patriot who silently endures the contempt of his son, his brothers and his neighbors while he poses as a loyal Communist, it tosses off dangerous innuendos and creates some ugly bugaboos in the process of sifting the details of how the Communists bore from within.

For instance, in glibly detailing how the Communist foment racial hate and labor unrest in this country, it colors its scenes so luridly that the susceptible in the audience might catch a hint that most Negroes and most laborers are "pinks." It raises suspicion of school teachers by introducing one as a diligent "party member" at the outset. (After she meets the hero and falls for him, she breaks away.) And, all the way through, it drops suggestions—always from the villains' oily tongues—that people who embrace liberal causes, such as the Scottsboro trial defense, are Communist dupes.

Critic Bosley Crowther reviewing I Was a Communist for the FBI, *in Crowther " 'Communist for F.B.I.,' New Picture at Strand Threatre,"* New York Times, *May 3, 1951, p. 34.*

Stop knocking football. God help this country if we didn't play football. . . . General Eisenhower came to West Point with his greatest desire to play football.

Colonel Earl H. Blaik, coach of the Army football team, in defense of his players who were expelled during summer 1951 for cheating at West Point, in Eric F. Goldman, The Crucial Decade—and After: America, 1945–1960, *p. 190.*

The whole world was watching our negotiation, Li Kenong [China's chief negotiator] said. We were prepared to put forward three principles as our first step to solve the Korean problem peacefully. These principles were consistent with a hope for peace by the people of the whole world, including the American and British people. The other side had already expressed a possible acceptance of our basic points. Our three principles were that both sides should stop fighting immediately; that both sides withdraw from the 38th parallel in order to establish a non-military zone, and that all foreign armies withdraw from the Korean Peninsula. For the first two points, Li continued, though both sides had some disagreements, the basic points were not unworkable. For the last point about foreign troops' withdrawal, the other side did not want to discuss it right now; they, however, agreed to talk about "gradual withdrawal" in the future. Although both sides had a big difference over the last point, there was still room for discussion and a possibility for reaching an agreement. However, it would not be an easy task for us to deal with the American imperialists. We needed to think about all possible difficulties. Therefore, our task required all the Chinese and Korean comrades to unite together under the leadership of Chairman Mao Zedong and Premier Kim Il Sung and work with collective wisdom and concerted efforts for the best result.

Chai Chengwen, political counselor at the Chinese embassy to Korea and a member of the Chinese negotiation team, describing the Chinese negotiating position in June 1951, in Chai, Banmendian Tanpan *(1989), pp. 135–37.*

Native Son, a novel stemming from passion, conviction and genius and a work that a decade ago was translated into a shattering and compelling drama, has emerged as a sincere but strangely unconvincing film. Perhaps Mr. Wright, who is the ill-fated hero of this screen transcription . . . is less of an actor than he is a novelist and playwright.

Obviously, his cast does not, by and large, attain the stature of his glowing words and thoughts. For their speeches merely relate this story of a sensitive Negro's revolt against social maladjustment and bigotry without depth and true feeling. And its murder melodramatics are muscular and only occasionally professional.

Critic A. H. Weiler reviewing Native Son, *in Weiler, "Richard Wright Plays Hero in Movie Adaptation of His Novel,"* Native Son, *New York Times, June 18, 1951, p. 19.*

We had this teacher . . . that took us there [the Museum of Natural History] damn near every Saturday. Sometimes we looked at the animals and sometimes we looked at the stuff the Indians had made in ancient times. Pottery and straw baskets. . . . I get very happy when I think about it. . . . They were always showing Columbus discovering America. . . . Nobody gave too much of a damn about old Columbus, but you always had a lot of candy and gum and stuff with you, and the inside of that auditorium had such a nice smell. . . .

The best thing, though, in that museum was that everything always stayed right where it was. Nobody'd move. You could go there a hundred thousand times, and that Eskimo would still be just finished catching those two fish. . . . Nobody'd be different. The only thing that would be different would be *you.* . . . You'd have an overcoat on this time. Or the kid that was your partner in line the last time had got scarlet fever and you'd have a new partner. . . . Or you'd heard your mother and father having a terrific fight in the bathroom. Or you'd just passed by one of those puddles in the street with gasoline rainbows in them. I mean you'd be *different in some way.* . . .

Certain things they should stay the way they are. You ought to be able to stick them in one of those big glass cases and just leave them alone. I know that's impossible, but it's too bad anyway.

Teenager Holden Caulfield musing on life's impermanence, in J. D. Salinger, The Catcher in the Rye *(1951), pp. 121–22.*

You figured most of them [girls] would probably marry dopey guys. Guys that always talk about how many miles they get to a gallon in their goddam cars. Guys that get sore and childish if you beat them at golf. . . . Guys that are very mean. Guys that never read books.

Holden Caulfield regretting the fate of women, in J. D. Salinger, The Catcher in the Rye *(1951), p. 123.*

You must not ask the President of the United States to get down in the gutter with a guttersnipe.

Nobody, not even the President of the United States, can approach too close to a skunk, in skunk territory, and expect to get anything out of it except a bad smell.

If you think somebody is telling a big lie about you, the only way to answer is with the whole truth.

Author John Hersey recollecting Truman's remarks at a high-level meeting at Blair House, in Washington, D.C., held in late summer 1951 in response to Senator Joseph McCarthy's attacks on members of the administration, in Hersey, Aspects of the Presidency *(1980), pp. 137–38.*

Today—August 1, 1951—the Nylon War enters upon the third month since the United States began all-out bombing of the Soviet Union with consumers' goods, and it seems time to take a retrospective look. Behind the initial raid of June 1 were years of secret and complex preparations, and an idea of disarming simplicity: that if allowed to sample the riches of America, the Russian people would not long tolerate masters who gave them tanks and spies instead of vacuum cleaners and beauty parlors. The Russian rulers would thereupon be forced to turn out consumers' goods, or face mass discontent on an increasing scale.

From David Riesman's satire "Nylon Wars," which is set in August 1951, in Stephen J. Whitfield, The Culture of the Cold War *(1996), p. 72.*

We have desired good, and we have done some! But we have also done great evil. The confession [of Whittaker Chambers] in itself is nothing, but without the confession there could be no understanding, and without the understanding of what the Hiss case tries desperately to declare, we will not be able to move

from a liberalism of innocence to a liberalism of responsibility.

Critic Leslie Fiedler commenting on the Alger Hiss case in August 1951, in Allen Weinstein, Perjury: The Hiss-Chambers Case *(1978), p. 458.*

We had needed a straight man . . . but Max Liebman was dedicated to some very fixed ideas, one of which was that a straight man always had to be taller than the comic. *Why* . . . I'll never know. . . .

This made it difficult for us, since I am six feet one. God forbid, a fine actor would show up and he was only five feet eleven. . . . Then, fortunately, Carl Reiner came along. He is six two. . . .

Sid Caesar recalling Your Show of Shows *in fall 1951, in Caesar,* Where Have I Been? *(1982), p. 107.*

I then went to another stage review . . . which began to develop problems. Who should be called in as a play doctor but Max Liebman.

From left to right: Sid Caesar, Imogene Coca, and Carl Reiner starred in *Your Show of Shows. (Photofest)*

The first thing he asked me was how tall I was. Then he had me meet with him and Sid. . . .

The writers were all crammed into Max's office, some of them overflowing into the toilet, and the actors all had to wait out in the hall. We were only called in when there was something to rehearse. I decided I had to get out of the hall and into the inner office.

> *Carl Reiner recalling when he joined Sid Caesar's* Your Show of Shows *at the beginning of its second season in fall 1951, in Caesar,* Where Have I Been? *(1982), pp. 108–9.*

Branca pitches and Bobby takes a strike called on the inside corner. Branca throws, there's a long fly. It's gonna be, I believe—the Giants win the pennant! The Giants win the pennant! The Giants win the pennant! The Giants win the pennant! The Giants win the pennant! Bobby Thomson hit it into the lower deck of the left-field stands. The Giants win the pennant, and they're going crazy! Waaa-hooo!

> *Radio announcer Russ Hodges describing Bobby Thomson's pennant-winning home run on October 3, 1951— "the shot heard 'round the world"—in David J. Halberstam, "Thomson's 'Shot' Heard 50 Years Ago,"* Miami Herald, *October 3, 2001, p. 2D.*

I went over to Japan barnstorming with Lefty O'Doul in 1951. Lefty O'Doul was God over in Japan. He was the one that got baseball introduced to the Japanese. . . . He could've run for emperor over there and he would've won.

> *Mel Parnell describing postseason activity in fall 1951, in Larry Moffi,* This Side of Cooperstown *(1996), pp. 143–44.*

During the 1950–51 season New York saw almost 30 new ballets presented by five different companies. Three came from Europe—the Sadler's Wells, the Marquis de Cuevas's Grand Ballet and Roland Petit's Ballets de Paris; two were American—the New York City Ballet and Ballet Theatre. . . . None of the new ballets presented by the Sadler's Wells and the Grand Ballet is likely to be seen here again. . . .

Ballet Theatre . . . is no longer a dance organization with a unified purpose; since its return from Europe last winter, it has become, more than anything else, a booking agency for outside talent. . . . Only one of the Ballet Theatre's eight new works originated within the company itself. . . . All eight ballets, in one way or another, were failures. . . .

The New York City Ballet danced for ten weeks at the City Center in New York. . . . Jerome Robbins is extraordinary among American-born choreographers. Devising dramatic movement to a sequence of music is no problem to him (nor is devising movement to silence, as in the most impressive parts of his Age of Anxiety). But Robbins must have a non-dramatic, non-dance idea to compel him to devise this movement. His ballets thus become dance demonstrations of ideas to be found in the program notes. The virtue of his new ballet is that the movement he has created dramatizes the idea at hand beyond all question. Its fault is that its drama does not extend beyond the non-dramatic vacuum of its program note; it is a mere curiosity.

> *Critic Francis Mason, Jr., reviewing the New York ballet season in fall/winter 1951, in Mason, "Ballet Chronicle,"* Hudson Review *(Autumn 1951), pp. 464–65.*

If poetry makes us more conscious of the complexity and meaning of our experience, it may have an eventual effect upon action, even political action. The recognition of this truth is not an achievement of our own age; it is very old. Our contribution to it I take to be a deviation from its full meaning, an exaggeration and loss of insight. Because poetry may influence politics we conclude that poetry is merely politics, or a kind of addlepated politics, and thus not good for anything. . . .

Philosophers, scientists, and politicians have by and large assumed that they had no special responsibility for the chaos of the modern world. Mr. Einstein not long ago warned us that we now have the power to destroy ourselves. There was in his statement no reference to his own great and perhaps crucial share in the scientific progress which had made the holocaust possible. If it occurs, will Mr. Einstein be partly to blame, provided there is anybody left to blame him? Will God hold him responsible?

> *Poet Allen Tate reflecting on the political responsibilities of poets, in Tate, "To Whom Is the Poet Responsible?"* Hudson Review *(Autumn 1951), pp. 326–27.*

Count a bewitching French lassie by the name of Leslie Caron and a whoop-de-do ballet number, one of the finest ever put upon the screen, as the most commendable enchantments of the big, lavish musical film that Metro obligingly delivered to the Music Hall yesterday. *An American in Paris,* which is the title of the picture, likewise the ballet, is spangled with pleasant little patches of amusement and George Gershwin tunes. It is also blessed with Gene Kelly, dancing and singing his way through a minor romantic complication in the usual gaudy Hollywood gay Paree. But it is the wondrously youthful Miss Caron and that grandly pictorial ballet that place the marks of distinction upon this lush technicolored escapade.

Critic Bosley Crowther reviewing An American in Paris, *in Crowther, "An American in Paris Arrival at Music Hall," New York Times, October 5, 1951, p. 24.*

There is no question that drugs are already on hand (and new ones are being produced) that can destroy integrity and make indiscreet the most dependable individual. . . . [These should be tested] under threat conditions beyond the scope of civilian experimentation.

From a CIA memo, dated October 21, 1951, pertaining to Operation ARTICHOKE, which oversaw the experimentation of LSD for intelligence and counterintelligence application, in Martin A. Lee and Bruce Shlain, Acid Dreams *(1985), p. 13.*

We are impressed by a medium through which a man sitting in his living room has been able for the first time to look at two oceans at once. . . . [N]o journalist age was ever given a weapon for truth with quite the scope of this fledgling television.

Edward R. Murrow on the opening broadcast of See It Now, *November 18, 1951, in Murrow,* In Search of Light: The Broadcasts of Edward R. Murrow *(1967).*

Dear Ike:

The columnists, the slick magazines and all the political people who like to speculate are saying many things about what is to happen in 1952.

As I told you in 1948 and at our luncheon in 1951, do what you think best for the country. My own position is in the balance. If I do what I want to do I'll go back to Missouri and *maybe* run for the Senate. If you decide to finish the European job (and I don't know who else can) I must keep the isolationists out of the White House. I wish you would let me know what you intend to do. It will be between us and no one else.

I have the uttermost confidence in your judgment and your patriotism.

President Harry Truman's letter of December 18, 1951, to General Dwight Eisenhower regarding the latter's potential candidacy in the 1952 presidential elections, in David McCullough, Truman *(1992), p. 888.*

Now that Arthur Miller's *Death of a Salesman* has been brought by Stanley Kramer to the screen and Frederic March has been given the opportunity to play its difficult leading role, a great many more million people, not only in this country but in the world, will have a chance to see this shattering drama at what is probably its artistic best. . . .

For, in every respect, this transference to the motion picture form enhances the episodic structure and the time-ranging nature of the play—which, in short, tells a grim, reflective story of a man and the tragic upset that his faking works on his wife and sons. . . . Past and present are run together with perfect smoothness and striking clarity in the film

Furthermore, Mr. Kramer's production is so faithfully transcribed and well designed that it stands as a nigh exact translation of Mr. Miller's play, both in its psychological candor and its exhibit of a bleak bourgeois milieu.

Critic Bosley Crowther reviewing Death of a Salesman, *in Crowther, "'Death of a Salesman,' with Fredrick March and Mildred Dunnock, at Victoria," New York Times (December 21, 1951), p. 21.*

[Bao Dai's French-supported government of South Vietnam] is in no sense the servant of the people. It has no grass roots. It therefore has no appeal whatsoever to the masses. It evokes no popular support because the nature of its leaders tends to an attitude that this would be a "concession." . . . Revolution will continue and Ho Chi Minh will remain a popular hero so long as "independence" leaders with French support are simply native mandarins who are succeeding foreign mandarins. . . . The present type of government in Vietnam is a relic of the past as much as French colonialism.

Senior American aid official R. Allen Griffith reporting on the situation in Vietnam in late 1951, in Stanley Karnow, Vietnam: A History *(1983), p. 188.*

4

"I Like Ike"
1952

At the beginning of 1952, the United States was beset by labor strife, approaching the apex of the Red Scare, and mired in a war in Korea that promised no quick resolution. Moreover, a polio epidemic was ravaging the country. Allegations from 1951 of corruption within the Truman administration persisted, and cold war tensions between the United States and the Soviet Union continued to intensify. Although The Revised Standard Version of the Holy Bible was issued to great acclaim—it sold 2 million copies in its first year—commentators throughout the social and political spectrum decried the breakdown of morality and the distortion of personal values within American society. In this tumultuous time, the presidential election in November ended in defeat for the Democrats, after 20 years of leadership.

THE COLD WAR AND INTERNATIONAL POLITICS

The Cold War Abroad

THE KOREAN WAR

The increasingly unpopular war became a campaign issue in the 1952 presidential campaign, because Truman's policy of limiting the conflict to Korea was creating a stalemate that many Americans found frustrating and wasteful of American lives. The Republican candidate, Dwight Eisenhower, appealed to that frustration throughout his campaign and promised to go to Korea to bring the conflict to an end.

On-again, off-again peace talks failed to show progress, and the fighting, which had moved up and down the peninsula in 1950 and 1951, remained confined throughout 1952 to mostly along the 38th parallel, which divided the two Koreas. In June, a controversial U.S. air raid against North Korean power plants close to the Chinese border outraged India's prime minister Jawaharlal Nehru, who had been quietly trying to broker a truce. It also alarmed the UN allies, who feared the unilateral American action would drag them into an expanded war with China that they had not agreed to fight. In response to their objections, the U.S. government apologized to Great Britain and other allies who had not been consulted in advance. Throughout the summer, U.S. planes bombarded the North Korean capital, Pyongyang.

The heaviest action occurred in late October and early November, when UN forces repulsed a Chinese armored offensive along two-thirds of the front line. The legendary struggle for Pork Chop Hill took place during this two-week battle, in which some 23,000 Chinese soldiers died. Afterward, the stalemate along the border resumed.

The peace talks, which had begun in late 1951, were impeded by a fundamental disagreement over the fates of Chinese and North Korean prisoners of war (POWs). The communists insisted that all prisoners should be repatriated, and they strenuously objected when the UN command began asking the 170,000 POWs on Koje Island if they would prefer to return to their communist homelands or immigrate to South Korea or Taiwan. This issue became extremely contentious. In February, communist POWs rioted at the compound and had to be suppressed by military force. In May, they captured the U.S. general in charge and held him for 78 hours, until they were given the right to establish a communist organization and provided telephones and mimeograph machines for running it. A month later, U.S. paratroopers invaded the compound, killing 30 communists who had reportedly been killing POWs complying with the UN command. In December, some 3,600 communist prisoners, more than a third of the total population, rioted on the prison island of Pongam. The uprising was suppressed only after UN guards fired on the POWs, killing 84 and wounding 120.

Ultimately, the United Nations ignored China and North Korea's objections and permitted roughly half of the prisoners, many of whom had been unwillingly drafted, to emigrate. This disagreement remained a sticking point for the peace process throughout the war. In late November, after five weeks of debate, the UN General Assembly voted overwhelmingly to support India's proposal to create a neutral "umpire" to decide which prisoners should be repatriated and which should be allowed to emigrate. However, the plan failed after it was denounced by the Soviet Union, which had submitted its own proposal, and by China's foreign minister, Zhou Enlai.

A typhus epidemic had decimated many Chinese units in 1951, and on February 22, 1952, North Korea formally accused the United States of practicing germ warfare. The charges were quickly reiterated by other communist countries throughout the world; for example, the Chinese government accused America of launching a germ-warfare assault of even greater proportions against China. It organized a massive "Hate America" campaign, in which the Chinese people took preventive measures to kill flies, mosquitoes, fleas, and rats, and to clean up garbage. The government supported its accusations with confessions by 38 American POWs who had been subjected to months of solitary confinement, deprivation, and torture. When the Soviet Union reiterated the charges before the United Nations General Assembly, the United States called for a commission to investigate both the communist accusations of germ warfare and the U.S. contention that China and North Korea were torturing and brainwashing UN POWs, a charge that persisted throughout the conflict (and was the basis for Richard Condon's best-selling 1959 novel, *The Manchurian Candidate*). In response to the U.S. counterproposal, the Soviets dropped the entire matter.

OTHER COLD WAR DEVELOPMENTS

One other major cold war development of 1952 arose on November 6, when a team of U.S. scientists under the leadership of the Hungarian-born physicist Edward Teller successfully tested the first hydrogen bomb. Although the H-bomb reasserted U.S. nuclear superiority for a short while, and its development was generally supported by the public, which regarded it as necessary for national security, the "superbomb" also significantly raised the stakes in the cold war and intensified anxieties over nuclear confrontation. For the first time in human history, the H-bomb introduced sufficient destructive capacity to destroy all, or most, of the human race, although the arsenals and delivery mechanisms were not sufficient for effecting such an apocalypse until the end of the decade. Consequently, on the one hand the hydrogen bomb sparked some public reassurance by reasserting America as the dominant nuclear power; on the other hand, it deepened fears about the consequences of a nuclear war and rendered problematic the very concept of "winning" such a conflict.

The H-bomb was awesome. It had an explosive power equivalent to more than 5 million tons of TNT, as compared with 120,000 tons for the atomic bombs that destroyed Hiroshima and Nagasaki or 20,000 tons for the largest conventional bombs used in World War II. The explosion completely obliterated Eniwetok Island, its test site in the Pacific Ocean, and left a hole that extended several hundred feet deep into the ocean floor. The test of the hydrogen bomb returned the United States to a position of undisputed nuclear superiority for the first time since the Soviet Union developed its atomic bomb in 1949. However, America's status as the world's sole owner of the hydrogen bomb was short lived, as the Soviets detonated their first H-bomb in August 1953. Five weeks earlier, Great Britain became the world's third nuclear power when it exploded its first atomic bomb.

As the arms race mushroomed, U.S.-Soviet relations remained cold, and in October, the Soviets demanded the recall of Ambassador George Kennan, one of the chief architects of the containment policy, after Kennan publicly likened life in Stalin's police state to living in a Nazi internment camp. Kennan, who began the job in April, had spent about six months in a Nazi camp following the U.S. entry into World War II.

As it would throughout the cold war, Germany remained a critical arena, especially after the failure of a Soviet proposal calling for a four-power conference on the reunification and rearmament of Germany. The United States, France, and Great Britain insisted that supervised free elections be a condition for reunification, but the Soviets refused to permit UN supervision of the elections. Following the collapse of these efforts, Germany moved quickly toward permanent partition into sovereign nations: the communist German Democratic Republic (GDR), or East Germany, as it was commonly known, and the Federal Republic of Germany (FRG), popularly called West Germany. These had existed as distinct German republics since 1949, but the Transition Agreement of May 26, 1952, also known as the Bonn Pact, established West Germany as a separate state, something short of the sovereign nation it became in 1955.

The following day, on May 27, West Germany, France, Italy, Belgium, the Netherlands, and Luxembourg established the European Defense Community to ensure peace along Germany's western borders and to protect the nations of

Western Europe from communist aggression from the east. The United States, Great Britain, and France then issued a tripartite declaration maintaining that any action that threatened the European Defense Community would be regarded as a threat to them. NATO also offered reciprocal guarantees, thereby formalizing the commitment of the United States and Canada to the defense of Western Europe and effectively codifying the containment of communism in Europe as national policy.

Subsequently, Great Britain and West Germany signed the London Debt Agreement to resolve Germany's reparation payments from World War I and thereby enable West Germany to receive economic aid from Britain to revive its economy. In June, shortly after West Germany's defense agreements were concluded, East Germany took a stronger military posture, too. It started to recruit a new "people's army," and by the end of the year, some 100,000 East Germans were serving in an army equipped with Soviet weapons. East Germany also became an even more closed society, effectively barring outsiders from the West.

As events developed in Germany, several important changes occurred within NATO. In January, the United States promised Great Britain that it would not launch an atomic attack against the Soviet bloc without British consent. In February, the alliance admitted Turkey and Greece. And at a meeting in Lisbon, Portugal, the NATO nations agreed to raise a 50-division army in Western Europe by the end of the year. In mid-April, NATO opened its new headquarters at the Palais de Chaillot in Paris. Shortly thereafter, General Eisenhower resigned his military appointment as supreme commander of NATO forces in Europe in order to seek the Republican nomination for president. He was replaced by another World War II veteran, General Matthew Ridgway, who in April 1951 had replaced General MacArthur as Supreme Commander of UN forces in Korea. General Mark Clark assumed command in Korea on May 12. In September, the Council of Europe approved the Strasbourg Plan to develop the European colonies as a bloc against Soviet influence in Africa and the rest of the underdeveloped world.

The Japanese Peace Treaty went into effect on April 28, and Japan again became a sovereign nation. Although Emperor Hirohito remained the titular head of state, the new constitution placed the real power in a democratically elected parliament that quickly aligned the country with the United States and the West in the cold war contest. A friendship treaty with the Nationalist Chinese on Taiwan further underscored Japan's opposition to the communist regime on the Chinese mainland. In August, the United States began new security talks with Australia and New Zealand.

The cold war lines were drawn deeper in Vietnam as the Soviet Union vetoed a French proposal to admit the pro-West Vietnamese government to the United Nations.

Other International Developments

Dr. Albert Schweitzer, a Christian theologian, musician, and medical missionary, captured the public imagination when he won the Nobel Peace Prize for his humanitarian work in Africa. Throughout the decade he remained a living and reassuring example of the ability of one person to make a positive impact on the world, despite the seemingly overwhelming complications of international politics.

King George VI of England died at age 56, a few months after the removal of a growth on his right lung. He was succeeded in the largely ceremonial office by his 25-year-old daughter, who was proclaimed Queen Elizabeth II. She was also named head of the Commonwealth, a new title. Her three-year-old son, Charles, became the crown prince and heir to the throne. The queen's coronation in February was broadcast live on television in the United States, and the pageantry was followed with close interest.

In Latin America, the United States agreed to give military aid to Peru, Colombia, and Ecuador. Bolivia moved to the left after revolutionary forces seized power, and after a bloody coup in which about a thousand people were killed, the new government nationalized three major tin companies. Puerto Rico gained self-rule and became the first U.S. commonwealth. Eva Perón, the powerful, popular wife of Argentina's president, Juan Perón, died of ovarian cancer at age 33. A champion of labor reform and women's causes, she was instrumental in obtaining women's suffrage in Argentina and for legalizing divorce there. Eva Perón had been widely adored within the large underclass from which she had risen.

On March 10, General Fulgencio Batista, who had been Cuba's dictator between 1933 and 1944, regained power in a military coup that overthrew the government of President Prío Socarrás. Batista immediately suspended constitutional liberties and canceled presidential elections in which he was participating but was expected to lose.

In the Middle East, tensions remained high in Egypt as popular protests mounted against British authority over the region. In response to the civil unrest, martial law was imposed. In July, a military coup placed Mohammed Naguib Bey in power. Naguib nullified the constitution and established a civilian cabinet that, for the first time in Egypt's history, included a member of the Moslem Brotherhood, which was dedicated to shaping public and private life around Islamic principles and practices.

Iran severed ties with Britain as part of an oil dispute that began in 1951, and in Jordan, Prince Hussein was crowned king. The 17-year-old Hussein, who attended school in England and spoke fluent English, replaced his mentally ill father, King Talial. Israel's founding president, Chaim Weizmann, died in November. Albert Einstein declined an offer to succeed him, and the post was subsequently filled by Itzhak Ben-Avi.

The African National Congress (ANC) organized protests throughout South Africa after the government refused to revoke its policy of apartheid, which officially relegated black South Africans to second-class status. Although the protests were initially peaceful, they became violent in November, prompting the government to ban the assembly of more than 10 blacks. Britain continued to face pressure from independence movements in former colonies that ultimately brought about the disintegration of the British empire. Mau Mau tribespeople in Kenya began a campaign of terror that employed voodoo and other strategies designed to drive out white settlers. Britain sent troops to suppress the rebellion, and by the end of 1954, 30 European civilians and some 1,800 native Africans were killed. Other anti-British movements sprang up in territories worldwide.

The United Nation's first convention on women's rights hinted at a nascent interest in issues that had received little international attention prior to the second half of the 20th century. In the 1950s and afterward, women's issues acquired increasing importance in the United States and Canada, as the roles of women in those societies continued to evolve and expand beyond their previously constrained boundaries.

The Cold War at Home

Election-year politics made it difficult for legislators to oppose anticommunist legislation, lest they be branded procommunist or "soft" on communism. In this political environment, the McCarran-Walter Immigration Bill passed over Truman's veto. The law revised U.S. immigration, naturalization, and nationality laws, eliminating race but retaining national origin as a criterion for legal immigration. It also gave the government greater power to exclude and deport aliens. The authors used the 1920 census to determine immigration quotas, but critics charged that the 32-year-old census underrepresented Asians and eastern, central, and southern Europeans, as most of the immigrants from those regions had arrived since 1920. These regions were popularly believed to be more sympathetic to communism; moreover, a sizable number of Americans who originated from western Europe looked down on immigrants from these more impoverished and less technologically advanced regions. Senator Pat McCarran, a Democrat from Nevada, defended the 1920 census by warning against allowing an influx of Asians into the country—at a time when the United States was battling China and North Korea. Truman vetoed the bill, insisting that the law would worsen the repressive and inhumane aspects of U.S. immigration procedures, but Congress overrode the veto.

Senator Joseph McCarthy continued to gain national prominence by railing against the Truman administration, which he accused of complicity with communists both internationally and domestically, and HUAC continued its investigation of the entertainment industry. Playwright Lillian Hellman refused to testify, invoking her Fifth Amendment rights rather than "bring bad trouble to people who, in my past association with them, were completely innocent of any talk or any action that was disloyal or subversive."[1] Claiming that she would not "cut my conscience to fit this year's fashions," Hellman, who describes her ordeal in her autobiography, *Scoundrel Time* (1976), suffered blacklisting for her refusal to cooperate.

Among those who did testify were actor Edward G. Robinson, writer-director Abe Burrows, director Elia Kazan, and writer-director Clifford Odets. Robinson and Burrows appeared at their own request. Robinson wanted to assert under oath that he was a liberal Democrat who had never been a communist or "fellow traveler" and was shocked to learn that others whom he believed were sincere liberals had proven actually to be communists. He did not identify anyone known to him as a communist. On the other hand, Kazan and Odets named former associates as communists and admitted belonging to the party briefly during the Great Depressions, when, according to Kazan, there was no clear opposition of national interests between the United States and the Soviet Union, and it was not fully evident the American Communist Party was taking its orders from the Soviet Union. Both men had been members of the Group Theater, where they were recruited into the party, and both quit the party in the mid-1930s after becoming disaffected. Kazan was America's preeminent director in 1952, and many liberals were upset at his testimony, as they believed he could have broken the blacklist by refusing to cooperate with the committee. But Kazan defended his action by pointing to the extensive communist threat in the nuclear age.

In addition to the activity in the legislative branch of government, the Truman administration banned the Soviet periodical *Amerika* and other Soviet information bulletins, and the Supreme Court rejected the appeals of Julius and Ethel Rosenberg, clearing the way for their execution in 1953. In New York, eight public school teachers were fired for alleged communist activities.

CIVIL RIGHTS

Although not as compelling as the Korean War or the threat from communism, civil rights was a campaign issue in 1952. Despite opposition from southerners in his own party, Adlai Stevenson, the Democratic presidential nominee, praised the steps toward integration that had been achieved during Truman's presidency, citing in particular the admission of African Americans into graduate and professional schools run by state universities that had previously denied them access. Stevenson asserted that civil rights meant "the right to equal opportunity for education, employment and decent living conditions. It means that none of these rights shall be denied because of race or color or creed." Furthermore, he advocated federal legislation "when states fail to act and inequalities of treatment persist."[2]

Eisenhower, the Republican candidate, was less forthcoming on the issue. He opposed using political or economic power to enforce segregation but pointed to his record of promoting racial integration within the army during the closing days of World War II. Where a specific issue clearly fell under federal jurisdiction, such as in the administration of federal programs and institutions, Eisenhower favored using executive power to end segregation. On the other hand, he did not believe that legislative action was an appropriate or effective means for ending discrimination, and he was reluctant to overstep what he believed were the proper bounds of federal authority to address it. During the campaign, Eisenhower rarely went out of his way to discuss civil rights, although in September, he warned white southerners that they could lose their own rights if they failed to protect the rights of black Americans.

In 1952, the country made some modest progress in granting equal rights. For the first time since 1881, there were no reports of lynching in the United States. Moreover, black Americans gained greater opportunities and recognition in professional sports and entertainment. Jackie Robinson became the highest paid player in Brooklyn Dodgers history. Dorothy Manor, a noted soprano who sang at Truman's inauguration, became the first black artist to perform at Constitution Hall since 1939, when the Daughters of the American Revolution, who owned the hall in Washington D.C., refused to permit Marian Anderson to sing there. Groton, an exclusive boys' preparatory school in Massachusetts, admitted its first black student, and Phoenix, Arizona, opened a restricted cemetery to permit the burial of an African-American war veteran.

But race-based restrictions at the Miami Springs country club were upheld when the Florida Supreme Court ruled that the city-owned facility could limit access for black golfers to one day a week. The U.S. Supreme Court declined to hear an appeal because it maintained that the decision did not center on a federal issue. It did, however, uphold a decision barring segregation on interstate railways.

A three-judge federal district court panel upheld the separate-but-equal doctrine in the case of *Davis v. County School Board of Prince Edward County.* However, the NAACP's Legal Defense Fund appealed the verdict to the Supreme Court, and, along with *Bolling v. Sharpe* and *Gebhart v. Belton,* the Davis case was joined with *Brown v. Board of Education of Topeka.* Presiding before a packed audience, the Supreme Court first heard arguments on these landmark cases on December 9. After lengthy deliberations that lasted into spring 1953, the judges scheduled new arguments for the fall 1953 session.

GOVERNMENT AND SOCIETY

Domestic politics were dominated by presidential and congressional elections, but for many Americans the development of a vaccine for polio (poliomyelitis, or infantile paralysis) was the most important event of the year. The nationwide polio epidemic afflicted some 50,000 Americans in the early 1950s, especially children. It killed many and paralyzed many others. Some people were able to recover completely, but others remained impaired for life by this disease that debilitates the muscles. When the damaged muscles are those necessary for the proper function of the brain, the lungs, or the heart, serious harm or death can ensue. "Iron lung" machines were used to help polio victims breathe when their lungs were weak, and one of the dominant recollections from the early 1950s is of friends or family members in iron lungs, and the general fear that one's children, or oneself, might contract the disease. The development in 1952 of a vaccine by Dr. Jonas Salk, therefore, offered hope and relief to a nation that was coping with a war abroad and a terrible epidemic at home. Mass inoculations of children began in 1954, and the epidemic ended soon thereafter.

In the presidential election of 1952, the Democrats, who had held the presidency since 1933, campaigned on the achievements of Franklin D. Roosevelt and Harry S. Truman: notably winning World War II, bringing about social improvements, and ending the Great Depression. The Republicans, on the other hand, complained about the stalemate in Korea, the infiltration of communists into the government, and the general need for fresh faces and a new start. The citizenry overwhelmingly sided with the Republicans.

After Truman decided not to seek reelection, he encouraged Supreme Court chief justice Fred M. Vinson to seek the Democratic nomination, which Truman guaranteed he could secure. But Vinson, who died in 1953, declined, pleading poor health and reservations about using the Supreme Court as a stepping stone to the presidency. Some controversy exists over whether Truman next offered the nomination to Eisenhower, who was then commanding NATO forces in Europe and was one of the most respected Americans alive. Truman and Eisenhower met on November 5, 1951, and two days later Arthur Krock reported in the *New York Times* that Truman had made the offer but Eisenhower had turned him down, claiming, "You can't join a party just to run for office. . . . You know I have been a Republican all my life and that my family have always been Republicans." Krock later cited his source as Supreme

Court justice William O. Douglas, but both Truman and Eisenhower publicly and privately denied that the offer had been made.[3] In either case, Truman spoke highly of Eisenhower, even after the general announced on January 7, 1952, that he would accept the Republican nomination if it were extended to him. Truman approved of his candidacy, because Eisenhower shared his conviction that the United States needed to support NATO and the defense of Western Europe, and he feared that if Eisenhower did not run, Senator Robert Taft of Ohio, a strong isolationist and champion of the Republican Party's right wing, would win the Republican nomination. If Taft, who was known popularly as "Mr. Conservative," were to win the general election, Truman feared he would abandon the efforts to contain worldwide communism that had been the cornerstone of Truman's foreign policy.

Of the possible Democratic contenders, Truman endorsed Illinois governor Adlai Stevenson, even though he judged presidential adviser Averell Harriman the most able. Truman believed that Harriman, a Wall Street banker and railroad tycoon who had never run for office, could not be elected on a Democratic ticket, and that Vice President Alben Barkley was too old for the job. The president distrusted Senator Estes Kefauver, whose televised hearings into organized crime and political corruption had made him a public figure, and whom the president privately called "Cowfever."[4]

But Truman was impressed by Stevenson's political instincts—he won the governorship by a large majority in 1948, in his first bid for public office—and by the fact that Stevenson's grandfather had served as Grover Cleveland's vice president. Truman first met with Stevenson on January 22 and after cementing his good opinion of the governor, asked him to seek the Democratic nomination, which Truman guaranteed. Flattered and surprised by the offer, Stevenson initially declined, believing Eisenhower was unbeatable and that, given Truman's decline in popularity, being his handpicked candidate might be more of a liability than an asset. Truman briefly reconsidered his own decision not to run, but on March 29, he publicly announced that he would not be a candidate, and Stevenson went on to secure the nomination. Senator John Sparkman of Alabama was selected as his running mate to balance the ticket between the North and South.[5]

The Republican convention, which opened in Chicago on July 7, was the first presidential convention to receive significant television coverage, and millions of Americans were engaged by viewing an arena filled with energized partisans from throughout the nation fighting passionately, both figuratively and sometimes even literally, for their candidates. Eisenhower and Taft were the leading candidates, although California governor Earl Warren also ran as a "favorite son" candidate with an outside hope of prevailing if the contest between Eisenhower and Taft deadlocked. As expected, Eisenhower won the nomination easily, defeating Taft on the first ballot, even though Taft entered the convention with a greater number of committed votes. Taking the advice of Thomas Dewey, the party's nominee from 1948 who wanted to stop Taft, Eisenhower appeased the party's right wing by selecting as his choice for vice president California senator Richard Nixon, an anticommunist who had come to prominence by championing Whittaker Chambers in the Alger Hiss dispute. Prior to the convention, Eisenhower had never before met Nixon and knew little about him.

The Democratic nomination was less straightforward. Still holding out for Stevenson, Truman declined to endorse any of the other candidates: Kefauver, Harriman, Barkley, or Senator Richard B. Russell, Jr., of Georgia. An eloquent speaker, Stevenson made a strong impression when he gave the welcoming address at the convention. As the selection promised to become deadlocked, he allowed his name to be entered in nomination, with Truman's approval, the day before the balloting began. The first two ballots were inconclusive, but Stevenson prevailed on the third, after Harriman released his delegates to him, at Truman's request.

Both nominees hailed from the Midwest (Eisenhower grew up on a small farm in Kansas, and Stevenson was raised in Illinois), but they were very different personalities. Although World War II had proven Eisenhower to be both a capable leader and gifted politician, he projected the image of a down-to-earth political outsider, the son of farmers who was guided by common sense and plain tastes and who stood apart from the governing establishment. Even the use of his nickname in his campaign slogan, "I Like Ike," projected familiarity and lack of pretension. Although by no means ignorant—Eisenhower was a West Point graduate—he did not come across as a figure of great learning or culture. Stevenson, on the other hand, grew up in a wealthy, politically connected family, attended an Ivy League university (Princeton), and spoke with great eloquence, wit, and erudition. He was also divorced at a time when it was still rare in America and when many considered it a personal, and perhaps moral or spiritual, shortcoming.

The candidates differed on domestic policies, but both were moderates, and their approaches to foreign policy were similar. Consequently, for many voters the election came down to a choice between a war hero of humble, rural origins and few personal pretensions and an "intellectual" from an elite, urban family. Thus, as in the late 1940s when a similar contrast in personal backgrounds and styles colored the public opinion about whether Whittaker Chambers or Alger Hiss was more trustworthy, the differences in the presidential candidates' styles and personalities influenced how Americans chose the man they would trust to lead the nation through a dangerous period. Indeed, Senator McCarthy played off this similarity when he famously called Stevenson "Alger," instead of "Adlai," and pretended that it was a slip of the tongue. Columnist Stewart Alsop also played on the general citizenry's suspicion of intellectuals when he referred to Stevenson as "the Egghead," a label that entered the lingo as a derisive term for smart people who enjoy working with ideas. As in 1948 when voters selected the plainspoken Missourian, Harry Truman, over the high-profile governor of New York, Thomas Dewey, voters in 1952 overwhelmingly trusted the man who was more plainspoken, with humbler origins, plainer tastes, and seemingly less lofty intellectual aspirations.

The Republican campaign centered on the U.S. response to the domestic and international threat of communism, the Korean war, corruption within the Democratic administration, and claims that 20 years of Democratic administrations had harmed the nation. In mid-September Eisenhower met with Taft, whose endorsement he felt was necessary to secure the votes of the Republican right wing, which in turn were essential to winning the general election. Eisenhower agreed to support Taft's call for a smaller federal budget, greater restrictions on organized labor, and opposition to "creeping socialism," while

Taft, an isolationist, supported Eisenhower's plans to contain communism and forge a strong defense of Western Europe.

Shortly after winning Taft's endorsement, Eisenhower encountered a new obstacle, when a September 18 exposé in the *New York Post* revealed that Nixon was enjoying the benefits of an $18,000 fund to cover his expenses. Eisenhower's first impulse was to drop Nixon from the ticket, but he soon reconsidered, as he believed Nixon's appeal to the Republican right was critical for winning the general election. Instead, he agreed to let Nixon make his case to the public in a nationally televised appearance, which Nixon did on the evening of September 23. In his so-called Checkers speech, named after his pet cocker spaniel, Nixon cited his humble origins, attacked the Democrats, and insisted that he would never disappoint his children by returning the dog that had been given to him as a gift from a political supporter. The speech was an overwhelming success, as the Republican National Committee received thousands of letters, telegrams, and phone calls urging that Nixon be retained. The next day, Eisenhower warmly endorsed him.

Another problematic moment for Eisenhower came on October 3, when he stopped in Milwaukee to campaign with McCarthy, who was running for reelection to the Senate. Among those whom McCarthy most viciously smeared in his accusations against the Truman administration was George Marshall, who had been Truman's secretary of state and, more recently, his secretary of defense. During World War II, Marshall had been the army's chief of staff—its highest-ranking officer—and he had been responsible for Eisenhower's meteoric rise through the chain of command. Eisenhower detested McCarthy's reckless demagoguery, and he especially resented the attacks on Marshall; therefore, he planned to add a paragraph in his Milwaukee address praising Marshall. He was dissuaded by his advisers, however, who argued that, as a matter of politics, he could not attack McCarthy in his home state. Subsequently, Eisenhower was criticized for his failure to defend his mentor, and, according to historian Geoffrey Perret, the event haunted him the rest of his life.[6]

Shortly before the election, in a speech televised nationally from Detroit, Eisenhower focused on and criticized the Truman administration for failing to resolve the Korean War and declared that if elected, he would go to Korea. Stevenson meanwhile defended the record of the Truman administration and pointed out the areas of growth, development, and prosperity the nation had enjoyed during the previous 20 years of Democratic rule. Moreover, he distinguished himself from Eisenhower by urging stronger government action in support of civil rights; promoting a labor-friendly revision of the Taft-Hartley Act and other measures supporting unions and collective bargaining; and advocating price subsidies for farmers. He also called for governmental management of publicly owned land and cattle ranges; conservation of natural resources; development of science, technology, and peaceful uses of atomic energy; and a bipartisan foreign policy.

While attacking communism, which he maintained "is committed to the destruction of every value which the genuine American liberal holds most dear," Stevenson dismissed the Red Scare rhetoric of the Republican right and insisted that the threat of subversion from domestic communists, while real, was greatly exaggerated.[7] Furthermore, Stevenson lashed out against the vicious Republican attacks against George Marshall, which he knew embarrassed

Eisenhower. Like Eisenhower, Stevenson favored maintaining a strong military and resisting communist aggression internationally, but he criticized as "dangerous, reckless, [and] foolish" suggestions by some Republicans to foment revolutions within the Soviet satellite countries.[8]

On November 4, Eisenhower won handily, receiving 442 electoral votes to Stevenson's 89, and 55 percent of the popular vote: 33.8 million, as compared to Stevenson's 27.3 million. The Republicans also gained six seats in the Senate and 19 in the House of Representatives to seize control of both houses of Congress by narrow margins. The party, however, suffered a major upset when Representative John F. Kennedy defeated the powerful Republican incumbent, Henry Cabot Lodge, in the Massachusetts senatorial race. The two men squared off again in 1960, when Kennedy ran successfully as the Democratic presidential candidate, and Lodge opposed him on the Republican ticket as Nixon's vice presidential candidate.

Six weeks after the election, Eisenhower spent three days in Korea reviewing battlefields, receiving briefings from field commanders, and meeting with South Korea's president, Syngman Rhee, and other diplomats. On his return to the United States, the president-elect also conferred with his incoming secretary of state, John Foster Dulles, and General MacArthur, now retired. Truman dismissed the trip as a mere play to public opinion and publicly doubted that either Eisenhower or MacArthur knew how to end the war; indeed, Eisenhower concluded at the end of his visit that there were "no panaceas, no trick solutions," but "much can be done and will be done."[9]

Of course, the election was not the only significant development in U.S. society. In more pedestrian matters, Don't Walk signs and three-color traffic lights were first introduced in New York City. A newspaper's spot check showed that eight of every 10 pedestrians obeyed the crossing signals that were first introduced in Times Square. In January, Truman dedicated the Hungry Horse Dam in Montana. At 564 feet, the dam was the third largest in the world at the time. The Chesapeake Bay Bridge became the third-largest bridge in the world when it opened. It cost $45 million to construct and reduced by several hours the driving time between the mainland in Virginia and the peninsula of Maryland's eastern shore. These monuments of construction were offset on March 22 by a series of tornadoes that killed some 200 people, injured 2,500 more, and destroyed entire towns in Missouri, Tennessee, Arkansas, Alabama, and Mississippi. During the summer, a severe drought plagued the East Coast.

The coronation of Queen Elizabeth II of England was followed with great interest throughout the United States, and it sparked a revival of collars, tiaras, and jeweled velvet dresses that had been the fashion during the reign of the first Queen Elizabeth at the end of the 16th century. Colleen Hutchens was crowned a different sort of queen when she became the first blond to win the Miss America contest in 13 years. Twenty-five years old, five feet 10 inches tall, and 143 pounds, Hutchens was also the oldest, tallest, and heaviest woman to win the beauty crown.

The much-needed renovation of the White House, which had begun in December 1949, was completed in spring 1952, at a final cost of $5.832 million.[10] Truman, along with a congressional committee, oversaw the work and made decisions about the design and decorations. The White House was reopened to the public on April 2; 5,444 people visited that day.[11]

BUSINESS

The war continued to undermine the economy and interfere with normal business operations. Citing the national wartime emergency, Truman ordered the government to seize steel mills that were about to be closed by strikes in early April. The act sparked a constitutional crisis in which Truman was ultimately rebuked by the Supreme Court. The president maintained that the impending strike would debilitate both the war effort in Korea and U.S. efforts to reinforce critical NATO defenses in Europe, that his action was necessary for national and worldwide security, and that any curtailment of steel production would endanger the lives of soldiers on the front lines. Moreover, Truman sympathized with the workers, who had not had a pay raise since 1950. Their union, the United Steel Workers (USW), which was part of the Congress of Industrial Organizations (CIO), had requested a 35¢-per-hour increase in November 1951. When the companies refused to negotiate, the USW issued a strike deadline to coincide with the expiration of their contract on December 31. When, on December 22, the president referred the matter to the wartime Wage Stabilization Board, the workers agreed to work without a contract and defer the strike until April 8.

After conducting hearings, the board recommended a 26¢-per-hour increase, but the companies rejected the recommendation, unless they were also authorized to raise the price of steel by $12 a ton. Truman, who was amenable to a more modest price increase of about $4.50 a ton, regarded the companies' proposal as tantamount to profiteering. In addition, he feared it would be inflationary and significantly increase the cost of fighting the war. He could have postponed the strike by an additional 80 days by invoking the Taft-Hartley Act, but he did not think such an act would change the outcome, and he acknowledged that the workers had already worked without a raise for three months since their contract had expired. So, on April 8, just hours before the strike was due to begin, he signed Executive Order No. 10340, placing the steel mills under the control of Secretary of Commerce Charles Sawyer.

Truman's unprecedented exercise of executive power sparked strong opposition. One congressman called for his impeachment, Truman was harshly attacked in most of the influential newspapers and magazines, and the steel companies immediately challenged him in federal court. In late April, Judge David A. Pine declared the action illegal and restored control to the companies. Subsequently, some 600,000 workers walked off the job. A higher court temporarily returned control to the government, pending a final ruling by the Supreme Court. That ruling came on June 2, when Judge Pine's decision was sustained by a 6–3 vote that stood out as a major political defeat for Truman.

As soon as control of the mills reverted to the companies, the workers immediately went back on strike, reducing normal steel production from some 300,000 tons daily to 20,000 tons. The 600,000-man strike, which idled another 1.4 million workers in other industries, did not end until July 24, 53 days later, after the workers received a 21¢-per-hour pay raise and the price of steel was increased by $4.50 a ton, the same amount the government had earlier approved, plus an additional 70¢ a ton for increased freight charges. Overall losses from the strike included 21 million tons of steel, $400 million in wages, and a reduction by one-third of the steel output for military purposes.[12]

In 1950, Truman had exercised his emergency wartime powers by placing certain railways under control of the army in order to circumvent a strike that would have impeded the nation's industrial capacity. In May 1952, the 21-month-long labor dispute was resolved, and two days later Truman restored the railroads to their owners. Earlier in the year, telegraph and telephone workers went on strike, and in October, soft-coal miners struck for a week in protest of a government order reducing their $1.90 pay increase by 40¢. The full amount of the pay raise was restored shortly after they returned to work.

In other labor-related matters, the American Federation of Labor (AFL) broke its long-held tradition of maintaining political neutrality and endorsed Democratic candidate Adlai Stevenson for president. It also initiated a drive to ban gangsters from union membership, and George Meany succeeded William Green as president, after Green died. Walter Reuther was elected president of the CIO, which merged with the AFL in 1955 to form the AFL-CIO. The Screen Guild signed its first TV actor-producer contract.

Significant corporate developments included the introduction of automobile air conditioning by General Motors; the invention of fiberglass, nylon stretch yarn, and "acrilan," an acrylic synthetic fiber; and Sony's release of the first pocket-sized transistor radio, which soon made it possible for teenagers to carry their rock 'n' roll with them and for workers and students to listen to critical baseball games while they worked. The newly invented transistors also figured in the manufacture of a hearing aid to replace those that relied on bulkier vacuum tubes.

Other new products to enter the market included the power lawn mower, which was introduced to serve the needs of the new suburban homeowners; the 16-mm home movie projector; the adjustable shower head; automatic "pin boys" for bowling alleys; plastic vinylite swimming pools; Kellogg's Sugar Frosted Flakes cereal; and *Mad* comic books, the predecessor of *Mad* magazine.

General MacArthur accepted the chairmanship of the Remington Rand Corporation, and Goodyear became the first rubber company to report annual sales in excess of $1 billion. TWA introduced tourist class service on its flights, and in May, British Overseas Airways launched the first commercial jet flight between London and Johannesburg, South Africa. The jet plane reduced the travel time to 18 hours and 40 minutes, some nine hours faster than propeller-plane service. By the end of the year, 37 airlines were offering international jet flights. The last major U.S. city was connected to a coaxial cable hookup for television network broadcasts, while the FCC lifted a three-year wartime ban on new stations. The U.S. Post Office introduced mail and parcel post deliveries by helicopter in New York City.

As the 1950s housing boom continued, Buckminster Fuller introduced the strong but lightweight geodesic dome house. The dome relied on a framework of aluminum triangles covered by a weatherproof plastic skin. The living areas were suspended by cables from the framework. The inexpensive, compact, and portable dome promised to provide affordable housing in situations where such housing was then unavailable. A 49-foot dome house erected in Canada required only 45 hours to assemble. The complete framework could fit into a steamer trunk and required no special tools.

Chlorophyll, the component that makes plants green, was introduced into numerous products, ranging from chewing gum and toothpaste to cough drops and dog food, with the promise of freshening the breath and body odor of its users. The fad died out, however, after the American Medical Association debunked the claim.

The Federal Reserve Board eliminated restrictions on installment credit purchases, and the state of New York revised a policy dating from 1935 and raised the legal ceiling on interest dividends from savings and thrift deposits from 2 percent to 2.5 percent. The year's inflation rate was 1.7 percent; the Dow Jones Industrial Average fluctuated on the New York Stock Exchange between 232 and 252, and unemployment was calculated at 3 percent. More than 6 million televisions were produced; two-thirds of American homes had telephones; and a quart of Fleischmann gin cost $3.55. The U.S. Post Office raised the price of mailing a postcard from 1¢ to 2¢, and a complete Chinese dinner for one in New York's House of Chan cost $1.50.[13]

SCIENCE AND TECHNOLOGY

As they had throughout the first half of the 20th century, science and politics continued to clash when a group of 34 leading scientists claimed that the government's policy of restricting visas to and from communist nations imperiled the free flow of ideas on which science sustained itself. The policy remained intact, but as science and technology continued to play greater roles in weaponry, communications, information processing, and other areas critical to the nation's defense during the decade, scientists' need for a free flow of information and ideas conflicted more and more frequently with the secrecy requirements of national security.

The decade saw many major life-saving medical developments, and the life expectancy in the United States rose from about 47 years at the beginning of the century to more than 68 years in 1952,[14] the same year as the first use of a mechanical heart on a human patient. The device sustained a 41-year-old steelworker during an operation, and it was deemed successful, even though the patient died of unrelated causes. Treatment of heart disease further advanced when Dr. Forest Dewey Dodrill of Detroit performed the first mitral valve heart operation; Charles Hufnagel of Georgetown University implanted the first artificial heart valve, and Harvard's Paul Zoll first used electric shock to treat cardiac arrest (heart attacks).

The decade also saw important advances in the field of genetics. The most famous of these was the discovery in 1953 of the structure of the DNA molecule, which enabled scientists to learn how the genetic material replicates itself. That crucial discovery was preceded by critical breakthroughs in 1952, as Linus Pauling and Robert Corey revealed the molecular structure of certain proteins; Joshua Lederberg demonstrated that viruses transmit genetic material between bacteria; and Alfred Hershey and Martha Chase confirmed that DNA contains genetic material with hereditary data.

Scientists learned more about other human biological systems as well. British researchers Alan Hodgkin and Andrew Huxley developed the theory of nerve excitation based on the passage of sodium and potassium through the nerve cells, and Eugene Asterinsky discovered the phenomenon of rapid-eye movement (REM) in sleeping individuals. REM was later associated with dreaming. In matters related to reproductive science, a contraceptive pill made from hesperidin, a citrus derivative, was introduced; Douglas Bevis developed amniocentesis, the practice of extracting amniotic fluid from the womb to test for abnormalities in the fetus; and in a procedure that furthered genetic engineering, a cow was artificially inseminated with frozen semen. A more sensational development occurred when Dr. K. Hamburger of Denmark completed the first human sex change: American George Jorgenson, a former soldier, returned from Copenhagen as Christine Jorgenson following 2,000 hormone injections and six operations. Jorgenson sold her life story to *American Weekly* for $30,000.

In physics, Donald Glaser discovered the presence of cosmic ray tracks in a bubble chamber. Glenn Seaborg discovered in the residue from the first hydrogen bomb test a new artificial element with an atomic number of 99. He named it einsteinium.

As the new science of rocketry and the persistent rumors of flying saucers and other extraterrestrial visitations provoked the nation and the world to direct more of their attention to outer space, the field of astronomy also progressed rapidly thanks to the advent of powerful new telescopes, computers capable of performing complex calculations, and other new technologies. Astronomer Milton Humason used data about runaway stars collected from a powerful telescope at the Palomar Observatory in Southern California to support the theory of an expanding universe; Martin Schwarzchild used graphs of star clusters to reveal new understandings of how stars evolve; Adriaan Blaauw proved that new stars are continually being created in the Milky Way; and Walter Baade discovered an error in the Cepheid luminosity scale that revealed galaxies to be twice as distant as previously believed. James van Allen developed the "rockoon," a balloon-launched rocket used to study the physics of the upper atmosphere.

Looking backward into the space-time continuum from a more terrestrial point of view, W. F. Libby of the University of Chicago set the date of Stonehenge at 1842 B.C.; Kenneth Oakely created a worldwide sensation when he revealed that the fossil remains of the Piltdown man, which had been presented in 1912 as the "missing link" in human evolution, were a fraud; and Michael Ventris deciphered Linear B, the oldest known form of Greek, dating from the time of the Trojan War. This made possible the translation of ancient texts that hitherto had been indecipherable.

SPORTS, ENTERTAINMENT, AND THE ARTS

Sports

International politics played into the 1952 Olympics. Nationalist China withdrew from the Olympics in protest of a plan to admit the People's Republic of China, and when the Summer Games convened in Helsinki, Finland, the Soviet Union participated for the first time ever. Cold war rivalries were very much present when the superpowers met in the finals of the men's basketball tournament, in which the United States prevailed. America dominated the track-and-field competitions, but the Soviets won the men's and women's gymnastic events, rowing, wrestling, and the women's discus throw. Future heavyweight champion Floyd Paterson, an American, won the gold medal for boxing, and Bob Richards, who later appeared on cereal boxes of Wheaties, "the Breakfast of Champions," won the pole-vault competition. Neither the United States nor Soviet Union fared well in the Winter Games, held in Oslo, Norway, but skier Andrea Mead Lawrence became the first American to win two winter events.

As attendance at other major sports declined or remained static, horse racing gained popularity. Almost 46 million Americans attended races in 1952, compared with slightly less than 41 million for baseball.[15] But baseball remained the popularly acclaimed "national pastime," and the New York Yankees won their third consecutive World Series when they defeated the Brooklyn Dodgers in seven games.

Football's Detroit Lions defeated the Cleveland Browns 17-7 to claim the NFL championship. Michigan State won the college football title; Oklahoma's Billy Vessels received the Heisman Trophy. Minneapolis defeated New York in seven games to take the NBA basketball championship, and the University of Kansas won the college championship. Its star, Clyde Lovellette, was named Player of the Year. Philadelphia's Paul Arizin, Minneapolis's George Mikan, Boston's Bob Cousy and Ed McCauley, and Bob Davies of Rochester were named to the NBA's All-Pro First Team. The Detroit Red Wings won hockey's Stanley Cup, and Frank Sedgman and Maureen Connolly prevailed in the men's and women's competitions at both Wimbledon and the U.S. Open. Julius Boros won the USGA Open golf title at age 37.

Boxing was also a popular sport in the 1950s, and weekly bouts were routinely televised, often sponsored by beer companies. "Jersey" Joe Walcott became the oldest heavyweight champion when he successfully defended his crown against Ezzard Charles in 15 rounds. But Walcott was deposed in September by Rocky Marciano, who had previously knocked out Lee Savold for his 39th consecutive victory. In the middleweight division, "Sugar" Ray Robinson defeated Rocky Graziano to retain his title.

Television

By 1952, television news was beginning to come into its own as a major medium for current events. The first full network coverage of a presidential election took place in 1952. The three networks shipped some 30 tons of equipment and 1,000 workers to the Republican and Democratic conventions, and approximately 70 million U.S. viewers tuned in. Walter Cronkite, who went on to become the most respected TV news reporter of his time, covered the gatherings for CBS, where his superiors criticized him for talking too much. Richard Nixon, the Republican vice presidential nominee, successfully defended himself before some 56 million viewers on September 23, in his nationally televised Checkers speech. On October 24, less than two weeks before the election, Eisenhower made a national television address in which he described Korea as a burial ground for 20,000 dead Americans and promised that, if elected, "I shall go to Korea."[16] Other televised events with cold war implications occurred on April 22 and May 1, when millions of Americans watched the largest atomic tests up to that time in the Nevada desert.

A friendlier atmosphere prevailed on May 3, when Truman led network announcers on a televised tour of the newly restored White House. He explained the decor and furnishings and provided anecdotes about former presidents who had resided in the building. Some 30 million citizens watched as their president gave an impromptu performance of Mozart's Ninth Sonata on the East Room's Steinway piano. He then added a few bars on an American-made Baldwin piano as well.

Among the most popular programs to premier in 1952 was *The Jackie Gleason Show,* an hour-long variety revue that Gleason introduced with a humorous monologue and then followed with sketches that derived from his vaudevillian background and from characters he had developed between 1950 and 1952 during his regular appearances on the DuMont network's *Cavalcade of Stars.* These characters included the stuck-up tycoon Reggie Van Gleason III, Joe the Bartender, Charley the Loudmouth, Pedro the Mexican, and the Poor Soul. Gleason's revue also featured regular performances by the strikingly costumed and carefully choreographed June Taylor Dancers. But the highlight of the weekly show was a half-hour skit called "The Honeymooners," which Gleason had first introduced on *Cavalcade of the Stars.*

Starring the portly Gleason as loud-mouthed bus driver Ralph Kramden; Audrey Meadows as his strong-willed, self-possessed wife, Alice; and Art Carney as his best friend and upstairs neighbor, Ed Norton, a sewer worker, *The Honeymooners* became one of the most enduring and best-loved television programs of the 1950s. Much of the activity centers around Ralph's ill-conceived attempts to rise above his working-class origins and become an admired figure of power and influence. By contrast, Alice seeks happiness by accepting their working-class status and acting wisely, responsibly, and with financial restraint. Although his dreams are never realized, and Alice's pragmatism routinely prevails over his foolish get-rich schemes, Ralph's spirit is never crushed. Instead, it is routinely revived by his recognition that his love for his wife and her love for him matter more than riches, despite their frequent clashes of will. Finally, it is their love that enables them to transcend the deprivations of their sparsely furnished Brooklyn apartment and accept the circumstances of their life.

Although Ralph and Ed are often the butt of the humor, they nonetheless emerge as likable and decent characters who possess fundamentally good values and retain dignity and self-esteem, despite their ridiculous foibles. In this regard, Ralph is a much larger version of Charlie Chaplin's immensely popular Little Tramp character from the 1920s and 1930s, who also is repeatedly defeated by business and society but never allows his spirit to be crushed or his dreams dashed. On the other hand, by ridiculing Ralph's proclivity for equating the trappings of success with its essence, the show reinforces traditional middle-class values of hard work, self-discipline, and fiscal responsibility. Like such earlier literature as Shakespeare's comedies, it derives humor by exposing the absurd pretensions of ignorant laborers. It further challenges aspirations of upward mobility and implies instead that members of the working class are better off accepting their status than trying to rise above it.

Omnibus, which was hosted by British-born Alistair Cooke, was the first major television show underwritten by the Ford Foundation, which subsequently offered it to commercial advertisers. The effort to bring high culture to television endured until May 1959, although the show changed networks twice during its seven-year run. Its offerings ranged from dramas to documentaries to musicals and operas. Among the presentations during its first season were a

From left to right: Jackie Gleason, Art Carney, Audrey Meadows, and Joyce Randolf starred in *The Honeymooners*. *(Photofest)*

serial adaptation of James Agee's *Mr. Lincoln;* plays by Anton Chekhov, George Bernard Shaw, and Maxwell Anderson; and Johann Strauss's comic opera *Die Fledermaus,* with Eugene Ormandy conducting the Metropolitan Opera Orchestra.

The *Today* show, television's first early-morning program and its longest-running daytime network program, debuted on January 14. The popular show still remains in production. Produced by NBC's Sylvester Weaver, who also developed Sid Caesar's *Your Show of Shows, Today* was the first program designed for an audience that was not expected to view it continuously from beginning to end. Instead, the format was tailored to viewers who could watch only intermittently as they prepared for their day. The two-hour program, therefore, was subdivided into small, discrete segments. It offered a news summary every half-hour, which was followed by short reports on sports and weather, interviews with newsmakers and celebrities, and brief features on topics of special interest. Its host, radio broadcaster Dave Garroway, remained on the show through July 1961. Garroway had a relaxed, conversational manner that appealed to listeners who were beginning their day. His signature sign-off for each show was "Peace."

Placed in direct competition with Milton Berle's *Texaco Star Theater,* which remained one of the most popular shows on television, *The Ernie Kovacs Show* premiered in December 1952 but only survived through April 1953. Nonetheless, the hour-long comedy-variety show, starring Ernie Kovacs and his wife, singer Edie Adams, featured some of early television's most imaginative comedy. An exceptionally innovative and versatile performer who frequently satirized other shows and commercials, Kovacs pioneered the use of blackouts and trick photography in television comedy. He introduced a playful element of whimsy and the absurd in such characters as German disc jockey Wolfgang Sauerbraten, Chinese songwriter Irving Wong, and the Nairobi Trio, a group of instrumentalists who performed in ape suits.

In 1952, a priest, minister, and rabbi appeared on *I Love Lucy* to give blessings to the main character Lucy Ricardo, who like star Lucille Ball, was pregnant. That year, *I Love Lucy* displaced *Arthur Godfrey's Talent Scouts* and Mr. Television, Milton Berle, as TV's top-rated program, a ranking it held through 1955. Bishop Fulton J. Sheen's religious show, *Life Is Worth Living,* debuted in 1952 in head-on competition with Berle. Sheen won the year's Emmy Award for outstanding television personality and soon attracted an audience larger than Berle's. *Life Is Worth Living* also inspired Sheen's best-selling book of the same title in 1953. It ran through 1957 and, at its peak, was broadcast by 170 U.S. and 17 Canadian stations and had more than 25 million viewers each week.[17] It was eventually canceled due to a conflict between Sheen and his superior, Cardinal Francis Spellman, but Sheen returned to television from 1961 to 1968 in *The Bishop Sheen Program.*

Ernie Kovacs and Edie Adams, a popular television couple in 1952, married in 1954. *(Photofest)*

Comedies remained among the year's most popular shows. In addition to established hits like *I Love Lucy,* Berle's *Texaco Star Theater,* Groucho Marx's *You Bet Your Life,* and *The Colgate Comedy Hour,* which featured such guest hosts as Dean Martin and Jerry Lewis, Bob Hope, and Jimmy Durante, new comedies from the 1952–53 season included *I Married Joan,* a domestic sitcom patterned after *I Love Lucy* that starred Jim Backus as a level-headed judge and Joan Davis as his zany wife; *My Little Margie,* starring Charles Farrell as a womanizing widower and Gale Storm as his meddlesome daughter; *Mr. Peepers,* starring Wally Cox as a diminutive, gentle science teacher; *Our Miss Brooks,* starring Eve Arden as an English teacher and Gale Gordon as her principal; and *The Adventures of Ozzie and Harriet,* television's longest-running situation comedy, which aired through September 1966. It depicted the benign, minor complications that upset the otherwise tranquil home life of mild-mannered bandleader Ozzie Nelson, his wife, singer Harriet Hilliard, and their sons, David and Ricky. The boys grew up on the show, and Ricky went on to become a popular teenage rock 'n' roll star.

Other shows that debuted in 1952 included *The Liberace Show,* a popular musical variety program hosted by pianist Guy Liberace, who dressed in flashy sequined suits and placed a candelabra atop his piano as he performed flamboyantly; *Arthur Godfrey Time,* a successful hour-long variety show hosted by ukulele-playing pitchman Arthur Godfrey, who was one of the most popular figures on television in the early 1950s; *This Is Your Life,* a human-interest show hosted by Ralph Edwards that featured guest celebrities and ordinary citizens who were pleasantly surprised by the unexpected appearance of people from their past; *I've Got a Secret,* a 20 questions–type quiz show hosted by Garry Moore in which celebrity panelists had to guess the guest contestant's secret; and *Death Valley Days,* an anthology of western dramas introduced by Stanley Andrews, in the costumed persona of the Old Ranger. In 1965, Ronald Reagan succeeded Andrews in the role, a career decision that increased Reagan's public visibility before he stepped down in 1966 to run successfully for governor of California.

After the 1950–51 Kefauver investigations, crime dramas began to gain popularity. *Dragnet,* a realistic-looking police series that claimed to be based on actual cases, became one of the top shows of the year. Jack Webb, who owned an interest in the show, directed most of the episodes and starred as the humorless, almost painfully professional Sergeant Joe Friday, who also narrated the episodes. Its musical theme, "dum-de-dum-dum," quickly caught on as a popular way for signaling imminent trouble, and Friday's oft-repeated line, "Just the facts, ma'am," delivered in a dry, clipped manner, became part of the public lingo.

Movies

The year's big technological advance in cinema was the introduction in Hollywood of 3-D movies, following the invention in 1951 of the polarized glasses that permitted images on the screen to appear in three-dimensions. Arch Oboler's *Bwana Devil* (1952), starring Robert Stack in a story of African railroad workers terrorized by murderous lions, was Hollywood's first 3-D movie. It was later followed by Andre de Toth's *House of Wax* (1953), which established Vincent Price as a horror-film star, and Jack Arnold's *It Came from Outer Space* (1953) and *Creature from the Black Lagoon* (1954), which remains the most famous of the genre.

The studios introduced the 3-D effect to counter competition from the growing television industry. Moviemakers hoped that by offering knife attacks, flying arrows, stampedes, and actresses' protruding busts they could make available entertainment possibilities that far exceeded those of television. Initially, the novelty of seeing images in three dimensions attracted sizable audiences. However, the glasses were cumbersome to wear and sometimes induced headaches, the process required reluctant theater owners to make costly upgrades to their equipment, and the 3-D effect was never really used to significant artistic advantage. Alfred Hitchcock shot *Dial M for Murder* in 1954 for 3-D projection, but by then the process had so fallen into decline that he released the movie for two-dimensional viewing, which did not require special projection. The 3-D version was finally released in 1983.

Although they appeared in only two dimensions, the top films of 1952 also relied on visual effects that television could not match, employed lavish sets and costumes, and otherwise presented stunning and exciting images. Cecil B. DeMille's circus epic *The Greatest Show on Earth* won the Academy Award for best picture and best story, but Gene Kelly and Stanley Donen's *Singin' in the*

Rain has proved to be the most enduring film of 1952. Still much beloved, this musical love story provides splendid dance sequences by Kelly and Donen, highlighted by Kelly's performance of the title song.

The Greatest Show on Earth stars Charlton Heston, Betty Hutton, and Cornel Wilde and celebrates the Ringling Brothers Circus. The large-scale production draws much of its appeal from the photography, costuming, theatrics, and other visual effects. Richard Thorpe's *Ivanhoe* also attracted viewers with its lavish sets and costumes. The costliest movie ever made in England at that time, *Ivanhoe* is based on Sir Walter Scott's novel and stars Robert Taylor, Elizabeth Taylor, and Joan Fontaine. The love story, set during the rule of England's King Richard I (the Lionhearted), received nominations for best picture and best cinematography.

Also produced in England, John Huston's *Moulin Rouge* is another historical film. Starring José Ferrer as deformed artist Henri Toulouse-Lautrec, the biographical film features a spectacular performance of the cancan dance. The movie won Academy Awards for best art direction and costume design and received nominations for best picture, best director, and best supporting actress. Ferrer, who plays most of the film on his knees, was nominated for best actor.

John Ford won the award for best director, and Winton Hoch and Archie Stout for best cinematography in *The Quiet Man,* which stars John Wayne as an American boxer who moves to Ireland to start his life anew and Maureen O'Hara as his love interest. Joseph Mankiewicz's *Five Fingers,* starring James Mason, is a factually based story of a valet to the British ambassador in Turkey who sells secrets to the Germans during World War II. The real-life spy on whom Mason's character is based actually sold 35 authentic top-secret documents to the Nazis, who did not act on any of them.

In addition to *Ivanhoe,* several other major films of 1952 were adapted from novels or plays. Michael Redgrave and Michael Denison star in British director Anthony Asquith's particularly well made adaptation of Oscar Wilde's comedy *The Importance of Being Earnest,* and Shirley Booth won an Academy Award for her performance of Lola Delaney in Ketti Frings's adaptation of William Inge's play *Come Back, Little Sheba.* Also starring Burt Lancaster, *Come Back, Little Sheba* explores the quietly unfulfilling relationship between a mild-mannered alcoholic and his extroverted wife. Henry King's adaption of Ernest Hemingway's *The Snows of Kilimanjaro* stars Gregory Peck as a semiconscious writer who reviews his love life while recovering in Africa from a gangrene infection. Susan Hayworth and Ava Gardner costar as the women in the writer's life, which spans the American Midwest, Paris between the world wars, and the Spanish Civil War. Fred Zinnemann adapted Carson McCuller's 1950 Broadway hit, *The Member of the Wedding,* a story about a disturbed adolescent that stars Ethel Waters, Julie Harris, and Brandon De Wilde.

Several films from 1952 have Red Scare associations. Gary Cooper won the Academy Award as best actor for his performance in the Zinnemann adult western *High Noon,* which tells the story of a sheriff who must stand alone against a recently released killer who is arriving on the noon train to seek revenge against the man who sent him to jail. Abandoned by his friends and community, then by his fiancée (Grace Kelly), who as a Quaker, does not believe in violence, the sheriff refuses to run from danger. The movie received additional nominations for best picture, director, score, and song. Dimitri Tiomkin and Ned Washington's ballad "Do Not Forsake Me," sung by Tex Ritter, became a classic of its genre. In addition, Carl Foreman was nominated for best screenplay.

Foreman, who quit the Communist Party in 1942, claimed to have written *High Noon* to express his feeling of abandonment by the film community when he was subpoenaed to testify before HUAC. The film was in production while Foreman was planning out his strategy for his testimony, and *High Noon* reflects his sense that no one would stand up with him against the committee. According to Foreman, even his business partner and the film's producer, Stanley Kramer, turned on him by forcing him from his own company. Kramer recounted the episode differently.[18] Foreman refused to inform on people he had met during his years as a communist and was subsequently blacklisted. The film, which symbolically equates HUAC with the outlaws, celebrates such traditional American values as courage, integrity, and doing the right thing. But John Wayne, then president of the politically conservative Motion Picture Alliance for the Preservation of American Ideals, attacked the film's depiction of the cowardly townspeople as un-American.[19]

Charlie Chaplin, who had been one of the most widely recognized and well loved people in the world in the 1920s and 1930s, was another victim of the Red Scare. A British citizen who had resided for many years in America, he was denied a visa to return to the United States after he went to England for the premiere of *Limelight,* which he directed and starred in with Claire Bloom, who became an overnight star after the screening. The American-made movie, which won the Academy Award for best score, tells the story of an aging theater star who takes in a desperate young actress and nurtures her health and career, as his own decline.

While Chaplin was en route to England for the opening there, Attorney General James McGranery revoked his permit to reenter the United States, citing a code that allowed for the exclusion of aliens based on morals, health, or insanity, or for advocating communism or associating with communist or pro-communist organizations. In 1947, Chaplin had informed HUAC via telegram that he was not a communist and had never belonged to any political party. But the Democratic attorney general, under attack from Nixon and other Republicans for mismanaging the Chaplin case, ordered him to appear before the Immigration and Naturalization Service to ascertain if he was eligible for readmission to the United States. Chaplin, whose affairs with underage women were also under scrutiny along with his left-wing political sentiments, refused to return to the United States until 1972, when he received a special Academy Award and was honored at the Lincoln Center Film Society in New York City.

Elia Kazan's *Viva Zapata!* was released before the director testified before HUAC. Starring Marlon Brando, Jean Peters, and Anthony Quinn and written by John Steinbeck, who adapted Edgcumb Pinchon's novel *Zapata the Unconquered,* the movie tells the story of Emiliano Zapata's peasant rebellion in Mexico early in the 20th century. It stands out as one of the very few 1950s Hollywood films to present a favorable view of something as closely linked to communism as the violent overthrow of landowners and their government by an insurgent movement whose main goal is land reform and redistribution of wealth. Kazan, who attacked anti-Semitism in *Gentlemen's Agreement* (1947) and racial discrimination in *Pinky* (1949), regarded himself an anticommunist liberal, and he testified before HUAC that *Viva Zapata!* was an anticommunist picture.[20]

Another film with Red Scare implications was Edward Ludwig's *Big Jim McClain*. Starring Wayne and James Arness, it celebrates the work of HUAC investigators and attacks the communist infiltration of labor unions. Leo McCarey's *My Son John* centers on a bookish younger son with an overly protective mother and homosexual traits who rejects his country and religious faith to become a communist spy, while his older, less cerebral but more manly brothers fight patriotically in Korea. McCarey was a fervent anticommunist who testified as a friendly witness before HUAC in 1947, and *My Son John* unites the anti-intellectualism, fear of homosexuality, and fear of women, especially of strong mothers, that were often ingrained within the Red Scare sensibility. Alfred L. Werker's *Walk East on Beacon* presents the FBI cracking a communist spy ring in Boston. Suggested by FBI director J. Edgar Hoover's *Crime of the Century,* produced in cooperation with the bureau, and filmed in documentary style, the movie depicts communists as both cruel and incompetent.

Harry Horner's *Red Planet Mars* stars Peter Graves in an attack on international communism from outer space. The science fiction film offered wish fulfillment to audiences who were frustrated by the cold war stalemate and longed for some divine or extraterrestrial intervention that would overthrow the communist governments and restore Christian society. For many Americans, Christianity stood as a bulwark against communism, and the cold war was as much a moral crusade as a political struggle. These viewers were heartened by the movie's dramatic conclusion, in which highly advanced Martians inspire the overthrow of the Soviet government via religious radio broadcasts.

The year's top box office attractions were the comedy team of Dean Martin and Jerry Lewis, Cooper, Wayne, Bing Crosby, Bob Hope, James Stewart, Doris Day, Peck, Susan Hayworth, and Randolph Scott. Among those to make their first major Hollywood appearances were Marilyn Monroe (*Niagara*), Grace Kelly (*High Noon*), Richard Burton (*My Cousin Rachel*), and Debbie Reynolds (*Singin' in the Rain*).

Literature

The general pessimism and cynicism that pervaded the political environment found expression in many of the important books of 1952. But like the American people themselves, many of whom managed to maintain a sense of humor and find private ways to lift their spirits, much of the literature strove toward personal growth and fulfillment in a hostile or indifferent world.

One of the most significant and enduring American novels from 1952 is Ralph Ellison's *Invisible Man,* about an idealistic young black man from the segregated South who moves to a more integrated New York City but becomes disillusioned by the false promise of true equality in the North. His innocence is manipulated by virtually everyone he encounters, from every strata of society, both black and white, and he finally concludes that he is "invisible" because no one will see him for who he is. They see only the identity they project onto him, based on what they want or expect him to be. One of the most powerful scenes shows a "battle royal" in which blindfolded black boys fight each other for the amusement of the white civic leaders in a small southern town. Horrifying as the event is in its own right, it foreshadows the far more devastating New York race riot that concludes the story. Agents of the Brotherhood (i.e., the Communist

Party), who had ostensibly been working on behalf of the oppressed minority, instigate the riot on orders from party headquarters, which is more concerned with making the United States look bad in the international arena than with helping the people suffering on the streets. Like the overt southern racists viewing the battle royal, the communist leaders watch with satisfaction as the black residents of Harlem blindly flail against one another, but instead of merely cutting and bruising themselves, and giving each other fat lips and black eyes, they loot their own stores and destroy their own homes.

Ernest Hemingway's *The Old Man and the Sea* won the Pulitzer Prize for 1952. It centers on an old Cuban fisherman who battles a giant marlin, catches it after a mighty struggle, then watches helplessly as sharks devour it before he can take it home. The novel portrays the struggle between man and nature and examines the problem of meaningful, even valiant, action in an indifferent universe. John Sturges directed the film adaptation, starring Spencer Tracy, in 1958. John Steinbeck's *East of Eden* follows the fates of three generations of family members, from the 19th century into the 20th, who have settled in California's Salinas Valley. Steinbeck, himself, acts as narrator, and his grandfather is the patriarch who begins the saga. In 1955, Kazan made the story into a film starring James Dean in his first major cinematic role.

Mary McCarthy satirizes knee-jerk liberal academics in *The Groves of Academe,* in which a self-serving, egotistical cynic manipulates the good intentions of his liberal colleagues in order to preserve his job—at the expense of theirs and of the career of the college's liberal-minded president. Kurt Vonnegut, Jr.'s, first novel, *Player Piano,* centers around a supercomputer capable of waging totally efficient war. The story addresses a fear then shared by a growing number of North Americans that science and technology would spin out of control and threaten to destroy all life. Like much of Vonnegut's subsequent work, *Player Piano* also suggests that humans are fundamentally stupid and

Actor Spencer Tracy (left) and author Ernest Hemingway converse on the set of *The Old Man and the Sea,* adapted in 1958 from the 1952 Pulitzer Prize–winning novella. *(Photofest)*

unable or unwilling to learn from their mistakes. Vonnegut's point of view became more widely shared throughout the decade, as an impending nuclear confrontation appeared more and more inevitable. Another science fiction novel of interest is *The Space Merchants* by Frederik Pohl and C. M. Kornbluth. The futuristic story of a United States dominated by advertising agencies and ruled by a small business class highlights the dangers of consumer capitalism, a view safer to publish in science fiction than in mainstream literature during the 1950s Red Scare, because at the time, science fiction was rarely regarded as a meaningful, serious form of literature.

Bernard Malamud's *The Natural* is a baseball story patterned to some extent on the medieval legend of the Fisher King and Holy Grail. (The same legend is at the heart of T. S. Eliot's 1922 poem, "The Waste Land.") Unlike Barry Levinson's optimistic Reagan-era film adaptation starring Robert Redford (1984), in Malamud's original story slugger Roy Hobbs fails to fulfill his promise of becoming the grail knight who will lead his team from their wasteland of losing seasons, because he allows himself to be seduced by sex and corrupted by material distractions. *The Natural* was written at the dawn of consumer capitalism, a state in the evolution of corporate capitalism in which manufacturers aggressively sought not simply to fill existing demands for material goods but to create new ones, and Malamud communicated the sense of waste and squandered opportunity that results when people prize fortune, fame, and sensual gratification more than personal growth and integrity. Thus, like F. Scott Fitzgerald in *The Great Gatsby* (1925), Malamud shows how the hero of a rags-to-riches American dream debases himself and fails his community because he values self-indulgence more than self-knowledge. Read as a metaphor for the nation at large, the book further suggests that the United States might easily possess the resources and talent to lead the world out of its postwar waste land but is instead squandering that potential on superficial attractions.

Other notable fiction from the year included William Styron's *The Long March,* Wright Morris's *The Works of Love,* and Flannery O'Connor's *Wise Blood,* which follows a mentally disturbed teenager and a nihilistic, evangelical southern preacher who establishes "the Church without Christ." As in much of her fiction, O'Connor, a committed Catholic, uses a grotesquely comical story to assert that spiritual salvation is always possible, even along the most unlikely avenues.

Among the year's best-sellers were *East of Eden* and *The Old Man and the Sea;* Frances Parkinson Keyes's *Steamboat Gothic,* which examines the choice between a comfortable, secure marriage and an exciting but unstable one; Frank Yerby's *The Saracen Blade;* Daphne du Maurier's *My Cousin Rachel;* Edna Ferber's *Giant,* a story of two generations of Texans that George Stevens adapted in 1956 into an Academy Award–nominated film starring Elizabeth Taylor, Rock Hudson, and James Dean; and Herman Wouk's *The Caine Mutiny,* the 1951 Pulitzer Prize–winning naval story.

Archibald MacLeish's *Collected Poems: 1917–1952* won the Pulitzer Prize for poetry. Eliot also published his *Complete Poems and Plays,* and Adrienne Rich, Wallace Stevens, Robert Creeley, W. S. Merwin, and early Beat writer Kenneth Rexroth all issued volumes of poetry. Although William Carlos Williams was appointed consultant in poetry to the Library of Congress, he was unable to serve because a note in his FBI file suggested he might be a security risk. The FBI agent, who described Williams as "a sort of absent minded professor type" speculated that his "expressionistic" style might be a form of secret code. The post remained vacant until 1956.[21]

The Revised Standard Version of the Bible was issued to considerable public interest and acclaim; it sold more than 2 million copies in its first year and topped the nonfiction best-seller list through 1954. Also released was the first English translation of the complete Torah, the first five books of the Old Testament that are the basis of Judaism. Other nonfiction from 1952 included *Witness*, Whittaker Chambers's autobiographical account of the Alger Hiss case and of Chambers's experience as an American communist in the 1930s; Van Wyck Brooks's social history *The Confident Years: 1885–1915*; William Shirer's *Midcentury Journey*; progressive theologian Reinhold Niebuhr's *The Irony of American History*; Norman Vincent Peale's influential *The Power of Positive Thinking*; and David Riesman and Nathan Glazer's *Faces in the Crowd*, a follow-up of their 1950 study of the culture of corporate America, *The Lonely Crowd. Anne Frank: Diary of a Young Girl*, the autobiography of a Jewish World War II Holocaust victim, was first published in the United States, where it was widely read and discussed and was later adapted into a Broadway play. Less intellectual but perhaps equally popular was the initial publication of the tell-all tabloid *Hollywood Confidential*, which was inspired by the vast public interest in the sordid details revealed by the Kefauver committee.

Spanish-born, Harvard-educated philosopher, poet, and literary critic George Santayana died in a convent in Italy at age 88. Italian socialist philosopher Benedetto Croce also died, at age 86.

Theater, Music, and the Visual Arts

The most enduring and influential play of 1952 was Samuel Beckett's masterpiece of the Theater of the Absurd, *Waiting for Godot*, which debuted in Paris. A comic play in which nothing happens, it is typically read as a metaphor for humanity's unfulfilled desire for God to appear on Earth.

In American theater, 1952 is best remembered for initiating the tradition of arty and experimental productions south of New York City's 42nd Street and the Broadway area that became known as Off Broadway. These began in April when Geraldine Page starred in a production of Tennessee Williams's *Summer and Smoke* at the Circle Theater in the Square in Sheridan Square. Openings on Broadway included Joseph Kramm's *The Shrike*, starring Jose Ferrer and Judith Evelyn, which won the Pulitzer Prize for 1952. Helen Hayes and Brandon De Wilde starred in Mary Chase's *Mrs. McThing*; Rex Harrison and Lilli Palmer appeared in Christopher Fry's *Venus Observed*; Shirley Booth starred in Arthur Laurents's *The Time of the Cuckoo*; and African-American playwright Alice Childress premiered *Gold through the Leaves*.

Two new plays that were later made into popular films were *The Seven-Year Itch*, George Axelrod's domestic comedy, and *Dial "M" for Murder*, Frederic Knott's tale of a husband who frames his wife for murder after failing to have her killed. Among the musicals to premiere were Vernon Duke and Ogden Nash's *Two's Company*, starring Bette Davis; Harold Rome's *Wish You Were Here*; a one-woman performance entitled *An Evening with Beatrice Lilli*; and June Carroll and Arthur Siegal's *New Faces of 1952*, which featured among others Carol Lawrence, Eartha Kitt, and Paul Lynde.

Robert Joffrey founded the American Ballet Center in New York City. The New York City Ballet debuted George Balanchine's *Harlequin Pas de Deux, Metamorphoses,* and *Scotch Symphony.* Working with his own dance company, experimental choreographer Merce Cunningham produced experimental composer John Cage's *Suite by Chance* and *Symphonie pour un homme seul.* Cage also premiered his *Water Music,* whose title plays off of George Frideric Handel's famous composition but whose sound is derived from pouring water from one receptacle to another at very precise moments. Cage also composed *Imaginary Landscapes No. 5,* which was created from splicing tapes, and perhaps his most famous piece, *4'33"*—four minutes and 33 seconds of silence that frame the random sounds of the environment in which the silence is "performed." Cage's *Collage* features 43 jazz recordings played simultaneously. In all of these works Cage asks his audiences to pay attention to and think about sound in ways apart from their ordinary experiences of it.

Charlie "Bird" Parker, Miles Davis, Charles Mingus, Ella Fitzgerald, Sarah Vaughan, Louis Armstrong, Duke Ellington, Stan Getz, George Shearing, Oscar Peterson, and Dizzy Gillespie remained the dominant figures in jazz. After a hiatus of several years due to drug addiction, Billie Holiday, whom saxophonist Lester Young dubbed "Lady Day," slowly returned to the performance circuit. Ellington celebrated his 25th year of musical performance by giving two concerts at Carnegie Hall in New York City that included Holiday, Parker, Gillespie, and Getz. Famed classical composer and conductor Leonard Bernstein also expressed himself through jazz. His opera *Trouble in Tahiti* debuted in 1952, and Bernstein hosted a symposium on jazz at Brandeis University in which Davis, Mingus, and pianist John Lewis explored the interplay between bop and traditional styles. Later in the year, Lewis, vibraphonist Milt Jackson, bassist Percy Heath, and drummer Kenny Clarke formed the influential Modern Jazz Quartet, which garnered a large following and remained productive for several decades. Meanwhile, the new West Coast "cool" jazz began to make an impact in the East. The Latin American influence on jazz remained evident in the music of Machito.

Rock 'n' roll first burst onto the national stage when Bill Haley and His Comets released the energetic song "Rock the Joint," which sold 75,000 records. Although rock 'n' roll did not have a major impact on American culture until 1954, when Haley, a Pennsylvania disc jockey, and his group recorded "Rock Around the Clock," with "Rock the Joint" he became the first white rock performer to reach a young, broad, middle-class audience with music whose origins were rooted in black rhythm and blues.

Additional popular hits from the year included the title song from the movie *High Noon* and the soundtrack from *Singin' in the Rain.* Other hits were Peggy Lee's "Lover," Leroy Anderson's "Blue Tango," Jo Stafford's "You Belong to Me," Karen Chandler's "Hold Me, Thrill Me, Kiss Me," Eddie Fisher's "Wish You Were Here," Georgia Gibbs's "Kiss of Fire," "Tell Me Why" by the Four Aces, and "Glow Worm" by the Mills Brothers. Country hits included Hank Thompson's "Wild Side of Life" and Carl Smith's "Let Old Mother Nature Have Her Way." Irving Berlin's "They Like Ike" became a hit during the presidential campaign, and it inspired the popular "I Like Ike" slogan that appeared on bumper stickers and buttons throughout the nation.

In the visual arts realm, Pablo Picasso, in an effort to placate critics who accused him of deviating from Soviet principles in his work, signed a statement

Bill Haley and His Comets made rock 'n' roll's first hit record, "Rock the Joint." *(Photofest)*

for the French Communist Party affirming his faith in socialist realism. The New York Metropolitan Museum of Art named its first two female trustees.

Experimental, purely expressive art featuring shapes, color, movement, and emotion continued to dominate the New York galleries, and its leading practitioner, Jackson Pollock, produced his abstract work "Convergence." Notable works of architecture completed in 1952 included the sleek, modern-looking United Nations headquarters in Manhattan, which was built on an $8.5-million tract of land donated by John D. Rockefeller, Jr.

At the other end of the fine arts spectrum, the Palmer Paint Company of Detroit first marketed the popular paint-by-numbers-kits, which consisted of color-coded canvases with predrawn figures that allowed anyone to produce more or less acceptable-looking copies of famous paintings or other designs. A kit of "The Last Supper," complete with an "antique" gold frame, cost $11.50, and some 12 million similar kits were sold. One received third prize in a San Francisco art competition for original art.[22]

CHRONICLE OF EVENTS

1952

January 5: British prime minister Churchill arrives in Washington, D.C., to confer with Truman.

January 5: In a nationwide crackdown on narcotics, federal agents arrest more than 500 people accused of selling marijuana and heroin.

January 5: The United States signs a five-year agreement giving India $50 million for economic development.

January 7: In Paris, General Eisenhower agrees to accept the Republican nomination if it is offered to him, but he says he will not campaign for it.

January 10: Churchill agrees to allow U.S. military bases on British soil.

January 26: Egypt is placed under martial law following anti-British riots. Premier Mustafa Nahas is removed the following day for failing to maintain order.

February 6: Great Britain's king George VI dies in his sleep.

February 13: Rocky Marciano gains his 39th consecutive victory by knocking out Lee Savold.

February 14: The Winter Olympic Games open in Oslo, Norway.

February 15: Elizabeth II is coronated queen of England in an internationally televised ceremony.

February 18: Greece and Turkey join NATO.

February 20: In Lisbon, Portugal, NATO convenes its ninth conference. Concerned with deterring aggression from the Soviet bloc, the alliance agrees to raise a 50-division army in Western Europe by the end of the year.

February 22: The United States agrees to give military aid to Peru.

February 26: The United States agrees to give military aid to Ecuador.

February 26: Britain announces that it has developed an atomic bomb and has the capacity to produce more.

February 27: UN committees hold their first meetings in the new headquarters, based in New York City.

February 29: The deadline that the African National Congress (ANC) has given the government of South Africa for eliminating apartheid passes. Subsequently, the ANC begins organizing protests throughout the country.

The United Nations Building opened in New York City in 1952. *(Photofest)*

February 29: The first electronic pedestrian street-crossing signs are installed in New York City. The signs flash "Walk" and "Don't Walk."

March 3: The Supreme Court upholds New York's Feinberg law banning communists from teaching in public schools.

March 4: North Korea accuses UN forces of practicing germ warfare.

March 7: The United States agrees to give military aid to Cuba.

March 10: General Fulgencio Batista overthrows the government of President Prío Socarrás of Cuba.

March 10: The Soviet Union proposes a four-power conference on the reunification and rearmament of Germany. The Soviets refuse to permit UN-supervised elections throughout Germany, and the proposal dies.

March 11: In the New Hampshire primary, Eisenhower defeats Taft and Kefauver beats Truman. The outcome helps convince Truman not to seek reelection.

March 15: The United States agrees to give military aid to Brazil.

March 20: Senator William Benton likens Senator Joseph McCarthy to Adolf Hitler. Six days later, McCarthy sues Benton for libel and conspiracy. He later drops the charges, claiming he can find no one who believes Benton's claims.

March 22: A string of tornadoes kills some 200 people and injures 2,500 more in Missouri, Tennessee, Arkansas, Alabama, and Mississippi.

March 25: The United States, Britain, and France reject a Soviet proposal for a rearmed, reunified, neutral Germany.

March 27: The Trumans move back into the newly restored White House.

March 29: Truman announces that he will not seek reelection.

April 1: The United States begins its third series of atomic-bomb tests.

April 4: The United States agrees to give military aid to Chile.

April 4: The UN Security Council holds its first meeting in the New York City headquarters.

April 10: Elia Kazan, preeminent theater and film director of the late 1940s and 1950s, testifies before HUAC in executive session and identifies several former associates as communists.

April 10: Gene Kelly and Stanley Donen's film musical, *Singin' in the Rain,* premieres.

April 11: General Eisenhower announces that, effective June 1, he will retire from active duty. This is a necessary step for him to run for election.

April 12: Kazan takes out an advertisement in the *New York Times* defending his testimony before HUAC. He argues that communism now poses a grave threat to America and urges others to cooperate with the committee.

April 13: The FCC terminates a three-year ban on new television stations.

April 13: Edward R. Murrow's *See It Now* airs the first television documentary of the filming of a movie when it presents a feature on the making of *Hans Christian Anderson.*

April 16: "Sugar" Ray Robinson retains his middleweight title by knocking out Rocky Graziano in the third round.

April 16: NATO opens its new headquarters at the Palais de Chaillot in Paris.

April 17: The United States agrees to give military aid to Colombia.

April 22: Television audiences witness the explosion of the largest atomic bomb yet.

April 24: Tennessee Williams's *Summer and Smoke,* starring Geraldine Page, opens at the Circle in the Square Theater in New York's Sheridan Square, becoming the first major theatrical performance below 42nd Street in 30 years.

April 28: The Japanese Peace Treaty ends U.S. occupation of Japan, and Japan establishes its own government.

April 28: The Supreme Court upholds the constitutionality of New York's released-time program for religious instruction of public school students.

May 1: TWA begins tourist-class service.

May 2: British Overseas Airways inaugurates the first commercial jet service. The first flight is between London, England, and Johannesburg, South Africa. The jet reduces travel time to 18 hours and 40 minutes, some nine hours faster than propeller-plane service.

May 6: Egypt's king Farouk proclaims himself a direct descendant of the prophet Muhammad.

May 9: Communist POWs on Koje Island capture the prison camp's commander, General Dodd. They hold him for 78 hours until some of their demands are met.

May 12: The United States receives its first female ambassador, India's Shrimati Vijaya Lakshmi Pandit.

May 12: General Mark Clark assumes command of UN forces in Korea.

May 13: The United Nations announces the existence of a huge plague of desert locusts in the Middle East.

May 15: Wernher von Braun, the head of the U.S. rocketry program, suggests that it is now time to begin thinking about space exploration and travel to Mars.

May 19–20: Playwright Clifford Odets testifies before HUAC and names former communist associates.

May 21: Playwright Lillian Hellman appears before HUAC but invokes the Fifth Amendment and refuses to identify others as communists or associates of communists. She is subsequently blacklisted in Hollywood.

May 21: Actor John Garfield is found dead of a heart attack that his friends believe resulted largely from agitation caused by his blacklisting in 1951 for his leftist political association.

May 23: Truman orders that the railroads he placed under army control in 1950 be returned to their owners, following the resolution of the labor dispute that provoked the action.

May 26: West Germany is established as a separate state.

May 27: West Germany, France, Italy, Belgium, the Netherlands, and Luxembourg establish the European Defense Community.

May 29: Greece gives women the right to vote.

May 30: Eisenhower steps down as supreme commander of NATO forces. He is replaced by General Matthew Ridgway, the supreme commander of UN forces in Korea.

June 3: Six thousand U.S. paratroopers storm the Koje POW camp and forcefully remove communist leaders who had defied orders. Thirty prisoners are killed in the action.

June 4: Britain joins the United States in condemning the purge of South Korea's Assembly by President Syngman Rhee.

June 15: Anne Frank: Diary of a Young Girl, the influential diary of a teenage Holocaust victim, is first published in the United States.

June 16: Soviet jets shoot down a Swedish air force plane over international waters in the Baltic Sea.

June 20: Truman signs a $6.5 billion mutual security bill.

June 23: More than 500 UN airplanes bomb five of North Korea's largest hydroelectric plants.

June 25: In Olympia, Greece, the Olympic torch is lit at the ancient Temple of Zeus.

June 26: One hundred fifty nonwhites are arrested for protesting apartheid in South Africa.

June 27: Congress overrides Truman's veto to pass the McCarran-Walter immigration bill.

July 7: The American passenger liner *United States* sets a new speed record for an Atlantic crossing.

July 12: Eisenhower wins the Republican nomination for president.

July 14: General Motors announces that it will offer air-conditioning in some of its 1953 model cars.

July 15: The United States bans the Soviet periodical *Amerika,* along with Soviet information bulletins.

July 15: Seventeen-year-old Maureen Connolly becomes the youngest player in the 20th century to win the Wimbledon women's singles tennis championship.

July 16: Congress approves a new G.I. Bill for Korean War veterans, granting them benefits similar to those given veterans of World War II.

July 17: Anti-Western Iranian premier Mossadegh is removed from office.

July 19: The Summer Olympic Games open in Helsinki, Finland.

July 22: Mossadegh is restored to power, following five days of riots.

July 24: U.S. steelworkers receive a pay raise and end their 53-day strike.

July 25: Puerto Rico gains self-rule and becomes the first U.S. commonwealth.

July 26: Illinois governor Adlai Stevenson receives the Democratic nomination for president.

July 26: Eva Perón, the powerful wife of Argentine president Juan Perón, dies at age 33.

July 26: In an army coup, Mohammed Naguib Bey seizes power in Egypt.

July 30: The Chesapeake Bay Bridge opens.

August 1: Alabama, Kentucky, Mississippi, Georgia, South Carolina, Tennessee, Massachusetts, and Maine are declared disaster areas and made eligible for federal assistance as a severe drought causes extensive crop failures in the South and East.

August 4: After praising the new Japanese peace treaty, Secretary of State Acheson opens security talks with Australia and New Zealand.

August 8: Iran demands a large indemnity from the British-owned Anglo-Iranian Oil Company.

August 11: Seventeen-year-old Prince Hussein is crowned king of Jordan.

August 15: The AFL vows to eliminate gangsters from its union membership.

August 16: Truman receives Faisal II, the 17-year-old king of Iraq.

August 17: Stalin receives China's premier, Zhou Enlai, in Moscow.

August 19: The United Nations convention on women's rights opens.

August 22: A severe earthquake destroys much of the business district in Bakersfield, California.

August 22: Bernard Malamud's novel *The Natural* is published.

August 25: Virgil Trucks of the Detroit Tigers becomes the third pitcher in Major League Baseball to throw two no-hitters in a single season.

August 29: UN bombers strike Pyongyang in the heaviest air attack of the war to date.

August 30: Buckminster Fuller displays his new geodesic-dome home at New York City's Museum of Modern Art.

September 3: Eisenhower warns white southerners that they endanger their own rights by failing to protect the rights of black Americans.

September 7: Frank Sedgman and Maureen Connolly win the men's and women's tennis titles at the U.S. Open at Forest Hills, New York.

September 11: Eritrea, a former Italian colony currently under British administration, is joined with Ethiopia.

September 23: Republican vice presidential candidate Richard Nixon defends himself against charges of abusing campaign funds in a televised appeal to the nation. The legendary address becomes known as the "Checkers speech."

September 23: Prize-fighter Rocky Marciano claims the heavyweight boxing title by knocking out 38-year-old "Jersey" Joe Walcott in the 13th round.

September 26: Spanish-born philosopher-poet George Santayana dies.

September 30: Cinerama, the wide-screen movie projection system, is first introduced.

October: The first *Mad* comic book is published. Billing itself as "Humor in a Jugular Vein," the publication is printed on newsprint paper but changes to a slick-papered magazine format in 1955, after the 1954 Comics Code imposes too many restrictions on its content for *Mad* to remain effective as satire in comic-book format.

October: Beginning in early October, Mau Mau insurgents in Kenya begin attacking white farmers and coffee planters, slaughtering their livestock, setting fires, and otherwise instituting a campaign of terror designed to drive white settlers from the British colony. Britain subsequently declares a state of emergency and imposes martial law.

October 3: Great Britain explodes its first atomic bomb.

October 7: The New York Yankees win the World Series by defeating the Brooklyn Dodgers 4-2 in the seventh game. Stan Musial, of the St. Louis Cardinals (.335) and Ferris Fain of the Philadelphia Athletics (.327) win the National and American Leagues batting titles, respectively, and Pittsburgh's Ralph Kiner and the Chicago Cubs's Hank Sauer lead the major leagues in home runs, with 37 apiece. Hoyt Wilhelm of the New York Giants (15-3) and Bob Shantz of the

Athletics (24-7) are the top pitchers in the National and American Leagues, respectively. Sauer and Shantz are voted Most Valuable Player (MVP) in their respective leagues.

October 8: Korean truce talks break down and are suspended indefinitely.

October 10: *The Adventures of Ozzie and Harriet* debuts on television.

October 12: Thirty-four leading scientists issue a statement denouncing the U.S. visa policy restricting suspected communists from entry into the country.

October 13: The Supreme Court rejects the Rosenbergs' appeal of their conviction for stealing atomic secrets.

October 14: The UN General Assembly meets for the first time in its new headquarters in New York City. It selects Canada's Lester Pearson as its president.

October 16: Charlie Chaplin's *Limelight* opens.

October 20: Soft-coal miners strike in protest of a government order cutting 40¢ from their $1.90/hour

Ozzie and Harriet Nelson's *The Adventures of Ozzie and Harriet,* television's longest-running situation comedy, debuted on October 10, 1952. *(Photofest)*

pay raise. The strike ends seven days later, and on November 1, the government restores the full $1.90 raise.

October 23: Eight New York City teachers are fired for alleged communist activities.

October 24: In a nationally broadcast television address, Eisenhower attacks the Truman administration's handling of the Korean War and vows that, if elected, he will go to Korea.

October 25: The UN General Assembly refuses to seat the communist People's Republic of China (PRL) for the third time since it was declared in October 1949.

October 29: Attorney General James P. McGranery announces he has revoked the reentry permit of British-born actor Charles Chaplin.

October 31: The United States explodes its first thermonuclear device, a 12-megaton hydrogen bomb.

October 31: Bolivia nationalizes three tin companies.

November 5: Republican Dwight Eisenhower is elected, ending 20 years of Democratic presidents, and Republicans gain control of both houses of Congress.

November 8: Greek opera soprano Maria Callas wins great acclaim in her first performance in London.

November 9: Israel's first president, Chaim Weizmann, dies.

November 10: The Supreme Court upholds a decision barring segregation on interstate railways.

November 10: Trygve Lie resigns as UN secretary general, largely because of opposition to him from the Soviet Union, which objects to his support of the UN intervention in Korea and his opposition to expelling Nationalist China in favor of seating the PRC. In 1950, however, Lie had supported admission of the PRC, in addition to Nationalist China.

November 12: Writer-director Abe Burrows voluntarily testifies before HUAC. He denies membership in the Communist Party but admits extensive associations with communists and communist-front organizations during World War II and shortly afterward. He avoids directly identifying party members but acknowledges that he assumes that certain individuals whom the committee identifies had been members.

November 18: Albert Einstein declines an offer to become Israel's next president.

November 20: President-elect Eisenhower chooses John Foster Dulles for secretary of state, General Motors president Charles Erwin Wilson for secretary

President-elect Dwight D. Eisenhower was all smiles on election night. *(Photofest)*

of defense, and Oregon governor Douglas McKay for secretary of the interior.

November 20: Italian socialist philosopher and historian Benedetto Croce dies at age 86.

November 24: Agatha Christie's murder mystery *The Mousetrap* opens in London. It goes on to become one of the longest-running plays in history.

November 25: George Meany becomes president of the AFL following the death of William Green.

November 26: Arch Oboler's *Bwana Devil,* the first 3-D movie, premieres.

November 28: Following antiapartheid riots in which 14 people were killed, South Africa bans meetings of more than 10 blacks.

November 29: The first international organization promoting birth control opens in Bombay, India.

December 2: Eisenhower begins a three-day tour of Korea, fulfilling his campaign promise.

December 4: Walter Reuther is elected president of the CIO.

December 9: The Supreme Court hears initial arguments on four civil rights cases challenging the separate-but-equal doctrine. Joined under the name of the case first heard by the court, *Brown v. Board of Education of Topeka, Kansas,* the litigation ultimately results in the landmark 1954 decision that rejects the separate-but-equal doctrine and leads to the integration of public schools and facilities.

December 10: Dr. Albert Schweitzer receives the Nobel Peace Prize for his humanitarian work in Gabon, in French Equatorial Africa.

December 12: The navy's *Viking 9* rocket reaches a record altitude of 135 miles.

December 17: Yugoslavia severs relations with the Vatican.

December 18: "Sugar" Ray Robinson retires as middleweight boxing champion.

December 22: Milt Jackson and John Lewis rename their group the Modern Jazz Quartet.

December 25: Restaurateur James "Dinty" Moore dies.

December 28: The Detroit Lions defeat the Cleveland Browns (17-7) to win the National Football League championship. Los Angeles Rams Norm Van Brocklin and Dan Towler lead the league in passing and rushing, respectively, and Mac Speedie of the Cleveland Browns leads in receiving yardage. The Washington Redskins's famed quarterback, Sammy Baugh, retires after the season ends.

EYEWITNESS TESTIMONY

So my task was one of revealing the human universals hidden within the plight of one who was both black and American, and not only as a means of conveying my personal vision of possibility, but as a way of dealing with the sheer rhetorical challenge involved in communicating across our barriers of race and religion, class, color and region . . . that were designed, and still function, to prevent what would otherwise have been a more or less natural recognition of the reality of black and white fraternity. And to defeat this national tendency to deny the common humanity shared by my character and those who might happen to read of his experience, I would have to provide him with something of a world view, give him a consciousness in which serious philosophical questions could be raised. . . . Most of all, I would have to approach racial stereotypes as a given fact of the social process and proceed ..to reveal the human complexity which stereotypes are intended to conceal.

*From Ralph Ellison's 1981 introduction to his 1952
novel,* Invisible Man, *in Ellison,* Invisible Man
(1995), p. xxii.

I am invisible, understand, simply because people refuse to see me. Like the bodiless heads you sometimes see in circus sideshows, it is as though I have been surrounded by mirrors of hard, distorting glass. When they approach me they see only my surroundings, themselves, or figments of their imaginations—indeed, everything and anything except me.

The anonymous black narrator in Ralph Ellison's Invisible Man *in Ellison,* Invisible Man *(1995), p. 3.*

The New Criticism seems to have triumphed pretty generally, *PR's* [*Partisan Review*] view of American life is indeed partisan, and a large portion of writers, intellectuals, critics—whatever we may care to include in the omnibus—have moved their economic luggage from the WPA [Roosevelt's depression-era Works Progress Administration] to the Luce chain as a writer for *Time* or *Life* once remarked. Among the major novelists, Dos Passos, Farrell, Faulkner, Steinbeck, and Hemingway have traveled from alienation to varying degrees of acceptance, if not outright proselytizing for the American Century.

*Norman Mailer commenting in 1952 on the state of
American literature, in Thomas Hill Schaub,* American
Fiction in the Cold War *(1991), p. 50.*

A girl who reaches the middle twenties without a proposal [of marriage] ought to consider carefully whether she really wishes to remain single. If she does not, she should try to discover why marriage hasn't come her way, and perhaps take steps to make herself more interesting and attractive.

*From a 1952 pamphlet, "Health for Girls," in
Lary May, ed.,* Recasting America: Culture and
Politics in the Age of the Cold War
(1989), p. 157.

Certain younger [college] teachers had been courting popularity by winking at gross infringements of the rules, allowing the punch to be spiked, hip-flasks to be produced on the dance-floor, necking to go on unchecked; on one occasion, even, marijuana had been smoked on the steps of the gymnasium during intermissions, with the tacit, shrugging, knowledge of the faculty-member present. . . . [E]very year there were rumors of seduction, homosexuality, abortion, lesbian attachments, and what shocked the students about these stories .. was the fact that they appeared to take place in a moral vacuum, to leave no trace the morning after . . . the student's grade . . . showed no improvement for the encounter.

*Mary McCarthy describing life at a fictional progressive
college in 1952, in McCarthy,* The Groves of
Academe *(1992), pp. 23–24.*

What the founder had had in mind was a utopian experiment in so-called "scientific" education; by the use of aptitude tests, psychological questionnaires, even blood-sampling and cranial measurements, he hoped to discover a method of gauging student-potential and directing it into the proper channels for maximum self-realization—he saw himself as an engineer and the college as a reclamation project along the lines of the Grand Coulee or the TVA [Tennessee Valley Authority]. . . . The founder had the sincere idea of running his college as a laboratory; failure in an individual case he found as interesting as success. . . .

It was the mixture of the sexes, some thought, that had introduced a crude and predatory bravado into the campus life; the glamour was rubbed off sex by the daily jostle in the soda-shop and barroom and the nightly necking in the social rooms, and this, in its turn, had its effect on all ideals and absolutes. Differences were leveled, students of both sexes had the wary disillusionment and aimlessness of the battle-hardened Marines.

Mary McCarthy describing the aims of progressive education in 1952, in McCarthy, The Groves of Academe *(1992), pp. 61–64.*

Our modern liberal culture, of which American civilization is such an unalloyed exemplar, is involved in many ironic refutations of its original pretensions of virtue, wisdom, and power. Insofar as communism has already elaborated some of these pretensions into noxious forms of tyranny, we are involved in the double irony of confronting evils which were distilled from illusions, not generically different from our own...

In the liberal world the evils in human nature and history were ascribed to social institutions or to ignorance or some other manageable defect in human nature or environment. . . . [This led to man's] confidence in his power over historical destiny . . [and the rejection of] the Christian idea of the ambiguity of human virtue. . . .

[The "grace" of America has been its common sense, which has kept the United States from trying to] cut through the vast ambiguities of our historic situation and thereby bringing our destiny to a tragic conclusion by seeking to bring it to a neat and logical one.

Theologian Reinhold Niebuhr in his book The Irony of American History, *published in 1952, in Thomas Hill Schaub,* American Fiction in the Cold War *(1991), p. 11.*

[Robert] Harrison had conceived the idea for the magazine [*Hollywood Confidential*] after watching the daily televised Kefauver crime investigations. When he observed that these journalistic reports on vice, crime and prostitution eclipsed all other programs in the ratings, he deduced that the public was hungry for gossip and that a publication that presented such material in a spicy manner and did, in effect, name names, would go over big.

Writer Kenneth Anger commenting in 1975 on the conception of the tell-all tabloid Hollywood Confidential, *which was first published in 1952, in Darden Asbury Pyron,* Liberace: An American Boy *(2000), p. 216.*

I resented the scene where the marshal ripped off his badge and threw it on the ground. That was like belit-

tling a Medal of Honor. . . . It's the most un-American thing I've ever scene in my whole life.

Actor John Wayne complaining about the ending of the movie High Noon, *which was written by blacklisted screenwriter Carl Foreman in 1952, in Stephen J. Whitfield,* The Culture of the Cold War *(1996), pp. 148–49.*

I'll never regret having helped run Foreman out of this country.

Actor John Wayne commenting in 1971 on his role in the blacklisting of screenwriter Carl Foreman in 1952, in Stephen J. Whitfield, The Culture of the Cold War *(1996), p. 149.*

The lie is the specific evil which man has introduced into nature. All our deeds of violence and our misdeeds are only as it were a highly-bred development of what this and that creature of nature is able to achieve in its own way. But the lie is our very own invention, different in kind from every deceit that the animals can produce. A lie was possible only after a creature, man, was capable of conceiving the being of truth. It was possible only as directed against the conceived truth. In a lie the spirit practices treason against itself.

It has been asked why there is no prohibition against lying in the Decalogue [the Ten Commandments]. It is prohibited; but it appears only as a prohibition of the lying witness. For the Decalogue is concerned with the establishment and securing of the inner bonds of a community, and therefore every injustice is considered from its social aspect. . . .

This is a Psalm [Psalm 12] in which this feeling is at once heightened and differentiated. The speaker no longer suffers merely from liars, but from a generation of the lie, and the lie in this generation has reached the highest level of perfection as an ingeniously controlled means of supremacy.

The two basic qualities, on which men's common life rests, well-wishing or the good will—that is, the readiness to fulfill for the other what he may expect of me in our relationship with one another—and loyalty or reliability . . . have gone. They have disappeared so completely that the basis of men's common life has been removed. The lie has taken the place, as of form of life, of human truth, that is, of the undivided seriousness of the human person with himself and all his manifestations.

. . . [T]his element of the lie now dominates human intercourse.

> *Philosopher Martin Buber writing about the biblical Psalm 12 in Buber,* Good and Evil *(1952), pp. 7–9.*

I am just as fond of General Eisenhower as I can be. I think he is one of the great men produced by World War II. . . . I don't want to stand in his way at all, because I think very highly of him, and if he wants to get out and have all the mud and rotten eggs thrown at him, that's his business.

> *President Harry Truman's remarks on January 10, 1952, at a press conference following General Dwight Eisenhower's announcement that he would accept the Republican presidential nomination, in David McCullough,* Truman *(1992), p. 889.*

Adlai, if a knucklehead like me can be President and not do too badly, think what a really educated smart guy like you could do in the job.

> *President Harry Truman, in a private White House meeting on January 22, 1952, with Illinois governor Adlai Stevenson, in David McCullough,* Truman *(1992), p. 891.*

On the evening of January 28, 1952, the General Headquarters of the [Chinese] Volunteers informed us in a circular that the enemy's aircraft [had dropped flies and insects]. . . . The circular asked us to pay close attention and to organize sanitary departments to conduct tests and, at the same time, mobilize troops to eliminate these insects.

On January 29, the enemy airplanes came to drop another batch of flies and fleas over Inchon. On February 11, four enemy airplanes flew over our headquarters. A milky mucus was dropped on the sleeve of my uniform. Subsequently, a report arrived from Sokbyonri: batches of flies and milky mucus stuck on paper packs and sheets and graphic cards had been found in Songnydong and villages in the surrounding area. Our troops also made reports of a similar discovery.

Medical officers tests showed that those insects were carrying cholera germs and other types of germs. This was indeed very critical information. We at once reported to the General Headquarters and simultaneously asked the sanitary department to apply emergency measures.

The General Headquarters told us that they had also found insects such as fleas, flies, mosquitos, crickets, spiders, and sand flies, all dropped by enemy aircraft in the areas of Cholwon, Pyongyang, and Soknyong. Laboratory tests identified more than ten types of insect-borne germs and viruses which might cause diseases such as plague, cholera, typhoid, dysentery, meningitis, encephalitis, and so on. The General Headquarters asked us to start preventive work and extinguish the insects simultaneously. . . .

The American imperialists had launched against us a special warfare—bacteriological warfare! We encountered many obstacles at the early stage of dealing with germ warfare. The main problem was that we lacked mental as well as material preparations, nor did we have any experience [with handling biological warfare].

> *Chinese general Yang Dezhi describing reports of U.S. biological warfare made in late January 1952, in Yang, Yang Dezhi Huiyilu (1993), pp. 606–11.*

Contrary to what everyone believes, when you're on television you're not playing to tens of millions of people. Your audience is really small groups: families sitting around in their living rooms, or play rooms or people in beds in hospitals. Maybe it's not a group at all. Your audience may be just one lonely person.

So you see, television is not one huge audience. It is a huge number of small audiences. These are people you are playing to, personally. You are alone with them in their homes. When you are entertaining them, you are their guest. It's a very personal kind of thing, and it's that personal sort of entertainment that you gave us this evening. If you can produce this kind of show on television you'll be holding lightning in a bottle. . . .

> *Pianist Guy Liberace recalling in 1973 the advice that station manager Don Fedderson gave him shortly before the debut of* The Liberace Show *on February 3, 1952, in Darden Asbury Pyron,* Liberace: An American Boy *(2000), p. 143.*

The audience was not the sophisticated, intellectual element that had a kind of snobbish attitude about all popular entertainment anyway, and so had nothing but sneers for TV. It was the solid backbone of America. The ones who did the work, kept things going and were ready to be friendly to anyone who was friendly to them.

> *Pianist Guy Liberace recalling in 1973 his own thoughts about the audience shortly before the debut of* The Liberace Show *on February 3, 1952, in Darden Asbury Pyron,* Liberace: An American Boy *(2000), pp. 143–44.*

Guy Liberace sought to project elegance and style by always performing in elaborate costumes, with a candelabra atop his piano. *(Photofest)*

Soft lights, sweet strings, brother George—smiling and silent, and plenty of closeups of Liberace and his candelabra.

An early newspaper review of The Liberace Show, *which premiered on February 3, 1952, in Darden Asbury Pyron,* Liberace: An American Boy *(2000), p. 140.*

[*Your Show of Shows*] was a continuing success. I was awarded my first Emmy on February 18, 1952—the day my son, Rick, was born—and the awards came in clusters after that. . . . Since Max Liebman and I believed that writing was the key to everything else, our writers got the highest pay in the industry. Max added Neil Simon (we all called him "Doc") and his talented brother, Danny Simon.

My attorney . . . kept negotiating salary increases for me. I ended up earning . . . just less than a million dollars annually. Those figures were unheard of in show business those days. I don't think even Clark Gable made that much. . . .

Sid Caesar recalling his first Emmy Award on February 18, 1952, in Caesar, Where Have I Been? *(1982), pp. 128–29.*

The President has the power to keep the country from going to hell.

President Harry Truman discussing with his staff his decision on April 6, 1952, to seize the steel mills, in David McCullough, Truman *(1992), p. 897.*

The plain fact of the matter is that the steel companies are recklessly forcing a shutdown. They are trying to get special, preferred treatment. . . . And they are apparently willing to stop steel production to get it. As President of the United States it is my plain duty to keep this from happening. . . . At midnight the Government will take over the steel plants.

President Truman in a nationally broadcast address on April 8, 1952, in David McCullough, Truman *(1992), p. 898.*

Seventeen and a half years ago I was a twenty-four-year-old stage manager and bit actor, making $40 a week, when I worked. At that time nearly all of us felt menaced by two things: the depression and the ever growing power of Hitler. The streets were full of unemployed and shaken men. I was taken in by the Hard Times version of what might be called the Communists' advertising or recruiting technique. They claimed to have a cure for depressions and a cure for Nazism and Fascism.

I joined the Communist Party late in the summer of 1934. I got out a year and a half later.

I have no spy stories to tell, because I saw no spies. Nor did I understand, at that time, any opposition between American and Russian national interest. It was not even clear to me in 1936 that the American Communist Party was abjectly taking its orders from the Kremlin.

What I learned was the minimum that anyone must learn who puts his head into the noose of party "discipline." The Communists automatically violated the daily practices of democracy to which I was accustomed. They attempted to control thought and to suppress personal opinion. They tried to dictate personal conduct. They habitually distorted and disregarded and violated the truth. All this was crudely opposite to their claims of "democracy" and "the scientific approach."

To be a member of the Communist Party is to have a taste of the police state. It is a diluted taste but it is bitter and unforgettable. It is diluted because you can walk out.

I got out in the spring of 1936.

Director Elia Kazan defending his decision to testify before HUAC on April 10, 1952, in a paid advertisement in the April 12, 1952, edition of the New York Times, *in Eric Bentley, ed.,* Thirty Years of Treason *(1971), p. 483.*

I believe that the contemplated strike, if it came, with all its awful results, would be less injurious to the public than the injury which would flow from a timorous judicial recognition that there is some basis for this claim to unlimited and unrestrained Executive power.

Federal district judge David A. Pine's April 1952 ruling against President Truman's seizure of the steel mills, in David McCullough, Truman *(1992), p. 900.*

Nothing has happened for quite a long time as admirable as the new production at the Circle in the Square. . . . Tennessee Williams' *Summer and Smoke* opened there last evening in a sensitive, highly personal performance. . . . Geraldine Page's portrait of the lonely, panicky spinster of Glorious Hill, Mississippi, is truthful, perceptive and poignant. . . . Although *Summer and Smoke* was acted beautifully uptown four years ago, the Sheridan Square production is more intimate and penetrating.

Critic Brooks Atkinson's review in the New York Times *of Tennessee Williams's* Summer and Smoke, *which instituted the tradition of Off-Broadway theater when it opened on April 24, 1952, in Stuart W. Little,* Off-Broadway: The Prophetic Theater *(1972), p. 24.*

Dramatists who write with Broadway in mind have more and more abandoned the traditional forms of realistic drama in favor of plays that, whatever their ostensible subject, are full of jokes; plays intended for a star actor and fashioned to show their star in a variety of situations, at any cost in consistency and logic; and, of course, musical plays, which very often have the best plots these days because [they are]

based on old plays that were written when plots were in fashion.

Critic Henry Popkin bemoaning the state of theater in 1952, in Popkin, "Theatre Letter," Kenyon Review *(Summer 1952), p. 493.*

We were in New Orleans, and the president of the [minor] league was there. ["Windy"] McCall's pitching, [Jimmy] Piersall's in center field, I'm at shortstop. We used to leave our gloves in the field back in those days. And Piersall, before he'd go out to center field, he'd stop and talk to me and tell me how to play shortstop. . . .

So McCall's warming up and he turns around and sees Piersall talking to me. He tells Piersall, "Get your blankety blank out in center field where you belong."

And Piersall . . . tells him, "Blankety blank, yourself. . . ." Well, Piersall hadn't reached his glove yet. So McCall takes the ball and throws it at him, and Piersall ducks and the ball rolls all the way to the center field fence. The umpire, at second base, says, "Jimmy, go get the ball."

"Hell, no!" he says. "I didn't throw it. Let McCall go get it." . . .

Finally, Piersall picked up his glove and saunters out there. He gets to the ball and throws it to the guy on the scoreboard. So McCall throws another ball at him. And Piersall turns around and throws it to the guy on the scoreboard.

Guess who they threw out of the ball game for throwing the balls away?

About a half-hour later, maybe less, we saw Piersall up in the stands. They had the knot-hole gang back then, where they let kids in free and they all sit together. Jimmy's leading them in cheers: "We want Piersall."

Milt Bolling describing his experience playing baseball in summer 1952 in the minor leagues, in Larry Moffi, This Side of Cooperstown *(1996), p. 229.*

Today, a kindly President uses the seizure power to effect a wage increase and to keep the steel furnaces in production. Yet tomorrow another President might use the same power to prevent a wage increase, to curb trade unionists, to regiment labor as oppressively as industry thinks it has been regimented by this seizure.

Justice William O. Douglas in support of the Supreme Court's ruling of June 2, 1952, against the government's seizure of the steel mills, in David McCullough, Truman *(1992), p. 901.*

We cannot with faithfulness to our constitutional system hold that the Commander in Chief of the Armed Forces has the ultimate power as such to take possession of private property in order to keep labor disputes from stopping production. This is a job for the Nation's lawmakers, not for its military authorities.

Justice Hugo L. Black stating his opinion supporting the Supreme Court's June 2, 1952, ruling against the government's seizure of the steel mills, in David McCullough, Truman *(1992), p. 901.*

The real pressure is a continuous day-by-day affair which has the effect of rewarding mediocrity, cowardice and sycophancy, and silencing independent and creative talent. . . .

Let me give one example which came my way. An American citizen who worked closely with the [Roosevelt] Administration during the war was recently asked to deliver a four weeks' course of lectures for a thousand dollars to an institute of higher learning. . . . He received a fourteen-page questionnaire which, he was informed, must be completed in every detail before he could be allowed to give the lectures. There were about 800 questions. They included medical inquiries . . . about whether he had "ever had terrifying nightmares" or was addicted to bed-wetting!

British visitor to the United States Kingsley Martin commenting in 1954 about the effects of the Red Scare on American life and culture, in Martin, "The American Witch-Hunt," New Statesman and Nation *(July 5, 1952), pp. 5–6.*

[The Republican Party deplores the] immoral policy of 'containment' which abandons countless human beings to a despotism and godless terrorism.

From the Republican Party platform at the presidential nominating convention that began July 7, 1952, in Edward H. Judge and John W. Langdon, A Hard and Bitter Peace *(1996), p. 112.*

The story is that Marilyn Monroe is being groomed by Twentieth Century-Fox for razzle-dazzle stardom on the assumption, we are told, that she is the hottest number to hit Hollywood in years. There may be some grounds for that assumption, but if they also expect her to act, they're going to have to give her a lot of lessons under an able and patient coach. At least, that's one man's opinion after seeing *Don't Bother to Knock.*

Critic Bosley Crowther reviewing the movie Don't Bother to Knock, *in Crowther, "Don't Bother to Knock,"* New York Times, *July 19, 1952, p. 8.*

But, our Republican friends say it [20 years of Democratic administrations] was all a miserable failure. For almost a week pompous phrases marched over this landscape in search of an idea, and the only idea they found was that the two great decades of progress in peace, victory in war, and bold leadership in this anxious hour were the misbegotten spawn of socialism, bungling, corruption, mismanagement, waste and worse. They captured, tied and dragged that ragged idea in here and furiously beat it to death.

After listening to this everlasting procession of epithets about our misdeeds I was even surprised the next morning when the mail was delivered on time! I guess our Republican friends were out of patience, out of sorts and, need I add, out of office.

From Adlai E. Stevenson's welcoming address to the Democratic Party nominating convention on July 21, 1952, in Stevenson, Major Campaign Speeches of Adlai E. Stevenson, 1952 *(1953), p. 4.*

[Adlai] Stevenson met Alger Hiss in 1933, in Washington when they were both employed by the Government. He also had contacts with Hiss during Hiss' service with the United Nations. . . . During the Hiss trial a deposition by Stevenson on behalf of Hiss' good character was read into the record by the Defense Counsel. . . .

IV. Association with Front Groups

Stevenson has allowed his name to be used as a sponsor by some groups which have been Communist controlled or infiltrated. They include a move to furnish economic aid to civilians of Loyalist Spain, 1938. . . . In 1944, his name was discussed as a possible chairman of the Chicago Council of American Soviet Friendship, as a "progressive-thinking fellow." . . .

In the April 1952, issue of *Harper's Magazine* Bernard DeVoto in a laudatory article . . . [stated] the "independent voter sees in him just such a younger spokesman of liberal democracy as a compelling need demands."

Alleged Sexual Perversion

In April, 1952, the New York Office received confidential information from a detective of the New York

District Attorney's office to the effect that Adlai Stevenson and David B. Owen, President, Bradley University, Peoria, Illinois, were two officials in Illinois who caused a great deal of trouble to law enforcement officers.

The detective had gone to Peoria to bring back basketball players who had been indicted in New York. The basketball players told the detective that the two best-known homo-sexuals in Illinois were Owen and Stevenson. According to the report, Stevenson was known as "Adeline."

From an informal, internal memorandum, dated July 24, 1952, written by FBI supervisor Milton Jones to FBI assistant director Louis Nichols, summarizing the FBI files on Democratic presidential nominee Adlai Stevenson, in Anthony Theoharis, ed., From the Secret Files of J. Edgar Hoover (1993), p. 285.

Too small for their jobs, too big for their breeches and too long in power.

Dwight Eisenhower's description of the Democrats in power, made in a stump speech he gave during his whistlestop train campaign that began shortly after Labor Day 1952, in Geoffrey Perret, Eisenhower (1999), p. 412.

Adlai [Stevenson is] the appeaser . . . who got his Ph.D. from Dean Acheson's College of Cowardly Communist Containment.

Republican vice presidential candidate Richard Nixon during the campaign in fall 1952, in Lois Gordon and Alan Gordon, American Chronicle (1999), p. 495.

I find myself constantly blackmailed by the virtual certainty that we shall have a first-class fascist party in the United States if the Republicans don't win. The real need for a change in this country arises, not from the decay of the Democrats, but from the need to give the Republicans the sobering experience of responsibility.

Columnist Joseph Alsop in a letter to Isaiah Berlin in fall 1952, in Porter McKeever, Adlai Stevenson: His Life and Legacy (1989), p. 235.

If one had read and understood [Herman] Melville one would not vote for [the left-wing Progressive Party's 1948 presidential candidate] Henry Wallace. I still believe this to be true . . because Melville presents his reader with a vision of life so complexly true that it exposes the ideas of Henry Wallace as hopeless-

ly childish and superficial. Literature tells us that life is diverse, paradoxical, and complicated, a fateful medley of lights and darks. . . . It warns us that the tendency of modern liberal politics has been to bleed political ideas white, to deny them their roots in natural reality, to deny them their extension over the possible range of human experience.

Literary critic Richard Chase critiquing liberal idealism, in Chase, "A Novel Is a Novel," Kenyon Review (Autumn 1952), in Thomas Hill Schaub, American Fiction in the Cold War (1991), p. 23.

Before the affair of the call girls passes into history, I want to say a few words about it. Prosecutions of this kind [prostitution] are supposed to reflect the upsurge of an outraged morality, and it is the moral side that interests me.

I want to deal first with the morality of the newspapers. They went to town on the story, complete with pictures. No editor in town seems to have asked himself whether it was fair to shame a lot of girls in this way. . . .

The truth everybody knows but nobody admits. The newspapers expose this kind of wickedness for the same reason that Minsky's used to expose Gypsy Rose Lee. The public gets a big kick out of it. This is synthetic sin.

Social commentator I. F. Stone in his newspaper column of September 7, 1952, "The Crusade against the Call Girls," in Stone, The Truman Era (1953), pp. 173–74.

I have had to spend the entire day with that slimy skunk. If he'd grabbed my arm one more time I would have hauled off and slugged him.

Dwight Eisenhower's reaction to campaigning on September 9, 1952, for the reelection of right-wing Indiana senator William Jenner, who had earlier gained notoriety by calling Eisenhower's mentor, former secretary of state George Marshall, a "front man for traitors," in Geoffrey Perret, Eisenhower (1999), p. 413.

It looks like Taft lost the nomination but won the nominee.

Adlai Stevenson commenting in mid-September 1952 on Eisenhower's acceptance of Taft's domestic policies in return for Taft's support of his presidential campaign, in Stevenson, Major Campaign Speeches of 1952 (1953), p. 126.

Democratic presidential candidate Adlai Stevenson could not compete with Eisenhower's national stature or the national mood for change after 20 years of Democratic rule. *(Photofest)*

All the eggheads are for Stevenson, but how many eggheads are there?

John Alsop in a telephone conversation in mid-September 1952 with his brother Stewart Alsop, a journalist who subsequently popularized egghead *as a derisive term for intellectuals in his syndicated column, in Eric F. Goldman,* The Crucial Decade—And After: America, 1945–1960 *(1960), p. 223.*

Eggheads of the world unite. You have nothing to lose but your yokes.

Adlai Stevenson 1952 presidential campaign, in Lois Gordon and Alan Gordon, American Chronicle *(1999), p. 502.*

So long as man remains a little lower than the angels, I suppose that human character will never free itself entirely from the blemish of prejudice, religious or racial. . . .

But I do not attempt to justify the unjustifiable, whether it is anti-Negroism in one place, anti-Semitism in another—or for that matter, anti-Southernism in many places. And neither can I justify self-righteousness anywhere. Let none of us be smug on this score, for nowhere in the nation have we come to that state of harmonious amity between racial and religious groups to which we aspire.

From Adlai Stevenson's campaign speech of September 20, 1952, in Richmond, Virginia, in Stevenson, Major Campaign Speeches of 1952 *(1953), p. 155.*

I come before you tonight as a candidate for the vice presidency and as a man whose honesty and integrity have been questioned. . . .

I am sure that you have read the charge and you've heard that I, Senator Nixon, took $18,000 from a group of my supporters. Now, was that wrong? . . .

I say that it was morally wrong if any of that $18,000 went to Senator Nixon for my personal use. I say that it was morally wrong if it was secretly given and secretly handled. And I say it was morally wrong if any of the contributors got special favors for the contributions that they made.

And now, to answer those questions, let me say this: Not one cent of the $18,000 or any other money of that type ever went to me for my personal use. Every penny of it was used to pay for political expenses that I did not think should be charged to the taxpayers of the United States. . . .

And so I felt the best way to handle these necessary political expenses of getting my message to the American people . . . of exposing this administration, the communism in it, the corruption in it . . . was to accept the aid which the people in my home state of California contributed to my campaign and who continued to make these contributions after I was elected were glad to make.

And let me say I am proud of the fact that not one of them has ever asked me for a special favor . . . [or] to vote on a bill other than my own conscience would dictate. . . .

I was born in 1913. Our family was one of modest circumstances, and most of my early life was spent in a store out in East Whittier [California]. . . .

I worked my way through college and to a great extent through law school. . . . I married Pat, who is sitting over there. We had a rather difficult time after we were married, like so many of the young couples who may be listening to us. . . .

Let me say that my service record was not a particularly unusual one. I went to the South Pacific. I guess I'm entitled to a couple of battle stars. I got a couple of letters of commendation . . . then I returned. . . .

Well, that's where we started when I got into politics. Now, what I've earned since I went into politics? Well, here it is. . . . [Nixon gives a detailed accounting of his assets and debits.]

Well, that's about it. That's what we have and that's what we owe. It isn't very much, but Pat and I have the satisfaction that every dime that we've got is honestly ours. I should say this: that Pat doesn't have a mink coat, but she does have a respectable Republican cloth coat. And I always tell her that she'd look good in anything.

One other thing I should probably tell you, because if we don't they'll probably be saying this about me too. . . . A man down in Texas heard Pat on the radio mention the fact that our two youngsters would like to have a dog. And believe it or not, the day before we left on this campaign trip we got a message . . saying they had a package for us. . . . It was a little cocker spaniel dog in a crate that he'd sent all the way from Texas. Black and white spotted. And our little girl—Tricia, the six-year-old—named it Checkers. And you know, the kids, like all kids, love the dog, and I just want to say this right now that regardless of what they say about it, we're gonna keep it. . . .

And now, finally, I know that you wonder whether or not I am going to stay on the Republican ticket or resign. Let me say this: I don't believe that I ought to quit, because I'm not a quitter. . . .

Regardless of what happens I'm going to continue this fight. I'm going to campaign up and down America until we drive the crooks and the communists and those that defend them out of Washington. And remember, folks, Eisenhower is a great man. . . . And a vote for Eisenhower is a vote for what's good for America.

Republican vice presidential candidate Richard Nixon delivering his so-called Checkers speech defending charges of abuse of campaign contributions on September 23, 1952, in Nixon, "The 'Fund Crisis' Speech" (2001).

The General [Eisenhower] condemns the Secretary of State's excluding Korea from our defense perimeter in 1950. But the General fails to point out that this defense perimeter was a line developed by the military authorities themselves. Twice in 1949 General MacArthur, then our top commander in Pacific, defined our defense perimeter in the terms later used by the Secretary of State.

From Adlai Stevenson's campaign speech of September 27, 1952, in Louisville, Kentucky, in Stevenson, Major Campaign Speeches of 1952 (1953), p. 184.

Sixty thousand Europeans cannot expect to hold all the political power and to exclude Africans from the legislature and from the Government. The end of that will be to build up pressures which will burst into rebellion and bloodshed.

You are suspicious and critical of what you term in a pejorative sense 'Colonial Office rule'. When, as the result of over-conservative or traditional policies you provoke an explosion, you are not slow to ask the British Government and the Colonial Office, which at other times you attack, for troops, aeroplanes and money to suppress a rebellion.

I warn you that one day you will be let down, and therefore besides force, which must now be used and which we will furnish, you must turn your minds to political reform, and to measures which will gradually engage the consent and help of the governed.

The security of your homes, the security of the money, hard work and skill which you have lavished upon your farms, and upon the industries which you have begun to build, cannot rest upon battalions of British troops: it can only rest upon the building of a multi-racial society.

Colonial secretary Oliver Lyttelton in an address to white settlers during the Mau Mau rebellion in Kenya, which began in early October 1952, in Martin Gilbert, A History of the Twentieth Century, vol. 3 (2000), p. 19.

The Bedford-Stuyvesant area is the Harlem of Brooklyn. Its schools are dilapidated. . . .

Mrs. Mildred Flacks proved one of the few [teachers who stayed]. She went to Public School 35 as a substitute in 1931 . . . and has been there ever since. . . .

[According to one witness, Mrs. Flacks] "had to deal with many problem children . . . but though they were problem children when they came to her they weren't when they left. . . . She loved every one of her children."

Why is a teacher with a reputation of this kind on trial? Mrs. Flacks is the first of eight teachers put on trial for refusing to answer questions about their political beliefs. . . . The *World-Telegram and Sun* says parents have a right to be protected against teachers "whose continuing Communist allegiance permits them to find subtle ways of injecting Communist-influenced ideology even into classrooms."

Are the writers prepared honestly to look at the facts in these cases? . . . [Mrs. Flacks] has always taught first and second grade. Are there hysterics so idiotic they believe she managed to inject Marxism-Leninism into minds grappling with alphabet blocks and how-to-do-sums-without-fingers?

Social commentator I. F. Stone in his newspaper column of October 3, 1952, "The Schools Besieged," in Stone, The Truman Era *(1953), pp. 201–2.*

FRANKIE THROWS AVA OUT

Headline in the New York Post, *October 21, 1952, announcing the marital rift between Frank Sinatra and Ava Gardner, in Earl Wilson,* Sinatra *(1976), p. 100.*

FRANKIE, AVA KISS AND MAKE UP

Newspaper headline following the reconciliation of Frank Sinatra and his wife, Ava Gardner, at a public rally for presidential candidate Adlai Stevenson on October 28, 1952, in Earl Wilson, Sinatra *(1976), p. 100.*

Jazz saxophonist Stan Getz was one of several pioneers of modern jazz who suffered from abuse of narcotics and other substances. *(Photofest)*

A jazz concert was presented at Carnegie Hall last evening . . featuring Duke Ellington and his Orchestra; Stan Getz, tenor saxophonist; Ahmad Jamal and his Three Strings; Dizzie Gillespie, trumpeter; Charlie Parker, alto saxophonist; and Billie Holiday, vocalist.

As usual on such occasions there was a great deal of music, some of it very fine and some of it routine. The playing of Mr. Getz and his ensemble, in particular, soon became tiresome, being the same thing over and over in the thinnest of disguises.

Mr. Jamal's trio was more rewarding. . . . Their playing was very easy and spontaneous.

As usual, also, it was Mr. Ellington's band that made the most lasting impression. The band's playing, despite its fame and long experience, retains a fresh, improvisational quality. . . . Especially impressive is the ease with which the ensemble handles tricky syncopations and the cross-rhythms of two-against-three and three-against-four.

Review of a Carnegie Hall jazz concert, in "Specialists in Jazz Team for Concert," New York Times, *November 15, 1952, p. 14.*

The generation which went through the last war . . . seems to possess a uniform, general quality which demands an adjective. It was John [sic] Kerouac . . . who finally came up with it. . . . One day he said, "You know, this is really a *beat* generation."

Clellon Holmes first introducing the term beat generation *in Holmes, "This Is the Beat Generation,"* New York Times Magazine *(November 16, 1952), p. 10.*

5

New Leadership in Washington and Moscow
1953

The world's political situation changed greatly between 1950 and 1953. By the beginning of March 1953, the leaders who had presided over the two superpowers since the end of World War II had been replaced, and in July, the Korean War concluded—and with it the state of national emergency that had prevailed since the middle of 1950. By the end of the year, America's monopoly on the hydrogen bomb had ended, and the nuclear stalemate that would characterize most of the cold war had begun.

The conclusion of the Korean War allowed many Americans to get their lives back on track, as wartime restrictions on consumer goods were lifted, the television industry expanded and introduced new technologies, and the economy generally stabilized. Rock 'n' roll began to find a wider audience, although its exuberant spirit, well suited to postwar euphoria, did not exert a strong national presence until 1954. But a frenetic, more consciously antiestablishment sensibility was already finding voice in the literary and social Beat movement whose adherents opposed the constraints of excessively cerebral formalism in literature and denounced the "spirit-killing," middle-class conformity in society.

THE COLD WAR AND INTERNATIONAL POLITICS

The Cold War Abroad

THE KOREAN WAR

Eisenhower had pledged during the 1952 presidential campaign to go to Korea, and he did so in December, meeting with troops, reviewing battlefields, receiving briefings, and meeting with allied leaders. After his inauguration in January 1953, he pressured China by threatening to use nuclear weapons against it and by removing the U.S. Seventh Fleet from the Formosa Straits—thereby eliminating the buffer that prevented Chinese Nationalists on Taiwan from attacking the mainland. Eisenhower also pressured South Korea's president, Dr. Syngman Rhee, to soften his stance against North Korea in the hope of reaching an accommodation; however, Rhee continued to oppose a cease-fire, and when the armistice was finalized on July 27, South Korea boycotted

the signing ceremony. Rhee nonetheless agreed to observe the cease-fire for a limited time, and he was further mollified when the United States and South Korea signed a mutual defense pact in August.

Many historians discount the effectiveness of Eisenhower's actions and maintain that the death of Joseph Stalin in early March had the greatest impact in breaking the longstanding deadlock in the peace negotiations. The U.S. entanglement in the Korean stalemate served Soviet interests, if not necessarily those of North Korea and China, and during his reign Stalin exercised considerable power over the other communist regimes. His demise, therefore, gave North Korean and Chinese negotiators new flexibility to strike a deal. On July 27, after resolving the contentious issue of repatriating POWs, the warring parties signed an armistice at Panmunjom, on the North Korean side of the 38th parallel. The cease-fire concluded the fighting but did not establish a political solution, or even an agreement to permanently end hostilities. The settlement allowed communist prisoners who did not want to be repatriated to be released to neutral countries, and it called for a conference on the reunification of Korea to begin in 90 days. But those talks yielded no results. As at the outset of the hostilities, the 38th parallel, now designated as a demilitarized zone, continued to serve as the boundary line between the two Koreas, and the country remains so divided as of this writing. The fighting, which continued until the 10 P.M. deadline, took the lives of some 2 to 4 million civilians and soldiers, including more than 33,000 U.S. men and women.

OTHER INTERNATIONAL COLD WAR DEVELOPMENTS

The two dominant cold war developments in 1953 took place in the Soviet Union. Stalin died on March 5 from a cerebral hemorrhage, and the USSR

President Eisenhower meets with the country's top military leaders. *In the front row, from left to right:* Air Secretary Harold E. Talbott, Deputy Defense Secretary Roger M. Kyes, Eisenhower, Defense Secretary Charles E. Wilson, Navy Secretary Robert B. Anderson, and Army Secretary Robert T. Stevens *(Photofest)* announced on August 14 that it had exploded its first hydrogen bomb. Earlier, the United States had successfully tested an atomic cannon, a tactical nuclear weapon with a seven-mile range, perfected another device for delivering an atomic bomb overseas, and exploded the largest atomic bomb to date, twice as powerful as the one that destroyed Hiroshima.

Stalin's death created, for the first time since he assumed full power in 1925, an opening for substantial change in Soviet domestic and cold war policy. Georgi Malenkov, Stalin's second in command, briefly emerged as both premier of the Soviet Union and secretary of the Communist Party, but within two weeks Nikita Khrushchev replaced him in the latter post, a weighty appointment that was made permanent in September. In June, Malenkov and Khrushchev succeeded in ousting one of their most powerful rivals, Lavrenti Beria, the greatly feared head of internal security and the secret police. For the next two years, the nation was governed jointly by the two men, until Khrushchev emerged as the undisputed leader in 1955.

Compared with Stalin, both men were moderates, and they inaugurated softer domestic and foreign policies. To better attend to the country's failing economy, Malenkov and Khrushchev resolved some Soviet international conflicts by abandoning claims to territory in northeast Turkey and improving relationships with Iran, Greece, Israel, and Yugoslavia. Moreover, they backed off from communist ideology that insisted war between the communists and capitalists was inevitable. Domestically, they diminished Stalin's push to increase the Soviet Union's industrial capacity at all costs. They increased production of consumer goods, otherwise improved the standard of living, and granted a general amnesty to all short-term prisoners in Soviet jails. Only prisoners serving terms for counterrevolutionary crimes, thievery, and premeditated murder remained in custody.

Stalin's death also probably spared millions of Soviet Jews, as charges in January of subversion against a group of Jewish doctors were widely regarded as the prelude to and justification for massive purges of both Jews and the Soviet leadership. (Ironically, while their detractors in the United States had long accused Jews of involvement in an international communist conspiracy, Soviet anti-Semites, such as Beria, accused them of participating in subversive, procapitalist conspiracies, such as the American Jewish Joint Distribution Committee.) The charges in the so-called Doctors' Plot were dropped after Stalin's death, and the doctors were later publicly exonerated. According to historian Martin Gilbert, "those present had no doubt that a trial of the Jewish doctors would be used as a general accusation against all the Jews of the Soviet Union—more than two million—and that mass deportations to Siberia, where new camps were already believed to have been prepared, and even some sort of bloodbath, might well follow."[1]

The death of Stalin at first heightened tensions between the East and West and then spurred unrest within several of the communist nations in Eastern Europe. In early March, Denmark seized a Russian-built Polish military jet that had landed on the Baltic island of Bornholm; in return, Poland detained seven Danish fishing boats that had sought shelter from a storm in Polish waters. Less than a week later, a Czech jet shot down a U.S. fighter plane flying over East Germany, en route to Berlin. The American pilot safely bailed out, but two days after that, on March 12, Soviet jets downed a British bomber also flying into Berlin, killing six of the seven crew members.

The international tensions created by these incidents subsided after a few months, as the regimes in the Soviet satellite nations faced new internal challenges. In Poland, where in February the government had assumed the right to make and terminate all appointments within the Catholic Church and to obtain loyalty oaths from the clergy, the editor of the Catholic newspaper was fired by the government for refusing to eulogize Stalin. Prior to Stalin's death, Czechoslovakia's president and founder of the Slovak Communist Party, Klement Gottwald, denounced independent farmers who resisted collectivization as "kulaks" (excessively wealthy farmers), taxed them, and withheld their food rations and clothing coupons. But Gottwald contracted pneumonia while attending Stalin's funeral and died five days later. The resulting power vacuum emboldened factory workers to strike against food and housing shortages, and demonstrators rioted in Plzeň, where busts of Lenin and Stalin were destroyed and portraits of anticommunist leaders who had become "nonpersons" were prominently displayed. The government dispersed the rioters with tanks and imprisoned many of the demonstrators. In subsequent months, charges of forced labor in Poland and Czechoslovakia were levied. Professor Marek Korowicz, a leading delegate to the United Nations who defected in October, maintained that there were at least 73 forced-labor camps in Poland and about 300,000 conscripts, about 30 percent of whom were women.[2] On May 28, a Czech law required all citizens to donate 12 days per year of unpaid service to the state.

Great disruption leading to the largest uprising in Eastern Europe took place in East Germany. Within three months after Stalin's death, more than 180,000 East Germans escaped the communist regime by crossing into West Berlin, where they received political asylum. Altogether, some 305,000 East Germans migrated to West Germany in 1953, approximately 1.7 percent of the population.[3] (The Berlin Wall was not built until 1961, when it was erected to stem a similar exodus of asylum seekers.) In May, the East German government reduced food rations for nonworkers and imposed an increased workload on laborers. In response, on June 17, workers in East Berlin went on strike and organized street protests. When East German police sympathetic to the demonstrators refused to disperse them, Soviet tanks and troops were called in. Riots broke out in which protestors torched Communist Party buildings and tore down the Red Flag hanging over the Brandenburg Gate separating East and West Berlin. The Soviet commanders in Berlin declared a state of emergency and instituted summary courts in which several hundred demonstrators were swiftly charged, tried, and executed. The action succeeded in suppressing the Berlin uprising.

Despite, or because of, the political instabilities following Stalin's death, in December Eisenhower appeared before the United Nations General Assembly to present his "Atoms for Peace Plan." Under the plan, both the United States and the Soviet Union would donate fissionable material to an International Atomic Energy Agency of the United Nations for agricultural, medical, and other peaceful uses throughout the world. Eisenhower hoped that, in addition to developing constructive uses for nuclear energy and improving living conditions throughout the world, the plan would establish a precedent of cooperation between the superpowers that might later broaden into an avenue for slowing or reversing their nuclear arms race. He also wanted to encourage other countries to recognize the potential benefits to them of nuclear energy and to show Americans that "they had not poured their substance into nuclear development with the sole purpose of using it for world destruction."[4] Consequently, although the Soviet Union did not endorse the plan, and the proposal did not manifest as envisioned, the United States gained some public relations benefits from making the offer, and it did eventually offer limited amounts of nuclear material to some allies for peaceful purposes.

Other International Developments

In an event that proved to have long-term implications for the United States, lawyer Fidel Castro began his revolution against Cuba's dictator, Fulgencio Batista, by leading a summer attack against a military barracks in Santiago de Cuba, the capital of the island's eastern province of Oriente. The raid failed, and Castro was captured and sentenced to 15 years in prison. He was released two years later and granted exile in Mexico, where he planned his successful revolution of 1959.

Other regions of Latin America also suffered from political instability in 1953. A military coup deposed Colombia's dictator, Laureano Gómez, and established General Gustavo Rojas Pinilla as the new president. The revolutionary regime that seized power in Bolivia in 1952 consolidated its power after suppressing two attempts to overthrow it. Despite its failure to compensate U.S. stockholders for the tin mines it nationalized, the Bolivian government continued to receive technical and financial assistance from the United States. Argentina's president, Juan Perón, signed economic agreements with the leaders of Chile, Paraguay, and Ecuador in order to counterbalance the enormous influence of what he called "dollar imperialism." But by the end of year, Perón sought and received technical and financial assistance from the United States to increase Argentina's industrial and oil capacity. On the other hand, the reform government of Guatemala's Jacobo Arbenz Guzmán antagonized the United States by openly seeking aid from communist nations and expropriating some 234,000 acres of uncultivated land from the American-owned United Fruit Company. These acts provoked the CIA-backed coup that deposed Arbenz in 1954 and replaced his government with a military regime friendlier to U.S. interests.

In Europe, a crisis erupted in late summer and fall when Italy and Yugoslavia confronted each other over the status of the free city of Trieste, which was under an allied military government. When Italy threatened to claim the city, Yugoslavia's Marshal Tito demanded that Trieste be internationalized and its hinterland absorbed into Yugoslavia. He further rejected an Italian plan for an election to decide the outcome of the entire area. In November, British and American troops quelled riots in which thousands of protestors tried to raise the Italian flag over the city's town hall. The situation was finally resolved when it was decided that Trieste would remain under allied military rule.

After fleeing to Baghdad, Iraq, following an unsuccessful attempt to remove Iran's anti-Western prime minister, Mossadegh, Shah Reza Pahlevi returned to power when troops loyal to him overthrew Mossadegh. The shah, who was assisted by the CIA, immediately outlawed Iran's communist party and implemented policies sympathetic to the West. General Naguib of Egypt, who had seized power the year before, dissolved all opposition parties, abolished the monarchy that had ruled the country since 1805, and proclaimed Egypt a republic, with himself as president and premier. Colonel Gamal Abdel Nasser, who had organized the 1952 coup that brought Naguib to power, was named deputy premier and minister of the interior, with control over the police. Tunisia's crown prince was assassinated in July, and French authorities temporarily assumed control of police operations. Civilian control was restored in October following pressure from Tunisian nationalists. The sultan of Morocco was overthrown in August and replaced by a regime that also sought greater autonomy from France.

At the other end of the continent, the South African parliament continued to tighten laws enforcing the apartheid that relegated nonwhites to second-class status. Calling for violent resistence against apartheid and other repressive government actions, lawyer Nelson Mandela emerged in 1953 as a vocal leader of the African National Congress.

The Islamic Republic of Pakistan, which was instituted on November 2, made Islamic principles the basis for government and law. In North Vietnam, French paratroopers captured the village of Dien Bien Phu, thereby setting the stage for the devastating defeat that drove the French from the region in 1954.

The Cold War at Home

In June, Julius and Ethel Rosenberg were executed for having given secrets about the atomic bomb to the Soviet Union during World War II. Their deaths stirred the passions of Americans on both the Right and Left. Many cheered the execution of the convicted spies who, according to Irving Kaufman, the judge who presided over their trial in 1951, had enabled the Soviet Union to acquire an atomic bomb prematurely and thereby sponsor the Korean War. Others protested either the Rosenbergs' innocence or the severity of the sentence. Some maintained that the couple were victims of anti-Semitism. Before leaving office in January, Truman declined to hear their appeal for a stay of execution, and after assuming office, Eisenhower turned down the request, despite mass rallies on the Rosenbergs' behalf and appeals from international figures as diverse as Albert Einstein and Pope Pius XII. This was the first time U.S. civilians had ever received the death penalty for espionage.

The government announced in October that during the previous four months, 1,456 people had been removed from federal jobs for security reasons. Later in the year, the Atomic Energy Commission withdrew the security clearance of J. Robert Oppenheimer, the "father of the atomic bomb." Oppenheimer, who had overseen the Manhattan Project that developed the A-bomb in 1945, was accused of having communist associations that he had concealed. He was also accused of deliberately obstructing development of the hydrogen bomb, which he had opposed on scientific grounds. Oppenheimer's case later became the subject for a popular play by German playwright Heinar Kipphardt, *In the Matter of J. Robert Oppenheimer* (1964). It is one of history's ironies that both Oppenheimer and Andrei Sakharov, who headed the Soviet program to develop the hydrogen bomb, were eventually cast out by the governments they had served.

Once out of office, Truman was subpoenaed by the House Un-American Activities Committee, but he refused to testify, citing the separation of powers doctrine within the Constitution. In return, Senator Harold H. Velde, the committee chairman, accused Truman and former secretary of state Acheson of fostering communism, and Senator McCarthy added that the Truman administration "crawled with Communists." Truman replied by warning of "the onslaught of fear and hysteria which are being manipulated in this country purely for political purposes."[5]

In April, McCarthy's top aides, Roy Cohn and David Schine, took a highly publicized 17-day, seven-country tour of the State Department's European libraries. Claiming the libraries contained some 30,000 books by "pro-communist" writers, they removed and in some cases burned books by about 40 authors. The works of 20 other authors who had not been forthright in Senate hearings were banned pending further examination. Among the authors whose works were removed were historical novelist and Communist Party member Howard Fast; African-American activist and writer W. E. B. DuBois, an outspoken advocate of communism as a means of eliminating economic disparities between the races; black poet and civil rights activist Langston Hughes; detective writer and Communist Party member Dashiell Hammett (author of *The Maltese Falcon* and *The Thin Man,* among others); Theodore White, whose *Thunder Out of China* (1946) argued against continued support of Chiang Kai-shek and the Chinese Nationalists; and French existentialist Jean-Paul Sartre, an avowed communist. Even earlier works by authors such as Herman Melville were taken off the shelves.[6] Eisenhower subsequently criticized "book-burners" but took no further action, and many public librarians within the United States were pressured to remove texts written by communists, accused communists, and communist sympathizers. In San Antonio, Texas, it was proposed that such books be branded with a red stamp.

Indifferent to Truman's criticism, HUAC continued its hearings into the communist influences in American society. Among the friendly witnesses who testified and named others who had been active in the Communist Party in the 1930s was former communist Daniel J. Boorstin, a noted historian who argued against the hiring of communists by universities. Others included literary and cultural critic Granville Hicks; choreographer Jerome Robbins, who later, in 1957, produced *West Side Story* in collaboration with Leonard Bernstein and Stephen Sondheim; and actor Lee J. Cobb, who in 1949 had starred in Elia Kazan's theatrical production of Arthur Miller's *Death of a Salesman.* Actor Lionel Stander appeared as an unfriendly witness in 1953, and Bishop G. Bromley Oxnam, a fervent anticommunist, testified at his own request to clear himself of charges by California congressman Donald L. Jackson that he "has been to the Communist front what Man o' War was to thoroughbred horse racing."[7]

Elsewhere, the Indiana State Textbook Committee charged that communists were promoting the story of Robin Hood, "because he robbed the rich and gave to the poor."[8] General Electric pledged to fire all communist workers, and the Screen Actors Guild adopted a by-law banning communists from membership.

GOVERNMENT AND SOCIETY

The conclusion of the war and the new presidential administration created a spirit of renewal within the country. Eisenhower was a popular figure, Stalin was dead, and the country could return to a peacetime economy. Moreover, it was the first year that worldwide per-capita food production reached pre–World War II levels, specifically that of 1939.[9] The swelling ranks of the baby boom generation also continued to remind Americans of new beginnings, even though the large numbers of children created several logistical problems. The government announced that some 30 million children would enter school in the fall, 10 million more than could easily be handled by existing facilities.

The U.S. government reported a budget deficit of $9.4 billion. Because the Korean War had been a "police action," this was officially the largest peacetime deficit in U.S. history. Congress passed new legislation transferring rights to offshore oil from the federal government to the individual states. It also created the Department of Health, Education and Welfare, whose secretary assumed a position in the cabinet. The Connecticut state senate once again debated a longstanding law forbidding the use of contraceptives, even for married couples. The law, which enjoyed the support of the state's large Catholic population, provided for a $50 fine and a prison sentence of not less than 60 days and not more than one year.

Tornadoes were especially destructive in 1953. On May 12, they struck Waco, Texas, killing 124 people; on June 8, another 139 in the Midwest were killed; and the following day 92 people in New England lost their lives to the storms.

Few new developments occurred in the arena of civil rights, although in a case filed against a Washington, D.C., restaurant, the Supreme Court ruled that dining establishments could not refuse service to black patrons. In September, Chief Justice Fred Vinson died, and arguments on *Brown v. Board of Education of Topeka* were delayed until after Eisenhower appointed California's governor, Earl Warren, as the new chief justice. The change was significant, because Vinson was believed to favor retaining the separate-but-equal doctrine, while Warren's views on school desegregation were unknown. The court heard the arguments in December but did not rule until May 1954.

BUSINESS

The conclusion of the Korean War ended the state of emergency, and the wage and price restrictions that controlled the economy during the first part of the decade were lifted, stirring economic prosperity. The GNP rose by 5 percent, inflation was just 0.6 percent, and the unemployment rate was a low 2.9 percent. The nation's gold reserves at Ft. Knox were audited and valued at $30,442,415,581.70. A postcard cost 2¢ to mail, and a Coronado refrigerator with nine cubic feet of space cost about $200.[10]

The burgeoning frozen-food industry allowed retailers to cater to suburban homemakers who were increasingly pressed for time. During the year, they sold a record 3.38 billion pounds of frozen food and grossed $1.2 billion, despite problems transporting the perishable goods that were especially popular among higher income groups. By 1953, some 64 percent of retail grocery stores were equipped with frozen-food cabinets.[11] Clarke and Gilbert

Swanson, who had introduced frozen pot pies to the national market in 1951, began selling complete frozen dinners in sealed aluminum trays in 1953. They called these meals TV dinners, because they could be easily consumed in front of the television set.

Publisher Walter Annenberg released the first issue of *TV Guide* in April, also with the intent of capitalizing on the burgeoning enthusiasm for television. The weekly publication, which listed daily television programming, brief descriptions of the episodes, and articles about television and TV celebrities, was an instant hit.

Another immediate success was *Playboy* magazine, which featured Marilyn Monroe, then a rising Hollywood star, as its first nude centerfold. By 1954, circulation reached 100,000, and by 1956, it reached 600,000. Its rising sales demonstrated the existence of a substantial market for an upscale sexually oriented magazine, despite condemnation by clergy, government leaders, and other leaders of the middle class, who viewed the publication as an assault on the fundamental Christian values that many Americans regard as the nation's bulwark against atheistic communism.[12]

Playboy projected an image of the modern, successful man as tasteful, knowledgeable, cultured and urbane; he was also frankly open about, accepting of, and confident in his sexuality. In addition, he was well accoutred with high-end consumer products. Publisher Hugh Hefner personally cultivated this image, as did the men depicted in advertisements and featured in the fiction, such as the suave, debonaire, fictional, super spy, Ian Fleming's James Bond, who first appeared in print in 1953 and whose stories were later published in the magazine. By publishing other fiction by top writers and articles by leading intellectuals, usually with a liberal political orientation, and by using glossy paper, *Playboy* distinguished itself from low-end "girlie" magazines and tabloids and marketed itself as a respectable publication that appealed to the intellect as well as the libido. Although later criticized as demeaning toward and exploitive of women, *Playboy*'s promotion of sexual and personal liberation extended to women, too. Its ideal young woman was upscale, self-assured, self-directed, and often college educated. She felt confident about herself sexually and expressed her own personal interests, goals, and aspirations.

Other new products from the year included tufted plastic carpeting, Sugar Smacks breakfast cereal, Schweppes bottled tonic water, and a burglar alarm operated by ultrasonic or radio waves.

Labor relations improved in the steel industry, where they had been contentious during the Truman industry. U.S. Steel, which in 1953 recorded its largest earnings since 1917, awarded its workers a pay increase of 8.5¢ per hour. But not all labor problems disappeared, and Eisenhower invoked the Taft-Hartley Act to stop a dock strike on the Atlantic coast. However, on December 1, longshoremen defied the injunction and struck, crippling ports along the coast. That strike lasted until April 2, 1954, when the longshoremen returned to work following an ultimatum by the National Labor Relations Board.

SCIENCE AND TECHNOLOGY

In the early 1950s, genetics was still a relatively new field, and the roles and functions of such genetic material as DNA were only beginning to be appreciated. A major advancement in human understanding of how DNA works occurred in April, when American James D. Watson and Englishman Francis H. C. Crick published an article in the scientific journal *Nature* demonstrating that the DNA molecule's structure was a double helix. This discovery, which Watson described in his popular book *The Double Helix* (1968), explained how the DNA molecule replicated itself and thus passed on genetic material and information. It proved to be a crucial development in the study of genetics that made possible the sophisticated genetic engineering that followed in subsequent decades. Although the general public did not immediately recognize the significance of the discovery, its magnitude became more fully appreciated in 1962, when the scientists won the Nobel Prize in physiology and medicine.

Dr. John Gibbon, Jr., performed the first open-heart surgery using a heart-lung machine, the first correlation between heart disease and a high-fat diet was demonstrated, and physicians Ernest Wynder and Evarts Graham showed that tobacco tars cause cancer in mice. In England, George Clemo demonstrated that urban air pollution contains a compound related to benzopyrene, a known carcinogen. The first tests of the vaccination against polio were begun for children, and scientists first identified and photographed the polio virus.

Pope Pius XII approved the use of psychoanalysis, calling it another tool for healing, but warned against committing sins that create a sense of guilt and against substituting psychoanalysis for religious practice. Meanwhile, Dr. Alfred C. Kinsey, whose *Sexual Behavior in the Human Male* (1948) revolutionized the way Americans regarded sexual practice, published his companion study, *Sexual Behavior in the Human Female*, which concluded that women's sex drive is less intense than men's and that women engage less frequently in forbidden sexual activity. After interviewing 5,940 American women, Kinsey and his staff revealed that 95 percent had petted before the age of 18, half of the married women born after 1900 had had sex before marriage (for many their only premarital partner was their future husband), and 69 percent of women who had had premarital sex did not regret it.[13] The report shocked many Americans who were appalled by the suggestion that women were much more sexually active than the public had commonly believed. The report eventually made a significant contribution to the growing recognition and acceptance of female sexual desire and conduct within society.

The same year, scientists from the University of Iowa achieved the first human pregnancies from artificial insemination using deep-frozen sperm. Dr. Virginia Apgar developed the Apgar score for evaluating the health of newborn babies.

University of Chicago archaeologists discovered a 10,000-year-old American Indian village at Prairie du Rocher, Illinois. Thirty-four-year-old New Zealand adventurer Edmund Hillary and his Nepalese Sherpa guide, Tenzing Norgay, were admired throughout the world after they became the first humans to reach the summit of Mount Everest, the world's highest mountain at more than 29,000 feet above sea level.

Jacqueline Cochran, a lieutenant colonel in the U.S. Air Force Reserves who had been decorated for her wartime service, became the first woman to exceed the sound barrier when she flew a Canadian-built F-86 Sabre jet fighter at more than 760 miles per hour. In December Charles Yeager set a new world speed record of 1,650 miles per hour in an experimental Bell X-1A rocket plane. (In 1947, Yeager became the first human to break the sound barrier.)

In subatomic physics, the atomic nucleus was demonstrated to be smaller than previously believed and twice as dense.

SPORTS, ENTERTAINMENT, AND THE ARTS

Sports

The enduring popularity of baseball was attested to by the introduction into the popular lingo of such expressions as "getting to first base" and "scoring a home run" to refer to sexual activity.[14] Boston's National League franchise, the Boston Braves, moved to Milwaukee before the baseball season began, becoming the first franchise to change location in the 20th century. The New York Yankees, guided by manager Casey Stengel, defeated the Brooklyn Dodgers in six games to win their record fifth straight World Series.

In football, the Detroit Lions defeated the Cleveland Browns to clinch the NFL title. Maryland won the college football title, and Notre Dame's running back John Lattner received the Heisman Trophy.

Minnesota defeated New York in five games to claim the NBA title, and Indiana won the college basketball title. The University of Washington's Robert Houbregs was selected Player of the Year, while Philadelphia's Neil Johnston, Minneapolis's George Mikan, Boston's Bob Cousy and Ed McCauley, and Adolph Schayes of Syracuse were named to the NBA's All-Pro First Team. The Montreal Maple Leafs won hockey's Stanley Cup; golfer Ben Hogan won the USGA Open; for the third year in a row Maureen Connolly was women's tennis champion at the U.S. Open, while Tony Trabert won the men's title; and heavyweight Rocky Marciano retained his boxing title by knocking out "Jersey" Joe Walcott in a rematch from 1952.

Americans Tenley Albright and Hayes Alan Jenkins won the women's and men's figure-skating competitions. Seventeen-year-old Albright, who started skating at age nine but contracted polio and had to give up the sport for six years, first gained widespread public admiration when she won the silver medal in the 1952 Olympic Games.

Television

The end of the Korean War permitted further growth of the television industry, which had been restricted by the national state of emergency. In 1953, 231 new television stations opened, and in December, following some experimental broadcasts in New York, including a special Halloween evening airing of Georges Bizet's opera *Carmen,* the FCC authorized color television broadcasts. In addition, local television stations began broadcasting educational programming.

I Love Lucy, which had premiered in the 1951–1952 season, was the most popular show in 1953. On January 19, 92 percent of all viewers tuned in to see Lucy give birth to "Little Ricky" on TV, the same day that Ball's real-life son Desi Junior was born. The attention to the birth overshadowed Eisenhower's inauguration the following day, and the ratings achievement has never since been equaled on television. Ball and her husband and costar, Desi Arnaz, signed an unprecedented $8 million contract later in the year. The program's immense popularity enabled it to survive a potential scandal when columnist Walter Winchell revealed that in 1952 Ball admitted to HUAC that she had joined the Communist Party in 1936 to please her grandfather. The committee exonerated her, and because her ratings were so strong, her commercial sponsor, cigarette manufacturer Philip Morris, continued to underwrite the show. After the news of Ball's past affiliation broke, Arnaz pleaded her innocence before a live television audience, which cheered the comedienne as she came onstage to film the newest episode. *I Love Lucy* successfully weathered the storm.

Comedies remained the most widely viewed form of television, and five of the 10 top shows were comedies. Among the new comedies in 1953 were *Topper*, about young homeowners who are visited by the ghost of the previous owner; *Make Room for Daddy*, a family sitcom starring Danny Thomas; and the slapstick *Soupy Sales Show* for children. Variety debuts included *Coke Time with Eddie Fisher*, sponsored by Coca-Cola, and *The Jack Paar Show*, a daytime feature that moved to Saturday evenings in 1954. Paar went on to replace Steve Allen as the host of NBC's *Tonight Show* in 1957. New dramatic revues included the *U.S. Steel Hour; The General Electric Theater*, hosted by Ronald Reagan; and *A Letter to Loretta*, which was retitled *The Loretta Young Show* in 1954. Sweeping through a doorway in an elegant gown that swirled around her, Young introduced the short plays that made up the show. Each was written in response to a fan letter she had received while a movie star. The themes were always uplifting, and the stories demonstrated the nobler sides of human nature. Young would return at the close to read a few lines of poetry or a biblical passage that resonated with the show's theme.

Bob Hope hosted the first televised presentation of the Academy Awards, and CBS newscaster Walter Cronkite presented dramatic reenactments of history in *You Are There*. Fellow CBS newsman Edward R. Murrow introduced *Person to Person*, in which he interviewed various celebrities who were sitting in their homes while Murrow was in his East Coast studio. Interviewees during Murrow's six years as host included Fidel Castro, Speaker of the House Sam Rayburn, Senator John F. Kennedy, and movie stars Marilyn Monroe and Zsa Zsa Gabor. Murrow also continued to host his public affairs show *See It Now*, and in October he broadcast one of its more important episodes, "The Case against Milo Radulovich," about an air force officer who had been dismissed because his father and sister read communist newspapers. Radulovich was reinstated a few weeks after the broadcast.

Based on the best-selling 1952 nonfiction account by Herb Philbrick, the drama *I Led Three Lives* purported to be based on the real-life adventures of an undercover FBI agent who infiltrated a communist cell in New England. The show, which ran through 1956, had the support of FBI director J. Edgar Hoover, and Philbrick reviewed all the scripts, acted as consultant, and was otherwise closely involved in the show's production. Despite the improbability of some of the later scripts—in one episode communist agents plot to sabotage the U.S. guided-missile program by converting vacuum cleaners into bomb launchers—the show was taken seriously as a patriotic effort, and viewers sometimes wrote in to ask for investigations into communists in their own

CBS newsman Edward R. Murrow and actress Marilyn Monroe converse from opposite ends of the country on Murrow's *Person to Person. (Photofest)*

neighborhoods. The producers passed those letters on to the FBI. Local sponsors of the series received promotional information stating that they were members of "the businessman's crusade" against international communism.

Movies

The Robe, an Academy Award–nominated biblical epic directed by Henry Koster and starring Richard Burton, Jean Simmons, and Victor Mature, became the first feature film to use Cinemascope. First demonstrated to the public in 1952, the new projection technique gave cinema another competitive advantage over its rival, television. Cinemascope projects a wide-screen image that is especially effective for epics with large casts, westerns with expansive landscapes, and other genres that depict events on a vast scale.

Fred Zinnemann's *From Here to Eternity,* starring Burt Lancaster, Frank Sinatra, Deborah Kerr, Montgomery Clift, Donna Reed, Ernest Borgnine, and

Jack Warden, won Academy Awards for best picture, director, supporting actor (Sinatra), supporting actress (Reed), screenplay, cinematography, editing, and sound. Based on the 1951 novel by James Jones, the movie is set in the army base at Pearl Harbor just prior to the Japanese attack on December 7, 1941. The unflattering tale of the peacetime army presents an insulated society where power is cruelly abused and virtue capriciously punished, although, unlike in Jones's novel, the worst offender in the movie is ultimately held accountable. Sinatra's performance rescued his slumping career. He had to beg the president of Columbia Pictures, Harry Cohn, for the role and agreed to play it at a greatly reduced salary. (His efforts to land the part are fictionalized and exaggerated in Francis Ford Coppola's 1972 hit, *The Godfather*, in which the Mafia chief makes the movie mogul "an offer he can't refuse.")

Other significant film debuts were Walt Disney's animated *Peter Pan*, about a boy who never wants to grow up and his heroic battles against the nefarious Captain Hook, and Howard Hawks's *Gentlemen Prefer Blondes*, a musical comedy based on a story by Anita Loos. Starring Marilyn Monroe and Jane Russell, it features the popular song, "Diamonds Are a Girl's Best Friend." Sam Fuller's *Pickup on South Street* stars Richard Widmark as a pickpocket who inadvertently steals microfilm intended for communist agents. The cynical thief ultimately performs his patriotic duty and helps the FBI bust the communist spy ring. Other films of note included Billy Wilder's *Stalag 17*, about American POWs during World War II; William Wyler's *Roman Holiday*, starring Gregory Peck and Audrey Hepburn; Vincente Minnelli's *The Bad and the Beautiful*, starring Lana Turner and Kirk Douglas; and George Stevens's *Shane*, starring Alan Ladd. Hepburn won the Academy Award for best actress and William Holden was selected best actor for his role in *Stalag 17*.

By and large, the same stars who had been among the most favorite at the beginning of the decade were the top box-office attractions. Their personae reflect a mix of righteousness and humor, and most of the men were actors in their mid- to late forties whose roles demanded adult maturity. Gary Cooper, who turned 52 in 1953 and appeared in Hugo Fregonese's *Blowing Wild*, was the biggest star of the year, followed by the comedy team of Jerry Lewis and Dean Martin, John Wayne, Ladd, Bing Crosby, Monroe, James Stewart, Hope, Susan Hayward, and Randolph Scott. Among those making their first major Hollywood appearances were Hepburn (*Roman Holiday*), Tony Curtis (*Houdini*), Rosemary Clooney, Robert Wagner (*Titanic*), and Jack Palance (*Shane*).

Literature

Lawrence Ferlinghetti opened the City Lights Bookstore in San Francisco, which offered poetry readings and jazz concerts and quickly became a gathering place for leftist intellectuals, university students, and others with unconventional and antiauthoritarian sensibilities. City Lights was the first major bookstore in the United States to specialize in paperback books. It sold radical magazines that were not otherwise readily available for purchase, and it nurtured the antiestablishment Beat movement, whose pioneers included Ferlinghetti, fellow poets Gregory Corso and Allen Ginsberg, and novelist Jack Kerouac.

Notable fiction from the year included James Baldwin's *Go Tell It on the Mountain,* a largely autobiographical account of a young black boy with an abusive stepfather who experiences an ecstatic religious revelation; *The Adventures of Augie March,* Saul Bellow's breakthrough novel, a picaresque story of an adventuresome young runaway who experiences urban America; William Burroughs's *Junkie;* John Cheever's *The Enormous Radio and Other Stores,* a collection of the author's *New Yorker* short stories; *Nine Stories* by J. D. Salinger, another *New Yorker* author who wrote about dysfunctional suburban families; *The Ponder Heart,* Eudora Welty's comic novel about a dysfunctional southern family; *Nisei Daughter,* Monica Sone's personal narrative based on her experience growing up as a Japanese American; Henry Miller's *Plexus,* a story of sexual exploration; and Richard Wright's existential novel *The Outsider.*

Popular fiction included *The Long Goodbye,* a detective novel by Raymond Chandler, which Robert Altman spoofed in his 1973 film of the same title, and the baseball novel *The Southpaw* by Mark Harris. Ray Bradbury expanded an earlier short story into a full-length novel about futuristic book burners in *Fahrenheit 451,* which François Truffaut filmed in 1966. The release of the book roughly coincided with the book burnings conducted by Senator McCarthy's aides at the U.S. embassies in Europe.

Best-sellers included *The Bridges at Toko-Ri,* a Korean War story that James Michener wrote at the suggestion of editors at *Life* magazine and that Mark Robson adapted into a 1954 movie starring William Holden and Grace Kelly; *Battle Cry,* Leon Uris's story of U.S. Marines fighting in the Pacific theater during World War II that Raoul Walsh adapted to film in 1955; and Ernest Gann's *The High and the Mighty,* a story about passengers on an airplane that develops mechanical problems and seems certain to crash. William Wellman directed the 1954 film adaptation starring John Wayne as the pilot. British author and former intelligence agent Ian Fleming published the first of his popular James Bond spy novels, *Casino Royale.* Subsequently, the Bond series became the most successful series of spy stories and films in history. Fleming published 12 Bond novels between 1953 and 1965, and after his death John Gardner and other writers created additional Bond stories, which were also the basis for numerous films.

Bruce Catton won a Pulitzer Prize in U.S. history for his civil war study, *A Stillness at Appomattox,* and aviator Charles Lindbergh won for his autobiography, *The Spirit of St. Louis.* Other notable nonfiction from 1953 included B. F. Skinner's *Science and Human Behavior;* Peter Viereck's *Shame and Glory of the Intellectuals;* Russell Kirk's *The Conservative Mind;* Ashley Montague's *The Natural Superiority of Women;* James Bryant Conant's *Modern Science and Modern Man;* Alfred Kinsey's *Sexual Behavior in the Human Female;* Eric Bentley's *In Search of Theater;* Randall Jarrell's *Poetry and the Age;* Bishop Fulton J. Sheen's *Life Is Worth Living,* which grew out of his popular television show; and *The Captive Mind,* an internationally acclaimed account by émigré and future Nobel Prize winner Czesław Miłosz of why he left communist Poland. Miłosz also published a collection of poems entitled *Daylight* and the Polish edition of *The Seizure of Power,* an account of the communist ascension to power in Poland that was translated into English in 1955.

Among the collections of poetry published in 1953 were John Ashbery's *Turandot and Other Poems,* Conrad Aiken's *Collected Poems,* Wallace Stevens's

Collected Poems, Robert Penn Warren's *Brother to Dragons,* Mary Sarton's *The Land of Silence,* Archibald MacLeish's *This Music Crept by Me upon the Waters,* and Theodore Roethke's Pulitzer Prize—winning *The Waking: Poems 1933–1953.*

Marjorie Kinnan Rawlings, author of *The Yearling,* died at age 57; Welsh poet Dylan Thomas died at age 39.

Theater, Music, and the Arts

The most enduring play to debut in 1953 was Arthur Miller's *The Crucible,* whose original Broadway cast included Walter Hampden, Beatrice Straight, Arthur Kennedy, and E. G. Marshall. The play dramatized the 17th-century Salem witch hunts and centered around John Proctor, a good but flawed man who goes to his death rather than indict innocent people before a morally tainted tribunal. Like the hearings conducted by HUAC and McCarthy, which were motivated by political agendas that extended beyond the fact-finding missions they purported to be, the Salem witch hunts in *The Crucible* also have ulterior motives. They further the interests of wealthy citizens trying to obtain the land of the victims whom the tribunal condemns, and they permit other citizens to pursue vendettas against personal enemies. In the end, Proctor goes to his death rather than betray his values and his soul. Miller, who has always maintained that the Red Scare was the historical context of the play, not its theme, resisted reading his depiction of the Salem witch hunts as an allegory. But that interpretation was widespread at the time of the play's appearance, and it persists today. Other notable dramas to debut on Broadway were William Inge's *Picnic,* which won the Pulitzer Prize, Robert Anderson's *Tea and Sympathy,* and Tennessee Williams's *Camino Real.*

Among the musicals, *Kismet* featured music from Russian composer Alexander Borodin's *Prince Igor* (1890), to which lyrics for the popular song "Stranger in Paradise" were added. Other musicals included Leonard Bernstein's *Wonderful Town;* Cole Porter's *Can-Can;* and a revival of George and Ira Gershwin's *Porgy and Bess,* starring opera diva Leontyne Price and Cab Calloway. Playwright Eugene O'Neill died at age 65.

On January 12, pianist Vladimir Horowitz celebrated his silver jubilee to great acclaim with the New York Philharmonic. Nine days later, violinist Yehudi Menuhin performed the music of Béla Bartók at Carnegie Hall, and on February 26, composer Igor Stravinsky conducted his own work with the New York Philharmonic. His opera, *The Rake's Progress,* premiered at the Metropolitan Opera of New York. The New York City Ballet staged an unprecedented 12 new productions, including two by Jerome Robbins. Soviet composer Sergei Prokofiev completed his ballet, *The Tale of the Stone Flower,* before he died on March 5, the same day as Stalin. After Stalin's demise, Dmitri Shostakovich wrote and premiered his Tenth Symphony in St. Petersburg, Russia, his first symphony in eight years.

Benny Goodman's re-formed jazz band went on tour with Louis Armstrong's All Stars, but Goodman experienced a nervous breakdown, allegedly due to personality conflicts among the performers. Herbie Mann, Bud Shank, and Frank Wess introduced the flute to jazz; Count Basie, the Hammond organ; and Oscar Pettiford, the cello. Lionel Hampton's band toured Europe

Blues singer Billie Holiday plays the trumpet of jazz performer Louis Armstrong. *(Photofest)*

and enjoyed a revival of interest in big-band music there. Jimmy and Tommy Dorsey reunited, and Glenn Miller performed as a soloist.

Popular songs from the year included "I Love Paris," "That's Amore," and "Stranger in Paradise." Among the top singles were Tony Bennett's "Rags to Riches," Patti Page's "Doggie in the Window," Percy Faith's "Song from Moulin Rouge," Perry Como's "Don't Let the Stars Get in Your Eyes," and Hank Williams's country-western number, "Kaw Liga."

Abstraction, action painting, and other nonrepresentational approaches to image making continued to attract praise from visual arts connoisseurs, who felt they appreciated the innovations by such creators as Jackson Pollock, Willem de Kooning, Stuart Davis, Josef Albers, and David Smith. The experimental art provoked disdain, however, from much of the general public, which failed to understand, enjoy, or otherwise be engaged by it. The public was not entirely alone in its repudiation of modern art. Forty-four painters and sculptors signed a manifesto assailing the lack of content and accessibility of abstract art, and they criticized the Museum of Modern Art for promoting it.

CHRONICLE OF EVENTS

1953

January 1: Country music singer Hank Williams dies at age 29.

January 5: J. A. Topf and Son, of Wiesbaden, Germany, receives a patent extension for the crematorium furnace design that was used at the Auschwitz concentration camp during the Holocaust.

January 10: Convicted atomic bomb spies Julius and Ethel Rosenberg appeal to President Truman for a stay of execution. Truman declines to act.

January 13: Nine Jewish doctors are charged in the Soviet Union with working on orders from Zionist organizations and U.S. and British intelligence agencies to use their medical arts to harm Soviet leaders. Six more physicians are later charged in the so-called Doctors' Plot.

January 19: Lucille Ball, star of television's top-rated *I Love Lucy,* delivers a baby boy, Desi Junior. Her television character, Lucy, gives birth to "Little Ricky" the same day.

January 20: Dwight D. Eisenhower is inaugurated president. This is the first presidential inauguration to be broadcast live on television.

Outgoing President Harry S. Truman (left) greets incoming President Dwight D. Eisenhower. In the background Bess Truman (left) greets Mamie Eisenhower. *(Photofest)*

January 21: Dizzy Dean and Al Simmons are elected to Major League Baseball's Hall of Fame.

January 22: Arthur Miller's play *The Crucible* opens on Broadway.

January 24: The United Nations announces that the world has at least 900 cities with populations of 100,000 or greater.

January 30: Eisenhower announces that he will withdraw the Seventh Fleet from the Straits of Formosa, leaving mainland China vulnerable to an attack from Taiwan.

February 2: In his first State of the Union address, Eisenhower tries to pressure China into cooperating more fully in the Korean peace talks by announcing that the U.S. Seventh Fleet will no longer intervene to prevent Chiang Kai-shek's Nationalist Chinese from invading mainland China from Taiwan. Eisenhower also calls for accelerated training and arming of South Korean troops, continued military aid to Europe, improved civil defense measures, and a balanced budget.

February 3: French underwater explorer Jacques Cousteau publishes *The Silent World.*

February 5: Jazz performer Charlie Parker visits Montreal, where he appears on Canadian television.

February 10: Egypt's leader, General Neguib, receives dictatorial powers.

February 11: Walt Disney's animated movie *Peter Pan* debuts.

February 13: Guatemala expropriates 234,000 acres of uncultivated land from the U.S.-owned United Fruit Company.

February 17: Eisenhower rejects the Rosenbergs' bid for a stay of execution, despite an appeal from Pope Pius XII on February 13.

February 24: Robert La Follette, Jr., commits suicide. The former Democratic Wisconsin senator, who was the son of the famous Progressive senator "Fighting Bob" La Follette, lost his seat to Republican Joseph McCarthy in 1946.

February 28: Greece, Yugoslavia, and Turkey sign a five-year defense pact.

February 28: Supporters of Iran's shah drive Prime Minister Mossadegh from his home, as anti-Western mobs riot outside.

March 2: Dave Brubeck's jazz quartet records the album *Jazz at Oberlin* in conjunction with a highly acclaimed tour of American college campuses.

March 3: Clare Boothe Luce, wife of *Time* magazine publisher Henry Luce, is named ambassador to Italy.

March 5: Joseph Stalin dies from a brain hemorrhage suffered in the early morning of March 1. The next day, Georgi Malenkov succeeds as Soviet premier and party secretary.

March 5: Soviet composer Sergei Prokofiev dies.

March 9: Actress Marilyn Monroe receives *Photoplay* magazine's award for Fastest Rising Star of 1952.

March 10: A Soviet fighter plane shoots down a British bomber flying over East Germany en route to Berlin.

March 17: More than 2,000 U.S. Marines participate in a military exercise at the atomic testing ground at Yucca Flat, Nevada: Immediately following an atomic explosion, the Marines, who are not wearing protective clothing, are ordered to charge into the test site and occupy the defensive fortifications that have been destroyed by the blast.

March 18: Baseball's Boston Braves move their National League franchise to Milwaukee.

March 20: Nikita Khrushchev replaces Malenkov as first secretary of the Soviet Communist Party. He is permanently elected to the powerful post on September 13.

March 26: Dr. Jonas Salk reports in the *Journal of the American Medical Association* that his polio vaccine has been used successfully in a test involving 90 children and adults. Salk concludes that the tests are "very encouraging" but adds that more tests are needed to prove the vaccination's safety and effectiveness.

March 26: Eisenhower offers to increase aid to France in its war against communists in Vietnam.

March 28: The Soviet government grants a general amnesty to all of its short-term prisoners and orders the Justice Department to revise its entire criminal code.

March 28: Football star and Olympian Jim Thorpe dies at age 64.

March 31: In a compromise that accommodates both the Soviets and the Western powers, the UN Security Council selects Sweden's minister of state, Dag Hammarskjold, to succeed Trygve Lie as UN secretary general.

April 3: The first issue of *TV Guide* is published, featuring Lucille Ball's son, Desi Arnaz, Jr., born on January 19, on the cover. It sells more than 1.56 million copies in the first week, and by 1959, it sells 6 million copies weekly.[15]

April 3–21: Roy Cohn and David Schine, aides of Senator McCarthy, take a highly publicized 17-day, seven-country tour of the State Department's European libraries, during which they remove, and in some cases burn, books by alleged communists.

April 8: The bones of Lakota Indian leader Sitting Bull are returned from North Dakota to South Dakota after 63 years.

April 10: 3-D movie *The House of Wax* opens at New York's Paramount Theater. It is released nationally on April 25. Star Vincent Price establishes himself as a movie villain, a persona that persists throughout his career.

April 25: James D. Watson and Francis H. C. Crick publish an article in the scientific journal *Nature* describing the double-helix structure of the DNA molecule. This discovery proves to be critical in making possible genetic engineering and other advanced genetics research.

May 8: Eisenhower announces that the United States will give $60 million to France in military aid for its anticommunist efforts in Vietnam.

May 12: Tornadoes strike Waco, Texas, killing 124 people.

May 15: Charlie Parker, Dizzy Gillespie, Charles Mingus, and other American jazz musicians perform in Toronto's Massey Hall.

May 18: Lieutenant Colonel Jacqueline Cochran of the U.S. Air Force Reserve becomes the first woman to break the sound barrier.

May 19: An unexpected change in wind direction carries radioactive fallout 137 miles from an atomic bomb test in Yucca Flat, Nevada, to the town of Saint George, Utah, where director Dick Powell films *The Conqueror* later in the year. Approximately half of the townspeople eventually die of cancer, as do 91 members of the film crew, including Powell, producer Howard Hughes, and stars John Wayne, Susan Hayward, and Agnes Moorehead.[16]

May 22: Eisenhower signs an offshore oil bill giving coastal states control over submerged lands.

May 29: Edmund Hillary of New Zealand and his Sherpa guide, Tenzing Norgay, become the first humans to reach the summit of Mount Everest, the world's highest mountain, in the Himalayas.

May 31: Secretary of State John Foster Dulles warns of a possible "domino effect" if the communist-led Vietminh drive the French from Indochina. The domino theory, which asserts that the fall of one

country to communism will trigger the fall of its neighbors, later becomes the primary justification for U.S. intervention in the Vietnam War.

June 2: The Supreme Court bars restaurants from refusing service to black patrons.

June 8: Tornadoes in the Midwest kill 139 people.

June 9: Tornadoes in New England kill 92 people.

June 14: Alluding to the activities of McCarthy aides Cohn and Schine, Eisenhower condemns book burning as a form of thought control in a graduation address at Dartmouth College, in New Hampshire.

June 17–July 12: Anti-Soviet uprisings in East Berlin nearly topple East Germany's communist government. Martial law, which is declared on June 21, suppresses the workers' rebellion.

June 19: Ethel and Julius Rosenberg are executed for their role in an atomic spy ring. This is the first time U.S. civilians are put to death for espionage. Their internationally reported deaths are both widely protested and heartily cheered.

June 26: Lavrenti Beria, head of the Soviet Union's secret police, is denounced at a top-level meeting in the Kremlin and arrested as a traitor. He is tried and executed in December.

July 1: The U.S. government reports a budget deficit of $9.4 billion.

July 13: With only Guatemala absent, the Central American states agree to fight communism.

July 15: Howard Hawks's *Gentlemen Prefer Blondes,* starring Marilyn Monroe and Jane Russell, debuts.

July 20: Israel and the Soviet Union renew diplomatic relations.

July 21: The Soviet Union tells the United States to stop distributing free food to East Berliners. On July 27, 10,000 citizens of East Berlin cross into West Berlin to receive free food there.

July 22: In a mass ceremony at Yankee Stadium in New York, Jehovah's Witnesses baptize 4,640 people in a single day.

July 26: In an effort to topple Cuba's dictator, Fulgencio Batista, Fidel Castro leads an unsuccessful attack on a military barracks in the eastern province of Oriente. Six of Castro's 134 men are killed during the fighting; others are tortured and killed afterward. Captured while sleeping, Castro is imprisoned.

July 27: Despite last-minute impediments by the government of South Korea and a military offensive by communist forces, an armistice is reached that concludes the hostilities in Korea at 10 P.M. local time.

July 29: Soviet jets shoot down an American bomber near Vladivostok.

July 31: Senate majority leader Robert Taft of Ohio, known as Mr. Republican for his hardcore conservative positions, dies of cancer at age 63. The son of President William H. Taft, he had run unsuccessfully for the Republican presidential nomination in 1952.

August 1: George Stevens's film *Shane,* a western, debuts. The movie establishes Jack Palance as an actor with popular appeal.

August 5: Frank Sinatra's slumping career begins its resurgence with the release of the movie *From Here to Eternity.*

August 5: Under the terms of the armistice, communist authorities in Korea release the first 400 UN prisoners.

August 8: The United States and South Korea sign a mutual defense pact.

August 9: Officials in Miami announce that the first mass antipolio vaccinations are ready to be tried on children.

August 14: The Soviet Union announces that it has exploded its first thermonuclear device, a hydrogen bomb.

August 20: American author Ray Bradbury publishes his novel about futuristic book burners, *Fahrenheit 451.*

August 22: With assistance from America's CIA, troops loyal to the shah of Iran topple the government of Prime Minister Mossadegh following a pitched battle with Mossadegh's household guards.

August 27: Dr. Alfred Kinsey releases his report on female sexuality, *Sexual Behavior in the Human Female.* The report shocks many Americans by the suggestion that women are much more sexually active than commonly believed.

August 30: Hungary and Yugoslavia restore diplomatic relations.

September 12: Senator John F. Kennedy of Massachusetts marries Jacqueline Lee Bouvier in a highly publicized ceremony involving the rich and famous. Some 3,000 people reportedly attempt to crash the wedding in Newport, Rhode Island.

September 16: CinemaScope is introduced into the movies in the premiere of Henry Koster's *The Robe.* The wide-screen process is meant to offer audiences visual technology with which television cannot compete.

September 30: Eisenhower appoints California governor Earl Warren as chief justice of the Supreme Court.

October 5: The New York Yankees win an unprecedented fifth straight World Series, defeating the Brooklyn Dodgers in six games. Mickey Vernon of the Washington Senators is the American League batting champion (.337), Brooklyn's Carl Furillo leads the National League (.344). Milwaukee's Eddie Matthews leads the majors with 47 home runs, and the Yankees's Ed Lopat (16-4) and Brooklyn's Carl Erskine (20-6) are the top pitchers in their respective leagues. Cleveland's Al Rosen and Brooklyn's Roy Campanella are selected Most Valuable Player (MVP) of the American and National Leagues, respectively.

October 13: Senator McCarthy opens hearings to investigate allegations that the U.S. Army knowingly harbored communists at Fort Monmouth, New Jersey.

October 14: Eisenhower orders the immediate dismissal of any federal employee who invokes the Fifth Amendment before a congressional committee.

October 18: The Chicago Bears's Willie Thrower becomes the first black football player to play quarterback in the National Football League, when he enters a game as a substitute for starter George Blanda. Thrower completes three of eight passes for 27 yards, with one interception, in a 35-28 loss to the San Francisco 49ers. No black man plays quarterback again in the NFL for the next 15 years.

October 20: Edward R. Murrow airs "The Case Against Milo Radulovich," a documentary about an Air Force officer whose resignation is requested because his father and sister, who read communist newspapers and participate in other activities the Air Force deems "suspicious," are considered security risks.

November 2: The Islamic Republic of Pakistan is declared. Islamic religious laws and principles become the basis for government and law.

November 23: North Korea and China sign a 10-year aid pact.

November 26: French airborne troops capture the village of Dien Bien Phu in the north of Vietnam.

December: *Playboy* magazine publishes its first issue, with rising star Marilyn Monroe as its first nude centerfold. The issue sells out in days.

December 3: Scientists from the University of Iowa announce the first human pregnancies by artificial insemination using deep-frozen sperm.

Brooklyn Dodger star Jackie Robinson (right) was the first black player to integrate baseball. He was soon joined by teammate Roy Campanella (left), the National League's Most Valuable Player in 1953. *(Photofest)*

December 4–8: Eisenhower and Churchill confer at a summit meeting in Bermuda.

December 7–9: The Supreme Court hears new arguments on *Brown v. Board of Education of Topeka,* which challenges the "separate-but-equal" doctrine that allows racial segregation in the public schools.

December 8: Eisenhower presents his "atoms for peace" proposal for atomic energy to the United Nations General Assembly.

December 12: Test pilot Charles "Chuck" Yeager sets a new airspeed record of 1,650 miles per hour in an experimental X-1A rocket plane.

December 18: The FCC authorizes color television broadcasts.

December 23: With Eisenhower's approval, the Atomic Energy Commission withdraws the security clearance of J. Robert Oppenheimer, the "father of the atomic bomb."

December 27: The Detroit Lions win the NFL football championship, defeating the Cleveland Browns 16-10. During the regular season, Cleveland's Lou Groza kicks a record 23 field goals, while San Francisco 49er Burt Rechichar sets a new record for the longest field goal, at 56 yards. Cleveland's Otto Graham leads the league in passing. San Francisco's Joe Perry in rushing, and Philadelphia Eagle Pete Pihos in receiving.

EYEWITNESS TESTIMONY

I thought what was good for the country was good for General Motors and vice versa.

Charlie Wilson, president of General Motors, testifying before the Senate Armed Services Committee on January 15, 1953, during hearings for his confirmation as secretary of defense, in Dwight D. Eisenhower, The White House Years, *vol. 1 (1963), p. 110.*

Almighty God . . .

Give us, we pray, the power to discern clearly right from wrong, and allow all our words and actions to be governed thereby, and by the laws of this land. Especially we pray that our concern shall be for all the people regardless of station, race, or calling. . . .

My fellow citizens:

The world and we have passed the midway point of a century of continuing challenge. We sense with all our faculties that forces of good and evil are massed and armed and opposed as rarely before in history. . . .

This trial comes at a moment when man's power to achieve good or to inflict evil surpasses the brightest hopes and the sharpest fears of all ages. We can turn rivers in their courses, level mountains to the plains. Oceans and land and sky are avenues for our colossal commerce. Disease diminishes and life lengthens.

Yet promise of this life is imperiled by the very genius that has made it possible. Nations amass wealth. Labor sweats to create—and turns out devices to level not only mountains but also cities. Science seems ready to confer upon us, as its final gift, the power to erase human life from this planet.

At such a time in history, we who are free must proclaim anew our faith. . . .

President Dwight Eisenhower in his inaugural speech, January 20, 1953, in Eisenhower, "First Inaugural Address" (2001).

You know, Paul, I really don't disagree at all with the Acheson policies, or those policies you've worked on. I'm in general agreement with what you and Acheson have been trying to do. The one quarrel I have is the way in which Acheson has handled the Congress. I don't think he did it well, and I think I can do it much better. But as far as policy is concerned, I have no quarrel with you.

Incoming secretary of state John Foster Dulles speaking to Paul Nitze, outgoing policy planning chief for the Truman State Department, on inauguration day, January 20, 1953, in Leonard Mosley, Dulles *(1978), p. 307.*

It was not only the rise of McCarthyism that moved me, but something which seemed more weird and mysterious. It was the fact that a political, objective, knowledgeable campaign from the far Right was capable of creating not only a terror, but a new subjective reality, a veritable mystique which was gradually assuming even a holy resonance.

Playwright Arthur Miller writing about The Crucible, *which debuted on January 22, 1953, in Miller,* Collected Plays *(1957), p. 39.*

It is worth one more try to crack at least one of the Rosenbergs [to obtain a confession of atomic spying]. . . . Cracking the Rosenbergs is not a "third degree" problem, but a psychiatric problem. Therefore, would it not be possible to get some really skillful Jewish psychiatrist, say Dr. Karl Binger, to attempt to insinuate himself into their confidence during these next 30 days, and if they did show signs of coming along, a stay of execution for another 30 or 60 days could be arranged while the work progressed.

Special adviser to the president for psychological warfare Charles Douglas Jackson in a hand-delivered letter to Attorney General Herbert Brownell, dated February 23, 1953, in Frances Stonor Saunders, The Cultural Cold War: The CIA and the World of Arts and Letters *(2000), pp. 182–83.*

I think a member of the Communist Party should not be employed by a university. I would not hire such a person if I were a university president.

Historian Daniel J. Boorstin testifying before the House Un-American Activities Committee on February 27, 1953, in Eric Bentley, ed., Thirty Years of Treason *(1971), p. 611.*

For the last twelve hours the lack of oxygen became acute. His face and lips blackened as he suffered slow strangulation. The death agony was terrible. He literally choked to death as we watched. At what seemed like the very last moment, he opened his eyes and cast a glance over everyone in the room. It was a terrible

Girls pretend to see evil spirits in a production of Arthur Miller's *The Crucible. (Photofest)*

glance, insane or perhaps angry, and full of fear of death. . . . [And then] he suddenly lifted his left hand as though he were pointing to something up above and bringing down a curse on all. The gesture was incomprehensible and full of menace.

Svetlana Stalin describing the final moments of her father, Joseph Stalin, on his deathbed, on March 5, 1953, in Robert Conquest, Stalin: Breaker of Nations *(1992), p. 312.*

On 5 March 1953, I walked the streets of a town, a free but exiled man. An old deaf woman woke me up one morning and forced me to go out and listen to a communique broadcast by the local radio station. Stalin's death was announced. It was my first day of freedom.

Author and political prisoner Alexander Solzhenitsyn recounting his sentiments on learning of Stalin's death on March 5, 1953, in Martin Gilbert, A History of the Twentieth Century, *vol. 3 (2000), p. 35.*

For the time being, intimate comedies or small scale, domestic stories should be put aside and no further monies expended on their development. . . . [Instead, the studio] will concentrate exclusively on subjects suitable for CinemaScope.

Darryl F. Zanuck, head of 20th Century-Fox, in a memo dated March 12, 1953, in Harry Haun, The Cinematic Century *(2000).*

Dear Max,

Thank you very much for your recent letters. We were quite interested in your account of the [Linus] Pauling seminar. The day following the arrival of your letter, I received a note from Pauling, mentioning that their model had been revised, and indicating interest in our model [of the DNA structure]. . . . Until now we have preferred not to write him since we did not want to commit ourselves until we were completely sure that . . . all aspects of our structure were . . . feasible. I believe now that we have made sure that our structure can be built and today we are laboriously calculating out exact atomic coordinates.

Our model (a joint project of Francis Crick and myself) bears no relationship to either the original or to the revised Pauling . . models. It is a strange model and embodies several unusual features. However since DNA is an unusual substance we are not hesitant in being bold. The main features of the model are (1) The basic structure is helical—it consists of two intertwining helices . . . (2) the helices are not identical but complementary so that if one helix contain[s] a purine base, the other helix contains a pyrimidine—this feature is a result of our attempt to make the residues equivalent and at the same time put the purines and pyrimidine bases in the center. . . .

In the next day or so Crick and I shall send a note to *Nature* proposing our structure as a possible model, at the same time emphasizing its provisional nature and the lack of proof in its favor. Even if wrong I believe it to be interesting since it provides a concrete example of a structure composed of complementary chains. If by chance, it is right then I suspect we may be making a slight dent into the manner in which DNA can reproduce itself.

> *Scientist James D. Watson in a March 12, 1953, letter to Max Delbrück describing the newly proposed double-helix structure of the DNA molecule, in Watson,* The Double Helix *(1968), pp. 228–34.*

Considering the popular reputation of a girl known as Salome, who had something to do with the unhinging of John the Baptist's head, and considering the wide-eyed admiration in which Rita Hayworth is held, it is not surprising to find the two young ladies brought together and exploited in a film.

Columbia's *Salome* . . . is a flamboyant, Technicolored romance, based vaguely on a Biblical tale, wherein the highly regarded Miss Hayworth plays the legendary dancer at Herod's court. It is also a lush conglomeration of historical pretenses and make-believe, pseudo-religious ostentation and just plain insinuated sex.

> *Critic Bosley Crowther reviewing the film* Salome, *in Crowther, "Salome,"* New York Times, *March 25, 1953, p. 37.*

After fourteen years, such is the hypnotic power of the press that misconceptions still exist about the investigation G. David Schine and I made of the State Department's Information Program in Europe. We were derided as snoopers, Rover Boys, Innocents Abroad, and junketeering gumshoes. . . . [M]any denounced us as "book burners" because we discovered that more than thirty thousand works by Communists, sympathizers, and unwitting promoters of the Communist cause were on the shelves of our overseas libraries.

The information program that caused such bitter controversy consisted of American libraries and reading rooms set up in foreign countries. They weren't intended to function as public or general libraries but to house reading matter about our country, its people, and their way of life. They were Cold War products whose purpose was to win friends.

My question was and is a simple one: Wasn't it self-defeating to stock the shelves with anti-American books? Why should we sponsor the propaganda of our socialist adversaries at this critical time? . . .

When David Schine and I went to Europe to look into charges of inefficiency and disloyalty in the information service, we considered the trip routine. . . . What we failed to foresee was the propaganda uses to which our critics would put the journey. David Schine and I unwittingly handed Joe McCarthy's enemies a perfect opportunity to spread the tale that a couple of young, inexperienced clowns were bustling about Europe, ordering State Department officials around, burning books, creating chaos wherever they went, and disrupting foreign relations. . . .

In Vienna we went through the U.S. Information Library, then to the Soviet sector and went through theirs. We discovered that some of the same books—for example, the works of Howard Fast—were stocked by both. One of us—the United States or the Soviet Union—had to be wrong.

> *McCarthy aide Roy Cohn describing his tour with fellow aide David Schine of U.S. State Department libraries in Europe, April 3–21, 1953, in Cohn,* McCarthy *(1968), pp. 75–92.*

I must speak of that issue that comes first of all in the hearts and minds of all of us—that issue which most urgently challenges and summons the wisdom and the courage of our whole people. This issue is peace. In this spring of 1953 the free world weighs one question above all others: the chances for a just peace for all peoples.

To weigh this chance is to summon instantly to mind another recent moment of great decision. It came with that yet more hopeful spring of 1945, bright with the promise of victory and of freedom. The hopes of all just men in that moment too was a just and lasting peace.

The 8 years that have passed have seen that hope waver, grow dim, and almost die. And the shadow of fear again has darkly lengthened across the world. Today the hope of free men remains stubborn and brave, but it is sternly disciplined by experience. It shuns not only all crude counsel of despair but also the self-deceit of easy illusion. It weighs the chances for peace with sure, clear knowledge of what happened to the vain hopes of 1945. . . .

The nations of the world [have since] divided to follow two distinct roads. . . . The way chosen by the United States was plainly marked by a few clear precepts, which govern its conduct in world affairs.

First: No people on earth can be held, as a people, to be an enemy, for all humanity shares the common hunger for peace and fellowship and justice.

Second: No nation's security and well-being can be lastingly achieved in isolation but only in effective cooperation with fellow-nations.

Third: Every nation's right to a form of government and an economic system of its own choosing is inalienable.

Fourth: Any nation's attempt to dictate to other nations their form of government is indefensible.

And fifth: A nation's hope of lasting peace cannot be firmly based upon any race in armaments but rather upon just relations and honest understanding with all other nations.

President Eisenhower delivering a speech before the press on April 16, 1953, in Eisenhower, "The Chance for Peace" (2001).

The following books have been withdrawn from the USIA library in Paris and in the provinces: Howard Fast, *The Proud and the Free, The Unvanquished, Conceived in Liberty;* Dashiell Hammett, *The Thin Man;* Theodore Haff, *Charlie Chaplin;* Langston Hughes, *Weary Blues, Ways of White Folks, Big Sea, Fields of Wonder, Montage of a Dream Deferred, Not Without Laughter, Histoires des Blancs.*

A telegram message dated April 20, 1953, from the U.S. Embassy in Paris to the State Department, in Frances Stonor Saunders, The Cultural Cold War: The CIA and the World of Arts and Letters *(2000), p. 193.*

Now we can see it [victory in Vietnam] clearly—like light at the end of a tunnel.

French general Henri Navarre, who assumed command in the war against the Vietminh in May 1953, in Stanley Karnow, Vietnam: A History *(1983), p. 189.*

[I] spoke to [Herbert] Brownell and urged him to play war of nerves with Rosenbergs, including if necessary [a] temporary stay of execution by the President. Brownell advised that the warden, matron, prison doctor, and anybody else involved should have impressed upon them the subtleties of the situation and the game that was being played, rather than let them play it by ear. This was no longer a police matter. Brownell agreed to do something along these lines.

Special adviser to the president for psychological warfare Charles Douglas Jackson describing his efforts to extract a confession from the Rosenbergs in a "memo for the file" dated May 27, 1953, in Frances Stonor Saunders, The Cultural Cold War: The CIA and the World of Arts and Letters *(2000), p. 183.*

Almost the moment I got to Stanford I fell in love and got engaged. My fiancé . . . was joining the navy and . . . he was sent to sea . . . so we had to postpone the wedding.

During my junior year, while I was trying very hard to be a loyal fiancée, I got involved in . . . this big Stanford show. . . . Well, this was all pretty intense. . . . Terrifically exciting. All this time I was getting these letters from my guy on this destroyer . . . in Korea, and they seemed so distant from my real life. But I dutifully answered every letter, feeling guiltier and guiltier. . . . [On opening night, she had sex with the director and became pregnant.]

Ken [her fiancé] was coming in on his ship from Korea and this gigantic, elaborate wedding was being planned. By this time I barely remembered why I was marrying him, but so much machinery had been set in motion and I was in kind of a daze. So here I turn up pregnant and the world comes crashing down. . . . I simply couldn't tell him [her father]. I truly believed he would have killed me.

I went to my uncle . . . hoping he could find me a regular doctor who could give me an abortion . . . [but] no one would touch me. So my mother and I went down to the Mexican section of L.A., to this dirty little house where I literally had to lie down on a kitchen table! This guy—I don't even know if he was a doctor—packed my cervix with something and told me I'd have to wait a few days. . . .

No sooner had I recovered from the abortion than Ken arrives—fresh-faced, clean-shaven, all ready for his wedding. . . . Mr. Clean meets Miss Dirty. I felt absolutely like a filthy, soiled creature. . . . I had to tell him I couldn't go through with the wedding, but I couldn't tell him why. Everyone was furious with me. . . .

Barbara Tuttle describing her abortion shortly before her scheduled marriage in June 1953, in Brett Harvey, The Fifties: A Women's Oral History (1993), pp. 24–25.

At one point, Senator McCarthy insisted that the government get rid of all the books in our overseas libraries that he decided were subversive and un-American. Informed of this while on a visit to Dartmouth College, I seized the opportunity in an impromptu talk to deplore the ignorance and stupidity of "book burners." I told the audience that there was no hope of eliminating evils—such as Communism—until we were able to learn exactly what Communism was. To hide our heads in the ashes of ignorance, I asserted, would, far from defeating Communism, merely contribute to our own confusion and defenselessness. . . .

Of one thing I was certain: McCarthyism antedated the appearance of Joseph McCarthy of Wisconsin and would last longer than the man's power or publicity.

Lashing back at one man . . . was not as important to me as the long-term value of restraint, the due process of law, and the basic rights of free men.

That is why I condemned book-burning, rather than bandying about the names of the men of the moment who would burn the books.

President Eisenhower remarking on his speech of June 14, 1953, in which he condemned the practice of burning books, in Eisenhower, The White House Years, vol. 1 (1963), pp. 320–21.

It looks very much as though someone is trying to out-bulldoze Mickey Spillane in Twentieth Century-Fox's *Pickup on South Street.* . . . For this highly embroiled presentation of a slice of life in the New York underground not only returns Richard Widmark in a savage, arrogant role, but uses Jean Peters

blandly as an all-comer's human punching-bag. Violence bursts in every sequence, and the conversation is slangy and corrupt. Even the genial Thelma Ritter plays a stool-pigeon who gets her head blown off.

Indeed, the climate is so brutish and the business so sadistic in this tale of pickpockets, demireps, informers, detectives and Communist spies that the whole thing becomes a trifle silly as it slashes and slambangs along, and the first thing you know its grave pretenses are standing there, artless and absurd.

Critic Bosley Crowther reviewing Pickup on South Street, in Crowther, "Pickup on South Street," New York Times, June 18, 1953, p. 38.

To paraphrase T. S. Eliot, *It Came From Outer Space* burst into Loew's State yesterday with a bang and went out with a whimper. Despite its three-dimensional, wide-screen, stereophonic, science-fiction trappings and Richard Carlson's awesome opening observation that this is "the biggest thing that ever happened in our time," the adventure in which he is involved is merely mildly diverting, not stupendous. The space ship and its improbable crew, which keep the citizens of Sand Rock, Ariz., befuddled and terrified, should have the same effect on customers who are passionately devoted to king-sized flying saucers and gremlins.

Critic A. H. Weiler reviewing It Came from Outer Space, in Weiler, "It Came from Outer Space," New York Times, June 18, 1953, p. 38.

Always remember that we were innocent and could not wrong our conscience.

Julius and Ethel Rosenberg writing to their sons, Robert and Michael, on the morning of their execution, June 19, 1953, in Frances Stonor Saunders, The Cultural Cold War: The CIA and the World of Arts and Letters (2000), p. 180.

It was a queer, sultry summer, the summer they electrocuted the Rosenbergs, and I didn't know what I was doing in New York. I'm stupid about executions. The idea of being electrocuted makes me sick, and that's all there was to read about in the papers—goggle-eyed headlines staring up at me on every street corner. . . . It had nothing to do with me, but I couldn't help wondering what it would be like, being burned alive all along your nerves.

I thought it must be the worst thing in the world. . . .

I kept hearing about the Rosenbergs over the radio and at the office till I couldn't get them out of my mind. It was like the first time I saw a cadaver. For weeks afterward, the cadaver's head—or what was left of it—floated up behind my eggs and bacon at breakfast . . . and pretty soon I felt as though I were carrying that cadaver's head around with me on a string, like some black, noseless balloon stinking of vinegar.

Poet Sylvia Plath in her memoir set at the time of the execution of Julius and Ethel Rosenberg, June 19, 1953, in Plath, The Bell Jar *(1971), p. 1.*

When two innocents are sentenced to death, it is the whole world's business. . . . [Fascism is defined not] by the number of its victims but by the way it kills them. . . . [The executions were] a legal lynching that has covered a whole nation in blood.

French existentialist Jean-Paul Sartre commenting on the execution of Julius and Ethel Rosenberg on June 19, 1953, in Frances Stonor Saunders, The Cultural Cold War: The CIA and the World of Arts and Letters *(2000), pp. 180–81.*

I was told only at the last minute that [Lavrenti] Beria was being arrested and that we were to escort the convoy carrying him. I was shocked. This was the most powerful man after Stalin. But I was told that he was an enemy of the people. Orders are orders.

Major Hiznyak Gurevich, senior Kremlin guard, describing the arrest on June 26, 1953, of the head of the Soviet secret police and internal security, Lavrenti Beria, in Martin Gilbert, A History of the Twentieth Century, *vol. 3 (2000), p. 38.*

We cannot screen [books and other works of culture] without looking like a fool or a Nazi. Can be done quietly if enough time and intemperate souls were taken out. Definite intention now to select new books to conform with law.

Handwritten notes from a presidential cabinet meeting on July 10, 1953, in Frances Stonor Saunders, The Cultural Cold War: The CIA and the World of Arts and Letters *(2000), p. 195.*

In the midst of a little war and a big Korean monsoon, things were not looking all that bad. As a 22-year-old junior infantry officer serving with some really great fellow soldiers, the decrease in the sights and sounds of hostile action was most welcomed. Then I was suddenly summoned to report to Colonel Nathan.

"Here's the deal, Nick," the colonel told me. "The area commanders want to use the lull in the fighting to boost the troops' morale. You know, like entertainment, and bringing in some of the goodies they haven't seen for a while. Your job is to go down south and pick up sodas, beer, candy, cookies, even cameras and film—the works. . . . Whatever you need in terms of equipment and personnel, you've got. But you need to be very careful Nick, because with trucks for stores, GIs for clerks, and cigar boxes for cash registers, you're going to have to watch out for pilfering at all times. Major Clark at the depot is expecting you."

I grew uneasy as the details unfolded. On Wednesday, two days hence at 0700 hours, I was to leave the depot with the shipment. I was the accountable officer, meaning that if anything happened to the cargo of $45,000 worth of goods, I would be personally, and financially responsible. Of course in 1953, military troops paid ten cents for beer, soft drinks and cigarettes, five cents for candy and gum—so the total shipment required 27 trucks.

Major Clark warned me that dishonesty and theft were rampant within his realm. "These guys know all of the tricks," he cautioned. Then he added that I needed to be especially alert for subterfuges like honeycombing.

"What the hell is honeycombing?" I wondered, and Major Clark described a common practice of putting empty containers in the middle of a shipment, and surrounding them with full ones to deceive whoever was signing for the goods.

This was not reassuring news, and soon I began to see beady eyes everywhere—including the major's. It seemed I was to be personally, and fiscally, responsible for a cargo that was warehoused in a den of thieves. But orders are orders, and I had little choice. On Wednesday morning at 0645 hours, the 27 trucks were fully loaded. Standing by were 47 potential salesclerks in combat uniforms, with their loaded weapons and bayonets. I don't know why, but even that didn't seem funny to me at the time. Soon my senior sergeant informed me that we were ready to roll at my command.

Just as I was about to give the order, Major Clark appeared, running toward us shouting and waving his

An audience wears special polarized glasses to watch movies in three dimensions. *(Photofest)*

arms. Suddenly, he fell forward and slid for a good five feet in the mud. We did our best not to laugh as he got up and kept coming undeterred. Despite his mud bath and lost hat, he was excited and happy.

"It's over, the war is over!" he shouted. "Report back to your unit. We have 24 hours to pull back from the line."

Soon we were on our way, while those trucks remained behind. The news spread rapidly and soldiers and civilians alike were celebrating heartily. But as for me, I can't tell you how happy and relieved I was, savoring the thought that my financially dangerous assignment had miraculously been canceled. The war was over, and, well, gee, that was really nice too.

Psychologist Nicholas Mason describing his experiences during the final days of the Korean War, which concluded July 27, 1953, in private correspondence with the author, September 3, 2001.

Multi-channel sound, in films, in radio transmission, and in home music reproduction, has been this year's sensation under a collection of highly confusing terms at the whim of publicity—biaural, stereophonic, 3-D, wide-screen sound, etc. The easy parallel with the new types of film photography helps a bit to untangle the terminology for phonograph owners. The obvious difference between those movies which *don't* require glasses and those which do is a good clue to the difference that divides into two distinct categories all of the sound systems using more than one recording at a time. To put it simply, one requires earphones, the other doesn't; it uses loudspeakers.

Don't expect to make sense of present terminology, even the official sort. The kind of picture (still or movie) that brings a separate image exclusively to each eye, via a hand-viewer or polaroid glasses, is a relatively accurate means of reproducing your actual two-eyed vision—each eye sees exclusively through one lense of the double camera. *Stereo (stereo-scopic)* is the official term. "3-D" (three-dimension) is in this case at least technically accurate.

The corresponding sound system that brings two recordings separately to your two ears and produces an analogous effect of realism is called *binaural*. Just as glasses or viewers are used for visual separation, so earphones must be used to separate the two recordings . . . one going exclusively to each ear. . . .

Wide-screen movies, sometimes projected from three films (Cinerama), make use of no glasses and are not stereo, though their effect is often very wonderful. Both eyes see the entire projection; there is no separation. In sound there is a similar system too, where a number of simultaneous recordings . . . are played through spaced-out loudspeakers, to recreate a strong sense of the original spatial arrangement, left to right.

Edward Tatnall Canby describing the year's new technologies, in Canby, "The New Recordings: 3-D Sounds," Harper's Magazine (August 1953), p. 104.

[Author James Jones] wrote a [film] treatment, and he ruined his book. He was worried about censorship—everyone was—and in his treatment, the captain's wife . . . is his sister! No movie. And the captain didn't apply the "treatment" to Prewett. He [the captain] was a nice fellow and when he found out about the treatment, he got furious.

I read the novel and thought, How the hell are you going to make a movie? And my wife and I were driving and I just sort of *saw* this movie. I went to Eve Ettinger and said I thought I could lick it. She got me in to see Buddy Adler. . . . In no time I was in Harry Cohn's bedroom. This is where he liked to have his meetings.

I said, "I'll give you two ideas. The first one is, instead of Maggio just petering out and being discharged and sent back to Brooklyn, Maggio should be just the way he is [eventually portrayed] in the film." And the moment in the book when Prew played "Taps" had no reason. I said, "It's when Maggio dies! You've got a great second-act curtain." And I said you should intercut the two love stories, but they should never meet. The audience will get the impression that somehow they are related. . . .

I asked for 2½ percent profit participation—which was really the first time a writer had done that. I believe they went with it because they never thought it would happen! We're never going to get anywhere with this movie, so give him whatever he wants! Cohn, I think, had got discouraged about it. He paid $85,000 for the book, and . . . the New York office was laughing at him. They thought, with all the "fucks" all over the book, you can't do it. They didn't stop to think you don't need the word.

Screenwriter Daniel Taradash commenting on the screenplay for From Here to Eternity, *which premiered on August 5, 1953, and for which Taradash won an Academy Award, in Pat McGilligan, ed.,* Backstory 2: Interviews with Screenwriters of the 1940s and 1950s *(1991), pp. 316–17.*

The Chicago Board of Health prohibited the re-use of glasses for viewing three-dimensional movies.

Herman M. Bundesen, president of the board, said the action was taken "to safeguard the public" after he had received complaints from a number of physicians about the increasing prevalence of eye infections after using the glasses.

Dr. Bundesen said bacteriological examinations of glasses presumed to have been sterilized showed they are still contaminated and "are therefore dangerous to the public health." . .

Two types of glasses are used in viewing 3-D movies. In one the viewing lense is held in a plastic frame while the other uses a cardboard frame. The cardboard ones are used only once. Dr. Bundesen expressed no objections to that type.

Public health officials questioning the safety of recycling the special glasses used for viewing 3-D movies, in "Chicago Health Board Bans Re-Use of Glasses for Viewing 3-D Films," Wall Street Journal, August 5, 1953, p. 10.

Lucille Ball is no Communist. Lucy has never been a Communist, not now and never will be. . . . She's as American as Barney Baruch and Ike Eisenhower. Please, ladies and gentlemen, don't believe every piece of bunk you read in today's papers. . . . And now I want you to meet my favorite wife—my favorite red-head—in fact, that's the only thing red about her, and even *that's* not legitimate.

Actor-singer Desi Arnaz introducing his wife and costar of "I Love Lucy," Lucille Ball, to a television audience following an article in fall 1953 by Walter Winchell pointing out that she had joined the Communist Party in 1936 to please her grandfather, in Stephen J. Whitfield, The Culture of the Cold War *(1996), p. 169.*

They never told us it was a "practice." Or maybe they just assumed we understood the meaning of the word "drill." Or maybe I was the only one among the classroom of five- and six-year-olds who didn't understand that the air raid exercise was not in preparation for a *real* and *imminent* attack. In any case, the underside of my little first grader's desk seemed inadequate refuge for what they described: "It could come at any time, at any moment. Attack! Bombs! The Enemy! Total Destruction! And don't forget to clasp your fingers over your neck!"

The moment I got home from school that day, I raced for my bedroom and crawled under the bed. Covering my neck with my little girl hands, I screamed and screamed for my mother. She was down the street in an afternoon *tête-a-tête* with the other neighborhood mothers. No one heard me. In almost all ways, I was a very quiet little girl. On this day, I wouldn't stop screaming.

When at last she coaxed me out from under the bed, my mother explained that "they" weren't actually coming—not that moment, not that day. Her words did little to stop the quaking inside my body, a feeling like shaken dice. Unthrown but unstoppable, their shaking was already too viscerally imprinted to be calmed.

An earlier event in my life, also at school, had similarly hurled me into a state of terror. But that one was individual, personal, isolated. It too had left me running for cover, but in deepest silence, forever misinterpreting my responsibility for my family's safety and well being. This time I understood that everyone, everywhere, was in imminent danger. But unlike that first innocence-obliterating calamity, this one offered

no belief that I could shelter myself, my little brother, my parents, my dogs, or my friends. The first terror, while leaving me limp with impotence, had implanted the delusion of my power, my responsibility to save all those I love. This one left me with no illusions—its danger was omnipresent. It could find me, find us, anywhere—even in the bosom of my own family, even in my own bed.

Eventually, the two terrors melded, and denial, that greatest of all human drives, returned me to a state, erratic as it would forever be, of function. I spent a good part of my adult life consciously recovering and examining the first calamity, the individual attack. But I'd all but repressed the terror of that air raid drill (and the others that followed throughout my elementary school years). Its threat was far too big: I needed to believe that I could be safe at least in my own bed. Then a terrorist attack against America came from the skies on September 11, 2001. As I tried to grasp the inconceivable, I came to recognize a sensation. Inside, my body was quaking like shaken dice.

Author Laura Cerwinske recounting her experience of an air raid drill in November 1953, in private correspondence with the author, September 13, 2001.

If you think you can run this operation without United Fruit [Company], you're crazy.

CIA operative Colonel Albert Haney recalling in 1973 the warning in November 1953 of Colonel Joseph Caldwell King, head of the CIA's Latin American division, concerning efforts to topple the leftist government in Guatemala, in Peter Grose, Gentleman Spy: The Life of Allen Dulles *(1994), p. 37.*

We had to cross mountains and jungles, marching at night and sleeping by day to avoid enemy bombing. We sometimes slept in foxholes, or just by the trail. We each carried a rifle, ammunition, and hand grenades. . . . We each had a week's supply of rice, which we refilled at depots along the way. We ate greens and bamboo shoots that we picked in the jungle, and occasionally villagers would give us a bit of meat. I'd been in the Vietminh for nine years by then, and I was accustomed to it.

Cao Xuan Nghia, an infantryman in the communist Vietminh, describing his journey to Dier Bien Phu in November and December 1953, in Stanley Karnow, Vietnam: A History *(1983), p. 191.*

If you had to sum up the idea of *Playboy,* it is anti-puritanism. Not just in regard to sex, but the whole range of play and pleasure.

Publisher Hugh Hefner describing the philosophy of his new Playboy *magazine, which first appeared in December 1953, in James S. Olson,* Historical Dictionary of the 1950s *(2000), p. 225.*

[The Soviet Union under Khrushchev is] a woman of the streets. Despite bath, perfume or lace, it [is] still the same old girl.

President Eisenhower remarking on the post-Stalin USSR to Britain's prime minister Winston Churchill during a summit meeting in Bermuda December 4–8, 1953, in Martin Gilbert, A History of the Twentieth Century, *vol. 3 (2000), p. 53.*

I know that the American people share my deep belief that if a danger exists in the world, it is a danger shared by all—and equally, that if hope exists in the mind of one nation, that hope should be shared by all. . . .

I need hardly point out to this assembly, however, that this subject is global, not merely national in character. On July 16, 1945, the United States set off the world's first atomic test explosion. Since that date in 1945, the United States has conducted forty-two test explosions. . . .

During this period, the Soviet Union has exploded a series of atomic devices, including at least one involving thermonuclear reactions.

If at one time the United States possessed what might have been called a monopoly of atomic power, that monopoly ceased to exist several years ago. Therefore, although our earlier start has permitted us to accumulate what is today a great quantitative advantage, the atomic realities of today comprehend two facts of even greater significance. First, the knowledge now possessed by several nations will eventually be shared by others, possibly all others. Second, even a vast superiority in numbers of weapons, and a consequent capability of devastating retaliation, is no preventive, of itself, against the fearful material damage and toll of human lives that would be inflicted by surprise aggression. . . .

My country wants to be constructive, not destructive. It wants agreements, not wars, among nations. It wants, itself, to live in freedom and in the confidence that the people of every other nation enjoy equally the right of choosing their own way of life. So my country's purpose is to help us move out of the dark chamber of horrors into the light, to find a way by which the minds of men, the hopes of men, the souls of men everywhere, can move forward toward peace and happiness and well-being. . . .

President Eisenhower delivering his Atoms for Peace Plan speech before the United Nations General Assembly on December 8, 1953, in Eisenhower "Atoms for Peace" *(2001).*

6

Separate Is Not Equal
1954

All years contain events that transform a nation's (and sometimes the world's) history, but 1954 was especially rich in such developments for the United States. When the Supreme Court struck down the 1896 *Plessy v. Ferguson* decision permitting racial segregation of public facilities and ordered the integration of public schools, it set in motion one of the most profound changes in U.S. politics and culture: the integration of American society. Although full implementation of the Court's 1954 ruling arguably remains incomplete, the decision transformed the country to an extent that exceeds almost any other verdict the Court ever issued. *Brown v. Board of Education of Topeka, Kansas* not only energized the civil rights movement and encouraged the demonstrations, both peaceful and violent, that characterized the late 1950s and 1960s; in the long run it made the United States a much more racially integrated nation than it ever had been, and thereby transformed everyday life for all American people in many significant ways.

The year also contained several other events that carried long-term implications for the United States and the world. The defeat of French forces in Vietnam led to France's military withdrawal from the region and created a power vacuum in Southeast Asia. U.S. efforts to fill that vacuum and prevent the spread of communism eventually evolved into the Vietnam War, in which the United States committed military troops between 1965 and 1973 and suffered more than 50,000 combat deaths. In Europe, the World War II Allies agreed to end their postwar occupation of Germany; East Germany declared itself a sovereign nation, and West Germany rearmed and joined the NATO alliance, a development that significantly altered the military and political dynamics in Europe and provoked the creation in 1955 of the Warsaw Pact, a Soviet-dominated military alliance of Eastern European nations. In domestic U.S. politics, although McCarthyism remained strong, the first sign of an abatement of the Red Scare occurred when Senator McCarthy, himself, fell from power and was denounced by the U.S. Senate.

Based on his experiences in World War II, Eisenhower believed that having the capacity to move troops and supplies expeditiously throughout the country was essential for defending against an enemy invasion. He thus proposed to build a system of interstate highways across the country. Congress funded the plan in 1956 with bipartisan support, and in the following decades the interstate highways not only contributed to the national defense, they also greatly facilitated trade and travel and played a major role in making the United States an especially mobile society. Eisenhower authorized construction of the St. Lawrence Seaway between Montreal and Lake Erie and hailed the opening of the New York Thruway as both an economic boon and an aid to national defense. Also of great national consequence were the massive field tests on schoolchildren that demonstrated the efficacy of Jonas Salk's polio vaccine, thereby providing the means to eradicate the polio epidemic then ravishing the country.

THE COLD WAR AND INTERNATIONAL POLITICS

The Cold War Abroad

In his State of the Union address on January 7, Eisenhower declared that U.S. policy would emphasize economic policies, peaceful uses of atomic energy, and new, scientifically informed defenses "to reduce the communist menace without war." Nonetheless, on January 11, Secretary of State John Foster Dulles announced the doctrine of massive retaliation that called for an instant and intense response to communist aggression anywhere in the world. The use of nuclear weapons was implied by the declaration. In response, Adlai Stevenson, Eisenhower's Democratic opponent in the 1952 and 1956 elections, questioned whether this policy would leave the nation with extreme choices between "inaction and thermo-nuclear holocaust."[1]

On March 1, the United States tested a hydrogen bomb that was hundreds of times more powerful than any previous weapon. The blast, estimated to be 600 times more potent than the Hiroshima bomb, was so immense that scientific instruments could not measure its full strength. Radioactive debris extended far beyond the designated safety zone, and exposed 264 native people of the Marshall Islands, 28 Americans, and the crew of the *Lucky Dragon,* a Japanese fishing boat, to dangerous levels of radiation. A second test was conducted three weeks later, and on April 1, a third H-bomb was detonated. That explosion was the first test of a hydrogen bomb to be nationally televised. On June 14, Americans participated in a national civil defense exercise to prepare for a nuclear attack. Another exercise was conducted in November, the same month that the United States and Canada cooperated on the construction of a 3,000-mile chain of radar stations across Canada at the 55th parallel and a Distant Early Warning radar system in the Arctic Circle that extended from Alaska to Greenland. The latter became known popularly as the DEW line. In January, the United States launched the submarine *Nautilus,* the world's first nuclear-powered ship, and at the end of the year, the United States commissioned the *Forrestal,* the world's largest aircraft carrier to date.

The exposure of the crew of the *Lucky Dragon* eventually killed one crew member and triggered an international incident. The United States later paid $2 million in reparations, but this event and the antinuclear demonstrations that followed did not impede a mutual defense treaty that the United States and Japan signed a week later. In September, Japanese meteorologists reported that the islands were being subjected to radioactive rainfall resulting from Soviet nuclear tests in the southern Urals. These tests were conducted without concern for the safety of nearby Russian inhabitants, the 44,000 Soviet soldiers who were ordered to advance to ground zero immediately after the blast, or the Japanese. By the end of the year, after two incidents that directly affected the uninvolved country, the National Anti–Bomb Council of Japan collected some 15 million signatures, which became the beginning of a worldwide "ban the bomb" campaign.[2]

The superpowers did explore some possibilities for reducing the nuclear threat. In December 1953, Eisenhower proposed the establishment of an international agency to promote peaceful uses of nuclear power—his "atoms for peace" plan—and in January 1954, Secretary of State Dulles met with Soviet ambassador Georgi Zarubin to discuss the issue. But the Soviets would not agree to international verification of compliance, and the United States refused to halt atomic weapons production without that assurance. Consequently, the talks yielded no substantive results.

In late January 1954, at the Berlin Conference, foreign ministers from the United States, the Soviet Union, France, and Great Britain met to discuss German reunification, arms control, admission of the People's Republic of China (PRC) into the United Nations, and a Soviet proposal for abandonment of a European defense community. However, the conference, whose venue moved between West and East Berlin, yielded few results, as the Soviets rejected British foreign secretary Anthony Eden's plan to hold national elections throughout the country, and the Western powers rejected the Soviet proposals on China, arms control, and European defense. The Eden plan was the last significant attempt to reunite Germany during the cold war, and in March, the Soviets recognized East Germany as a sovereign nation. In October, West Germany joined the NATO alliance and the Western European Union, and the Soviets and Allied powers agreed to conclude the post–World War II occupation of Germany, which officially ended in May 1955, when West Germany became a sovereign state. (The United States did not formally recognize East Germany until 1974; in 1955, the Soviets and the Western powers recognized West Germany.)

Following Chinese Nationalist attacks in August on gunboats from the PRC, and a subsequent threat from the PRC to invade the Nationalist stronghold on Taiwan, Eisenhower pledged that the United States would oppose any invasion of Taiwan by Communist China, and he committed the Seventh Fleet to that end. The situation intensified in September when the PRC shelled Jinmen (Quemoy), an island off Taiwan, and the Nationalists responded by bombing the communist-held island of Tateng and later attacked a communist oil tanker. Additional provocations by both sides continued through the fall, and in early December, the United States signed a mutual defense pact with Taiwan.

Other International Developments

After suffering a crushing defeat in May at the battle of Dien Bien Phu, French troops withdrew from North Vietnam. Under the terms of the Geneva peace treaty, which was brokered by China's foreign minister Zhou Enlai and signed in July, Vietnam was divided at the 17th parallel. South Vietnam remained affiliated with France, which retained some troops there, while North Vietnam was ruled by a communist regime based in Hanoi and headed by Ho Chi Minh. According to the peace agreement, this division was to last for two years, at which time nationwide elections were to unify the country. In the interim, the communist Vietminh government agreed to remove its forces from the south and from Laos and Cambodia. The conclusion of the peace agreement was followed by a mass exodus from North to South Vietnam of refugees fearful of communist rule.

A participant in the Geneva talks, the United States refused to accept the final terms of the agreement but agreed not to disrupt them either. However, Eisenhower, who had declined a French request to intervene with atomic weapons at Dien Bien Phu or to furnish other substantial military aid, apart from air transport of French troops, declared that the United States would view any new communist aggression in the south with concern, and he authorized plans for intensively training South Vietnamese forces. South Vietnam's head of state, Emperor Bao Dai, also refused to abide by the Geneva agreements, as did his successor in 1955, Ngo Dinh Diem. Consequently, neither the United States nor the Saigon government felt bound to honor the call for the 1956 election. These election never took place, as U.S. and South Vietnamese officials feared Ho Chi Minh would win easily.

Elsewhere in Asia, the United Nations withdrew its last troops from Korea, despite the failure of the Geneva Conference to formulate an acceptable plan to reunify the country, or even officially conclude hostilities. A conference of Asian countries meeting in Ceylon called for peace in Indochina, a cessation of atomic testing, and the termination of colonialism in the region. Following the final end of Dutch rule in Indonesia and the partitioning of Korea and Vietnam, the United States, Great Britain, Australia, France, New Zealand, Pakistan, the Philippines, and Thailand formed the Southeast Asia Treaty Organization (SEATO) to oppose communist gains in Southeast Asia. Kashmir's assembly voted to accept reunification with India, and in China, Chairman Mao Zedong instituted drastic rural reforms involving the creation of more than 100,000 collective farms. China's alliance with the Soviet Union further strengthened— it was even included in the preamble of China's new constitution—and the Soviet Union returned Port Arthur (Lushun) to the Chinese.

The French defeat in Indochina caused the ruling government in France to collapse, and in June a new government was formed under Premier Pierre Mendès-France, who negotiated the peace settlement in Vietnam. The United States loaned $100 million to the European Coal and Steel Community for modernization of colliery installations and construction of power stations. Cypriots seeking unification with Greece began a four-year campaign of bombing and terrorism, and Yugoslavia steered a middle course between the East and West, as it rejected both Soviet-style centralized government and economy and U.S.-style democracy. Sweden, Norway, Denmark, and Finland announced a plan to form a common Scandinavian market, and they signed an agreement creating a common labor market giving equal employment opportunities in each country to citizens of all four nations.

In the Middle East and Africa, Colonel Gamal Abdel Nasser, a proponent of pan-Arab unity, overthrew General Mohammed Naguib to become Egypt's new dictator. Nasser negotiated the agreement that concluded Britain's 72-year occupation of the country and ceded the Suez Canal to Egypt. Long-smoldering Arab-Israeli tensions exploded in March when 11 Israelis were machine-gunned to death near Beersheba, in the worst violence since an Israeli raid killed 53 Jordanians in October 1953. In July, President Mendès-France offered autonomy to Algeria, but not independence; this did not satisfy Islamic nationalists, whose independence movement intensified, despite a devastating earthquake that killed more than 1,000 Algerians. In the fall, the nationalists launched more than 60 attacks on French civilians and police. In response to the violence, France increased its military presence in the country. France also sent its Foreign Legion into Morocco to suppress rioting by nationalist forces there.

South Africa strengthened its policies of apartheid by empowering the government to remove nonwhite settlements it considered too close to or too closely connected with white areas. The government also forbade whites and nonwhites to belong to the same trade unions and thereby work together for their common interests as laborers, and it transferred authority for the education of native Africans to the government and away from the more liberal church missionaries who had assumed most of that responsibility. In Kenya, the British began a major effort to suppress the nationalist Mau Mau revolt.

Guatemalan president Jacobo Arbenz Guzmán, whose reform government had become increasingly receptive to communist influences and overtures, was deposed by a right-wing military coup that the CIA secretly aided. Under the new military regime of Colonel Carlos Castillo Armas, more than 2,000 suspected communists were arrested, and the government pursued policies more favorable to U.S. political and business interests, including those of the United Fruit Company, whose lands Arbenz had nationalized in 1953. Juan Perón won reelection in Argentina and promptly arrested four opposition leaders; a military junta seized control in Paraguay; and Brazil's dictator, President Getúlio Vargas, committed suicide following scandals involving financial corruption and other matters.

The Cold War at Home

Senator McCarthy's fall from power began after he accused the army of complicity with communists. Whereas his earlier charges had been directed mostly against liberals, leftists, intellectuals, and entertainers, the attack on the army struck much closer to home for many middle Americans. Not only had the army played a decisive role in winning World War II, it was also the institution from which Eisenhower had risen to power and in which hundreds of thousands of Americans had proudly served. So, in confronting the army, McCarthy risked alienating the political center of the country, as well as antagonizing the leader of his own party.

In October 1953, McCarthy charged that the army had attempted to conceal communist activity at the Fort Monmouth Army Signal Corps Center in New Jersey. Then, in January 1954, he accused it of coddling the communists when it approved the routine promotion at Camp Kilmer, also in New Jersey, of an officer with leftist sympathies, Captain Irving Peress. During hearings into the situation at Camp Kilmer, McCarthy accused General Ralph Zwicker, a World War II hero, of shielding communists and declared that the general was unfit to be an officer. He also attacked Secretary of the Army Robert Stevens so savagely that Stevens offered to resign. McCarthy's treatment of Zwicker later became one of the charges of his official misconduct, although it was not included in the Senate's final condemnation of him in December.

In March, under Eisenhower's direction, the army accused McCarthy of blackmail for his threats to conduct further investigations unless it commissioned one of his top aides, David Schine, who had recently been drafted. The pressure to do this came from another top McCarthy aide, Roy Cohn, who promised to "wreck the Army" if it did not comply with his request.[3] On April 22, the Senate opened new hearings to investigate the army's charges. Whereas in previous investigations, McCarthy had assumed the role of interrogator, in these hearings he was, for the first time, placed on the defensive, and the television cameras gave the American public a prolonged view of his bullying style, threats, incessant use of points of order and points of personal privilege to confuse his opponents, and his incoherent rambling. The carefully controlled, soft-spoken manner of army counsel Joseph Welch, a Republican lawyer from a well-established Boston law firm, further contrasted McCarthy's unrestrained emotion. The hearings climaxed when Welch challenged Cohn to give the FBI the names of the communists and possible spies whom Cohn and McCarthy had alleged were at Fort Monmouth. As Welch implored Cohn to give the names before the sun went down McCarthy interrupted with an unrelated accusation that a member of Welch's law firm had been a member of an alleged communist-front organization. Welch's dramatic reply to McCarthy's character assassination made a strong impression on the public audience watching the hearings: "Have you no sense of decency, sir, at long last? Have you no sense of decency?"[4]

Even though the Republican-controlled Senate ultimately exonerated McCarthy, the hearings led to his political downfall and that of Cohn, who resigned shortly after the investigation concluded. McCarthy subsequently wanted to open his own hearings into alleged communist infiltration of the CIA and nuclear power plants, but Eisenhower squelched the investigation. McCarthy's conduct at the army hearings, along with questionable financial dealings and other improprieties, provoked the Senate, which fell under Democratic control after the November elections, to condemn him on December 2. Afterward, McCarthy ceased to exert significant influence in American politics.

However, McCarthy's troubles did not terminate anticommunist activity within the government. In August, Congress passed the Communist Control Act, which strengthened the 1950 McCarran Internal Security Act by providing severe penalties for communist and communist-dominated organizations that refused to register the names of their members and supporters with the federal government. The Communist Control Act revoked the rights to collective bargaining of communist-dominated unions and denied the rights, privileges, and immunities of the Communist Party as a legal organization. By October, some 2,600 civil service employees were dismissed under the act.[5]

Congress further outlawed the Communist Party in the United States, and passed legislation revoking the U.S. citizenship of anyone convicted of conspiring to overthrow the government by force. The World War II–era Smith Act had already been used to convict communist leaders because they endorsed the teachings of Lenin, who preached the necessity of violently overthrowing governments—notably in the 1949 Foley Square trial. In 1954, many individual states also passed "little Smith Acts" that required loyalty oaths of state employees and denied communist candidates places on election ballots. Congress also voted to institute the death penalty for espionage during peacetime, and the Supreme Court ruled that membership in the Communist Party was sufficient grounds for deporting aliens.

CIVIL RIGHTS

The Thirteenth, Fourteenth, and Fifteenth Amendments to the Constitution freed the slaves, made them citizens, and guaranteed their voting rights after the Civil War. The 1896 Supreme Court ruling on *Plessy v. Ferguson* declared that separate-but-equal facilities for blacks and whites were constitutional and thereby upheld the so-called Jim Crow laws mandating separate treatment of blacks. Then, on May 17, 1954, occurred the most significant legal development in American civil rights since the 1896 decision; the U.S. Supreme Court issued its landmark ruling on four civil rights cases heard as *Brown v. Board of Education of Topeka, Kansas.* In that unanimous ruling, the Court reversed *Plessy v. Ferguson* and ordered the desegregation of public schools and other public facilities. In 1955, it amplified on the decision by ordering school desegregation to take place "with all deliberate speed."

Although the Court was initially split on *Brown v. Board of Education,* newly appointed Chief Justice Earl Warren worked behind the scenes to provide a unanimous decision, which he believed was necessary to ensure compliance. Even so, the first response of many public officials in the South, including some U.S. senators, was to condemn the decision and declare their refusal to abide by it. In Mississippi, voters approved an amendment to the state constitution that would permit the abolition of public schools if there were no other way to avoid desegregation, and South Carolina's governor, Strom Thurmond, was elected to the U.S. Senate after pledging to oppose it. He was the first U.S. senator ever elected by a write-in vote. This resistance to desegregation both threatened a constitutional crisis within the country and set the stage for the civil rights protests that marked the second half of the 1950s and the 1960s. Eisenhower signaled his administration's implicit support of desegregation in August, when he invited Assistant Secretary of Labor James Wilkins, an African American, to attend a presidential cabinet meeting. Wilkins thus became the first African American to participate in that policy-making body.

GOVERNMENT AND SOCIETY

Even before the Supreme Court issued its edict on desegregation, the rapid-pace national and world events provoked a feeling that the country was undergoing a period of explosive change. That explosiveness was made literal on March 1, when five U.S. congressmen were wounded, one seriously, by Puerto Rican nationalists who opened fire in the chamber of the House of Representatives. The four assailants were arrested and sentenced to maximum prison terms. Although unrelated to cold war or Red Scare issues, the assault threw one more log on the fire of fear already burning throughout the nation.

The conclusion of the Korean War in 1953 meant that industrial factories, steel, and labor that had been dedicated to the war effort were now available for producing consumer goods, and the suburbanization of America encouraged development of a culture centered around the automobile, as there were few stores and places of entertainment people could easily walk to in the new housing developments. By 1954, some 47 million passenger cars were registered in the United States.[6] The freedom, independence, and flexibility that the flashy cars afforded average citizens sparked satellite industries along popular roadways, such as motels and diners, drive-in restaurants and movies, and roadside attractions. Drag racing and "cruising" downtown areas while listening to rock 'n' roll on the radio became popular pastimes for teenagers and young adults, often to the dismay of elders. Although the large American cars of the 1950s were rarely fuel efficient or durable (they were designed with "planned obsolescence" in mind to encourage future sales), they were typically exuberant in their design and suggested a sense of power, freedom, and good feeling to adults and teenagers alike. The roomy back seats also afforded young men and women a place to be alone together without parental supervision and thereby contributed significantly to the sexual revolution that began in the 1950s and blossomed in the 1960s.

However, as the nation enjoyed greater material prosperity, underwent social changes that challenged traditional values, and otherwise became increasingly secular in its institutions and practices, Americans identified themselves more and more closely with religion. Indeed, much of the attraction of religion can be attributed to the sense of stability, sense of greater purpose in life, and the source of respectable authority it offered during unstable times. Affiliation with an established church was higher in the 1950s than at any other time during the century; in 1954, some 90 percent of Christians reported that they believed Jesus Christ to be a divine being, and about two-thirds stated that they believed in the existence of the devil.[7] To further emphasize the nation's religious foundation, which many secular and religious leaders maintained was key to its past success and future preservation, Congress changed the language in the pledge of allegiance from "one nation indivisible . . ." to "one nation, under God, indivisible. . . ."

In more secular matters, Eisenhower also signed a bill extending Social Security coverage to an additional 10 million more Americans, but Congress defeated his proposal to allow 18-year-olds to vote and his proposal to build 140,000 units of public housing over the next four years. An international convention concluded with a worldwide agreement to curb the practice of ships dumping oil into the ocean.

In the midterm elections on November 2, Democrats regained control of both the Senate and the House of Representatives. Future president Lyndon Johnson became the powerful majority leader in the Senate, and fellow Texan Sam Rayburn became speaker of the House, where he also exerted considerable influence. Johnson's and Rayburn's willingness to work cooperatively with Eisenhower on foreign policy played an important role in the nation's ability to formulate and sustain a largely bipartisan cold war policy throughout the 1950s. On the other hand, the fact that the Democrats took control of the

Senate no doubt made possible that body's official condemnation in December of McCarthy, a Republican.

Legendary baseball star Joe DiMaggio, the "Yankee Clipper," married Hollywood star and sex symbol Marilyn Monroe on January 14. The wedding of the two "superstars" sparked great interest throughout the nation; however, Monroe sued for divorce in October, citing conflicting career demands.

The 1954 murder of Marilyn Sheppard, who was bludgeoned to death in her home, became a national sensation after it was revealed that her husband, the prominent doctor Samuel Sheppard, was having an extramarital affair. Sheppard claimed that he fell asleep on the downstairs couch, awoke to screams upstairs, struggled with a "white figure," and then passed out. During his trial, Sheppard was widely vilified in the press, and the judge told columnist Dorothy Kilgallen that the doctor was "guilty as hell." Sheppard was convicted and sentenced to life in prison; however, attorney F. Lee Bailey later learned of the judges's remark to Kilgallen and appealed the conviction on the grounds of judicial misconduct and prejudice. The Supreme Court set aside the conviction in 1964, thereby establishing Bailey's reputation, and it granted Sheppard a new trial in 1965, in which he was acquitted. As an innocent doctor wrongly accused of murdering his beloved pregnant wife, Sheppard became the inspiration for the television series *The Fugitive* (1963–67), which in 1993 was adapted into a film starring Harrison Ford and Tommy Lee Jones. Sheppard died in 1970. In 1996, his son obtained a confession to the murder from a convict imprisoned for a different killing. However, in a civil trial in 2000, in which Sheppard's family sought to have him declared innocent instead of merely "not guilty," a jury declared that Sheppard was "not innocent" of the murder.[8]

Influenced by the Beat poets who were beginning to gather at San Francisco's City Lights Bookshop and in New York's Greenwich Village, young women began sporting a "raccoon look" that featured heavy, dark eye makeup.

Toronto opened Canada's first subway line.

BUSINESS

Although the year began with a small recession, overall the U.S. GNP rose 5 percent to a record $365 billion, or $1 billion a day; the New York Stock Exchange had its most active year since 1933, trading 573.4 million shares; and the London gold market reopened for the first time since the outbreak of World War II in 1939. Inflation was at 0.4 percent, and the Dow Jones Industrial Average fluctuated between 279 and 404. Ten percent of U.S. households were headed by women, who accounted for almost a third of the labor force. The nation claimed to have 154 millionaires, and a Gallup poll reported that a family of four could live on $60 a week. A record $3.135 billion was spent on new housing starts. Alligator handbags ranged between $115 and $185 at Saks Fifth Avenue; wing-tip shoes cost $27.95, and imported ski boots cost $17.98 at Macy's.[9]

Among the new products to appear on the market were the gas turbine car, automatic coffeemakers, newspaper vending machines, a language-translation machine, automatic toll collectors, and Levi's faded blue denim jeans. IBM announced development of a computer capable of performing more than 10 million operations an hour, which it planned to rent for $25,000/month, beginning in 1955. IBM also released an all-transistor calculator that required only 5 percent of the power consumed by electronic calculators.

Once an almost exclusive province of the wealthy, jet travel became quicker, easier, and more accessible to the general public as Boeing introduced its 707 passenger jet, which was capable of cruising at 600 miles per hour. Boeing also conducted initial flights on its B-52A bomber, and the air force authorized development of the B-58, the first supersonic bomber. Color television made its first significant appearance, as RCA, which owned the NBC network, initiated mass production of color televisions with 12-inch screens at a cost of $1,000.

The booming car industry was helped along when U.S. oil companies introduced premium-grade gasoline, which they hailed as the greatest innovation in their product since the introduction of tetraethyl lead in the 1920s. U.S. and European oil companies resumed production in Iran for the first time since former premier Mossadegh nationalized the industry there in 1951. Americans spent some $65 billion on automobiles, approximately 20 percent of the GNP.[10] General Motors celebrated the production of its 50 millionth car, Chevrolet introduced the powerful V-8 engine, and manufacturers Studebaker and Packard agreed to merge.

In labor relations, an ultimatum by the National Labor Relations Board ended the five-month strike by longshoremen that had begun in December 1953. U.S. Steel and the CIO signed a two-year agreement that raised wages and provided welfare benefits.

SCIENCE AND TECHNOLOGY

The awareness that the world had truly entered an atomic age capable of unleashing, and sometimes also harnessing, energy at levels never before possible became more acute when in January, the United States launched the world's first atomic-powered ship, the submarine *Nautilus*. A priority project of Admiral Hyman Rickover, who promoted its development despite considerable opposition from within the military establishment, the $55 million *Nautilus* could cruise at a top speed of 30 knots and travel around the world without surfacing, because its atomic engine required no air. The atomic reactors served as prototypes for large, civilian, nuclear power plants that promised a bright future filled with bountiful supplies of inexpensive atomically produced electricity. In March, the Atomic Energy Commission awarded the first contract to build a nuclear power plant, a 60,000-kilowatt plant for Pittsburgh. The Soviet Union opened a 5,000-kilowatt plant in June. On August 30, Eisenhower signed the Atomic Energy Act, which permitted private development of nuclear power.

The multinational Center for Nuclear Research (CERN) was founded in Geneva, Switzerland, and the MASER (Molecular Amplification by Stimulated Emission of Radiation) was invented. A French bathysphere descended to a record 13,284 feet in the Atlantic Ocean. The Arctic and Antarctic became more open to human exploration: Two U.S. icebreakers became the first vessels to complete the trip through the Northwest Passage from the Atlantic to the Pacific, the Soviet Union set up survey stations in the Arctic Circle to study weather and ocean currents, and the United States established a series of scientific bases in Antarctica, including one at the South Pole, to study magnetic storms, cosmic rays, movement of polar ice, and weather patterns. Archaeologists in Egypt discovered the 4,800-year-old Khufu (Cheops) boat at the side of the Great Pyramid of Khufu at Giza.

Mass field tests of polio vaccinations for schoolchildren began in February. Positive results on the 440,000 students inoculated in 44 states led to approval in 1955 of a nationwide program of immunization.[11] Development of oral contraception, which later played a significant role in changing sexual practices within the country, took a step forward when G. C. Pincus introduced an early form of the oral contraceptive pill after field tests in

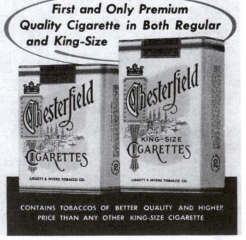

Contradicting the American Cancer Society, singer Perry Como claims that scientific evidence shows the safety of Chesterfield cigarettes. *(Photofest)*

Haiti and Puerto Rico. Vincent du Vingeaud synthesized two pituitary hormones: vasopressin, which raises blood pressure and stimulates the kidneys to retain water, and oxytocin, which causes the uterine muscles to contract during childbirth. Chlorpromazine (Thorazine) was developed for treating mental disorders. In Toronto, Canada, Dr. William Mustard performed the first successful open-heart surgery aided by hypothermia, and surgeons in Boston performed the first successful kidney transplant between identical twins. Humans were shown to have 46 chromosomes instead of 48, as previously believed. Linus Pauling won the Nobel Prize for demonstrating the nature of the chemical bond and its application to the structure of complex substances.

The dangers of tobacco smoking became increasingly apparent throughout the decade, and in 1954 the sixth international congress on cancer at São Paulo, Brazil, announced a definite link between cigarette smoking and cancer. That conclusion was based on a statistical study by the American Cancer Society in which, of 187,000 male smokers between the ages of 50 and 70, 5,000 died of cancer within two years—a rate far greater than any other cause of death among nonsmokers.[12] But the Tobacco Industry Research Committee reported "no proof . . . that cigarette smoking is a cause of lung cancer."[13] Smog, which remained a growing problem, was demonstrated to result from automobile emissions, and the dangers of radioactive waste became publicly known. In Britain, a clean-air act was passed, and in California, the governor temporarily closed oil refineries following the 16th consecutive day of smog. Meanwhile, Bell Labs introduced the first solar battery capable of converting solar energy into electricity.

Among the agricultural advancements that greatly enhanced humanity's capacity to feed its worldwide population, E. R. Sears manipulated the genes of grains to create hybrid forms of wheat more resistant to drought and disease, and the agricultural insecticide paraquat was invented. Italian-born Enrico Fermi, a major figure in the development of nuclear energy who orchestrated the first self-sustaining atomic chain reaction at the University of Chicago in 1942, died of cancer at age 53.

SPORTS, ENTERTAINMENT, AND THE ARTS

Sports

Recognizing the growing national passion for professional and collegiate sports, Henry Luce, publisher of *Time* and *Life* magazines, presented the first issue of *Sports Illustrated,* which proved to be a great success. During its initial years, the magazine covered a wide range of sports, but by the end of the decade it found that it could attract the largest percentage of its target audience—middle-class men—by concentrating on baseball, football, basketball, auto racing, boxing, horse racing, and golf.

On May 6, England's Roger Bannister ran a mile in three minutes, 59.4 seconds, breaking the four-minute barrier that many believed would never be crossed. Less than two months later, Australian John Landy broke Bannister's mark by a second, and within a year several other runners had crossed the four-minute threshold.

Baseball's Cleveland Indians won a record 111 games, led by pitchers Bob Lemon, Early Wynn, Mike Garcia, and Bob Feller, but they lost the World Series to the New York Giants, whose centerfielder, Willie Mays, made one of the most famous defensive plays in the history of the game—an over-the-shoulder basket catch that robbed Vic Wertz of a home run. The spectacular play apparently demoralized the Indians for the remainder of the series, and they lost in four games. Mays and New York Yankees catcher Yogi Berra were the Most Valuable Players (MVP) of the National and American leagues, respectively. Milwaukee Braves outfielder Hank Aaron, who went on to hit more home runs in his career than anyone in Major League history, made his debut in the majors.

In football, Philadelphia Eagles quarterback Adrian Burk tied a record by throwing seven touchdowns in a single game. The Cleveland Browns avenged their defeat in the 1953 championship game by trouncing the Detroit Lions, 56-10. Ohio State University was named the top college team, and University of Wisconsin running back Alan Ameche, who went on to star with the Baltimore Colts, received the Heisman Trophy.

The National Basketball Association introduced the 24-second shot clock to speed up the game and make it more offense oriented. Minneapolis defeated Syracuse in seven games to win the NBA championship. The NBA All-Pro First Team included Philadelphia's Neil Johnston, Baltimore's Ray Felix, Minneapolis's George Mikan, and Boston's Ed Macauley and Bob Cousy. The University of Kentucky won the college basketball title, and LaSalle's Tom Gola was named Player of the Year.

The Detroit Red Wings won hockey's Stanley Cup, and in June, Rocky Marciano defeated Ezzard Charles in 15 rounds to retain the heavyweight boxing title. Marciano also won a rematch on September 17, for his 47th consecutive victory. Ed Furgol won the USGA Open golf tournament, and Tony Trabert and Doris Hart prevailed in the men's and women's championships in the U.S. Open tennis championship.

Television

On March 9, Edward R. Murrow presented a special segment entitled "A Report on Senator Joseph R. McCarthy" on his news show, *See It Now*. Primarily a collection of film clips showing the senator contradicting himself, bullying a witness, and making inaccurate statements and accusations, the show represented the first time that network television directly addressed McCarthy's reckless demagoguery. The following month, the senator received free air time to respond; however, rather than address the contents of Murrow's show, McCarthy attacked the broadcaster personally, calling him a communist and "the leader and the cleverest of the jackal pack which is always at the throat of anyone who dares expose individual communists or traitors." Although the owners of CBS initially feared the network might lose its license because of Murrow's report, it did not suffer any debilitating repercussions, and the "Report on Senator Joseph R. McCarthy" has since come to be regarded as one of the high points in television journalism, even though, at the time, the majority of viewers interviewed responded more favorably to the senator than to Murrow. Other important political "firsts" televised in 1954 included a hydrogen bomb test on April 1 and a cabinet meeting on October 25. CBS's *Face the Nation* debuted in 1954, featuring interviews of well-known politicians, foreign dignitaries, and other public figures.

Among the shows to premiere was Walt Disney's *Disneyland,* the first major investment in television production by a Hollywood movie studio. The popular show went on to become the longest-running prime-time series in network history. A mixture of cartoons, live-action adventure stories, documentaries, and nature stories, the program opened each broadcast with a fireworks display over Cinderella's castle that promoted Disney's new California theme park, also called Disneyland. In its premiere season, the show aired the first of a highly successful series of episodes starring Fess Parker as frontiersman Davy Crockett. Subsequently Disney made a movie in response to the character's popularity, whose coonskin cap, along with other Davy Crockett paraphernalia, quickly became a fashion rage among children. "The Ballad of Davy Crockett" (the "king of the wild frontier" who "killed him a b'ar [bear] when he was only three") became a musical hit in 1955.

Although comedies still predominated, crime shows and variety programs gained in popularity. The most popular programs were *I Love Lucy, The Jackie Gleason Show, Dragnet, You Bet Your Life,* and Ed Sullivan's *Toast of the Town,* all established programs from earlier seasons. But *Disneyland* placed sixth for 1954 and rose to fourth in 1955 and 1956, before dropping out of the top 10. Among other new shows was *Father Knows Best,* a situation comedy starring Robert Young and Jane Wyatt. Along with *Leave It to Beaver,* which debuted in 1957 and also enjoyed a long run on television, it came to represent an idealized version of 1950s white America, in which virtue always triumphed,

Host Ed Sullivan banters with singer Eartha Kitt on his popular television show *Toast of the Town. (Photofest)*

parental authority was respected, and the most serious problems were minor domestic conflicts. Father was a wise, caring, if somewhat distant authoritarian figure; Mother was intelligent, competent, and loving. Concerns about national or international current events played no apparent role in these households.

Private Secretary, starring Ann Southern, was another new sitcom, as was *December Bride,* one of the few network shows of any era to revolve around an older woman. The 10th most popular show of the year, *December Bride* starred Lily Ruskin as an attractive, admirable widow for whom her married daughter, son-in-law, best friend, and neighbor continually try to find a suitable mate. Another premiere for the year, *Lassie* starred George Cleveland as a farm boy who had many adventures with his pet dog, a collie.

Like Groucho Marx's successful *You Bet Your Life,* Art Linkletter's *People Are Funny* was ostensibly a quiz show, but its appeal was comedy. Good-natured volunteers from the audience would become involved in zany stunts and often be doused with water, hit with pies, or subjected to other mild forms of humiliation. "Little man" comedian George Gobel, known as Lonesome George, introduced his comedic variety show. *The Jimmy Durante Show,* in the same comedic vein, was set in a small nightclub ostensibly owned and operated by Durante, a comedian with a trademark raspy voice and large "schnozzola" (nose) who would audition the talent. He closed each episode with the famous tag line, "Good night, Mrs. Calabash, wherever you are." In November, Ed Sullivan signed a 20-year contract with CBS to host *Toast of the Town* under a new title, *The Ed Sullivan Show.*

One effort to broadcast high culture over a mass communications medium was *Producer's Showcase,* a new dramatic anthology of lavish 90-minute plays that aired through 1957. It appeared every fourth Monday on NBC and featured major stars in such productions as *Petrified Forest* (starring Humphrey Bogart and Lauren Bacall in their television dramatic debuts) and *State of the Union* (starring Joseph Cotten). Memorable episodes from later years included *Peter Pan,* with Mary Martin (1955 and 1956), and a 1955 musical version Thornton Wilder's *Our Town,* with Paul Newman, Eva Marie Saint, and Frank Sinatra as the singing stage manager. *Producer's Showcase* also featured entertainment from other countries, for example, the ballets *Sleeping Beauty* and *Cinderella,* which starred prima ballerina Margot Fonteyn and Michael Somes.

Movies

Elia Kazan's *On the Waterfront,* starring Marlon Brando, Lee J. Cobb, Karl Malden, and Eva Marie Saint, won the Academy Award for best film; Brando won for best actor and Kazan for best director. The movie also won for best story and screenplay (Budd Schulberg), cinematography (Boris Kaufman), editing, and art direction. Leonard Bernstein was nominated for his jazz-influenced musical score. *On the Waterfront* tells the story of a washed-up boxer who, prompted by the love of a sweet girl, overcomes his reluctance to become a "stool pigeon" and brings down the corrupt union boss who controls the longshoremen on the docks. Apart from its innate dramatic power, the film is notable for its relationship to contemporary events. It is based on Malcolm Johnson's series of Pulitzer Prize–winning articles in the *New York Sun* about corruption on the docks of New York harbor. Audiences also associated the story with revelations of union ties to organized crime that surfaced during the widely viewed 1950–51 Kefauver Senate investigations. Moreover, a longshoremen's strike crippled the shipping industry on the nation's east coast during the beginning of 1954, making the public more aware of the power and importance of the union.

However, the film's most controversial topical associations deal with HUAC investigations into communist activity within the entertainment industry. In 1952, despite strenuous efforts to dissuade him by his former collaborator, playwright Arthur Miller, Kazan testified before HUAC and named several former associates as communists. Miller's 1953 play, *The Crucible,* is commonly viewed as his response to Kazan's act of informing. Cobb and *Waterfront's* screenwriter, Schulberg, also named names before HUAC during the early 1950s, and the movie can be regarded as their effort to validate their action. Its dramatic climax comes as Brando's character, who "could have been a contender" for the boxing title but for the labor leader's corruption, overcomes his misguided loyalties and testifies before a government commission. As a result, the docks are cleaned up, murder and other wrongs are avenged, and everyone but the boss and his thugs are better off.

Brando also starred in 1954 as an alienated, misunderstood motorcyclist in Laslo Benedek's *The Wild One.* The first of the Hollywood biker movies, and possibly the best, *The Wild One* was based on an incident in 1947, when a gang of motorcyclists took over the town of Hollister, California, during the Fourth of July weekend and destroyed it. Brando's tough, antiauthoritarian attitude struck a responsive chord among teenagers and other rebellious youth, and many took to wearing black leather jackets like the one he wears in the movie, to make a fashion statement. Brando's silent, tough but sensitive character anticipated the persona that made James Dean famous the following year.

Humphrey Bogart was nominated best actor for his portrayal of the paranoid Captain Queeg in *The Caine Mutiny.* Directed by Edward Dmytryk and based on the best-selling novel by Herman Wouk, the Oscar-nominated film shows both Queeg's abuses of his authority on the World War II destroyer he commands and the self-serving manipulations of those who would depose him. In particular, the liberal intellectual who instigates the mutiny, played by Fred MacMurray, proves to be cowardly, self-serving, and manipulative. Bogart also starred that year in Billy Wilder's *Sabrina,* along with Audrey Hepburn, who played the title role of the daughter of the chauffeur to a wealthy businessman. She falls in love with Bogart's playboy brother (William Holden) but eventually switches her affections to the more responsible Bogart. Hepburn and Wilder received Oscar nominations. In addition, Bogart starred with Jennifer Jones and Italian sex symbol Gina Lollobrigida in John Huston's screwball comedy *Beat the Devil,* and he appeared with Ava Gardner in Joseph L. Mankiewicz's *The Barefoot Contessa,* about a director who manipulates the career of a Spanish dancer, whom he turns into a Hollywood star.

Grace Kelly won the Academy Award for best actress for her role in *The Country Girl* as the codependent wife of a dapper alcoholic, played by Bing Crosby. Crosby and George Seaton received nominations for best actor and director, respectively, and the movie, which won for best original screenplay, was nominated for best film. Alfred Hitchcock's *Rear Window* also starred Kelly, along with James Stewart and Raymond Burr. The story centers around efforts by a voyeuristic photojournalist with a broken leg and his high-society girl-friend to verify his suspicion that his neighbor has committed murder. Another Hitchcock movie of 1954, *Dial M for Murder,* also featuring Kelly, is about a woman whose husband (played by Ray Milland) frames her for the murder of the man he has, unbeknownst to her, hired to kill her. Actor Spencer Tracy and director John Sturges received Oscar nominations for *Bad Day at Black Rock,* about a one-armed stranger who uncovers a dangerous secret in a western town filled with racial prejudice.

Judy Garland and James Mason received Oscar nominations for their roles in George Cukor's remake of the musical *A Star Is Born.* Ira Gershwin wrote the lyrics for this story about the decline of an alcoholic Hollywood star (Mason) who cannot deal with the success of his wife and protegée (Garland). Garland's performance is regarded as one of the finest in her career. Irving Berlin wrote the title song of Michael Curtiz's *White Christmas,* which stars Bing Crosby, Danny Kaye, and Rosemary Clooney. Another outstanding musical from the year is Stanley Donen's robust *Seven Brides for Seven Brothers,* which won the Academy Award for best score. Jean Negulesco's musical *Three Coins in the Fountain,* which won awards for best song and cinematography, is a love story about three young American women living in Rome. Dorothy Dandridge was nominated as best actress for her role as Carmen in Otto Preminger's *Carmen Jones,* a modern-day version of Georges Bizet's opera *Carmen,* played with an all-black cast. Harry Belafonte costars as the upstanding young soldier whom Carmen corrupts with her beauty and sensuality; opera soprano Marilyn Horne sang for Dandridge.

Made in association with the International Union of Mine, Mill and Smelter Workers, Herbert Biberman's *Salt of the Earth* is a simulated documentary that sympathetically portrays a 1951–52 strike by Mexican-American zinc workers in New Mexico. Biberman, who was one of the Hollywood Ten, producer Paul Jarrico, actor Will Geer, and scenarist Michael Wilson had all been blacklisted by the Hollywood studios for their politics. Jarrico and Biberman therefore created an independent film company to employ blacklisted artists and make films that portray groups typically not represented in Hollywood movies; however, *Salt of the Earth* was their only production. It is notable for its inclusion of Chicanos and its depiction of the central role women played in the labor movement; indeed, some critics argue that the film concentrates more on gender oppression than on inequities among the social classes. During the filming in 1953, anticommunist groups picked fights with crew members and shot their cars, and local merchants refused to conduct business with anyone involved with the film. Technicians and laboratories refused to perform postproduction work; members of the International Alliance of Theatrical Stage Employees were also prohibited from working on the film, and its projectionists were not allowed to screen it. Although it was well received in Europe, *Salt of the Earth* appeared only briefly in 10 U.S. cities. It was rereleased and more widely distributed in 1965, when it became a rallying point for counterculture activism.

The top Hollywood box office draws of 1954 were John Wayne, the comedy team of Jerry Lewis and Dean Martin, Gary Cooper, Stewart, Marilyn Monroe, Alan Ladd, Holden, Crosby, Jane Wyman, and Brando. Rod Steiger and Eva Marie Saint, who later starred with Cary Grant in Hitchcock's *North by Northwest,* made their first major Hollywood appearances in *On the Waterfront.*

Notable foreign films included Federico Fellini's *La Strada,* which stars Giulietta Masina and Anthony Quinn in the story of a dim-witted, well-intended girl whose family sells her to a brutish circus strong man to be his wife. Akira Kurosawa's *The Seven Samurai* centers on a group of Japanese samurai who agree to defend an unprotected town from marauding bandits in exchange for food. The basis for Sturges's *The Magnificent Seven* (1960), *The Seven Samurai* is a powerful tale when taken at face value, but it can also be viewed as an allegory that implicitly questions the relationships between standing cold war armies and the citizens they serve. Inoshiro Honda's *Godzilla, King of the Monsters,* like the U.S.-made *Them!,* which also appeared in 1954, was among the first monster movies to present destructive creatures that had mutated from the nuclear fallout from atomic testing. *Godzilla,* which was released in the United States in 1956, and its imitator, *Rodan* (1957), metaphorically equated the powerful and destructive monsters with the atom bombs dropped on Japan to conclude World War II. In the 1959 sequel, *Godzilla Raids Again,* atomic testing reawakens the monster, which goes on to devastate the city of Osaka. In later sequels, however, Godzilla changes from Japan's nemesis to its protector, much as the U.S. nuclear force that destroyed Hiroshima and Nagasaki went on to protect Japan from possible threats from North Korea, China, and the Soviet Union.

Literature

Established authors who earned their reputations before World War II received the highest honors in 1954, as Ernest Hemingway won the Nobel Prize in literature, and William Faulkner won the 1954 Pulitzer Prize and National Book Award for *A Fable,* which retells the Gospel as a tale of mutiny in the trenches of France during World War I. Other fiction by notable American authors included John Hawkes's experimental *The Goose on the Grave,* Shirley Jackson's *The Bird's Nest,* Anaïs Nin's sexually charged *A Spy in the House of Love,* and John Steinbeck's *Sweet Thursday.*

British writer, linguist, and literary scholar J. R. R. Tolkien published *The Fellowship of the Ring* and *The Two Towers,* the first two novels in an adventure trilogy that was a sequel to his 1937 novel, *The Hobbit.* The final book in the trilogy, *The Return of the King,* was published in 1955. Later collected as *The Lord of the Rings* (1966), the popular series was inspired by composer Richard Wagner's Ring Cycle operas and Norse mythology. It presented a struggle between good and evil set in a mythological place and time and in a world populated by wizards and small humanlike creatures called "hobbits." The horror genre was also hugely popular in 1954; in one month some 20 million horror novels were sold.[14]

Future Nobel Prize winner William Golding, another British author, published *Lord of the Flies,* about a group of British schoolboys whose plane crashes on an isolated Pacific island while they are seeking a haven in anticipation of a nuclear war. Initially the boys conform to their upper-class upbringing, but soon the thin veneer of civilization wears off and they degenerate into a primitive society led by the dominant male. The book demonstrates the inability of a

Winners of the 1954 National Book Award were (from left to right) Joseph Wood Krutch (nonfiction), William Faulkner (fiction), and Wallace Stevens (poetry). *(Photofest)*

rational worldview to succeed in a barbaric environment and suggests that a postnuclear environment will produce the death of a social ego that mediates between communal desires for order and individuals' basic impulse toward violence and destruction.

Other popular fiction included Irving Stone's *Love Is Eternal,* Daphne du Maurier's *Mary Anne,* Frances Parkinson Keyes's *The Royal Box,* Frank Yerby's *Benton's Row,* Taylor Caldwell's *Never Victorious, Never Defeated,* and Mac Hyman's comic story of a country bumpkin in the peacetime army, *No Time for Sergeants,* which Mervyn LeRoy made into a 1958 film starring Andy Griffith, Myron McCormick, Nick Adams, and Don Knotts. Philip Wylie's *Tomorrow!* imagines the nuclear destruction of a Midwestern city that has failed to take civil defense precautions. Wylie, who in the best-selling *A Generation of Vipers* (1942) introduced the term *momism* to refer to overbearing, emasculating mothers, served as a consultant to the Federal Defense Administration from 1949 to 1954. He concluded that U.S. defense planning failed to anticipate the panic and other psychological consequences of a nuclear attack. In *Tomorrow!,* he places much of the blame for the city's lack of preparation on middle-class mothers, whom he depicts as self-righteous, hypocritical, sexually repressed, and emasculating.

Set during the Korean War, James Michener's *Sayonara* is an updated version of *Madame Butterfly* that addresses the racial prejudice inherent in the official U.S. military policy that forbade marriages between American soldiers occupying Japan and Japanese women. The book explores the ramifications of the policy, which some 10,000 U.S. servicemen—including Michener—knowingly violated in order to marry according to their own wishes. In 1957, Joshua Logan adapted it into a popular film starring Brando, Red Buttons, James Garner, and Patricia Owens.

In his nonfiction book *Seduction of the Innocent*, Frederic Wertham charged that America's youth are being corrupted by comic books that undermine their moral values. It sparked enough outcry that the comic book industry developed a Comic Code later in the year to establish standards of "morality and decency." Other significant nonfiction included William F. Buckley's defense of Senator McCarthy, *McCarthy and His Enemies: The Record and Its Meaning;* James Rorty and Moshe Decter's *McCarthy and the Communists;* Ben Hecht's *A Child of the Century;* George F. Kennan's *Realities of American Foreign Policy;* Adlai Stevenson's *Call to Greatness;* Aldous Huxley's *The Doors of Perception,* which later inspired Jim Morrison and his 1960s rock band The Doors; Frank Lloyd Wright's *The Future of Architecture;* David Riesman's *Individualism Reconsidered;* and *Betty Crocker's Good and Easy Cook Book.* The Revised Standard Version of the Holy Bible and Norman Vincent Peale's *The Power of Positive Thinking* remained on the best-seller list from earlier years. Literary and social critic Joseph Wood Krutch won the National Book Award for his *The Measure of a Man.*

Although the First Amendment greatly restricted the extent to which the government could censor literature, self-censorship during the Red Scare was not uncommon. For instance, when African-American poet Langston Hughes published his collection of biographical essays, *Famous American Negroes,* he omitted, at the request of his publisher, the essay on W. E. B. DuBois, one of the country's most influential black intellectuals, because DuBois supported communism as a way of achieving economic parity for African Americans and was perceived as a fellow traveler. Hughes, whose writings Cohn and Schine had removed from State Department libraries in Europe in 1953, was himself dropped from later textbooks because he, too, became perceived as too radical.[15]

Among the poetry released during the year was Louise Bogan's *Collected Poems, 1923–1953,* e. e. cummings's *Poems 1923–1954,* Robinson Jeffers's *Hungerfield and Other Poems,* W. S. Merwin's *The Dancing Bears,* William Carlos Williams's *The Desert Music and Other Poems,* and *The Collected Poems of Wallace Stevens,* which won the National Book Award.

Theater, Music, and the Visual Arts

Theater audiences in 1954 were treated to dramas that ranged from escapism to the exploration of serious matters of authority and values. *The Pajama Game* was a musical love story set among labor strife in a pajama factory starring John Raitt, Janis Paige, Eddie Foy, Jr., and Carol Haney. Featuring hit songs "Hernando's Hideaway," "Steam Heat," and "Hey There," it went on to enjoy a run of 1,063 performances and was adapted to film in 1957 by Stanley Donen. Other musicals included *The Boyfriend,* starring Julie Andrews; *Fanny,* starring Ezio Pinza, Walter Slezak, and Florence Henderson; and Kurt Weill and Bertolt Brecht's *The Threepenny Opera,* which introduced the hit song "Mack the Knife." Bobby Darin made the song even more famous in 1959, when he recorded a jazzy rendition of it. John Patrick's *The Teahouse of the August Moon* won both the Pulitzer Prize and the Tony Award. New dramatic productions included Herman Wouk's adaptation of his novel *The Caine Mutiny Court Martial,* starring Henry Fonda; Maxwell Anderson's *The Bad Seed;* Agatha Christie's murder mystery *Witness for the Prosecution;* Jean Giraudoux's *Ondine,* starring Audrey Hepburn and Mel Ferrer; N. Richard Nash's *The Rainmaker,* starring Geraldine Page and Darren McGavin; Clifford Odets's *The Flowering Peach;* and T. S. Eliot's *The Confidential Clerk,* starring Claude Rains.

Maria Callas made her U.S. debut in a performance of *Norma* during the Lyric Opera of Chicago's first season, and in Venice, Benjamin Britten conducted the premiere of his opera *The Turn of the Screw,* which is based on the story by Henry James. The New York City Ballet staged George Balanchine's choreography of Tchaikovsky's *The Nutcracker,* the Ballet Theatre performed Valerie Bettis's dance adaptation of *A Streetcar Named Desire,* and Paul Taylor formed his own company. Eighty-seven-year-old conductor Arturo Toscanini concluded his 68-year career with an all-Wagner performance with the NBC Symphony Orchestra at Carnegie Hall, Fritz Reiner became the principal conductor of the Chicago Symphony, and German conductor Wilhelm Furtwangler died.

Rock 'n' roll truly became a national phenomenon as Bill Haley and His Comets released "Rock Around the Clock." In 1955, Richard Brooks introduced it to thousands in *The Blackboard Jungle,* and "Rock Around the Clock" subsequently became the best-selling single record to date. Haley also scored a big hit with "Shake, Rattle, and Roll." Although still an obscure figure, Elvis Presley made his first commercial record, "That's All Right Mama," and Folkway Records released a four-record album of 94 songs by black folksinger Leadbelly (Huddie Ledbetter), who died in 1949. Among the hits on the album were "Irene Good Night," "Jailhouse Blues," and "On Top of Old Smokey."

Along with singer Celia Cruz, bandleader Tito Puente (shown here) brought Cuban music to America in the 1940s and 1950s. *(Photofest)*

Other hit songs from the year included "Three Coins in the Fountain" the Academy Award–winning song from the movie, and "Hernando's Hideaway" "Hey There," and "Steam Heat" from *The Pajama Game.* The ongoing Latin influence on American mainstream music resurfaced in the growing popularity of the mambo, as evidenced in the popularity of "Papa Loves Mambo" and "Mambo Italiano."

Jazz continued to find a wider, more mainstream audience, as George Wein organized the first American jazz festival in Newport, Rhode Island (later known as the Newport Jazz Festival). In addition, several leading American jazz performers, including Billie Holiday and Count Basie, made their first European tours. The popularity of the emotionally restrained West Coast, or "cool," jazz spread throughout the country, as the Chet Baker Quartet released "My Funny Valentine" and "But Not for Me" on its *Standards* album, and Dave Brubeck appeared on the cover of *Time* magazine. In New York, saxophonist Stan Getz and blind pianist George Shearing also popularized the style, which Miles Davis had first inspired in his 1949 album, *Birth of Cool*. Louis Armstrong and other jazz musicians had given jazz even wider national and international exposure in 1953 when they performed in Anthony Mann's Oscar-nominated movie *The Glenn Miller Story,* but the musical form suffered a setback in 1954 with the attempted suicide and subsequent deterioration of legendary saxophonist Charlie "Bird" Parker, who was depressed over his daughter's death.

In sculpture, the Iwo Jima monument in Washington, D.C., was dedicated to the Marines who captured the Pacific island during World War II, and in architecture, Eliot Noyes introduced Bubble prefab houses in Hobe Sound, Florida. On Miami Beach, Morris Lapidus opened his curvaceous, elegant, upscale Fontainebleau Hotel. Suggesting glamour, luxury, and wealth (it was featured for those reasons in the 1964 James Bond movie, *Goldfinger*), the Fontainebleau became the flagship of the Miami Beach hotels, even though it was rivaled almost immediately, in 1955, by its new next-door neighbor, the Eden Roc.

Surrealist painter Salvador Dalí sued Mrs. William Woodward for $7,000 after she refused to accept delivery of his portrait of her and instead walked away from it as though she were "walking away from a monster."[16] Abstraction and nonrepresentational art continued to dominate the New York art scene, while in the Soviet Union, works of modern art, such as futuristic and cubist paintings that were hidden from the Nazis during World War II, and then suppressed because they were deemed politically incorrect under Stalin, were displayed at the Hermitage in Leningrad. Henri Matisse, leader of the Fauves (wild beasts), an artistic movement that experimented with expressionistic uses of color at the beginning of the century, died at age 84.

CHRONICLE OF EVENTS

1954

British authorities begin removing femur bones from dead children, without their parents' knowledge or consent, to measure radiation levels from atmospheric testing of hydrogen bombs. Between 1954 and 1970, about 4,000 femurs are removed. Australia also removes bones from dead children for similar tests during the same time period. Results from the tests contribute to the decision in 1963 to stop atmospheric testing of nuclear devices.[17]

January 7: The Vatican issues an announcement reminding Catholics that viewing televised masses does not fulfill religious requirements.

January 8: In celebration of his 19th birthday, Elvis Presley, then an obscure singer, pays a Memphis recording studio $4 to record "Casual Love" and "I'll Never Stand in Your Way."

January 8: IBM presents the first language-translation machine.

January 11: Secretary of State John Foster Dulles announces that the U.S. defense policy is now based on instant and massive retaliation against any aggressor. The use of nuclear weapons is implied in the phrase "massive retaliation."

January 13: Dulles meets with Soviet ambassador Georgi Zarubin to discuss the possibility of pooling atomic energy resources.

January 14: Sex icon Marilyn Monroe marries baseball legend Joe DiMaggio.

January 21: The United States launches the submarine *Nautilus,* the world's first atomic-powered ship.

January 25–February 18: The Berlin Conference of foreign ministers from the United States, Soviet Union, France, and Great Britain meets to discuss German reunification, arms control, admission of the PRC into the United Nations, and a Soviet proposal for abandonment of a European defense community. The conference does not yield substantive results.

February 6: The New York City Ballet premieres George Balanchine's *The Nutcracker.*

February 6: Folkway Records releases a four-record album of songs by the late folksinger Leadbelly.

February 17: The Tobacco Industry Research Committee is formed by 14 major cigarette companies to address claims that smoking causes cancer.

February 23: The first mass polio vaccinations are administered in Pittsburgh. Their success leads to a nationwide program of mass immunization for children in 1955.

March 1: Radioactive debris from nuclear testing on the Pacific Bikini atoll inadvertently falls on the Japanese fishing boat *Lucky Dragon,* causing radiation sickness among members of the crew, killing one, creating panic in Japan, and provoking an international incident. In 1955, the United States pays Japan $2 million in damages.

March 1: Four Puerto Rican nationalists open fire in the U.S. House of Representatives, wounding five congressmen.

March 1: The United States convenes the Organization of American States (OAS) to address the threat of communism.

March 1: Reverend Billy Graham begins a three-month religious crusade in England.

March 8: Japan and the United States sign a mutual-defense agreement.

March 9: Television newsman Edward R. Murrow broadcasts his "Report on Senator Joseph R. McCarthy" on *See It Now.*

March 10: President Eisenhower calls McCarthy a peril to the Republican Party.

March 11: The United States admits that its atomic testing in the Pacific has exposed 264 native people of the Marshall Islands and 28 Americans to excessive radiation.

March 14: The Vietminh, under the leadership of General Giap, initiates the decisive battle of Dien Bien Phu in North Vietnam. The French outer perimeter, the Gabrielle Line, falls the following day.

March 16: CBS launches its *Morning Show,* hosted by Walter Cronkite, to compete with NBC's *Today Show.*

March 18: Billionaire Howard Hughes purchases all of the remaining stock of the RKO film studio, becoming the first individual ever to become the sole owner of a major movie production company.

March 26: The Soviet Union recognizes East Germany as a sovereign nation.

April 1: The first televised hydrogen bomb test is broadcast nationwide.

April 1: The U.S. Air Force Academy is established in Colorado Springs, Colorado.

April 4: Famed orchestra conductor Arturo Toscanini concludes his career with a final performance at Carnegie Hall.

April 5: Nicaragua declares a state of martial law following an assassination attempt on President Anastasio Somoza.

April 6: McCarthy attacks Murrow personally in his rebuttal on *See It Now* for Murrow's report on the senator one month earlier.

April 7: Reiterating Secretary of State Dulles's 1953 warning of a "domino effect," Eisenhower cautions that a communist victory in Vietnam will spark a chain reaction that will spread throughout Southeast Asia.

April 7: The United States and Canada announce plans to establish a chain of radar stations across Canada along the 55th parallel for early detection of Soviet air attacks.

April 12: Bill Haley and His Comets make their energetic hit single "Rock Around the Clock" at Decca Records's recording studio in New York.

April 15: Activist Margaret Sanger becomes the first woman to address the Japanese Diet. She speaks on the issue of birth control.

April 16: The Detroit Red Wings defeat the Montreal Canadians to win hockey's Stanley Cup.

April 17: Three thousand U.S. troops return from Korea.

April 20: U.S. planes begin flying French paratroopers into Vietnam.

April 22–June 17: In nationally televised Senate hearings, the army charges that Senator McCarthy tried to blackmail the army into commissioning David Schine, one of his aides who has recently been drafted.

May 2: Stan Musial of baseball's St. Louis Cardinals hits five home runs in a doubleheader.

May 4: Governor General Charles Vincent Massey becomes the first Canadian leader to address both houses of the U.S. Congress.

May 6: In the 10th revolution since 1948, a military junta seizes control of Paraguay.

May 6: Roger Bannister, an English medical student at Oxford University, runs a mile in 3:59.4 minutes to become the first person on record to complete a mile in less than four minutes.

May 7: The communist-led Vietminh defeat the French army at Dien Bien Phu. Peace talks begin on May 10.

May 11: The United States declares that Indochina is important but not essential to the security of Southeast Asia.

May 13: The musical *The Pajama Game* opens on Broadway.

May 17: In its landmark ruling on four civil rights cases heard as *Brown v. Board of Education of Topeka, Kansas,* the Supreme Court strikes down the separate-but-equal doctrine that permitted racial segregation of public schools and other facilities.

May 24: IBM announces development of a computer capable of performing more than 10 million operations an hour.

May 28: Alfred Hitchcock's movie *Dial M for Murder* opens.

May 29: The late Pius X becomes the 70th pope to be canonized.

June 6: The current pope, Pius XII, opens an eight-nation television network, Eurovision.

June 10: Ten leading southern politicians declare their intention to refuse to comply with the Supreme Court ruling calling for integration of public schools.

June 14: The United States conducts a nationwide test of civil defense preparedness against an atomic attack.

June 14: On Flag Day, Eisenhower signs a bill adding the phrase "under God" to the Pledge of Allegiance.

June 16: Ngo Dinh Diem returns from exile to South Vietnam. Two days later, South Vietnam's head of state, Bao Dai, appoints Diem prime minister.

June 17: Rocky Marciano defeats Ezzard Charles in 15 rounds to retain the heavyweight boxing title.

June 18: The CIA covertly aids a military coup in Guatemala aimed at removing the leftist reform government of Jacobo Arbenz Guzmán that had become increasingly open to communist influence.

June 18: Following the fall of the French government, after the defeat of Dien Bien Phu, a new government is formed under Premier Pierre Mendès-France.

June 24: The New York State Thruway opens.

June 25: Guatemala's president, Arbenz Guzmán, steps down and is replaced by a right-wing regime led by Colonel Carlos Castillo Armas.

June 29: J. Robert Oppenheimer loses his final appeal to retain his security clearance at the Atomic Energy Commission (AEC), despite a finding that he had been "loyal" in handling U.S. secrets. The AEC justifies its decision because of what it perceives are "fundamental defects" in his character. In 1963

Oppenheimer is "rehabilitated" when President Johnson presents him with the Fermi Award.

July 3: Marilyn Sheppard, the pregnant wife of Dr. Samuel Sheppard, is bludgeoned to death in her home. When allegations of his extramarital affair become public, the story becomes a scandal that dominates the news.

July 5: Elvis Presley makes his first commercial recording, "That's All Right (Mama)."

July 12: Eisenhower proposes the establishment of an interstate highway system that will serve the needs of both national defense and the general public.

July 13: The United States recognizes the new military government of Guatemala.

July 18: Howard Hughes sells his recently acquired RKO film studio and its film backlog to General Teleradio for a $23.5-million profit.

July 19: The first Boeing 707 passenger jet makes its maiden flight.

July 20: A peace agreement between France and the Vietminh calls for the temporary creation of North and South Vietnam, which are to be unified within two years by national election results. The agreement also requires the withdrawal of communist Vietminh forces from South Vietnam. The United States and South Vietnam refuse to sign the accords, and the elections are never held.

August 2: Eisenhower signs the Housing Act to provide 35,000 new housing units, a setback for Eisenhower, who had requested a commitment to build 140,000 units over a four-year period. Furthermore, restrictions within the bill make it unlikely that all 35,000 units can be built.

August 4: Alfred Hitchcock's film *Rear Window,* a murder mystery, premieres.

August 12: The last UN forces withdraw from Korea.

August 16: Henry Luce, publisher of *Time* and *Life* magazines, puts out the first issue of *Sports Illustrated* to appeal to the growing national interest in professional and collegiate sports. The cover features slugger Eddie Matthews of baseball's Milwaukee Braves.

August 17: Eisenhower declares that the United States will stop any invasion of Taiwan by Communist China, and he commits the U.S. Seventh Fleet to this end. This announcement follows the sinking by the Nationalist Chinese of eight communist gunboats off Taiwan and a subsequent threat by the PRC to attack Taiwan.

August 17: Pope Pius XII authorizes U.S. clergy to deliver sacraments in English.

August 18: Assistant Secretary of Labor James Wilkins becomes the first African American to attend a presidential cabinet meeting.

August 22: The 83rd Congress adjourns to prepare for mid-term elections.

August 24: The Communist Control Act strengthens the 1950 McCarran Internal Security Act by designating the Communist Party "a clear, present and continuing danger to the security of the United States." It provides severe penalties for communist and communist-dominated organizations that refuse to register the names of their members or to divulge the identity of their supporters within the federal government. The act effectively outlaws the party, but not individual membership, by depriving it of "all rights, privileges, and immunities attendant upon legal bodies."[18]

August 27: Two U.S. icebreakers become the first vessels to sail completely through the Northwest Passage from the Atlantic to the Pacific.

August 30: Eisenhower signs the Atomic Energy Act, which permits private development of nuclear power.

September 5: Chinese communists attack Jinmen (Quemoy), an island near Taiwan.

September 8: In Manila, the United States, Great Britain, Australia, France, New Zealand, Pakistan, the Philippines, and Thailand form the Southeast Asia Treaty Organization (SEATO) to oppose further communist gains in Southeast Asia.

September 12: Lassie, a popular, heartwarming series about a boy and his pet collie, makes its television debut.

September 14: The Soviet Union begins a series of hydrogen bomb tests in the southern Urals, near the town of Totskoe. Radioactive rain falls on Japan, causing panic.

September 17: India outlaws bigamy.

September 17: Heavyweight boxer Marciano wins a rematch against Charles for his 47th straight victory.

September 27: Construction begins on a second joint U.S.-Canada early warning radar network known as the DEW line. Located in the Arctic Circle, it extends from Alaska to Greenland.

September 29: In a critical situation during the World Series against the Cleveland Indians, who won

From left to right: Senate minority leader Lyndon Johnson, Vice President Richard Nixon, and Senate majority leader William Knowland wave good-bye as the 83rd Congress adjourns on August 22, 1954. *(Photofest)*

a record 111 games in the regular season, San Francisco Giants outfielder Willie Mays makes a sensational over-the-shoulder basket catch to rob first baseman Vic Wertz of a home run. The catch is one of the most memorable plays ever made in Major League Baseball. San Francisco goes on to win the World Series, defeating the Indians in four games. Mays wins his league's batting championship (.345) and is named the National League's Most Valuable Player (MVP). New York Yankee catcher Yogi Berra is the American League MVP. Cleveland's Bobby Avila is the American League's top hitter (341). Although Stan Musial of the St. Louis Cardinals set a Major League record when he hit five home runs in a doubleheader on May 2, Cincinnati's Ted Kluszewski leads the majors

with 49 home runs for the year. Giants pitcher John Antonelli (21-7) and Sandy Consuegra (16-3) of the Chicago White Sox are the top National and American League pitchers, respectively.

October 2: West Germany is admitted into the NATO alliance.

October 3: The television sitcom *Father Knows Best* premieres.

October 4: Marilyn Monroe and Joe DiMaggio divorce after only nine months of marriage.

October 8: Communist-led Vietminh soldiers occupy Hanoi as the French evacuate the city in accordance with the Geneva peace agreement.

October 10: Ho Chi Minh emerges from eight years of hiding to assume leadership of North

Vietnam. Meanwhile the victorious Vietminh, under the leadership of General Giap, parade through the streets of Hanoi, following the evacuation of French troops.

October 12: NBC's highly rated dramatic series *Fireside Theater* broadcasts "The Reign of Amelika Jo," which *TV Guide* maintains in probably the first all-black show ever to be shown on network television (although the cast also includes some Asians). Capitalizing on the popularity of the long-running Broadway hit *South Pacific,* the drama is set in the South Pacific during World War II and is based on a true story.

October 14: The movie *White Christmas,* starring Bing Crosby and Danny Kaye, opens.

October 19: Egypt and Great Britain sign the Suez Canal treaty giving control of the canal to Egypt.

November 1: Steve Allen introduces *The Tonight Show* to national television after several successful local broadcasts.

November 2: Democrats regain control of both houses of Congress in midterm elections.

November 13: In a military coup, Colonel Gamal Abdel Nasser, a proponent of pan-Arab unity who engineered the withdrawal of Britain from Egypt and secured the Suez Canal treaty, ousts General Mohammed Naguib and assumes control of Egypt. Nasser and Naguib had conducted an ongoing power struggle throughout the year.

November 20: Ed Sullivan, host of the popular television variety show *Toast of the Town,* signs a 20-year contract with CBS to host the program under a new title, *The Ed Sullivan Show.*

November 22: The Soviet ambassador to the United Nations, Andrei Vishinsky, dies from a sudden heart attack while preparing a speech for the General Assembly's debate on the U.S. "atoms for peace" proposal. Vishinsky had been Stalin's chief prosecutor during the Soviet purge trials of the 1930s.

November 27: Alger Hiss, a former top official in the Roosevelt administration, is released from prison after serving 44 months for lying about his affiliation with the Communist Party.

December 1: The United States and Nationalist China sign a mutual security pact.

December 2: By a vote of 67-22, the U.S. Senate condemns McCarthy for his behavior toward the

Actor Fess Parker ignited a Davy Crockett fad and a Disney marketing bonanza when he starred in Walt Disney's television and movie stories about the famous American frontiersman. *(Photofest)*

Senate elections subcommittee that was investigating his finances and his behavior during the army-McCarthy hearings, and for his behavior toward the full Senate during the subsequent censure proceedings. All 44 Democrats vote to condemn him, along with one independent and 22 Republicans.

December 10: Ernest Hemingway wins the Nobel Prize in literature and Linus Pauling wins it in chemistry.

December 12: The United States launches the *Forrestal,* the world's largest aircraft carrier to date.

December 15: The first of the "Davy Crockett, Indian Fighter" episodes appears on *Disneyland.*

December 26: The Cleveland Browns win the NFL title by defeating the Detroit Lions 56-10. Los Angeles Rams quarterback Norm Van Brocklin leads the league in passing, San Francisco's Joe Perry in rushing, and Philadelphia's Pete Pihos in receiving.

EYEWITNESS TESTIMONY

It is true that parental or relatives' approval wasn't sought. We assume that parents weren't asked because it wasn't the norm at the time.

Beth Taylor, spokesperson for Britain's Atomic Energy Authority, commenting in 2001 on the practice that lasted from 1954 to 1970 of removing femur bones from dead children in order to test levels of radiation from atomic testing, in "Children's Bones Were Secretly Tested," Miami Herald, October 1, 2001, p. 6A.

The great traitors of the past have swung battles, but not wars. The situation is different today. An Alger Hiss, critically situated, can, conceivably, determine the destiny of the West. A Klaus Fuchs can deliver to "the thirteen scheming men" what may well be the key to world conquest. . . .

By 1950 . . . , the era was past when Americans needed to be educated about the threat of Communism.

But a new era arrived, the dominant characteristic of which was—and remains—indecision. . . . The evolution from pro-Communism in the direction of anti-Communism seemed to have ground to a halt in an intermediary stage . . . *anti*-anti-Communism.

This, then, was the overriding problem when Senator McCarthy made his entrance on the national stage: having acknowledged the nature and immediacy of our peril, how might we get by our disintegrated ruling elite, which had no stomach for battle, and get down to the business of fighting the enemy in our midst? . . .

As regards one of the two fundamental questions we have been asking (Are McCarthy's specific charges warranted in the light of his evidence?), it is clear that he has been guilty of a number of exaggerations, some of them reckless; and perhaps some of them have unjustly damaged the persons concerned. . . .

As regards the other standard for determining whether smearing has been a characteristic of McCarthy's method (Does the evidence McCarthy presents justify calling into question his targets' loyalty?), the case-by-case breakdown clearly renders a verdict extremely favorable to McCarthy. With the two exceptions of [newspaper columnist] Drew Pearson and [former secretary of state and secretary of defense] George Marshall, not a single person was accused by McCarthy whose loyalty could not be questioned on the basis of a most responsible reading of official records. And this is the only test that seems to be relevant for deciding whether McCarthy "habitually smears people."

Conservative editor and author William F. Buckley, Jr., defending Senator McCarthy's actions, in Buckley, McCarthy and His Enemies: The Record and Its Meaning (1954), pp. 3–4, 277.

When the Soviets showed the first signs of enclosing, in Soviet secrecy, mere scientific principles like those of the bomb, we Americans could and should have seen that Russian secrecy would instantly compel American secrecy. We should have seen that an America thus suddenly made secret . . . would no longer be free, and its democratic people could no longer be informed. Hence Russia's Iron Curtain would have been seen as what it was and is and always will be: a posture of intolerable aggression against American freedom. . . .

We have always had the cause, to challenge Soviet power earlier, in the name of liberty, brotherhood, justice, human integrity and decency. . . . We were feeble-minded in ideals and ideology: our vision of freedom was myopic. . . .

If the McCarthys should remove from U.S.A. every single Communist and Communist suspect, the present danger to us all—so clear, so terrible—*would not be measurably altered.* . . . America would be Communist-free, spy-free, to be sure. But half a billion people elsewhere in the world, Communists all or slaves of Communists, would *still* be undeterred and laboring day and night to destroy liberty on earth and the United States in particular. . . . That is the measure of the cosmic *unimportance* of the Senator from our sister state. And that is the measure of the foolishness of those who hold the credulous notion that the McCarthys are accomplishing work of primary importance in the matter of our imminent doom.

Civil defense proponent Philip Wylie attacking McCarthyism for distracting Americans from the much-greater threat of international communism, in his novel Tomorrow! (1954), p. 102.

The bombing had proved an ultimate blessing by furnishing a brand-new chance to build a world brand-new—and infinitely better. . . . Then the Bomb would be no catastrophe at all, but pure benefit. "End of an era," they would say. "Good thing, too," they'd add. "Can't imagine how they stood those old cities" [with their confining architecture and stifling urban design] they'd assert. "Barbaric." "Positively medieval."

> *Survivors in the Midwest expressing gratitude for the opportunity to create society anew in the aftermath of a fictional atomic war, in Philip Wylie,* Tomorrow! *(1954), pp. 284, 286.*

[*Batman* comic books present] a wish dream of two homosexuals living together.

> *Social critic Frederic Wertham, pointing to perceived immorality in comic books in* Seduction of the Innocent *(1954), in Jack Mingo, ed.,* The Whole Pop Catalogue *(1991), p. 66.*

Dr. Jonas Salk invented the vaccine that brought to an end the polio epidemic of the early 1950s. *(Photofest)*

I was amazed, and impressed, that a famous author had written a story about an unmarried girl getting a diaphragm (described in frank and sometimes humorous detail), and that it was published in the most highbrow literary journal of the known (to me) world, the periodical whose pages carried the words of Lionel Trilling, Irving Howe, Philip Rahv, and William Phillips, high priests of intellectual life in New York. (In fact, the magazine looked to me like some kind of holy missal, the list of titles and authors on the cover seeming to give it the weight and authority of a prayerbook.)

> *Writer Dan Wakefield describing his reaction to the publication of Mary McCarthy's story "Dottie Makes an Honest Woman of Herself," which appeared in* Partisan Review, *January–February 1954, in Wakefield,* New York in the Fifties *(1992), pp. 233–34.*

I was nine when my childhood ended. We had celebrated my birthday the day before, which was a Saturday, and it hadn't gone well. . . . had a feeling that had become familiar to me during those last weeks: that I was watching everything from a great distance. My mother had taken me to a number of doctors, but they could find no reason for the fatigue or the insomnia that now plagued me. . . .

I was sitting on a low wall. . . . I pushed myself off the wall and a surprise pain, a bad one, shot through my legs, back, and neck as I dropped straight down onto the pavement. As my friends crowded around, I tried to laugh. I was mortified. It was my birthday and I couldn't even get up. . . .

After entering the hospital, I was abruptly taken away from my parents, without explanation, and wheeled into an elevator. That was when I came apart. I screamed all the way upstairs. . . . I was beyond terror. Everything hurt—my back, neck, legs, arms, and chest; it even hurt to breathe. . . .

It was supposed to be a children's ward, but the iron lungs that lined the halls must have contained some adults too. I could hear men's voices wheezing and shouting in the night. When my turn came to be in the iron lung, I kept calling out, I'm okay . . but nobody came, and you can't even scratch your own nose. . . .

If polio marked the end of my childhood, it also left me with embryonic survival skills. I discovered that whatever your losses, you can still for the most part choose your attitude. If you have your health, a little courage, and imagination, then you have the internal resources to build a new life, and maybe even a better one.

Actress Mia Farrow describing in her autobiography how she came down with polio on her ninth birthday, February 9, 1954, in Farrow, What Falls Away *(1998), p. 1.*

As a police reporter many years ago, I was irked by eyewitnesses who had heard shots only as "backfiring automobiles," "blowouts" and "firecrackers." But this time I too thought that firecrackers were going off, and I thought it was a Latin demonstration.

But only for a moment. I saw two men and a woman, in the second row of the Ladies Gallery, pumping at pistols. The two men appeared to be aiming at the desk of representative Charles A. Halleck of Indiana, the Republican Floor Leader.

The woman had her pistol high, working it with both hands, and was apparently shooting at the ceiling or at areas along gallery rails. When she had emptied it, she handed it to a companion, apparently for reloading, and waved a Puerto Rican flag, shrieking, "freedom for my country." . . .

A glance at the floor, at which the bullets had poured at almost machine-gun rapidity, showed most members feeling themselves to see if they had been hit. The number who threw themselves to the floor was astonishingly small. But several could not get up and other House members hovered over them. . . .

The woman, crying out about "freedom" again waved her flag, then threw it into the gallery row in front of her. . . .

Outside the gallery door a man was prone, held down by so many persons that news photographers had to fight their way through to get a picture. A second man had been pinned to a wall.

The man on the floor still had a pistol in his hand and was defying attempts to make him let go. Finally, Representative James E. Van Zandt, Republican of Pennsylvania, a Naval Reserve captain with a long South Pacific war record, and others broke the man's hold on the pistol.

Reporter C. P. Trussell describing the attack by Puerto Rican nationalists on members of Congress in the Capitol on March 1, 1954, in Trussell, "Witness Describes Shooting, Capture," New York Times, *March 2, 1954, pp. 1, 16.*

They put a tiny turd on every one of your lines.

Actor-director Orson Welles commenting to writer Abe Burrows about changes made to his script for the film adaptation of Guys and Dolls, *the rights to which producer Samuel Goldwyn paid $1 million on March 4, 1954, in Harry Haun,* The Cinematic Century *(2000).*

[McCarthy] dons his war paint. He goes into his war dance. He emits his war whoops. He goes forth to battle and proudly returns with the scalp of a pink Army dentist. We may assume that this represents the depth and seriousness of Communist penetration in the country at this time.

Republican senator Ralph E. Flanders in a speech on the Senate floor on March 9, 1954, responding to McCarthy's criticism of the promotion and honorable discharge of a left-wing dentist, Major Irving Peress, who was based at Camp Kilmer, in Martin Gilbert, A History of the Twentieth Century, *vol. 3 (2000), p. 61.*

Our working thesis tonight is this quotation: "If this fight against communism is made a fight between America's two great political parties, the American people know that one of these parties will be destroyed, and the Republic cannot endure very long as a one-party system." We applaud that statement, and we think Senator McCarthy ought to. He said it 17 months ago in Milwaukee [on October 3, 1952]. . . .

But on February 4, 1954, Senator McCarthy spoke of one party's treason. . . . "The issue between Republicans and Democrats is clearly drawn. It has been deliberately drawn by those who have been in charge of twenty years of treason. Now, the hard fact is . . . that those who wear the label Democrat . . . wear it with the fame of a historic betrayal." . . .

On one thing the senator has been consistent. Often operating as a one-man committee, he has traveled far, interviewed many, terrorized some, accused civilian and military leaders of the past administration of a great conspiracy to turn over the country to communism, investigated and substantially demoralized the present State Department, made varying charges of espionage at Ft. Monmouth. The Army says it has been unable to find anything relating to espionage there. He has interrogated a varied assortment of what he calls Fifth Amendment communists. . . .

[On February 22, 1954, McCarthy] reviewed some of the General Zwicker testimony and "proved" he hadn't abused him. [Murrow shows film of McCarthy speaking:] "There is nothing more serious than being a traitor to his country as part of the communist conspiracy. . . . After he [Zwicker] said that he wouldn't remove that general from the Army who cleared the communist major, I said to him, '. . . General, you should be removed from any command. Any man who has been given the honor of being promoted to general and who says, "I will protect another general who protects communists" is not fit to wear that uniform, General.'" [applause] . . .

"And wait until you hear the bleeding hearts scream and cry about our methods of trying to drag the truth from those who know or should know who covered up a Fifth Amendment communist major. But they say, 'Oh, it's alright to uncover them, but don't get rough doing it, McCarthy.'" . . .

[Murrow states,] Senator McCarthy claims that only the left-wing press criticized him on the Zwicker case. Of the fifty largest circulation newspapers in the country . . . the ratio is about three to one [against McCarthy. Murrow then reads several headlines in prominent papers criticizing McCarthy]. . . .

[Murrow:] Two of the staples of his diet are the investigations, protected by immunity, and the half truth. We herewith submit samples of both. . . .

[Murrow concludes:] The line between investigating and persecuting is a very fine one, and the junior senator from Wisconsin has stepped over it repeatedly. His primary achievement has been in confusing the public mind as between the internal and the external threats of communism. We must not confuse dissent with disloyalty. We must remember always that accusation is not proof and that conviction depends upon evidence and due process of law. . . . We will not be driven by fear into an age of unreason, if we dig deep in our history and our doctrine. . . . This is no time for men who oppose Senator McCarthy's methods to keep silent, or for those who approve. . . . We cannot defend freedom abroad by deserting it at home.

Journalist Edward R. Murrow's "Report on Senator Joseph McCarthy," on his television show, See It Now, *March 9, 1954, in Murrow,* In Search of Light: The Broadcasts of Edward R. Murrow *(1967).*

You may have cost us the network.

CBS president Frank Stanton to Fred Friendly, the producer of Edward R. Murrow's See It Now, *after Murrow broadcast his "Report on Senator Joseph McCarthy" on March 9, 1954, in Stephen J. Whitfield,* The Culture of the Cold War *(1996), p. 165.*

The Senate Investigating Committee has forced out of government and out of important defense plants communists engaged in the Soviet conspiracy. And, you know, it's interesting to note that the viciousness of Murrow's attacks is in direct ratio to our success in digging out communists. . . . Murrow is a symbol, the leader, and the cleverest of the jackal pack which is always found at the throat of anyone who dares to expose individual communists and traitors. I am prepared to say to you, in fact, that Mr. Edward R. Murrow, as far back as twenty years ago, was engaged in propaganda for communist causes.

Senator Joseph McCarthy rebutting Edward R. Murrow's "Report" on the senator, which aired March 9, 1954, on See It Now, *April 16, 1954.*

I am not afraid of being thought a sentimentalist when I stand here tonight and tell you that I believe natural beauty has a necessary place in the spiritual development of any individual or society. I believe that whenever we destroy beauty, or whenever we substitute something man-made and artificial for a natural feature of the earth, we have retarded some part of man's spiritual growth.

I believe this affinity of the human spirit for the earth and its beauties is deeply and logically rooted. As human beings, we are part of the whole stream of life. We have been human beings for perhaps a million years. But life itself passes on something of itself to other life—that mysterious entity that moves and is aware of itself and its surroundings. . . . [I]ts living protoplasm is built of the same elements as air, water, and rock. To these the mysterious spark of life was added. Our origins are of the earth. And so there is in us a deeply seated response to the natural universe, which is part of our humanity. . . .

I believe that it is important for women to realize that the world of today threatens to destroy much of that beauty that has immense power to bring us a healing release from tension. . . .

We see it [the destruction] in small ways in our own communities, and in larger ways in the community. We see the destruction of beauty and the suppression of human individuality in hundreds of suburban real estate developments where the first act is to cut down all the trees and the next is to build an infinitude of little houses. . . .

We see the destructive trend on the national scale in proposals to invade the national parks with commercial schemes such as the building of power dams. . . .

Environmentalist Rachel Carson decrying the adverse
spiritual consequences of environmental destruction in a
speech in Columbus, Ohio, April 21, 1954, in Carson,
Lost Woods: The Discovered Writing of Rachel
Carson *(1998), pp. 160–62.*

I'm just a lil' ole singles hitter. Besides, I prefer four singles to one homer any day in the week. I don't mean to say that I'll refuse the home run championship if I should win it. But I certainly have no intention of trying for it. . . .

When I try to hit the long ball, I never do. . . . I'm sure I told you . . . the story of how I hit thirty-nine homers in 1948 without trying to hit even one. So I deliberately went for the fences the next year. Not only did I stop hitting homers. I also stopped hitting singles. That's when I quit as a slugger. I haven't tried for a home run since. . . . Oops!. . . I forgot. I did shoot for the moon a couple of weeks ago. It was in that double-header with the Giants. After I'd hit my fourth home run in the same afternoon, the announcer boomed out the news that I'd just tied a record. Until then, I hadn't been paying any attention to my homers. I'd just met the ball solidly four times and each went for the distance.

That's when I determined to try for a fifth homer. Hoyt Wilhelm was pitching and I never had hit him particularly well. He threw me a knuckler and—oh boy—that fifth homer was the best shot of them all. It went all the way over the roof in right center. Wow! What a belt! . . .

When I got home that night. . . . my son, Dickie, remarked, "Gee, dad, those pitchers must have fed you a lot of fat pitches today." How do you like that for hero worship?

Baseball player Stan Musial of the St. Louis Cardinals
describing when he hit five home runs in a single day,
May 2, 1954, in Arthur Daley, "Just a Singles
Hitter," New York Times,
May 20, 1954, p. 42.

For America, detente with Cuba should be time of confession and catharsis, a time when America comes to understand the self-destructive delusions of the Imperial mentality.

But instead of self-understanding, America is anxious merely to resume trade and forget the whole thing. . . .

So I entered the library and ordered the microfilms of the local newspaper. . . .

May 3, 1954. Hanoi, Indochina. (AP) The red-led masses of the Vietminh unleashed a new assault on Dien Bien Phu, overran three strong points and occupied part of a fourth today in their attempt to wipe out France's Gibraltar of the Jungle. . . .

May 3, 1954. Rochester's high-school youth will play an important part in the civil defense of the city in the event of an emergency attack by serving as stretcher bearers for the Emergency Medical Services of Civil Defense. . . .

May 3, 1954: WINGS BOW TO HAVANA 3–1

(Dugout Diggins). . . . "This is really a beautiful ballpark," said Coco Bacallao . . . road secretary of the Cubans. "It's the greenest grass I've seen in any stadium."

This was just a day like any other, where history could be pursued in any direction. Involvement in Southeast Asia, cold-war fears of enemy attack, baseball. But it was also a special day. This was the day of the first game played on American soil by the Havana Sugar Kings, also called the Cubans. I remember the oldest and loudest of the regular fans who sat in my section. . . . He was . . reading from this little bit of paper and shouting at the top of his, the most powerful of all lungs, *"Napoleon, a qui Napoleon, a qui!"* He was attempting to call the Havana manager, "Nap" Reyes, in his native tongue. It was not an incident. I remember nothing else about the game.

Author Howard Senzel recalling the events of May 3,
1954, in Senzel, Baseball and the Cold War
(1977), pp. 37–40.

These cases come to us from the states of Kansas, South Carolina, Virginia, and Delaware. They are premised on different facts and different local conditions, but a common legal question justifies their consideration together in this consolidated opinion.

In each of the cases, minors of the Negro race . . . seek the aid of the courts in obtaining admission to the public school of their community on a nonsegregated basis. In each instance, they had been denied admission to schools attended by white children under laws requiring or permitting segregation according to race. This segregation was alleged to deprive the plaintiffs of the equal protection of the laws under the Fourteenth Amendment. . . .

In the first cases in this Court construing the Fourteenth Amendment, decided shortly after its adoption [in 1868], the Court interpreted it as proscribing all state-imposed discriminations against the Negro race. The doctrine of "separate but equal" did not make its appearance in this Court until 1896 in the case of *Plessy v. Ferguson, supra,* involving not education but transportation. In this Court, there have been six cases involving the "separate but equal" doctrine in the field of public education. . . . In none of these cases was it necessary to re-examine the doctrine to grant relief to the Negro plaintiff. . . .

Here, unlike *Sweatt v. Painter,* there are findings below that the negro and white schools involved have been equalized, or are being equalized, with respect to buildings, curricula, qualifications and salaries of teachers, and other "tangible" factors. Our decision, therefore, cannot turn on merely a comparison of these tangible factors. . . . We must look instead to the effect of segregation itself on public education.

In approaching this problem, we cannot turn the clock back to 1868 when the Amendment was adopted. . . . We must consider public education in the light of its full development and its place in American life throughout the Nation. Only in this way can it be determined if segregation in public schools deprives these plaintiffs of the equal protection of the laws.

Today, education is perhaps the most important function of state and local government. . . . It is the very foundation of good citizenship. Today, it is a principal instrument in awakening the child to cultural values, in preparing him for later professional training, and in helping him to adjust normally to his environment. In these days, it is doubtful that any child may reasonably be expected to succeed in life if he is denied the opportunity of an education. Such an opportunity . . . is a right which must be made available to all on equal terms.

We come then to the question presented: does segregation of children in public schools solely on the basis of race, even though the physical facilities and other "tangible" factors may be equal, deprive

the children of the minority group of equal educational opportunities. We believe that it does. . . .

The effect of this separation on their educational opportunities was well stated by a finding in a Kansas case by a court which nevertheless felt compelled to rule against the Negro plaintiffs:

"Segregation of white and colored children in public schools has a detrimental effect upon the colored children. The impact is greater when it has the sanction of law, for the policy of separating the races is usually interpreted as denoting the inferiority of the negro group. A sense of inferiority affects the motivation of a child to learn. Segregation . . . therefore, has a tendency to [retard] the educational and mental development of negro children and to deprive them of some of the benefits they would receive in a racial[ly] integrated school." . . .

We conclude that in the field of public education the doctrine of "separate but equal" has no place. Separate educational facilities are inherently unequal. Therefore, we hold that the plaintiffs and others similarly situated . . . are, by reason of the segregation complained of, deprived of the equal protection of the laws guaranteed by the Fourteenth Amendment.

Chief Justice Earl Warren delivering the opinion for the unanimous Supreme Court ruling on Brown v. Board of Education of Topeka, *issued on May 17, 1954, in Warren, "Opinion of the Supreme Court of the United States" (2001).*

The South will not abide by nor obey this legislative decision by a political court.

Mississippi senator James O. Eastland responding to the landmark Brown v. Board of Education of Topeka *ruling of May 17, 1954, in Sanford Wexler,* An Eyewitness History of the Civil Rights Movement *(1999), p. 39.*

My oath of office requires me to accept it as the law. . . . I urge all Southern officials to avoid any sort of rash or hasty action.

Louisiana senator Russell B. Long commenting on the Brown v. Board of Education of Topeka *ruling of May 17, 1954, in Sanford Wexler,* An Eyewitness History of the Civil Rights Movement *(1999), p. 39.*

The men who should have the most credit for a unanimous decision were those men who came out of the South [Justices Hugo Black, Stanley Reed, and Tom Clark].

Supreme Court chief justice Earl Warren commenting on the Brown v. Board of Education of Topeka *ruling of May 17, 1954, in Sanford Wexler,* An Eyewitness History of the Civil Rights Movement *(1999), p. 38.*

I had my first "date" when I was nine years old. I had no idea what to do on a date, or what to talk about, but I had read somewhere that a girl should talk about either sports or politics. As I knew nothing about sports, I chose politics. So when my date, a little nine-year-old boy, arrived at my door, I looked earnestly into his eyes and asked, "What do you think of the McCarthy hearings?"

Professor Peggy Endel recollecting the impact of the army-McCarthy hearings, which began in spring 1954, when she was a little girl, in private correspondence with the author, September 7, 2001.

Miami Beach has experienced more than its share of ups and downs. Carl Fisher took a virtually deserted island off the Miami coast in the early 1900s and converted it into a lush resort rivaling Palm Beach, St. Petersburg, and St. Augustine in elegance. In the 1920s and early '30s oceanfront hotels sprang up on Ocean Drive all the way to 16th Street.

The stock market crash of 1929 dealt a heavy blow to the Miami area, and tourism, the bedrock of business, slumped disastrously. However, World War II boosted the economy, as hotels were requisitioned to house service personnel, and by 1950, the boom was back in full swing. Tourists returned in ever-increasing numbers and ex-GIs who trained in the Miami area returned to settle down and establish roots. The building boom resumed in full vigor with sky-scraper hotels being built in ever-increasing numbers. The Saxony, the Sans Souci, the Fontainebleau, the Eden Roc, the Cadillac, to name a few—all opened their doors in the 1950s. The expansion created all sorts of new jobs in the local economy, including an opportunity for someone like me to go into business for himself making brochures for and otherwise promoting some of the smaller, new hotels that were opening farther up along the strip.

Robert I. Schwartz recalling when he became a self-employed advertising agent in summer 1954, in private correspondence with the author, September 30, 2001.

What 3-D [3-dimensional film projection] adds, then, to the movies' classic potencies is an increased kinaesthetic sensation. Cinerama's rival, Cinemas-cope, offered a decisive sample: a racing car smashed up apparently under one's nose. The privilege conferred on every single patron of 3-D, then, is that conferred at an actual auto race only on the very limited few who have to dodge the swerving racer as it careens toward the sidelines. One is "on the spot" (marked X) during nature's and man's most significant, or at least violent, behavior.

It is logical to conclude that, with the patron of the 3-Ds assailed more effectively than ever with the temptation to see reality in terms of unreality, his whole view of life, inside and outside the place of entertainment, will be increasingly tinged with chimericalness. . . . The classic "alienation" of our times has thus acquired an extra dimension via the screen "depth." . . . The two-dimensional screen was always a guarantee against the optical feeling of depth. It was a formal barrier. . . . The concrete evidence that it is physically penetrable proposes not so much greater opportunities for artistic effects as greater opportunities for its patrons to judge all existence as compact with the *illusion* of three-dimensional space. So the 3-Ds tend to rob life itself of its third dimension.

Critic Parker Tyler discussing the impact on cinema of three-dimensional film projection in Tyler, "Movie Note: The 3-D's," Kenyon Review *(Summer 1954), pp. 468–72.*

When you find there are Communists and possible spies in a place like [Fort] Monmouth, you must be alarmed, aren't you? I don't want the sun to go down while they are still in there. Will you not, before the sun goes down, give those names [of alleged communists at the fort] to the FBI?

Army special counsel Joseph Welch to Senator McCarthy's aide, Roy Cohn, on June 9, 1954, during the army-McCarthy hearings, in This Fabulous Century *(1970), p. 126.*

Mr. J. Edgar Hoover and his men know a lot better than I. . . . I do not propose to tell the FBI how to run its shop.

Roy Cohn replying to Counsel Joseph Welch's request to give names of alleged communists in the army to FBI, on June 9, 1954, in This Fabulous Century *(1970), p. 126.*

I think we should tell Mr. Welch that he has in his law firm a young man named Fisher who has been for a number of years a member of an organization named as the legal bulwark of the Communist Party [Fisher had once belonged to the National Lawyer's Guild]. . . . Mr. Welch, I just felt that I had a duty to respond to your urgent request that before sundown, when we know of anyone serving the Communist cause, we let the agency know. . . . I have been rather bored with your phony requests to Mr. Cohn here that he personally get every Communist out of government before sundown.

Senator Joseph McCarthy's retort to Counsel Joseph Welch on June 9, 1954, after Welch pressed Roy Cohn to furnish the names of the alleged communist spies in the army, in This Fabulous Century *(1970), p. 128.*

Until this moment, Senator, I think I never really gauged your cruelty or your recklessness. Fred Fisher is starting what looks to be a brilliant career. . . . Little did I dream you could be so reckless and so cruel as to do an injury to that lad. I fear he shall always bear a scar needlessly inflicted by you. . . . Let us not assassinate this lad further, Senator. You have done enough. Have you no sense of decency, sir, at long last? Have you no sense of decency?

Army counsel Joseph Welch's response to Senator Joseph McCarthy's attack of June 9, 1954, on Fred Fisher during the army-McCarthy hearings, in This Fabulous Century *(1970), p. 130.*

That which was missing [from the Pledge of Allegiance] was the characteristic and definitive factor in the American way of life. Indeed, apart from the mention of the phrase, 'the United States of America,' it could be the pledge of any republic. In fact, I could hear little Muscovites repeat a similar pledge to their hammer-and-sickle flags in Moscow with equal solemnity. . . . Russia also claims to be indivisible.

Reverend George M. Docherty urging in a sermon attended by President Eisenhower and members of Congress that the phrase "one nation under God," be added to the Pledge of Allegiance, an addition that Eisenhower signed into law on June 14, 1954, in Stephen J. Whitfield, The Culture of the Cold War *(1996), p. 89.*

These negotiations appear to have gone underground, and we have little reliable knowledge of what is really in the minds of the French government. . . . We fear that the French may in fact, without prior consultations with us . . . agree to a settlement that . . . contains such political clauses and restrictions that Laos, Cambodia, and southern Vietnam will almost surely fall in a few months under Communist control.

Secretary of State John Foster Dulles commenting on a private meeting on June 23, 1954, between China's foreign minister, Zhou Enlai, and France's president, Pierre Mendès-France, during the peace talks following the French defeat at Dien Bien Phu, in Stanley Karnow, Vietnam: A History *(1983), p. 202.*

Well, we tried three or four things. . . . [A]ll of a sudden Elvis started singing a song, jumpin' around and just acting the fool too, and you know, I started playing with them.

Musician Sam Phillips describing the recording session on July 5, 1954, that produced Elvis Presley's first commercial record, "That's All Right (Mama)", in Paul Friedlander, Rock and Roll: A Social History *(1996), p. 44.*

Resolved, that the conduct of the Senator from Wisconsin, Mr. McCarthy, is unbecoming a Member of the United States Senate, is contrary to Senatorial traditions, and tends to bring the Senate into disrepute, and such conduct is hereby condemned.

The motion calling for the censure of McCarthy, introduced on July 30, 1954, by Republican senator Ralph Flanders of Vermont, in Dwight Eisenhower, The White House Years, *vol. 1 (1963), p. 329.*

Now, I believe, is the moment for parley at the summit [between the United States and Soviet Union]. All the world desires it. In two or three years a different mood may rule either with those who have their hands upon the levers, or upon the multitude whose votes they require. . . . Fancy that you and Malenkov should never have met, or that he should never have been outside Russia, when all the time, in both countries, appalling preparations are being made for measureless mutual destruction. . . . After all, the interests of both sides is survival and, as additional attraction, measureless material prosperity of the masses.

Britain's prime minister, Winston Churchill, in a letter dated August 8, 1954, to President Dwight Eisenhower, in Martin Gilbert, A History of the Twentieth Century, *vol. 3 (2000), pp. 53–54.*

The Soviet high command did not drop its bomb directly on to the 44,000 troops assembled for the Totskoe exercise. They were grouped in attack formation three miles to the south. Film shot at the time showed soldiers ducking into trenches as the shock wave swept over them. Forty minutes after the blast, the order to advance was given and the lead elements reached the epicenter two hours later. No thought was given to the deadly health effects.

Anatol Lieven, correspondent for the London Times, *recalling the Totskoe nuclear exercise of September 1954, in Martin Gilbert,* A History of the Twentieth Century, *vol. 3 (2000), p. 59.*

Those who today oppose this peacekeeping exercise should remember 1954, when the whole population for eighteen miles around were kicked out of their homes and had to hide in ditches. It was a barbaric event, threatening the destruction even of our own people.

Russian minister of defense Pavel Grachev recalling Soviet nuclear tests that began on September 14, 1954, in an address at a combined U.S.-Russian military exercise in Totskoe in 1994, in Martin Gilbert, A History of the Twentieth Century, *vol. 3 (2000), p. 58.*

It was October of 1954, I was ten years old and watching with great excitement the first game of the World Series on our old Philco black and white TV. The Indians were winning, I believe, in a close game, and my favorite player, first basemen Vic Wertz, was at bat. There were runners on first and second, and Wertz crushed a ball to straight away center. It looked like a home run for sure. Suddenly, Willie Mays ran straight back, and, with his face to the wall, reached out, caught the ball over his head, and turned around and fired it back. I couldn't believe it. After that, everything went downhill: the great pitchers, Wynn, Lemon and Garcia, faltered; Dusty Rhodes hit a game-winning home run against us that was less than 300 feet, and the next thing I knew, it was all over. In just four games. And my father had tickets to take me to the fifth game!! What an experience.

Historian Howard Rock recalling Willie Mays's pivotal over-the-shoulder catch in the first game of the World Series between the San Francisco Giants and the Cleveland Indians on September 29, 1954, in private correspondence with the author, September 5, 2001.

He wanted the average guy to feel he was driving a baby Cadillac.

Automobile designer Bob Cadaret commenting on Ed Cole, the General Motors executive who assembled the team that developed the revolutionary V-8 engine for the 1955 Chevrolet, which appeared on the market in October 1954, in David Halberstam, The Fifties *(1993), p. 495.*

No man can excel at two national pastimes.

Comedian Oscar Levant's quip about the breakup on October 4, 1954, of the marriage between movie star Marilyn Monroe and baseball hero Joe DiMaggio, in Harry Haun, The Cinematic Century *(2000).*

I would have the American people recognize the fact that the Communist party has now extended its tentacles to the United States Senate. It has made a committee of the Senate its unwitting handmaiden.

Senator Joseph McCarthy's statement on November 9, 1954, the day prior to the debate by the full Senate of the recommendation of the Select Committee, chaired by Republican Arthur Watkins of Utah, that McCarthy be censured for contempt of the Senate; in Dwight Eisenhower, The White House Years, *vol. 1 (1963), p. 329.*

If there were a competition of saints in which liberals could bid, George Orwell would be their man; he satisfies at once the liberal nostalgia for action and their resignation to despair.

Critic Philip Rieff, characterizing liberals in his article, Rieff, "George Orwell and the Post-Liberal Imagination," Kenyon Review *(Winter 1954), p. 49.*

[LSD can] produce serious insanity for periods of 8 to 18 hours and possibly longer. [Therefore, I do] not recommend testing in the Christmas punch bowls usually present at Christmas office parties.

From an internal Central Intelligence Agency security memo dated December 15, 1954, in response to reports of a planned gag to spike the punch at the annual CIA office Christmas party, in Martin A. Lee and Bruce Shlain, Acid Dreams, The Complete Social History of LSD *(1985), p. 29.*

7

Disneyland and Cold War Angst
1955

As both the United States and Soviet Union continued to test increasingly more powerful nuclear weapons, scientists worldwide warned that if used en masse in a large-scale war, these devices could potentially wipe out the human race. Moreover, they cautioned, even the testing itself was harmful to the survival of the species, as the radioactive fallout from the aboveground tests was shown to cause significant genetic damage at distances far from the test sites. At the same time, cold war antagonisms between the superpowers intensified as Congress authorized Eisenhower to go to war to defend Taiwan against communism, and the Soviet-dominated Warsaw Pact formed to oppose a NATO that now included a rearmed, newly independent West Germany.

The growing recognition of the dangers of nuclear war—to winners and bystanders as well as to losers—and the sharpening of the East–West division contributed to a cultural angst that was sometimes expressed overtly in angry antinuclear demonstrations and in antiauthoritarian public performances by the Beat poets and others. However, more often cold war anxieties remained unspoken, and the brisk economy; advances in science, medicine, travel, and technology; and the ever-increasing variety of consumer goods and entertainment opportunities created an outward veneer of good times. These perhaps found their strongest expression in the opening of Disneyland in California. The world's first modern theme park resonated strongly with Americans by re-creating the wonder and delight of youthful innocence, promoting a patriotic and noble view of America's past, and imagining a bright future made better and easier by science and modern technology.

Nonetheless, feelings of fear, hopelessness, vague despair, and inability to control life found expression not just in the translated writings of the French existentialists that were becoming more widely available in the United States, but also in America's own popular culture. Several of the year's top movies feature characters who lead lives of quiet desperation, including the Motion Picture Academy's selection for best film, *Marty*. The ongoing personal and spiritual crises within the United States's new, comparatively affluent, suburban families, depicted in such best-selling fiction as Sloan Wilson's *The Man in the Gray Flannel Suit,* also resonated with the public. But dissatisfaction with the

American status quo was voiced most strongly, and angrily, by the emerging, antiestablishment Beat poets, who gave their first major public reading in San Francisco.

Empowered by the 1954 Supreme Court ruling that struck down the separate-but-equal doctrine, activists ushered in a new era of civil rights and legal challenges to the institutions of segregation in the South. The arrest in December of Rosa Parks in Montgomery, Alabama, sparked a successful boycott there of public transportation and brought Dr. Martin Luther King, Jr., to the forefront of the civil rights movement.

The social protest provoked many Americans to question the fairness of the nation's institutions and social norms. Although their dissatisfaction was less politically directed, young people, especially, found inspiration in antiauthoritarian figures such as movie star James Dean, who died in an automobile accident shortly after rising to fame. Teenagers and young adults also distanced themselves from convention and authority by embracing fast-paced, energetic rock 'n' roll, which continued to grow despite opposition by adults who could not appreciate the music form, feared its origins in black rhythm and blues, and/or recognized the sexual energy that it tapped into and believed it was inappropriate, or even dangerous. The point of view of these adults was better represented in best-sellers such as Herman Wouk's *Marjorie Morningstar* and newly introduced television westerns such as *Gunsmoke,* which endorsed traditional values and defended social authority against those who would violate it.

THE COLD WAR AND INTERNATIONAL POLITICS

The Cold War Abroad

Although the danger of human extinction from nuclear war was becoming increasingly apparent, cold war antagonisms remained strong during 1955. Tensions grew between the United States and the communist People's Republic of China (PRC), and the Soviet Union joined with other Eastern bloc nations to form the Warsaw Pact, in opposition to NATO. Throughout the year, new attention was directed to the immediate dangers of nuclear testing and to the ultimate potential of a nuclear war to exterminate all human life. In June, the U.S. Atomic Energy Commission acknowledged that radioactive fallout from nuclear testing could produce genetic mutations in humans, although it downplayed the extent of the risk. In July, a group of Nobel Prize winners warned that "science was giving mankind the means with which to destroy itself," and that nuclear weapons could "contaminate the world with radioactivity to such an extent that entire nations may be wiped out."[1]

Nonetheless, governments continued to develop and test nuclear weaponry that was increasingly potent. In February, Great Britain announced that it had the capability to make a hydrogen bomb, although it did not actually test one until 1957. Applying results from the nuclear tests conducted in the Pacific during 1954, the United States developed a range of new hydrogen-based weapons during the first six months of the year, and in June, the Atomic Energy Commission announced it could build inexpensive hydrogen bombs of virtually limitless size. Eisenhower believed that a strong economy was the best defense against communism, and that excessive military spending would undermine the economy; therefore, he preferred to place a larger share of national defense in nuclear weaponry, which was more cost efficient than maintaining a large, standing conventional military force. In popular lingo, his policy of relying upon less-expensive nuclear armaments was known as "getting a bigger bang for the buck."

The United States also developed a prototype of a guided missile capable of delivering an atomic warhead, and it continued to conduct aboveground tests of nuclear weapons, which Eisenhower threatened to use in case of war. In November, the USSR detonated its most potent weapon to date, a one-megaton hydrogen bomb. While calling for effective international control of nuclear weaponry, Nikita Khrushchev, first secretary of the Communist Party, maintained that the Soviet government would continue to develop and test new atomic devices in order to guarantee national security.

Within that context, war threatened to break out between the PRC and the United States early in the year, until tensions eased in the spring. Antagonism between mainland China and the United States and its ally Nationalist China had escalated during fall 1954 and intensified during the early months of 1955, as the communists raided Nationalist positions on islands surrounding Taiwan. In January, Congress authorized Eisenhower to mobilize the United States for war to defend Taiwan from a communist attack, and in February, Eisenhower ordered the Seventh Fleet to the Tachen Islands, west of Taiwan, following communist raids on the Nationalist outposts there. In February, shortly after the PRC prepared for war by instituting mandatory military service, the Chinese Nationalists, assisted by the U.S. Navy, completed their evacuation of those islands.

There was international concern that the situation might erupt into a major war, but Eisenhower pressured Nationalist leader Chiang Kai-shek not to exploit the situation by drawing the United States into a larger conflict. The crisis finally centered on whether the U.S. commitment to defend the Nationalists extended to Jinmen (Quemoy) and Mazu (Matsu) two small Nationalist-held islands close to China's mainland. The PRC claimed these as its territory, and throughout the United States and the world, people debated whether protecting Nationalist sovereignty over these distant islands was worth going to war. Tensions eased some in March and April, after the United States announced that it would not assist Nationalist aggression against mainland China and China's foreign minister Zhou Enlai, while still denouncing the United States, announced at the Afro-Asian Bandung Conference in Indonesia that China did not seek war with the United States and hoped to negotiate a solution to the current dispute. The United States agreed in late May to negotiate directly with the PRC, without the presence of the Nationalists, whom the communists refused to recognize. By the end of the year, China had released several captured American pilots, freed the remaining U.S. civilians in its custody, and settled the crisis. Jinmen and Mazu remained under Nationalist control; however, the dispute was revived in 1958, when the communists again bombarded the islands and Eisenhower declared his country's commitment to defending them. The debate over the extent to which America should be willing to protect Nationalist control over these islands also reemerged as a campaign issue in the 1960 Kennedy-Nixon presidential debates.

Also in February, Congress solidified U.S. opposition to the spread of communism in Asia by ratifying U.S. membership in the newly formed Southeast Asia Treaty Organization (SEATO), and Turkey and Iraq signed the Baghdad Pact to resist communism in the oil-producing sections of the Middle East. Pakistan, Iran, and Great Britain later joined the alliance. For their part, the Soviets agreed to sell weapons to Egypt, which was involved in border fights in Gaza with Israel during the summer. In October, Egypt, Syria, and Jordan agreed to form a unified military command against Israel. To keep pace with the Soviet Union, in September, the United States also offered military assistance to Egypt and conducted talks about funding the proposed Aswan Dam across the Nile.

In May, the Allied occupation of West Germany officially ended, and the Federal Republic of Germany was declared. A member of NATO since October 1954, West Germany was allowed to rearm but forbidden to produce nuclear weapons. The Soviet and Allied occupation of Austria also concluded in May, and a treaty among Austria, the Soviet Union, and the United States established Austria as a neutral country forbidden to enter into military alliances with either side or to permit foreign soldiers on its soil. Free from foreign occupation for the first time since 1938, Austria was permitted to rebuild its army. Moreover, the Soviets renounced their claims to Austrian oil fields. The nation was excused from paying war reparations and generally held to be not responsible for the outbreak or prosecution of World War II.

The rearmament of West Germany and its expected admission into NATO spurred the Soviet Union to establish the Warsaw Pact within two weeks after the formation of the new German state. A military alliance of Eastern European nations under communist control and Soviet domination, the Warsaw Pact included Albania, Bulgaria, Czechoslovakia, Hungary, Poland, Romania, the Soviet Union, and East Germany, which was permitted to remilitarize in 1956. Thus, 11 years after Germany's surrender in World War II, the nation was not only allowed to rearm, it was also, in its bifurcated form, encouraged to participate in military alliances with its former enemies.

In February, Soviet party secretary Khrushchev consolidated his power by replacing his rival Georgi Malenkov with his own choice for premier, Nikolai Bulganin. Concerned by the remilitarization of West Germany, one of their first acts together was to visit Yugoslavia in late May to repair the damaged relations with its leader, Marshal Tito. They apologized to Yugoslavia for past Soviet behavior, which they blamed on another of Khrushchev's former political rivals, Lavrenti Beria, the former head of the Soviet secret police who was arrested and executed after Stalin's death in 1953. As a further gesture to Tito, the Soviets dissolved COMINFORM, the international communist organization that had expelled Yugoslavia in 1948.

In return for agreeing to withdraw from Austria and accepting the independence and rearmament of West Germany, the Soviets insisted upon a summit conference. Consequently, in July, the first Geneva summit conference took place among the leaders of the United States, Soviet Union, France, and Great Britain. The goal of the conference was to reduce cold war tensions, but a subsequent conference in the fall failed to implement the directives from the July summit, and it accomplished little.

Although still aligned with the West and a partner in America's missile defense pact, Canada pursued a more independent course of economic engagement. It granted to and received from the Soviet Union most-favored trade status.

Other International Developments

The middle of the decade saw Europe's colonial powers become increasingly challenged by independence movements in Africa and Asia. France's premier, Pierre Mendès-France, who had negotiated the French military exit from Vietnam in July 1954, was forced to resign in March after accommodating some requests for greater autonomy by native Algerians and for negotiating with nationalist Algerian rebels. His critics argued that this conciliatory approach would weaken the French republic. A month later, the new French government, under Edgar Faure, declared a state of emergency in Algeria to deal with the increasingly violent independence movement. As author Albert Camus sent back newspaper dispatches and editorials from Algeria, the violence increased during the summer, along with internal dissent in France against the nation's growing military involvement. France also faced violent civil unrest in Morocco and placed the city of Casablanca under martial law following an outbreak of Bastille Day bombings in July. Negotiations during the fall finally led to a treaty in which Morocco received first self-government, then independence. France also accorded internal autonomy to Tunisia, but maintained a defense agreement and retained rights to setting its foreign policy.

Winston Churchill stepped down as Britain's prime minister and was replaced by Anthony Eden, another Conservative. Eden, too, had to contend with nationalist insurgencies within the empire. Encouraged by Archbishop Makarios, head of Cyprus's Greek Orthodox Church, Greek nationals on Cyprus seeking union with Greece intensified their uprising. Following a series of autumn attacks on British servicemen and institutions, the colonial governor declared a state of emergency, banned public meetings, and enacted severe penalties for terrorist activities. Turkey, whose nationals comprised a minority on the island, also opposed the effort to align it with Greece, and the developments on Cyprus further antagonized relations between Greece and Turkey. Britain also struggled to suppress the ongoing Mau Mau uprising in Kenya.

Behind the Iron Curtain, Hungary's liberal premier, Imre Nagy, was removed at the behest of the Soviet Union and replaced by a more hard-line regime. Nagy returned during the Hungarian uprising of 1956 but was later executed for his role in it. In a further break from Stalin's legacy, Khrushchev introduced new policies within the Soviet Union aimed at easing building shortages and satisfying the demand for more consumer goods. He also implemented agricultural reforms, including plans to increase the output of corn and to send "volunteers" to cultivate the barren wilderness of Kazakhstan, where the crop yields proved disappointing.

Argentina's president, Juan Perón, who had ruled the country since 1945, was deposed in September by a military junta. Perón was exiled first to Paraguay, then to Spain until 1971. The U.S.-backed government in Guatemala suppressed a coup attempt and imposed a state of siege, and tensions flamed between Nicaragua and Costa Rica after Nicaraguan president Somoza supported rebel air attacks against Costa Rican villages close to the border. The

Organization of American States (OAS) established a buffer zone to ease the situation. A military coup seized power in Brazil, and Peru gave women the right to vote.

Following a violent power struggle between South Vietnam's emperor, Bao Dai, who ruled in absentia from France with support of the French government, and his prime minister, Ngo Dinh Diem, who enjoyed U.S. backing, a referendum established the Republic of South Vietnam under Diem's leadership. As events developed, the United States increased its military assistance to South Vietnam.

At the Bandung Conference in April, delegates from 29 African and Asian nations not aligned with either cold war superpower called for independence, an end to colonialism, and membership in the United Nations. Elsewhere, South Africa's enforcement of strict apartheid laws, including the expulsion of some 60,000 black Africans from their homes in Johannesburg, provoked international protest. Declaring that the United Nations was forbidden to intervene in the domestic affairs of any nation, the South African delegation walked out in protest when the UN Human Rights Committee sought to investigate its racial policies. The forced resettlement, which took place under the supervision of thousands of armed policemen after 13 days of peaceful protest, led Nelson Mandela, a leader of the African National Congress (ANC), to conclude that nonviolent protest was fruitless and that "in the end, we had no alternative to armed and violent resistance."[2]

The Cold War at Home

With the fall from power of Senator McCarthy in late 1954, the Red Scare began to diminish but did not die out completely. Radio raconteur John Henry Faulk filed a lawsuit in 1955 that eventually brought an end to blacklisting by holding the creators of blacklists financially responsible for the consequences of misrepresenting people on their lists. Faulk claimed that Aware, Inc., had erroneously identified him as having communist associations and thereby caused his blacklisting. Seven years later, a jury awarded a large sum to Faulk (later reduced), put Aware out of business, and signaled new financial dangers for would-be blacklisters.

A federal judge dismissed a long-standing indictment against Professor Owen Lattimore, whom McCarthy had accused in 1950 of being the top Soviet espionage agent in the country. (Lattimore's book, *Ordeal by Slander* [1950], responds to the charge and describes his experience of being denounced. A Senate subcommittee investigating the accusation in 1950 found no evidence that Lattimore was a spy.) The Supreme Court ordered the reinstatement of a medical professor at Yale University who had been fired after allegations of communist connections. The Court also struck down the government policy of denying accused communists the right to travel abroad. And the New York Court of Appeals ruled that the New York Housing Association could not require a loyalty oath as precondition for renting apartments.

Republicans, who for years had vilified President Roosevelt for selling out U.S. interests to the communists at the 1944 Yalta conference, revived that argument by making the government release a report containing secret documents from the talks. Churchill condemned the report, which he said was riddled with errors, and the controversy over whether Roosevelt acted pragmatically or caved in to Stalin remained a passionate, but unsettled, issue for many Americans.

HUAC continued to investigate and expose communist influences in the entertainment industry. Among those who testified before HUAC were folksinger Pete Seeger, an unfriendly witness who resisted answering questions about any communist membership or affiliation but did offer to discuss his song "If I Had a Hammer." He was convicted of contempt of Congress and sentenced to one year in jail, but successfully appealed the case after a legal battle lasting several years. Comedian Zero Mostel denied being a communist at the time but took the Fifth Amendment repeatedly when asked about past affiliations. Both Seeger and Mostel were blacklisted in the television and film industries. After his testimony, Mostel declared, "I am a man of many faces, all of them blacklisted."[3]

CIVIL RIGHTS

On August 28 in Money, Mississippi, 14-year-old Emmett Till, a black youth visiting from Chicago, was brutally murdered for "talking fresh" to a white woman tending a store. Roy Bryant, the woman's husband, and J. W. Milam, his half brother, were arrested and quickly brought to trial. But despite testimony connecting them to the crime, they were rapidly acquitted by a local all-white jury. Afterward, Bryant and Milam admitted in a paid interview in *Look* magazine that they killed Till. Till's murder and the failure of the all-white jury to bring his killers to justice fueled the nascent civil rights movement, which had been energized the year before by the Supreme Court's ruling to desegregate the public schools and would be furthered by the Court's follow-up ruling in May 1955 that desegregation take place with "all deliberate speed" and be overseen by federal courts.

The next major development in the civil rights movement was the successful 13-month bus boycott in Montgomery, Alabama. The prolonged action demonstrated to the nation the protesters' resolve to gain equal rights. The boycott resulted in the elimination of discriminatory practices on public transportation in Montgomery, and brought Dr. Martin Luther King, Jr., to public prominence. It was also the first time King successfully employed the nonviolent, passive protest methods used by Mohandas Gandhi in gaining India's independence.

The boycott, which leaders of the white community angrily denounced, began in early December, four days after Rosa Parks, a black woman, was arrested for refusing to give her seat on a public bus to a white rider. Charged with violating a city ordinance intended to "separate the white people from the Negroes,"[4] Parks agreed to become a test case for the National Association for the Advancement of Colored People (NAACP), despite fears that she might be lynched for trying to reverse the local segregation law. This concern, after the murder of Till and the acquittal of his killers, seemed especially well grounded. E. D. Nixon, a former head of the Alabama chapter of the NAACP then organized a bus boycott for Monday, December 5, and he invited King to address a group of supporters at the Holy Street Baptist Church that evening. Following King's stirring speech, Parks was introduced, and the group voted to continue to boycott the public buses until African Americans were treated courteously, black drivers were hired for predominantly black routes, and all riders were seated on a first-come, first-served basis, with blacks filling the bus from the rear and whites from the front. These demands were rejected by the city on December 8, and the strike continued. Its organizers arranged car pools and settled in for the long haul until December 1956, when the Supreme Court sided with the protestors.

In other civil rights–related developments, contralto Marian Anderson became the first black American to sing at the New York Metropolitan Opera, when she played Ulrica, the high priestess in Verdi's *A Masked Ball*. The Interstate Commerce Commission (ICC) forbade segregation of commercial trains and buses that crossed state lines; the Maryland National Guard was ordered to desegregate; and an all-white Methodist congregation in Mystic, Connecticut, installed an African American as its pastor. Walter White, executive secretary for the NAACP who had worked with Truman and Roosevelt on race-related issues, died at age 61 and was succeeded by Roy Wilkins.

GOVERNMENT AND SOCIETY

The nation experienced a new, unexpected source of anxiety on September 23, when Eisenhower suffered a mild heart attack (coronary thrombosis), less than a month before his 65th birthday. He was given morphine to treat the pain and was then hospitalized through early November, during which time Vice President Richard Nixon presided over cabinet meetings but did not assume full powers of the presidency. Although the normal working of the government was not seriously disrupted and the nation revealed no weakness to its cold war enemies, Eisenhower's incapacity generated concern about the constitutional provisions for enabling a sitting vice president to temporarily replace a living president. The experience later became one of the major justifications for the Twenty-fifth Amendment to the Constitution, which establishes procedures for dealing with such circumstances. Eisenhower's illness also became a campaign issue in 1956 but did not preclude him from seeking and winning reelection.

Among Eisenhower's initiatives for 1955 was a proposed $101 billion highway development plan, a third of which would be financed by the federal government. Republicans were frustrated, however, when Wayne Morse of Oregon became the first U.S. senator to switch political parties when he became a Democrat.

The role of women in the clergy was a matter of some controversy, and in 1955, the U.S. Presbyterian Church voted to allow women to become ministers. The question of whether men and women from different religions should marry was also debated throughout the decade, as interfaith marriages became somewhat more frequent, although not common. Of special concern was the kind of religious upbringing the children from such unions would receive. In a related issue, in 1955 the Supreme Court upheld a state law that forbade a Jewish couple to adopt twin Catholic children. Weekly church attendance in the United States was estimated to be 49 million—including half of the adult population.[5]

But the high level of religious affiliation did not preclude Americans from indulging in more frivolous activities, including adult and children's comic books. A survey conducted at the University of California in 1955 revealed that from the late 1940s through 1953, 1 billion comic books were printed each year, at a total cost of $100 million, four times the total book budgets of all the public libraries in the country.[6] The study followed the publication in 1954 of Frederic Wertham's influential book, *Seduction of the Innocent,* which charged that comic books were corrupting America's youth and undermining their values.

Weather catastrophes included a string of tornadoes that killed 29 people in Mississippi in February and another that killed 121 in the South on May 27. August floods killed 179 in the Northeast, and in September, hurricane Ione's 107 mile-per-hour winds caused millions of dollars of damage, destroyed crops, and upset telephone communication and transportation all along the Carolina coast.

BUSINESS

Overall, 1955 was a good year for business. The housing market remained strong, and the GNP rose by 9 percent. Inflation was well under control, at a rate of -0.3 percent. The Dow Jones Industrial Average fluctuated between 391 and 488, and unemployment remained low, at 4.4 percent. A long-playing record album (33⅓ rpm) cost $3.98, an Annie Oakley cowgirl outfit cost $4.90, an English-made bicycle cost $47.50, and a round-trip flight on National Airlines from New York to Havana could be purchased for $176.50.[7]

The number of women in the workforce rose from about 16 million in 1950 to 22 million in 1955—an increase of almost 40 percent. However, most were employed in low-paying fields, such as teaching, nursing, and secretarial work that had traditionally been reserved for women.[8]

The most significant development in labor was the merger of the American Federation of Labor (AFL) with the Congress of Industrial Organizations (CIO). The union of the AFL-CIO, headed by AFL president George Meany, ended two years of intense rivalry between two of the nation's largest labor unions and created a new, powerful organization to represent the needs of industrial workers. Elsewhere, some 600,000 steelworkers received a 15¢-per-hour pay raise after a 12-hour strike, and the federal government raised the minimum wage to $1 per hour.

In July, Walt Disney opened Disneyland in Anaheim, California. The first large-scale, modern theme park cost some $17 million to construct and employed 2,500 construction workers. Disneyland was built on a 160-acre site and contained four individual theme parks: Fantasyland, Frontierland, Adventureland, and Tomorrowland. Offering innovative rides and attractions, the park as a whole appealed to the imaginations of middle Americans; offered a safe, clean, friendly environment for their young children, the baby boomers; and enabled adults to escape into socially acceptable, optimistic fantasy worlds that eliminated the anxieties of contemporary life. Although skeptics had predicted that the venture would fail because America's amusement parks had largely fallen into disrepair and were often seedy hangouts for derelicts and delinquents, Disneyland succeeded beyond imagination, drawing more than 1 million visitors to its Anaheim location during the first six months of operation.

Much of Disneyland's success also owed to its pioneering state-of-the-art forms of entertainment and corporate marketing. The theme park benefited from free, weekly national advertising when a splendid fireworks display exploded over Cinderella's castle at the opening of each episode of *Disneyland*. The park, in turn, presented characters like Davy Crockett, Mickey Mouse, and Donald Duck, who were based on characters from *Disneyland* and Disney films. This cross-fertilization of enterprises proved to be an enormous financial success, as it generated larger audiences for Disney movies and TV programs, while enabling Disneyland to earn $10 million in 1956, its first full year of operation, and more than $200 million by 1965, by which time Disney enterprises became the world's largest entertainment operations.

The Disney characters found broad appeal in popular culture and in consumer markets in other ways, too. Inspired by the Davy Crockett episodes on *Disneyland,* coonskin caps and other Crockett paraphernalia became an instant fad in late 1955. In 1956, "The Ballad of Davy Crockett" was made into 17 different recordings. Altogether, Disney licensed more than 3,000 Davy Crockett–related items, including lunch boxes, T-shirts, comic books, and toothbrushes.[9]

Other new products from 1955 included the popular word game Scrabble, and Crest toothpaste, roll-on deodorant, no-smear lipstick, and the Dreyfus Fund. DuPont introduced Fantasique, a fast-drying, wrinkle-resistant Dacron fiber that promised to make life easier for homemakers, and Chase National and Bank of Manhattan agreed to merge to form the second-largest bank in the United States. RCA developed the first music synthesizer.

As Americans spent more of their time working, commuting, and raising children, fast food became an increasingly attractive option, and in 1955 two major chains were introduced: Colonel Sanders's Kentucky Fried Chicken (now called KFC) and McDonald's, which introduced the concept of franchising fast-food restaurants nationwide. The chain started as a roadside stand run by Richard and Maurice McDonald in San Bernardino, California. In April, Ray Kroc, a distributor of a milkshake-making machine who had observed their successful assembly-line style operation, opened his own hamburger stand in Des Plaines, Illinois, outside of Chicago. In hopes of selling more of his milkshake machines, Kroc obtained the right to license the McDonald's name and production methods across the country, and from there, he developed the practice of fast-food franchising. By 1961, the company had 200 franchises around the country. In addition, the same year that McDonald's appeared in the United States, the Wimpy Hamburger chain introduced the hamburger to Europe. Home-prepared fast foods also catered to the faster pace of life in the 1950s, and frozen dinners helped satisfy a growing demand for quick and easy meals. In 1954, TV dinners were first introduced, and in 1955 Gorton's Fish Sticks entered the market.

SCIENCE AND TECHNOLOGY

Outer space and aeronautics continued to attract the scientific imagination, and major advances occurred that even a decade earlier would have been dismissed as pure science fiction. Promising to share its scientific data with the world at large, the United States announced plans to develop a space satellite capable of going 200–300 miles beyond Earth's atmosphere. Meanwhile, scientists in the Soviet Union established a permanent commission for interplanetary communications. B. B. Burk discovered that Jupiter emits radio waves. The United States tested self-guided missiles, and Bell Aircraft demonstrated a fixed-wing plane capable of taking off vertically.

In addition to the promise of inexpensive nuclear energy, the sun was also identified as a potential source for satisfying the nation's energy needs, which were growing enormously in the consumer-driven decade. Bell Telephone first employed solar energy to power telephone calls, and other firms demonstrated a solar-powered automobile and a solar-heated and radiator-cooled house.

Britain's Christopher Cockerell developed the first viable hovercraft, which rides across water on a cushion of air; scientists at Columbia University developed an atomic clock accurate to one second in 300 years; researchers at the Massachusetts Institute of Technology developed uses for ultrahigh frequency (UHF) waves; Narinder Kapary of Great Britain produced the first optical fibers; Clyde Cowan and Frederick Reines made the first observation of neutrinos, whose existence theorist Wolfgang Pauli had earlier predicted; and Owen Chamberlain and Emilio Segrè discovered the antiproton, a subatomic particle that was the second form of antimatter to be demonstrated. The researchers won the 1959 Nobel Prize in physics for their discovery, which quickly led to the demonstration of additional particles of antimatter. In 1956, they demonstrated the existence of antineutrons.

Medical advances also continued to offer greater human control over their physical lives—and thereby contributed to the sentiment that became more and more widely embraced that, given resources and time, science could solve most human problems. In the field of eye care, the modern tonometer, still in use as of this writing, was developed to detect the disease glaucoma. Researchers discovered the structure of insulin, a pancreatic hormone that regulates the body's blood sugar levels. Despite concerns by Secretary of Health, Education, and Welfare Oveta Culp Hobby that free distribution of the polio vaccine to poor children would introduce socialized medicine "by the back door," a nationwide immunization program for children was initiated and quickly terminated the polio epidemic, although it did not altogether wipe out the disease.[10]

Albert Einstein, who developed the theory of relativity in 1905 and later went on to pioneer quantum physics and general relativity, died of heart failure at age 76. Shortly before his death, Einstein made a radio appeal to halt the arms race and joined other Nobel Prize winners who signed a statement pointing out the danger of nuclear weapons to the survival of the human race. Alexander Fleming, the British biologist who discovered penicillin, died at age 73.

SPORTS, ENTERTAINMENT, AND THE ARTS

Sports

By mid-decade, golf, once the exclusive preserve of the wealthy, had become a popular outlet for middle-class Americans, too, and in 1955, some 3.8 million Americans were playing on 5,000 courses that covered 1.5 million acres.[11] The appeal of the sport no doubt was enhanced by the enthusiasm with which Eisenhower played it, and the president was often photographed and even interviewed while on the golf course. Among the professionals who dominated the sport in the 1950s were Arnold Palmer, Ben Hogan, and Jack Nicholas, who earned celebrity status for their prowess and were typically followed by legions of fans as they played their rounds. Jack Fleck won the USGA Open in 1955.

In the World Series, the Brooklyn Dodgers lost the first two games to the New York Yankees but went on to win in seven games—the first time any team had overcome such a deficit. Dodgers catcher Roy Campanella and Yankees catcher Yogi Berra were subsequently named the Most Valuable Players (MVP) of the National and American Leagues, respectively. After the season concluded, Leo "the Lip" Durocher, who managed the Dodgers from 1939 to 1947 and the New York Giants from 1948 to 1955, retired from baseball to enter private business, and during the year, pitcher Cy Young, who recorded 511 wins during his career, died at age 88. In his honor, the Cy Young Award was introduced in 1956; it is given each year to the best pitcher. Honus Wagner, one of the finest shortstops of the early days of the sport, died at age 81.

The Cleveland Browns repeated as NFL champions, defeating the Los Angeles Rams 38–14. The Chicago Bears's Harlon Hill was named the league's MVP, the first time the award was given. John Unitas, one of the outstanding quarterbacks in the history of professional football, had his rookie season after the Baltimore Colts hired him as a free agent. University of Oklahoma was picked as the top college team, after it defeated the University of Maryland in the Orange Bowl, and Ohio State's Howard Cassady won the Heisman Trophy. Other college All-Americans included running backs Tommy McDonald of Oklahoma and Paul Hornung of Notre Dame, who went on to star for the Green Bay Packers.

Syracuse defeated Fort Wayne in seven games to claim the NBA basketball championship. The NBA All-Pro First Team included Philadelphia's Neil Johnston and Paul Arizin, Milwaukee's Bob Petit, Fort Wayne's Larry Foust, and Boston's Bob Cousy. University of San Francisco won the college basketball title, and its center, Bill Russell, was named Player of the Year.

The Detroit Redwings won hockey's Stanley Cup. "Sugar" Ray Robinson came out of retirement to knock out Bobo Olson and regain the world middleweight title, and Rocky Marciano retained his heavyweight boxing championship by knocking out Archie Moore in the fifth round. Women's tennis champion Maureen Connolly retired, and Willie Shoemaker, who went on to become a preeminent horse jockey, rode Swaps to victory in the Kentucky Derby. Willie Hartack, another dominant jockey of the 1950s, rode Nashua to win the Preakness and the Belmont Stakes. In France, the worst accident to that

Bob Cousy, an early standout on the Boston Celtic team that dominated professional basketball for a decade, appeared prominently on boxes of Wheaties cereal, "the breakfast of champions." *(Photofest)*

date in the history of auto racing occurred on June 11 at the Le Mans raceway outside Paris, when three cars collided. One skidded out of control and smashed into the grandstand, killing 80 people and injuring nearly 100 more. The race, however, was not canceled.

Television

In 1955, RKO Studios sold its entire film back catalog for $15 million to a corporation that planned to sell broadcast rights to television networks and studios. This move greatly enhanced television's ability to air the product of its greatest competitor, the motion picture industry.

Revlon introduced the big-money TV quiz show when it sponsored *The $64,000 Question* during prime time. The program, which showed contestants sweating in "isolation booths" as they pondered questions, was an immediate smash hit; it supplanted *I Love Lucy* as the nation's number-one show, a position *Lucy* had held since 1952. If contestants answered correctly, they could cash in or risk everything by attempting a more difficult question that was worth more money. The pot doubled until the contestant arrived at the top challenge, "the $64,000 question," a phrase that entered the general lingo. The show spawned several imitators, such as *Dotto* (1958) and *Twenty-One* (1956–58), and the big-money quiz format remained popular until 1958, when some shows were uncovered as dishonest and a major scandal shut them down.

Apart from the top-rated *$64,000 Question,* the most popular shows of the 1955–56 season were mostly holdovers from previous seasons: *I Love Lucy;* the renamed *Toast of the Town, The Ed Sullivan Show; Disneyland; The Jack Benny Show; December Bride; You Bet Your Life;* and *Dragnet. The Millionaire,* the only other new program to become one of the 10 most widely viewed, starred Marvin Miller as Michael Anthony, the personal secretary of an eccentric, off-screen billionaire who each week would select a different unsuspecting person to award a million dollars. Anthony delivered the money with a highly professional demeanor, and the audience then watched how the unexpected windfall either enhanced or destroyed the recipient's life. Although ostensibly about the consequences of unexpected good fortune, it often served as a moral parable in which proper uses of the money generated happiness but attempts to spend it unwisely or insensitively brought about misfortune. In this regard, the show appealed to the inherent conflict between traditional Protestant values of humility, thrift, hard work, and compassion on the one hand and on the other, the notion promulgated by consumer capitalism that happiness can be found through material acquisition—a basic conflict that surfaced throughout the culture in various ways during the decade.

Although not an immediate success, *Gunsmoke,* television's first adult western, went on to become America's longest-running prime-time dramatic series with a continuous cast of characters. Its 20 prime-time seasons have been surpassed only by *Disneyland,* which was an anthology without recurring characters; *The Ed Sullivan Show,* a variety show; and *Monday Night Football. Gunsmoke,* which began in 1952 as a radio program, starred James Arness as Marshal Matt Dillon, the earnest and just guardian of law and order in Dodge City. William Conrad had played Dillon on the radio series, and CBS first offered the television role to John Wayne. Wayne, who did not want to commit to a weekly series, recommended Arness, his friend and costar in *Big Jim McClain* (1952). Milburn Stone costarred as Dillon's sensible friend and sometimes adviser Doc Adams; Dennis Weaver played Chester, the helpful deputy who walked with a limp and spoke with a twang; and Amanda Blake was Miss Kitty, the saloon proprietor with a soft heart beneath her tough exterior who was also Dillon's friend and unrequited love interest. Although during the 1960s the show addressed such topical issues as the rights of minorities, social protest, and crimes against women, during the 1950s it projected essentially conservative values that endorsed respect for authority and preservation of order. By standing tall against outlaws who attempted to undermine these values, Dillon implicitly projected America's dutiful and self-sacrificing view of itself in the cold war, opposing the forces of godless communism that sought to spread revolution and undermine social stability and democratic institutions. Another adult western to debut in 1955 was *The Life and Legend of Wyatt Earp,* starring Hugh O'Brian.

The Phil Silvers Show was a sitcom set during peacetime in an army barracks in Kansas. Originally titled *You'll Never Get Rich,* it starred Silvers as the fast-talking, opportunistic Sergeant Bilko, who made the men in his squad assist him in his never-ending get-rich schemes. The slang term *bilked* (i.e., swindled) comes from the Bilko character. Jackie Gleason's *The Honeymooners* became a half-hour sitcom in its own right, after being presented since 1952 as a popular skit on Gleason's variety show.

Playing off the movie director's reputation for making psychological thrillers, *Alfred Hitchcock Presents* consisted of stories of terror, horror, suspense, and the bizarre. Although he did not direct the episodes, Hitchcock introduced each week's offering in an understated manner that often dripped with morbid irony. *The Alcoa Hour* also featured original dramas, although these were more highbrow in their appeal. The show, which ran through 1957, attracted some of the best actors of the era, including Walter Matthau, Joanne Woodward, Sal Mineo, Helen Hayes, Eddie Albert, Maureen Stapleton, and British performer Laurence Harvey in his U.S. television debut. A syndicated show entitled *Confidential File* featured dramatic treatments of topics of current interest. One episode, entitled "Lysergic Acid," addressed the use of LSD on schizophrenics and showed an artist who used the drug.

Among other new programming was *The Lawrence Welk Show,* a folksy, Bavarian-style musical variety show with a regular cast of performers that included the wholesome-looking and sweet-sounding Lennon sisters and spirited accordionist Myron Floren. Two influential children's shows debuted: *Captain Kangaroo,* starring Bob Keeshan as the friendly captain; and *The Mickey Mouse Club,* a Disney production that starred Annette Funicello and the other "Mouseketeers," who wore caps with mouse ears and

Phil Silvers (right) starred as the ever-conniving Sergeant Ernie Bilko in *The Phil Silvers Show.* Maurice Gosfield costarred as the always loyal, if not too bright Private Doberman. *(Photofest)*

introduced and participated in the various segments. Each day of the week focused on a different theme, such as Fun with Music Day, Guest Star Day, and Anything Can Happen Day, and each episode featured a newsreel or short documentary film, a sketch or production number, an episode from a serial story, and a Disney cartoon. Like *Captain Kangaroo* and much of the other children's programming of the decade, the show tried to educate children about their world and inculcate good values, as well as entertain them.

Navy Log, which ran through 1958, was an anthology of military dramas based on official navy files and produced with the cooperation of the Navy Department. The show focused on individual seamen or airmen, usually in a battle setting, but some episodes addressed personal issues, such as the plight of a mentally disturbed veteran. One episode featured an account of the sinking of John F. Kennedy's PT-109 in the South Pacific. Senator Kennedy, the future president, appeared as a special guest.

Other noteworthy television moments occurred on January 19, when Eisenhower gave the nation's first televised presidential press conference, and on May 11, when Kiyoshi Tanimoto, a Japanese minister and Hiroshima survivor, appeared on *This Is Your Life,* a human-interest show that surprised unsuspecting participants with recollections and people from their past. Told only that he was appearing on a local television show that could help him raise money for his cause, Tanimoto was unsuspectingly introduced to Captain Robert Lewis, the copilot of the plane that dropped the atomic bomb. Lewis described the mission to Tanimoto before a national audience. He claimed to have written in his log book, "My God, what have we done?" Afterward, Tanimoto was more happily surprised by the appearance of his family, whom the producers had flown in from Japan, and by two of the Hiroshima Maidens, on whose behalf Tanimoto had come to the United States to raise money. The maidens were 25 women who had been disfigured by the atomic attack in World War II and had come to the United States to receive reconstructive surgery that was paid for by private American donations.[12]

Movies

Several of the year's top movies dealt with loneliness and alienation, including *Marty,* which won the Academy Award for best film, director (Delbert Mann), actor (Ernest Borgnine), and screenplay (Paddy Chayefsky). A short, low-budget, black-and-white film, it was also nominated for best supporting actor and actress, cinematography, and art direction. Starring Borgnine and Betsy Blair, *Marty* tells the story of a lonely, unattractive Bronx butcher who lacks direction or meaning in life and is dominated by his possessive mother. He spends most evenings wondering with his few pals what to do that night. At a dance, after he strikes out with other, more attractive women, Marty meets Clara, a homely schoolteacher. They soon fall in love, but his pals call her ugly and his mother derides her. Marty lacks the self-esteem and personal courage to choose Clara over the opposition of his mother and friends, who feel threatened by her. Consequently, he abandons Clara and resumes his empty life. But now he must live with the pain of knowing that his existence might have been happier and more fulfilling had he been strong enough to choose differently.

Frank Sinatra received an Academy Award nomination for his performance in another story of personal despair, *The Man with the Golden Arm,* Hollywood's first serious treatment of drug addiction. Otto Preminger adapted Nelson Algren's best-selling 1949 novel about a heroin addict who returns home after spending six months in rehabilitation. He had worked as a crooked card dealer but now wants to go straight and become a jazz drummer; however, his bitter, crippled wife insists that he return to his old job, where he faces the temptations of sex, money, and drugs. In addition to an excellent performance by Sinatra, the film is notable for its jazz score, which also received an Academy Award nomination.

Teen idol James Dean, who projected restless, misunderstood youth, died in a car accident in September, shortly after catapulting to fame in Elia Kazan's *East of Eden* and before the release of Nicholas Ray's *Rebel Without a Cause.* *East of Eden* tells a Cain and Abel story about two sons of a wealthy, devoutly religious lettuce farmer in California's Salinas Valley. Dean's self-destructive character, Cal, mistakenly believes that his good, well-adjusted brother is his father's favorite. Cal challenges all authority, especially that of his father, and in his despair he ultimately engineers a family tragedy.

Costarring Natalie Wood, Sal Mineo, and Jim Backus, *Rebel Without a Cause* also demonstrates the damage done by bad parenting. Appearing when juvenile delinquency was attracting national attention, techniques of proper parenting were widely debated, and professional experts were gaining greater authority within the culture, the film further suggests that professional counselors often know better how to deal with teenagers than do parents. (Incidentally, the teens who were the subject of the nation's concerns about juvenile delinquency at the time were not postwar baby boomers; instead, they were born before World War II, and many went through their formative years without their fathers, who were serving in the military during the war.)

In *Rebel Without a Cause,* Jim (Dean), the new kid in school, feels torn apart because his mother and father keep sending him mixed signals. His father (Backus) is dominated by Jim's mother and grandmother and is incapable of providing the strong male role model Jim needs. Meanwhile, the father of the adoring Judy (Wood) rejects her expressions of love, which he feels she has outgrown, and at the same time refuses to acknowledge or accept that she is on the cusp of becoming a woman, with sexual desires. Mineo's wide-eyed, diminutive character, a bright boy nicknamed Plato who has been essentially abandoned by both of his divorced parents, seeks attention by acting destructively. When Jim shows him some sympathy, Plato becomes infatuated with him. Plato creates a fantasy about their friendship and seeks to create a new family with Jim and Judy as his surrogate parents. (There are strong suggestions of a homosexual attraction on Plato's part, but not Jim's.) Without parental direction or support, the threesome must negotiate their way through a threatening world of teenagers who are coming of age, trying to find their identities, and asserting their dominance. That year Dean also acted in George Stevens's adaptation of Edna Ferber's *Giant,* which was released posthumously in 1956. A film biography of the actor, *The James Dean Story,* was released in 1957.

Richard Brooks's *The Blackboard Jungle* also centers on out-of-control youth. Starring Glenn Ford, Sidney Poitier, and Vic Morrow, it presents the story of an inner-city high school that is dominated by a gang of tough students who intimidate the teachers and reject adult authority. Poitier, who was the first black actor to become a Hollywood star, came to fame in this movie as one of the wayward boys; he later starred as the teacher in a film with a similar premise, *To Sir, With Love* (1967). The film is also notable for its rock 'n' roll soundtrack, which made Bill Haley's "Rock Around the Clock" a number-one hit. In fact, the jazz in *The Man with the Golden Arm* and *The Glenn Miller Story* (1954) and the rock 'n' roll in *The Blackboard Jungle* not only made these films stand out as fresh and innovative, they introduced these forms of music to wider, more mainstream audiences and helped create a broader market for them.

Anna Magnani won the best actress award for her performance in *The Rose Tattoo,* Daniel Mann's adaptation of Tennessee Williams's play about a Sicilian widow who is unable to move on with her life until she discovers the truth about her dead husband. Williams wrote the screenplay for the movie, which costars Burt Lancaster. It also won Oscars for black-and-white cinematography and art direction and was nominated for best picture, supporting actress, score, editing, and costume design.

Alfred Hitchcock's *To Catch a Thief* stars Cary Grant as an infamous former cat burglar who clears his name by catching a jewel thief who imitates his modus operandi on the French Riviera. The movie features a famous love scene between Grant and Grace Kelly that is intercut with a lavish fireworks display. Kelly, who plays a sexually aggressive American debutante, was a top box office draw, and she met her future husband, Prince Rainier II of Monaco, while making the film. Robert Burks won the Academy Award for color cinematography.

Other notable films included Henry King's *Love Is a Many-Splendored Thing,* starring William Holden and Jennifer Jones, a retelling of the *Madame Butterfly* story set in China against the background of the struggle between the communists and Nationalists, and Mark Robson's adaptation of James Michener's Korean War novel, *The Bridges at Toko-Ri,* starring Holden and Kelly. James Stewart and June Allyson star in Anthony Mann's *Strategic Air Command,* about a baseball player who is recalled to active duty in the air force. The film showcases the Strategic Air Command (SAC), which always kept nuclear-armed planes in the air near its targets, ready to respond in the event of a communist attack. The air force's newest jets are prominently featured, and the patriotic film suggests that, despite the complications that the requirements for national security introduce into the personal and professional lives of U.S. military personnel, the nation's nuclear fleet is in safe and responsible hands, and SAC's capacity for retaliation leaves the nation secure from nuclear attack.

Holden also stars in Joshua Long's Academy Award–nominated adaptation of William Inge's play *Picnic,* about a handsome drifter who comes to a small American town and attracts several women there, including the fiancée of his friend. John Ford's adaptation of the Broadway hit *Mr. Roberts* tells the story of officers on a World War II cargo ship. It stars Henry Fonda, James Cagney, and Jack Lemmon, who was named best supporting actor for his role as Ensign Pulver. Cagney also stars with Doris Day in *Love Me or Leave Me,* Charles Vidor's biography of 1920s singer Ruth Etting, who is victimized by her manipulative, gangster husband.

Three notable film musicals appeared in 1955: *Oklahoma, Guys and Dolls,* and *It's Always Fair Weather.* Fred Zinnemann directed *Oklahoma,* a love story set in Oklahoma shortly before the territory became a state that starred Gordon McRae and Shirley Jones and featured music by Richard Rodgers and Oscar Hammerstein II. Based on the Broadway hit by Damon Runyon and directed by Joseph L. Mankiewicz, *Guys and Dolls* featured Marlon Brando, Sinatra, Stubby Kaye, and Jean Simmons in a comic tale of a high-rolling gambler who falls in love with a Salvation Army worker. Stanley Donen and Gene Kelly, who had collaborated on *Singin' in the Rain,* directed *It's Always Fair Weather* on wide-screen CinemaScope. It starred Kelly, Dan Dailey, and Cyd Charisse in a satire of television advertising, which although still a relatively new phenomenon, had by 1955 become a prominent feature in American life.

The top draws at the box office continued to be older men who projected strong characters and moral righteousness: Stewart, Wayne, Holden, Gary Cooper, Humphrey Bogart, and Clark Gable. Younger actors Brando and the comedy team of Dean Martin and Jerry Lewis were also top draws, as were actresses Kelly and June Allyson. Among those to make their first major Hollywood appearance were Dean (in *East of Eden*), Woods (in *Rebel Without a Cause*), Kim Novak (in *The Man with the Golden Arm*), and Jack Lemmon (in *Mr. Roberts*).

In Sweden, Ingmar Bergman released a comedy—a rarity for the director—*Smiles of a Summer's Night,* which is loosely based on Shakespeare's *A Midsummer Night's Dream.* It later became the basis for the musical *A Little Night Music* and, to some extent, Woody Allen's *A Midsummer Night's Sex Comedy* (1982). In France, Alain Resnais premiered *Night and Fog,* a documentary about the Nazi extermination camp at Auschwitz. Jules Dassin, who directed such examples of Hollywood film noir as *Brute Force* (1947), *Naked City* (1948), and *Thieves Highway* (1949), moved to France after being blacklisted for alleged communist affiliations. He shared the prize for best director at the Cannes Film Festival for *Rififi,* about the aftermath of a jewel theft in Paris.

Literature

One of the year's most controversial yet enduring works of fiction was Vladimir Nabokov's *Lolita,* a comically perverse tale of a college professor who becomes infatuated with a prepubescent girl, a "nymphet." As a result of controversy over Nabokov's treatment of the taboo subject and his depiction of the young girl's sexual power over adult men, the novel was not published in the United States or Britain until 1958. In 1962, Stanley Kubrick released a film adaptation starring Peter Sellers, James Mason, and Sue Lyon, and in 1992, Adrian Lyne remade it with Jeremy Irons, Frank Langella, and Dominique Swain.

Other significant American fiction included Robert Penn Warren's *Band of Angels,* about a mulatto girl who learns of her mixed-race background at her father's funeral; Norman Mailer's *The Deer Park,* which explores the sordid actions and motivations of Hollywood power brokers, the complications of their sexual and personal relations, and their responses to the anticommunist blacklist; William Gaddis's self-reflective, philosophical exploration, *The Recognitions;* and Eudora Welty's minor work, *The Bride of Innisfallen.* Flannery O'Connor's short story collection, *A Good Man Is Hard to Find,* presented perverse, darkly humored tales of the American South in which the possibilities for Christian salvation are present in the most unlikely situations. J. D. Salinger published his long story "Franny," which in 1961 was published as a book with a related novella, "Zooey" (1957).

The story of a returning World War II veteran, Sloan Wilson's best-selling *The Man in the Gray Flannel Suit* explores many of the social changes that occurred in U.S. society during the 1950s, including development of the suburbs, the rise of the advertising industry, child support for illegitimate war babies fathered overseas, problems for veterans trying to adapt to postwar America, and the growing phenomenon of divorce. A best-selling historical novel was MacKinlay Kantor's *Andersonville,* a Pulitzer Prize–winning historical novel of life in a Confederate Civil War prison camp. Herman Wouk's *Marjorie Morningstar,* as his *The Caine Mutiny* (1951) had done, made the case for subordinating individual will to institutional authority. Leigh Brackett's *The Long Tomorrow* was one of the first novels to envision life after a nuclear attack. Written three years after the development of the hydrogen bomb, it is initially set in a Mennonite community in the aftermath of a nuclear war. The novel explores the proper role of science in a postnuclear society, and like other postapocalyptic science fiction, such as *A Canticle for Leibowitz* (1959), it pictures human recovery from a nuclear armageddon as a progression from the new Dark Ages in which the dominant religious authority is capricious, superstitious, and hostile to science, to a new Enlightenment in which science, now used responsibly, reemerges.

Poet Lawrence Ferlinghetti, who in 1953 opened the City Lights bookstore, started his own publishing company to give fuller voice to Beat writers and other antiestablishment writers and intellectuals. City Lights Books went on to publish Allen Ginsberg, Gregory Corso, Jack Kerouac, Denise Levertov, Frank O'Hara, and other important authors and poets. Ferlinghetti's own *Pictures of a Gone World* was the press's first publication. It accuses the capitalist system of being dehumanizing and portrays its leaders as unimaginative and emotionally disconnected. The first major reading of Beat poets took place during the year at San Francisco's Six Gallery.

Other significant works of poetry from 1955 included Adrienne Rich's *The Diamond Cutters and Other Poems,* A. R. Ammons's *Ommateum,* Howard Nemerov's *The Salt Garden,* William Carlos Williams's *Journey to Love,* and Elizabeth Bishop's *North and South—A Cold Spring,* which won the Pulitzer Prize.

Influential works in American nonfiction included R. W. B. Lewis's *American Adam,* which challenged the pessimism of the New Liberalism, a 1950s political movement that in Lewis's view, properly began as a corrective to America's belief in its fundamental innocence but degenerated into a cult of original sin. In the epilogue, entitled "Adam as Hero in the Age of Containment," Lewis recognized a vital dynamic between innocence and sin. Another influential book was James Baldwin's *Notes of a Native Son,* a personal memoir about being an African-American man in the United States. Its title alludes to *Native Son* (1940), Richard Wright's novel about a black man who accidentally kills the drunken daughter of his white employer. Other civil rights–related nonfiction included Wright's *Black Power* and C. Vann Woodward's *The Strange Career of Jim Crow.* Ernest Jones's *The Life and Work of Sigmund Freud* offered a biographically based study of the work of the great psychoanalyst, and Edmund Wilson's *The Scrolls from the Dead Sea* discussed the ancient Old Testament texts found in Israel in 1947.

Politically oriented nonfiction included *A Democrat Looks at His Party*, by Dean Acheson, who had been President Truman's secretary of state. Truman published the first volume of his memoirs, *Year of Decisions*, which was a best-seller. The second volume, *Years of Trial and Hope*, appeared in 1956. Richard Hofstadter's *The Age of Reform: From Bryan to FDR* won the Pulitzer Prize for U.S. history.

Two new magazines encouraged expression from different sides of the political spectrum. William F. Buckley, Jr., founded the *National Review* to provide a national forum for the right-wing views he was having difficulty airing in the mainstream press. The magazine eventually became an important conservative outlet that helped the political career of Ronald Reagan and the more extreme form of conservatism he and his followers represented. The *Village Voice*, on the other hand, served the more liberal interests of the artists, poets, and other creative people who gathered in New York City's Greenwich Village during the 1950s.

A noteworthy work of foreign literature was *The Quiet American*, by British author Graham Greene. It told the story of a CIA agent in Vietnam who became deceived by his own well-intended deceptions. His anticommunist counterterrorist activities kill and maim innocent civilians, and the narrator characterizes him, and by extension U.S. policy in Southeast Asia, as "impregnably armoured by his good intentions and his ignorance." Greene based the character partly on CIA agent Colonel Edward Lansdale, who also inspired the character of Colonel Edwin Hillandale in Eugene Burdick and William Lederer's *The Ugly American* (1958). Joseph L. Mankiewicz adapted *The Quiet American* to film in 1958. While the book argued for the necessity of disloyalty in the face of misapplied idealism, the movie presented a more sympathetic treatment of American efforts. In the latter version, the main character works for a private U.S. aid mission instead of the CIA, and the ending transforms Greene's anti-American sentiments into an anticommunist statement. Several book reviewers have speculated that Greene's attack on U.S. policy was partly motivated by the attorney general's decision to ban him from the United States in 1952, because he had briefly joined the Communist Party in 1923. In 1954, the year of the French defeat in Vietnam, Greene wrote a nonfiction article on the Southeast Asian country for the *New Republic* entitled "Indo-China."

Other foreign literature included British author Evelyn Waugh's *Officers and Gentlemen* and French writer Alain Robbe-Grillet's experimental "new novel," *The Voyeur.* French anthropologist Claude Lévi-Strauss, who founded structural anthropology, which in turn spawned the school of literary theory known as structuralism, published his influential *Tristes Tropiques*. The Universal Copyright Convention of 1955 extended copyright protections to authors throughout the world. Poet and novelist James Agee died at age 45; Dale Carnegie, author of the best-selling *How to Win Friends and Influence People*, died at 64; German novelist and Nobel Prize winner Thomas Mann died at 80; and Spanish philosopher José Ortega y Gasset died at 72.

Theater, Music, and the Visual Arts

Among the major plays to premiere were Tennessee Williams's *Cat on a Hot Tin Roof*, which explores the dynamics among members of a wealthy southern family whose patriarch is dying, and Arthur Miller's *A View from the Bridge,* a tragedy about an immigrant who informs on an illegal alien and consequently dies because of it. Like *The Crucible* before it, Miller's play implicitly attacks those who appeared before HUAC and accused former associates of having communist ties. The waterfront setting further suggests a specific allusion to Miller's former collaborator, director Kazan, who named names before HUAC in 1952 and later justified acts of informing in his film *On the Waterfront* (1954). Jerome Lawrence and Robert E. Lee's *Inherit the Wind* starred Tony Randall, Paul Muni, and Ed Begley in the story of attorney Clarence Darrow's defense of John T. Scopes in the famous Scopes Monkey Trial about teaching evolution in public schools. Thornton Wilder's *The Matchmaker* starred Robert Morse and Ruth Gordon in a farce that celebrates the excitement of ordinary life. Like many of the movies from the year, William Inge's play *Bus Stop* shows the isolation and alienation of individuals. Frances Goodrich and Albert Hackett adapted for stage *The Diary of Anne Frank,* the real-life diary of a young Jewish girl who was a Holocaust victim.

Cole Porter's musical *Silk Stockings* adapted Ernst Lubitsch's movie *Ninotchka* (1939), about a female Soviet official who falls in love with an American capitalist in Paris. Richard Adler and Jerry Ross's *Damn Yankees* was a musical comedy about a fan of the lowly Washington Senators who sells his soul to the devil in order to become a baseball star capable of breaking the New York Yankees's hold on the American League pennant.

The New York City Ballet premiered George Balanchine's *Pas de Dix,* and the Chicago Opera Ballet had its debut. Pierre Boulez introduced his classical composition *Le Marteau sans maître,* and classical pianists Glenn Gould and Alicia de Larrocha made their professional debuts. *Porgy and Bess* became the first American opera to be performed in Milan's famed La Scala theater, and the U.S. government sent conductor Eugene Ormandy and the Philadelphia Symphony Orchestra on an international tour to demonstrate the wide range of American culture. The State Department rejected complaints by musicians' unions that Berlin Philharmonic conductor Herbert von Karajan was an ex-Nazi. It permitted the Berlin Philharmonic to make its first performance in Washington, D.C.

Dale Evans, the real-life and television wife of singing cowboy Roy Rogers, wrote the song, "The Bible Tells Me So," which became a gospel music standard. Its refrain repeats, "How do I know? The Bible tells me so." Other popular songs included "The Ballad of Davy Crockett," "Dance with Me, Henry," "Whatever Lola Wants" from *Damn Yankees,* and "Love Is a Many-Splendored Thing" and "Love Me or Leave Me" from the movies by the same titles. Also popular were Tennessee Ernie Ford's "Sixteen Tons," "Only You" by The Platters, and "The Yellow Rose of Texas" by Mitch Miller and his orchestra, which eventually sold more than 22 million copies.

Jazz innovator and saxophonist Charlie "Bird" Parker died at age 34 from pneumonia and cirrhosis of the liver while watching big-band performers Jimmy and Tommy Dorsey on television. Despite Parker's passing, jazz continued to thrive with such hits as Count Basie's "Everyday"; Oscar Pettiford's album incorporating rhythms of American Indians, *Bohemia After Dark;* and Duke Ellington's *Night Creature,* which was performed at Carnegie Hall with a full symphony. Other major jazz performers of the year included the Modern Jazz Quartet, Stan Getz, Ella Fitzgerald, Frank Sinatra, and Sammy Davis, Jr.

Rock 'n' roll continued to come of age with such songs as Chuck Berry's "Maybelline," Fats Domino's "Ain't That a Shame," and "Rock Around the Clock" by Bill Haley and His Comets. Elvis Presley further established himself by signing a record contract with RCA Victor.

The United Nations tried to create greater harmony among people and countries when it hosted a 69-nation photo exhibit, *The Family of Man,* which stressed the commonality of all people by showing them in familial and intimate (but not sexually explicit) situations. The photos were reproduced in a widely distributed book.

The opulent Eden Roc opened to rival the Fontainebleau as the flagship hotel on Miami Beach, one of the nation's premier winter vacation spots. In Olympia, Greece, where the Olympic Games had been held in antiquity, German archaeologists discovered the molds used to cast a giant statue of Zeus.

Salvador Dalí painted one of his major works, *The Lord's Supper,* and 25-year-old Jaspar Johns, one of the most accomplished American artists to come into prominence during the 1950s, began to make his presence felt in the New York art scene with mixed media

Rock 'n' roller Chuck Berry had an affinity for songs with lyrics fraught with sexual innuendo. *(Photofest)*

pieces inspired by Marcel Duchamp, the former dadaist who was a proponent of anti-art. Johns's work in 1955 included *Flag* and *Target with Four Faces,* a mixed media blue-green and yellow bull's-eye target on newspaper and canvas, framed by sculptures of four eyeless faces. Along with Robert Rauschenberg, whose *Satellite* appeared in 1955, Johns helped to popularize pop art, a whimsical form of artistic creation that rejected the esoteric elitism of abstract art and the realism of traditional representation. Part of its program was to open art to a broader, less aesthetically refined audience than the then-dominant abstract art attracted and to create art that does not take itself so seriously.

CHRONICLE OF EVENTS

1955

January 1: The United States gives $216 million in military aid to South Vietnam.

January 7: Contralto Marian Anderson becomes the first black American to sing at the New York Metropolitan Opera.

January 10: A fleet of about 100 airplanes from the PRC attacks Nationalist forces on the Tachen Islands.

January 13: Chase National and Bank of Manhattan agree to merge.

January 19: Eisenhower gives the first televised presidential press conference.

January 19: The March of Dimes holds its "Pumping for Polio" campaign by soliciting contributions at gasoline stations.

January 28: Congress passes the Formosa Doctrine, authorizing Eisenhower to mobilize the country for war if communist China attacks Taiwan.

February 1: Congress ratifies U.S. participation in the newly formed Southeast Asia Treaty Organization (SEATO).

February 1: Tornadoes kill 29 people in Mississippi.

Dressed as a gas station attendant, Vice President Richard Nixon wipes windshields to raise money for the March of Dime's "Pumping for Polio" campaign on January 19, 1955. *(Photofest)*

February 5: Eisenhower orders the Seventh Fleet to the Tachen Islands off Taiwan.

February 8: Soviet party secretary Nikita Khrushchev consolidates his power by replacing his rival, Georgi Malenkov, with his personal choice, Nikolai Bulganin, as premier.

February 8: Eisenhower proposes a three-year, $7-billion school construction program.

February 8: American Machine and Foundry Company announces plans to build the first nuclear reactor entirely owned and operated by private industry.

February 9: Military service becomes obligatory in communist China.

February 9: The American Federation of Labor (AFL) and the Congress of Industrial Organizations (CIO) agree to merge and form the AFL-CIO.

February 9: South Africa concludes its forced expulsion of some 60,000 black Africans from their homes in Johannesburg to a settlement in the meadowlands outside town.

February 22: The United States tests its first prototype of a guided missile capable of carrying an atomic warhead.

February 28: A railway line linking Hanoi, Beijing, Moscow, and East Berlin opens.

March 7: Mary Martin stars in Jerome Robbins's televised production of *Peter Pan.*

March 9: The movie *East of Eden* opens, and James Dean becomes an instant star.

March 11: Director David Lean films the spectacular destruction of the bridge for *The Bridge on the River Kwai.*

March 12: Jazz innovator and saxophonist Charlie "Bird" Parker dies at age 34.

March 20: Richard Brooks's film *Blackboard Jungle* opens. By July, Bill Haley's rock 'n' roll song, "Rock Around the Clock," which is featured prominently on the soundtrack, becomes the top-selling single record in the country.

March 22: Radioactive fallout from a nuclear test reaches Las Vegas and falls on 2,000 Marines positioned near the test site.

March 24: Tennessee Williams's play *Cat on a Hot Tin Roof* opens on Broadway. Elia Kazan directs the production.

March 31: France declares a state of emergency in Algeria.

April 5: Sir Winston Churchill resigns as Great Britain's prime minister. Declining an offer from the

Mary Martin (flying) brought Peter Pan to life, first on Broadway and then before millions on television's *Producer's Showcase* in 1955 and 1956. *(Photofest)*

queen to become a member of the aristocracy, the 80-year-old Churchill remains a member of the House of Commons. He is succeeded the next day by Sir Anthony Eden, also of Churchill's Conservative Party.

April 14: An armed Nike guided missile accidentally launches itself and explodes in flight.

April 18: Albert Einstein dies at age 76. FBI director J. Edgar Hoover officially closes the investigation of Einstein eight days later. (An FBI interview in February with Einstein's personal secretary, Helen Dukas, debunked a long-standing, anonymous charge that Einstein's office in Berlin had been used by communists prior to World War II.)

April 18–27: Delegates from 29 "nonaligned" African and Asian nations meet in Bandung, Indonesia, where they call for an end to colonialism, independence, and membership in the United Nations.

May 3: The United States and Turkey conclude an "atoms for peace" agreement to exchange data and material necessary for nuclear energy.

May 5: West Germany becomes a sovereign state—the Federal Republic of Germany—and Eisenhower officially ends the U.S. occupation there.

May 5: The musical *Damn Yankees* opens on Broadway.

May 6: The United States tests the ability of an American residential community to survive an atomic attack by exploding an atomic bomb within two miles of 10 model homes built in the Nevada desert. The blast, with a force equivalent to 35,000 tons of TNT, destroys three of the houses, but the rest are reported to suffer only minimal damage, including broken windows and damaged furnishing. Dalmatian dogs left in bomb shelters in the houses are unharmed.

May 7: Reverend George Lee, a black grocery-store owner from Belzoni, Mississippi, who had threatened to file a legal suit after the local sheriff refused to accept his poll tax and allow him to vote, is killed while driving alone. Despite powder burns on Lee's face and shotgun pellets in his car, the sheriff initially maintains the cause of death was an automobile accident. Then he theorizes that Lee was having a sexual liaison and was killed in a crime of passion. No perpetrator is ever arrested.

May 8: Twenty-five Hiroshima Maidens, women who had been disfigured by the atomic attack of World War II, arrive in the United States for reconstructive surgery, which is paid for by donations from Americans.

May 14: The Warsaw Pact for military defense is signed by Albania, Bulgaria, Czechoslovakia, East Germany, Hungary, Poland, Romania, and the USSR in response to the remilitarization of West Germany and in opposition to the NATO alliance.

May 15: The Soviet Union and United States sign an agreement with Austria to end its post–World War II occupation and establish the country as a neutral buffer state between the East and West.

May 31: The U.S. Supreme Court issues *Brown II,* an enforcement decree for *Brown v. Board of Education.* The decree calls for desegregating public schools "with all deliberate speed" and orders lower federal courts to oversee the process.

June 15: The U.S. government conducts a civil defense test in which top officials are moved into 30 separate shelters.

July 1: The United States gives an additional $216 million in aid to South Vietnam.

July 11: The Air Force Academy opens in Colorado and admits its first cadets.

July 16: Premier Diem declares that South Vietnam is not bound by the 1954 Geneva accords that arranged the French withdrawal and called for nationwide elections in 1956.

July 18: The first Geneva summit conference aimed at reducing cold war tensions is held among leaders of Britain, France, the Soviet Union, and United States.

July 18: Walt Disney, the head of Disney motion picture studios and producer of the popular ABC television show *Disneyland,* opens the first modern theme park, Disneyland.

July 27: Austria formally regains autonomy.

July 29: The United States announces plans to develop a satellite capable of going 200 to 300 miles into outer space.

August 1: The PRC frees 11 captured U.S. airmen as it begins talks with the United States.

August 2: Congress votes to fund 45,000 additional public housing units.

August 25: Fourteen-year-old Emmett Till, a black youth from Chicago who is visiting his cousin in Money, Mississippi, accepts a dare from one of the local boys to talk to the white woman behind the counter. Till goes inside, buys some candy, and, as he leaves, whistles and says "Bye, baby." Three days later, on August 28, two white men come in the middle of the night to his great-uncle's house and forcibly remove the boy, striking his great-aunt on the head with a shotgun as she tries to protect him. Three days after that, Till's body is found badly mutilated, with one eye gouged out, a portion of his skull crushed, and a bullet in his head.[13]

September 7: Peru grants voting rights to women.

September 19: Following four days of civil war, a military coup deposes Argentine president Juan Perón, who has ruled the country since 1945. Perón's successor is General Eduardo Lonardi.

September 19: Hurricane Ione strikes the North Carolina coast, with winds up to 107 miles per hour.

September 23: Eisenhower suffers a mild heart attack and is hospitalized until November. Vice President Nixon assumes some presidential responsibilities.

September 30: Actor and teenage idol James Dean dies at age 24 in a car accident when his Porsche Spider careens off the road between Los Angeles and Salinas. Dean becomes the only person to receive two posthumous Academy Award nominations, for his roles in *East of Eden* and *Giant.*

October 1: France boycotts the UN General Assembly after it votes to deliberate the crisis in Algeria.

October 4: The Brooklyn Dodgers defeat the New York Yankees to win baseball's World Series in seven games. The Dodgers had lost all eight of their previous World Series appearances, including five in a row against the Yankees. Dodgers pitcher Don Newcombe (20-5) finishes the season at the top of his league. Yankees pitcher Tommy Byrne (16-5) leads the American League. Philadelphia's Richie Ashburn hits .338 to lead the National League; Detroit's Al Kaline is the American League batting champion at .340. New York Giant Willie Mays leads the majors with 51 home runs, and St. Louis star Stan Musial becomes only the 12th player in Major League Baseball to hit 300 home runs in a career. Brooklyn's catcher, Roy Campanella, and Yankee catcher Yogi Berra are subsequently named the Most Valuable Players (MVP) of the National and American Leagues, respectively. It is Berra's second consecutive year to win the honor.

October 5: *The Diary of Anne Frank* opens on Broadway, directed by Frances Goodrich and Albert Hackett and starring Joseph Schildkraut and Susan Strasberg.

October 6: The U.S. Army commissions its first male nurse.

October 13: Beat poet Allen Ginsberg gives his first public reading of his influential poem "Howl" at Gallery Six in San Francisco.

October 27: A follow-up meeting to the July summit conference in Geneva convenes among the foreign ministers of Britain, France, the Soviet Union, and United States; however, the conference fails to yield substantive results for defusing cold war tensions.

November 11: Eisenhower leaves the hospital after his late-September heart attack and resumes some of his duties.

November 11: A military coup seizes power in Brazil.

November 13: Argentina's leader, General Eduardo Lonardi, in charge for under two months, is deposed in a bloodless coup led by General Pedro Aramburu.

November 14: Conservative writer and editor William F. Buckley, Jr., publishes the first issue of the *National Review.*

December: In communist North Vietnam, landlords are brought to trial before people's tribunals. Many are purely vindictive and send the "guilty" to their execution.

December 1: Rosa Parks, a black woman, refuses to surrender her seat on a public bus in Montgomery, Alabama, to a white rider. Her arrest prompts the bus boycott that on December 5, initiates the civil rights social protests of the 1950s and 1960s and brings Dr. Martin Luther King, Jr., to the forefront of the movement.

December 15: The New York Thruway is completed with the opening of the Tappan Zee Bridge.

December 26: The Los Angeles Rams win football's NFL title, defeating the Cleveland Browns 38-14. Cleveland's Otto Graham retires at the end of the season, after leading the league in passing. Baltimore's Alan Ameche is the top rusher, and Philadelphia's Pete Pihos the leading receiver, for the second straight year.

EYEWITNESS TESTIMONY

After all, this is only the first wife, first car, first house, first kids—wait 'til we get going.

An anonymous man expressing his enthusiasm for the emerging consumer culture in a 1955 interview in Better Homes and Gardens, *in Lary May, ed.,* Recasting America: Culture and Politics in the Age of the Cold War *(1989), p. 187.*

The harbor of New York makes the city of New York and the city of New York is the capital of America, no matter what our civics teachers say. Eight billion dollars of world trade makes this the heart-in-commerce of the Western world. Oh, you simple Hendrik Hudson in your simple little ship . . . look at your harbor now!

The narrator marveling over the port of New York, in Budd Schulberg, Waterfront *(1955), p. 5.*

Brother, we've got another first century on our hands, and converts to reconvert. Man redeemed must be redeemed again. My God, what a different place Bohegan would be if these harps really knew in the innermost depths of their beings what it means to take Christ's Flesh and Blood as food and drink. Let the Commies talk about their revolution, economic salvation by purge trials and forced labor camps. What a revolution we could make if Christians in name should ever develop into Christians in deed.

Father Pete Barry, a character in Budd Schulberg, Waterfront, *expressing a belief commonly held in the 1950s that true, heartfelt Christian belief was a bulwark against communism, in Schulberg's* Waterfront *(1955), pp. 82–83.*

The [*Village*] *Voice* was more significant than anything else at the time in giving a sense of community to writers, but that first couple of years I felt its positions were not adventurous enough, then I left and that improved. Sometimes you get what you want by no longer being there—your ghost gets you farther than if you were still around.

The *Voice* changed the nature of American journalism. People like Pete Hamill came out of it, and James Wolcott. Of course, Jimmy Breslin was an enor-mous influence on journalism too. Breslin and the *Voice* were big influences of the time.

Author Norman Mailer, who was one of the original writers for the Village Voice, *which first appeared in 1955, in Dan Wakefield,* New York in the Fifties *(1992), p. 146.*

By the time they had lived seven years in the little house on Greentree Avenue in Westport, Connecticut, they both detested it. There were many reasons, none of them logical, but all of them compelling. For one thing, the house had a kind of evil genius for displaying proof of their weaknesses and wiping out all traces of their strengths. The ragged lawn and weed-filled garden proclaimed to passers-by and the neighbors that Thomas R. Rath and his family disliked "working around the place" and couldn't afford to pay someone else to do it. . . .

The Raths had bought the house in 1946, shortly after Tom had got out of the army and . . . become an assistant to the director of . . . an organization which an elderly millionaire had established to finance scientific research and the arts. They told each other that they would probably be in the house only one or two years before they could afford something better. It took them five years to realize that the expense of raising three children was likely to increase at least as fast as Tom's salary at a charitable foundation. . . .

"I hear we've got a new spot opening up in our public-relations department," Bill, who wrote promotion for United Broadcasting, said. . . .

"How much would it pay?" . . .

"If you try for it, ask fifteen. I'd like to see somebody stick the bastard good."

It was fashionable that summer to be cynical about one's employers, and the promotion men were the most cynical of all.

"You can have it," Cliff Otis, a young copy writer . . . said. "I wouldn't want to get into a rat race like that."

Tom . . . said nothing. Maybe I could get ten thousand a year, he thought. If I could do that, Betsy and I might be able to buy a better house.

Character Tom Rath exemplifying a typical 1950s white-collar suburbanite, in Sloan Wilson's novel, The Man in the Gray Flannel Suit *(1955), pp. 1–4.*

Over and over again, we had used all the non-violent weapons in our arsenal—speeches, deputations, threats, marches, strikes, stay-aways, voluntary imprisonment—all to no avail, for whatever we did was met by an iron hand.

A freedom fighter learns the hard way that it is the oppressor who defines the nature of the struggle, and the oppressed is often left no recourse but to use methods that mirror those of the oppressor. At a certain point, one can only fight fire with fire.

Nelson Mandela explaining his decision to resort to violent opposition following the forced expulsion, under armed guard, of some 60,000 black Africans from their neighborhoods in Johannesburg, South Africa, on February 9, 1955, in Martin Gilbert, A History of the Twentieth Century, *vol. 3 (2000), p. 90.*

[The testimony of Helen Dukas] in itself tends to discredit the allegations by G-2's [army intelligence] source, who furnished the information that Einstein's office had a staff of secretaries and typists. . . . It is believed that additional investigation is not warranted in view of the long lapse of time since Einstein's office was allegedly used by the Soviets, the lack of corroborating information, and the fact that personnel involved are scattered in many countries and in many cases are deceased.

FBI internal memorandum from mid-February 1955 following an interview with Helen Dukas, Albert Einstein's longtime personal secretary, about alleged communist use of Einstein's Berlin office, in Richard A. Schwartz, "The F.B.I. and Dr. Einstein," Nation *(September 3–10, 1983), p. 170.*

We live in a period, happily unique in human history, when the whole world is divided intellectually and to a large extent geographically between the creeds of Communist discipline and individual freedom, and when, at the same time, this mental and psychological division is accompanied by the possession by both sides of the obliterating weapons of the nuclear age.

Sir Winston Churchill's remarks to Parliament on March 1, 1955, in Martin Gilbert, A History of the Twentieth Century, *vol. 3 (2000), p. 155.*

Bird lives!

Graffito that appeared in New York shortly after the death of jazz performer Charlie "Bird" Parker on March 12, 1955, in Thomas Owens, Bebop: The Music and Its Players *(1995), p. 45.*

Beginning with a banal situation, William Inge has written a fresh and illuminating drama. *Bus Stop* is the work of an expert craftsman. But it is also the work of a writer who has wistful awareness of the loneliness of human beings. Exuberant and hilarious on the surface, *Bus Stop* . . . expresses a point of view about the hunger people have for companionship and understanding.

Critic Brooks Atkinson reviewing William Inge's play Bus Stop, *in Atkinson, "Mr. Inge in Top Form,"* New York Times, *March 13, 1955, sec. 2, p. 1.*

[The stock market boom is due mainly to the] dramatic expansion and improvement of so many industries . . . [the confidence of people in business and] the cumulative effects of inflationary policies [of the government over the past 15 years]. . . . If any economic danger threatens today . . . it will be found not in the stock market but in this inflationary heritage. . . .

The impression has been built up that the stock market is the cause of booms and busts. Actually, it is the thermometer, not the fever. . . . The thermometer should not be blamed for reflecting all the uncertainties [of the world situation and business climate]. . . . The reason stock fluctuations today are so puzzling is that both [confidence in the future and fear of inflation] . . . are so active. . . .

No form of regulation that may be proposed can take the place of sound government policy. . . . If this [inflation] has been the central economic problem of our lifetime, it is mainly because during the whole of the last 40 years this country has either been going into a war or coming out of one. . . .

What kind of dollars is one to use to measure the price of stocks? If inflation is to persist, many stocks may be under-priced today. . . .

If our general economic and security policies are sound, the stock market will adjust to them and we will not need to worry about a possible collapse. If we do not preserve our national security and national credit, then nothing can have lasting value.

Bernard Baruch testifying before the Senate Banking Committee, in "Baruch Says Inflation's Effects, Not Stock Prices, Pose Whatever Danger Is Ahead," Wall Street Journal, *March 24, 1955, pp. 3–4.*

[The intention of these hearings] is to embarrass the Eisenhower Administration and undermine confidence in business by trying to paint a picture that aspects of the [economic] situation are the same now as those leading up to the crash of 1929.

> *Senator Homer Capehart, a Republican from Indiana, criticizing the Democratic-controlled Senate Banking Committee hearings into the state of the economy, in "Baruch Says Inflation's Effects, Not Stock Prices Pose Whatever Danger Is Ahead,"* Wall Street Journal, *March 24, 1955, pp. 3–4.*

I remember the fear of going to public pools because of polio. Children with braces on their legs and crutches were commonplace. Then the first vaccine was a liquid you drank out of a little paper cup.

At the swimming pools, you always had to step into an antiseptic solution before entering the water, and girls had to wear those awful bathing caps. So they came out with ones with plastic flowers on them.

Saturdays were the day you washed your hair, because it took hours to dry if you wore it long, which most of us did. And you used pin curls to curl your hair. You always wrapped it with a scarf to make it look better. The introduction of the hair dryer changed women's lives significantly. At first dryers were only available at salons, then when they first came into the home, they were big, like the ones in the salons. Later they became more portable with plastic head covers.

We wore our cardigans backwards to give a smooth look in front with a detachable collar to dress it up. Bras were made from cotton, and we would starch and iron them to a point so they would project well.

Fads went in and out of fashion. For a while, we wore skirts with lots of crinolines, sometimes as many as seven or eight. Then the hoops came with several crinolines over the hoops. It was a disaster to try to sit in a desk at school and was quickly abandoned. Winter brought long skirts with kick pleats in the back, with bobby socks and loafers worn with the reverse cardigans and collars mentioned above. On Sundays, the ladies always went to church with a hat and short gloves. Evening attire was incomplete without elbow-length gloves and garter belts and seams in the back of your nylons (no pantyhose yet).

Guys wore penny loafers and put horseshoe taps on their shoes. I still remember the sound they made in church when the altar boys would walk in unison across the marble floor.

Everyone knew how to do the Lindey, or jitterbug; in our area it was called the Manual Hop, after our high school. Every part of the country had a different name for it, not the kind you see in the movies with all the acrobatics. And it was quite okay for two girls to dance the jitterbug together.

We always knew there would be someone at the corner drug store. The guys would be wearing Levi's pulled down on the hips as far as possible, making the seat bag.

Anybody who had a car was lucky; we never cared how old it was. Gas was cheap, but teenagers had very little money to just drive. So we'd have to pay for the gas if we wanted to go in the guy's car. When we'd go to a drive-in movie, we'd take a collection for gas and two tickets. Then everyone else had to hide in the trunk. We'd hold our breath 'till we got through the ticket booth. Afterward, everyone would pile out and get inside the car. It was great fun. The speakers at the drive-in were always missing due to vandals or because someone forgot to take it off their car window before they pulled away.

Marriage at young ages was the norm. With no method of birth control for girls, pregnancies were not uncommon. A girl would disappear for a few months to "visit a sick aunt" and then reappear to finish school. Abortions weren't legal, so they would usually give the baby to relatives to raise or give them up for adoption. There were homes for wayward girls and boys. One of the great ironies is that our mothers used to threaten to call HRS [Housing and Human Resources] on us if we didn't behave. Now, kids threaten to report the parents to the same agency. Back then, spanking was the norm. Neither a switch, garnered by mother from a bush outside, nor a razor strap used by dad, had to be employed very often. Once a year was usually enough for most.

Before we got a TV, we used to watch the radio. *The Shadow, Inner Sanctum, The Creaking Door, The Lone Ranger.* When we did get television, we watched shows like *Studio One, The Loretta Young Show,* Sid Caesar, Red Skelton, Art Linkletter, *Ozzie and Harriet,* and *I Love Lucy.*

When television came, the movie theaters were sure they would go broke. But just as today we wanted to go see the movies on the big screens with peers, not parents. Movies were mostly 25 cents, but your folks would complain about how expensive it was, because it had been ten cents in their day. The movie theaters were beautiful where I was from. The seats were velvet and the decor was very ornate. I guess they were a carry over from vaudeville. I don't know. The first 3-D was *The Wax Museum* and we had to wear the special glasses. The musicals were great: *Showboat, The Greatest Show on Earth,* etc. We still cried at the movies.

The radio usually was a combination with a 78 rpm record player, and music was a big part of our lives, just as for kids today. Some of the really cool records—they're collectors' items now—had pictures printed on them. Then came the 45's for teenagers. Juke boxes were everywhere. When you went out to eat, you had one right at your booth. Or the big Wurlitzer was somewhere in the room. A great many of us really loved the black musicians like Fats Domino and the Platters, just to name a couple. We didn't know they weren't allowed to stay at the hotels where they played. Our parents were quite upset with our music.

Maezel Brown, who graduated from high school in Missouri in spring 1955, recalling her impressions of the times, in private correspondence with the author, September 9, 2001.

With the production of *Cat on a Hot Tin Roof,* Tennessee Williams has completed his first decade on Broadway. *The Glass Menagerie* introduced his unique talents to New York on March 31, 1945.

There has never been any reason to temper the rejoicing that greeted his first play. For the succeeding plays have revealed the same insight into troubled recesses of the human spirit and the same poetic command of the theatre. . . .

In *Cat on a Hot Tin Roof,* Mr. Williams has emerged from the period of experimentation. The new play is the work of a mature artist who effortlessly dominates the characters and the theatre.

Critic Brooks Atkinson reviewing Tennessee Williams's play Cat on a Hot Tin Roof, *in Atkinson, "Williams' 'Tin Roof,'"* New York Times, *April 3, 1955, p. 11.*

We invite you to . . . join the American Legion . . and take a poll of the customers as they buy Kraft products. For instance, a questionnaire could be drafted reading, "Do you want any part of your money spent for Kraft products, to help subsidize anyone who had directly or indirectly contributed in any way toward helping the Communist Con-

spiracy in the United States? Indicate in the appropriate box YES or NO."

The Veterans Action Committee of Syracuse Super Markets in an April 1995 letter to the Kraft Foods Company, whose hiring of two entertainers associated with communist-front organizations for its TV show was opposed by the committee, in John Cogley, Report on Blacklisting *(1956), p. 67.*

A man should shave every day, clean his fingernails every day, keep his teeth and breath fresh and clean all the time, bathe often to prevent underarm and other body odors and use a deodorant. . . . Personnel with bad teeth, severe skin blemishes or tattoos should not be stationed at service windows. Your windowmen and outside order takers must impress customers as being "All American boys." They must display such desirable traits as sincerity, enthusiasm, confidence, and a sense of humor.

From an early operations manual for workers at McDonald's hamburger restaurants, which first opened in April 1955, in Jane Stern and Michael Stern, Encyclopedia of Pop Culture *(1992), pp. 312–13.*

Let's get that word "honest" out of there. It would depend on the decree. The white people would not send their children to school with Negroes.

S. E. Rogers, representing Clarendon County, South Carolina, on April 12, 1955, in response to Chief Justice Earl Warren's query whether the county would make an "honest attempt" to abide by whatever decree the Supreme Court might issue to enforce its 1954 ruling calling for school desegregation, in Luther A. Huston, "High Court Hears South Will Defy Quick End to Bias," New York Times, *April 13, 1955, p. 1.*

Charles E. Wilson, Secretary of Defense, defended today his directive for control of defense information, denying that it was "censorship."

He said in a news conference that the widespread publication of technical information in the hydrogen bomb age made national security a "greater problem than ever before in history."

He declared he would be willing to pay hundreds of millions of dollars to get the same kind of information about the Soviet Union as that country gets about the United States in its newspapers and periodicals.

The Secretary outlined a dilemma created by the great outpouring of technical information in a free and highly industrialized society. He said "our top folks" felt too much was being published as a result of rivalries between corporations with defense contracts and between the armed forces, and of the enterprise of a free press and the historical tendency of scientists to report all the latest developments.

> *Secretary of Defense Charles E. Wilson defending restrictions on the availability of technical information, in Anthony Leviero, in "Censorship Move Denied by Wilson," New York Times, April 13, 1955, p. 1.*

A Nike guided missile, misguided, supersonic, and loaded to kill, ran away from its launching platform at nearby Ft. Meade, MD. . . . The explosion occurred about three miles away. . . . The giant missile streaked into the sky, burning a sergeant as it blasted off, and blew apart over a sparsely populated area. . . .

The Nike, named after the winged Greek goddess of victory, was loaded with its warhead of high explosives. . . . An automatic detonator assured the explosion high in the air. . . . A ground explosion would have caused havoc near the heavily traveled new highway between Washington and Baltimore.

> *Description of a runaway guided missile on April 14, 1955, in Anthony Leviero, "Rogue Nike Missile Runs Away,' Explodes in Flight," New York Times, April 15, 1955, pp. 1, 11.*

My experience this morning shows conclusively that women can stand the shock and strain of an atomic explosion just as well as men. . . . It also proved that with the proper precautions, entire communities can survive an atomic bombing.

> *Jean Wood Fuller, director of women's activities in the Federal Civil Defense Administration, describing her experience as a "female guinea pig" in a trench 3,500 feet from ground zero of an atomic test, in a Los Angeles Times article of May 6, 1955, in Lary May, ed., Recasting America: Culture and Politics in the Age of the Cold War (1989), p. 160.*

As shiny as a new baseball and almost as smooth, a new musical glorifying the national pastime slid into the Forty-sixth Street Theatre last night. As far as this umpire is concerned you can count it among the healthy clouts of the campaign.

> *Critic Lewis Funke reviewing the musical Damn Yankees, in Funke, "'Damn Yankees' Tells of Witchery," New York Times, May 6, 1955, p. 17.*

The so-called Attorney General's list is compiled at the direction of the President . . . for the guidance of the heads of the Federal executive departments and agencies for use in connection with requests for investigation regarding employment or retention . . . of Federal employees. Its content becomes public information because it is published in the Federal Register. . . .

The nature and extent of membership in a designated organization is but one factor to be considered. . . .

The Attorney General's list is issued solely for the purpose of [apprising] the heads of executive departments and agencies . . . of the names of organizations, membership in which would warrant requesting a full field investigation in connection with the Federal Employee Security Program. . . . No official compilation of Communists is maintained by the Executive Branch of the Government.

> *William F. Tompkins in a letter of May 11, 1955, to John Cogley, quoted in Cogley, Report on Blacklisting (1956), p. 219.*

[Senator Joseph McCarthy's aide] Don Surine told me in confidence that in 1944 General Eisenhower wrote a personal letter to General [George] Marshal[l] . . . asking Marshal's advice as to what effect a divorce would have upon General Eisenhower's personal career. This occurred at a time when General Eisenhower was allegedly having an affair with Kay Summersby, the British WAC [who was Eisenhower's chauffeur, aide, and secretary during World War II].

> *FBI assistant director Louis Nichols in an internal, informal memorandum dated May 13, 1955, to FBI associate director Clyde Tolson, in Athan Theoharis, ed., From the Secret Files of J. Edgar Hoover (1993), p. 57.*

What the hell are you doing? Can't you see I'm having a *real* moment? Don't you *ever* cut a scene while I'm having a real moment. What the fuck do you think I'm here for?

> *Method actor James Dean chewing out director Nicholas Ray, who, on May 22, 1955, temporarily stopped the filming of a knife fight in Rebel Without a Cause to attend to Dean, who was cut during the take, in Harry Haun, This Cinematic Century (2000).*

In spite of the horror of the situation, I did not judge that the race should be interrupted. Even when a tragedy happens, the sport should be guided by its own laws.

The director of the Le Mans speedway justifying his decision to continue an auto race after 80 fans were killed on June 11, 1955, when a car went out of control and skidded into the grandstand, in Clifton Daniel, ed., The Twentieth Century Day by Day (2000), p. 769.

As Stan Musial strode to the plate in the twelfth inning today, Harry Walker, his manager on the St. Louis Cardinals, called out to him from a box alongside the dugout.

"Let's end this now, Stan," he exhorted. "I'm getting hungry."

Stan the Man must have been hungry too. But at least he was obedient. He swung at the first pitch. The resounding crack of the bat was engulfed in the roar of the crowd. Through the shadows, which were settling over the field, shot the ball. Then it shone in glistening white resplendency as it burst into the sunshine, headed for the bleachers. It was a home run.

Thus ended a gripping dramatic All-Star game with the Nationals the winners after an uphill climb, 6 to 5. It was only the second overtime affair the midsummer classic has offered and the pattern is now firmly established. A Cardinal player always wins extra inning All-Star shindigs with home runs. Red Schoendienst did it in 1950 in the fourteenth....

The tremendously popular Musial was greeted by the entire National League squad as he jammed his spikes on the plate with a joyous, bouncing leap.... He showered and had a much earlier dinner than he expected....

"I haven't hit a homer in this park all year," said [Duke] Synder to [Ted] Williams before the game. "Every time I belt one, Bill Burton leans over the center field fence to rob me."

In the seventh inning, Williams understood exactly how he felt. Ted shot a towering blast over the fence in right center. But Willie Mays leaped up, reached over the parapet and made a miraculous one-handed catch to rob the Boston slugger of a sure homer.

Arthur Daley describing the All-Star Game on July 12, 1955, in Daley, "Gazing at the Stars," New York Times, July 13, 1955, p. 29.

Investigation of Einstein instituted 1950 based upon information that he was affiliated with over 30 Com-

munist-front organizations. Investigation reflected he sponsored entry into U.S. of numerous individuals with pro-Communist backgrounds. . . . Extensive investigation in U.S. showed Einstein affiliated or his name extensively associated with literally hundreds of pro-Communist groups. No evidence of C.P. membership developed.

FBI internal memorandum of July 27, 1955, summarizing the bureau's investigation of Albert Einstein, in Richard Schwartz, "The F.B.I. and Dr. Einstein," Nation (September 3–10, 1983), p. 172.

We was going to Money, Mississippi to have a good time. . . . My grandfather in Mississippi was a preacher. He had a church and he had a little raggedy '41 Ford. . . . While he was in the pulpit preaching, we get the car and drive to Money. Anyway, we went into this store to buy some candy. Before Emmett went in, he had shown the boys round his age some picture of some white kids that he had graduated from school with, female and male. He told the boys . . . there

Stan "the Man" Musial of the St. Louis Cardinals celebrates his 300th home run. *(Photofest)*

must have been maybe ten or twelve youngsters there—that one of the girls was his girlfriend. So one of the local boys said, "Hey, there's a white girl in that store there. I bet you won't go in there and talk to her." So Emmett went in there. When he was leaving out the store, after buying some candy, he told her, "Bye, baby."

I was sitting out there playing checkers with this older man. Next thing I know, one of the boys came up to me and said, "Say, man, you got a crazy cousin. He just went in there and said 'Bye, baby,' to "that white woman." This man I was playing checkers with jumped straight up and said, "Boy, you better get out of here. That lady'll come out of that store and blow your brains off." . . .

That was Wednesday. . . . [On Saturday night about 3:30 A.M.] I was awakened by a group of men in the house. . . . [T]hey told him [grandfather] to get the one who did the talking. My grandmother was scared to death. She was trying to protect Bo [Emmett]. They told her to get back in bed. One of the guys struck her with a shotgun side of the head. When I woke up the next morning, I thought it was a dream.

Curtis Jones explaining the events leading up to the murder of his cousin, 14-year-old Emmett Till, outside Money, Mississippi, on August 28, 1955, in Henry Hampton, Steve Fayer, and Sarah Flynn, eds., Voices of Freedom: An Oral History of the Civil Rights Movement from the 1950s through the 1980s *(1990), pp. 3–4.*

Have you ever sent a loved son on vacation and had him returned to you in a pine box so horribly battered and waterlogged that this sickening sight is your son—lynched?

Mamie Bradley speaking about the murder of her son, Emmett Till, outside Money, Mississippi, on August 28, 1955, in David Halberstam, The Fifties *(1993), p. 436.*

What else could we do? He [Emmett Till] was hopeless. I'm no bully; I never hurt a nigger in my life. I like niggers in their place. I know how to work 'em. But I just decided it was time a few people got put on notice. As long as I live and can do anything about it, niggers are going to stay in their place. Niggers ain't gonna vote where I live. If they did, they'd control the government. They ain't gonna go to school with my

kids. And when a nigger even gets close to mention sex with a white woman, he's tired of livin'.

J.W. Milam, who admitted his guilt in Look *magazine, January 24, 1956, explaining why he and his brother-in-law, Roy Bryant, killed Emmett Till on August 28, 1955, in David Halberstam,* The Fifties *(1993), p. 435.*

We've sued Milam a couple of times for debt. He's bootlegged all his life. He comes from a big, mean, overbearing family. Got a chip on his shoulder. That's how he got that battlefield promotion in Europe; he likes to kill folks. [But] hell, we've got to have our Milams to fight our wars and keep the niggahs in line.

Attorney J. J. Breland explaining why he defended J.W. Milam, who killed Emmett Till on August 28, 1955, in David Halberstam, The Fifties *(1993), p. 434.*

Although no Soviet data are available on LSD-25, it must be assumed that the scientists of the USSR are thoroughly cognizant of the strategic importance of this powerful new drug and are capable of producing it at any time.

From the conclusion of "An OSI Study on the Strategic Medical Significance of Lysergic Acid Diethylamide (LSD-25)," dated August 30, 1955, in Martin A. Lee and Bruce Shlain, Acid Dreams *(1985), p. 16.*

General Snyder arrived shortly thereafter, and gave me some injections, one of which, I learned later, was morphine. This probably accounts for the hazy memory I had—and still have—of later events in the night.

President Dwight D. Eisenhower's recollection of his heart attack on the evening of September 23, 1955, in Eisenhower, The White House Years, *vol. 1 (1963), p. 237.*

["Howl"] is a tragic custard-pie-comedy of wild phrasing, meaningless images for the beauty of abstract poetry of mind, running along, making awkward combination (of images) like Charlie Chaplin's walk, long saxophone-line chorus lines I knew [Jack] Kerouac would hear *sound* of—taking off from his own inspired prose line, really a new poetry.

Beat poet Allen Ginsberg describing the composition of "Howl," which he first performed at Gallery Six in San Francisco on October 13, 1955, in Barry Miles, Ginsberg: A Biography *(1989), p. 188.*

I've always played lugubrious, heavy things and neglected this side of the entertainment business. Song and dance is part of an actor's trade; he should be able to dance a jig or tell a joke as part of his bag of tricks. It's just as important as telling a story poignantly and beautifully, with some kind of grace and power.

Actor Marlon Brando commenting on his decision to star in the film adaptation of the musical Guys and Dolls, *which premiered in early November 1955, in David Downing,* Marlon Brando *(1984), p. 38.*

Davy Crockett makes what presumably will be a triumphant return over the American Broadcasting Company television network on Wednesday, Nov. 16, from 7:30 to 8:30 P.M.

In the new Crockett episode of the *Disneyland* series, Davy will be confronted by one Mike Fink, a legendary hero, river brawler and boatman who was known as the king of the Ohio and Mississippi Rivers.

As any viewer of *Disneyland* knows, Davy Crockett died at the Alamo last Feb. 23. This little incident, however, has not stopped Walt Disney from producing more Crockett films, which he has labeled as fiction. . . .

"King of the River," a song by George Brun and Tom Blackburn, who wrote "The Ballad of Davy Crockett," will be introduced in the new episodes.

Val Adams previewing a Davy Crockett episode, in Adams, "Davy Crockett Returning to TV," New York Times, *November 2, 1955, p. L 70.*

I don't think any segregation law angered black people in Montgomery more than bus segregation. . . .

I knew they [the NAACP] needed a plaintiff who was beyond reproach. . . . But that is not why I refused to give up my bus seat to a white man on Thursday, December 1, 1955. I did not intend to get arrested. If I had been paying attention, I wouldn't even have gotten on that bus. . . .

When I got off from work that evening . . . I didn't look to see who was driving. . . . It was the same driver who had put me off the bus back in 1943, twelve years earlier. . . . And he was still mean-looking. . . . Most of the time if I saw him on a bus, I wouldn't get on it.

I saw a vacant seat in the middle section of the bus and took it. . . . The next stop was the Empire Theater, and some whites got on. They filled up the white seats, and one man was left standing. The driver . . . looked back at us. He said, "Let me have those front seats." . . . Didn't anybody move. We just sat there, the four of us. . . .

The man in the window seat next to me stood up . . . and then I looked across the aisle and saw that the two women were also standing. . . .

I thought back to the time when I used to sit up all night and didn't sleep, and my grandfather would have his gun right by the fireplace, or if he had his one-horse wagon going anywhere, he always had his gun in the back of the wagon. People always say that I didn't give up my seat because I was tired, but this isn't true. I was not tired physically. . . . No, the only tired I was, was tired of giving in . . . I chose to remain.

Rosa Parks describing her arrest for refusing to give her seat to a white rider on December 1, 1955, which sparked the beginning of the Montgomery Bus Boycott, in Parks, Rosa Parks: My Story *(1992), pp. 108–16.*

Nearly a quarter-century ago, concluding a moral evaluation of the wage contract, Pope Pius XI wrote: "We consider it more advisable . . . in the present condition of human society that, so far as is possible, the work-contract be somewhat modified by a partnership-contract."

What the Holy Father had in mind were certain improvements in the ordinary labor contract that would enable workers "to become sharers in ownership or management or participate in some fashion in the profits received."

Whether or not the men who founded the Council of Profit Sharing Industries were aware of Pope Pius' thought, they have succeeded in a brief eight-year period in demonstrating its practicality and effectiveness. To the 800 delegates . . . [attending] the council's annual convention, Cardinal McIntyre was able to say, "You have won not only the hands of your men but . . . their hearts."

Recalling an earlier period in our history when ruthless industrialists exploited the needs of immigrant labor, "to the grave detriment of justice," the Cardinal hailed the progress that U.S. labor and management have made. . . .

For the ills of industrial society, profit sharing is no panacea, nor was it so proposed by Pius XI. But sincerely practiced, it can in many cases make labor-management relations a mutually rewarding adventure.

Labor-management relations as a moral and religious issue, in "Profit Shares in Los Angeles," America: National Catholic Weekly Review (December 3, 1955), p. 262.

But there comes a time when people get tired. We are here this evening to say to those who have mistreated us so long that we are tired—tired of being segregated and humiliated, tired of being kicked around by the brutal feet of oppression. We have no alternative but protest. For many years, we have shown amazing patience. We have sometimes given our white brothers the feeling that we liked the way we were being treated. But we come here tonight to be saved from that patience that makes us patient with anything less than freedom and justice. . . .

One of the greatest glories of democracy is the right to protest for right. . . . These organizations [the Ku Klux Klan and the White Citizens Councils] are protesting for the perpetuation of injustice in the community, we are protesting for the birth of justice in the community. Their methods lead to violence and lawlessness. But in our protest there will be no cross burnings. No white person will be taken from his home by a hooded Negro mob and brutally murdered. . . . We will be guided by the highest principles of law and order. . . .

Our method will be that of persuasion, not coercion. We will only say to people, "Let your conscience be your guide. . . . [O]ur actions must be guided by the deepest principles of our Christian faith. Love must be our regulating ideal. Once again we must hear the words of Jesus echoing across the centuries, 'Love your enemies, bless them that curse you, and pray for them that despitefully use you.'" If we fail to do this our protest will end up as a meaningless drama on the stage of history, and its memory will be shrouded with the ugly garments of shame. . . . As Booker T. Washington said, "Let no man pull you so low as to make you hate him."

Dr. Martin Luther King, Jr., addressing a mass meeting on December 5, 1955, the first day of the Montgomery, Alabama, Bus Boycott, in Leon Friedman, The Civil Rights Reader (1968), pp. 40–41.

The NSC [National Security Council] has determined that such covert operations shall to the greatest extent practicable, in light of U.S. and Soviet capabilities and taking into account the risk of war, be designed to:

a. Create and exploit troublesome problems for International Communism, impair relations between the USSR and Communist China and between them and their satellites, complicate control within the USSR, Communist China and their satellites, and retard the growth of the military and economic potential of the Soviet bloc.

b. Discredit the prestige and ideology of International Communism, and reduce the strength of its parties and other elements.

c. Counter any threat of a party or individuals directly or indirectly responsive to Communist control to achieve dominant power in a free world country.

d. Reduce International Communist control over any areas of the world.

e. Strengthen the orientation toward the United States of the peoples and nations of the free world, accentuate, wherever possible, the identity of interest between such peoples and nations and the United States as well as favoring, where appropriate, those groups genuinely advocating or believing in the advancement of such mutual interests, and increase the capacity and will of such peoples and nations to resist International Communism.

f. In accordance with established policies and to the extent practicable in areas dominated or threatened by International Communism, develop underground resistance and facilitate covert and guerrilla operations and ensure availability of those forces in the event of war, including wherever practicable provision of a base upon which the military may expand these forces in time of war within active theaters of operations as well as provide for stay-behind assets and escape and evasion facilities.

The U.S. government authorizing covert operations against communist regimes, in National Security Council directive NSC-5412/2, issued on December 28, 1955, in John Prados, Presidents' Secret Wars: CIA and Pentagon Covert Operations from World War II through the Persian Gulf (1996), pp. 112–13.

8

Ike and Elvis, Budapest and Suez

1956

The year 1956 began on a note of hope, as Communist Party secretary Nikita Khrushchev modified Marxist doctrine and declared that violent confrontation with the West was not inevitable; instead, he suggested that the superpowers might enjoy "peaceful co-existence." Moreover, at a closed session of the 20th Congress of the Soviet Communist Party, Khrushchev denounced Stalin's personality cult and introduced a number of domestic reforms. These reforms generated some optimism that the new Soviet leadership might be fundamentally different from Stalin and might negotiate in good faith for a diplomatic resolution of the differences between the East and West. But those hopes were dashed after Khrushchev brutally suppressed a populist, anticommunist uprising in Hungary in the fall. At the same time, a crisis erupted in the Suez as combined Israeli, French, and British forces invaded Egypt following Egypt's seizure of the Suez Canal. While both of those international events were unfolding, Americans opted for stability and reelected Eisenhower in a landslide, but Democrats held control of both houses of Congress. Court-mandated desegregation of the South began, but not without strenuous and sometimes violent opposition.

Passions also ran high as more and more young people enthusiastically embraced sexually charged rock 'n' roll, while many of their elders opposed it. Despite the controversy, expressions of sexuality became more widely tolerated, even embraced by some, and certainly more profitable. When Elvis Presley swung his hips on national television, he won fans as much for his sex appeal as for his voice; Elia Kazan's film *Baby Doll* provoked censure from the pulpit but drew large audiences with its steamy story; and Grace Metalious's *Peyton Place* became a best-seller with its frank treatment of sex in staid, small-town New England. Moreover, if Presley's gyrations challenged middle America's morality, Beat poetry such as Allen Ginsberg's "Howl" outright assaulted it, as did James Baldwin, albeit in a more restrained style, when he wrote sympathetically about homosexuality in *Giovanni's Room*. On the other hand, Cecil B. DeMille found a large, receptive audience for his final directorial effort, *The Ten Commandments,* which celebrates the moral codes in the Bible. And, in a popular effort to establish more firmly the connection between religion and the national interest, Congress made "In God We Trust" the nation's official motto. The phrase also appeared on a red-white-and-blue postage stamp.

The debates over contemporary morality did nothing to impede the influence of big business on "the organization man" or to slow the pace of scientific discovery and technological innovation: The first computer programming language was developed, as was videotape recording; astronomers first viewed the birth of stars; and for the first time individual atoms were seen under a microscope. Nonetheless, the prevailing themes of much of the serious fiction of the year were in one way or another personal despair and dysfunctional family life.

THE COLD WAR AND INTERNATIONAL POLITICS

The Cold War Abroad

Cold war tensions eased in January and February, when Khrushchev stated that he believed Eisenhower was sincere in his desire for peace. Then, at the opening of the 20th Congress of the Soviet Communist Party on February 14, Khrushchev announced that communism could exist without violence. More dramatically, at the final, closed-door session of the congress, on February 25, he called for peaceful coexistence with the capitalist democracies and shocked his audience by attacking Stalin's policies and personality cult. He subsequently introduced a number of reforms designed to improve the standard of living and provide somewhat greater, but still restricted personal liberties and artistic freedom.

Despite these reforms, Khrushchev retained Stalin's practice of censoring ideas and restricting the flow of information to the public. Although his speech was leaked to the U.S. State Department, which published the full text within months of its delivery, the Soviet public received only a much less critical version that condemned only Stalin's practice of establishing a personality cult. The full speech was not released inside the Soviet Union until 1989. Khrushchev also blamed Stalin for creating the rift that drove Yugoslavia from the Soviet bloc, and in a gesture aimed at restoring relations with Marshal Tito, the Soviets dissolved COMINFORM, the international alliance of communist parties that had expelled Yugoslavia in 1948, after Tito removed the Stalinists from Yugoslavia's army and governing bodies.

In a move aimed at improving East-West relations, Khrushchev and Soviet premier Nikolay Bulganin went to London to meet with Prime Minister Eden, but the talks also included a warning that the Soviet Union was developing an intercontinental ballistic missile (ICBM) capable of delivering a nuclear warhead. The United States unveiled its Lockheed Starfighter, a jet capable of flying at 1,500 miles per hour and carrying a hydrogen bomb, but the Defense Department conceded that the Soviet Union had a greater number of planes capable of delivering nuclear weapons. In Europe, East Germany rearmed and established the People's Army, after the United States installed its first long-range Nike missiles in West Germany.

Communism's harsher side surfaced in Poland and Hungary, where workers and students were demanding greater freedoms, akin to those being granted in the Soviet Union. On June 28, workers in Poznan rioted in protest and seized the headquarters of the secret police, but the Polish government suppressed the uprising by sending troops and tanks into the city center and opening fire, killing 38. But new demonstrations occurred that fall, provoking Khrushchev and three other Soviet leaders to fly to Warsaw in October and warn that the protests must stop. Soviet warships were ordered to the Polish coast, and Soviet troops based in the country were positioned around the outskirts of Warsaw; however, two days later, on October 21, Khrushchev relented and appointed reform-minded Wladyslaw Gomulka as first secretary of the Polish Communist Party. Gomulka ended forced farm collectivization and permitted greater freedom of speech, but he was careful to uphold Poland's fundamental alignment with the Soviet Union and insist that his more nationalistic vision was a variety of communism, not a repudiation of it. Gomulka's cautious approach enabled him to modify the election laws in January to permit voters greater choice.

The Hungarian Uprising

By contrast to the situation in Poland, the greater challenge to Soviet supremacy in Hungary provoked a more extreme response from Khrushchev. For years to come, Americans pointed to his brutal suppression of the Hungarian revolt as proof of the Soviet Union's willingness to use terror and raw power to impose its will on any country that fell under its influence, and it seemingly confirmed the need to continue the cold war.

The changes in Poland inspired dissidents in Hungary, and immediately after Gomulka announced his reforms in October, students and workers in Budapest, Pécs, and Szeged began agitating for greater freedoms in their country, too. Among their demands were free elections and representative government, Hungary's withdrawal from the Warsaw Pact, freedom of the press, independent courts, the right to strike, free communication with the West, an end to forced collectivization of farms, cessation of uranium deliveries to the Soviet Union, and reinstatement of Imre Nagy, the former prime minister who had been removed in 1955 and replaced by hard-liner Andreas Hegedus.

On October 22, a group of students delivered their demands to Hegedus, and on the following day, violent demonstrations erupted throughout Budapest. To appease the rioters, Nagy was reinstated on October 24. He promised immediate reforms, and the Soviet troops stationed in Budapest began to evacuate the city; however, on that same day, a full-fledged uprising ensued, and after heavy street fighting, the Soviet forces withdrew fully from Budapest. The next day, demonstrators sought assistance from the United States and Britain, and many misconstrued Eisenhower's statement that "the heart of America goes out to the people of Hungary" as a pledge of support. Ultimately, however, despite Secretary of State Dulles's earlier advocacy of a liberation policy to free Eastern Europe from Soviet domination, Eisenhower respected the Soviet sphere of influence and refused to involve the United States in the Hungarian rebellion.

Nagy formed a new government on October 27 that included several noncommunists. He also freed some 5,000 political prisoners. In response, on November 1, a Soviet force of more than 75,000 troops and 2,500 tanks crossed into Hungary and advanced on the capital. By November 5, they had crushed the rebellion, but only after heavy street fighting that pitted Russian tanks against civilians, often children, armed with hand grenades or Molotov cocktails (bottles filled with gasoline and corked with a fuse). It was estimated that some 7,000 Soviet soldiers and 25,000 Hungarians were killed, and as many as 200,000 additional Hungarians—almost 2 percent of the population—fled the country into Austria. Many of these, who included some of Hungary's brightest and most creative thinkers and artists, subsequently relocated in Britain, France, Norway, Canada, West Germany, and the United States, which accepted some 28,000 refugees.

Of those who remained in Hungary, thousands were arrested and deported to camps inside the Soviet Union. A new government led by hard-liner János Kádár was installed, and when workers called a general protest strike in early December, Kádár declared martial law and ordered the arrest of all who demonstrated. In January 1956, the government made strikes and protests punishable by death. After the Soviet invasion, Nagy took refuge in the Yugoslav embassy but was later arrested by Soviet police after being given assurances of safe passage. He was placed in custody of the Kádár regime, which later tried and executed him.

Although Khrushchev succeeded in squelching the rebellion, the brutality of the Soviet response alienated many communists and communist sympathizers around the world—existentialist philosopher Jean-Paul Sartre among them—and impeded Khrushchev's efforts to seek peaceful coexistence with the West and defuse the cold war.

THE SUEZ CRISIS

As the events in Hungary transpired in October, Israel preempted an anticipated Egyptian attack by invading Egypt. This precipitated what became known as the Suez crisis. As prearranged, Israel was soon joined by Great Britain and France, who were intent on retaking the Suez Canal, which Egypt had nationalized in July. However, Eisenhower was angered that the allies had failed to consult him before invading, and the United States did not support this effort. Nonetheless, Eisenhower announced that a threatened missile attack by the Soviet Union against France and Britain would provoke a U.S. nuclear response and lead to global war. Canada played a major role in brokering the UN armistice in November that defused the crisis. The armistice arranged for British and French troops to be replaced by an international peacekeeping force, and it left the United States as the sole superpower in the region. Israeli forces remained in the Gaza Strip before yielding to UN troops in early March 1957. The UN peacekeepers were then almost immediately forced to withdraw by superior Egyptian forces.

Although the military expedition fulfilled Israel's goal of forestalling an Egyptian attack, it failed to accomplish the main objective of the British and French, which was to topple the Nasser regime and reestablish international control over the canal. Furthermore, the crisis damaged the already deteriorating U.S.-French alliance, and its unpopularity in Britain was one of the factors, in addition to ill health, that led Prime Minister Anthony Eden to retire in January 1957. Egypt agreed to repay the shareholders of the canal but continued to deny Israeli ships passage through it, which was one of the provocations of the invasion. Sunken ships and destroyed bridges closed the canal until March 1957. Following the resolution of the conflict, some 25,000 Egyptian Jews were forced to leave the country, even though their families had been there for generations, after Egypt made Islam its official state religion. About half immigrated to Israel under the 1950 Law of Return that allows any Jew arriving in Israel to become a citizen.

Other International Developments

The deportation of Archbishop Mikhail Makarios for supporting terrorist acts by the Cypriot separatist movement sparked anti-British riots and a general strike in Cyprus, where violent opposition against British rule by Greek nationals intensified. Sudan gained its independence from Britain, and Morocco and Tunisia from France, but violence flared in Algeria, where, despite offers from the French government to hold free elections, hard-line nationalists insisted that the 1.2 million French nationals living there be treated as foreigners in an independent Algeria if they did not convert to Islam. This position was unacceptable to France, and Algeria, which was already under martial law, moved closer to outright civil war. In South Africa, the government relocated the stands of Indian traders away from town centers, now reserved for whites only, and it arrested 156 members, including Nelson Mandela, of the anti-apartheid African National Congress.

South Vietnam's Diem regime, which enjoyed the support of the United States, won its first election in the National Assembly, and North Vietnam's Ho Chi Minh began a program of land reform that ensured full communist control over the countryside. Some 100,000 wealthy peasants and small landowners were arrested, tried, and executed; agricultural production dropped drastically. Pakistan was established as the first Islamic republic on February 29, although it remained part of the British Commonwealth. Britain also agreed to grant independence to Malaysia within two years. China briefly became more tolerant of divergent ideas, as Mao Zedong introduced his Hundred Flowers Campaign. Its theme was "Let a hundred flowers bloom/let a hundred schools of thought contend."[1] However, when criticism of the Communist Party became too strong, Mao terminated the policy.

Fidel Castro and 82 followers landed in Oriente Province in Cuba in an unsuccessful attempt to overthrow Batista's military government. Most of the group were killed or captured, and Castro, himself, was reported dead. But the reports of his demise proved inaccurate, and the survivors, including Ernesto "Che" Guevara, formed the nucleus for his successful revolution two years later. In Nicaragua, General Anastasio Somoza was assassinated and succeeded by his son.

The Cold War at Home

Anticommunist activity abated within the United States during the election year, although the Internal Revenue Service briefly seized property from the American Communist Party headquarters, citing nonpayment of income taxes. The property was returned the following week after the party paid $1,500. The HUAC hearings focused investigations on foreign travel and improper use of passports by communists and communist sympathizers. Testifying as hostile witnesses before the committee were singer Paul Robeson, a pro-Soviet black performer whose passport had been rescinded in 1950, and

Director J. Edgar Hoover of the FBI led the fight against domestic communism. *(Federal Bureau of Investigation)*

playwright Arthur Miller, an outspoken critic of HUAC. Citing the First Amendment, which the Supreme Court had already ruled could not be used to avoid testimony, Miller answered questions about his own activities but refused to comment on anyone else's. He was later found guilty of contempt of Congress, fined $500, given a 30-day suspended sentence, and had his passport revoked, but the conviction was overturned on appeal in 1958. Also appearing before HUAC was Willard Uphaus, a leader of the World Fellowship, Inc. He came to the committee's attention after being named by J. B. Matthews in a 1953 article in the *American Mercury* that claimed, "the largest single group supporting the communist apparatus in the United States today is composed of Protestant clergymen."[2]

FBI director J. Edgar Hoover initiated a counterintelligence program (COINTELPRO) after federal courts made prosecuting communists increasingly difficult under existing laws. Designed to undermine the Communist Party in the United States, COINTELPRO involved leaking accurate and inaccurate information to the press about communist activities, sending anonymous letters to employers of communists demanding that they be fired, and otherwise harassing party members and disrupting their work. In 1975, the Senate's Church Committee (named after Senator Frank Church) revealed the COINTELPRO operations and other illegal wiretaps, burglaries, and mail openings during the Eisenhower era. The committee also reported that Hoover had informed the president, the White House staff, and attorney general, and no one had objected.

The FBI had been seriously infiltrating the American Communist Party since the early days of the cold war, and party membership fell from about 31,000 in 1950 to just a few thousand in 1956, a large number of whom were FBI agents. According to writer Howard Fast, an ex-communist who left the party in 1956, "The Communist Party of the United States, in fact, at that moment, was practically a branch of the Justice Department." William Colby, who later headed the CIA, has also expressed his belief that the dues provided by FBI infiltrators were, by 1956, sustaining the party.[3]

CIVIL RIGHTS

Violence erupted in scattered regions throughout the South as black children began to enroll in all-white public schools. Early in the year, in an effort to circumvent the Supreme Court ruling calling for desegregation, Virginia sanctioned state funding of private schools. Autherine Lucy, the University of Alabama's first black student, was suspended after riots on campus threatened her safety in early February; she was later expelled for criticizing the university officials. In June, Alabama outlawed the National Association for the Advancement of Colored People (NAACP). In April, singer Nat "King" Cole was attacked while performing before a white audience in Birmingham, but in November NBC gave him his own 15-minute television variety show on Monday evenings, before the network news. In the summer of 1957, he received a half-hour time slot at 10 P.M., but the show was canceled in December 1957, reportedly because sponsors feared a southern boycott.[4] Cole became the third, and last, black performer to host a television variety show during the 1950s. He was preceded by Hazel Scott (DuMont, 1950) and Billy Daniels (ABC, 1952), but neither of those shows remained on the air for more than three months.

In Montgomery, emotions surrounding the bus boycott became increasingly passionate. In late January, Martin Luther King, Jr.'s front porch was bombed, as was the home of his colleague E. D. Nixon a few days later. In February, King and 88 others were indicted for violating a 1921 law prohibiting boycotts. King was tried and convicted in March and sentenced to pay a $500 fine. In June, a federal district court declared that the segregationist bus policies were unconstitutional, but Montgomery officials appealed the decision to the Supreme Court, which upheld it in November, ruling that the practice of segregating public transportation is unconstitutional, even for travel that occurs solely within a state. The boycott continued until December 21, 1956, when the ruling officially arrived in Montgomery and activists King, Nixon, Glenn Smiley, and Ralph Abernathy boarded the city's first integrated bus. However, a bus boycott in Tallahassee, Florida, that began in May continued through 1958, as local officials refused to desegregate the buses, despite the court's ruling.

On March 12, southern senators and congressmen issued the so-called Southern Manifesto, declaring their opposition to the Supreme Court's intrusion into what they regarded as a state, not federal, matter. Refusing to sign the document were Democratic senators Al Gore, Sr., of Tennessee, Estes Kefauver of Tennessee, and Lyndon Johnson of Texas, the Senate majority leader.

GOVERNMENT AND SOCIETY

The dominant public issue in 1956 was the presidential election. The Republicans naturally renominated their popular incumbent president, Eisenhower, and Illinois governor Adlai Stevenson defeated Senator Kefauver for the Democratic presidential nomination. In turn, Kefauver, who campaigned wearing a coonskin cap that had been made popular that year by *Disneyland*'s Davy Crockett, beat out Senator John F. Kennedy of Massachusetts for the vice presidential nomination, despite Kennedy's impressive keynote speech. The contest between Eisenhower and Stevenson was a rematch of 1952's, and the results were similar. Despite Eisenhower's heart attack the previous year and his surgery in June for an intestinal complication that was more serious than commonly acknowledged, he was overwhelmingly expected to prevail, and he did. Apart from the matter of Eisenhower's health, Stevenson's only major campaign issue was a proposal to ban aboveground nuclear testing, which Eisenhower dismissed as unrealistic.

Running on his administration's record for the previous four years, Eisenhower claimed credit for the conclusion of the Korean War and the elimination of wartime wage and price controls, a modest budget surplus, growth in personal income, extension of Social Security coverage to an additional 10 million people, a large tax cut in 1954, initiation of an interstate highway system and the St. Lawrence Seaway, and a record of curtailing communist expansion in Iran, Guatemala, and elsewhere around the world, while still remaining at peace.[5]

There was some question as to whether Eisenhower would retain Richard Nixon as his vice president, but despite pressure from the party leadership to step down in favor of former navy secretary Robert Anderson or Ohio's Democratic, Roman Catholic governor, Frank Lausche, Nixon insisted on remaining on the ticket, even after Eisenhower offered him a cabinet position in which he could exert more direct influence on policy and establish a reputation for executive ability. Although Eisenhower won by a margin of 9 million popular votes and carried 41 of the 48 states, the Democrats prevailed in both houses of Congress.

Soon after the election, Eisenhower signed the $33.4 billion highway bill that funded construction of the interstate highway system. This had immense long-term consequences for the nation, greatly facilitated commerce and leisure travel, positively affected industry, and made possible the further expansion of the suburbs. He also signed a farm bill authorizing the government to store agricultural surpluses and the Colorado River Bill that allocated $760 million for electrical power and irrigation.

Other, less political matters of social interest included the wreck of the Italian ocean liner, the *Andrea Doria,* on July 25, in which 51 people were killed but more than 1,600 were rescued. Launched in 1951 to help the Italian oceangoing fleet regain its former glory after the loss of the *Rex* and *Conte di Savoia* during World War II, the *Andrea Doria* sank after colliding with the Swedish liner *Stockholm* in heavy fog off Nantucket Island. As with the *Titanic* earlier in the century, the loss of the *Andrea Doria* was especially unsettling because it was not only the fastest and most luxurious ship in the Italian fleet, it was also supposed to be the safest. It had a double hull, 11 water-tight compartments, and radar to warn of nearby vessels.

M. E. Tower of Syracuse, New York, became the first woman to be ordained as a Presbyterian minister; former first lady Eleanor Roosevelt received the first Woman of Valor award; and the last Union army veteran of the Civil War died. In Schenectady, New York, closed-circuit television was used for the first time to teach students in public school.

At least two celebrity marriages captured the public imagination and garnered immense publicity: the wedding of movie star Marilyn Monroe and playwright Arthur Miller and the more enduring, seemingly fairytale union of actress Grace Kelly and Prince Rainier II of Monaco. Kelly, who retired from acting after she married, met Rainier while she was filming Alfred Hitchcock's *To Catch a Thief* in Monaco in 1955. Gene Kelly became the first movie actor to appear on a U.S. postage stamp.

BUSINESS

The economy was strong during 1956, despite a steel strike in July that slowed the economy and forced the railways to lay off some 30,000 workers. The GNP increased by 5 percent, inflation rose at only 1.2 percent, unemployment remained a low 4.3 percent, and the Dow Jones Industrial Average fluctuated between 462 and 521. Thirty-four percent of high school graduates went on to college. The number of drive-in movie theaters rose to 7,000, and the price of tickets in regular movie theaters rose to $2 in New York City and $1.50 in Los Angeles; women's bathing suits could be purchased for $8.95; a Georg Jensen gold brooch cost $60; and a Tiffany sports watch cost $47.[6]

While meeting with Western ambassadors at the Kremlin in Moscow, Khrushchev boasted of the economic superiority of the communist system, claiming "History is on our side. We will bury you!"[7] Although the context was the economy, the quote was widely perceived among the American public as a military threat against the United States. In turn, Eisenhower, then campaigning for reelection, praised the U.S. labor force for creating an economy so strong that it was "the terror of any who would be our enemies."[8]

One of the most significant business developments was the introduction of standardized shipping containers that could be stacked aboard ships and trains. These revolutionized the shipping industry by making goods easier to load on and off, in turn making the movement of goods throughout the world vastly more efficient. Ford Motor Company went public, selling more than 10 million shares worth $650 million to more than 250,000 investors. Crest introduced the first fluoridated toothpaste to prevent tooth decay, and Procter & Gamble developed disposable Pampers after discovering that women changed babies' diapers some 25 billion times a year.[9]

Other new products included Comet cleansing agent, Raid insecticide, Imperial margarine, Midas mufflers, and Salem cigarettes. Among the more enduring new advertising slogans was the question posed, with sexual double entendre, "Does she or doesn't she?" in a Clairol hair-dye ad.

SCIENCE AND TECHNOLOGY

The year saw significant progress in the understanding of genetics: Scientists announced that radiation harms the descendants of those exposed to it, the first human cells were cloned in a test tube, the DNA molecule was first photographed, and other advances in the study of DNA and RNA for genetic research were made. In other medical developments, the first prefrontal lobotomy for treating mental illness was performed, and a machine for kidney dialysis and a biopsy capsule for collecting intestinal tissue were developed. Dr. Albert B. Sabin of the University of Cincinnati developed an oral vaccine against polio.

Technological advances expanded the applications for computers and simplified their use considerably. These included the development of FORTRAN, the first computer programming language, and Lisp (List Processor), the computer language of artificial intelligence. The Ampex company introduced the era of modern video recording with a machine that could store and replay video images on magnetic tape, and Bell Telephone demonstrated a "visual telephone" capable of transmitting pictures and sound simultaneously. The first trans-Atlantic telephone cable was completed; it stretched from Nova Scotia to Scotland and spanned 2,250 miles.

The United States tested its first rocket for sending a humanmade satellite into orbit. It ascended 125 miles and reached speeds of 4,000 miles per hour. The birth of stars were photographed for the first time; the largest telescope to date was dedicated at Harvard University, and solar flares were discovered to be a source of X rays. Oceanographers discovered the Mid-Oceanic Ridge, and Jacques Cousteau photographed the Atlantic Romance trench at a depth of some 4.5 miles.

E. W. Mueller invented the field-ion microscope, the first instrument capable of showing individual atoms; American scientists discovered the antineutron, a new particle of antimatter; and the neutrino was first observed. Irène Joliot-Curie, the Nobel Prize–winning daughter of French Nobel Prize winners Pierre and Marie Curie, died from radiation-induced leukemia at the age of 59. Like her famous parents, Joliot-Curie and her husband, Frédéric, who died in 1958, performed research on the behavior of radioactive materials.

SPORTS, ENTERTAINMENT, AND THE ARTS

Sports

The Winter Olympics opened in January in Cortina d'Ampezzo, Italy, and the Summer Olympics took place in November in Melbourne, Australia; where the Soviet Union won more gold medals than the United States for the first time. Westerners complained to no avail that the Soviet athletes were essentially professionals competing in amateur games, as they had benefited from government subsidies and training programs. The much-publicized courtship of American gold medalist hammer-thrower Harold Connolly and Soviet discus champion Olga Fikotova captured the public imagination, as it gave a hopeful human face to cold war antagonisms. The couple subsequently married, but divorced nine years later.

On October 8, New York Yankees player Don Larsen pitched the only perfect game ever recorded during a World Series. The Yankees went on to defeat Brooklyn in seven games to vindicate their loss from the previous year. Brooklyn's Don Newcombe became the first recipient of the Cy Young Award, which is given to the year's most outstanding pitcher. It was named in honor of Cy Young, one of the best pitchers in baseball history, who died the previous year. Newcombe and Yankees outfielder Mickey Mantle were their leagues' Most Valuable Players (MVP).

The New York Giants crushed the Chicago Bears 47-7 in the NFL championship game. Giant Frank Gifford was named the league's MVP. Chicago's Ed Brown and Rick Casares led the league in passing and rushing, respectively, and San Francisco's Billy Wilson was the top receiver. Coached by Bud Wilkinson, the University of Oklahoma went undefeated for the second year in a row to repeat as the number-one college football team and extend its winning streak to a still-unequaled 40 games. The Sooners won seven more games the following year before losing to Notre Dame. Between 1948 and 1958, the team won 107 games, lost eight, and tied two. Notre Dame's Paul Hornung, all-American in 1955 and future star running back for the Green Bay Packers, won the 1956 Heisman Trophy.

Philadelphia defeated Fort Wayne in five games to claim the NBA basketball championship. Chosen for the NBA's All-Pro First Team were Philadelphia's Paul Arizin and Neil Johnston, Boston's Bob Cousy and Bill Sharman, and St. Louis's Bob Pettit, who was the league's MVP. The University of San

Roberto Clemente (left) and Henry Aaron (right) surround Willie Mays. The trio are among the National League's premier outfielders. *(Photofest)*

Francisco repeated as the number-one college basketball team, and its star center, Bill Russell, repeated as MVP. Russell, who led the U.S. basketball team to an Olympic gold medal, also made his debut with the Boston Celtics, where he went on to become one of the league's most dominant players. The Montreal Canadians won hockey's Stanley Cup, to begin an impressive streak of five consecutive championships that extended through 1960.

In a decade when boxing was featured regularly on television and the sport was especially popular, Rocky Marciano achieved special acclaim when he retired in April as an undefeated heavyweight boxing champion, after compiling a lifetime record of 43 knockouts and three decisions. Floyd Paterson claimed the vacant title by scoring a technical knockout over Marciano's last challenger, Archie Moore.

Ken Rosewall and Shirley Fry won the men's and women's single's tennis championships in the U.S. Open, and Cary Middlecoff won golf's USGA Open.

Television

At age 21, Elvis Presley made his television debut on January 28, on Jimmy Dorsey's *Stage Show,* where he performed "Shake, Rattle, and Roll," "Flip, Flop, and Fly," and "I Got a Woman." The audience responded enthusiastically, and he reappeared on the program five more times over the ensuing eight weeks. Presley also appeared twice on Milton Berle's show. His sexy performance of "Hound Dog" created a national furor, and when Presley performed that summer on the new *Steve Allen Show,* Allen spoofed the critics by having Presley dress in a tuxedo, eliminate his sexy gestures, and sing "Hound Dog" to a basset hound. That episode had higher ratings than *The Ed Sullivan Show,* which had perennially been the most popular of its time slot.

Although Sullivan had once vowed that Presley would never appear on his program, he subsequently paid the singer $50,000 for three appearances, which was more money than any performer had ever received to appear on a network variety program. By September 9, when he first appeared with Sullivan, Presley already dominated the music charts, mostly due to sales to teenagers and young adults. His appearance on the Sullivan show gave him wider exposure among adults and to middle America in general. During Presley's third appearance, on January 6, 1957, Sullivan introduced Presley as a fine, wholesome young man but appeased critics of the singer's "lascivious" hip-grinding by filming the performer from only the waist up.

Although the message was mixed, Sullivan's personal endorsement no doubt made Presley's new, provocative style more acceptable in middle America. On the other hand, the controversy surrounding his hip gyrations and raw sexual energy intensified his appeal to young people and sparked public debate about the state of the nation's morality. Many citizens regarded America's self-proclaimed moral superiority to be its chief virtue and the decisive factor in its struggle against atheistic communism, so the impact of rock 'n' roll's effect on the country's moral fabric became the topic of serious debate.

After a year's hiatus, *I Love Lucy* returned as the number-one show in America. It was followed by *The Ed Sullivan Show, General Electric Theater, The $64,000 Question, December Bride,* and *Alfred Hitchcock Presents.* Of the top 10 programs, none made its debut in the 1956–57 season, and all but the ninth, *The Perry Como Show* (NBC), appeared on CBS. This was the first time since 1950, when NBC aired eight of the top 10 shows, that one network so dominated network programming. Such dominance did not occur again until the 1963–64 season, when CBS broadcast 14 of the 15 most widely viewed programs. *Gunsmoke,* which debuted in 1955 and went on to become the top show for the rest of the decade, rose to eighth place in 1956–57.

Game shows and quiz shows appealed to audiences because they offered real-life, real-time drama, with hefty sums at stake. They appealed to the networks because they were both popular and comparatively inexpensive to produce. Following the instant success in 1955 of *The $64,000 Question,* CBS added *The $64,000 Challenge,* which pitted winners from *The $64,000 Question* against one another. NBC responded with *Twenty-One,* which became the source of controversy in 1957, when a losing contestant charged that certain participants were given the answers in advance. An investigation revealed that most of the quiz shows were similarly rigged, and the ensuing scandal led to the cancellation of the big-money quiz shows in 1958. More enduring were the

Singer Dinah Shore debuted as hostess of the variety program *The Chevy Show,* sponsored by Chevrolet ("See the U.S.A. in your Chevrolet"). Perry Como, who also hosted a popular television show, released a top hit record, "Hot Diggity" ("Dog ziggity, ooh what you do to me"). *(Photofest)*

lower stakes game shows that debuted in 1956: *The Price Is Right,* in which contestants had to guess the value of various consumer goods, and *Tic Tac Dough,* a variant on the game tick-tack-toe in which players won the right to place Xs or Os by answering questions correctly.

Other new shows included a reprise of *The Steve Allen Show,* a variety program that NBC pitted against Ed Sullivan. It debuted in the summer, and in addition to Presley, it featured such high-profile guests as Sammy Davis, Jr., Kim Novak, and Vincent Price. Allen's show was more humorous than Sullivan's, and it regularly featured comic routines. One, a mock interview with a man on the street, played by Tom Poston, became an ongoing feature.

Presenting original plays for television, *Playhouse 90* was one of the medium's most ambitious dramatic series. Its first show, *Forbidden Area,* starred Charlton Heston, Tab Hunter, Diana Lynn, Jackie Coogan, and Price. It was written by Rod Serling, who also wrote the second episode of *Playhouse 90,* the critically acclaimed *Requiem for a Heavyweight,* which starred Jack Palance as a broken-down boxer. Serling went on in 1959 to create the popular science-fiction anthology *The Twilight Zone.* CBS also introduced television's first daytime soap operas: the long-running *As the World Turns* and *The Edge of Night,* so-named because of its late-afternoon time slot.

Chet Huntley and David Brinkley first paired up on NBC's *The Huntley-Brinkley Report,* which quickly became the top-rated news program and remained so during most of its 14-year duration. Introduced by the dramatic opening notes of the second movement of Beethoven's Ninth Symphony, the team played Huntley's direct, no-nonsense manner against Brinkley's dry wit. The contrast produced an appealing on-camera chemistry, even though the two men were based in different cities and rarely saw each other in person. On November 30, their competition on CBS, *Douglas Edwards with the News,* took advantage of the newly developed videotape technology to become the first network news show to be recorded for rebroadcast in the Western time zones.

Movies

Many of the top hits of the year appealed to audiences' interest in faraway places and distant times. This was due in part to the film industry's desire to offer the public a level of grand splendor and exoticism that small-screen television could not convey. The lavish costumes, grand-scale sets, and wide-screen vistas and panoramas, in particular, enabled the movies to distinguish themselves from their growing competitor. In addition, the remote settings stimulated and indulged viewers' imaginations while affording them a chance to escape from their everyday worlds.

The Academy Awards selection for best picture, cinematography, adapted screenplay, editing, and musical score was Lindsay Anderson's *Around the World in Eighty Days,* starring David Niven, Shirley MacLaine, and Mexican comedian Cantinflas. Based on the 1873 novel by Jules Verne, the adventure story celebrates the faraway places visited by British gentleman Phileas Fogg and his bumbling valet, and the adventures they have while trying to win a bet in 1872 that they can travel around the world in 80 days. The plot has Fogg traveling by train, ship, hot-air balloon, and elephant across two oceans and four continents, rescuing a princess and evading a detective along the way. Shot in 100 locations and 140 special sets, the movie features 46 famous personalities; it introduced the practice of presenting celebrities in cameo roles.[10]

Another hit set in a faraway land was Walter Lang's musical *The King and I,* starring Yul Brynner as the king of Siam and Deborah Kerr as his children's British schoolteacher, Anna. Brynner won the Academy Award for best actor and Kerr was nominated for best actress. The movie also won best musical score, sound, and art direction. Based on the hit Broadway musical by Richard Rodgers and Oscar Hammerstein II, which in turn was based on Margaret Landon's novel *Anna and the King of Siam,* the story shows how the arrogant, chauvinistic, all-powerful king reluctantly learns compassion, respect, and sensitivity from Anna, who astounds him by challenging his decisions—something no one else, especially no woman—would do. The king falls in love with her while in the process of having his consciousness raised, and through his transformation, he becomes a worthy partner for Anna. Brynner made the role famous when he introduced it on Broadway in 1951.

Cecil B. DeMille's *The Ten Commandments* also stars Brynner as a king—this time Pharaoh Rameses I of Egypt, whom Moses (Charlton Heston) confronts in his effort to gain freedom for Jewish slaves. This movie, a remake of DeMille's 1923 silent film, likewise appealed to the public's taste for adventure in a distant place, with exotic costumes and magnificent settings. DeMille's last directorial effort, *The Ten Commandments* tapped into the strong religious sentiments of the time, also evident in the introduction that year of the national motto "In God We Trust." The extravaganza employs huge sets and a "cast of thousands" as it tells the biblical story of Moses leading his people out of bondage. Furthermore, DeMille dazzled audiences with special effects that enabled him to re-create the burning bush, the parting of the Red Sea, and other miracles.

In addition, *The Ten Commandments* makes an overt appeal to cold war sympathies. The theme of resisting tyranny by accepting Judeo-Christian values had cold war overtones that DeMille made explicit in his personal prologue. Filmed stepping before a gold curtain, DeMille introduces the moving by stating, "The theme of this picture is whether men are to be ruled by God's law—or whether they are to be ruled by the whims of a dictator. . . . Are men the property of the state? Or are they free souls under God? This same battle continues throughout the world today." Moreover, like other epic films of the era, *The Ten Commandments* uses its grand scope, spectacular effects, and vast scale to impress viewers at home and abroad with America's wealth, abundance, and capacity to achieve extraordinary things on an almost unimaginable scale.

Also set in a different land, at a different time, two other extravagant films appealed to America's interest in Russia prior to communism. King Vidor's *War and Peace,* starring Audrey Hepburn, Mel Ferrer, and Henry Fonda, adapts Leo Tolstoy's novel (1869) of Russia's war with Napoléon. And Ingrid Bergman won the Academy Award for her portrayal of a woman who claimed to be the daughter of the last czar, in Anatole Litvak's *Anastasia.* The film also stars Brynner.

Lust for Life, Vincente Minnelli's biography of painter Vincent Van Gogh, stars Kirk Douglas and Anthony Quinn, who received the Academy Award for best supporting actor as Van Gogh's friend and fellow artist, Paul Gauguin. Based on Edna Ferber's novel, James Dean's last film, *Giant,* was released posthumously. It costars Rock Hudson and Elizabeth Taylor in the story of two rival families in Texas. Hudson was nominated for best actor, and George

Stevens won for best director. Gary Cooper, Dorothy McGuire, and Anthony Perkins star in William Wyler's *Friendly Persuasion,* about a Quaker family that is drawn into the Civil War. Perkins plays the son who chooses to fight because he fears he is a coward hiding behind his religion. Joshua Logan adapted William Inge's play, *Bus Stop,* about the interactions among a group of people stranded overnight in a diner. It stars Marilyn Monroe, who sings "That Old Black Magic" in one of her better performances. Alfred Hitchcock remade his 1934 film *The Man Who Knew Too Much.* Retaining the original title, the 1956 version stars James Stewart and Doris Day as an innocent couple that becomes entangled in an assassination plot. Day's rendition of "Que Será Será" received the Academy Award for best song and became a top-selling recording. John Ford directed John Wayne, Jeffrey Hunter, Vera Miles, Natalie Wood, and Ward Bond in *The Searchers,* about a white man looking for his niece who was abducted by Indians and raised as one of them. The morally ambiguous movie is one of Ford's best directorial achievements and Wayne's finest acting performances.

In *Baby Doll,* Elia Kazan adapted Tennessee William's play *27 Wagonloads of Cotton.* Starring Karl Malden and Carroll Baker, it became the most controversial Hollywood film of the year. For some critics, its sexual suggestiveness, like that of Presley's grinding hips, represented a decline in American morals that made the United States vulnerable to communism. Nonetheless, the film generated enough interest that much of the town of Benoit, Mississippi, where it was filmed on location, tried out as extras.[11] By more recent standards, the film is not sexually explicit, but in 1956, *Time* magazine called it "possibly the dirtiest American picture ever legally exhibited," and Francis Cardinal Spellman condemned it from the pulpit, although he did not personally view it. Moreover, he ordered priests to stand in the theater lobbies and write down the names of parishioners who attended it under "pain of sin."[12] The Catholic Legion of Decency also declared that *Baby Doll* "dwells upon carnal suggestiveness."

The movies continued to create worldwide audiences for the developing musical sounds of rock 'n' roll and jazz. Presley capitalized on his rapid rise to fame by starring in Robert D. Webb's *Love Me Tender,* whose title song topped the charts. And jazz star Louis Armstrong is prominently featured in Charles Walters's *High Society.* Starring Frank Sinatra, Bing Crosby, and Grace Kelly, the musical remake of 1940's *The Philadelphia Story* shows three men vying for the same high-society woman: her ex-husband, her priggish upper-crust fiancé, and a magazine reporter assigned to cover her upcoming wedding. This was Kelly's last film, as she retired after marrying Prince Rainier II of Monaco.

Donald Siegel's *Invasion of the Body Snatchers,* starring Kevin McCarthy and Dana Wynter, is one of the most enduring of the Red Scare science fiction movies. Based on Jack Finney's 1955 novel, *The Body Snatchers,* the movie shows how seed pods from outer space take over the bodies and identities of the inhabitants of a small California town and transform them into unfeeling automatons. The movie contains a subtext that plays out Senator McCarthy's right-wing claims about communist infiltration of American institutions. Like the members of the far Right, who believed that they perceived events accurately and were being unfairly branded as insane and paranoid for shouting the truth, the film's protagonist, Dr. Miles Bennell, opens the movie arguing before a

Although his family life was tumultuous, Bing Crosby projected a warm, stable, fatherly image to the public. *(Photofest)*

disbelieving audience of doctors and psychiatrists that he is fleeing from the treacherous pod people. Moreover, the pod people exhibit the stereotypical characteristics often associated with communist cadres: They are emotionless, immune to the attachments of family or love, totally devoted to their cause, and come from large pods, which are seed cells, just as fifth-column communists—American saboteurs who were secret communist agents—were known to work in revolutionary cells for security reasons. More important, like the communists who, according to McCarthy and his supporters, were advancing their quest for world domination by infiltrating the top levels of the U.S. government and military, the pods seize control of the local community by first transforming the mayor and police force into unfeeling pod people. Right-wing distrust of psychiatry also figures in the film. At the conclusion, the right-wing fantasy is shown to be true: Dr. Bennell is proven sane and correct, and J. Edgar Hoover's FBI is called in to save the day.

In the opposite vein, Bette Davis, Brian Keith, and Kim Hunter star in Daniel Taradash's *Storm Center,* one of the few Hollywood films to directly criticize the Red Scare and the practices of censoring books and smearing intellectuals and liberals for pre–cold war political activities. It tells the story of a meddlesome small-town librarian who refuses to remove a copy of *The Communist Dream* after the local city council bans it from the shelves. The film makes clear that the librarian is a civil libertarian and not a radical or a communist; nonetheless, she is accused of being a danger to society and shunned for insisting that, although the book is preposterous, it is influential and should be available, like Adolf Hitler's *Mein Kampf,* to readers. Her antagonists tend to be not only anticommunist but also anti-intellectual, and they associate high culture with "pinkos." After her opponents denounce the librarian for her membership in World War II–era communist-front groups, she is fired, and eventually a child burns down the entire library. *Storm Center* was written secretly and required five years of interrupted filming to make.

Once again, older, mature men whose personae projected responsibility and moral virtue were the top box office draws of the year—with the exception of James Dean, who in *Giant* tapped into a latent sympathy for the misunderstood, young rebel. The leading female stars were much younger and appealed primarily for their sexuality. The leaders at the box office were William Holden, Wayne, Stewart, Burt Lancaster, Glenn Ford, Dean Martin and Jerry Lewis, Gary Cooper, Monroe, Kim Novak, and Frank Sinatra. Yul Brynner (in *The King and I* and *The Ten Commandments*) made his first major Hollywood appearances. Paul Newman had his first starring role in Robert Wise's *Somebody Up There Likes Me,* a biography of Rocky Graziano, who rose from the New York slums and a life of petty crime to become the middleweight boxing champion of the world. (James Dean had originally been cast for the part.)

Notable foreign films included Swedish director Ingmar Bergman's *The Seventh Seal,* a story of existential angst set during the Middle Ages as the black plague scourged the land. Its deep, philosophical questioning of the meaning of life and the problem of living in an uncertain, possibly atheistic universe made the movie the quintessential 1950s art film for many, including Woody Allen, who has spoofed it often but regards it as "the definitive work on the subject" of death.[13] Moreover, Bergman intended that the plague also be understood as a metaphor for the nuclear bomb, as during both points in history, death seemed to constantly hover overhead, capable of wiping out entire communities overnight. The film starred Max von Sydow, Gunnar Björnstrand, Nils Poppe, and Bibi Andersson.

Literature

If movies offered escapism by featuring faraway places and distant times, much of the important fiction from 1956 placed people in the here and now, in internal states of vaguely recognized despair. *Further Fables of Our Time,* by *New Yorker* humorist James Thurber, presents a bleak view of life in which ordinary people are defeated by their environment. *Seize the Day,* by Canadian-born Saul Bellow, tells the story of a desperate man whose life collapses on him and whose family turns against him. Like *The Floating Opera,* John Barth's first novel (also released in 1956), *Seize the Day* centers on the flawed communication between a father and son and on the son's inability to sustain close personal relationships. However, where Bellow's novel is a traditional, realistic narrative, Barth employs a more experimental, loosely connected structure in which a series of apparent digressions come together to form a cohesive whole. *The Floating Opera* is narrated by Todd Andrews, a brilliant but depressed and emotionally detached lawyer who concludes that life has no intrinsic meaning. So, after deducing through a progression of logical syllogisms that there is no reason to live, Andrews sets about to blow up himself and his entire community. Barth thereby suggests that very smart people become dangerous to themselves and their societies when they become disconnected from their own feelings and detached from the rest of humanity. The near-apocalyptic ending, which Barth had to soften for the novel's debut publication, and the use of McCarthyism to drive part of the plot establish the cold war as an unspoken presence in the background. But unlike Bellow's *Seize the Day,* whose only expression of hope comes in the Buddhist-like suggestion that suffering can give birth to empathy and human connection, Barth's *The Floating Opera* is darkly funny. It plays with language, surrenders to the temptations of digression, and revels in eccentric characters and absurd situations. This narrative self-indulgence generates a comic pleasure that enables readers and the author, if not the protagonist, to celebrate life, even if these pleasures of storytelling cannot negate the reasons for despair in the modern world. Thus, as in Barth's other work from the period, the comic energy itself becomes the meaning of life and a means for coping with the inherent nihilism that results from living in a world that seems to be moving inexorably toward self-destruction.

Wright Morris also explores the psychological functions of storytelling in *The Field of Vision,* about an old man who tells stories to keep his perception of his personal past and the Old West alive. In Mark Harris's *Bang the Drum Slowly,* a teammate tells the story of a baseball player who dies young. Nelson Algren followed *The Man with the Golden Arm* (1949), a tale of heroin addiction, with another story of the down-and-out, *A Walk on the Wild Side*. In *Giovanni's Room,* James Baldwin, inspired by his own problems of coming to terms with his homosexuality, describes the conflict of a young man who recognizes but cannot accept that he is gay. It is one of the few books to deal openly with homosexuality, which in the literature and the political and religious discourse of the 1950s, was typically viewed as a form of perversion and often associated with communists and people of weak character.

Although usually more upbeat than "serious" literature, the best-selling fiction of 1956 presented a jaded view of life. Grace Metalious's controversial *Peyton Place,* for example, highlights the hypocrisy lurking below the wholesome surface of small-town America. All the major publishing houses rejected the manuscript, largely because they feared the public would object to the graphic sex scenes and sordid view of contemporary life, but when Dell issued the paperback edition, it sold 12 million copies and established Dell as an important paperback publisher. Mark Robson adapted *Peyton Place* into a 1957 film starring Lana Turner and Hope Lange, and in 1964, it became the first prime-time soap opera to air on TV since the earliest days of the medium, and the first to be a success.

One of the most influential works of nonfiction from the year was W. H. Whyte's *The Organization Man,* which employs an analytical approach to spotlight the corporate culture of exploiting employees and suppressing individual creativity—a topic the Beat poets were also expressing but in a different way, to a largely different audience. Senator John F. Kennedy, who unsuccessfully sought the Democratic vice presidential nomination, published his Pulitzer Prize–winning account of crucial moments in American politics, *Profiles in Courage.* Eric F. Goldman explored the social, cultural, and political developments that shaped a decade in *The Crucial Decade: America 1945–1955.* Goldman updated his findings in 1960, when he rereleased it as *The Crucial Decade—And After: America, 1945–1960.* Sponsored by the Fund for the Republic, a Catholic organization, John Cogley published his *Report on Blacklisting,* a carefully documented study of how blacklisting worked, who was behind it, and HUAC's role in it. He was subsequently interrogated by HUAC about the report. Personal human relations were the subject of literary and cultural critic Lionel Trilling's *Freud and the Crisis of Our Culture,* psychologist Erich Fromm's *The Art of Loving,* and philosopher Herbert Marcuse's *Eros and Civilization.*

Lawrence Ferlinghetti's publishing company, City Light Books, released Allen Ginsberg's *Howl and Other Poems.* The best known and most influential of the Beat poems, "Howl" attacks middle-class values and lifestyles and American institutions. It was informed by the poet's incarceration in the Columbia Psychiatric Institute in 1949, and it is dedicated to Carl Solomon, a fellow inmate whom Ginsberg called a "lunatic saint." Motivated by fellow Beat writer Jack Kerouac's free-flowing prose, Ginsberg wanted to create a new kind of poetry that could replicate in language the spontaneity, emotion, and energy of the improvisational jazz of the period.

Although "Howl" eschews the formal conventions of more traditional poetic forms, it remains poetry, not prose, because it is fundamentally concerned with the rhythms and sounds of the language. The speaker begins by describing the best minds of his generation destroyed by madness and drug addiction; he then goes on to depict corporate, industrialized American society as the ancient pagan god Moloch that consumed children sacrificed to it. The poem reportedly was inspired by Ginsberg's peyote-induced vision of San Francisco's Sir Frances Drake Hotel as the Canaanite god. Other works of poetry included Donald Hall's *Exiles and Marriage,* John Ashbery's *Some Trees,* Marianne Moore's *Like a Bulwark,* Elizabeth Bishop's *Poems,* and Richard Wilbur's Pulitzer Prize–winning *Things of This World.*

Appalled by the brutal suppression of the Hungarian uprising, French existentialist Jean-Paul Sartre quit the Communist Party in November and dedicated an issue of his *Modern Times* magazine to the revolutionaries who died in Hungary. Writer, editor, and social critic H. L. Mencken died at age 75, and A. A. Milne, the British author of the Winnie the Pooh stories, died at age 74.

Theater, Music, and the Visual Arts

The most enduring new plays to open on Broadway were musicals. Leonard Bernstein, playwright Lillian Hellman, and poet Richard Wilbur adapted *Candide,* Voltaire's story from 1759 of a youth who becomes subjected to the brutality of human existence but clings to his innocent belief that this is the best of all possible worlds. The musical overture to *Candide* remains in the classical repertoire. For their Pulitzer Prize–winning musical *My Fair Lady,* Alan Jay Lerner and Frederick Loewe adapted George Bernard Shaw's play *Pygmalion* (1913). Starring Julie Andrews and Rex Harrison and featuring such hits as "I Could Have Danced All Night," "On the Street Where You Live," and "All I Want," *My Fair Lady* tells the story of a professor, a confirmed bachelor, who wagers that by improving the diction and command of the English language of a Cockney flower girl, he can transform her into a woman who can pass as a lady of culture. He wins the bet but in the process falls in love, in spite of himself. One of the most successful plays in Broadway history, *My Fair Lady* inspired a late Edwardian-era influence on fashion and decor. Harrison costarred with Audrey Hepburn in George Cukor's 1964 film adaptation.

Other musicals included Jule Styne, Betty Comden, and Adolph Green's *Bells Are Ringing,* starring Judy Holliday; Frank Loesser's *The Most Happy Fella;* and Gene de Paul and Johnny Mercer's *Li'l Abner,* a theatrical adaptation of Al Capp's satirical comic strip about ignorant hillbillies living in Dogpatch, U.S.A. *L'il Abner,* which starred Edie Adams, Peter Palmer, and Julie Newmar, caught the public imagination and also spawned fashion spin-offs.

Other Broadway debuts included Eugene O'Neill's autobiographical portrayal of a dysfunctional family, *Long Day's Journey into Night,* which starred Frederic March, Florence Eldridge, Bradford Dillman, Katharine Ross, and Jason Robards, Jr. Paddy Chayefsky's *Middle of the Night* starred Edward G. Robinson and Gena Rowlands; and Jerome Lawrence and Robert E. Lee's *Auntie Mame,* the story of an eccentric woman based on the best-selling 1955 novel by Patrick Dennis, featured Rosalind Russell and Peggy Cass. *Waiting for Godot,* Samuel Beckett's comic depiction of existential absurdity, made its Broadway debut; it was first performed in France in 1952. Alan Schneider directed the American premiere at the Coconut Grove Playhouse in Miami. The Actor's Workshop in San Francisco gave the American premiere of *Mother*

Courage by Bertolt Brecht, who died in August. *Look Back in Anger* debuted in England; the first play by John Osborne, one of England's so-called Angry Young Men, it celebrates the working class and rails against the smug superiority of the middle and upper classes.

The spirit of peaceful coexistence that Khrushchev said he wanted to foster between the superpowers found early expression in cultural exchanges. The Boston Symphony Orchestra performed in the Soviet Union, and Russia's famous Bolshoi Ballet made its first appearance in the West, when it danced to great acclaim in London. A planned return visit to Moscow by the Sadler's Wells Ballet was canceled, however, in response to the brutal Soviet suppression of the Hungarian uprising. But Sadler Wells's performance of *Sleeping Beauty* was televised in the United States and viewed by 30 million people. Other classical performers who toured abroad included opera star Jan Peerce, violinist Isaac Stern, the New Orleans Orchestra, the Los Angeles Philharmonic, and the Juilliard String Quartet, which celebrated its 50th anniversary by commissioning works by Roger Sessions and Walter Piston, among others.

In addition to using culture to pursue a better relationship with the Soviet Union, the State Department also sponsored goodwill music tours to other parts of the world. Jazz was often chosen because of its international appeal and because it is a purely indigenous American art form. Named an "ambassador of jazz" and sponsored by the State Department, Dizzie Gillespie formed a new big band to tour the eastern Mediterranean, the Middle East, Pakistan, and South America. While on tour in Thailand, Benny Goodman struck up an impromptu jazz session with King Bhumibol Adulyadej. Louis Armstrong toured Europe and Africa. Likewise, Nat "King" Cole, who was the first male jazz singer since Louis Armstrong to gain worldwide fame, reached millions of listeners with his weekly 15-minute television show on NBC.

Jazz continued to evolve and to make an impact on the nation's culture. Drummer Art Blakey and his Jazz Messengers band popularized "hard bop," characterized by powerful, driving rhythms that are strongly linked to the blues. Charles Mingus broke new ground in free ensemble improvisation in his album *Pithecanthropus Erectus;* Ella Fitzgerald recorded a collection of songs by Duke Ellington; Ellington, himself, appeared on the cover of *Time* magazine after his band's spectacular performance of "Diminuendo and Crescendo in Blue" at the Newport Jazz Festival; and Billie Holiday published her autobiography, *Lady Sings the Blues.* Pianist Art Tatum, trumpeter Clifford Brown, and trombonist Tommy Dorsey, the "Sentimental Gentleman of Swing" who helped launch Sinatra's career, died.

While religious leaders condemned rock 'n' roll and a Connecticut psychiatrist labeled it "a communicable disease,"[14] Presley gyrated to national fame. More through his personal style, rich voice, energetic performance, and raw sex appeal than the lyrics of his songs, he dominated the music charts by introducing middle-class teenagers, and later middle-class adults, to a more overtly sexual kind of music—although the lyrics were not usually risqué. Certainly Presley was not the first performer to project sexuality in his music—jazz and much black rhythm and blues did this before him—but Presley presented it to middle America at a time when it was ready to hear and respond to rock 'n' roll. In 1956, Presley made his television debut and had his first number-one song, "Heartbreak Hotel." In the same year, he also had number-one hits with

Singer Vic Damone poses with friends. *(Photofest)*

"I Want You, I Need You, I Love You," "Don't Be Cruel," "Hound Dog," and "Love Me Tender." "Anyway You Want Me," "I Was the One," "When My Blue Moon Turns Gold Again," and "Blue Suede Shoes" were among the top 20.

Other top songs of the year included "Hot Diggity" (Perry Como), "Que Será Será" (Doris Day, from *The Man Who Knew Too Much*), "Wonderful, Wonderful" (Johnny Mathis), "Why Do Fools Fall in Love" (Frankie Lyman and the Teenagers), "The Great Pretender" (The Platters), and "On the Street Where You Live" (Vic Damone, from *My Fair Lady*). Blacklisted folksinger Pete Seeger released his album *Love Songs for Friends and Foes,* which included "Autherine," a ballad about Autherine Lucy's plight when she tried to become the first black student at the University of Alabama. Harry Belafonte, who was born in Harlem of Jamaican parents, created an interest in Caribbean music when he released his *Calypso* album, which featured such hits as "Jamaica Farewell" and "The Banana Boat Song (Day-O)." In 1959, it became the first American long-playing (LP) album to sell a million copies.

The unbounded possibilities of the modern age found expression in Frank Lloyd Wright's design for a mile-high skyscraper, which was never built. He did, however, begin construction on the Solomon R. Guggenheim Museum in New York City, which also expressed a radical, contemporary look. More than 2.25 million people attended the "World Masterpieces Show" at the National Gallery, and the Museum of Modern Art exported American abstract expressionism by lending its exhibit "Modern Art in the U.S." to the Tate Gallery in London. The exhibition included works by Willem de Kooning, Mark Rothko, Franz Kline, and Jackson Pollock, who died in a car crash in August at age 44.

CHRONICLE OF EVENTS

1956

January 1: Sudan is proclaimed an independent republic.

January 5: The United States installs its first long-range Nike missiles in West Germany.

January 9: In an effort to circumvent the Supreme Court ruling calling for the desegregation of public schools, the Virginia legislature votes to permit state funding of private schools.

January 10: Great Britain sends 1,600 paratroopers to Cyprus to quell anti-British violence by rebels seeking the island's union with Greece.

January 10: Twenty-one-year-old Elvis Presley records "Heartbreak Hotel" and "I Want You, I Need You, I Love You" at RCA's recording studios in Nashville, Tennessee.

January 12: The FBI identifies and arrests six of the perpetrators of the Great Brinks Robbery of 1950, in which 11 men stole $2.7 million from the Brinks company headquarters.

January 13: Syria and Lebanon sign a mutual-defense pact against Israel.

January 14: Christian evangelist Billy Graham meets with Secretary of State John Foster Dulles to clarify that U.S. foreign policy does not endorse colonialism. Dulles's reference to Portuguese provinces in

Prior to traveling to India for a month-long evangelical tour, Reverend Billy Graham (left) met with Secretary of State John Foster Dulles. *(Photofest)*

the Far East had prompted the government of India, where Graham will travel on a month-long tour, to accuse the United States of supporting Portuguese control of Goa. Graham leaves the meeting satisfied that United States policy does not in any way support colonialism.

January 16: Egypt declares Islam the state religion.

January 18: East Germany creates the People's Army.

January 26: The Winter Olympics open in Cortina d'Ampezzo, Italy. Tenley Albright of the United States wins the gold medal in women's figure skating.

January 28: Presley makes his debut on national television on Jimmy Dorsey's *Stage Show.* He appears on other variety shows throughout the year, including those of Milton Berle, Steve Allen, and, in September and October, Ed Sullivan.

January 29: Writer, editor, and social critic H. L. Mencken dies.

January 30: White supremacists firebomb the home of Dr. Martin Luther King, Jr., in Montgomery, Alabama.

February 1: President Eisenhower and British prime minister Anthony Eden issue the Declaration of Washington, warning Africans and Asians against seeking political or economic aid from the Soviet Union.

February 4: Autherine Lucy becomes the first black student admitted to the University of Alabama; however, she is suspended two days later after anti-integration rioting threatens her safety.

February 8: Britain sets August 1957 as the date for Malayan independence.

February 8: Writer Albert Camus resigns from *L'Express* after the newspaper, for which he has been writing dispatches from Algeria, endorses Algerian nationalists who sponsor violent protest against French rule. Camus has advocated moderation from both sides.

February 21: A grand jury in Montgomery, Alabama, indicts 115 black Americans, including Martin Luther King, Jr., for boycotting the public bus system, in violation of a city ordinance prohibiting boycotts.

February 24: Reverend Ralph Abernathy declares a National Deliverance Day of Prayer to protest the mass arrests of protestors boycotting the Montgomery public buses. Abernathy calls for a mass pilgrimage through the streets of Montgomery in support of the ongoing boycott.

February 25: At the closing session of the 20th Congress of the Soviet Communist Party, Secretary Khrushchev delivers a speech advocating greater freedoms for Soviet citizens and denouncing the hardline policies of Stalin.

February 25: In Schenectady, New York, closed-circuit television is introduced for teaching students in public school.

February 29: A federal court reinstates Autherine Lucy and orders the University of Alabama to provide adequate protection for her. The next day, the university expels Lucy after accusing her of making libelous accusations about college officials. She does not return to the university.

March 12: Southern senators and congressmen issue their Declaration of Constitutional Principles, also known as the Southern Manifesto, opposing the Supreme Court rulings calling for desegregation.

March 15: Alan Jay Lerner and Frederick Loewe's musical *My Fair Lady* opens on Broadway. Starring Rex Harrison and Julie Andrews, the play runs for 2,717 performances.

March 21: Delbert Mann's *Marty* becomes the only movie adapted from television to win an Academy Award for best film. Paddy Chayefsky wrote both the teleplay and screenplay.

March 22: Martin Luther King, Jr., is found guilty of violating Montgomery's ordinance forbidding boycotts. He is fined $500 but appeals the conviction.

April 10: Singer Nat "King" Cole is attacked while performing before a white audience in Birmingham, Alabama.

April 17: In a gesture aimed at mending relations with Yugoslavia, the Soviet Union disbands the international alliance of communist parties, COMINFORM.

April 18: The first steps are taken to establish an international "atoms for peace" agency with a 12-nation agreement that includes both the United States and the Soviet Union.

April 19: Actress Grace Kelly marries Prince Rainier II of Monaco in a high-profile ceremony with 1,200 guests.

April 23: The U.S. Supreme Court endorses a lower-court ruling striking down a South Carolina law requiring racial segregation on public buses.

April 23: Radioactive mud is mixed with rain that falls on Rome. According to Italy's National Council for Nuclear Research, the mud is a product of dust from Africa and contains radioactive elements that can be absorbed by living organisms.

April 25: Presley's "Heartbreak Hotel" becomes his first number-one hit song.

April 26: For the first time since the beginning of the cold war, the United States eases restrictions on trade with the Soviet Union and Eastern Europe.

May 21: The United States explodes the first airborne hydrogen bomb, demonstrating the country's capability against an enemy.

May 27: A bus boycott begins in Tallahassee, Florida, in protest of segregating riders.

June: The U.S. State Department releases a copy of Khrushchev's speech denouncing Joseph Stalin.

June 1: Alabama outlaws the NAACP.

June 9: Eisenhower undergoes successful surgery to relieve an intestinal obstruction after complaining of persistent stomach discomfort. He returns to the White House on June 15.

June 12: Performer Paul Robeson appears before HUAC, where he invokes the Fifth Amendment in response to questions about a noncommunist affidavit he signed as a requirement for his passport application.

June 13: Britain ends its 72-year occupation of the Suez Canal zone.

June 21: Playwright Arthur Miller testifies before HUAC, where, like Paul Robeson, he is questioned about the noncommunist affidavit he signed for a passport application.

June 28: The largest anticommunist uprising since 1953 takes place in Poland, when workers riot at an industrial fair in Poznan. In November, Poland and the Soviet Union sign an agreement allowing Poland greater economic and political freedom, but Soviet troops remain on Polish soil.

June 29: Eisenhower signs a $33.4 billion highway bill that authorizes construction of an interstate highway system.

June 29: Actress Marilyn Monroe marries Arthur Miller in a civil ceremony. A rabbi performs a religious ceremony on July 2.

July 19: The United States and Great Britain refuse to finance Egypt's proposed Aswan Dam project because of Egypt's ties with the Soviet Union.

July 20: A nationwide Operation Alert tests how federal agencies react during a simulated atomic attack.

July 25: The Italian ocean liner *Andrea Doria* sinks after colliding with the Swedish liner *Stockholm* in heavy fog off Nantucket Island. Fifty-one people die, but some 1,600 are rescued.

July 26: Egypt's Gamal Nasser nationalizes the British-owned Suez Canal, proposing to use revenues from it to finance the Aswan Dam. Nasser also denies Israeli ships use of the canal. He expels British oil and embassy officials in August and increases border raids against Israeli territory.

August 7: Mechanics and Farmers Savings Bank opens the nation's first drive-through teller.

August 11: Action painter Jackson Pollock dies in a car crash at age 44.

August 14: Leftist playwright Bertolt Brecht dies in Berlin, East Germany.

August 16: Demonstrators stage a march in England protesting nuclear arms and the dangers of radiation.

August 17: Democrats nominate Adlai Stevenson again as their presidential candidate. Senator Estes Kefauver of Tennessee narrowly edges out Massachusetts senator John F. Kennedy for the vice presidential nomination.

September: Grace Metalious publishes her best-selling novel *Peyton Place,* which exposes a sexy, seamy underside of American small-town life.

September 9: Presley appears on *The Ed Sullivan Show,* where he enthralls teenagers and scandalizes adults with his frenetic, hip-grinding performance.

September 25: The first regular transatlantic telephone service is inaugurated after the completion of a 2,500-mile underwater cable from Nova Scotia to Scotland.

October 8: Don Larsen becomes the only person ever to pitch a perfect game in a World Series contest, as the New York Yankees defeat the Brooklyn Dodgers 2-0. The Yankees go on to win the deciding, seventh game of the series on October 10. Brooklyn's Don Newcombe (27-7) receives the Cy Young Award as Major League Baseball's best pitcher; Yankee Whitey Ford (19-6) is the top American League pitcher. Yankee outfielder Mickey Mantle leads the majors with 52 home runs, and he bats .340 to lead in hitting, too. Milwaukee outfielder Hank Aaron (.328) is the National League batting champion. Newcombe and Mantle are their league's Most Valuable Players (MVP).

October 19: Khrushchev flies to Warsaw to demand that anti-Soviet protests cease and orders troops to surround the city.

October 21: Khrushchev relents, appoints reform-minded Wladyslaw Gomulka as Communist Party secretary of Poland, and makes some concessions to Polish demands for greater liberties.

October 23: A popular anticommunist revolution in Hungary briefly overthrows the government in Budapest and installs a neutral government.

October 29: Preempting an anticipated Egyptian attack, Israel invades Egypt and precipitates the Suez crisis.

October 29: Soviet troops evacuate Budapest.

October 31: In response to the popular uprising in Hungary, the Soviet Union installs Imre Nagy as the new premier and János Kádár as first secretary.

October 31: Intent on reclaiming the Suez Canal, Britain and France invade Egypt.

November 4: After Premier Nagy declares that Hungary will quit the Warsaw Pact and seek neutral status, Khrushchev sends tanks and troops into Budapest. Nagy and other prominent figures are later executed.

November 6: Eisenhower defeats Adlai Stevenson again in the presidential elections, but Democrats win a majority in both houses of Congress.

November 7: The United Nations achieves an armistice in the Suez crisis, replacing the British and French troops with an international peacekeeping force.

November 13: The U.S. Supreme Court rules that segregation of public transportation is unconstitutional.

November 22: The Summer Olympic Games open in Melbourne, Australia. For the first time ever, the Soviet Union garners the largest number of gold medals.

November 26: The "Sentimental Gentleman of Swing," jazz trombonist and band leader Tommy Dorsey, dies.

November 29: The United States offers political asylum to Hungarian freedom fighters.

December 2: Fidel Castro lands in Cuba with 82 exiles intent on overthrowing the military regime of Fulgencio Batista. Most of the group are killed or captured, but the survivors form the nucleus of Castro's successful revolution two years later.

December 12: The United Nations votes to censure the Soviet invasion of Hungary by a vote of 55 to 8.

December 12–13: Art Blakey records his influential jazz album *Hard Bop.*

December 16: Francis Cardinal Spellman denounces Elia Kazan's soon-to-be-released movie *Baby*

Comedians Lou Costello (center) and Bud Abbott (right) clown around with the New York Yankees's popular king of home runs, Mickey Mantle. *(Photofest)*

Doll from the pulpit and assigns priests to go to the theaters and record the names of parishioners who attend.

December 18: Japan is admitted to the United Nations.

December 20: The Supreme Court decision forbidding segregation of public transportation is officially delivered to government leaders in Montgomery, Alabama, bringing to an end the city's year-long bus boycott.

December 21: Martin Luther King, Jr., Reverend Ralph Abernathy, and activists Glenn Smiley and E.

D. Nixon are the first black Americans to ride a desegrated bus in Montgomery.

December 23: The comedy team of Dean Martin and Jerry Lewis officially breaks up, although the schism between the comedy stars had been apparent for more than a year.

December 30: The New York Giants win the NFL football championship after defeating the Chicago Bears 47-7. New York's Frank Gifford is the league's MVP. Chicago's Ed Brown and Rick Casares lead the league in passing and rushing, respectively. San Francisco's Billy Wilson is the leader in pass receptions.

EYEWITNESS TESTIMONY

But the very Industrial Revolution which this highly serviceable ethic begot [the Protestant work ethic that promotes industriousness and thrift] in time began to confound it . . . [By] the 1880s the corporation had already shown the eventual bureaucratic direction it was going to take. . . . One of the key assumptions of the Protestant Ethic had been that success was due neither to luck nor to the environment but only to one's natural qualities—if men grew rich it was because they deserved to. But the big organization became a standing taunt to this dream of individual success. Quite obviously to anyone who worked in a big organization, those who survived best were not necessarily the fittest but, in more cases than not, those who by birth and personal connections had the breaks. . . .

How can the organization man be thrifty? Other people are thrifty *for* him. He still buys most of his own insurance, but for the bulk of his rainy-day saving, he gives his proxy to the financial and personnel departments of his organization. . . . The same man who will quote from Benjamin Franklin on thrift for the house organ would be horrified if consumers took these maxims to heart and started putting more money into savings and less into installment purchases. . . . Few talents are more commercially sought today than the knack of describing departures from the Protestant Ethic as reaffirmations of it. . . .

I have been talking of the impact of organization on the Protestant Ethic; just as important, however, was the intellectual assault. In the great revolt against traditionalism that began around the turn of the century, William James, John Dewey, Charles Beard, Thorstein Veblen, the muckrakers and a host of reformers brought the anachronisms of the Protestant Ethic under relentless fire, and in so doing helped lay the groundwork for the Social Ethic.

Sociologist William H. Whyte, Jr., discussing the inherent conflict between the Protestant ethic and consumer capitalism in Whyte, The Organization Man *(1956), pp. 16–20.*

So, I begin each day with a gesture of cynicism, and close it with a gesture of faith[,] . . . begin it by reminding myself that, for me at least, goals and objectives are without value, and close it by demonstrating that the fact is irrelevant. A gesture of tempo-

rality, a gesture of eternity. It is in the tension between these two gestures that I have lived my adult life.

Narrator Todd Andrews asserting his philosophy of life in John Barth, The Floating Opera *(1956), p. 51.*

The subscription agency was sympathetic to communism. You give money to the agency; therefore you're sympathetic to communism. It's like saying that if you give money to a Salvation Army girl who happens to be a vegetarian you're sympathetic to vegetarians.

Narrator Todd Andrews explaining a logical flaw in McCarthyism, in John Barth, The Floating Opera *(1956), p. 96.*

On this particular evening . . . the notes I took . . . I intended to be my last

I. Nothing has intrinsic value.

II. The reasons for which people attribute value to things are always ultimately irrational.

III. There is, therefore, no ultimate "reason" for valuing anything. . . .

Now I added *including life,* and at once the next proposition was clear:

IV. Living is action. There's no final reason for action.

V. There's no final reason for living. . . .

[Todd then proceeds to attempt to blow up a visiting showboat on which he and many of the people of his community are watching a minstrel show; however, for some unknown reason, the effort fails.]

Alone in my room, then, I sat on the window sill and smoked a cigar for several minutes, regarding the cool night, the traffic below . . and the black expanse of the sky, the blacker as the stars were blotted out by storm clouds. . . . How like ponderous nature, so dramatically to change the weather when I had so delicately changed my mind! I remembered my evening's notes, and going to them presently, added a parenthesis to the fifth proposition:

V. There's no final reason for living (or for suicide).

Narrator Todd Andrews questioning the meaning of life in John Barth, The Floating Opera *(1956), pp. 223–228, 250.*

Not that to be a professor was in itself so great. How could anyone bear to know so many languages? . . . Did Artie love his languages, and live for them, or was he also, in his heart, cynical? So many people nowadays were. No one seemed satisfied, and Wilhelm was especially horrified by the cynicism of successful people. Cynicism was bread and meat to everyone. And irony too. Maybe it couldn't be helped. It was probably even necessary.

Protagonist Tommy Wilhelm considering the cynicism of successful people, in Saul Bellow's novel Seize the Day *(1956), pp. 16–17.*

I stand here ironing, and what you asked me moves tormented back and forth with the iron.

"I wish you would manage the time to come in and talk with me about your daughter." . . .

"Who needs help?" Even if I came, what good would it do? You think because I am her mother I have a key, or that in some way you could use me as a key? She has lived for nineteen years. There is all that life that has happened outside of me, beyond me. . . .

She was two. Old enough for nursery school they said, and I did not know then what I know now—the fatigue of the long day, and the lacerations of group life in the kinds of nurseries that are only parking places for children.

Except that it would have made no difference if I had known. It was the only place there was. It was the only way we could be together. The only way I could hold a job. . . .

The old man living in back once said . . . "You should smile at Emily more when you look at her." What was in my face when I looked at her? I loved her. There were all the acts of love. . . .

She starts up stairs to bed. "Don't get me up with the rest in the morning." "But I thought you were having midterms." "Oh, those . . . in a couple of years when we'll all be atom-dead they won't matter a bit."

She has said it before. She *believes* it. . . .

Let her be. So all that is in her will not bloom—but in how many does it? There is still enough left to live by. Only help her to know . . . that she is more than this dress on the ironing board, helpless before the iron.

Writer Tillie Olsen describing the experience of being a single mother in her 1956 story "I Stand Here Ironing," in John G. Parks, ed., American Short Stories since 1945 *(2002), pp. 37–42.*

A classic American folk opera overcame strange surroundings . . to find a warm, emotional reception in the hearts of an opening-night Moscow audience.

Porgy and Bess brought high Soviet officials, foreign diplomats and other first nighters to their feet for more than eight minutes after the final curtain fell on Catfish Row. Some spectators wept; others shouted and stomped their feet but many were still almost hypnotized by the melodies of George Gershwin. The first American opera to come to this country since the Bolshevik Revolution was intellectually incomprehensible to many Russians present tonight. But emotionally it evoked spontaneous enthusiasm from an audience desperately eager to welcome foreign theatre.

Welles Hangen describing a performance of the American opera Porgy and Bess *in the Soviet Union under a superpower cultural exchange program, in Hangen, "'Porgy' Is Hailed in Moscow Debut,"* New York Times, *January 11, 1956, p. 36.*

Communist China of the near future, unified, industrialized and militarily up-to-date, may exert a profound, political influence far beyond its borders. In particular, that influence is likely to be greatest in precisely those countries and continents which today are regarded as "undeveloped" but tomorrow may be the world's decisive areas.

Indeed, the process has already begun on a serious scale, for the Chinese impact upon the thought of the Communist parties of the world is already becoming evident. China's political message is being heeded by growing numbers of people in India, Japan, and other parts of Asia, in the strategically important areas of the Middle East and in the vast continent of Africa, which is just beginning . . . to put its foot inside the modern world.

In Tokyo some time ago I visited a Communist bookshop. . . . In the days when I was a Communist leader, more than half the books and pamphlets . . . would have come from Russia, approximately 25 per cent from local sources and the remainder from various foreign sources. But in that bookstore in Tokyo probably half the reading matter . . . came from China. A quarter, I would guess, had its origins in the Soviet Union. The rest was produced either by the Communist party in Japan or came from the publishing house of its sister parties abroad.

The bookshop was crowded with keen, alert young students and workers, most of whom appeared to be as impecunious as they were intelligent. . . . And the books they read were political dynamite. They told . . . when and how revolutions should be made, taught them the art of insurrection and the principles of guerrilla warfare. All over the world today . . . the restless minds of frustrated, sensitive young men and women are being fed in this way—and from the same Chinese source.

> *Douglas Hyde, former editor of the London communist newspaper* The Daily Worker, *describing the growing influence of Chinese communism among Asian students and intellectuals in Hyde, "How Red China Takes Over,"* America: National Catholic Weekly Review *(January 21, 1956), p. 450.*

Neither Comrade Mikoyan nor Comrade Molotov would be here today [if Joseph Stalin had not died suddenly in 1953]. . . .

[In the executions of thousands of Soviet citizens that Stalin ordered in the political purges of the 1930s] we see no wisdom but only a demonstration of the brutal force which had once so alarmed V. I. Lenin.

> *Secretary Nikita Khrushchev of the Communist Party denouncing Stalin at the closing session of the 20th Congress of the Soviet Communist Party on February 25, 1956, in Clifton Daniel, ed.,* 20th Century Day by Day *(2000), p. 782.*

The nearly 1,500 delegates sat in total silence, interrupting only occasionally with cries of outraged indignation. They seemed to see a ghost standing at the shoulder of the speaker. The more Khrushchev revealed, the clearer the image of the ghost. It was a moment of rare historic significance. Only hours before the speech, no one could have predicted that the stagnant and deformed party would be capable of performing this genuinely civic feat.

> *General Dmitri Volkogonov recollecting Nikita Khrushchev's denunciation of Joseph Stalin before the 20th Congress of the Soviet Communist Party on February 25, 1956, in Martin Gilbert,* A History of the Twentieth Century, *vol. 3 (2000), p. 104.*

"Ye gods, what in the world is *that* supposed to be?" "Oo-oooh, isn't it *ugly?*" "Mama—let's get *out* of here." Would it be unfair to entitle those snatches of museum-talk "Average American's Three-Phase Reaction to Modern Art"? Let's face it, it is a mystery for most of us. How can those assemblages of grotesque shapes be called beautiful. Would anyone claim for them the *claritas* St. Thomas demands in the

beautiful. El Greco, Vermeer, Rembrandt we can understand . . . but why do these follows have to be so obscure? . . .

But can those general remarks [about St. Thomas's theory of beauty] be brought to closer grips with the problems of today's museumgoer? . . . [I]t means sharpening our notion of beauty . . . then seeing how the artist "translates" beauty into the language of his medium, and what the syntax of that language is. Finally, it means asking ourselves honestly, have we really understood Vermeer after all, or Rembrandt or the rest?

Just to set your prejudices on edge, it seems the modern artist can teach us a lot about his predecessors, too.

Talk about art and you talk about beauty: that's the way it is. But it is unfortunate. That unhappy word "beauty" has been clouded with so much confusion, is actually so much more misleading than helpful, that it seems time to sideline it for a while. . . .

We have lost the realization the beauty is *being:* being laid bare to our searching souls, not tinseled up for our roving eye by some Max Factor of the cosmos whom we call an artist. Beauty is *being,* the radiance of mystery, the hidden "inscape" that will "leap out like flaming from shook foil," if only we sensitize ourselves to perceive it through the half-concealing, half-revealing shell of sense-appearances. Its root is intelligible *form,* that elusive stamp of God's transcendent creativity in every being.

> *Critic Robert J. O'Connell defending experimental art, in O'Connell, "Modern Art Isn't All Crazy,"* America: National Catholic Weekly Review *(March 24, 1956), p. 693.*

I do not believe there is a debatable point between us. We both agree in advance that the position you will take is right morally, legally, and ethically. If it is not evident to you that the position I take in asking for moderation and patience is right practically then we will both waste our breath in debate.

> *Writer William Faulkner answering African-American writer and activist W. E. B. DuBois's challenge in April 1956 to a debate on racial integration, in The Mississippi Writers Page,* William Faulkner *(2001).*

"It's just like what Elbert Hubbard said," says Governor Hodges of North Carolina. . . . "'If I had but two loaves, I would sell one and buy white hyacinths to feed my soul.' Our people must be given more than the material things in life."

But even so it is extraordinary that a state legislature should have passed a measure to spend a million dollars of taxpayers' money to start a state art collection, a feat which no other state has achieved.

Betty Chamberlain discussing North Carolina's unprecedented investment in the fine arts, in Chamberlain, "How to Get and Spend a Million Dollars for Art," ARTnews (April 1956), p. 37.

When we speak of humanity we mean a quality, and it is interior. It is a quality of light that proceeds from the light of the world, the light of the universe, light as it is. . . . But I don't think it's outside of yourselves, a mystery that someday you're going to inherit. I think that all you'll see of it you've got right now. And the thing for you to do is to look, listen, and conform to that. It's the only conformity I would suggest to you. It's different for each of you. . . .

Stronger in spirit is the only strength that this country, or any country, or any man needs . . . [T]oday by way of scientific invention we can do a hundred to one anything man ever did, but how about *him*. . . . Is *he* any stronger? Is he any more competent to beautify his life—and no man can beautify his life without beautifying the life of others. . . .

In architecture we want a humane architecture. We don't want buildings that simply say things by rhyme or without reason, nor by rhyme and reason, even, without a soul. We want the thing to be extremely humane, of the spirit. . . . And when we say that the reality of the building consists of the space within to be lived in, don't you see that philosophically we have abandoned all exterior thought, idea— that anything outside it matters. It all must come from within. That is what gives charm and grace and beauty and integrity to the buildings that we build. And the more you can strengthen your own natures, the more of a break you give it, the more respect you pay to it, the more powerful you will be in making things beautiful.

Architect Frank Lloyd Wright addressing his students on April 15, 1956, in Robert Torricelli and Andrew Carroll, eds., In Our Own Words (1999), pp. 205–6.

Over 1200 guests attended, including dignitaries from 25 nations. The groom wore a uniform of his own design, a black suit with gold cuffs. The bride wore ivory taffeta and a 125-year-old lace veil. The gown will be sent to the Museum of Art in Philadelphia, the bride's hometown.

From a news report on the wedding of Grace Kelly and Prince Rainier II of Monaco on April 19, 1956, in Clifton Daniel, ed., 20th Century Day by Day (2000), p. 780.

I thought it was a mistake when Joe Louis tried a comeback. Barring poverty, the ring has seen the last of me.

Rocky Marciano, the undefeated heavyweight champion, announcing his retirement from boxing on April 25, 1956, in Clifton Daniel, ed., 20th Century Day by Day (2000), p. 779.

Under no conditions would I think of signing any such affidavit [certifying that he is not a communist], that is a complete contradiction of the rights of American citizens. . . .

Would you like to come to the ballot box when I vote and take out the ballot and see [if Robeson is a communist]? . . .

Could I say that the reason that I am here today, you know, from the mouth of the State Department itself, is: I should not be allowed to travel because I have struggled for years for the independence of the colonial peoples of Africa. . . . I can say modestly that

Heavyweight boxing champion Rocky Marciano retired undefeated after 46 fights: 43 knockouts and three decisions. *(Photofest)*

my name is very much honored all over Africa, in my struggles for their independence. . . .

Another reason that I am here today, again from the State Department . . . is that when I am abroad I speak out against the injustices against the Negro people of this land. . . .

I know Jackie Robinson, and I am sure that in his heart he would take back a lot of what he said about me. . . . I was taken by [baseball commissioner] Landis by the hand, and I addressed the combined owners of the American and National Leagues, pleading for Robinson to be able to play baseball, like I played professional football.

Performer Paul Robeson testifying before HUAC on June 12, 1956, in Eric Bentley, ed., Thirty Years of Treason *(1971), pp. 773–79.*

I would have made a statement that I had been affiliated from time to time with organizations that were cited as communist-dominated organizations, but I would have certainly taken an oath at any time in my life that I was never under the discipline of the Communist Party or communist cause.

Playwright Arthur Miller testifying before HUAC on June 21, 1956, in Eric Bentley, ed., Thirty Years of Treason, *p. 786.*

Pinko Playwright Weds Sex Goddess
Newspaper headline announcing the marriage on June 29, 1956, of playwright Arthur Miller and actress Marilyn Monroe, in Stephen J. Whitfield, The Culture of the Cold War *(1996), p. 117.*

Whatever pictorial magnificence *The King and I* may have had upon the stage—and goodness knows it had plenty . . . it has twice as much in the film version. . . .

It has, first of all, the full content of that charmingly droll and poignant "book" that Mr. Hammerstein crystallized so smartly from Margaret Landon's *Anna and the King of Siam.* Every bit of the humor and vibrant humanity that flowed through the tender story . . . is richly preserved in the screen play that Ernest Lehman has prepared. And it is got onto the screen with snap and vigor under the direction of Walter Lang.

It has, too, the ardor and abundance of Mr. Rodgers's magnificent musical score, which rings out as lyrically and clearly as Siamese bells. . . .

Also, it has the advantage of a handsome and talented cast, headed by the unsurpassed Yul Brynner and lovely Deborah Kerr. The King is the heart and soul of this story, and Mr. Brynner makes him vigorous and big. But Kerr matches him boldly.

Critic Bosley Crowther reviewing The King and I, *in Crowther, "The King and I,"* New York Times, *June 29, 1956, p. 15.*

His [actor Yul Brynner's] imaginative suggestions and instructions were responsible for turning *The King and I* into a great movie. If not for him it would have wound up being just another pleasant Hollywood musical. He had a wonderful way of handling actors—got things out of them they never realized they possessed. Nothing escapes him—he was interested in the most minor scene. I will always be grateful to him for making me look better than I really am.

Actress Deborah Kerr describing the contributions of her costar, Yul Brynner, to their hit film The King and I, *which opened in late June 1956, in Rock Brynner,* Yul: The Man Who Would Be King *(1989), p. 88.*

There is nothing to be said against Elvis—and many people have said it—except that when placed in front of a microphone, he behaves like an outboard motor. . . .

Nonetheless, we all watched with interest last week when one of our number, Steve Allen, made a public attempt to neutralize, calm, or de-twitch Elvis Presley, the lively singer.

Allen did this, one assumes, in what he personally considers the best interests of civilization. . . . Civilization today is sharply divided into two schools which cannot stand the sight of each other. One school, Allen's . . . believes in underplaying, or underbidding, or waiting 'em out. The other, Presley's, is committed to the strategy of open defiance, of confusing 'em, of yelling 'em down. The hips and the Adam's apple . . . must be quicker than the eye. . . .

When Allen made his move last week to mute and frustrate Presley . . [he] was nervous, like a man trying to embalm a firecracker. Presley was distraught, like Huckleberry Finn, when the widow put him in a store suit and told him not to gap or scratch.

Allen's ethics were questionable from the start. He fouled Presley . . . by dressing him like a corpse, in white tie and tales. This is a costume often seen on star performers at funerals, but only when the deceased has specifically requested it in his will. Elvis made no such request—or for that matter, no will. . . .

"Who was that lady I seen you with last night, Elvis?" said Allen . . . , sticking his thumb in the victim's eye and turning it slowly around.

"That was no lady, that was my git-tar," said Elvis morosely.

Now, I do not claim that that was exactly the gag that was used; but . . . it was a gag from which no ordinary twitching vocalist, or rabbit singer, could be expected to recover.

John Lardner reviewing Elvis Presley's appearance on The Steve Allen Show, *in which Presley allowed himself to be made fun of by dressing in a tuxedo and a cowboy outfit, for the July 16, 1956, issue of* Newsweek, *in Kevin Quain, ed.,* The Elvis Reader *(1992), pp. 43–45.*

All of a sudden, the fog started rolling in. The ship's alarm went off and we had to go back downstairs. All you could see was solid white fog. Everybody started to worry, "What's happening?" . . . All of a sudden, there was a loud crash. The engines stopped immediately and the ship was strangely quiet until passengers, flooding the hallways, began screaming. Like the Titanic, they had hit an iceberg, some said. . . . By the time I got out of bed, the ship was already listing. When I opened the door to our cabin, it swung into the passageway. There was a lot of confusion. People were yelling, "Where's my baby? Were is my son?"

My father and brother—we didn't know where they were, or whether they were alive or dead. We didn't know whether we were going to make it or not. . . . You could tell they [his family members whom he'd found after the rescue] had been through hell.

Louis Bellamo's firsthand account of the wreck of the Andrea Doria *on the night of July 25, 1956, as reported to the* Virginian-Pilot & Ledger-Star, *in* Andreadoria.org, "Bellomo Recollection" *(2001).*

Nowadays experienced travelers travel light.

Fortunately modern clothes, as well as modern luggage, make it easy to pack enough for two weeks—or two months—in one suitcase of reasonable size.

At this season of the year, the first things I'd pack are two suits of tropical weight, one dark (say charcoal grey or navy blue) and one light (say natural or medium tan). These will make your wardrobe flexible.

In cities you can wear them as complete suits, and the dark one will serve for dinner and dancing even in smart metropolitan restaurants.

In the country you can mix them, using the jacket of one with the trousers of the other, or you can wear either pair of trousers with sport shirts.

I've found Palm Beach suits very satisfactory because the jackets are well balanced and special construction makes the collars hug your neck. . . .

Next we come to shoes. . . . Norwegian moccasins such as the Bass "Weejuns" are popular, comfortable, and don't take up much room.

Those wash-and-wear shirts, made of dacron and cotton fabrics which require no ironing, are a great help. So are stretch nylon socks and underwear. . . .

Many men who'd never consider driving an old jalopy, don't seem to realize how much they are judged by their luggage. If they did they wouldn't travel around with beat-up old bags when smart luggage is so inexpensive.

Columnist Dermod Kenedy advising men on fashion in his Night Shift column in the men's magazine The Dude, *in Kenedy,* The Dude *(August 1956), p. 65.*

[Jackson] Pollock was the most famous of the artists who have come into prominence since 1940. His death [in a car accident on August 11, 1956] is tragic not only because his career is cut short but because it is logical: similar logic seems to hint that it need not have happened. Pollock's was the tragic, logical death of a man whose greatness and strength are precisely the qualities that led him to a death that could have been avoided if he had not been so strong, or had been willing to compromise, or step backwards, or hold some strength in reserve—in other words, if he had not been Jackson Pollock. . . .

Literally thousands of painters—more in Europe, by now, than in America—have adapted, in some way or other, the superficialities of the look of freedom which he was able to give to paint on canvas. They use his necessities as if they were tricks of commercial art or ways of jazzing-up academic compositions or devices to produce safe-and-sane spectacular abstractions. . . .

Pollock's true influence was felt elsewhere. . . . He was the first successfully to liberate painting from the dominant conventions of the School-of-Paris *cuisine.* When the interior evolution of his style led him to work with the canvas lying on the floor and, later, to toss and splash pigment on the picture—to throw the picture on the floor and attack it in a violent dance . . . a new approach was opened to painters and a new appearance was made possible for pictures . . .

Pollock's career was brief. Like Rimbaud's, it involved an excess of violence which always was colored by tough laughter and never was tainted by sentimentality; like Caravaggio's or van Gogh's, it was filled with moments of stupendous creative activity, as if the artist knew how little time he had to paint in.

Eulogy for artist Jackson Pollock, who died on August 11, 1956, in "Jackson Pollock: 1912–56," ARTnews *(September 1956), p. 44.*

To a tourist these towns look as peaceful as a postcard. But if you go beneath that picture, it's like turning over a rock with your foot—all kinds of strange things crawl out.

Author Grace Metalious talking about the setting of her best-selling novel Peyton Place, *which was published in September 1956, in Jane Stern and Michael Stern,* Encyclopedia of Pop Culture *(1992), p. 382.*

This library does not carry *Peyton Place.* If you want it, go to Salem.

A sign in the Beverly, Massachusetts, library repudiating Peyton Place, *which was published in September 1956, in Jane Stern and Michael Stern,* Encyclopedia of Pop Culture *(1992), p. 382.*

[The U.S. government] now has decided not to sponsor any further international shows including oil paintings executed after 1917 because one of them might be by a Communist or an artist suspected of Communist sympathies. For some strange reason watercolors, graphics and photographs are exempt from this ban. . . . [H]ow can artists contemplate future collaboration with the Government on any project? This, and the fact that American painting is one of our greatest contributions to modern culture, and is recognized as such abroad, may further encourage private foundations and dealers to export it—to their and to the artists' own credit. . . .

Two exhibitions of contemporary American art, scheduled for tours abroad under the sponsorship of the U.S. Government, have recently been canceled. The first, "Sport in Art," was to have gone to Australia this autumn during the Olympic Games there. The second was to have been one of this country's most ambitious official efforts: one hundred pictures rang-

ing in style from realistic to non-objective, painted by Americans of this century, were to tour Europe. The USIA [United States Information Agency] had asked the American Federation of Arts to make the selection; the selection was duly made and half the pictures were in warehouse awaiting shipment when the USIA discovered that ten of the chosen artists were, the agency said, "social hazards."

The USIA asked the Federation to withdraw these paintings; the Federation refused, stating that it could make selections only on the basis of merit. It did not wish to know the names of the ten or the charges against them. Decision as to whether or not to call off the show lay with Theodore Streibert . . . [who] felt the whole operation of the USIA might be put in jeopardy. . . .

In July, Streibert queried the White House. The decision was to cancel the exhibition.

Charlotte Devree discussing an impact of the Red Scale on the arts, in Devree, "The U.S. Government Vetoes Living Art," ARTnews *(September 1956), p. 34.*

Eisenhower and Stevenson were supposed to debate, and then the president didn't want to do it, as you know, in '56, feeling it would be a soliloquy. That's what everyone thought. At the end, the president could take an examination.

Canadian-born comedian Mort Sahl making fun of the perception in fall 1956 that Democratic presidential candidate Adlai E. Stevenson was much better educated and better spoken than President Dwight D. Eisenhower, in Sahl, The Next President *(1960), side 1.*

He's just one big hunk of forbidden fruit.

A female fan's assessment of Elvis Presley's appeal to teenagers after his first performance on The Ed Sullivan Show, *on September 9, 1956, in Clifton Daniel, ed.,* 20th Century Day by Day *(2000), p. 786.*

Why, no. I did just like I always do. Had a few beers and went to bed around midnight.

New York Yankees pitcher Don Larsen stating that he did nothing special the night before he pitched a perfect game in the World Series against the Brooklyn Dodgers on October 8, 1956, in Clifton Daniel, 20th Century Day by Day *(2000), p. 789.*

We worked from four-thirty in the morning until night-fall with only a brief rest for lunch. . . . For three years we were allowed no books, no paper, no pencils, no radio, no newspapers. We could have no visitors, no mail, no parcels of food, and we were not permitted to tell our families where we were. We did not know for how long we were there, nor for what reason. We lived a life of blank terror.

Ferenc Gabor describing his existence in a Hungarian prison camp for political prisoners prior to the antigovernment uprising that began October 23, 1956, in James Michener, The Bridge at Andau *(1957), p. 119.*

Somewhere, the doors of a military barracks were forced open. It was from there they got their arms . . . [T]he guards tried to keep them back with a fire hose. . . . The situation became more and more tense. . . . Now the slogan was, "Occupy the Radio Station!"

Zoltan Pal describing the attempt to take over the state-run radio station in Budapest, one of the pivotal events of the Hungarian uprising on October 23, 1956, in James Michener, The Bridge at Andau *(1957), p. 65.*

The United States considers the development in Hungary as being a renewed expression of the intense desire for freedom long held by the Hungarian people. . . .

The United States deplores the intervention of Soviet military forces which under the Treaty of Peace [1947] should have been withdrawn and the presence of which in Hungary, as now demonstrated, is not to protect Hungary against armed aggression from without, but rather to continue an occupation of Hungary by the forces of an alien government for its own purposes.

President Dwight Eisenhower addressing the nation about the crisis in Hungary on October 25, 1956, in Eisenhower, The White House Years, *vol. 2 (1965), p. 65.*

After eleven years of "people's democracy" it had come to this: that the security police was so remote from the people, so alien to them, so vicious and so brutal that it turned its weapons on a defenseless crowd and murdered the people who were supposed to be the masters of their own country.

Peter Fryer, a correspondent for the British Communist Party's newspaper The Daily Worker, *commenting on the massacre of 87 Hungarians by communist troops on October 26, 1956, during the Hungarian uprising, in Martin Gilbert,* A History of the Twentieth Century, *vol. 3 (2000), pp. 120–21.*

I later found out from [Lord] Mountbatten that the British government gave the chiefs the order like that—snap. Without time for preparation.

Admiral Arleigh H. Burke, chief of naval operations for the U.S. Navy, commenting on the joint British-French invasion of Egypt on October 31, 1956, in Leonard Mosley, Dulles *(1978), p. 419.*

Who's the enemy?

Captain "Cat" Brown, commander of U.S. naval forces in the Mediterranean, upon being told by Admiral Arleigh H. Burke to be prepared for an action against either a land or sea force, following the joint British-French invasion of Egypt on October 31, 1956, in Leonard Mosley, Dulles *(1978), p. 418.*

Tell your friends to comply with the goddam cease-fire or go ahead with the goddam invasion. Either way we'll back them up if they do it fast. What we can't stand is their goddam hesitation, waltzing while Hungary is burning.

Chester Cooper, CIA liaison officer to British intelligence on November 1, 1956, in Peter Grose, Gentleman Spy: The Life of Allen Dulles *(1994), p. 440.*

At this moment there is silence. It may be the silence before the storm.

We have almost no weapons. . . . We haven't any kind of heavy guns.

The people are jumping at the tanks, throwing in hand grenades and closing the drivers' windows. The Hungarian people are not afraid of death. It is only a pity that we can't stand for long. . . .

The tanks are nearing, and the heavy artillery. . . . It can't be allowed that people attack tanks with their bare hands. What is the United Nations doing? Give us a little encouragement. . . .

Russian plane just fired a machine-gun burst. We don't know where, just heard and saw it.

The building of barricades is going on. The Parliament and its vicinity are crowded with tanks. We don't know why, but it certainly is not a good sign. Planes are flying overhead, but can't be counted, there are so many. . . .

They just brought us a rumor that the American troops will be here within one or two hours. . . .

Send us any word you can about world action in Hungary's behalf.

Hungarian news reporter Jozsef Boulevard's on-the-scene dispatches from Budapest to the Associated Press office in Vienna on November 4, 1956, in James Michener, The Bridge at Andau *(1957), p. 99.*

If I'd known what the outcome would be, I would probably have refused to run.

President Eisenhower to Senator Styles Bridges after the national election on November 6, 1956, in which Eisenhower was overwhelmingly reelected president but Democrats won majorities in the House and Senate, in Geoffrey Perret, Eisenhower *(1999), p. 541.*

The theme of this picture is whether men are to be ruled by God's law—or whether they are to be ruled by the whims of a dictator. . . . Are men the property of the state? Or are they free souls under God? This same battle continues throughout the world today.

Cecil B. DeMille's spoken prologue to his epic film The Ten Commandments, *which had its world premiere on November 8, 1956.*

Yul Brynner is the most powerful personality I've ever seen on the screen: a cross between Douglas Fairbanks, Sr., Apollo, and a little bit of Hercules.

Film director Cecil B. DeMille commenting on actor Yul Brynner, star of The Ten Commandments, *which opened on November 8, 1956, in Rock Brynner,* Yul: The Man Who Would Be King *(1989), p. 81.*

I knew from experience that [DeMille] wouldn't tolerate the slightest interference. Why, he'd stomp off the set if anyone dared to raise their voice. But it was very different in the case of Brynner. It was as if DeMille was paying close attention to a very intelligent favorite child. . . . The old man took [Brynner's] advice without a murmur. Later the script called for a mob to try and tell Pharaoh its troubles—almost one at a time. Yul thought it would be more striking if they all babbled simultaneously. DeMille agreed and reshaped the entire scene.

Cameraman Sam Cavanaugh describing the relationship between director Cecil B. DeMille and actor Yul Brynner during the filming of The Ten Commandments, *which premiered on November 8, 1956, in Rock Brynner,* Yul: The Man Who Would Be King *(1989), p. 81.*

Charlton Heston stars as Moses in Cecil B. DeMille's extravagant remake of *The Ten Commandments*. (Photofest)

My first reaction [to the Hungarian uprising], anguish; there was this unbelievable error; the request for intervention by Russian troops, and no one knew as yet whether it was the last Rakosi-ist or the new Hungarian government which was responsible. After a few days, anguish gave way to hope and even joy; although the Russian command—which we had just learned was called in by Gero—had committed the criminal clumsiness of answering this call, it had then withdrawn its troops from Budapest.

We saw Soviet regiments withdrawing before the insurgents rather than fire on them; Russian soldiers deserting. The Kremlin seemed hesitant: it seemed as if the insurgents were going to win. Perhaps . . the Soviet Union wanted to resort to negotiations like those in Poland.

The anguish returned immediately after, more intense each day. . . .

The crime, for me, is not *only* the attack on Budapest by the tanks, it is that it was made possible

Ike and Elvis, Budapest and Suez 311

and perhaps necessary (from the Soviet point of view naturally) by twelve years of terror and stupidity. If the right was predominant among most of the insurgents it is because they all shared one passion, completely negative: hatred of the Soviets and Rakosiism. . . .

The sad reality today, for me, is that the French left risks extinction by these events unless there is a change in its parties, and unless the minorities take things in hand. . . . The Communists are dishonored, the Socialists are plunging themselves into the mire. . . . If, as everything seems to indicate, the honest and sincere Communists are agitated, let them look for support among the working classes. . . . As for the right, it has no right to make claims. Those who did not protest against the tortures in Algeria and against Suez have no right to protest against the events in Hungary.

Leftist, existentialist philosopher Jean-Paul Sartre reacting to the Soviet suppression of the Hungarian uprising in the Paris Express, *November 9, 1956, in Barney Rosset, ed.,* Evergreen Review Reader: 1957–1961 *(1979), pp. 29–35.*

I went to see *Love Me Tender* last night, and I liked it enormous. Elvis Presley isn't a bit obscene or lewd; he's just *different*. He certainly stood out from everybody else in the picture—it takes place back in the Civil War times when they didn't hardly have no rock'n' roll yet—and not only because of his singing and virileness; but also because of his acting.

Elvis didn't just *memorize* his lines. He seemed to sense, deep down inside somewhere, what almost every word meant. That's why his portrayal of Clint, a nice Southern boy who helps his mother around the house, and does bumps and grinds to raise money for the new school, and then all of a sudden goes insane with jealousy, was so moving.

But that Debra Paget! She's so *vapid*. Elvis and her are married and everything, but she likes the brother. . . . I don't mean that Debra and Richard Egan (he's the brother) *do* anything, but *still*. She and Vance (he's Richard Egan) had gone around with each other before the war. The minute, however, she hears he was killed, she marries Elvis who was too young to fight. But the brother wasn't really killed, and when he comes back she still has a thing about him. For a long time Elvis doesn't suspect nothing, but finally it dawns on him. . . .

But the best scene was the one where Elvis dies this tragic death. It was so poignant. A lot of movies they don't make you feel crumby when the hero dies, but this one you really do, like when Laurence Olivier dies in *Hamlet,* the famous play by William Shakespeare. Elvis doesn't die slowly, but he doesn't die quickly either. He dies just right, whimpering and grasping and drooling. He dies in Debra's arms.

Critic Janet Winn's satirical review of Love Me Tender, *in Winn, "A Star Is Borne,"* New Republic *(December 24, 1956), p. 22.*

9

Sputnik and Little Rock
1957

The Soviet launching of *Sputnik,* the first human-made satellite whose name means "companion," marked the beginning of a space age that both excited the public imagination with new possibilities of exploration and provoked new fears of nuclear weapons that could rain down from outer space. The Soviet triumph with *Sputnik* also prompted charges that American public schools were asking too little of their students and especially were failing to provide adequate science education. New programs were subsequently introduced to improve the quality of science education, and bright young men and women were encouraged to pursue careers in the sciences. The importance of science was brought to the forefront of society in a way it never had been before, and the position of science as the premier source of authority within the society became substantially strengthened during and after 1957.

It was a year of new beginnings in other aspects of American life, too. Congress passed the first federal civil rights legislation in more than 80 years, and Eisenhower called out the army to enforce school integration in Little Rock, Arkansas. The fan base for professional baseball widened, and the East's domination of American culture showed serious signs of weakening as the Brooklyn Dodgers and New York Giants completed their last seasons in those cities before relocating to California. The era of the television western hit full stride, as *Gunsmoke* topped the ratings; scientists discovered a new element; and even typesetting, which had not seen a major technological innovation in 400 years, entered a new period with the introduction of phototypesetting. The era of miniaturized technology came of age when Sony introduced the pocket-size transistor, which was first used to produce popular, handheld, portable radios.

THE COLD WAR AND INTERNATIONAL POLITICS

The Cold War Abroad

The year's most far-reaching cold war developments, and the developments with the greatest impact on the public imagination, were the Soviet Union's successful test of an intercontinental ballistic missile (ICBM) that could travel as far as to the United States and its successful launch of *Sputnik I,* the first human-made satellite to orbit Earth. In August, the Soviets successfully tested an ICBM with a range of about 5,000 miles. This altered the critical balance of power, because although the United States had bases in Europe and had long been able to send missiles deep within Russia, the Soviet Union could never before comparably strike the American heartland.

The new Soviet missile capability had the immediate effect of rendering U.S. policy of massive retaliation problematic—as the Soviets could now strike the U.S. mainland in reply to any attack against it. As a result, a new policy of mutually assured destruction (MAD) gradually came to dominate cold war nuclear politics. The Soviets' recent successes also created a mistaken impression that they possessed missile superiority. That inaccurate belief persisted until satellite observation in the early 1960s debunked it; nonetheless, by November 1957, Secretary Nikita Khrushchev felt so confident that he challenged the United States to a rocket-range shooting match. After several failures throughout the year, the United States successfully tested its own Atlas ICBM in December. Before that, in October, it successfully fired its first intermediate-range ballistic missile (IRBM), which had a range of about 2,000 miles. The United States then quickly agreed to base IRBMs in Europe under U.S. control. Although the Soviet lead in missile technology was brief and never decisive, and the "missile gap" that later became the focus of public debate was largely illusory, Khrushchev's belief in Soviet missile superiority emboldened him to take more aggressive action in Berlin between 1958 and 1961.

Even more upsetting to most Americans was the Soviet Union's launch on October 4 of *Sputnik I.* Then on November 3, the Soviets launched *Sputnik II,* which carried a dog named Laika into space. The *Sputnik* launches sparked fear among Americans that the Russians had gained a huge cold war military advantage. In addition to heightening the climate of cold war anxiety, this new fear pushed President Eisenhower to advance the U.S. space program, something he had been reluctant to do earlier because he feared the cost would undermine the robust health of the economy, which he believed was the nation's strongest defense against communism. Fears of Soviet supremacy in space also created an immediate demand for improved science education in U.S. schools. On a slightly more hopeful note, the International Atomic Energy Commission was created to develop peaceful uses for atomic energy throughout the world.

The debacle of the 1956 Hungarian uprising soiled the Soviet Union's image and diminished its support throughout the world. It also briefly weakened Khrushchev and his program of reform. For instance, in January, hardliner Andrei Gromyko was appointed Soviet foreign minister, a position he held until 1985. Then on July 4, U.S. Independence Day, Khrushchev suppressed a coup attempt by hard-liners Georgi Malenkov, Vyacheslav Molotov, and Lazar Kaganovich, who were publicly linked to Stalin. The challengers were expelled from the Central Committee of the Communist Party. After suppressing the insurrection, Khrushchev consolidated his power base. In October 1957, Khrushchev removed Marshal Georgi Zhukov, a World War II hero under Stalin, from his post as defense minister and stripped him of his top positions in the Communist Party. Zhukov's celebrated wartime achievements were belittled, and the general was accused of self-aggrandizement at the expense of the Soviet people. Khrushchev continued his program of domestic reforms to improve the Soviet standard of living, declaring that "Marxist-Leninism will taste better with butter."[1] By 1958, he had forced out Premier Bulganin, whom he accused of supporting the coup, and assumed the top positions in both the government and the party.

Poland, which in 1956 avoided the fate of Hungary by maintaining a more conciliatory relationship with the Soviet Union while still pushing for greater individual freedoms, received a pledge in June from the United States for almost $50 million in surplus farm equipment. Poland's reform government then pledged to restore free-market agricultural trade for peasants. Popular protests for additional personal liberties later in the year, however, provoked more stringent responses by the government. Yugoslavia's Marshal Tito met with Khrushchev and pledged closer ties between Yugoslavia and the Soviet Union, something Khrushchev had been trying to achieve since coming to power to counterbalance the threat from NATO.

In the Suez region, the 1956 military adventure resulted in Britain largely withdrawing from the Middle East, the United States and Soviet Union moving to fill the resulting power vacuum, and a larger role for cold war politics in the region. Eisenhower believed that the Soviets wanted to take control of the Suez Canal and the oil-rich Middle Eastern countries to place a stranglehold on the West's supply of energy resources. Therefore, on January 5, he issued the Eisenhower Doctrine, in which he asked Congress for authority to employ military force and send military and economic aid to protect Middle Eastern countries from communist aggression. He received that authority in March, and in June, the United States joined Turkey, Iraq, Iran, Pakistan, and Britain in the Baghdad Pact, formed in 1955 to protect the oil-producing states against communism. Meanwhile, Egypt and Syria, who formed an economic union in September, drew closer to the Soviet Union, repudiated the Western powers, and promoted pan-Arabic unity.

In January, Egypt, Syria, and Saudi Arabia agreed to replace British aid to Jordan, but in April, after Jordan's king, Hussein, removed the pro-Soviet premier, pro-Egyptian elements tried to overthrow him. Assured of the loyalty of his army, Hussein squelched the conspiracy, declared martial law, denounced Egypt and Syria, purged the Egyptian sympathizers from his government, and formed a new, pro-Western government. Thus Jordan, like Lebanon, Saudi Arabia, and Iraq, strengthened its cold war ties to the United States and distanced itself from Nasser's pan-Arabism. Hussein's new government was vulnerable, however, and in response to a request from President Camille Chamoun of Lebanon to take decisive action in support of Hussein, Eisenhower, using the powers Congress recently had granted him, sent the U.S. Sixth Fleet to the eastern Mediterranean to stabilize the situation. Eisenhower also authorized a $10-million grant in economic aid for Jordan, and the crisis passed.[2]

The Soviet Union denounced the U.S. involvement, calling it blatant interference with Jordan's internal affairs. At the same time, the Soviet Union cultivated closer ties to Syria, and when communist sympathizers took over the government in August, the Soviets hosted a Syrian delegation in Moscow and offered military aid. Perceiving a threat from Syria, Turkey then massed troops on their common border. The situation in October seemed ready to erupt into a major international confrontation after the USSR threatened Turkey on Syria's behalf. In response, Secretary of State Dulles made a thinly veiled threat against the Soviet Union, itself, stating that the United States would not restrict itself to a defensive response if the Soviets attacked Turkey, which was a member of NATO. Although Khrushchev accused the United States of practicing "brinkmanship"—going to the brink of nuclear war—he soon mollified his position toward Turkey. Soon after the conflict was resolved, thousands of Palestinians in Damascus called for the death of Hussein, who had sided with the West against the pan-Arab Syrian-Egyptian coalition.

In March, Israel acquiesced to UN and U.S. pressure and withdrew its troops from land it had occupied in the Gaza Strip during the 1956 Suez incursion. Despite a promise to UN secretary general Hammarskjold that Egypt would not reoccupy the region, Egyptian president Nasser immediately forced out a small UN peacekeeping force, and Egypt regained control of the territory, from which it had launched raids on Israel before the Suez crisis. Nasser further reiterated his refusal to permit Israel use of the Suez Canal, and he rejected a UN revenue-shaping proposal for the canal. Saudi Arabia briefly barred Israeli ships from the Gulf of Aqaba but was later persuaded by U.S. diplomacy to reopen the port. The Saudis also signed an agreement with the United States to receive military aid in return for allowing a U.S. airbase in Dhahran.

Despite growing public concern about the safety of nuclear testing, both superpowers continued to explode weapons in the atmosphere. In July, the Soviets tentatively agreed to a Western plan to halt the testing, and in August, Eisenhower offered to suspend nuclear testing for two years. But disarmament talks in London in September broke down. However, in an effort to reduce the dangers from atmospheric testing, the United States conducted its first underground tests, and it announced plans to reduce its military force by 100,000 troops. It also successfully tested a supersonic B-58 bomber. The United States further announced a plan to install new Nike Hercules missiles with nuclear warheads in sites defending major U.S. cities. Missile sites around New York City included the Kensico Reservoir near White Plains, Fort Tilden in Queens, and Monmouth County in New Jersey. In July, an army Redstone ballistic missile was put on display in New York City's Grand Central Station.

Other International Developments

An important era in European history began when, on March 25, France, West Germany, Italy, Luxembourg, Belgium, and the Netherlands signed the Treaty of Rome, thereby forming the European Economic Community, better known as the Common Market. The purpose of the economic alliance was to create a common market for all products and services, especially coal and steel. It equalized import taxes among the member nations, with the long-term goal of eliminating all trade barriers. The Treaty of Rome also created the European Investment Bank to assist underdeveloped nations with aid and credit, the European Atomic Energy Authority, and the European Court of Justice.

In January, Harold Macmillan, the leader of the right wing of Britain's Conservative Party, replaced Anthony Eden, another Conservative, as prime minister. He and Eisenhower subsequently formed a good working relationship. When

John Diefenbaker became Canada's prime minister in June, conservative parties took control of all three of the English-speaking, North Atlantic governments for the first time since before World War II. In 1957, Diefenbaker appointed Canada's first female cabinet minister, Ellen Fairclough, and in 1958, he named James Gladstone Canada's first Native senator.

The extent to which West Germany had moved beyond its World War II legacy just 12 years after the fighting ended became evident in January, when a West German general, Hans Speidel, was appointed commander in chief of the Central Sector of NATO in Europe. Speidel had been Nazi general Erwin Rommel's chief of staff during the Normandy invasion in World War II; the Gestapo arrested him a month later for complicity in the assassination attempt against Hitler. On September 6, West Germans reelected Konrad Adenauer as their chancellor. Adenauer, who had been an early opponent of Hitler, led West Germany in its various states of sovereignty from 1949 to 1963, and he was one of the driving forces behind the formation of the Common Market. Although he established relations with the Soviet Union, he refused to recognize East Germany, because he hoped for an eventual German reunification. In November, West Germany broke off relations with Yugoslavia in retaliation for the latter's recognition of East Germany.

The struggle for Algerian independence broke into outright war in late January, when France greatly increased its military presence; the military's use of systematic torture to combat terrorism raised public outcry in France and turned world opinion against the colonial power. In July, Senator John F. Kennedy of Massachusetts called on Eisenhower to discontinue U.S. support of "colonial repression" and instead work to help achieve Algerian independence.[3] Tunisia was proclaimed a republic independent from France; the West African territory of Guinea rejected a proposal to join a new French Commonwealth, and instead established itself as an independent nation. Among the members of the French Commonwealth were territories in Equatorial Africa, Madagascar, Somalia, the Comoros, Polynesia, New Caledonia, and St. Pierre and Miquelon.

Ghana became an independent nation in March, and Nigeria, another British territory, also received autonomy. The white-supremacist government of South Africa distanced itself further from Britain and continued to harden its policies of apartheid, despite appeals from the United Nations to reconsider them.

In September, Fidel Castro led another uprising against Cuba's dictator, Fulgencio Batista. Although this rebellion was also suppressed, for the first time the rebel forces included members of the military. In response to the unrest, Batista suspended the constitution. A military coup in Haiti installed François Duvalier (Papa Doc) as president, and in Guatemala, Colonel Carlos Castillo Armas, was assassinated. With secret U.S. assistance, Castillo Armas had overthrown the reform government of Jacobo Arbenz Guzmán in 1954. During his three years in power, although Castillo eradicated communist influences from the government, he also imprisoned thousands of political prisoners, disenfranchised three-fourths of the voting citizenry, and denied other democratic freedoms. He was followed by two temporary governments before Ydígoras Fuentes became president in March 1958.

Eisenhower met in Washington with South Vietnam's president, Diem, and the leaders pledged to work together to resist the spread of communism in Southeast Asia. A military coup seized power in Thailand; and Malaya, the last of Britain's major Asian colonies, was granted independence in August and subsequently allowed to join the British Commonwealth and the United Nations. Although Kashmir was admitted as a state within India, its controversial unification with India provoked periodic opposition from both Pakistan and Kashmiri independence groups that has persisted into the 21st century.

PRC chairman Mao Zedong halted the campaign of "One Hundred Flowers," which had been instituted the year before to allow broader criticism of the government and the party. Later in the year, Mao instituted the "Great Leap Forward" in which peasant men were conscripted for large irrigation and water-control projects. Within a few months, more than 100 million peasants had been removed from their farms to work on these enormous undertakings. In their absence, women assumed responsibility for raising the crops, and centralized programs were developed to provide child care and food preparation while they were in the fields.[4]

The Cold War at Home

The specter of internal communist subversion resurfaced when police in Brooklyn, investigating what they initially believed was a case of immigration violation, discovered suspicious radio and photographic equipment in Rudolf Abel's apartment and arrested him for spying for the Soviet Union. Abel was convicted in October of operating a spy network for nine years in America. In 1962, the United States exchanged him for Francis Gary Powers, a U-2 reconnaissance pilot who was shot down while flying over Soviet airspace in 1960.

The same year that saw Senator Joseph McCarthy die from ailments related to his alcoholism also saw some of the excesses that he championed reversed by Supreme Court decisions. These rulings played a substantial role in diminishing the Red Scare, which nonetheless persisted in varying degrees of intensity through the rest of the decade and beyond. Noting that the accused never explicitly advocated overthrowing the U.S. government, in *Sweezy v. New Hampshire* the Court overturned the contempt conviction of a college professor who had admitted belonging to the left-wing Progressive Party but refused to identify other members before a state legislature. For similar reasons, the conviction of an admitted member of the American Communist Party who would not name other members before HUAC was reversed in *Watkins v. United States*. In *Yates v. United States* the Court distinguished between speech and advocacy to overturn the Smith Act conviction of an avowed communist. In doing so, it rejected the government argument that because communist doctrine calls for the eventual toppling of capitalist governments by the workers, all Communist Party members necessarily endorse the violent overthrow of the U.S. government and are therefore inherently guilty of violating the Smith Act, which prohibits such advocacy. In *Service v. Dulles,* the Court declared that Secretary of State Dulles acted arbitrarily and violated constitutional guarantees of due process and free speech when he fired William Service for expressing political viewpoints his superiors considered excessively liberal. Prior to the firing, the State Department's Internal Loyalty Board had investigated and determined that Service was not a security risk, but Dulles rejected that finding. The Court also ruled that FBI reports used to secure convictions must be made available to defendants in criminal cases and that Congress can investigate only matters related to potential legislation or governmental oversight; it cannot hold hearings simply for the purposes of exposing citizens' beliefs or behaviors.

The rulings stirred great controversy. Praised by liberals and civil libertarians, they were condemned by hard-line anticommunists, who referred to June 17, the day the decisions were handed down, as Red Monday. FBI director J. Edgar Hoover went so far as to accuse the Court of promoting the communist cause in the United States. Nonetheless, the FBI had become so effective at infiltrating the American Communist Party during the 1950s, that by 1957, party membership was down from a high of about 75,000 during World War II to some 10,000 or less.[5] Moreover, the percentage of party members who were actually FBI infiltrators was so great that Hoover reportedly considered taking control of the party, by having all of his informants support one faction at the Communist Party national convention.[6]

The hazards of exposure to radiation resulting from weapons testing became a growing matter of political controversy and debate. Edward Teller, known popularly as the "Father of the Hydrogen Bomb," reported that scientists had succeeded in reducing radioactive fallout by more than 95 percent, and he claimed that its effect on human life was negligible. Other leading scientists warned that fallout was collecting beneath the high-altitude jet stream, and Linus Pauling, who had won the 1954 Nobel Prize in chemistry, maintained that some 10,000 people were dying or had died from leukemia contracted as a result of the tests. Albert Schweitzer, another Nobel Prize winner, also weighed in against nuclear testing when he urged the Nobel committee to mobilize world opinion against it. As the possible dangers from fallout became more widely known, grassroots opposition against nuclear testing and the arms race also galvanized private citizens. Among the new opposition groups was the influential Committee for a Sane Nuclear Policy, founded by *Saturday Review* editor Norman Cousins. Cousins also published numerous articles in his magazine that advocated nuclear nonproliferation and international efforts to promote peaceful uses of atomic energy.

CIVIL RIGHTS

The major civil rights developments were the passage of the Civil Rights Act of 1957 and the crisis over school integration in Little Rock, Arkansas. Although considerably weaker than originally proposed, the Civil Rights Act established a division of civil rights within the Justice Department and a national Commission on Civil Rights. It also enacted penalties for violating the voting rights of any U.S. citizen. The act, which survived a record-setting 24-hour-and-18-minute filibuster by Senator Strom Thurmond of South Carolina, was the first federal civil rights legislation since 1875.

The Little Rock crisis threatened to create a constitutional emergency, as at its height, Eisenhower had to call in the army to force the governor of Arkansas to comply with a federal court order. The situation began on September 2, when Governor Orval Faubus announced he would call out the National Guard to block enrollment of black students at Little Rock's Central High School. A federal judge then directed the U.S. Justice Department to file an injunction insisting that Faubus comply with the desegregation order; however, the next day the guard blocked nine African-American students from entering the school. On September 14, Faubus met with Eisenhower, who maintained that he had no objection to the presence of the guard, but insisted that they must protect the black students, not bar them. He turned down Faubus's request to defy the Supreme Court edict to act with "all deliberate speed" by ordering a year's delay in the desegregation program. Faubus then appeared to be willing to comply with Eisenhower, but on September 20, after being ordered by the federal court to remove the guard and allow the integration to proceed, Faubus made a radio broadcast asking black students to remain home until he could implement a peaceful integration program. He then withdrew the guard and left town to attend a conference.

The following Monday, September 23, the nine students evaded a crowd of more than 1,000 white protestors and entered the school by a side entrance. When their presence inside was discovered, the crowd became so unruly the police could barely contain it, and groups of white students left the building in protest. Fearful that the situation might erupt into uncontrollable violence, Mayor Woodrow Wilson Mann ordered that the black students be withdrawn until their safety could be guaranteed.

That night Eisenhower issued a "cease and desist" decree against those obstructing federal law; however, the following day, September 24, an even larger crowd appeared, and the students were unable to enter the school. In response, Eisenhower federalized 10,000 members of the National Guard and ordered 1,000 soldiers from the army's 101st Airborne Division to go to Little Rock. He explained his decision to the nation that evening in a televised broadcast. Before dawn the next day, paratroopers encircled Central High and faced the crowd with bayonets drawn as the students entered. The paratroopers left after two months, but the federalized guard remained throughout the school year.

The following year, after the citizens of Little Rock voted by more than 2–1 against integration, Faubus closed all of the public schools in Little Rock and tried to lease the public facilities to a private corporation that would run the schools as segregated facilities. A federal court, however, ruled that the practice was unconstitutional, and in 1959 the Little Rock public schools were integrated without serious incident.

Elsewhere opposition to desegregation was more narrowly focused but sometimes more violent. Four black churches and the homes of two black ministers were bombed on January 10 in Montgomery, Alabama, and on September 10, a public school in Nashville, Tennessee, that had admitted black students was bombed. The Georgia senate outlawed interracial athletic competitions, and the governor of Florida shut down the Tallahassee bus system rather than integrate it. In October, Eisenhower had to apologize to the finance minister of Ghana because a restaurant in Delaware had refused to serve him. On the other

Tennis star Althea Gibson received a ticker tape parade in Manhattan after becoming the first black woman tennis player to win at Wimbledon. *(Photofest)*

hand, the first black family moved into Levittown, an all-white suburb in New York, and Althea Gibson, the first black tennis player to win at Wimbledon, received an enthusiastic ticker tape parade upon her homecoming in New York City.

GOVERNMENT AND SOCIETY

In celebration of the 30th anniversary of the first trans-Atlantic flight, the *Spirit of St. Louis II* crossed the ocean in 6.7 hours. The historic achievement was also celebrated in Billy Wilder's *The Spirit of St. Louis,* which starred James Stewart as aviator Charles Lindbergh. The crossing of the *Mayflower* from Plymouth, England, to Plymouth Rock, Massachusetts, was reenacted, too.

In late November, Eisenhower suffered a mild stroke. Doctors reported him fully recovered on March 1, 1958. Several high-profile mafia figures were killed by rivals, including Frank Costello, who became a national figure during the 1950–51 Kefauver hearings; Frank Scalice, who was shot at a peach stand in the Bronx; and Albert Anastasia, the so-called Lord High Executioner of Murder, Incorporated, died in the barber shop of New York's Park Sheraton Hotel.

In December, 19-year-old Charles Starkweather committed the first of a series of highly publicized murders in Wyoming and Nebraska that outraged and alarmed the nation, when he robbed and killed a gas station owner. The next month, Starkweather visited his girlfriend, Caril Ann Fugate, argued with her, and murdered her parents. He also shot her two-year-old sister before fleeing with her in her parents' car. The couple then went on a robbery and murder spree until they were captured while struggling with a victim. At his trial, Starkweather pled insanity and Fugate maintained that he kidnapped her and forced her to assist him; however, both were convicted, and Starkweather was executed in 1959. Fugate received a life sentence but was paroled in 1977 after serving 18 years as a model prisoner.

San Francisco was hit by the strongest earthquake since 1906, and Lake Charles, Louisiana, was struck by a rare June hurricane that killed some 500 people along the Gulf of Mexico. An earthquake in Iran killed nearly 2,000 people near the Caspian Sea, and an outbreak of the so-called Asian flu produced the worst global epidemic since the end of World War I. Some 7,000 people died in Japan, 16,000 in Britain, and 70,000 in the United States, where it was first reported in early June and peaked in October, by which time approximately 7 million Americans had received vaccinations. Over a two-year period, the flu killed more than a million people worldwide. The very young and the elderly were the most likely to succumb.[7] Planned Parenthood estimated that between 200,000 and 1.2 million abortions took place each year within the United States. (The 1953 *Kinsey Report* reported that about 20 percent of sexually active single women interviewed in the study had had abortions.)[8]

BUSINESS

The economy did not change much from 1956, except that inflation rose from 1.2 percent to 2.9 percent. The Dow Jones Industrial Average fluctuated between a high of 520 and a low of 425 (compared with 521 and 462 in

1956), and the GNP grew at the same rate of 5 percent. Toward the end of the year, the economy experienced the first signs of a mild recession that manifested in 1958; nonetheless, during the Christmas shopping season, Macy's department store recorded its first $2-million day in store history. The average salary nationwide was $4,230: The average teacher earned $4,085, the average factory worker made $4,789, and medical doctors earned $22,100 on average. A four-piece Sloane's cherry bedroom set cost $524, a 55-inch hutch cabinet was $328, a Louis XIV dining table was $539, and a twin foam mattress set cost about $125. Some 21 million people spent more than $2 billion on fishing-related goods and services.[9]

Overall, labor relations were smooth. In February, the U.S. Senate conducted hearings investigating corruption in the Teamsters Union, and in March, Teamsters vice president Jimmy Hoffa was arrested by the FBI and indicted for bribery, conspiracy, and obstruction of justice. Hoffa was acquitted in July, however, and elected president of the Teamsters in October. Following his election, the AFL-CIO expelled the Teamsters due to the alleged rampant corruption within the union.

Two established popular magazines, *Collier's* and *Woman's Home Companion,* went out of business, in part due to the competition from television for visually oriented entertainment. Among the year's new products was Ford's latest automobile, the Edsel, named after founder Henry Ford's son. The car's unusual, ostentatious design, which was the result of intense market research, was widely ridiculed, and the heavily promoted model was discontinued in 1959, after was it recognized as a failure. On the other hand, Germany's Volkswagen sold 2,000 of the tiny Beetles that it introduced to America, and at the other end of the

The big American cars of the 1950s were roomy and stylish but neither fuel efficient nor meant to last long. *(Photofest)*

luxury scale, the Cadillac Eldorado added a lipstick vanity case and four gold cups to its dashboard. Ford also introduced a car with a retractable hardtop.

Sony's pocket-size transistor not only made possible the popular handheld transistor radios; it also anticipated the computer chip in its ability to miniaturize electronic circuitry. So did a new cryotron device developed to miniaturize computer technology. So small that 100 could fit into a thimble, the cryotron device went on to play a critical role in the development of the computer technology. The first commercial building to be heated by solar energy was completed in Albuquerque, New Mexico. The accidental overheating of the glass Fotoform led to the invention of ovenproof pyro-ceram domestic cook ware that was popularized as Pyrex.

The Broadway musical *Li'l Abner* created a demand for Dog Patch outfits, and the California-based Wham-O toy company introduced Fred Morrison's frisbee, an aerodynamic plastic disk that sails through the air like a flying saucer. Philip Morris spent $250,000 to develop a new, colorful cigarette package that would show up well in ads on color television. One of its competitors produced a simple jingle that caught the public's ear: "Winston tastes good like a cigarette should." The ad garnered even more attention as grammarians argued over the use of *like* instead of *as*.

SCIENCE AND TECHNOLOGY

Throughout the 1950s while some scientists developed increasingly sophisticated weaponry, others spoke out loudly about the dangers of those weapons. Unlike in the political realm, where cold war antagonisms had polarized the East and West, in the sciences there was still a generally cohesive and cooperative international community in the late 1950s, and as portrayed in the 1951 science fiction film *The Day the Earth Stood Still,* some scientists sought to use their community as a forum to address cold war issues. Scientists from the Eastern and Western bloc countries first met together in the village of Pugwash, Canada, to try to overcome political divisions and maintain meaningful dialogues among nuclear scientists on opposite sides of the nuclear arms race. The Pugwash conferences continued throughout the conflict and one of its founders, Joseph Rotblat, received the Nobel Peace Prize in 1995 for his efforts to reduce the danger of nuclear war. A different kind of connection between East and West was made when the British ship *Labrador* discovered a new northwest passage across the Arctic Circle.

A committee of experts appointed by the American Heart Association, the American Cancer Society, and the National Heart and Cancer Institutes concluded that scientific evidence had established beyond a reasonable doubt a direct relationship between cigarette smoking and the onset of lung cancer. Although the seven-member panel acknowledged that more research was necessary to study the exact nature of the connection, it maintained that the current studies were sufficient to justify public health measures against smoking.

In other developments in the biological and medical sciences, selenium was shown to be a trace element that is essential for life; interferon was identified for its role in building immunity against viruses; and giberellin, a growth-producing hormone was isolated. Anticoagulants were shown to reduce permanent damage in stroke victims, and the painkiller Darvon and the tranquilizer meprobamate were developed. An intensive study of birth control pills was begun in Puerto Rico. After the test results were positive, the pill was introduced to the public in 1960, and women then acquired access to a reliable form of contraception that was fully within their personal control—a development that contributed substantially to the sexual revolution of the 1960s, to the growing practice of family planning, and to the corresponding ability of women to enter more fully and advance within the workforce.

The first laser technology was invented. The Soviets opened a new particle accelerator for subatomic research, as did a joint European cooperative (the European Organization for Nuclear Research, or CERN) based in Geneva, Switzerland. Element 102 was discovered and named nobelium.

SPORTS, ENTERTAINMENT, AND THE ARTS

Sports

Some of the year's key developments in sports occurred in the courts and elsewhere off the field. The Supreme Court ruled that the National Football League (NFL) was subject to antitrust legislation; Major League Baseball, however, remained free from antitrust laws, which precluded athletes from becoming free agents who could sell their services to the highest bidder. The American Medical Association voted to study the use of stimulants in athletics.

The Milwaukee Braves defeated the New York Yankees in seven games to win the World Series. Milwaukee's Hank Aaron, who led the major leagues with 44 home runs, was the National League's Most Valuable Player (MVP). New York Yankee Mickey Mantle was the MVP for the American League. Prior to the start of the season, Boston's league-leading hitter, Ted Williams, became baseball's highest-paid player after signing a contract for $500,000, and Jackie Robinson, the Brooklyn Dodgers star who integrated Major League Baseball in 1947, retired. The Brooklyn Dodgers and New York Giants played their last seasons in those cities, before moving to Los Angeles and San Francisco, respectively, after the season ended, as baseball began its westward expansion, much to the elation of West Coast fans. For years afterward, however, many New York–based Dodgers and Giants fans expressed feelings of anger and betrayal at the loss of teams they had followed faithfully throughout their lives, especially as the teams were relocated not because of poor attendance or an unreliable fan base, but purely for other business considerations.

For the second year in a row, the Chicago Bears were humiliated in the NFL championship game, which they lost to the Detroit Lions 59-14. The Cleveland Browns's sensational rookie running back, Jim Brown, made his professional debut, and Baltimore Colts quarterback John Unitas was named MVP. Auburn had the top college football team. John Crow from Texas A&M won the Heisman Trophy.

The Boston Celtics defeated St. Louis to begin its era of domination over the National Basketball Association. Celtics standout Bob Cousy was MVP. Other members of the league's All-Pro First Team were Boston's Bill Sharman, Philadelphia's Paul Arizin, St. Louis's Bob Pettit, Syracuse's Dolph Schayes, and Fort Wayne's George Yardley. The University of North Carolina had the top college basketball team, and its star Len Rosenbluth was named Player of the Year. The Montreal Maple Leafs won hockey's Stanley Cup.

"Sugar" Ray Robinson came out of retirement to regain the middleweight boxing championship for the fourth time, but he was then defeated by Carmen Basilio. Floyd Patterson retained his heavyweight title by knocking out challenger Tommy Jackson in 10 rounds. Althea Gibson, a tennis player from Harlem, who was the first black to compete in the U.S. Open at Forest Hills (1950) and at Wimbledon (1951), defeated Darlene Hard to become the first black tennis player to win a championship at Wimbledon. She was heartily cheered when she returned home to her native New York City. She also won the U.S. Open, along with Mal Anderson, who won the men's competition. Dick Mayer won golf's USGA Open.

Television

Television expanded its role in the cold war when for the first time in history, the leader of an enemy country directly addressed an American audience. A panel of three reporters conducted a controversial, hour-long interview of Khrushchev on CBS's *Face the Nation.* The interview, in which Khrushchev announced that the Soviet Union was ready to seek disarmament, was broadcast from Moscow. The network was attacked for not abiding by the established American practice of following interviews of a communist spokesman with live panels of prominent anticommunists who responded to the communist leader. The Catholic War Veterans demanded that CBS cancel the show, and Eisenhower dismissed the interview as a stunt. In his opinion, "a commercial firm in this country [is] trying to improve its commercial standing."[10] CBS president Frank Stanton defended the program, claiming that it was important to demystify Khrushchev and to allow Americans an opportunity to see him and assess him for themselves. Another CBS special documentary report about the revolution in Cuba included an interview with Castro, who did not reveal himself as a communist.

Billy Graham, an evangelical minister, carried out four widely viewed "crusades" between 1957 and 1959, during which he held services every Saturday night for two to three months. On the opposite end of the spectrum of social respectability, Alan Freed, the disc jockey who coined the term *rock 'n' roll,* hosted *The Rock 'n' Roll Show,* an ABC special devoted to rock music and featuring Sal Mineo, the Clovers, Screamin' Jay Hawkins, and the Del-Vikings, among others. Freed later hosted a series of four half-hour summer specials entitled *The Big Beat,* which featured Connie Francis, Bobby Darin, Chuck Berry, Fats Domino, and others. These were the first prime-time network specials to showcase rock music, and they drew an enthusiastic audience of young people.

As videotape became more commonly employed during the 1957–58 season, the demise of live television began. Moreover, for the first time westerns, and not comedies, topped the ratings. That the country so readily looked to the distant past at a time when so many aspects of American society were entering new phases suggests a desire for some foundation of cultural stability on which the current wave of social change could stand. And even though their views of history were often inaccurate and/or clichéd, TV westerns offered the illusion of reassuring stability. The most widely viewed show was *Gunsmoke,* and among the top-10 Nielsen-rated programs, four others were also westerns: *The Life and Legend of Wyatt Earp* and the newcomers *Tales of Wells Fargo,* starring Dale Robertson; *The Restless Gun,* starring John Payne; and *Have Gun, Will Travel,* starring Richard Boone, about a professional gunman who uses his talents for good. Comedies still figured highly as the other top-rated programs, including *The Danny Thomas Show, December Bride,* and Groucho Marx's *You Bet Your Life.* But the decade's top-rated *I Love Lucy* went out of production at the end of the 1956–57 season, as stars Lucille Ball and Desi Arnaz dissolved their marriage. Although it did not strive to be as funny as *You Bet Your Life, I've Got a Secret* was another popular quiz show that drew its appeal from the clever repartee among the panel of celebrities. The remaining show among the top 10 was *General Electric Theater,* a dramatic anthology hosted by future president Ronald Reagan. Other westerns to debut included *Wagon Train, Bat Masterson,* and *Maverick,* starring James Garner and Jack Kelly as the smooth-talking, poker-playing, peace-loving Maverick brothers who preferred to use their wits rather than their guns but sometimes had to employ both.

Marshal Matt Dillon, portrayed by actor James Arness, was oblivious to the unrequited affection of Miss Kitty, the saloon keeper played by Amanda Blake in the top-rated western *Gunsmoke. (Photofest)*

Leave It to Beaver also debuted in 1957. It was one of several situation comedies from the late 1950s and early 1960s that presented an idealized view of the white, middle-class American family. Shown mostly from the point of the Beaver (Jerry Mathers), a seven-year-old boy, it presented American life as a series of minor trials and challenges, all of which were learning experiences. Beaver's parents, Ward and June Cleaver (Hugh Beaumont and Barbara Billingsley) provided guidance and insisted that their children always strive to do the right thing. As in *Father Knows Best,* the father was a caring, if somewhat distant authoritarian figure, but the mother was also intelligent, competent, committed, and loving, if deferential.

Perry Mason was a popular new show based on the successful novels by Erle Stanley Gardner about an unbeatable defense lawyer who saves his clients by figuring out the actual perpetrators. Raymond Burr starred as Mason; Barbara Hale as Della Street, his efficient and dedicated secretary; and William Hopper as his private detective, Paul Drake. William Talman was Hamilton Burger, the prosecutor whom Burr beat episode after episode.

American Bandstand, a rock 'n' roll show directed at teenagers and young adults, played an important role in helping rock music find a large, nationwide audience and in promoting the success of specific songs and performers. It aired weekday afternoons after school, although it also had a prime-time slot in fall 1957. The program featured young people dancing to the latest hits, and several of the dancers who regularly appeared developed their own followings among viewers. The two-year romance between dancers Bob Clayton and Justine Carrelli, in particular, appealed to television viewers. In addition to playing records, host Dick Clark also featured live performances by most of the top singers of the period, who benefited from their exposure on the show. These included Frankie Avalon, Chubby Checker, Fabian, and Bobbie Rydell. Notable exceptions were Elvis Presley and Ricky Nelson, who declined to perform. The team of Paul Simon and Art Garfunkel appeared as Tom and Jerry on the 1957 Thanksgiving show, when they sang their hit "Hey, School-girl." *American Bandstand* began as a local program in Philadelphia in 1952, and Clark, a radio disc jockey, took over as host in 1956. ABC picked it up as a network program in 1957 and it became ABC's longest-running series, lasting through 1987, and then two more years in syndication.

Other new shows from the season included *To Tell the Truth,* a game show, and situation comedies *Bachelor Father,* which starred John Forsythe as a care-free bachelor whose social life is complicated when his 13-year-old niece (Noreen Corcoran) comes to live with him, and *The Real McCoys,* which starred Walter Brennan, Richard Crenna, and Kathy Nolan in American television's first successful rural sitcom. Set in northern California, *The Real McCoys* depicted the trials, tribulations, and endearing moments experienced by a close-knit farming family headed by the irascible Grandpappy Amos (Brennan). Movie directors John Frankenheimer, George Roy Hill, and Arthur Penn made their television debuts on NBC's *The Tonight Show,* where Jack Paar replaced Steve Allen as host. Known for his displays of emotion, Paar also added another new dimension to the program by openly asserting his political views.

Movies

The top films of 1957 question misplaced authority, explore the growing awareness of abnormal psychology, and insist on the importance of acting in good faith and assuming full responsibility for decisions. David Lean's *The Bridge on the River Kwai,* starring Alec Guinness, William Holden, Jack Hawkins, and Sessue Hayakawa, won Academy Awards for best picture, director, actor (Guinness), cinematography (Jack Hildyard), editing (Peter Taylor), and score (Malcolm Arnold). The movie tells the story of British prisoners of war who build a railway bridge for the Japanese in Burma during World War II. They are driven not only by their captors but by their own colonel (Guinness), who becomes obsessed by the task, which he has embraced to maintain a sense of purpose among his troops and to demonstrate British character and toughness to the Japanese. The film costars Holden as an American assigned to destroy the bridge. Peter Boulle, who wrote the 1952 novel on which the film is based, was credited for the screenplay and won the Academy Award for it; however, the actual writers were Carl Foreman and Michael Wilson, who were blacklisted in Hollywood at the time and unable to receive credit for their work. In 1996, the Writers Guild of America officially credited them as cowriters.

Joanne Woodward won the Academy Award for best actress for her portrayal of a woman with multiple personalities in *The Three Faces of Eve.* The movie brought to the forefront the public's growing interest in abnormal psychology and mental health. Based on the best-selling 1956 novel by Grace Metalious, Mark Robson's *Peyton Place* airs the hidden scandals in a small, seemingly respectable New England town. Joshua Logan adapted *Sayonara,* James Michener's 1954 update of the *Madame Butterfly* story, this time set during the Korean War. Starring Marlon Brando, Red Buttons, and Miyoshi Umeki, it centers on a love story between an American military officer and a Japanese woman who are forbidden by official American policy to wed. Billy Wilder's *Witness for the Prosecution* stars Marlene Dietrich, Charles Laughton, and Tyrone Power in the adaptation of Agatha Christie's novel and play. The suspenseful courtroom drama climaxes with an ironic plot twist at the end. Wilder also directed Gary Cooper, Audrey Hepburn, and Maurice Chevalier in *Love in the Afternoon,* about a love affair between a wealthy, older American man and a shy French girl. Set in Paris, the movie features Chevalier as Hepburn's wise and worldly father. Laurence Olivier directed himself and Marilyn Monroe in *The Prince and the Showgirl,* a love comedy about a flighty showgirl who attracts the attention of a prince from eastern Europe who has come to London in 1911 for the coronation of King George V. Otto Preminger's adaptation of George Bernard Shaw's play *St. Joan* stars Jean Seberg as Joan of Arc. Graham Greene wrote the screenplay. Andy Griffith rose to fame in his film debut as a folksy, homespun philosopher with a dark side in Elia Kazan's *A Face in the Crowd.* Written by Budd Schulberg, who collaborated with Kazan in 1954 in *On the Waterfront,* the movie addresses the new capacity of television to create instant stars of people whom the public knows only by their exterior facades. It costars Patricia Neal, Walter Matthau, Lee Remick, and Anthony Franciosa.

Sidney Lumet's first movie, *Twelve Angry Men,* is notable for introducing television filming techniques to Hollywood. It stars Henry Fonda as a juror of sound reason and good conscience who insists on giving careful consideration to the arguments in favor of a Puerto Rican boy who upon a cursory review of the evidence, seems clearly guilty of killing his father. Lee J. Cobb, Ed Begley, Jack Warden, and E. G. Marshall costar as other jurors. Reginald Rose wrote the original television play, which aired in September 1954 on *Studio One.* Lumet, who began his career directing for theater and television, used a single static set—something that was never before done in a major Hollywood film, because it was assumed audiences would become bored. However, the technique was more permissible on television, which until 1957 had mostly been filmed live. Lumet made the movie dynamic and achieved visual variety and drama by employing 365 separate takes from multiple camera angles, another television technique.[11]

Burt Lancaster stars as a journalist seduced by power in Alexander Mackendrick's *Sweet Smell of Success.* Written by leftist playwright and screenwriter Clifford Odets, the movie takes an unusually critical view of American business and politics for a 1950s Hollywood movie. On the flip side, *Jet Pilot* is a patriotic spy film in which John Wayne not only resists the efforts of a Soviet female spy, played by Janet Leigh, to induce him to defect, he also wins her love and convinces her to defect to the United States. *Jet Pilot* was directed by Josef von Sternberg under the auspices of Howard Hughes. Based on George Kaufman's 1955 Broadway musical, *Silk Stockings* is a remake of the 1939 Greta Garbo movie *Ninotchka,* which likewise celebrates the virtues of capitalism over communism. Directed by Rouben Mamoulian, *Silk Stockings* stars Fred Astaire, Cyd Charisse, Janis Page, and Peter Lorre. Cole Porter wrote the music and the lyrics.

Sam Fuller, who directed the first Korean War movie, *The Steel Helmet* (1951), also directed one of the earliest Vietnam War films. Released eight years before U.S. military troops were introduced, *China Gate* revolves around a female Eurasian saloon keeper who helps a squad of soldiers from the French Foreign Legion destroy a communist supply depot. It was the first Hollywood film to show American soldiers fighting in Vietnam, although they do so under the auspices of the French. The movie, which stars Angie Dickinson and features Nat "King" Cole, was doubly topical in that it condemns both the Vietnamese communists and American racism.

Kirk Douglas stars in Stanley Kubrick's *Paths of Glory,* which shows the efforts of a French colonel (Douglas) during World War I to save the lives of three of his soldiers who are being sacrificed as scapegoats for the commanding general's incompetence. Although the offending officers are not American, few films during the Eisenhower years were so overtly critical of an ally's military behavior or the corruption of top-ranking figures of authority. Douglas also plays "Doc" Holliday to Lancaster's Marshal Wyatt Earp in John Sturges's *Gunfight at the O.K. Corral,* a western that presents the showdown between the forces of law and order, represented by Earp, and elements of lawlessness and selfish greed, represented by the Clantons. The confrontation between the Earps and Clantons had earlier been filmed in Allan Dwan's *Frontier Marshal* (1939) and John Ford's *My Darling Clementine* (1946), and Sturges treated it again in a 1967 sequel, *Hour of the Gun.* Frank Perry gave a different slant to the tale in *Doc* (1972), but in the 1957 treatment, the forces of civilization and order are called upon to protect the community against greedy, selfish forces of anarchy.

George Abbott and Stanley Donen adapted the hit Broadway musical *The Pajama Game* to film. Choreographed by Bob Fosse, it stars Doris Day and John Raitt in a love story set during a labor strike at a pajama factory. George Cukor directed Gene Kelly and Mitzi Gaynor is *Les Girls,* a musical comedy about the personal relationships within a European cabaret act, as seen from different points of view. Cole Porter wrote the music, which includes "Why Am I So Gone (About That Girl)," a spoof of Marlon Brando in *The Wild One* (1953). Orry-Kelly won the Academy Award for best costume design. Elvis Presley's second movie—and his first in color—was Hal Kanter's *Loving You,* a story about a country boy who is pushed into stardom by a persistent agent that has clear parallels to Presley's own career. He next starred as a convict who uses his guitar as a means of gaining freedom in Richard Thorpe's *Jailhouse Rock.* Presley was praised for his spirited choreography of the title song, which became a top hit, and the movie established his image as a rebel with a guitar.

Although male stars consistently commanded greater popularity than female stars in the United States throughout the decade, 1957 was the only year from that period when no women were among the 10 leading Hollywood box office draws. It was also a year when popular music performers exerted an especially strong appeal on moviegoers, and for the first time in several years, their popularity introduced some younger faces into the Hollywood pantheon of popular male actors. The top-10 box office draws were Rock Hudson, Wayne, Pat Boone, Presley, Frank Sinatra, Cooper, Holden, James Stewart, Jerry Lewis, and Yul Brynner. Humphrey Bogart died of throat cancer at age 57. He was survived by his wife and sometimes costar Lauren Bacall and their two children.

Notable foreign films included Charlie Chaplin's *A King in New York,* Ingmar Bergman's *Wild Strawberries,* and Roger Vadim's *And God Created Women.* Made in Britain, *A King in New York* fiercely satirizes HUAC, which had helped drive Chaplin from the country in 1952. Chaplin makes literal the metaphorical farce of the hearings when his character accidentally turns a fire hose on his interrogators. Subsequently, however, the sinister reality of the committee manifests, as the congressmen intimidate a little boy into becoming an informer who identifies several of his parents' political colleagues. The films ends as the once-spirited boy has been clearly traumatized and become frightened and withdrawn. *A King in New York* was not released in the United States until 1976.

Swedish-made *Wild Strawberries,* which received an Academy Award nomination for best original screenplay, stars Victor Sjöström as a self-important university professor who gains deep insight into life when he takes his daughter-in-law, whom he does not like, on a long car ride. In the process, he examines his life and reviews his past with her when they stop at his childhood home. The film costars Ingrid Thulin and Bibi Andersson.

Brigitte Bardot became an international sex symbol after her performance in French director Vadim's *And God Created Women,* about a newlywed 18-year-old girl in St. Tropez who becomes discontented in her marriage. Bardot's pouting lips, accentuated breasts, skimpy dress, and wild, erotic dancing not only established her career, they also introduced a more openly erotic direction in French cinema. Italian sex symbol Sophia Loren made her U.S. film debut in Jean Negulesco's *Boy on a Dolphin,* about an aquatic treasure hunt set in the Greek islands.

Literature

In March 1957, customs agents seized a shipment of Allen Ginsberg's poem "Howl," which they maintained was obscene. It had been first published in England in 1956 by Villiers. The American Civil Liberties Union contested the seizure, on the grounds that the poem was not obscene, and after the book editor of the San Francisco *Chronicle* defended the poem in a newspaper column, the U.S. attorney in San Francisco declined to initiate condemnation proceedings. However, the local police subsequently arrested publisher Lawrence Ferlinghetti, who had issued the first American edition in fall 1956 and sold the book in his City Lights Bookstore. But on October 3, Municipal Court judge Clayton Horn issued a 39-page ruling finding Ferlinghetti not guilty of publishing or selling obscene writings.

The legal ruling that Ginsberg's profanity-laden "Howl" is not obscene helped establish a precedent that enabled other writers to employ images and language hitherto forbidden in American literature. The *Evergreen Review,* which the Grove Press introduced in 1957, republished "Howl" that year, thereby giving it greater national exposure than Lawrence Ferlinghetti's City Lights Books was able to provide—although the court case generated more press coverage than the poem would otherwise have garnered. *Evergreen* quickly became a nationwide organ for the Beats and other alternative voices—its second issue was a special on the "San Francisco Scene"—and among the writers it published in its first year were Jack Kerouac, Albert Camus,

Samuel Beckett, Jean-Paul Sartre, Eugène Ionesco, Frank O'Hara, and poets Ferlinghetti, Charles Olson, Robert Duncan, and William Carlos Williams. Other poetry from 1957 included Denise Levertov's *Here and Now,* Theodore Roethke's *The Exorcism,* Richard Wilbur's *Poems 1943–1956,* James Wright's *The Green Wall,* and in England, Ted Hughes's first poetry collection, *The Hawk in the Rain.* Robert Penn Warren won the Pulitzer Prize for *Promises: Poems 1954–56.*

Beat writer Jack Kerouac published *On the Road,* which he wrote in three weeks while typing on a continuous roll of teletype paper. The autobiographical novel remains popular to the present, especially among college students. Like jazz and rock 'n' roll, which was truly hitting its stride in 1957, *On the Road* celebrates life force and raw, frenetic energy as it tells the story of Kerouac's travels across America in the late 1940s with his wild, unpredictable friend Neal Cassady. At the same time, it presents a largely sympathetic picture of America's underclass, without altogether championing it. Kerouac accepts the poor, working-class people with whom he comes into contact, some of whom are alcoholics, derelicts, and/or drug users, without either condemning their chaotic and often unstructured lives or presenting them as victims. *On the Road* introduces the automobile to the long-standing tradition of American stories about men who bond as they travel across the land. In so doing, it draws upon the promise of freedom, speed, and adventure that cars made available in the postwar era to middle- and working-class young Americans.

Another work of enduring American fiction from the opposite end of the political spectrum is *Atlas Shrugged* by Ayn Rand. Rand, author of *The Fountainhead* (1943), was a prominent anticommunist Russian émigré who fled to America as a young woman in 1926, shortly after Stalin came to power. In 1948, at the behest of the influential Motion Picture Alliance for the Preservation of American Ideals, she wrote *A Screen Guide for Americans,* which served as an early Hollywood production code. The *Screen Guide* spelled out what was and was not acceptable in the portrayal of businessmen; common people; poverty; social, political, and economic institutions; and anything else that might influence how viewers feel about communism and capitalism. Ironically, like *On the Road,* whose lawlessness and recklessness the conservative Rand doubtlessly deplored, *Atlas Shrugged* also rejects collective society in favor of radical individualism. However, Rand places greater emphasis on self-responsibility, as she explores the implications of and possibilities for individual freedom and self-reliance. The story, which was widely assigned as high school reading throughout the second half of the century, imagines a futuristic society based on the oath "I will never live for the sake of another man, nor ask another man to live for mine." It sold some 125,000 copies when it first appeared, and eventually more than 2 million copies were purchased.

Beat writer Jack Kerouac (right) poses with his friend Neal Cassady, whose escapades inspired *On the Road.* (Photofest)

Other works of fiction included Isaac Bashevis Singer's *Gimpel the Fool and Other Stories,* which were translated from the original Yiddish and mostly set in Jewish ghettos in Poland. J. D. Salinger published his novella, *Zooey,* a companion piece to his long short story "Franny" (1955), about a dysfunctional middle-class family. They were published together in 1961. Another *New Yorker* writer, John Cheever, also described dysfunctional middle-class life in his autobiographical novel, *The Wapshot Chronicle.* In *The Town,* William Faulkner returned to the poor, white, rural Snopes family he had introduced in *The Hamlet* (1940). He concluded the Snopes trilogy in 1959, when he published *The Mansion.* Vladimir Nabokov, a Russian émigré, published *Pnin,* about a Russian intellectual who comes to terms with his new life in America. Like Saul Bellow in *Seize the Day* (1956), Bernard Malamud, in *The Assistant,* tries to find redemption through the empathy and self-knowledge that derive from suffering. The tightly written novel has been praised especially for its almost poetic use of language.

British novelist Lawrence Durrell published *Justine,* the first volume of his *Alexandria Quartet,* an exploration of modern love set in Egypt. Nevil Shute, another British author, published *On the Beach,* a best-selling tale of the final days of human existence after a nuclear war in 1964 kills everyone in the Northern Hemisphere and issues a radioactive cloud that moves slowly but inevitably toward Australia, where it promises to kill everybody there, too. In 1959, Stanley Kramer adapted it into a film starring Gregory Peck, Ava Gardner, and Anthony Perkins. Other popular fiction included *The Cat in the Hat,* the first of the rhyming, whimsical, imaginatively illustrated children's books by Dr. Seuss, pen name of Theodore Geisel.

Among the notable nonfiction was *Nuclear Weapons and Foreign Policy* by Harvard professor Henry Kissinger, who later became Richard Nixon's national security adviser and secretary of state. Kissinger argues for a doctrine of limited nuclear war, in contrast to the prevailing belief that the Soviet Union must be opposed either by a policy that endorses full-scale nuclear war or by conventional military means that preclude nuclear weapons altogether. In making his argument, Kissinger underscores the importance of deterrence, which became the cornerstone of U.S. nuclear policy throughout the cold war. Deterrence worked on the assumption that the Soviets would restrain their actions if they truly believed that the United States was willing to react with weapons of mass destruction. One ironic result was that the more dangerous the weapons were, the less likely they were to be employed.

In *The Naked God,* Howard Fast describes his decision to leave the Communist Party. Fast had served time in federal prison for contempt of Congress as a result of his refusal in 1950 to give HUAC the names of antifascists who had contributed to a Spanish hospital in which Fast had worked during the Spanish Civil War. While in prison, he wrote *Spartacus,* which was probably the main reason why he was awarded the 1954 Stalin Peace Prize from the Soviet Union. But he became disaffected with the party and parted from it in 1956. Mary McCarthy published her autobiographical *Memories of a Catholic Girlhood,* and Norman Mailer published his influential essay, "The White Negro." Linguist Noam Chomsky introduced the notion of "deep structures" embedded within language in his *Systematic Structures.*

French existentialist novelist Albert Camus won the Nobel Prize in literature. Soviet author Boris Pasternak issued an indictment of the Soviet system in *Dr. Zhivago,* which he smuggled out of Russia and published in Italy. The novel had been first accepted but then rejected by the official Soviet publishing house. The story centers on Dr. Yuri Zhivago, a married man who falls in love with Lara, another man's mistress, during World War I. The story becomes a tale of frustrated love as the hardships they endure because of the Russian Revolution keep Yuri and Lara apart. Because of its unflattering portrayal of communism, the book was outlawed in the Soviet Union and praised in the United States, where it was published in English in 1958. In 1965, David Lean directed the Academy Award–nominated film adaptation, starring Omar Sharif, Geraldine Chaplin, and Julie Christie. Pasternak was awarded the 1958 Nobel Prize in literature but was not allowed to travel to Sweden to accept it. Instead he was expelled from the Soviet Writers Union and denounced as a traitor in official publications. To avoid being exiled from Russia he wrote to Khrushchev acknowledging his political weakness. He then endured internal exile at a writers' colony near Moscow, until his death in 1960.

Theater, Music, and the Visual Arts

Two Broadway musicals became major hits that remain in the repertoire. Meredith Wilson's Pulitzer Prize–winning *The Music Man* starred Robert Preston in the story of a fast-talking huckster who falls in love with a small-town Iowa spinster. The plot plays off a long-standing tradition in American humor centering on the confidence man, or con man, as he came to be called. Hit songs included "Seventy-Six Trombones," "Gary, Indiana" (which ironically celebrates the city built for the steel industry as though it were a small, rural town), and "Trouble" ("You've got trouble, right here in River City").

Leonard Bernstein composed the music and Stephen Sondheim wrote the lyrics for *West Side Story,* which Jerome Robbins choreographed. The Romeo and Juliet–type tale of a tragic love affair between an Italian boy and a Puerto Rican girl in New York City tapped into public concern about not only antagonisms between immigrant groups but also the problem of gangs and out-of-control youth, which increasingly became a subject of discussion throughout the 1950s and which also found expression in such films as *The Wild One* (1953), *Rebel Without a Cause* (1955), and *The Blackboard Jungle* (1955). Bernstein's score is influenced by his then-growing interest in jazz, and Robbins's choreography, by his interest in ballet and modern dance. Hit songs included "Tonight," "Maria," and "America." Also, Beatrice Lillie and Billy De Wolfe starred in Sammy Fain's *Ziegfeld Follies.*

Among the stage plays to premiere on Broadway were Ketti Frings's Pulitzer Prize–winning *Look Homeward, Angel,* which was based on Thomas Wolfe's autobiographical novel and starred Anthony Perkins; William Inge's *The Dark at the Top of the Stairs,* an examination of a conflicted personal relationship; Noël Coward's *Nude with Violin;* and Eugene O'Neill's *A Moon for the Misbegotten.* Maureen Stapleton and Cliff Robertson starred in Tennessee Williams's *Orpheus Descending,* which was a reworking of the playwright's earlier drama *Battle of Angels* (1940). Peter Ustinov wrote and starred in *Romanoff and Juliet,* a comedy about a Russian boy and American girl torn apart by the cold war. Ustinov also directed and starred in the 1961 film adaptation.

The spirit of experimentation was strong in all of the arts in the late 1950s, and this was evident when in a move to encourage new choreographers to push the limits of dance, the Ballet Theater, which changed its name to the American Ballet Theater, performed 15 new works without orchestral accompaniment or new scenery. Moreover, the dancers broke with convention by performing in their practice clothes. George Balanchine choreographed *Square Dance* and Igor Stravinsky's *Agon* for the New York City Ballet. In a more conventional performance, Margot Fonteyn and Michael Somes danced *Cinderella* with the Royal Ballet on television. Opera star Ezio Pinza, who had starred in *South Pacific* on Broadway, conductor Arturo Toscanini, and composer Jean Sibelius all died in 1957.

Several of the top jazz performers and innovators received national and international exposure on television and in the movies. In early December, Billie Holiday sang "Fine and Mellow" on a live television performance. Steve Allen hosted *All Star Jazz,* a late-December special that featured a number of important performers. Miles Davis wrote the soundtrack for French film director Louis Malle's thriller *Lift to the Scaffold,* and the Modern Jazz Quartet wrote the score for Vadim's *No Sun in Venice.* Among the important jazz albums released were Nat Cole's *Love Is the Thing,* John Coltrane's *Blue Train,* and Charles Mingus's *Tijuana Moods,* which draws upon Latin influences. In reaction to the so-called cerebral style, also known as symphonic jazz, which the Modern Jazz Quartet pioneered by combining jazz with forms from classical music, Mingus began to develop freer improvisational forms. The Modern Jazz Quartet, meanwhile, toured the British islands, making 88 performances in four months. Bandleader Jimmy Dorsey, who pioneered the big jazz bands in the 1930s and hosted his own television show, *Stage Show,* from 1954 to 1956, died in June, about half a year after his brother, Tommy, another prominent bandleader, passed away.

Culture wars between the generations were waged increasingly through music as the 1950s progressed. In 1957, Pat Boone, a straight-A Ivy Leaguer who projected Christian wholesomeness, rose to prominence as a socially conservative rival to hip-thrusting Elvis Presley, who lit up the stage with new songs such as "Jailhouse Rock" and made girls swoon with such sentimental numbers as "Loving You." Those were the title songs of the two movies in which Presley appeared in 1957. He also issued *Elvis' Christmas Album,* and his songs such as "All Shook Up!" inspired other musicians such as Jerry Lee Lewis, who electrified audiences with "Whole Lotta Shaking."

But if Presley challenged social convention with his open sex appeal and frenetic rock 'n' roll, Boone appeared to embody middle-class virtues of family, devotion, and clean living, and his music appealed to

Elvis Presley was "the King" of rock 'n' roll. *(Photofest)*

emotional sentiment, not pounding rhythms or raw sexual energy. The fact that a willing audience was anxious for the sound and image that Boone projected is evident in his million-selling hits of 1957: "I'll Be Home," "I Almost Lost My Mind," and "Ain't That a Shame." "Love Letters in the Sand" was another big hit from the year. Boone, who became a regular on Arthur Godfrey's *Talent Scouts* in 1954, was given his own television show in 1957, *The Pat Boone Show,* which lasted through the end of the 1959–60 season. He became one of the top box office draws of the year—beating out Elvis—after he made his movie debut in Harry Levin's *Bernardine* and then starred in Levin's *April Love.*

Although more sprightly than Boone, the Everly Brothers offered a less frenzied rock alternative to Elvis in such songs as "Bye Bye Love" and "Wake Up Little Susie," and Buddy Holly and the Crickets released their first single, "That'll Be the Day." But even their tame form of rock had its critics. "Wake Up Little Susie," a song about a teenage boy and girl who miss their curfew because they fall asleep at the movies, was banned in Boston, and a psychiatrist at Columbia University likened rock dancing to the medieval St. Vitus plague where victims could not stop dancing.[12] On the other hand, Bill Haley and His Comets, who pioneered rock 'n' roll, received an enthusiastic reception when they brought their fast-paced, energetic music to England on their first international tour.

Other hits from the year included "Maria" from *West Side Story,* Paul Anka's "Diana," Harry Belafonte's "Banana Boat Song," Debbie Reynolds's "Tammy," Fats Domino's "Blueberry Hill," and Little Richard's "Lucille."

An exhibition of 328 works by Pablo Picasso traveled to New York, Philadelphia, and Chicago in honor of the painter's 75th birthday, and the Art Institute of Chicago hosted a special Claude Monet exhibit. Mexican mural painter, Diego Rivera, and Romanian sculptor, Constantin Brancusi, both died.

CHRONICLE OF EVENTS

1957

January 4: *Collier's* magazine publishes its final issue. The cover features Grace Kelly, now Princess Grace of Monaco. The demise of *Collier's* anticipates the later failure of *Look* and *Life,* all of which are photo-oriented magazines that struggle to compete with television.

January 5: President Eisenhower asks Congress for authority to use force to protect Middle Eastern countries from communist aggression. This becomes known as the Eisenhower Doctrine.

January 6: Elvis Presley makes his final appearance on *The Ed Sullivan Show.* Although Sullivan defends Presley as a wholesome young man, he appeases the singer's critics by blacking out the screen from Presley's waist down so as not to show his hip gyrations.

January 10: Martin Luther King, Jr., helps organize the Southern Christian Leadership Conference to promote civil rights.

January 10: Harold Macmillan, leader of the right wing of Britain's Conservative Party, is sworn in as prime minister. He replaces Anthony Eden, another Conservative, who stepped down due to poor health.

January 10: Four black churches and the homes of two black ministers are destroyed by dynamite in Montgomery, Alabama.

January 11: Eisenhower proclaims a Bicentennial Day to honor the 200th birthday of Alexander Hamilton, one of the nation's Founding Fathers.

January 14: Movie star Humphrey Bogart dies from cancer of the esophagus at age 57.

January 16: Classical conductor Arturo Toscanini dies at age 89.

January 21: Eisenhower is sworn in as president for his second term.

January 30: The United Nations General Assembly calls upon South Africa to reconsider its policy of apartheid.

January 31: France makes a full military commitment to fight Algerian nationalists.

February 2: The United Nations calls on Israel to withdraw its troops from Gaza.

February 15: Hard-liner Andrei Gromyko is appointed Soviet foreign minister.

February 18: Playwright Arthur Miller is indicted for contempt of Congress for his uncooperative testimony before HUAC in 1956.

February 21: *The Spirit of St. Louis* opens. The film biography of aviator Charles Lingbergh stars James Stewart.

February 24: Pope Pius permits Catholics to use pain relievers "if advantage of higher worth" is achieved.[13]

March 1: Israel agrees to remove its troops immediately from Gaza. The region falls under UN control briefly before superior Egyptian forces compel the peacekeepers to yield.

March 6: Ghana, the former British African colony of the Gold Coast, achieves independence.

March 9: Congress approves the Eisenhower Doctrine, which establishes U.S. willingness to send military and economic aid to any Middle Eastern country requesting U.S. assistance against communism.

March 20: Eisenhower meets in Bermuda with new British prime minister Macmillan. The purpose of the summit is to restore relations that had been strained due to Britain's participation in the Suez military action of 1956.

March 22: San Francisco is struck by the strongest earthquake since 1906.

March 25: France, West Germany, Italy, Luxembourg, Belgium, and the Netherlands sign the Treaty of Rome to form the European Economic Community (popularly known as the Common Market), the European Investment Bank to assist underdeveloped countries, the European Atomic Energy Authority, and the European Court of Justice.

March 25: Customs agents seize a shipment of Allen Ginsberg's "Howl," which was first published in England by Villiers.

April 4: Cheryl Christina Crane, the 14-year-old daughter of movie star Lana Turner, stabs Johnny Stompanato, Turner's abusive boyfriend, to death while the couple is quarreling. The case attracts enormous publicity, but an inquest held on April 11, 1958, rules that the killing was justifiable homicide, and Crane is not charged with murder. Aspects of Woody Allen's film *September* (1987) are apparently inspired by the incident.

April 11: Nathan Juran's *Hellcats of the Navy* opens in San Diego. The film costars future-president Ronald Reagan and his future wife, Nancy Davis, in their first on-screen pairing.

April 14: Sidney Lumet's film *12 Angry Men* opens, starring Henry Fonda.

April 20: The *Mayflower II* sets sail from Plymouth, England, to reenact the crossing by the original ship that brought the Pilgrims to America in 1620.

April 23: Nobel Prize winner Albert Schweitzer urges the Nobel committee to mobilize world opinion against nuclear testing.

April 26: Eisenhower sends the Sixth Fleet to the Middle East to support King Hussein of Jordan, who squelches a conspiracy to overthrow him, declares martial law, and forms a new, pro–Western government.

May 2: Senator Joseph McCarthy dies at age 48.

May 4: Disc jockey Alan Freed hosts *The Rock 'n' Roll Show,* the first network television special devoted to rock music.

May 13: Virginia celebrates the 350th anniversary of the Jamestown settlement, the first permanent British settlement in the New World. Air force jets bring copies of the original charter from England; 114 ships from nations allied with the United States convene at the festival's naval review; and Eisenhower and Nixon make speeches.

May 15: Great Britain explodes its first hydrogen bomb.

May 17: Twenty-five thousand civil rights demonstrators join a prayer pilgrimage in Washington, D.C.

May 21: In celebration of the 30th anniversary of the first trans-Atlantic flight, the *Spirit of St. Louis II* crosses the ocean in 6.7 hours.

May 28: Major League Baseball grants the Brooklyn Dodgers and New York Giants permission to move their teams to Los Angeles and San Francisco, respectively, which they do after the conclusion of the 1957 season.

May 29: John Sturges's *Gunfight at the O.K. Corral,* starring Burt Lancaster and Kirk Douglas, opens.

June 1: The Soviet Union announces that it is prepared to launch its first satellite.

June 2: Secretary Khrushchev announces on U.S. television that the Soviet Union is willing to pursue a policy of disarmament with the United States.

June 3: The United States joins the Baghdad Pact to contain communist expansion in the Middle East.

June 5: The American Medical Association votes to study the use of stimulants in athletics.

Jerry Mathers (the Beaver) and Jeri Weil are cast as cute kids in *Leave It to Beaver. (Photofest)*

June 11: The first U.S. test of an intercontinental missile fails when the Atlas rocket explodes shortly after takeoff from Cape Canaveral.

June 13: Mayflower II arrives at Plymouth, Massachusetts.

June 17: John Diefenbaker is invited to become Canada's prime minister.

June 17: Ruling on several Red Scare–related civil liberties cases, the Supreme Court reverses earlier convictions and restricts the extent to which the government can punish an individual for maintaining radical political views. Civil libertarians and liberals praise the decisions, but hard-line anticommunists condemn it.

July 4: Khrushchev suppresses an attempt by Communist Party hard-liners Malenkov, Molotov, and Kaganovich to topple him.

July 5: Singer-actor Frank Sinatra and movie star Ava Gardner officially divorce.

July 6: Tennis star Althea Gibson becomes the first black player to win at Wimbledon.

July 11: Gibson is welcomed back to her home city of New York with a ticker tape parade.

July 20: Some 100,000 people go to Yankee Stadium in New York to listen to evangelist preacher

Billy Graham. On the platform with Graham is Vice President Nixon. The beginning of a six-week revival, the prayer meeting attracts the largest crowd in the stadium's history to that date.

July 30: Britain grants autonomy to Nigeria.

August 5: American Bandstand, hosted by Dick Clark, debuts on network television.

August 7: Rudolf Abel is indicted for spying for the Soviets.

August 26: The Soviet Union announces it has successfully tested an ICBM.

August 26: Ford Motor Company unveils its newest model, the Edsel, which turns out to be one of its greatest flops.

August 27: The jazz musical *West Side Story* opens on Broadway.

August 29: Congress passes the Civil Rights Act of 1957.

August 29: The film version of Broadway hit *The Pajama Game* opens. Directed by George Abbott and Stanley Donen, the movie stars Doris Day and John Raitt.

August 31: Malaya, the last of Britain's major Asian colonies, is granted independence and allowed to join the British Commonwealth.

September 1: Some 200,000 people attend services on the final day of Graham's evangelical revival in New York City.

September 2: The Little Rock, Arkansas, school crisis begins as Governor Orval Faubus calls in the National Guard to prevent black students from integrating Central High School.

September 4: In Britain, the Wolfenden report on homosexual offenses and prostitution recommends that homosexual acts between consenting adults no longer be considered criminal behavior.

September 4: Egypt and Syria form an economic union.

September 5: Fidel Castro leads an unsuccessful uprising in Cuba.

September 6: Disarmament talks between the United States and Soviet Union end without an agreement.

September 10: Segregationists bomb a public school in Nashville, Tennessee, that earlier admitted black students.

September 19: The United States conducts its first underground nuclear test.

September 22: The military junta that ruled Haiti for the previous three months installs François "Papa Doc" Duvalier as president.

September 24: Eisenhower orders the army's 101st Airborne Division to protect nine black students attempting to attend school at Little Rock, Arkansas's Central High School. He addresses the nation that evening to explain his action.

September 26: Nunnally Johnson's *The Three Faces of Eve* opens. Joanne Woodward later wins the Academy Award for her portrayal of a woman with multiple personalities.

October: Under direction from North Vietnam, communist insurgents in South Vietnam, later known as the Viet Cong, begin their campaign to overthrow the South Vietnamese government.

October 4: The Soviets launch *Sputnik I,* the first human-made satellite to orbit the Earth.

October 4: Jimmy Hoffa, who in July was acquitted on federal charges of corruption, is elected president of the Teamsters union.

October 4: Leave It to Beaver debuts on television.

October 10: The Milwaukee Braves defeat the New York Yankees to win baseball's World Series.

At 39 years old, Ted Williams of the Boston Red Sox became the oldest player ever to win Major League Baseball's batting championship in 1957. He won again in 1958. *(Photofest)*

Warren Spahn wins the Cy Young Award, although another Milwaukee pitcher, Bob Buhl, has the league's best win-loss record at 18-7. Yankee Tom Sturdivant and Chicago White Sox Dick Donovan tie for the best record in the American league at 16-6. St. Louis's Stan Musial (.351) and Boston's Ted Williams (.388) win the National and American League batting championships, respectively. Yankee Mickey Mantle repeats as the American Leagues MVP; Hank Aaron of the Braves is MVP of the National League.

October 10: Egypt sends troops to Syria, as border tensions between Syria and Turkey escalate.

October 16: Secretary of State Dulles warns that if the Soviets attack Turkey over its border dispute with Syria, the United States is prepared to take aggressive action against the Soviet Union. Khrushchev accuses Dulles of "brinkmanship"—going to the brink of nuclear war—but he soon tempers the Soviet position.

October 17: Queen Elizabeth II visits Eisenhower in Washington as part of a series of state visits to the United States and Canada.

October 22: The United States conducts its first successful test of an IRBM.

October 24: French fashion designer Christian Dior dies at age 52. Dior revolutionized the fashion industry in 1947 with his New Look.

October 26: Rudolf Abel is convicted as a Soviet spy.

November 3: The Soviets launch *Sputnik II,* carrying a dog, Laika.

November 5: For the first time, women in Britain are permitted to sit in the House of Lords.

November 15: Boasting of Soviet missile superiority, Khrushchev challenges the United States to a rocket-range shooting match.

November 19: Leonard Bernstein becomes the music director of the New York Philharmonic.

November 26: Eisenhower suffers a mild stroke.

December 1: Nineteen-year-old Charles Starkweather commits the first of a series of highly publicized murders in Wyoming and Nebraska.

December 6: The first U.S. attempt to launch a human-made satellite into outer space fails, as the Vanguard rocket carrying it explodes two seconds after liftoff.

December 16–19: NATO heads of state agree to establish a European-based nuclear missile force under U.S. command.

December 16: Macy's department store records its first $2-million day in store history.

Singer Nat "King" Cole's television show was canceled in December, possibly as fallout from the civil rights disturbances earlier in the year. *(Photofest)*

December 17: The United States successfully tests its first ICBM.

December 17: The *Nat King Cole* television show airs for the final time after failing to attract a major sponsor—due, in part, to advertisers' fears of a boycott of their products in the South.

December 29: The Detroit Lions win football's NFL championship by defeating the Chicago Bears 59-14. Cleveland's rookie running back, Jim Brown, leads the league with 942 yards, including a record-setting 237 yards in a single game. Brown, who starred in college at Syracuse, goes on to become one of the best, if not the best, rusher in NFL history. Cleveland quarterback Tom O'Connell leads the league in passing, and Baltimore Colt Raymond Berry in receiving. Baltimore's quarterback, Johnny Unitas, is named the MVP.

December 30: Steve Allen hosts an NBC special entitled *All Star Jazz* that features Louis Armstrong, Dave Brubeck, Paul Desmond, Duke Ellington, Woody Herman, Gene Krupa, Carmen McRae, and Charlie Ventura.

EYEWITNESS TESTIMONY

The greater the horror of our destructive capabilities, the less certain has it become that they will in fact be used.

> *Harvard professor and future secretary of state Henry Kissinger arguing for a policy of nuclear deterrence in* Nuclear Weapons and Foreign Policy *(1957), in Martin Gilbert,* A History of the Twentieth Century, *vol. 3 (2000), p. 164.*

I always believed the old adage that the FBI kept the Communist Party alive through their dues payments of their agents.

> *Former CIA director William Colby discussing in an interview in June 1994 the drop in membership in the American Communist Party from 31,000 in 1950 to just a few thousand by 1957, many of whom were FBI infiltrators, in Frances Stonor Saunders,* The Cultural Cold War: The CIA and the World of Arts and Letters *(2000), p. 191.*

The word "beat" originally meant poor, down and out, deadbeat, on the bum, sleeping in subways. Now that the word is belonging officially it is being made to stretch to include people who do not sleep in subways but have a certain new gesture, or attitude. . . . "Beat Generation" has simply become the slogan or label for a revolution in manners in America. Marlon Brando was not really the first to portray it on screen. Dane Clark with his pinched Dostoyevskyan face and Brooklyn accent, and of course Garfield, were the first. The private eyes were Beat, if you will recall. Bogart. . . .

I wrote *On the Road* in three weeks in the beautiful month of April 1951 while living in the Chelsea district in the lower West Side Manhattan, on a 100-foot roll and put the Beat Generation in words in there, saying at the point where I am taking part in a wild kind of collegiate party with a bunch of kids in an abandoned miner's shack[,] "These kids are great but where are Dean Moriarty and Carl Marx? Oh well I guess they wouldn't belong in this gang, they're too *dark,* too strange, too subterranean and I am slowly beginning to join a new kind of *beat generation*. . . ." [Italics Kerouac]

So then what horror I felt in 1957 and later 1958 naturally to suddenly see "Beat" being taken up by everybody, press and TV and Hollywood borscht circuit. . . .

And so now they have beatnik routines on TV, starting with satires about girls in black and fellows with snap-knives and sweat-shirts. . . .

But yet, but yet, woe, woe unto those who think that the Beat Generation means crime, delinquency, immorality, amorality. . . . [W]oe unto those who spit on the Beat Generation, the wind'll blow it back.

> *Novelist Jack Kerouac discussing in 1959 the term* beat, *which he popularized in 1957 with the publication of* On the Road, *in Stephen Ambrose and Douglas Brinkley, eds.,* Witness to America *(1999), pp. 435–36.*

I enjoyed only a glancing acquaintance with the Beat movement. Like others, I spent a lot of time in jazz clubs, nursing the two-beer minimum. I put on hornrimmed sunglasses at night. I went to parties in lofts where girls wore strange attire. I was hugely tickled by all forms of marijuana humor, though the talk back then was in inverse relation to the availability of that useful substance. In 1956, in Norfolk, Virginia, I had wandered into a bookstore and discovered . . . the *Evergreen Review,* then an early forum for Beat sensibility. It was an eye-opener. I was in the navy at the time, but I already knew people who would sit in circles on the deck and sing perfectly, in parts, all those early rock 'n' roll songs, who played bongos and saxophones, who had felt honest grief when Bird and later Clifford Brown died. By the time I got back to college, I found academic people deeply alarmed over the *cover* of the *Evergreen Review* then current, not to mention what was inside. It looked as if the attitude of some literary folks toward the Beat generation was the same as that of certain officers on my ship toward Elvis Presley. They used to approach those among the ship's company who seemed like likely sources— combed their hair like Elvis, for example. "What's his message?" they'd interrogate anxiously. "What does he want?"

We were at a transition point, a strange post-Beat passage of cultural time, with our loyalties divided. As bop and rock 'n' roll were to swing music and postwar pop, so was this new writing to the more established modernist tradition we were being exposed to then in college. . . .

On the negative side. . . . [the Beat] movement placed too much emphasis on youth, including the eternal variety.

Novelist Thomas Pynchon describing his early encounters with the Evergreen Review, *which first appeared in 1957, and with the Beat movement, in Pynchon,* Slow Learner *(1984), pp. 8–9.*

The gist of the [*Life* magazine] editorial was that in the last ten years this country had enjoyed an unparalleled prosperity, that it had come nearer to producing a classless society than any other nation, and that it was the most powerful country in the world, but that our novelists were writing as if they lived in packing boxes on the edge of the dump while they awaited admission to the poorhouse. . . .

I do not know that any . . . who answered considered the question specifically from the standpoint of the novelist with Christian concerns, who, presumably, would have an interest at least equal to the editors of *Life* in the "redeeming quality of spiritual purpose."

The Christian writer will feel that in the greatest depth of vision, moral judgment will be implicit. . . .

In the greatest fiction, the writer's moral sense coincides with his dramatic sense, and I see no way for it to do this unless his moral judgment is part of the very act of seeing, and he is free to use it. . . . [Belief in Christian dogma] frees the storyteller to observe. It is not a set of rules which fixes what he sees in the world. It affects his writing primarily by guaranteeing his respect for mystery. . . .

My own feeling is that writers who see by the light of their Christian faith will have, in these times, the sharpest eyes for the grotesque, for the perverse, and for the unacceptable. Redemption is meaningless unless there is cause for it in the actual life we live, and for the last few centuries there has been operating in our culture the secular belief that there is no such cause. . . .

Unless we are willing to accept our artists as they are, the answer to the question, "Who speaks for America today?" will have to be: the advertising agencies. . . .

Writer Flannery O'Connor in 1957 discussing her literary obligations as a Christian fiction writer, in O'Connor, Mystery and Manners *(1969), pp. 25–35.*

"Is anybody writing any kind of history about these times [in the aftermath of worldwide nuclear war]? . . ."

"There doesn't seem to be much point in writing stuff that nobody will read. . . ."

"The seismic records show about four thousand seven hundred [nuclear bombs were dropped]. . . ."

"The Russians never bombed Washington. . . . They proved that in the end. . . . I mean, the very first attack of all. . . ."

"Do you mean to say, we bombed Russia by mistake?"

"That's true. . . . The first one was the bomb on Naples. That was the Albanians, of course. Then there was the bomb on Tel Aviv. . . . Then the British and Americans intervened and made that demonstration flight over Cairo. Next day the Egyptians sent out all the serviceable bombers they'd got. . . . One got through to Washington, and two to London. . . . [T]hese aircraft were identified as Russian. . . ."

"But if it was a mistake, why didn't they get together and stop it? . . ."

"It's mighty difficult to stop a war when all the statesmen have been killed."

The scientist said, "The trouble is, the damn things got too cheap. . . . Every little pipsqueak country like Albania could have a stockpile. . . ."

"Another was the aeroplanes. . . . The Russians had been giving the Egyptians aeroplanes for years. . . . The big mistake was ever to have given them a long-range aeroplane. . . ."

A fictional exchange among the crew of the USS Swordfish *in the final days of human existence following a nuclear war in 1964, as portrayed in Nevil Shute's 1957 novel,* On the Beach, *(1974), pp. 73–77.*

"Couldn't anyone have stopped it [the nuclear war]?"

"I don't know . . . some kinds of silliness you just can't stop. . . . I mean, if a couple of hundred million people all decide that their national honour requires them to drop cobalt bombs upon their neighbour, well, there's not much that you or I can do about it. The only possible hope would have been to educate them out of their silliness. . . .

"You could have done something with newspapers. We didn't do it . . . because we . . . liked our newspapers with pictures of beach girls and headlines about cases of indecent assault. . . ."

Australian naval officer Peter Holmes explaining to his wife the cause of the fictional nuclear war, in Nevil Shute's 1957 novel, On the Beach *(1974), p. 268.*

Faith is the state of being ultimately concerned. . . . But man, in contrast to other living beings, has spiritual concerns—cognitive, aesthetic, social, political. Some of them are urgent . . . and each of them as well as the vital concerns can claim ultimacy for a human life or the life of a social group. If it claims ultimacy it demands the total surrender of him who accepts this claim, and it promises total fulfillment even if all other claims have to be subjected to it or rejected in its name. . . . The extreme nationalisms of our century are laboratories for the study of what ultimate concern means in all aspects of human existence. . . . Everything is centered in the only god, the nation—a god who certainly proves to be a demon, but who shows clearly the unconditional character of an ultimate concern.

But it is not only the unconditional demand made by that which is one's ultimate concern, it is also the promise of ultimate fulfillment which is accepted in the act of faith. . . .

Faith and culture can be affirmed only if the superego represents the norms and principles of reality. This leads to the question of how faith as a personal, centered act is related to the rational structure of man's personality which is manifest in his . . . ability to know the true and do the good, in his sense of beauty and justice. . . . Faith is not an act of any of his rational functions, as it is not an act of the unconscious, but it is an act in which both the rational and the nonrational elements of his being are transcended.

Faith as the embracing and centered act of the personality is "ecstatic." . . . [But] Faith is not an emotional outburst. This is not the meaning of ecstasy. . . . [It] is an act of the will.

Theologian Paul Tillich discussing problems of religious faith in the 20th century, in Tillich, Dynamics of Faith *(1957), pp. 1–9.*

The leaders of the Soviet Union, like the Czars before them, had their eyes on the Middle East. The Soviet goal was by no means merely the right to move ships through the Suez Canal, for less than 1 per cent of the Canal traffic was Russian. Neither was the goal Middle Eastern oil: the Soviet Union had no need for it and, indeed, exported oil itself. The Soviet objective was, in plain fact, power politics: to seize the oil, to cut the Canal and pipelines of the Middle East, and thus seriously to weaken Western civilization.

President Dwight Eisenhower commenting on the state of the Middle East in January 1957, in Eisenhower, The White House Years, *vol. 2 (1965), pp. 177–78.*

I went a few times. Most of his friends went, some almost every day, like Sinatra. Some were very loyal. He seemed to bring out the best in them all. He looked so awful, so terribly thin. His eyes were huge and they looked so frightened. They got bigger and bigger. It was real fear and yet there was always that gay, brave self. He'd have to be brought downstairs on the dumbwaiter and he'd sit and wait and wait for his Martini. He was allowed one, I think, or two. And that's how we used to find him, smoking and sipping that Martini.

Writer Truman Capote describing his visits with Humphrey Bogart prior to the actor's death on January 14, 1957, in Peter Bogdanovich, Pieces of Time *(1973), p. 97.*

Bogart is the man with a past. When he comes into a film, it is already 'the morning after'; sardonically victorious in his macabre combat with the angel, his face scared by what he has seen, and his step heavy from all he has learned, having ten times triumphed over his death, he will surely survive for us this one more time. . . . The Bogartian man is not defined by his contempt for the bourgeois virtues, by his courage or cowardice, but first of all by his existential maturity which little by little transforms life into a tenacious irony at the expense of death.

French film critic André Bazin writing in the journal Cahiers du Cinéma *in tribute to Humphrey Bogart upon the actor's death on January 14, 1957, in Peter Bogdanovich,* Pieces of Time *(1973), p. 85.*

Before all else, we seek, upon our common labor as a nation, the blessing of Almighty God. And the hopes in our hearts fashion the deepest prayers of our whole people.

May we pursue the right without self-righteousness.

May we know unity without conformity.

May we grow in strength without pride in self.

May we, in our dealings with all peoples of the earth, ever speak truth and serve justice.

And so shall America—in the sight of all men of good will—prove true to the honorable purposes that bind and rule us as a people in all this time of trial through which we pass.

The invocation to President Dwight Eisenhower's second inaugural speech of January 21, 1957, in Eisenhower, "Second Inaugural Address" (2001).

It doesn't make you a hoodlum just by wearing side-burns.

> *Acting student and future star Bruce Dern explaining on February 8, 1957, his decision to resign from the University of Pennsylvania track team rather than shave his Elvis Presley–style sideburns, in Clifton Daniel, ed.,* 20th Century Day by Day *(2000), p. 797.*

After thirty long years, the story of Charles A. Lindbergh's historic flight across the Atlantic from New York to Paris is re-enacted on the screen in Leland Hayward's and Billy Wilder's production of *The Spirit of St. Louis*. . . . And at last the magnificent achievement of the solo flier is dramatically portrayed in the medium most apt for its portrayal, with James Stewart playing the leading role.

As a straight-away visual re-creation of the background and facts of Lindbergh's flight . . . this picture would be hard to beat. It has drama, sentiment, humor, and a slight dash of destiny. It pictures the dogged perseverance of the youthful flier in simple, standard term. And it details his trans-Atlantic passage in exciting and suspenseful episodes.

> *Critic Bosley Crowther reviewing* The Spirit of St. Louis, *in Crowther, "The Spirit of St. Louis,"* New York Times, *February 22, 1957, p. 25.*

"Culture" is no longer a sissy word. A nation like ours can be virile. A nation like ours can be fantastically successful economically. But in a strange way the glue that holds things together is the nation's coefficient of idealism. . . . The tangible, visible, audible expression of national idealism is culture. Of all the expressions of present-day musical culture, the Boston Symphony Orchestra is the best.

> *Charles Douglas Jackson, special adviser to the president for psychological warfare, writing about the political uses of art and culture on March 26, 1957, in Frances Stonor Saunders,* The Cultural Cold War: The CIA and the World of Arts and Letters *(2000), p. 225.*

The question of what effect the Church has on the fiction writer who is a Catholic cannot always be answered by pointing to the presence of Graham Greene among us. One has to think not only of gifts that have ended in art or near it, but of gifts gone astray and of those never developed. In 1955, the editors of *Four Quarters* . . . printed a symposium on the subject of the dearth of Catholic writers among the graduates of Catholic colleges, and in subsequent issues published letters . . . in response. . . . These ranged from the statement of Mr. Philip Wylie that "A Catholic, if he is devout, i.e., sold on the authority of his Church, is also brain-washed, whether he realizes it or not" (and consequently does not have the freedom necessary to be a first-rate creative thinker) to the oft-repeated explanation that the Catholic in this country suffers from a parochial aesthetic and cultural insularity. . . .

If he [the Catholic writer] takes the Church for what she takes herself to be, he must decide what she demands of him and if and how his freedom is restricted by her. . . .

For the writer of fiction, everything has its testing point in the eye, an organ which eventually involves the whole personality and as much of the world as can be got into it. . . .

The fiction writer will discover . . . that he himself cannot move or mold reality in the interests of abstract truth. The writer learns . . . to be humble in the face of what-is . . . and . . . that fiction can transcend its limitations only by staying within them. . . .

The Catholic writer . . . will feel life from the standpoint of the central Christian mystery; that it has, for all its horror, been found by God to be worth dying for. But this should enlarge, not narrow his field of vision.

> *Fiction writer Flannery O'Conner discussing the relationship between literary fiction and factual truth in O'Connor, "The Church and the Fiction Writer,"* America: National Catholic Weekly Review, *March 30, 1957, pp. 733–35.*

A correspondent from Communist Czechoslovakia writes . . .

> I heard about rock 'n' roll. Is it a new style of jazz, or does it belong to popular music? I would be glad to hear it. How does Elvis Presley sing? I had lent a Canadian journal *Liberty*, issue from August 1956, and in this is a picture of Elvis Presley while singing and playing on guitar. He looks in ecstasy.

This came to me about the same time as a clipping from the *New York Times* ("Presley Records a Craze in Soviet Union") which stated that Elvis discs, cut on discarded hospital X-ray plates, are selling in Leningrad for $12.50 apiece. "Returning travelers report," wrote Harrison Salisbury, "that the singer is the latest craze of the Soviet zoot-suiters, or *stilyagi,* as they are called."

Yes, Virginia, there is an Elvis Presley.

Actually, from a strictly Marxist-Leninist viewpoint, you probably realize that he is a typical example of capitalist exploitation. Presley is an authentic folk-artist, in the tradition of the Negro blues-shouters, who has cleverly masqueraded as a *stilyagi* in order to capture the attention of the proletariat. Dismayed by his success, the American warmongers have urged their lackey intellectuals .. to discredit Presley. Only the jazz scholar John A. Wilson has had the courage to point out that Presley is merely "mixing a genuine musical heritage with a musical fad that was well under way long before he gained any prominence. . . ."

That's about the story to date, though it is rumored that the State Department—ever the servant of imperialism—is facilitating the anti-Presley campaign by importing large numbers of the calypso singers, by banana boat, from the American satellites in the Caribbean. If the situation becomes desperate . . . Presley will be drafted into the mercenary armies of Wall Street and deprived of his sideburns.

Magazine columnist "Mr. Harper" discussing Elvis Presley, in Harper, "Elvis the Indigenous," Harper's Magazine *(April 1957), p. 86.*

We are forced to regard every increase in the existing danger through the further creation of radioactive elements by atomic bomb explosions as a catastrophe for the human race, a catastrophe that must be prevented at all costs.

Nobel laureate Dr. Albert Schweitzer in a letter dated April 23, 1957, to the Nobel Prize committee, written in opposition to superpower nuclear testing, in Martin Gilbert, A History of the Twentieth Century, *vol. 3 (2000), p. 159.*

But as I began to watch Creole, I realized that it was Creole who held them all back. He had them on a short rein. Up there, keeping the beat with his whole body, wailing on the fiddle, with his eyes half closed, he was listening to everything, but he was listening to Sonny. He was having a dialogue with Sonny. He wanted Sonny to leave the shoreline and strike out for the deep water. He was Sonny's witness that deep water and drowning were not the same thing—he

had been there, and he knew. And he wanted Sonny to know. . . .

Creole started into something else, it was almost sardonic, it was *Am I Blue.* And, as though he commanded, Sonny began to play. Something began to happen. And Creole let out the reins. The dry, low, black man said something awful on the drums, Creole answered, and the drums talked back. . . .

Then Creole stepped forward to remind them that what they were playing was the blues. He hit something in all of them, he hit something in me, myself, and the music tightened and deepened, apprehension began to beat the air. Creole began to tell us what the blues were all about. They were not about anything very new. He and his boys up there were keeping it new, at the risk of ruin, destruction, madness, and death, in order to find new ways to make us listen. For, while the tale of how we suffer, and how we are delighted, and how we may triumph is never new, it always must be heard. There isn't any other tale to tell, it's the only light we've got in all this darkness.

An excerpt from James Baldwin's short story "Sonny's Blues," which appeared in Partisan Review *in summer 1957, in George Perkins and Barbara Perkins, eds.,* Contemporary American Literature *(1988), pp. 166–67.*

His dress is conservative and casual. He always wears loafers. . . . There is an electronic entertainment wall in his office, very much like the one featured in *Playboy's* Penthouse apartment, that includes hi-fi, AM-FM radio, tape, and television. . . . Brubeck, Kenton or Sinatra is usually on the turntable. . . . He is essentially an indoors man, though he discovered the pleasures of the ski slope last winter. He likes jazz, foreign films, Ivy League clothes, gin and tonic and pretty girls—the sort of things that *Playboy* readers like—and his approach to life is as fresh, sophisticated, and yet admittedly sentimental as is the magazine.

Playboy *publisher Hugh Hefner describing himself in the magazine's June 1957 issue, in David Halberstam,* The Fifties *(1993), pp. 574–75.*

[Soviet Communist Party secretary Nikita] Khrushchev and his views are of great importance to our world and the world of our children. The less this man . . . remains a myth or a dark legend or a mystery to the American people, the more certain they are to size him up correctly.

CBS president Frank Stanton defending the appearance of Khrushchev on Face the Nation *on June 2, 1957, in Stephen J. Whitfield,* The Culture of the Cold War *(1996), p. 162.*

I can't imagine any set of circumstances that would ever induce me to send Federal troops . . . into any area to enforce the orders of a federal court.

President Dwight Eisenhower's remarks in a press conference in July 1957, in Eisenhower, The White House Years, *vol. 2 (1965), p. 170.*

I have said that women are not sentimental, *i.e.*, not prone to permit mere emotion and illusion to corrupt their estimate of a situation. The doctrine, perhaps, will raise a protest. . . . But an appeal to a few obvious facts will be enough to sustain my contention, despite the vast accumulation of romantic rubbish to the contrary. . . .

Surely no long argument is needed to demonstrate the superior competence and effectiveness of women here [in the realm of monogamous marriage], and therewith their greater self-possession, their saner weighing of considerations, their higher power of resisting emotional suggestion. The very fact that marriages occur at all is a proof, indeed, that they are more cool-headed than men, and more adept in employing their intellectual resources, for it is plainly to a man's interest to avoid marriage as long as possible, and as plainly to a woman's interest to make a favorable marriage as soon as she can. . . . Which side commonly prevails? I leave the verdict to the jury. . . .

Women . . . are much more cautious about embracing the conventional hocus pocus of the situation. They never acknowledge that they have fallen in love, as the phrase is, until the man has formally avowed the delusion, and so cut off his retreat. . . . The theory, it would seem, is that the love of the man, laboriously avowed, has inspired it [the woman's love] instantly, and by some unintelligible magic; that it was non-existent until the heat of his own flames set it off. . . . A woman seldom allows herself to be swayed by emotion while the principal business is yet afoot and its issue still in doubt. . . . Such a confession would be an admission that emotion had got the better of her at a critical intellectual moment, and in the

eyes of women . . . no treason to the higher cerebral centers could be more disgraceful.

Social critic H. L. Menken comparing the sentimentality of men and women, in Mencken, "The Marriage Game," The Dude *(July 1957), pp. 51, 61.*

The eyebrows of filmland been swung to the ionosphere. It happened when Vicki Dougan, former New York fashion model . . ankled to the platform in a dress that reversed the famous plunge of Christian Dior. Her phone got busy the next day. . . . We quote columnist Kendis Rochlin: "Jayne Mansfield busted into the movie world, Vikki Dougan is backing into it!"

Review of model Vicki Dougan's dress, cut low in the back and worn at the Golden Globe Awards dinner, in "Of What Is Past, Passing, and to Come," The Dude *(August 1957), p. 37.*

[I began] with only a foggy notion of what the kids, the music, and the show were really about. . . . I don't understand this music.

Host Dick Clark telling a record promoter how he first came to American Bandstand, *which premiered on national television on August 5, 1957, in Jane Stern and Michael Stern,* Encyclopedia of Pop Culture *(1992), p. 16.*

Teens have nine billion dollars a year to spend.

Dick Clark commenting in Time *magazine about the success of* American Bandstand, *which premiered on national television on August 5, 1957, in Jane and Michael Stern,* Encyclopedia of Pop Culture *(1992), p. 16.*

My own theory about Communism is that it is master-minded by Satan. . . . I think there is no other explanation for the tremendous gains of Communism in which they seem to outwit us at every turn, unless they have supernatural power and wisdom and intelligence given to them.

Evangelical minister Billy Graham in September 1957, in Stephen J. Whitfield, The Culture of the Cold War *(1996), p. 81.*

I stood looking at the school—it looked so big! . . When I was able to steady my knees, I walked up to the guard who had let the white students in. He didn't move. When I tried to squeeze past him, he raised his bayonet and then the other guards moved in and they raised their bayonets. They glared at me with a mean look and I was very frightened and didn't know what to do. I turned around and the crowd came toward me. They moved closer and closer. Somebody started yelling, "Lynch her! Lynch her!"

Elizabeth Eckford, one of the nine black students trying to integrate Little Rock's Central High School, describing her experience on the first day of school, September 4, 1957, in Steven Kasher, The Civil Rights Movement: A Photographic History, 1954–68 *(1996), p. 54.*

In the Sunday paper, I saw a pitiful closeup photograph of Elizabeth [Eckford], walking alone in front of Central. . . . It pained my insides to see, once again, the twisted scowling faces with open mouths jeering, clustered around my friend's head like bouquets of grotesque flowers. It was an ad paid for by a white man. . . . "If you live in Arkansas . . . study this picture and know shame. When hate is unleashed and bigotry finds a voice, God help us all."

I felt a kind of joy and hope in the thought that one white man was willing to use his own money to call attention to the injustice we were facing.

Melba Patillo Beals, one of the nine black students who tried to integrate Little Rock's Central High School, on September 4, 1957, in Steven Kasher, The Civil Rights Movement: A Photographic History, 1954–68 *(1996), p. 52.*

Just as, more than any other novel of the Twenties, *The Sun Also Rises* came to be regarded as the testament of the "Lost Generation," so it seems certain that *On the Road* will come to be known as that of the "Beat Generation."

Gilbert Millstein reviewing Jack Kerouac's novel On the Road *in Millstein,* New York Times, *"Books of the Times," September 5, 1957, p. 27.*

When [the *New York Times*'s regular book reviewer Orville] Prescott . . . read my review of *On the Road* he was enraged. He hated the book. He even hated to *look* at it. That was the end of me in daily book reviewing for the *Times*. . . .

I was enchanted by him [Jack Kerouac]. The only word for him was sweet. He was a sweet man and he loved his mother. . . .

When he introduced me to people, he'd put an arm around me and say, "This is Gilbert Millstein—he made me."

Gilbert Millstein commenting on his review of Jack Kerouac's On the Road *on September 5, 1957, in Dan Wakefield,* New York in the Fifties *(1992), pp. 163–64.*

The crowd let out a roar of rage. "They've gone in," a man shouted. . . . A group of six girls . . started to shriek. . . . "The niggers are in our school." One of them jumped up and down. . . . "Come on out, come on out." Tears flowed down her face, her body shook in uncontrollable spasms.

New York Times *correspondent Benjamin Fine describing the forced integration of Little Rock's Central High School on September 23, 1957, in Steven Kasher,* The Civil Rights Movement: A Photographic History, 1954–68 *(1996), p. 54.*

"We may have to let the mob have one of those kids, so's we can distract them long enough to get the others out."

"They're children. What'll we do, have them draw straws to see which one gets a rope around their neck?"

Melba Patillo Beals recalling a conversation she overheard between Little Rock's Central High School administrators about how to evacuate the nine black students from school safely during integration, September 23, 1957, in Steven Kasher, The Civil Rights Movement: A Photographic History, 1954–68 *(1996), p. 55.*

To make this talk I have come to the President's office in the White House . . . [because] I felt that, in speaking from the house of Lincoln, of Jackson and of Wilson, my words would better convey both the sadness I feel in the action I was compelled today to take and the firmness with which I intend to pursue this course until the orders of the federal court at Little Rock can be executed without unlawful interference. . . .

Unless the President did so, anarchy would result. . . .

Mob rule cannot be allowed to override the decisions of our courts. . . .

President Dwight Eisenhower addressing the nation on September 24, 1957, about the desegregation crisis at the Little Rock, Arkansas, Central High School, in Eisenhower, "Federal Court Orders Must Be Upheld" (2001).

The prosecution put only two "expert witnesses" on the stand—both very lame samples of academia—one from the Catholic University of San Francisco and one a private elocution teacher, a beautiful woman, who said, "You feel like you are going through the gutter when you have to read that stuff. . . ." The University of San Francisco instructor said, "The literary value of this poem ["Howl" by Allen Ginsberg] is negligible. . . . This poem is apparently dedicated to a long-dead movement, Dadaism. . . . And, therefore, the opportunity is long past for any significant literary contribution of this poem." . . .

Legally, a layman could see that an important principle was certainly in the line drawn between "hard core pornography" and writing judged to be "social speech." But more important still was the court's acceptance of the principle that if a work is determined to be "social speech," the question of obscenity may not even be raised.

Poet Lawrence Ferlinghetti, who first published "Howl" in the United States, recalling his obscenity trial that concluded with his acquittal on October 3, 1957, in Barney Rosset, ed., Evergreen Review Reader *(1979), p. 135.*

The first part of "Howl" presents a nightmare world; the second part is an indictment of those elements of modern society destructive of the best qualities of human nature; such elements are predominantly identified as materialism, conformity, and the mechanization leading to war. . . . It ends with a plea for holy living.

Judge W. J. Clayton Horn ruling on October 3, 1957, that Allen Ginsberg's poem "Howl" is not obscene, in David Halberstam, The Fifties *(1993), p. 307.*

I was in first grade when Sputnik went up. I still remember going outside at night to watch it pass overhead. We didn't have streetlights on our block, and this was before cities introduced sodium vapor lights to deter crime, so the sky was starry and black. Our neighbors were out too. I remember feeling helpless and scared when Thomas Johnston, an engineer and former Seabee who seemed to embody competence and reason, pointed out the satellite as it inched across the sky. It may have been my first experience of awe.

A child's reaction to the October 4, 1957, launching of the Soviet satellite, Sputnik I, *in Richard Schwartz, "The Best Minds of My Generation,"* Journal of Evolutionary Psychology *(August 1997), p. 178.*

"[Robert E.] Lee was offered command of the Federal Army in 1861. . . . Lee decided to remain loyal to the people of his state.

"The democratic party of the North wants me to go along with them on the integration issue. I will remain with the people of Arkansas."

Arkansas governor Orval Faubus, on October 4, 1957, declaring his continued opposition to integration of the public schools, in Homer Bigart, "Faubus Compares His Stand to Lee's," New York Times, *October 5, 1957, p. 1.*

The country, Dr. Land thought, would reap a tremendous return if I could find ways of inspiring our youth to pursue a whole variety of scientific adventures. There must be some way he, he said, to give science the popular appeal in this country that it held in the Soviet Union. . . .

I questioned the assumption that the Russians were trying to inspire all their people to enter scientific pursuits. I thought instead . . . that they had adopted a practice of culling out the best minds and ruthlessly spurning the rest. . . . I said I would seek out every possibility for kindling more enthusiasm for science among young Americans, but I told the scientists that it was fatuous to think that one speech—or any one man—could do the job. There would be a need for an unlimited follow-through.

President Dwight Eisenhower recalling a meeting with scientists Isidor Rabi of Columbia University and E. H. Land, president of the Polaroid Corporation, in mid-October 1957, in Eisenhower, The White House Years, *vol. 2 (1965), p. 212.*

One of the most dramatic of memories I have took place soon after I moved from New York to Miami in late 1957. I was food shopping with my mother in Kwik Chek (now Winn-Dixie) [supermarket] and noticed in a corner two separate water fountains; one was labeled "Whites" and the other "Colored." I had a vague notion of the significance of those words—having seen images of Little Rock on television—but decided to check it out with my mother. When she verified my understanding and cautioned me about also paying attention to those signs on restroom doors lest I upset other people, I burst into tears, realizing that I had become part of the overt world of segregation and discrimination.

Film instructor Barbara Weitz recalling her first encounter with racial discrimination in late 1957, in private correspondence with the author (November 9, 2001).

The National Canine League is asking dog-lovers to observe a minute each day, with special thoughts for Laika's early and safe return to earth. Officers of the League will call at the Russian Embassy at 11 a.m. to lodge a protest.

One of several protests by animal lovers of the Soviets' sending a dog, Laika, into outer space on November 3, 1957, in Martin Gilbert, A History of the Twentieth Century, *vol. 3 (2000), p. 165.*

[*Sputnik 1* and *2* are] lonely . . . waiting for American satellites to join them in space.

Secretary Nikita Khrushchev gloating after the successful launching of Sputnik 2 *on November 3, 1957, in Lois Gordon and Alan Gordon,* American Chronicle *(1999), p. 547.*

The American satellite ought to be called Civil Servant. It won't work and you can't fire it.

A popular joke following America's failure on December 6, 1957, to launch a space satellite, in Lois Gordon and Alan Gordon, American Chronicle *(1999), p. 540.*

Credit Kirk Douglas with having the courage to produce and appear in the screen dramatization of a novel that has been a hot potato in Hollywood for twenty-two years. That is Humphrey Cobb's *Paths of Glory*, a shocking story of a shameful incident in World War I—the court-martial and execution of

The Soviet Union's *Sputnik 2*, the second human-made earth satellite, carried a dog named Laika into outer space. *(Photofest)*

three innocent French soldiers on charges of cowardice, only to salve a general's vanity.

Obviously, this is a story—based on an actual occurrence, by the way—that reflects not alone on France's honor but also on the whole concept of military authority. Yet Mr. Douglas has made a movie of it—an unembroidered, documentary-like account—with himself playing the role of an outraged colonel who tries vainly to intercede.

Bosley Crowther reviewing Stanley Kubrick's Paths of Glory, *in Crowther, "Paths of Glory," New York Times, December 26, 1957, p. 23.*

10

America Enters Outer Space
1958

As the United States followed the Soviet Union into outer space, it both celebrated its achievements and for the first time since World War II concluded, brooded that it had fallen behind in the competition for technological domination. By penetrating beyond the Earth's atmosphere and by learning to use nuclear fusion to produce a new, heavier atom from two lighter ones—in effect to change one element into another, which was the goal of ancient alchemists—American scientists were accomplishing feats that humans had been dreaming of since time immemorial. On the other hand, the Soviet advantage in missile technology led to accusations by American politicians and others that U.S. schools were failing to provide adequate science education, and that American students were falling behind their Soviet counterparts. As a result, changes were made in the curricula to provide more comprehensive and rigorous education in math and science, and the National Defense Education Act was created to encourage college students to major in those disciplines and to facilitate improved math and science instruction.

American confidence was also undermined by a mild recession that began this year. Eisenhower, however, initiated a massive public works program that by the end of the year stabilized the economy and reduced the unemployment rate, which had grown to its highest level since the Great Depression. The integration of public schools continued in the South, although rarely with the "deliberate speed" mandated by the Supreme Court and sometimes punctuated by bombings, beatings, and other violence. Arkansas governor Orval Faubus closed Little Rock's high schools for the year rather than integrate them; schools were similarly closed in Virginia.

The violence, anger, and social upheaval associated with desegregation appeared to generate greater levels of anxiety for many Americans. So, too, did the dawning of the age of space exploration, which was fraught with a slew of unknown challenges and possible dangers. Moreover, the beginning of a new era that included nuclear-armed ICBMs made all Americans vulnerable to nuclear assault, regardless of where they lived. This heightened anxiety seemed to dampen the national spirit and make it more serious minded. The remarkable shift from 1956 in the kinds of television shows and movies that became popular in 1957 and 1958 demonstrated a public preference in television programming that was more violent and earnest and movies that were more gritty, realistic, and attuned to topical events. For instance, such films as Stanley Kramer's *The Defiant Ones* challenged both social authority and racism, and John Barth's novel *The End of the Road* addressed the fallout from racial discrimination, emotional detachment, domestic abuse, and illegal abortion. Young people continued to express their spirit of rebellion through rock 'n' roll.

Even greater transformation undercut the established order in the rest of the world. The deepening Algerian crisis nearly provoked a military coup in France and brought Charles de Gaulle to power, Fidel Castro's revolution in Cuba toppled the Batista dictatorship, and other revolutions sprang up around the globe. For the first time since the Korean War, the United States deployed troops on a large-scale military mission as Eisenhower ordered U.S. Marines to Lebanon to support the pro-Western government there. Furthermore, by the end of the year the hopeful signs of superpower cooperation that had surfaced earlier faded, and 1958 concluded on a dangerous note when Soviet leader Khrushchev inaugurated the second Berlin crisis by demanding that the Western powers evacuate West Berlin.

THE COLD WAR AND INTERNATIONAL POLITICS

The Cold War Abroad

Cold War tensions abated at the beginning of the year but returned in the fall and winter after the United States and Britain intervened militarily in the Middle East, arms control talks failed, and Khrushchev demanded the Western allies pull out of West Berlin. In the initial half of 1958, the United States and Soviet Union issued voluntary moratoriums on nuclear testing; eased travel; created cooperative arrangements within the cultural, educational, technical, sports, and scientific fields; and made various other limited gestures of conciliation. In addition, Britain and France eased restrictions on trade with the communist-bloc countries and communist China. Following a U.S. troop reduction in 1957, the Soviets announced in January that they would downsize their armed forces by 300,000, and in February, Khrushchev requested a summit meeting with the United States. A month later Khrushchev returned the Soviet Union to one-man rule for the first time since Stalin's death, when he assumed the post of premier, in addition to his role as first secretary of the Communist Party. Following the conclusion of an extensive series of tests, Khrushchev declared a unilateral halt to nuclear testing in late March and called on the United States and Britain to do likewise. Eisenhower initially dismissed the gesture as a gimmick, but on April 8, he proposed that a verification system for enforcing a total test ban be established, and in July, the three nuclear powers—the United States, Britain, and the Soviet Union—met to discuss this possibility. The talks ultimately failed, and throughout the cold war, the superpowers remained divided over on-site verification of compliance, which the United States sought and the Soviet Union rejected.

Even while the talks were going on, both sides made preparations to continue the arms race. In early July, the United States and Britain signed a bilateral agreement to cooperate on the development of nuclear weapons, and in

September, the Soviets ended their moratorium on testing in order to catch up with the Western allies. In April, before the talks started, the United States test-fired the first nuclear-capable Polaris missile ever shot from a submerged submarine. In May, the United States and Canada established the North American Air Defense Command (NORAD), and in July the two nations established a new defense link at the cabinet level.

Despite the efforts to curb nuclear testing and the more conciliatory attitude that manifested early in the year, deep divisions between the two sides remained. In February, the United States placed 60 nuclear-armed IRBMs in Great Britain, an act that provoked the formation of Britain's grassroots Campaign for Nuclear Disarmament, which went on to exert substantial, but not decisive, political pressure during the next decade. The Soviets warned against placement of nuclear weapons in the Middle Eastern countries affiliated with the Baghdad Pact, which were receiving U.S. military aid. And in late November, Khrushchev initiated a second Berlin crisis by demanding that Western troops evacuate West Berlin and leave it as a demilitarized free city. NATO rejected this demand on December 16, and a tense three-year, on-again, off-again standoff began.

In August, tensions flared again between the United States and the PRC, after the Chinese bombarded Jinmen (Quemoy) and Mazu (Matsu), contested islands off of Taiwan. Eisenhower dispatched an aircraft carrier and four destroyers to defend them and declared that America was determined to defend the two islands by force, if necessary. Communist China resumed shelling on October 20, but the situation died down over the next few months. The degree to which the United States should be willing to defend these islands later became an issue in the 1960 Richard Nixon–John F. Kennedy presidential debates.

A growing number of scientists expressed their opposition to nuclear testing. In January, Linus Pauling headed a petition of some 9,000 scientists requesting the United Nations call for an end to the tests. In February, philosopher and pacifist Bertrand Russell addressed the inaugural meeting of Britain's Campaign for Nuclear Disarmament, which led an antinuclear rally of some 5,000 people in London in early April. On March 11, a U.S. B-47 bomber accidentally dropped an unarmed atom bomb on a South Carolina farm home, injuring six people, and in May, eight Nike missiles accidentally exploded at a base in New Jersey, killing 10 people.

U.S. Marines in Lebanon

On July 14, General Abdul Karim Kassem led a successful coup in Iraq and replaced the monarchy with a republic. King Faisal, whose family had fought with T. E. Lawrence (Lawrence of Arabia) during World War I and ruled the country ever since, was killed during the coup, along with at least 10 other members of the royal family. The coup in Iraq, which embraced the pan-Arabism promulgated by Egyptian president Nasser, sparked anti-Western riots in Jordan and in Beirut and Tripoli, where Muslims demonstrated for pan-Arabism. On July 15, the day after the Iraqi coup, Eisenhower invoked the Eisenhower Doctrine to send U.S. Marines to Lebanon in support of President Camille Chamoun, who remained sympathetic to the West. Two days later, Britain sent 2,000 troops to aid King Hussein in Jordan. The Soviets condemned the Western military support as open aggression, and they made their military "volunteers" available to serve in the Middle East. The situation eased on July 23, after Khrushchev accepted a U.S. proposal for a Middle East summit. Following a UN resolution and the succession of General Fouad Chehab to the Lebanese presidency, the marines began to depart on August 13 and completed their withdrawal on October 25. However, tensions among the feuding Arab states remained high, and in November, King Hussein claimed that his plane was attacked by Syrian jets while he was flying over Syria on his way back to Jordan.

THE SPACE PROGRAM

On the night of January 31, following a disappointing failure in December 1957, the *Explorer 1* satellite brought the United States into the space age. For both superpowers, space exploration was motivated not only by scientific inquiry but also by a desire to achieve cold war dominance. Apart from the potential military advantages that derive from orbiting weapons and observation satellites, humanity's entry into the heavens was an astounding accomplishment that generated enormous enthusiasm around the world. The achievement actualized a fantasy that had captured people's imaginations throughout the entire course of human existence but had never before been more than mythology or science fiction. The entry into outer space generated considerable respect among other nations, and each superpower strove to be perceived as the most technologically advanced country in the world, in part because that perception translated into real political capital.

The army's Jupiter-C rocket that carried *Explorer* into space was developed by a team headed by Wernher von Braun, a German scientist who had developed the V-2 rocket that the Nazis used against Britain at the end of World War II. After the war, von Braun was brought to the United States, along with other German scientists. Still others were taken to work for the Soviet Union. At the time of the satellite launch, he was director of the development operations division of the U.S. Army Ballistic Missile Agency, a position he held until after the United States sent its first man to the moon in 1969.

Despite the success of *Explorer 1,* a month after its launch von Braun announced that the United States's space program was several years behind that of the Soviets. Throughout the year, both nations sent several satellites into orbit, and in July, Eisenhower formed the National Aeronautics and Space Administration (NASA) to oversee the U.S. program. NASA announced an ambitious program to put men into space within two years (Project Mercury), to place a man on the moon in six to 10 years (Project Apollo), and to explore Mars within 10 to 15 years.

The Soviet rockets carried much heavier satellites (*Sputnik 3* weighed almost 3,000 pounds, compared with *Explorer 1*'s 30.8 pounds), but the American missiles flew deeper into space. In March, the United States announced its intention to orbit the moon, and in October it launched its first moon rocket, *Pioneer 1,* which failed to reach the moon but traveled some 79,000 miles into deep space. Later attempts to reach the moon made progress but failed to escape Earth's gravitational pull. In addition to simply breaking the space barriers, the U.S. satellites were sent to study cosmic rays, meteors, solar cells, and radiation 600 miles above the Earth. Eisenhower sent a prerecorded radio message to the entire world using a satellite radio relay that had been launched a week before. The first space-based message wished all the people on the planet, "Peace on earth, goodwill to men."

Other International Developments

The unpopular war in Algeria continued to influence French domestic politics, as on the one hand, French nationals in Algeria became more militant in their insistence that France support them, and on the other hand, atrocities by the French Algerian Army and a growing willingness to relinquish colonialism fueled domestic and international opposition to the war, which was beginning to spread to Tunisia as well. The threat of a military coup in France in late May provoked the collapse of the country's Fourth Republic and the resignation of President Pierre Pflimlin, whose policy of trying to accommodate the independence-minded Algerian nationalists was unacceptable to the French army. Charles de Gaulle, who had been the leader of the Free French during World War II and the first provisional president of France after its liberation, was much more satisfactory to the military, which supported his return to power. Outspoken in his support of the French army in Algeria, de Gaulle introduced a new constitution that was approved in the fall, and he was elected the first president of the Fifth Republic in December.

De Gaulle's appeal to hard-liners averted the coup; nevertheless, he too tried to reach a settlement with the Islamic nationalists in Algiers by making several concessions, including full French citizenship to Muslims as well as French nationals and a statement in France's new constitution recognizing the right of France's overseas territories to independence. However, the Algerian National Liberation Front refused his offer of a cease-fire. Other initiatives by de Gaulle included an agreement with Britain to ease trade restrictions with the communist powers. The United States, on the other hand, maintained its harder line and maintained embargos on trade with communist China, North Korea, and North Vietnam.

While still strengthening its alliance with NATO and the Western powers, West Germany, under Chancellor Konrad Adenauer, also improved its relations with the Soviet Union, when the two nations signed a trade agreement in April. Adenauer met with de Gaulle in September, and they formed a good working relationship after discovering that they shared similar aspirations for the future of Europe. Belgium, the Netherlands, and Luxembourg established an economic union that provided for the free flow of capital, services, and people among the three countries.

On the other side of the Iron Curtain, Poland's leadership took a harder line against labor dissent, making strikes illegal and requiring unions to submit to Communist Party rule. And Imre Nagy, who had headed the rebellious Hungarian government in 1956, was executed for his role in that uprising, along with the former minister of defense. The executions sparked international protests.

In February, Egypt and Syria merged as the United Arab Republic. The two anti-Western states were joined in March by Yemen and reorganized as the United Arab States. Jordan and Iraq, who were allied with the West, also formed a union in February. In May, Nasser established closer ties with the

Soviets, who agreed to help finance the construction of the Aswan Dam, Nasser's most ambitious domestic project.

European colonialism continued its collapse in Africa, as several new republics were declared, including Senegal, Chad, Gabon, Congo-Brazzaville (now the Republic of Congo) and Guinea. The year 1958 was also a turbulent one in the Caribbean and South America. Populist uprisings in Venezuela toppled the military dictatorship of General Marcos Pérez Jiménez in January. That spring, Eisenhower ordered U.S. troops to the region after Venezuelan mobs attacked Vice President Nixon on his goodwill tour of South America. Nixon had earlier sparked angry protests in Peru. Haitian president Duvalier suppressed a military revolt, after which he was granted authority to rule by decree for six months, making him a virtual dictator. A coup was also thwarted in Argentina, which was placed under martial law. A more peaceful development was Britain's creation of the West Indies Federation among its former colonies and territories.

The most enduring development in the Caribbean, with the greatest long-term impact on world events, was revolutionary Fidel Castro's populist military campaign that finally toppled Cuba's dictator Fulgencio Batista at year's end, despite limited U.S. support of Batista. Even before Castro took power and revealed his communist leanings, his relations with the United States were difficult, although he had many sympathizers within the American public (among them was Jack Paar, host of the popular late-night *Tonight Show* who on air denounced Batista and praised Castro). In March, the U.S. government stopped 35 New Yorkers who were traveling to Cuba to join the revolution. Subsequently, the United States embargoed arms shipments to Cuba and intercepted ships carrying weapons bound for the rebels on the island. In June, Castro's followers captured 28 marines and navy personnel near the U.S. naval base at Guantánamo Bay in retaliation for the alleged American practice of allowing government military planes to refuel at the base. The servicemen were freed in July, but two weeks later U.S. Marines were deployed in Cuban territory, with Batista's approval, to protect the water supply at the naval base, which had been threatened by the rebels.

Beginning in the mountains of Cuba's easternmost province of Oriente, Castro began his major offensive in September, a two-pronged attack that moved westward toward Havana. Batista fled on New Year's Eve to Miami, and the rebels entered the capital victoriously on New Year's Day 1959. According to Eisenhower, the CIA did not conclude that Castro was likely to form a communist government until the end of 1958, when the revolution was almost complete. At that time, Eisenhower rejected advice that the United States should fully back Batista as the lesser of two evils; instead, he maintained that "our only hope, if any, lay with some kind of non-dictatorial 'third force,' neither Castroite nor Batistiano."[1]

The PRC cracked down on separatist movements among the Mongol, Turkic, and Korean minorities and instituted a severe crackdown on Tibet. The Great Leap Forward stressed increased industrial production at the expense of agricultural output and abolished private plots of land in favor of large collective communes; however, the experiment produced famine and hardship throughout the nation. In December following the failure of his economic program, Mao Zedong stepped down as China's head of state, but not as leader of the powerful Communist Party. Mao returned to full power during the Cultural Revolution of the mid-1960s. Elsewhere in Asia, Eisenhower sought to create stronger relations with Afghanistan, and he met with the premier of Afghanistan, whose strategic importance to the Middle East he recognized.

The Cold War at Home

The worst excesses of the Red Scare continued to be reversed, as the Supreme Court ruled that passports could not be denied or withdrawn on the basis of suspected communist affiliation. Entertainer and political activist Paul Robeson, who had been forbidden to travel abroad for eight years—and who was blacklisted within the United States and therefore largely unable to work at home or abroad—was again permitted to ply his craft in Europe, where he remained popular. Playwright Arthur Miller also had his passport restored, and the Supreme Court overturned his earlier conviction for contempt of Congress for his 1956 testimony. Both men reappeared before HUAC, along with seven other entertainers who also refused to comment on their political beliefs and associations. Among them was Joseph Papp (Papirofsky), noted director of Shakespearean drama, who invoked the Fifth Amendment against self-incrimination when asked about communist affiliations prior to June 1955, although he maintained that he had not been a party member since that time. The American Communist Party's official newspaper, *The Daily Worker,* shut down after its editor, John Gates, resigned from the party. Gates complained that the Communist Party in the United States was "a futile and impotent political sect."[2]

CIVIL RIGHTS

The integration of public schools in the South remained a contentious issue. In Little Rock, Arkansas, Governor Orval Faubus closed the city's four high schools after the Supreme Court rejected his "evasive scheme" to privatize them and then have a private company enroll only white students. In Tennessee, Clinton High School, which had been integrated in 1956, was destroyed by dynamite. Also firebombed was a synagogue in Atlanta. The Supreme Court struck down Alabama's attempt to demand access to the membership rolls of the NAACP.

GOVERNMENT AND SOCIETY

The cold war and foreign relations dominated the nation's legislative agenda. Even the congressional action to admit Alaska as the 49th state, which Eisenhower signed in July and took effect in 1959, was promoted largely as a matter of national defense. Congress earlier passed Eisenhower's request for a $73-billion budget, of which 64 percent was for defense and foreign aid. Congress also passed an additional emergency appropriation of $1.3 billion for missile development and the space program, and it enacted the food additive amendment prohibiting the use of any additives that induced cancer in people or animals. In the off-year elections, the Democrats solidified their control of Congress, gaining 15 seats in the Senate and 48 in the House of Representatives. During the campaign, White House aide Sherman Adams resigned after a House committee revealed that he had received an Oriental rug and a vicuña coat from textile magnate Bernard Goldfine, for whom Adams made inquiries at two federal agencies. Adams called himself a victim of a political campaign to vilify him, and Eisenhower reluctantly accepted his resignation.

The Soviet advantage in space exploration in 1957 and 1958 sustained the demand for more rigorous science education in public schools. In the spring, *Life* magazine ran a widely discussed series entitled "Crisis in Education," which focused on matters of overcrowding, poorly paid teachers, inadequate curricula, and other problems encountered by public schools. Eisenhower introduced the National Defense Education Act, which allocated $4 billion of federal aid for four years to fund higher education, especially in the teaching of science, mathematics, and modern languages.

Religion remained a matter of considerable public interest. Pope Pius XII died on October 9. He was succeeded on October 28 by Cardinal Roncalli of Venice, who assumed the name Pope John XXIII; Americans Richard Cushing and John O'Hara were promoted to cardinals. More than 250,000 New Yorkers attended Jehovah's Witness conventions at Yankee Stadium and the Polo Grounds.

Unidentified soldiers from World War II and Korea were enshrined in the Tomb of the Unknown Soldier at Arlington National Cemetery; Colorado and Kansas were plagued by grasshoppers; and a Gallup poll showed that former first lady Eleanor Roosevelt was the most admired woman in the country—for the 11th consecutive year. The March of Dimes, which had been established by her husband, President Franklin D. Roosevelt, declared that its mission to combat polio had been successfully concluded, and it redirected its resources to treating birth defects and related infant health problems. The Mackinac Bridge, which links Michigan's upper and lower peninsulas, became the world's longest suspension bridge to that date when it was completed in June. Built at a cost of $100 million to stimulate industrial development on the isolated upper peninsula, the suspension portion of the Mackinac Bridge was 8,614 feet, some 2,000 feet longer than San Francisco's Golden Gate Bridge.[3]

BUSINESS

The early part of the year produced a small recession and high unemployment. In March, the jobless rate reached its highest mark since 1941, with some 5 million Americans out of work, despite a new three-year labor agreement between the United Auto Workers and Chrysler and General Motors. Black workers felt the effects especially hard. But in March, Eisenhower initiated a $3-billion program of public housing, highway construction, and land reclamation, and by the end of the year, the Roosevelt-like strategy of stimulating the economy through public works succeeded in ending the recession and providing jobs for more than 1 million workers.[4] Nonetheless, the unemployment rate for the year was 6.8 percent, and the GNP remained static at 0 percent growth rate, while the Dow Jones industrial average fluctuated between 451 and 583. On October 23, the national debt reached a record high of more than $280 billion. A new Oldsmobile cost $2,933; a French Renault automobile was $1,345; an Emerson 7.5-amp air-conditioner was $128; a pair of blue

Italian actress Gina Lollobrigida participates in the hula hoop craze while filming King Vidor's *Solomon and Sheba,* released in 1959. *(Photofest)*

jeans was $3.75; an economy-class round-trip ticket on Air France between New York and Paris was $489.60; and a year's tuition at Harvard University was $1,250.[5]

In the fall, international travel became considerably more convenient and less time consuming, as first British Overseas Airways, then Pan American introduced the first regularly scheduled transatlantic jet service. Regular domestic jet service between New York and Miami also began during the year.

During the summer, the Wham-O toy company introduced the hula hoop, which became an instant fad with nearly 100 million large, brightly colored, plastic hoops sold worldwide in a year, after which the demand plunged almost as rapidly as it rose. (It was perhaps not coincidental that the hula hoop captured the public imagination at the same time that Hawaii was moving toward statehood, which it was granted in 1959.) Both a game and a form of exercise, the hula hoop also offered a socially acceptable form of limited sexual expression, as the practitioner swung the hoop around his or her waist and kept it from falling by mimicking the gyrating motion of a Hawaiian hula dancer. Made of lightweight, injection-molded polyethylene, the hoop, three feet in diameter, sold for $1.98.

The success of the hula hoop also demonstrated the new power of television to create national, even global consumer and cultural phenomena. The hoops were initially promoted without any advertising budget. Local television news shows featured children playing in the public parks of Pasadena, California, where Wham-O distributed free samples to generate interest. Network news then picked up the coverage, and by Labor Day hula hoops were the rage throughout the country. By November, the *Wall Street Journal* announced that the craze was over in America, but interest spread throughout the world, where the fad persisted through 1959.

Other new products to appear included the Chevrolet Impala, Green Giant canned beans, Sweet 'n Low artificial sweetener, bifocal contact lenses, and a solid-state electronic computer. DuPont marketed Lycra, an artificial elastic that was the first of the Spandex fibers, which are stronger and longer lasting than rubber. In France, Mark Gregoire began producing nonstick Teflon frying pans. EMI and Decca record companies released the first stereophonic records, Pizza Hut opened its first franchise, and the first two-way moving sidewalk was introduced.

Certainly the charge card, however, introduced by American Express for travel-related expenses, had the broadest, deepest, and most enduring impact on the American and worldwide economies by facilitating increased personal and corporate expenditures on travel and entertainment. Although the American Express card required payment in full each month, it, along with the Diner's Club card introduced in 1950, paved the way for the credit card that Bank

America first issued in 1959 and that evolved into the Visa card, which enabled individuals to borrow money easily and thereby fueled spending by allowing consumers to exceed their budgets. Although department stores had for years been permitting installment purchases, the charge and credit cards, more than any other economic tool, challenged the virtues of thrift and living within a balanced budget that had been cornerstones of the Protestant ethic.

SCIENCE AND TECHNOLOGY

As they had throughout the decade, developments in medical care continued to advance with unprecedented speed. At the same time, psychology became accepted, and even embraced, by a growing portion of the public and medical community. John Eiders developed a measles vaccination, and in Britain ultrasound was first used to examine babies in the womb. Thalidomide, a medication sold in Europe, was determined to cause birth defects. Developed as a sleeping pill, it had also been prescribed to treat morning sickness. Arnold Lazarus coined the term *behavior therapy,* and Joseph Wolfe published *Psychotherapy by Reciprocal Inhibition,* which presented a behavioral approach to psychology.

British and American scientists teamed together to produce nuclear fusion in a controlled environment by inducing two light atoms to collide at high speeds, in 100-million-degree temperatures, to produce a new, heavier atom. The capacity to transform one element into another fulfilled the goal of ancient alchemists, who similarly sought to transmute one element (lead) into a different one (gold). But the down side of nuclear energy was also becoming increasingly apparent, and environmentalists obtained a court order stopping the construction of a nuclear-power plant at Badaga Head, California.

The revolution in electronics took a great leap forward with the invention of integrated circuitry, and Jack Kilby formulated the conceptual basis of the microchip that later made the personal computer possible. Scientists from Bell Labs applied for a patent on the first laser, which revolutionized industries as diverse as precision manufacturing, gemstone cutting, and medical care.

Terrestrial and extraterrestrial exploration continued to expand the very limits of imagination, as three British scientists developed the steady-state theory of the universe; John Van Allen used data collected from *Explorer* to describe two belts (named after him) of cosmic radiation around the earth; and Edmund Hillary of New Zealand, who with Nepalese Sherpa guide Tensing Norgay in 1953 became one of the first men to reach the summit of Mt. Everest, led an expedition to the South Pole. At the other end of the world, the American nuclear-powered submarine *Nautilus* sailed beneath the polar ice cap at the North Pole. Leaving Pearl Harbor, Hawaii, on July 23, it arrived in Iceland on August 7 and covered 1,830 miles in 96 hours.

In addition to the Soviet Union's achievements in outer space, the superpower sought to impress the nonaligned countries by building the world's largest hydroelectric dam on the Volga River. The project created huge lakes in the valley and led to environmental damage that included the steady shrinking of the Caspian Sea. The Soviet Academy of Science elected Americans Linus Pauling and Detlev Bronk as members. In addition to being a Nobel Prize winner, Pauling was also a vocal opponent of nuclear testing.

SPORTS, ENTERTAINMENT, AND THE ARTS

Sports

Major League Baseball underwent a major transformation when it expanded to the West Coast, as the Giants and Dodgers played their first seasons in San Francisco and Los Angeles, respectively. But the career of Roy Campanella was cut short when the standout Dodgers catcher, who was one of the first black players to integrate the game, was paralyzed in an automobile accident. In a particularly exciting World Series, the New York Yankees avenged their loss to the Milwaukee Braves from the previous year. Trailing three games to one, the Yankees came from behind to win the championship in seven games. Chicago Cubs shortstop Ernie Banks won the National League's Most Valuable Player Award (MVP), and Boston's Red Sox Jackie Jensen won in the American League.

Professional football enjoyed a strong surge in popularity after the Baltimore Colts won the NFL championship in a dramatic 23–17 overtime victory over the New York Giants. Colts quarterback John Unitas starred in the game, which is still regarded as one of the best championship football games ever played. But perhaps of even greater impact was the fact that it was the first NFL title game to be broadcast live from coast to coast. The drama of the widely viewed, sudden-death contest attracted large numbers of new fans to the game, which previously had been dominated by college rivalries. Cleveland's Jim Brown, who set a new single-season rushing record of 1,527 yards, was selected as the year's MVP. Louisiana State University (LSU) was the top college team, and Army's Pete Dawkins won the Heisman Trophy.

St. Louis defeated Boston in six games to win the NBA basketball title. Boston's star center Bill Russell was the MVP. The NBA All-Pro First Team included Detroit's George Yardley, Syracuse's Dolph Schayes, St. Louis's Bob Pettit, and Bob Cousy and Bill Sharman of Boston. The University of Kentucky won the college basketball title, and Seattle's Elgin Baylor was selected Player of the Year.

Montreal won hockey's Stanley Cup. "Sugar" Ray Robinson regained the middleweight boxing title for the fifth time. Arnold Palmer, a favorite among fans, was the top money-earner in professional golf ($42,607), but Tommy Bolt won the U.S. Open. Ashley Cooper and Althea Gibson won the men and women's singles tennis championships at the U.S. Open.

Television

Scandal rocked the television industry when serious accusations were made that most of the high-stakes quiz shows were fixed, including *Dotto, Twenty-One,*

"Sugar" Ray Robinson once again reclaimed his middleweight boxing title in 1958. *(Photofest)*

The $64,000 Question, and *The $64,000 Challenge.* The scandal was precipitated when Herbert Stempel complained in 1958 that, in 1957, the producers of *Twenty-One* had given his opponent, Charles van Doren, the answers to some of the questions prior to air time. Van Doren, a good-looking, engaging instructor at Columbia University, defeated Stempel, the unpopular reigning champion, after a series of tense ties. Van Doren then became a national celebrity, and for 14 weeks he clung to his title as he answered ever-more challenging questions. (After his success on the show van Doren went on to host the NBC show *Kaleidoscope.*) Following Stempel's charges, and those of others from other games, all of the high-stakes quiz shows were canceled in the fall. In 1959, after denying newspaper stories to the contrary, van Doren confessed to a congressional committee that the games had been dishonest and that the winners were predetermined. Van Doren, who was then working on his doctorate, claimed he had participated in the deceit because it was having such a good effect on the national attitude toward teachers, education, and the intellectual life. The revelation that the games were rigged deeply disillusioned many Americans—Eisenhower compared it to the so-called Black Sox scandal of 1919 in which the World Series was fixed—and the betrayal by television, which by 1958 had become a major source of trust and authority within the culture, was profoundly disturbing to many. The dishonesty provoked many public figures to express concern, even despair, over the state of public morality.

Paramount Pictures sold the television rights to its pre-1948 movies for $50 million, making television an even more significant venue for showing films. (In 1955, the much smaller RKO Studio sold the rights to all of its films to television.)

In an apparent shift in the national mood, action-packed westerns continued to replace comedies as the most widely viewed shows on television. Prior to 1957, comedies had been the main staple of prime-time programming throughout the decade. Whereas in the 1956–57 season, three of the top 10 shows were comedies and only one, *Gunsmoke,* was a western, in 1957–58 *Gunsmoke* replaced *I Love Lucy* as the number-one show, after *Lucy* went out of production. In addition, four other westerns were among the top 10. In the 1958–59 season, the top four most widely viewed shows were westerns—*Gunsmoke; Wagon Train; Have Gun, Will Travel;* and *The Rifleman*—and *Maverick, Tales of Wells Fargo,* and *The Life and Legend of Wyatt Earp* were among the top 10. The only comedies in the top 10 were *The Danny Thomas Show* and *The Real McCoys.* Of the highly rated westerns, only *The Rifleman* made its debut in 1958. It starred Chuck Connors as a widower raising his son on a ranch in lawless New Mexico. Other new westerns included *Wanted: Dead or Alive,* starring Steve McQueen; *Bat Masterson,* starring Gene Barry as a dapper ex-lawman who roamed the West with a gold-tipped cane that concealed a sword; *The Lawman,* starring John Russell; and *Tales of Texas John Slaughter,* which starred Tom Tryon as a Texas Ranger. The latter's opening song lyric appealed to middle America's preoccupation with maintaining law and order and perhaps served as an admonishment to rebellious youth: "With Texas John Slaughter, men did as they oughter, 'cause if they didn't they'd die."

Also debuting were several detective and crime shows, which were similarly action oriented, with a strong law-and-order theme. Several drew on the growing appeal of the upscale, cosmopolitan, well-accoutered, successful professional—a product of consumer capitalism that was then being promoted in television and magazine advertising and by such publications as *Playboy* magazine. These shows added polish, sophistication, and an up-to-date "with-it" appeal to the detective genre, which previously typically featured private eyes with working-class manners and tastes. 77 *Sunset Strip* starred Efrem Zimbalist, Jr., and Roger Smith as playboy private eyes based in Hollywood, and it costarred Edd Burns as Kookie, a hip-talking parking-lot attendant who was always combing his hair. In 1959, Burns and Connie Stevens recorded a popular song, "Kookie, Kookie (Lend Me Your Comb)," based on the character, who was a big hit among teenagers. *Peter Gunn* starred Craig Stevens as another debonaire private detective. The show was introduced by a memorable, jazzy musical score by Henry Mancini. John McIntire and James Franciscus starred in the more gritty *Naked City*, a police show filmed entirely on location in New York City. Based on the 1948 film noir movie of the same title, the program always ended, "There are 8 million stories in the naked city; this has been one of them."

The Donna Reed Show was a new sitcom set in a small-town, middle-class household. It starred Donna Reed as a wholesome, all-American mother who held together a family composed of her pediatrician husband (Carl Betz), son Jeff (Paul Petersen), and daughter Mary (Shelley Fabares). Petersen, who had been an original Mouseketeer on *The Mickey Mouse Club*, and Fabares launched singing careers based on their popularity on the show, which faltered in its first year but went on to become one of ABCs longest running prime-time series.

Partly to demonstrate social responsibility in the face of the quiz show scandals, the networks aired several special documentaries on world events, including the revolution in Cuba, the Great Leap Forward in China, and the situation in Berlin after Khrushchev issued his ultimatum that the Western powers leave the city. CBS also presented *Hiroshima*, one of the earliest documentaries about the first atomic bombing. Notable specials from 1958 included *Days of Wine and Roses*, starring Piper Laurie and Cliff Robertson, and a Thanksgiving Day special on General Electric Theater entitled *A Turkey for the President*, starring Ronald Reagan and Nancy Davis, who later married.

Movies

Just two years prior, the top films of 1956 offered escapism to exotic places far-away in space and time; many of the most influential films of 1958, however, had the opposite effect, making viewers confront a tough and gritty here and now. Like television, which turned from lighthearted comedy to earnest, action-driven westerns between 1956 and 1958, these movies suggest a shift in the national mood. They express a seriousness that rejects frivolous pretense and pomp and insists on heightened social awareness. For instance, Susan Hayward was named best actress for her role in Robert Wise's *I Want to Live*. She plays Barbara Graham, a real-life criminal from a broken home whose conviction and death sentence made her a controversial national figure. Vincente Minnelli directed Frank Sinatra, Shirley MacLaine, and Dean Martin in *Some Came Running*, a dark story about a returning World War II veteran who has difficulty readjusting to civilian life. The film exerted considerable influence on the French New Wave critics and filmmakers, who admired its sense of realism and believed the movie accurately depicted American culture. Montgomery Clift, Myrna Loy, and Robert Ryan star in another unhappy story, Vincent J. Donehue's *Lonelyhearts*. Adapted from Nathaniel West's novel *Miss Lonelyhearts* (1933), it tells the story of a man who uncovers a world of unhappy, lonely, pathetic people when he writes an advice column for the lovelorn under the female pseudonym, Miss Lonelyhearts. Clift also costars with Marlon Brando and Dean Martin in Edward Dmytryk's *The Young Lions,* an adaptation of Irwin Shaw's novel about three soldiers—one German, one Jewish American, and one Christian American—whose paths intersect during World War II. The film highlights anti-Semitism within the U.S. Army, as well as the Nazi atrocities that disillusion the once-enthusiastic German. Another film to tackle topical social controversy was Stanley Kramer's *The Defiant Ones,* which addresses racism in American society. Tony Curtis and Sidney Poitier star as white and black escaped convicts who are chained together. The movie, which won Academy Awards for best story and screenplay (Nathan E. Douglas and Harold Jacob Smith) and best cinematography (Sam Leavitt), features one of Curtis's finest performances as a southern racist, and it established Poitier as a major star.

Several of the top films of the year were adapted from hit Broadway plays. Minnelli's musical *Gigi* won the Academy Award for best film director, adapted screenplay (Alan Jay Lerner), cinematography (Joseph Ruttenberg), score (André Previn), song (Frederick Loewe), editing, art direction, and costume design. It stars Leslie Caron, Maurice Chevalier, and Louis Jourdan in a heart-warming story of a Parisian girl who is raised to become the mistress of a wealthy man. Mitzi Gaynor and Rossano Brazzi star in Joshua Logan's adaptation of *South Pacific,* about love on the Pacific islands during World War II. Rosalind Russell and Forrest Tucker star in another adapted Broadway hit, *Auntie Mame,* which Morton DaCosta directed. The movie tells the story of an eccentric woman who adopts an orphan boy and exposes him to an array of bizarre characters during the 1920s and 1930s. The Academy Award–nominated film stood out to 1950s audiences because it celebrates a strong, independent woman and, in the era of the "organization man," it shows the attractiveness of being unconventional. Richard Brooks directed Paul Newman, Elizabeth Taylor, and Burl Ives in a powerful treatment of Tennessee Williams's *Cat on a Hot Tin Roof,* about a wealthy but dysfunctional southern family whose members are clumsy, at best, in their ability to acknowledge and express love. David Niven was chosen best actor for Delbert Mann's adaptation of Terence Rattigan's *Separate Tables,* a drama about the interaction of a group of upper-class British men and women at a small hotel on the seashore.

Orson Welles directed and costars with Charlton Heston, Janet Leigh, and Marlene Dietrich in *Touch of Evil,* a twisting thriller set along the Mexican border, and Ingrid Bergman stars with Curt Jurgens and Robert Donat in Mark Robson's *Inn of the Sixth Happiness,* a drama about a missionary who leads children to safety in China during the 1930s. Among the notable foreign films was Ingmar Bergman's *The Magician,* starring Max von Sydow and Ingrid Thulin, about a traveling troupe of illusionists who come to a small Swedish town where people do not believe in magic.

Rock Hudson and Doris Day were voted the top male and female movie stars for 1958 and 1959. (*Photofest*)

Irvin Yeaworth's *The Blob,* starring Steve McQueen and Anita Corseaut, was one of the more notable creature-from-outer-space movies. The gelatinous creature slogs its way through a small American town, engorging everything in its path. It thus makes literal the common 1950s metaphor of "creeping communism." As in *Invasion of the Body Snatchers* (1956), *The Blob* centers on the protagonist's struggle to persuade his fellow citizens that a dangerous and imminent threat exists.

The top box office draws were a mix of established, older male stars and younger male and female stars, reflecting some of the shift toward youth that became more characteristic in American culture during the late 1950s and blossomed in the 1960s. The leading box office attractions were Glenn Ford, Taylor, Jerry Lewis, Brando, Rock Hudson, William Holden, Brigitte Bardot, Yul Brynner, James Stewart, and Frank Sinatra.

Literature

Authors have always felt freer than film directors or television producers to critique society and explore social dynamics and personal crises in an honest, deep fashion. This was particularly true in the 1950s, when the Red Scare and the movie code placed implicit and explicit limitations on what filmmakers could express, so anxiety and gloom were apparent in American fiction to a much greater degree than on television or in the movies. Much of the fiction from 1958 also articulates the harder edge that the other media were expressing.

For instance, John Barth's *The End of the Road* continued the author's questioning of the possibility, or impossibility, of meaningful action in a meaningless universe. Darkly comic, and harsher in tone than its companion piece from 1956, *The Floating Opera, The End of the Road* explored the possibility of living by a set of relative absolutes, in the absence of absolute truths. It further considered the consequences of racism, illegal abortion, and various levels of mental cruelty and mental illness. Truman Capote published a greatly admired story collection about characters living at the edge of society, *Breakfast at Tiffany's,* which Blake Edwards adapted into a 1961 film starring Audrey Hepburn and George Peppard. Although first published in 1955, Vladimir Nabokov's *Lolita* was not released in the United States until 1958, when the dark comedy about a professor infatuated with a prepubescent girl sold more than a million copies. Although not sexually titillating, the controversial novel, which was denounced as immoral, further addressed the nature of middle-class morality, personal delusion, abnormal psychology, and the sexual sophistication of young girls. More uplifting, but still very aware of life's struggles, Bernard Malamud's collection of short stories, *The Magic Barrel,* was praised especially for its mystical title story, and Jack Kerouac provided an affectionate account of some of his early love affairs in *The Subterraneans*. Kerouac's *The Dharma Bums,* also published in 1958, appealed to the growing interest in the Beat writers by providing accounts of some of the major figures.

William Lederer and Eugene Burdick's best-selling novel *The Ugly American* brought the United States political problems in Southeast Asia to the attention of the American public well before the introduction of U.S. combat troops to Vietnam. Set in Sarkhan, a mythical Southeast Asian country similar to Vietnam, the story focuses on the American ambassador whose failure to understand and appreciate local history, customs, and practices undermines his nation's well-intentioned efforts to improve the standard of living with advanced technology and improved agricultural methods. The novel criticizes State Department bureaucrats and political hacks who fail to learn the native languages and customs, insult local leaders, inhibit the constructive work of private individuals working in the villages, and allow their own egos, self-interest, and career aspirations to dominate their decisions. By contrast, the Soviet diplomatic corps appears dedicated, modest, self-sacrificing, well informed of local customs, linguistically fluent, and focused on its goal. The authors extol private Americans working directly with the local people in the villages, despite obstacles caused by government officials; these characters anticipate John F. Kennedy's Peace Corps volunteers. Eisenhower read it while on vacation. The book was adapted into a play in 1961, and Brando starred in George Eglund's film adaptation the following year.

One of the growing number of books that imagine life after a nuclear war, Alfred Coppel's *Dark December* considers who should lead a postapocalyptic society and what its values and aspirations should be. British author Peter George published *Red Alert,* which explores the possibility of unintended nuclear war in a story about a psychotic American general who sends a squadron of planes to attack Russia. The novel is best remembered as the basis for *Dr. Strangelove,* Stanley Kubrick's 1964 dark comedy about nuclear annihilation. Leon Uris's *Exodus* is a best-selling account of Jewish refugees from World War II who overcome obstacles to go to Palestine and help create the new nation of Israel. When Otto Preminger adapted it to film in 1960, he broke the Hollywood blacklist by crediting Dalton Trumbo with writing the screenplay. Trumbo was one of the blacklisted Hollywood Ten who had gone to jail for refusing to cooperate with HUAC in 1947.

The cold war also inspired some of the important nonfiction of the year. FBI director J. Edgar Hoover published *Masters of Deceit,* a best-selling handbook that educates Americans about communism. It sold some 250,000 copies in hardcover and 2 million copies in paperback. Ghostwritten by Louis B. Nichols, head of FBI public relations, *Masters of Deceit* went through 29 printings over 12 years and was

Truman Capote published *Breakfast at Tiffany's* in 1958. *(Photofest)*

frequently required reading in mandatory high school courses on Americanism versus communism.

Hoover's foreword begins, "Every citizen has a duty to learn more about the menace that threatens his future, his home, his children, the peace of the world—and this why I have written this book." He argues that American communists, aided by the Soviet Union, are actively, and illegally, acting to impose communism on America. He then provides a history of communism and explain the basic precepts of Marxism-Leninism, pointing out how Stalin employed mass terror, suspicion and distrust, illegal arrests, and a personality cult to consolidate and maintain power. Hoover then describes the history of communism in America, maintaining that its primary means of acquiring power is through thought control. He presents five categories of people who work on behalf of communism: acknowledged party members, secret party members, fellow travelers, opportunists, and dupes.

The book also describes how the American Communist Party is organized, how it operates, its strategies, and its tactics, which include mass agitation, infiltration, front organizations, appeals to minorities, and its "malicious" attempt to create a myth that Jews and communists share common interests. The book concludes by asserting that religion represents the strongest bulwark against atheistic communism.

Columnist Walter Lippmann traveled to the Soviet Union and received his first Pulitzer Prize for the series of articles he wrote about his experiences and observations. Nobel Prize winners Linus Pauling and Edward Teller, the "father" of the H-bomb, each published books expressing their opposing views on nuclear testing and arms development. Teller's *Our Nuclear Future,* coauthored with Albert Latter, argues that radioactive fallout from nuclear testing does not pose a serious threat to human life. The authors compare the risks from testing to ordinary dangers in everyday life, such as the possibility of developing lung cancer from smoking. The book was widely praised for its clear description of how atomic energy works, but it received mixed reviews for its political assessments. Pauling's *No More War!* describes the biological effects of radiation and other hazards from radioactive fallout and presents a scientist's perspective on the cold war nuclear threat. The appendix to *No More War!* includes the Mainau Declaration of Nobel laureates, a list of petitioners to the United Nations, and appeals by Albert Einstein and Albert Schweitzer to deal with the nuclear threat. Pauling was accused by book reviewers and members of Congress of contributing to the communist effort by promoting his pacifist position.

Economist John Kenneth Galbraith's best-selling *The Affluent Society* acknowledges that American capitalism, for the first time in history, has created a society in which most citizens enjoy a lifestyle rooted in prosperity instead of poverty. But Galbraith bemoans the vast disparity between the wealthy and the poor and argues for increased government investment in the public sector and greater government involvement in the management of the private economy, with the intention of reducing poverty, unemployment, and a deteriorating public infrastructure. Vilified by conservatives and embraced by liberals, the book influenced American economic thought for decades. Aldous Huxley also amplified upon the dangers of the current Western economic-political system in *Brave New World Revisited,* a commentary on his popular novel from 1932.

Lawrence Ferlinghetti's volumes of poems, *Tentative Description of a Dinner Given to Promote the Impeachment of President Eisenhower* and *A Coney Island of the Mind,* also have strong political agendas that were beginning to find a wider audience in 1958. *A Coney Island of the Mind* attacks religious hypocrisy in America that permits rampant commercial exploitation of Christ while remaining unmoved by the human suffering caused by the policies of the U.S. government. In that book, Ferlinghetti also condemns nationalism and the nation-state itself, as warfare and the nuclear bomb are their outgrowths. The title poem evokes images of cars falling from the trees and animals meeting terrible deaths to communicate the horror of the nuclear destruction. Beat poet Gregory Corso published *Gasoline.* One of the poems from that collection, "Don't Shoot the Warthog," depicts society as eating its young like cannibals— an image that mirrors Ginsberg's representation in his 1956 masterpiece, "Howl" of Moloch, the Canaanite god of fire who was believed to eat the children offered to him as sacrifices. Other significant poetry included Karl Shapiro's *Poems of a Jew,* e.e. cummings's *95 Poems,* Theodore Roethke's *Words for the Wind,* and Stanley Kunitz's Pulitzer Prize–winning *Selected Poems, 1928–1958.* Charges of treason against modernist poet Ezra Pound for his active support of fascism during World War II were dropped because Pound was ruled incompetent to stand trial. He was then released from the mental hospital where he had been incarcerated since the end of the war and allowed to return to Italy, where he died in 1972.

French anthropologist Claude Lévi-Strauss published his *Structural Anthropology,* which exerted enormous influence on several intellectual disciplines in the 1970s, including literary theory, which developed a branch called structuralism. Soviet writer Boris Pasternak, author of *Dr. Zhivago,* refused to accept the Nobel Prize in literature. Although Pasternak described his refusal as voluntary, he was pressured to do so by Soviet officials.

Theater, Music, and the Visual Arts

Archibald MacLeish's Pulitzer Prize– and Tony Award–winning play *J.B.* also questions how we should best cope with a hostile universe. The play presents an updated version of the biblical story of Job, whom God afflicts with many hardships as a test of his faith. In MacLeish's version, J.B. suffers from more modern afflictions, and false friends use contemporary clichés to express their insincere good wishes. Dore Schary's *Sunrise at Campobello* starred Ralph Bellamy as Franklin D. Roosevelt as a young man who experiences the onset of crippling polio. Bellamy and Greer Garson starred in Vincent J. Donahue's 1960 film adaptation. British actor John Gielgud performed a sequence of sonnets and scenes from Shakespearean plays in *Ages of Man* (the title comes from the "seven ages of man" speech in *As You Like It*). Eugene O'Neill's *A Touch of the Poet* had its Broadway debut. It was the first of a cycle of plays using American history as its background that the playwright left unfinished at his death in 1953. Britain's "angry young man," John Osborne, had two plays on Broadway: *Epitaph for George Dillon,* coauthored with Anthony Creighton, and *The Entertainer,* which starred Laurence Olivier and Joan Plowright. Henry Fonda and Anne Bancroft appeared in William Gibson's *Two for the Seesaw;* Alfred Lunt, Lynn Fontanne, and Eric Porter starred in Friedrich Dürrenmatt's absurdist comedy *The Visit.* The most enduring musical from the year was *Flower Drum Song* by Richard Rodgers and Oscar Hammerstein II.

The 75th anniversary of New York's Metropolitan Opera, celebrated by some 3,000 people, demonstrated that enthusiasm for the classical tradition of high culture remained alive, even while experimental forms of music and dance that depart from the traditions, trappings, and values of high culture continued to be pioneered. Alvin Ailey formed the American Dance Theater for modern dance; the New York City Ballet premiered George Balanchine's *Stars and Stripes;* Merce Cunningham produced John Cage's *Antic Meet;* and Martha Graham produced *Clytemnestra.* New cultural exchanges with the Soviet Union permitted the Moscow Moiseyev Dance Company to tour the United States, where it was enthusiastically received. In turn, four American composers were invited to the Soviet Union: Roger Sessions, Peter Mennin, Roy Harris, and Ulysses Kay. Moreover, in April pianist Van Cliburn won the Soviet Union's international Tchaikovsky competition in Moscow. Afterward, the *New York Times* ran a hopeful front-page headline proclaiming that Cliburn's victory had created an artistic bridge between the superpowers, and Cliburn returned to a hero's welcome in the United States. He went on to sign a contract with RCA, and his recording of the Tchaikovsky concerto became the first classical album ever to sell more than 1 million copies.

Jazz trumpeter Miles Davis made several important recordings: "On Green Dolphin Street" with pianist Bill Evans, large-ensemble arrangements of standards from George Gershwin's *Porgy and Bess* with pianist Gil Evans, and the album *Milestones,* which includes an early example of modal jazz in which improvisations are based on modes rather than conventional changes. At the end of the year, Davis predicted a new direction for jazz that would de-emphasize harmonic variation and accentuate melody. Peggy Lee's sexy recording of "Fever," Frank Sinatra's *Come Fly With Me* album, and a posthumous release of Tommy Dorsey's "Tea for Two Cha Cha" were among the other top jazz hits in the country.

The State Department continued to sponsor goodwill jazz tours around the world, promoting the indigenous American art form. Among those to serve as American "goodwill ambassadors" were Woody Herman (South America), Dave Brubeck (Middle East and India), and Jack Teagarden (Far East). Oscar Peterson performed in Amsterdam, and Duke Ellington played for Queen Elizabeth II at the Leeds Festival. Nat "King" Cole took the role of W. C. Handy, "Father of the Blues," in Allen Reisner's remake of *St. Louis Blues,* which also starred Ella Fitzgerald, Cab Calloway, and Mahalia Jackson. Handy died the same year, at age 84.

The world of rock 'n' roll was shaken up when Elvis Presley was drafted into the army on March 24. Although his induction anguished his many teenage fans, Presley, who had acquired a reputation as a rebel, performed his patriotic duty without protest and with grace. The fanfare over Presley's entry into military service later became the basis for the Broadway musical *Bye Bye, Birdie.* Prior to his induction, Presley had a hit single with "Hard-Headed Woman."

Ricky Nelson, who had gained national exposure on television's *The Adventures of Ozzie and Harriet,* released his album, *Ricky.* Other rock hits included "Bird Dog" and four playful songs that reflect some of the absurdist spirit found in the pop art and absurdist theater of the time: "Purple People Eater," "Pink Shoe Laces," "Witch Doctor," and "The Chipmunk Song," which was released in December, in time for Christmas, and sold some 3.5 million copies in its first five weeks. David Seville, who also recorded "Witch Doctor," created the Chipmunk trio of Alvin, Theodore, and Simon by recording the music at different speeds to produce a squeaky, high-pitched "chipmunk sound." In 1961, The Chipmunks made what some historians regard as the first music video when they appeared on their own weekly CBS television show.[6] Other top songs from 1958 were Perry Como's "Catch a Falling Star"; "Twilight Time" by the Platters; "Lollipop," a vaguely sexually suggestive song by the Chordettes; "Who's Sorry Now?" by Connie Francis; and "Gigi," from the movie.

The Kingston Trio brought folk music back into vogue with its song "Tom Dooley," about a man about to be executed, and Laurie London demonstrated the persistent appeal of gospel with her rendition of "He's Got the Whole World in His Hands." Johnny Cash's "Ballad of a Teenage Queen" was also a hit.

The Metropolitan Museum of Art in New York City featured Georgia O'Keeffe in a historical review of American art. O'Keeffe, who is best known for her work earlier in the century but who remained active through the 1950s and beyond, is famous for her luscious renditions of plants and animal artifacts that often suggest sexual movements and forms. The Museum of Modern Art celebrated the 70th anniversary of Marc Chagall, Georges Seurat, Amedeo Modigliani, and Jean Arp's paintings pioneering innovative, expressive uses of color, light, and abstraction. Major new works of modern architecture included New York's Seagram Building by Ludwig Mies van der Rohe and Philip Johnson and Johnson's Four Seasons restaurant, for which Mark Rothko created monumental paintings. Known for its austere, rectilinear design and its use of reinforced glass and other contemporary building materials, the Seagram Building is often pointed to as a premier example of modern architecture.

CHRONICLE OF EVENTS

1958

January 1: As per the 1957 Treaty of Rome, the European Economic Community (Common Market) comes into being.

January 13: Some 9,000 scientists from 43 countries petition the United Nations for an immediate international agreement to halt nuclear testing.

January 20: The Soviet Union warns the Baghdad Pact countries against introducing nuclear weapons and missile bases into the Middle East.

January 27: The United States and Soviet Union agree to expand cultural exchanges.

January 28: Baseball star Roy Campanella of the former Brooklyn, now Los Angeles Dodgers is paralyzed in a car accident.

January 28: Film stars Paul Newman and Joanne Woodward wed while filming *The Long, Hot Summer.* They later become only the second married couple in which both partners win an Academy Award.

January 29: The United States authorizes $10 million in aid to the Baghdad Pact nations.

January 29: Charles Starkweather and his girlfriend, Caril Ann Fugate, are captured after going on a robbery and murder spree that included the death of Fugate's parents and sister. Both are tried and convicted for murder.

January 30: Dore Schary's play about Franklin D. Roosevelt's struggle against polio, *Sunrise at Campobello,* opens on Broadway with Ralph Bellamy as Roosevelt and Mary Fickett as his wife, Eleanor. The Tony Award–winning play enjoys 558 performances, and in 1960, Vincent J. Donehue adapts it to film, starring Bellamy and Greer Garson.

January 30: In Paris, Yves Saint Laurent has his first fashion show. The 22-year-old is hailed as the successor to Christian Dior, who died in October 1957.

January 31: The United States launches its first space satellite, *Explorer 1,* into orbit at 10:48 P.M. (EST). The 30.8-pound satellite is propelled atop a military Jupiter rocket that has been modified by a team of scientists headed by Wernher von Braun. It orbits the Earth every 114 minutes and achieves a maximum altitude of 2,000 miles; its closest point to Earth is 230 miles. Scientific data collected by *Explorer* enable astronomer John Van Allen to identify two belts of cosmic radiation that circle the Earth.

February: To test the effects of LSD, the U.S. Army administers the drug on at least four occasions to 741 soldiers who believe they are volunteering for a test of equipment and clothing under conditions of chemical warfare. At least one of the soldiers, James Stanley, suffers long-term effects, including flashbacks, confusion and depression, and later sues the government. (The Supreme Court rules 5–4 against him in 1987, but an arbitration panel awards him $400,000 in 2001.)

February 2: Soviet president Bulganin requests a summit meeting with Eisenhower.

February 17: Organizers in Britain form the Campaign for Nuclear Disarmament (CND), which advocates unilateral nuclear disarmament. The CND becomes a significant, but never dominant, force in British politics through the mid-1960s.

February 22: The United States agrees to supply Great Britain with intermediate-range ballistic missiles capable of reaching the Soviet Union.

March 11: A U.S. B-47 bomber accidentally drops an unarmed atom bomb on a South Carolina farm home, injuring six people.

March 22: Film producer Mike Todd and screenwriter Art Cohn are killed in a plane crash when Todd's chartered plane, *The Lucky Liz,* crashes into a mountain near Albuquerque, New Mexico. Todd's wife, actress Elizabeth Taylor, misses the flight because she is bedridden with pneumonia and a high fever. Writer-director Joseph L. Mankiewicz, who is initially reported to be among those aboard, also misses the flight because his sister-in-law convinces him not to fly in the turbulent weather.

March 24: Elvis Presley is inducted into the U.S. Army.

March 27: Khrushchev replaces Bulganin as Soviet premier. Khrushchev retains his post as first secretary of the Communist Party, and the Soviet Union thus returns to one-man rule for the first time since Stalin's death in 1953. Bulganin is demoted in August to a provincial post.

March 31: Following the conclusion of an extensive series of tests, Khrushchev declares a unilateral halt to nuclear testing and calls on the United States and Britain to do likewise.

April 1: Eisenhower signs an emergency $1.8-million house-building bill to reinvigorate the sagging economy.

April 4: The Campaign for Nuclear Disarmament leads a rally of 5,000 people, who protest in London's Trafalgar Square against nuclear testing.

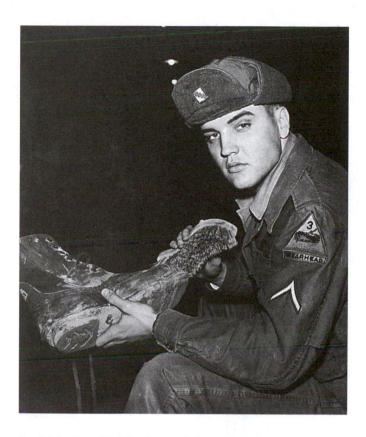

Rock 'n' roll star Elvis Presley was inducted into the U.S. Army as a private and served in Germany during the second Berlin crisis. *(Photofest)*

April 5: Castro declares all-out war against the Batista regime.

April 6: Arnold Palmer wins golf's Master's title.

April 13: Twenty-three-year-old American pianist Van Cliburn wins the Soviet Union's international Tchaikovsky piano competition, when a panel of 16 Soviet judges select him over eight other contestants, including three Russians. He returns to a hero's welcome in the United States, as Eisenhower hosts a special White House reception for him and New York City gives him a ticker tape parade.

April 27: Vice President Nixon begins his tour of South America in Trinidad.

May 1: Nasser signs an accord with the Soviet Union promising that Egypt will support Soviet foreign policy in return for Soviet work on behalf of the liberation of the people of Asia and Africa.

May 7: Nixon and his wife, Pat, are greeted by angry crowds in Lima, Peru, protesting U.S. influence in South American internal and economic affairs.

May 8: Secretary of State Dulles announces that the United States will regard an attack on West Berlin as an attack on the Western allies.

May 8: Eight Nike missiles explode at a New Jersey military base, killing 10 people.

May 13: French troops seize control of Algiers and demand the return of Charles de Gaulle to power within France. On May 19, de Gaulle gives a press conference in which he denies any intention to install himself as dictator.

May 13: Eisenhower orders U.S. troops to the Caribbean after Venezuelan mobs attack Nixon on his goodwill tour of South America. The tour ends prematurely the following day.

May 24: French army rebels seize power in Corsica and call for the return of de Gaulle.

May 26: Trumpeter Miles Davis records "On Green Dolphin Street" with pianist Bill Evans.

May 28: France's premier, Pierre Pflimlin, resigns to avert a military coup, and the Fourth Republic ends. The following day, de Gaulle is asked to form a new government and starts drafting a new constitution.

May 30: Unknown soldiers from World War II and Korea are enshrined at Arlington National Cemetery.

June 9: Eisenhower meets with British prime minister Macmillan in Washington to discuss world affairs. They agree to send jets to Iran, Jordan, and Lebanon, and Britain sends paratroopers to support the government in Lebanon.

June 16: The Supreme Court rules that it is unconstitutional to deny passports to suspected communists.

June 28: The world's longest suspension bridge to date is opened between Michigan's upper and lower peninsulas.

June 29: A bomb explodes outside the church of civil rights activist Reverend Fred Shuttleworth, in Birmingham, Alabama.

June 29: Castro's rebels capture 28 U.S. servicemen near the U.S. naval base at Guantánamo Bay, Cuba, in retaliation for U.S. cooperation with the Cuban government's military operations.

July 7: Eisenhower signs a bill admitting Alaska as the 49th state.

July 14: The royal family of Iraq is murdered in a military coup led by anti-Western general Abdul Karim Kassem, who proclaims Iraq a republic with himself as its head.

July 15: Eisenhower invokes the Eisenhower Doctrine to send U.S. Marines to Lebanon to support the presidency of Camille Chamoun, whose pro-West policies have sparked rebellion in Beirut in the aftermath of the anti–Western revolution in Iraq.

July 17: Britain sends two battalions of soldiers to support the pro-Western government of King Hussein of Jordan, in response to protests sparked by the anti–Western revolution in Iraq.

July 18: U.S. servicemen captured by Castro's rebels in Cuba are freed.

July 20: Khrushchev tells Egyptian president Nasser that Soviet volunteers are ready to serve in the Middle East.

July 23: The Soviet Union accepts a U.S. proposal for a summit meeting on the Middle East to be held at the United Nations.

July 28: Eisenhower sends a contingent of marines to Cuba, with the approval of the Batista regime, in order to protect the water supply to the U.S. naval base at Guantánamo Bay.

July 29: Congress passes legislation and funding to create the National Aeronautics and Space Administration (NASA) to implement the nation's program of space exploration.

July 31: Haiti's president, "Papa Doc" Duvalier, personally helps suppress a military revolt led by two former army captains. Following the aborted coup, Duvalier is granted authority to rule by decree for six months, making him a virtual dictator.

August 3: Some 250,000 people attend Jehovah's Witness rallies in New York's Yankee Stadium and Polo Grounds.

August 3: Khrushchev and Mao Zedong meet in Beijing.

August 4: Greek rebels on Cyprus call a truce with Turkey and Britain.

August 7: The Supreme Court reverses Arthur Miller's conviction for contempt of Congress during his 1956 testimony before HUAC.

August 13: Eisenhower removes 1,700 U.S. Marines from Lebanon.

August 14: Britain and France announce that they are relaxing trade restrictions with the Soviet Union, the People's Republic of China, and other communist nations.

August 18: Vladimir Nabokov's *Lolita* (1955) is published in the United States.

August 23: Communist China begins bombarding Jinmen (Quemoy) and Mazu (Matsu), contested islands near Taiwan.

August 26: Classical composer Ralph Vaughan Williams dies in London at age 86.

August 27: Eisenhower sends an aircraft carrier and four destroyers to defend Jinmen and Mazu.

August 27: The crew of the nuclear submarine *Nautilus* receives a ticker tape parade in New York City following its record-making voyage beneath the North Pole. Admiral Hyman Rickover, who was largely responsible for the formation of the nuclear submarine fleet, is also honored.

August 28: Accusations are first reported that the high-stakes quiz show *Twenty-One* is fixed.

August 29: Kirk Neumann's science fiction horror film *The Fly* premieres at more than 100 theaters in New York.

September 2: Eisenhower signs the National Defense Education Act to provide student loans, aid for technical education, and postsecondary education in mathematics and the sciences.

September 5: In Alabama, Dr. Martin Luther King, Jr., is arrested for loitering.

September 11: Eisenhower declares the U.S. determination to defend Jinmen and Mazu by force, if necessary.

September 12: Arkansas governor Faubus closes all four Little Rock high schools for the year rather than integrate them.

September 22: Denying any wrongdoing, White House aide Sherman Adams resigns after it is revealed that he received gifts from a textile magnate for whom he made inquiries at two federal agencies.

September 28: The former French territory of West Guinea is established as a new nation after rejecting admission into the French Commonwealth.

September 28: In a major victory for de Gaulle, French voters overwhelmingly approve a new constitution that gives expanded powers to the president. Algerians vote in the French elections for the first time, and Muslim women in Algiers first exercise the right to vote.

September 29: The Supreme Court bans "evasive schemes" to thwart school integration, such as that proposed by Arkansas's governor, Orval Faubus.

October 3: New York's Idlewild Airport (later renamed John F. Kennedy International Airport), opens to jet airliners.

October 4: After rules restricting noise levels are altered, at Idlewild, British Overseas Airways initiates the first regular transatlantic jet service between London and the United States.

October 5: Clinton High School in Tennessee is destroyed by a firebomb. The school was integrated in 1956.

October 9: Pope Pius XII dies.

October 10: The New York Yankees come from behind to defeat the Milwaukee Braves and win baseball's World Series in seven games. New York's Bob Turley wins the Cy Young Award with a record of 21-7. Milwaukee's Warren Spahn (22-11) and Lew Burdette (20-10) have the best records in the National League. At age 40, Boston Red Sox Ted Williams wins the American League batting title (.328), while Philadelphia Phillies centerfielder Richie Ashburn leads the National League (.350). Chicago Cub Ernie Banks, the National League's MVP, leads the major leagues with 47 home runs. Boston's Jackie Jensen is named the American League MVP. During the season Stan Musial has his 3,000th hit, and Ted Williams alienates fans across the nation when a bat he hurls in frustration flies into the stands and hits a fan.

October 11: The United States launches *Pioneer,* its first moon rocket. Although *Pioneer* does not attain its destination, due to an error in calculating the initial angle of takeoff, it travels more than 79,000 miles before gravity draws it back to Earth, where it crashes into the Pacific Ocean.

October 22: The U.S. national debt reaches a record high of more than $280 billion.

October 23: The Soviet Union agrees to lend approximately $100 million to Egypt for construction of the Aswan High Dam.

October 25: The last group of U.S. Marines leave Lebanon.

October 28: Cardinal Roncalli of Venice becomes Pope John XXIII.

October 31: Soviet writer Boris Pasternak, author of *Dr. Zhivago,* refuses the Nobel Prize in literature.

November 4: The United States, the Soviet Union, and Great Britain agree to a voluntary moratorium on nuclear testing.

November 10: King Hussein claims that Syrian jets attacked his plane while he was flying over Syria on his way home to Jordan.

November 10: Khrushchev initiates a second Berlin crisis by issuing an ultimatum for Western forces to leave West Berlin by threatening to sign a peace treaty with East Germany that will terminate all rights of the Western allies in Berlin.

November 27: Khrushchev agrees to postpone the peace treaty with East Germany, but insists that West Berlin must become a "free city" under UN authority and that all occupying military powers withdraw their forces. He adds that if such an agreement is not reached within six months, the Soviet Union will sign the treaty with East Germany, which will then insist that the Western troops leave.

December 1: Ninety people die in a school fire in Chicago.

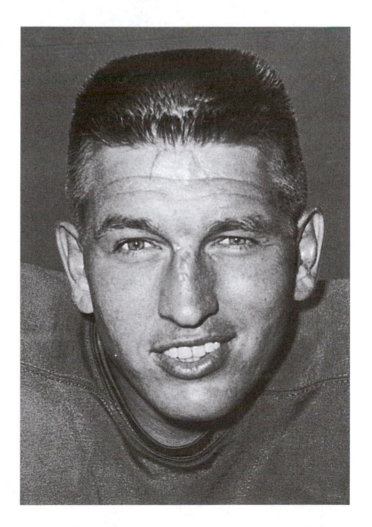

Quarterback John Unitas led the Baltimore Colts to an exciting, nationally televised, overtime victory in the NFL title game on December 28, 1958. *(Photofest)*

December 16: NATO rejects the Soviet-East German ultimatum.

December 17: Arms-control talks end without achieving significant progress.

December 17: Due to the failure of his economic programs in the Great Leap Forward, Mao Zedong steps down as China's head of state. Moderate reformer Liu Shaoqi succeeds him.

December 25: Eisenhower broadcasts a prerecorded Christmas message to the entire world using a satellite radio-relay station.

December 28: In what is still considered one of the finest football championship games ever played, the Baltimore Colts win the NFL title by defeating the New York Giants 23-17 in a dramatic overtime finish. Washington Redskin quarterback Eddie LeBaron leads the league in passing; Baltimore's Raymond Berry leads in receiving, and Cleveland's Jim Brown, the league's MVP, gains the most yardage rushing.

December 31: After losing a series of battles to Castro, Batista flees Cuba to Miami on New Year's Eve.

EYEWITNESS TESTIMONY

In light of what we have recently learned about animal behavior in general, and human behavior in particular, it has become clear that control through the punishment of undesirable behavior is less effective, in the long run, than control through the reinforcement of desirable behavior by rewards, and that government through terror works on the whole less well than government through the non-violent manipulation of the environment and of the thoughts and feelings of individual men, women and children. Punishment temporarily puts a stop to undesirable behavior, but does not permanently reduce the victim's tendency to indulge in it. Moreover, the psycho-physical by-products of punishment may be just as undesirable as the behavior for which an individual has been punished. Psychotherapy is largely concerned with the debilitating or anti-social consequences of past punishments.

The society described in *1984* is a society controlled almost exclusively by punishment and the fear of punishment. In the imaginary world of my own fable punishment is infrequent and generally mild. The nearly perfect control exercised by the government is achieved by systematic reinforcement of desirable behavior, by many kinds of nearly non-violent manipulation, both physical and psychological, and by genetic standardization. . . .

Meanwhile impersonal forces over which we have almost no control seem to be pushing us all in the direction of the Brave New Worldian nightmare; and this impersonal pushing is being consciously accelerated by representatives of commercial and political organizations who have developed a number of new techniques for manipulating, in the interest of some minority, the thoughts and feelings of the masses. . . . What are these forces? And why has the nightmare, which I had projected into the seventh century A.F. [After (Henry) Ford], made so swift an advance in our direction?

Aldous Huxley discussing the growing danger of subtle, psychological manipulation of the masses, in Huxley, Brave New World Revisited *(1958), pp. 5–8.*

Four things that I'm not impressed by . . . are unity, harmony, eternality, and universality. In my ethics the most a man can ever do is be right from his point of view; there's no general reason why he should even bother to defend it, much less expect anybody else to accept it, but the only thing he can do is operate by it, because there's nothing else. He's got to expect conflict with people or institutions who are also right from *their* points of view, but whose points of view are different from his.

Fictional character Joe Morgan discussing relative absolutes with The End of the Road's *narrator, Jacob Horner, in John Barth's novel* The End of the Road *(1958), p. 42.*

The more sophisticated your ethics get, the stronger you have to be to stay afloat. And when you say good-bye to objective values, you really have to flex your muscles and keep your eyes open, because you're on your own. It takes *energy*: not just personal energy, but cultural energy, or you're lost. Energy's what makes the difference between American pragmatism and French existentialism.—where else but in America could you have a cheerful nihilism, for God's sake?

Joe Morgan discussing the possibility of formulating a philosophy of life predicated on a "cheerful nihilism," in John Barth's novel The End of the Road *(1958), p. 44.*

What a man ends up doing is what he has to take responsibility for having wanted to do.

Joe Morgan expressing existentialist sentiments that were coming into vague in America in the late 1950s, in John Barth's novel The End of the Road *(1958), p. 104.*

Slowly the priest concluded that these Communist speeches were a form of secular ritual. The crude slogans were only symbols which meant much to the converted; the incredible promises of an abundant future were as real to them as the Stations of the Cross to a Catholic. . . . [The] faith of a Communist was no more shaken by news of a bloody purge of "right-wing deviationists" than is the faith of a Catholic by the news that the Inquisition was brutal.

William J. Lederer and Eugene Burdick describing the attraction of communism to its followers in their novel The Ugly American *(1958), p. 46.*

What in general has caused America's loss of prestige?

The Americans I knew in the United States were wonderfully friendly, unassuming, and interested in the world. . . .

For some reason, however, the Americans I meet in my country [Burma] are not the same as the ones I knew in the United States. A mysterious change seems to come over Americans when they go to a foreign land. They isolate themselves socially. They live pretentiously. They're loud and ostentatious. Perhaps they're frightened and defensive. . . .

In 1953 Burma was in critical need of money and technical assistance. Yet you terminated all United States aid. Why . . .?

In the first place we were offended by the superior airs and what even Americans call the "razzle-dazzle." . . . Second . . . although American money was flowing into Burma, it wasn't helping much. . . .

You implied earlier that the Russians who went abroad seemed to operate more effectively. . . .

The Russians are professionals. They keep many of their men in Burma for as long as five years. They all know Burmese. They study quietly and live quietly. They employ no Burmese servants, and hence there is nobody to spread gossip about them. All their servants are Russian. . . .

[Their economic aid] is much more obvious, and so more effective as propaganda [than America's]. . . .

Burmese journalist U Maung Swe answering questions about the United States's image in Southeast Asia, in William J. Lederer and Eugene Burdick, The Ugly American *(1958), pp. 145–51.*

Ol' Elvis Presley may be a better musician than most people dare to admit—and he might be offering the kids a commodity their parents can't recognize.

As a subject for polemic Elvis Presley has few peers, and too many people have experienced sudden shifts in blood pressure—either up or down—for him to be regarded as anything but an authentic barometer of the times. But, even now that he has been on the national scene for more than two years, he may be telling us more about ourselves than we would care to admit.

Presley's climb to fame, in the winter of 1955–56, followed upon the appearance of that raucous brand of popular music, primitive and heavy-footed, known as rock-and-roll. Untouched by subtlety, rock-and-roll seemed to signal a total collapse in popular taste, the final schism between a diminishing group sensitive to tradition and the great bulk of those who make entertainment to sell. Suddenly, there was Elvis, not merely a manifestation of rock-and-roll, but of lascivious gyrations of the torso that older generations quickly recognized—the classic bump and grind of the strip-teaser.

Television compounded the jeopardy: Elvis could come lurching into any living-room . . . the chorus of adolescent shrieks was swelled by shrieks from the parents. . . . the foot-spread stance and the unmistakable thrust—well, "The Pelvis" was going too far.

He went too far in every direction. Elvis was making millions of dollars, owning white Continental Mark IIs, getting into fights and reviving sideburns and being prayed over and building a house for his parents. The legend should have swallowed him out of sight, but it was all true—and furthermore, palpably American. . . .

By constantly reminding his teen-age listeners of what he so obviously was—a simple boy from Tupelo . . . Elvis somehow removed the sting from the sexuality that could easily have terrified them.

James Baxter and Annette Baxter discussing the popularity of Elvis Presley, in Baxter and Baxter, "The Man in the Blue Suede Shoes," Harper's Magazine *(January 1958), pp. 45–48.*

Since a hundred schoolchildren a year write me letters like yours—some writers get a thousand—the problem of what to do about classroom "projects" has become a serious one for all of us. If a writer answered all of you he would get nothing else done. When I was a baby goat I had to do my own research on projects, and I enjoyed doing it. I never wrote an author for his autograph or photograph in my life. Photographs are for movie actors to send to girls. Tell your teacher I said so. . . .

One of the things that discourage us writers is the fact that 90 percent of you children write wholly, or partly, illiterate letters, carelessly typed. You yourself write "clarr" for "class" and that's a honey, Robert, since *s* is next to *a*, and *r* is on the line above. Most schoolchildren in America would do a dedication like the following (please find the mistakes in it and write me about them):

To Miss Effa G. Burns

Without who's help this book could never of been finished it, is dedicated with gratitude by it's arthur.

Show that to your teacher and tell her to show it to her principal, and see if they can find the mistakes. . . .

Just yesterday a letter came in from a girl your age in South Carolina asking for biographical material and photograph. That is not the kind of education they have in Russia, we are told, because it's too much like a hobby or waste of time. What do you and your classmates want to be when you grow up—collectors? Then who is going to help keep the United States ahead of Russia in science, engineering, and the arts?

Please answer this letter. If you don't I'll write to another pupil.

Humorist James Thurber's letter of January 4, 1958, to grade-school student Robert Leifert complaining of intellectual sloppiness in Thurber, Selected Letters of James Thurber *(1981), pp. 205–6.*

Lewis Carroll's Alice would have found herself very much at home at the NATO meeting. Non-existent missiles in exchange for promissory bases. What a Wonderland bargain! Yet those who believe that the world's problems can be settled in some way other than through international hari-kari are grateful that NATO dealt exclusively in futures. It leaves time . . . for the build-up of public pressures which alone, it would seem, can force a genuine East-West negotiation. In this connection, there are two obvious points to be made. The first . . . is that Mr. [Secretary of State John Foster] Dulles, who has repeatedly announced that he does not believe in negotiation, is clearly not the man to negotiate. The second is that we ought to take a long, hard look at what it is we want to negotiate. Ten long years of negotiation on disarmament have proven futile mainly because burning political issues have devoured the mutual trust on which disarmament, to some extent, must be based. . . .

The Russians have offered their version of a solution for each of these problems: a complete embargo on arms to the Middle East; the neutralization of a united Germany; an anti-aggression pact between NATO and the Soviet bloc. This is not to say that the Russian solutions should be accepted in the terms in which they have been offered; it is only to say that they promise more in terms of negotiation than does disarmament. The arms race is a product of political conflict, and not the other way around. Negotiating on the political issues is negotiating on the heart of the matter.

Editorial on East-West negotiations in "Negotiate on What?" Nation *(January 4, 1958), p. 1.*

[Spain's dictator, Francisco Franco, has suggested that] NATO might find Spain's Canary Islands useful as a naval base. . . . [If Franco] could inveigle NATO into his part of North Africa, he could shift onto broader shoulders his present troublesome and costly war with Arab nationalists. Franco was never a fool.

Editorial on NATO's relations with Spain in "Franco Has a Job for NATO," Nation *(January 4, 1958), p. 1.*

Caril is the one who said to go to Washington State

by the time anybody will read this i will be dead for all the killings then they cannot give caril the chair . . . they got us Jan. 29, 1958.

kill 11 persons (Charlie kill 9) all men
(Caril kill 2) all girls

they have so many cops and people watching us leave I can't add all of them up

Mass murderer Charles Starkweather writing on his prison wall while incarcerated for killings committed by him and his girlfriend, Caril Ann Fugate, in Nebraska between December 1, 1957, and January 29, 1958, quoted in Jane Stern and Michael Stern, Encyclopedia of Pop Culture *(1992), p. 478.*

If I fry in the electric chair, Caril should be sitting in my lap.

Mass murderer Charles Starkweather, at the trial of his girlfriend, Caril Ann Fugate, for killings committed in Nebraska between December 1, 1957, and January 29, 1958, in Jane Stern and Michael Stern, Encyclopedia of Pop Culture *(1992), p. 478.*

Mr. T. S. Eliot is the Jayne Mansfield of the intellectuals. Miss Mansfield comprises all the arguments that there is a whole sex consisting entirely of women; and similarly, Mr. Eliot epitomizes one side of the great debate between left thinkers and right thinkers.

For he is Reaction in the flesh. He believes in original sin, in the fall of man, in the permanence of evil. . . . Whenever he hears the word "progress," he unscrews the cap of his fountain pen. . . .

The *Sweeniad* is a savagely satirical parody, in 66 pages, of Eliot's poem, "The Waste Land." . . .

When he is mocking Mr. Eliot, Dr. Purcell is very funny. . . . [But] a generation has passed since "The Waste Land" was written. The world has lived through Hitler, Stalin, Belsen, Auschwitz, as well as Hiroshima. It is surprising, indeed, to find anyone prepared to set down as pungent and devastating the naive variations on the theme of Progress as a Good Thing that are contained in the *Sweeniad.* . . . Dr. Purcell begins with a bang but he ends as a whimper.

> *Charles Curran reviewing* Sweeniad, *a parody of T. S. Eliot's* The Waste Land, *by Dr. Victor Purcell (a.k.a. Myra Buttle), in Curran, "The Bang and the Whimper,"* New Republic *(February 3, 1958), p. 19.*

Walter Reuther's collective-bargaining gimmicks have always been showy. A decade ago, he brightened the technology of collective bargaining by installing escalators with the result that wage increases tied to the cost-of-living index and "annual improvement factors" are now a feature of many agreements. (This idea came initially from the other side of the bargaining table when "Engine Charlie" of GM proposed an annual increase proportional to *productivity,* but Reuther revised the semantics and made the idea his own.) Then came his demand for a "guaranteed annual wage," and if g.a.w. in the final form of the contract was spelled s.u.b. (supplementary unemployment benefits), there was more of a relation than semantics might indicate.

This year's gimmick, profit-sharing in a three-way split, is even showier. His proposal is that the before-tax profits of the company, after 10 percent had been set aside, be divided 50 percent to shareholders and executives, 25 percent to purchasers of the year's new models as a consumer rebate, and 25 percent to the companies' workers. . . .

> *Labor-leader Walter Reuther's proposal for a profit-sharing plan being ridiculed, in "Reuther's Proposal for Profit-Sharing,"* New Republic *(February 17, 1958), pp. 6–7.*

MIKE TODD KILLED IN PLANE CRASH. Additional death by Art Cohn.

> *Screenwriter Harry Kurnitz's dark quip about the lowly status of writers in Hollywood, made after producer Mike Todd and writer Art Cohn were killed in a plane crash on March 22, 1958, in Harry Haun,* The Cinematic Century *(2000).*

It really pisses me off they called me a producer.

> *Film writer-director Joseph L. Mankiewicz remarking on an article in the* New York Times, *March 23, 1958, stating that he was among the victims of the airplane crash that killed Mike Todd and Art Cohn, in Harry Haun,* The Cinematic Century *(2000).*

Elvis was getting big the year I got married. I remember when he first performed on *The Ed Sullivan Show* that year [1956]. When he went into the army [in 1958], the most exciting thing was when they shaved his beautiful hair off, although they left his a little longer than most.

> *Maezel Brown recalling the induction of Elvis Presley into the U.S. Army on March 24, 1958, in private correspondence with the author, September 9, 2001.*

If I had an infinite amount of respect for the people who think I gave the greatest performance, then it would matter.

> *Actress Joanne Woodward commenting on the Academy Award she won on March 26, 1958, for her performance as the schizophrenic title character in* The Three Faces of Eve, *in Harry Haun,* The Cinematic Century *(2000).*

The theme [of Erich Kahler's *The Tower and the Abyss*]. . . is the leitmotif of our time: from Nietzsche to the Existentialists we have heard that the old order, the old values are gone (*really* gone) and the task of modern man is to reconstitute both "the shattered picture of the world" and the decent community of men. A good many people probably agreed with William Barrett [in *What Is Existentialism?*] that "the modern world, the modern city, has made it increasingly difficult for any person to lead a life that is really his own. The forces of advertising, mass culture, crowding, traffic congestion, standardization, regimentation in and out of war, beat upon us all, threatening to reduce our personalities to mere figments and shadows." . . . Undoubtedly a sizeable number of intellectuals still hold that the trend toward what Irving Howe calls a "sort of low-pressured, usually non-terroristic yet essentially unfree authoritarianism is a real "possibility." . . .

The question for [Kahler] remains . . . Will the supra-human collective of the future exclude or contain the human community of the past? The choice, he believes, is still our own to make. . . .

What we have in Mr. Kahler's work is a significant misreading of reality. It may be true, for example, that the old values have (in some sense) really disappeared, but how can we be certain that man is much the worse for it? It is difficult to imagine a question more loaded with subjective pitfalls than whether men are more anxious, less integrated and generally unhappier than they were in former times. . . . That life was more meaningful, more unified, more harmonious, when hierarchy and the Church ruled the world seems to be an unquestioned assumption among an astonishing number of intelligent people, both believers and non-believers, both liberals and conservatives. How can they possibly know?

C. Roland Wagner reviewing Erich Kahler's book The Tower and the Abyss: An Inquiry into the Transformation of the Individual, *in Wagner, "The Moral Perspective of Humanism,"* Hudson Review *(Spring 1958), pp. 140–41.*

[The Young Lions *was trying*] to show that Nazism is a matter of mind, not geography, that there are Nazis—and people of good will—in every country. The world can't spend its life looking over its shoulder and nursing hatreds. There would be no progress that way.

Marlon Brando discussing his role as Christian Diestl in The Young Lions, *which premiered in early April 1958, in David Downing,* Marlon Brando *(1984), p. 72.*

Most notable of its changes is in the character of the young Nazi [played by Marlon Brando] who . . . is central in Mr. [Irwin] Shaw's novel of World War II. In that large and sweeping saga, this young warrior is introduced as a fairly decent ski instructor who, under the hammering of Nazism and war, is molded into a monster, fired with militaristic madness and blood lust.

But in this prettier film version . . . this significantly unregenerate Nazi is changed into a very nice young man who never embraces Nazism with any apparent zeal. Indeed, he regards the whole business of war with sadness and disgust that become increasingly depressing as time and disasters pile up.

Film critic Bosley Crowther reviewing The Young Lions, *in Crowther, "The Young Lions,"* New York Times, *April 3, 1958, p. 23.*

Occasionally one comes across a book which delivers such a powerful jolt to the reader that he cannot remain neutral or indifferent before it. . . . Such a book is . . . Romano Guardini's *The End of the Modern World.* . . .

The gist of Guardini's message . . . [is that] in the coming new world of total power and unlimited scientific mastery over nature . . . all traditional landmarks of our culture, all the characteristic family traits of Western humanism, will be obliterated. As a result, this world will be more harsh and intense, more antihuman and antipersonalist, than any era in history. . . . To live genuine humanism, let alone a Christian humanism, in any kind of harmony with such a world will be extremely difficult, if not impossible. Even to be an authentic Christian at all will require rare courage and resistance to overwhelming social pressures.

What is the evidence for this bleak verdict? Guardini makes his case by sketching in broad outline the characteristic traits of Western man in the three great periods of his history up to the present, and then shows how the contemporary world is moving inexorably toward the almost total obliteration of all these "family traits" of the past. . . .

[The] central and most crucial [theme] . . . is the radical change which has taken place in man's relation to nature, both in his thinking and in his acting. . . .

Nature is now, Guardini says, about to become dependent on man and will have to plead with him, so to speak, to protect her and to take into his own hands the responsibility for her future.

But post-modern man will pay a heavy price for this new-found mastery. Having emancipated himself from the service of God and made nature herself his dependent, he will suddenly wake up to the awful loneliness and terrifying consequences of having to bear ultimate responsibility for ultimate power.

W. Norris Clarke reviewing Romano Guardini's book The End of the Modern World, *in Clarke, "The End of the Modern World?"* America: National Catholic Weekly Review *(April 19, 1958), pp. 106–7.*

Nine pacifists were arrested yesterday morning for refusing to take shelter during the air-raid drill.

After being booked at the West Fifty-fourth Street Precinct, they pleaded guilty. . . . Magistrate Kenneth M. Phipps sentenced them to thirty days in jail and then suspended the sentence, admonishing them to obey the law in the future.

The three were Miss Dorothy Day, 60 years old, publisher of *The Catholic Worker;* Ammon Hennacy, 65, associate editor, and Miss Deane Mowrer, 51, a writer for the paper. The rest . . . were Quakers and members of *The Catholic Worker.*

The nine marched together under the auspices of Non-Violent Action Against Nuclear Weapons, a group that has been protesting the proposed nuclear tests in the Pacific. . . .

Mr. Gilmore [the spokesman] told Magistrate Phipps they were opposed to air-raid drills "because they are a method of preparation for war" and there is no defense against nuclear weapons except a cessation of war." . . .

[In addition, in Rochester, New York] five young people . . defiantly stood in a public square near the heart of the city and refused to take cover during the Civil Defense alert.

Four of the group described themselves members of the Society of Friends. They said that as Quakers and pacifists they did not feel they could "participate in war or preparations for war such as air raids." . . .

No one asked the group to leave the square or interfered with its pamphlet distribution.

Protestors resorting to civil disobedience in opposition to air raid drills, in "9 Pacifists Seized in Defying Alert," New York Times, *May 7, 1958, p. 30.*

[Florida State Senator] Charlie Johns didn't have anything against the University of Florida, as such, he wasn't out trying to hurt the university. He was out on a mission by gosh that he had heard there were homosexuals on the faculty and he was going to get rid of them.

John Wayne Reitz, former president of the University of Florida, commenting in November 1983 on the Johns Committee (Florida senate) investigations of homosexuality at the university that began in summer 1958, in Bonnie Stark, McCarthyism in Florida: Charley Johns and the Florida Legislative Investigation Committee July 1956 to July 1965 *(1985), p. 1.*

The American equivalents of AYM [Angry Young Men] are no doubt the much-stigmatized and tsk-tsk'd San Francisco crowd. But the differences are very great indeed; and . . . they are all in favor of the West-Coast thunderbirds.

This is not to claim that Mr. Allen Ginsberg is the bardiest bard since Orpheus, or that Mr. Jack Kerouac is in line for the laurel-wreath of Cervantes. The sort of protest that these writers voice is liable, as some of them at least are aware, to its own sort of silliness. . . . About the San Francisco scallions, one can note approvingly that at least they are not ashamed to grow big and green and smelly: and it is never safe to blame an artist for choosing to be a scallion instead of a petunia. In setting out to gut the American bourgeois, the San Franciscans have not blinkered out of their vision everything but the bourgeoisie. Kerouac particularly is a man of high comic talent; he has a gift for grotesque free-wheeling which merits a good deal of what I can only call gratitude, and his wild, Faustian appetite for seeing every possible aspect of every situation sometimes builds to peaks of genuine intensity. He is in an old American tradition of living and writing big; and about this sort of thing, it's always premature . . . to say, "Nothing will ever come of it." . . .

A rather special quality of the AYM novels . . . is their recurrent attitude toward . . . anything artistic. They are truculent, downright, no-nonsense-about it. . . . Anything highbrow is probably phony. . . .

The West-Coast JD's are, thank God, a cut above this. Their protest has in it the indispensable ingredient of generous, not to say sincere, imagination; it involves their whole, unarmored beings, and it aspires to be something more than a cute, tired game played with smudgy counters.

Robert Martin Adams comparing Britain's Angry Young Men and San Francisco's Beat writers, in Adams, "Fiction Chronicle," Hudson Review *(Summer 1958), p. 288.*

The man largely responsible for construction of the world's first nuclear-powered submarine was not asked to the White House today to share her moment of triumph [sailing beneath the polar icecap at the North Pole].

Some thought was given to inviting Rear Admiral Hyman G. Rickover to the ceremony for the *Nautilus,* White House officials said. But only "top brass" had been asked and it was decided no exception could be made for him.

The skipper of the *Nautilus,* Comdr. W. R. Anderson, proved in the circumstances to be as bold a navigator in Navy politics as in the waters under the polar ice.

Commander Anderson went directly from the White House to Admiral Rickover's office . . . a few blocks away. There he paid his personal respects on the slight, frail figure whose tough-minded drive made the *Nautilus* a reality.

Hanson W. Baldwin describing the snub given to Admiral Hyman Rickover, the main promoter of the nuclear submarine fleet, after the success of the USS Nautilus, in Baldwin, "Nautilus' Skipper Helps to Mitigate a Snub to Rickover," New York Times, *August 9, 1958, p. 1.*

Secretary General Dag Hammarskjold proposed today that the United Nations step up its political and economic activities in the Middle East to stabilize the area.

Mr. Hammarskjold took the floor at the opening of the General Assembly's emergency special session on the Middle East to put forward his program....

The principal provisions of his plan are:

A declaration by the Arab states reaffirming their adherence to the principles of mutual respect for each other's territory, non-aggression and non-interference in each other's internal affairs.

The continuation and extension of present United Nations activities in Lebanon and Jordan.

Joint action by the Arab states, with support of the United Nations, in economic development. This would include arrangements for cooperation between "oil-producing and oil-transiting countries" and joint utilization of water resources.

Thomas J. Hamilton describing UN efforts to achieve harmony in the Middle East, in Hamilton, "Chief of U.N. Gives a Plan for Mideast," New York Times, *August 9, 1958, p. 1.*

Pedestrians waited for traffic lights and motorists waited for pedestrians yesterday as the police began enforcing New York's new safety law.

High officials of the Traffic and Police Departments were gratified at the extent of compliance by drivers and walkers.

Traffic Commissioner T. T. Wiley said: "My hat is off to New York. The reaction is wonderful."

He spoke after a tour of midtown Manhattan during which turning trucks waited for pedestrians and cab drivers not only waited but also shouted warnings to pedestrians starting to cross against lights.

"479 Get Jaywalking Summonses but Public Is Hailed on Response," New York Times, *August 9, 1958, p. 1.*

"Duck and Cover, Duck and Cover!" What a great opportunity to move from the torturous confinement of a seated position at my desk.... Squatting under the desk, wondering if anyone could see my underpants, doing a sniff test, and rotating my head to count the fossilized remains of years of illicit chewing gum deposits.

I don't remember much anxiety associated with the bomb scare.... There was always a conspiracy of silence in my family about controversy and unpleasant subjects. I do recollect clearly in the 4th grade that Fidel Castro was a hero in the U.S. and by the 5th grade he became our country's most despised villain. This may have been the beginning of my political awareness.

Horticulturist Patti Jacobs recalling her experiences of nuclear air-raid drills at school in fall 1958, in private correspondence with the author, September 30, 2001.

All Labor Day weekend, on the beach and at home, children were using them [hula hoops] as boomerangs or jump ropes, but most people were doing a hula inside them.... It takes a child five minutes to master the thing, but adults take longer; it all depends on the waistline.

A Newsweek article in early September 1958 discussing the hula hoop fad, in Jane Stern and Michael Stern, Encyclopedia of Pop Culture *(1992), p. 237.*

Well, modern architecture is anything built today. It's an ambiguous term, but "modern architecture" does not necessarily mean new architecture. The *new* architecture is organic architecture.... [It has] a natural influence.

[Isn't it an Oriental influence?]

No—except that the philosophy is perhaps Oriental. It was Tao who declared that the reality of the buildings did not consist in the walls and the roof, but in the space within to be lived in. The interior space was the reality of the building. Now that means that you build from within outward rather than from the outside in, as the West has been building. Insofar as that's Taoism, I suppose the philosophy is Eastern. But somehow only the West has ever built according to that philosophy. And our "organic" architecture happens to be the original expression of that idea. The space concept in architecture is organic, and "organic," as we use the term means "natural," it means "essential." It means *of* the thing instead of *on* it.

[How can you adapt this philosophy of "organic" architecture to the cities of today, which lack space?]

You can't. The city of today will have to run its course. It's being finished now by excess. Excess is ruining it. When we need a new city we're going to have to have it on our own "organic" terms and it will be more an agronomy, it will be part of the ground and it will be pretty nearly everywhere. The concentrations that are now cities are feudal survivals.

Schoolchildren participate in an air raid drill to prepare for a possible nuclear attack. *(Photofest)*

We've got to go forward and make better use of the ground. . . .

The skyscraper is responsible for the congestion, and is making the city of today impossible to use. The skyscraper piles the crowd up high, dumps it on the street, stuffs it in again, and the streets are not nearly wide enough. Paris is so beautiful today because it has that sense of space without the skyscraper.

Frank Lloyd Wright discussing modern architecture in an interview with Henry Brandon, in Brandon, "Flat on Our Faces: A Conversation with Frank Lloyd Wright," New Republic *(September 8, 1958), pp. 14–15.*

Since April . . . the situation in West Germany seriously deteriorated and took an unwelcome direction. . . .

The formation of Bundeswehr [a fully separate army of West Germany] goes on, atomic armament is now legalized. . . . Our joint task is to keep putting a braking influence on the formation of the Bundeswehr. . . . [Given good coordination between the Soviet Union and East Germany, this development] could be delayed by two to three years, which would be a serious gain for our mutual cause. . . . [We should] retaliate against the enemy's offensive by a counteroffensive on the part of the GDR [East Germany].

The Soviet ambassador in Bonn, A. Smirnov, in a message of October 5, 1958, to East German leader Walter Ulbricht, in Vladislav Zubok, "Working Paper #6: Khrushchev and the Berlin Crisis (1958–62)" (2001).

We are currently wealthy, fat, comfortable, and complacent. We have a built-in allergy to unpleasant or disturbing information. Our mass media reflect this. But unless we get off our fat surpluses and recognize that television in the main is being used to distract, delude, amuse, and insulate us, then television and those who finance it, those who look at it, and those who work at it may see a totally different picture too late.

I do not advocate that we turn television into a twenty-seven inch wailing wall, where longhairs constantly moan about the state of our culture and our defense. But I would like to see it reflect occasionally the hard realities of the world in which we live. . . .

This instrument can teach, it can illuminate—yes, it can even inspire. But it can do so only to the extent that humans are determined to use it to those ends. Otherwise it is merely wires and lights in a box. There is a great and perhaps decisive battle to be fought against ignorance, intolerance, and indifference. This weapon of television could be useful.

Stonewall Jackson, who knew something about the use of weapons, is reported to have said, "When war comes, you must draw the sword and throw away the scabbard." The trouble with television is that it is rusting in the scabbard during a battle for survival.

Television journalist Edward R. Murrow addressing the Radio and Television News Directors Association on October 15, 1958, in Murrow, In Search of Light: The Broadcasts of Edward R. Murrow *(1967).*

[Deleted name] claimed he learned that Rev. Martin Luther King, Jr., would leave Montgomery at 8:15 P.M. on 11/3/58 for Mobile. Also that King would travel alone in his automobile . . . implied that this would have been a good chance to kill or at least to do bodily harm to King. . . . said he would try to find out when King planned to return to Montgomery. . . .

[Deleted name] furnished the Birmingham Office an unsigned copy of a statement made on 12/8/58 . . . by the unidentified informant. . . . This statement . . . contained information regarding the collection of money to have some Negroes killed and noted that a list of ten names picked out of the air included Martin Luther King of Ala. It was also noted that the news that King was going to be killed had gotten out all over the country and the plans were stopped.

From FBI files on Martin Luther King, Jr., pertaining to plans to assassinate King in November and December 1958, in Kenneth O'Reilly, ed., Black Americans: The FBI Files *(1994), pp. 183–84.*

I'm the only director who ever made two pictures with [Marilyn] Monroe. It behooves the Screen Directors guild to award me a Purple Heart. . . . I have discussed this project with my doctor and my psychiatrist, and they tell me I'm too old and too rich to go through this again.

Director Billy Wilder, upon completing the filming of Some Like It Hot *on November 6, 1958, in reference to actress Marilyn Monroe's many absences from the set, which caused the film to go $500,000 over budget, in Harry Haun,* The Cinematic Century *(2000).*

Don't upset yourself. Life goes on.

Actor Tyrone Power counseling Gina Lollobrigida, his costar in Solomon and Sheba, *a few hours before he suffered a fatal heart attack while filming a duel on November 15, 1958, in Harry Haun,* The Cinematic Century *(2000).*

I think a movement in jazz is beginning away from the conventional string of chords, and a return to emphasis on melodic rather than harmonic variations. There will be fewer chords but infinite possibilities as to what to do with them.

Trumpeter Miles Davis commenting in December 1958 on the future of jazz, in Mervyn Cooke, The Chronicle of Jazz *(1997), p. 142.*

11

America Expands into the Pacific
1959

The United States concluded the decade by increasing its landmass, when for the first time since Arizona was admitted in 1912, a new state was added to the Union: Alaska, became the 49th state on January 3. Easily surpassing Texas as the largest state, Alaska increased the country's landmass by almost 20 percent, brought a wealth of natural resources to the nation, and established a U.S. state directly across the Bering Strait from the Soviet Union.

The United States then extended its domain farther into the Pacific on August 21, when Hawaii concluded its long campaign for statehood and was admitted as the 50th state, despite opposition from some southern politicians, who opposed adding the largely nonwhite, racially mixed population. The addition of Hawaii pushed U.S. boundaries more than 2,000 miles beyond the North American continent into the Pacific Ocean. The addition of the new states was motivated primarily by cold war security interests—Truman had recommended the action for that reason in 1950. At the same time that the expansion enhanced national defense, it also introduced greater ethnic diversity into the nation and contributed to the ever-evolving American identity. And combined with the intensified efforts at space exploration, the vast increase in sovereign American territory made the United States's dominance inescapable.

Cold war tensions eased as Vice President Nixon visited Moscow in the summer and Premier Khrushchev toured the United States in the fall, when he and Eisenhower came to some apparent understandings over the situation in Berlin and other matters. However, North Americans experienced some anxiety as Khrushchev boasted that the success of the Soviet space program had shifted the balance of power toward the USSR, and the popular culture of the year reflected an especially large concern about nuclear war. The United States intensified its efforts to improve science and math education in the public schools, and social critics decried the frivolous lifestyles of American youth, who spent their time listening and dancing to rock 'n' roll and participating in fads such as the hula hoop, while their Soviet counterparts were supposedly studying assiduously. Revelations in congressional hearings that television game shows had been fixed gave further ammunition to critics who maintained that the nation was being endangered by the erosion of traditional Judeo-Christian values upon which the country had been built.

The final year of the decade concluded therefore with vast material gains for individual American citizens and enormous territorial gains for the nation as a whole, but as was the case throughout the 1950s, these and other strides in the standard of living were offset by concerns that the nation was becoming frivolous and its materialism was causing it to stray too far from its moral center.

THE COLD WAR AND INTERNATIONAL POLITICS

The Cold War Abroad

The space race and the Berlin controversy were the headline grabbers of 1959, which generally saw an easing of tensions between the superpowers, as Khrushchev, despite his ultimatum about Berlin in late 1958, seemed genuinely interested in defusing the explosive political climate. The space race was important to the cold war both for the potential military advantages that orbiting weapons, communications satellites, and spy satellites could offer and for the international prestige that was acquired from the vast technological achievements of space exploration.

The early successes of the Soviet space program were impressive; in particular, the Soviets made significant gains in 1959 in their effort to reach the Moon. After *Lunik 1* narrowly missed the Moon at the beginning of the year, *Lunik 2* struck its target in September, and *Lunik 3* orbited the Moon and sent back pictures of its far, or "dark," side, which had never before been viewed by humans. In addition to demonstrating that human rockets could, in fact, reach the Moon, the Soviet missions gathered and transmitted information about its magnetic field, cosmic radiation, and interplanetary space. Meanwhile, the United States pushed forward with its program for manned space flight. NASA selected candidates for the first series of American manned space flights—Project Mercury—and it sent monkeys into deep space and returned them alive. The United States also established radio contact with Venus and placed the first weather station in outer space.

Back on Earth, Berlin had been an issue since World War II. Divided into a communist-controlled eastern sector and a western sector protected by the United States and its allies, the city was located entirely within communist East Germany. Emboldened by the Soviet gains in space, as well as by new ICBMs that could reach the U.S. heartland, Khrushchev insisted in November 1958 that Western forces vacate West Berlin within six months and leave it as a demilitarized city under UN control. Because West Berlin was isolated within East Germany, it was particularly vulnerable to hostile communist action, as it had been in 1948–49, when the Soviets blockaded land access and necessitated the Berlin airlift. Nonetheless, the allies refused to comply with the Soviet ultimatum and prospects for a major East–West military confrontation escalated. In late January 1959, Eisenhower ordered a quiet buildup of military forces in the region, and throughout the rest of the winter Khrushchev's language remained bellicose. However, a meeting in late May of foreign ministers provided him with a pretext for delaying action after the May 27 deadline passed. And in September, he met with Eisenhower and agreed to reopen the matter to negotiations, without a set time limit. In December, the NATO allies invited Khrushchev to a summit conference on Berlin to be held in April 1960, but that conference ended almost as soon as it had convened because a U.S. U-2 spy plane was shot down over Soviet territory. Subsequently, the Berlin crisis erupted into one of the most dangerous moments of the cold war: In October 1961, after East Germany erected the Berlin Wall to halt the flow of East Germans to the West and after the Soviet Union ended a voluntary moratorium on nuclear testing begun in 1958, U.S. and Soviet tanks faced each other across the divided city.

Khrushchev's concession on Berlin in 1959 came while he was in the United States on a goodwill tour. The cheerful, grandfatherly image he projected made a positive impression on the American public, and he was enthusiastically greeted in several U.S. cities. Eisenhower's perception was that public pessimism about the superpower confrontation had diminished as a result of the Soviet leader's trip, and Khrushchev alluded to the conciliatory "spirit of Camp David," referring to the presidential retreat in Maryland, where the two leaders had agreed to hold further talks on Berlin, broaden cultural exchanges, improve trade relations, and commit to resolving differences by peaceful means.[1] Khrushchev's visit followed Vice President Nixon's trip to Moscow in July, as part of the growing number of U.S.-Soviet cultural exchanges intended to foster greater cooperation and goodwill between the superpowers. While opening the American National Exhibition in Moscow, Nixon and Khrushchev engaged in an internationally viewed "kitchen debate," as Nixon showed off the attractive features of a model American home. Speaking before a video camera from the exhibition, Nixon extolled the virtues of capitalism and the desirability of being able to choose among several makes of products, while Khrushchev pointed to the great advances the Soviet Union had made in its short life as a nation. He boasted that within seven years it would equal the level of the United States; then he derisively waved good-bye, as he described the Soviets leaving America behind. Despite the obvious personal animosity between Nixon and Khrushchev, the U.S. vice president was subsequently permitted to address the Soviet people on television.

The other cold war development of lasting significance was Fidel Castro's assumption of power in Cuba at the beginning of the year. Initially perceived by many in the United States as a liberator overthrowing a corrupt dictatorship, Castro soon alienated Americans by consolidating military power, conducting wholesale arrests, executing supporters of the Batista regime, collectivizing agriculture, expropriating the holdings of all Cuban and foreign industries, and promoting close ties with communist countries. His rise to power spawned an exodus of well-educated, skilled middle- and upper-class Cubans to the United States, starting in 1959, and led to the creation of an influential Cuban enclave in Miami. In 1961, Castro openly declared himself a Marxist-Leninist and denounced U.S. imperialism; a year later Cuba became the focal point of the single most dangerous moment of the cold war. During the Cuban missile crisis of October 1962, the U.S. Navy intercepted Soviet ships delivering nuclear missiles to the island, and President Kennedy demanded that Khrushchev remove the nuclear weapons already deployed there.

Other International Developments

The decade concluded with greater autonomy for former European colonies. Although Charles de Gaulle came to power in France in 1958 as a champion of French settlers in Algiers, in September 1959, he offered to put the question of Algerian independence to a public referendum in which both French nationals and Islamic Arabs could vote. After three more years of conflict, the referendum was held, and Algeria gained independence in 1962.

Britain, Turkey, and Greece concluded the ongoing dispute over Cyprus in February, when they granted the Mediterranean island complete independence. Contrary to the wishes of Greek nationals on Cyprus, who sought affiliation with Greece, the agreement established a republic, with its own president and with the Greek and Turkish communities retaining a large degree of autonomy. Britain retained two military bases.

In Asia, China suppressed a rebellion in Tibet and drove the Dalai Lama, the Tibetan Buddhist spiritual leader, into exile in India. Although India's prime minister, Jawaharlal Nehru, who was anxious not to antagonize China, forbade the Dalai Lama from conducting political activities, he could not forestall a Chinese incursion across their common border in August. The crisis ended in November, when China agreed to negotiate a resolution to their border dispute. In June, the British colony of Singapore became self-governing; the new regime was committed to opposing the influence of the Chinese communism, as well as the "corrupting" influences of Western rock 'n' roll and sexual decadence.

In the Caribbean, Jamaica, another former British colony, obtained internal self-government within the West Indies Federation, which had been established in 1957.

The Cold War at Home

By the end of the decade, many of the worst aspects of the Red Scare had either been reversed by the Supreme Court or simply died out from a lack of perceived urgency, as the American Communist Party had been essentially eliminated as a viable political force within the nation. Senator McCarthy had died two years earlier, and, for the first time since 1951, HUAC conducted no hearings into communist activities within the entertainment industry. (It had begun its hearings in 1947 but suspended them from 1948 through 1950, pending a Supreme Court decision on the right of witnesses to invoke the First Amendment to avoid testifying.) Still, many laws remained that forbade communists from teaching in public schools and participating in other public activities. The Hollywood blacklist ending in 1960, and the blacklist in radio and television list ended in 1962, after a jury held blacklisters financially responsible for damages incurred by inaccurate listings.

With only a limited degree of accuracy, some public officials accused the growing civil rights movement of being inspired by communists who wanted to cast the United States in an unfavorable light before the nonwhite nations of Africa and Asia. Certainly, the Soviets were quick to point out to the international audience the racial inequities in the United States, and in the 1940s communists had instigated some racial disturbances, but there is no evidence to suggest that Martin Luther King, Jr., and the other leaders of the movement in the 1950s were motivated by a communist agenda. Nonetheless, some southern states attempted to deny rights to civil rights activists in manners similar to the way communists were barred from public positions. For instance, a law in Arkansas forbade the hiring of members of the politically active NAACP by any state or local government agency. (The law was subsequently struck down by a federal court.) In May, leaders of the National Council of Churches protested attempts to label NAACP members as *subversive*—a term commonly applied to communists—because of their opposition to segregation.

CIVIL RIGHTS

Integration continued, often grudgingly and despite ongoing protests by segregationists, throughout the South. The Southern Regional Council reported that 33 southern cities in nine states had desegregated their transit systems without incident, all of them voluntarily except for New Orleans; Atlanta; Columbia, South Carolina; and Montgomery, Alabama. And public libraries in cities in North Carolina, Arkansas, Florida, Louisiana, Virginia, and Georgia voluntarily permitted black patrons use of the facilities; however, they were refused such privileges in Savannah, Georgia. The Supreme Court struck down a Louisiana law prohibiting white and black boxers from fighting one another. A federal court voided an Arkansas law that allowed schools to close as a means to prevent integration, and in Tallahassee, Florida, four young white men received life sentences for raping a black woman. No white man had ever previously been convicted in Florida of raping a black woman. In Mississippi a law forbidding interracial cohabitation was struck down. Schools were reopened and integrated in Virginia and in Little Rock, Arkansas, where Eisenhower had called in the army in 1957 to enforce a federal court order, and where Governor Orval Faubus had closed the public high schools in 1958 rather than permit continued desegregation. When the president of the State College of Mississippi forbade the school's basketball team to participate in the racially integrated NCAA tournament despite a student vote that called for participation by a 6-1 margin, the students burned his effigy on campus. A federal court ruling overturned a law barring interracial athletic competition, and the NBA responded to complaints by black star players Bill Russell and Elgin Baylor by requiring that all teams receive assurances that their personnel will not be discriminated against in lodging and dining facilities.

At the federal level, under provisions of the Civil Rights Act of 1957, the U.S. Commission on Civil Rights came into existence. It conducted public hearings throughout the country into discrimination in the areas of voting rights and housing, and it exposed significant abuses within the nation. It also called for federal officials to monitor voting in the southern states. In addition, the U.S. Justice Department proposed a ban on federal funding to states that maintained segregated public schools. The Supreme Court, for the second time, voided a $100,000 fine levied against the NAACP by Alabama, in response to the organization's refusal to provide its membership and financial records to state officials.

On the other hand, impediments to integration remained strong. The Georgia legislature passed a series of anti-integration bills that, among other things, gave the governor power to close individual public schools that were integrated. In Little Rock, a black woman with a rare blood type almost died because of a new Arkansas law requiring that all donated blood be labeled by race. Although the law permitted the mixing of blood with the patient's consent, many white people did not respond to the citywide appeals because they erroneously believed that a black person would not be able to receive their blood. The director of Alabama's public libraries called for the removal of a children's book in which a black rabbit marries a white rabbit. And Louisiana passed a law forbidding black and white musicians to perform together. Jackie Robinson, the star player who had integrated Major League Baseball, was forbidden to use the white-only waiting room at the airport in Greenville, South Carolina, and the Eisenhower administration was embarrassed after an African diplomat to the United Nations and his son were denied membership in New York City's West Side Tennis Club because of their race. In the investigation that followed, it was revealed that the club, which sponsored the U.S. Open, had no black members and no Jewish members. And in Toronto, Canada, a black woman was barred from pledging a sorority that used an application form like those in the United States, which asked for the applicant's race.

BUSINESS

Unemployment rose by 1.4 million between May and July, and labor relations were uneasy, as workers became increasingly anxious about new threats to their job security posed by machines. Some 500,000 steelworkers struck in July, demanding a new contract that would provide higher wages and protections against changes in work rules that might permit companies to reduce jobs through automation. Citing national security and reports from the Department of Commerce that the strike was creating a harmful ripple effect in other industries and introducing delays in the construction of missile bases, in October Eisenhower invoked the Taft-Hartley Act to delay the strike for 80 days, and in November, the Supreme Court upheld his order and ended the strike after 116 days. A final settlement was reached on January 4, 1960, in which workers received a modest pay raise and guarantees that they would be protected against job loss due to automation through July 1962. Eisenhower also invoked the act to end a dock strike in October. In June, he raised the federal debt ceiling to $295 billion.

Despite the labor unrest, the economy recovered from the recession of 1958. Although there was a high rate of joblessness at the beginning of the year, by the end of 1959 unemployment had dropped to 5.5 percent, down 1.3 percent from the previous year. The GNP, which had been stagnant in 1958, grew by 8 percent, and the Dow Jones reached a high of 679, an increase of almost 100 points. The low was 574, as compared to 451 in 1958. Fears that higher wages and economic growth might produce inflation proved unfounded, as the inflation rate dropped from 1.9 percent to 0.7 percent. An average car cost $1,180, as compared to $1,300 in 1939; a Bell & Howell 8-mm movie camera could be purchased for between $19 and $48; a high-fidelity tape recorder cost $49.95, and a 15-day Caribbean cruise was available for $355, with seven ports of call.[2]

The expanding commercial applications of plastic and other inexpensively produced synthetic materials was evident in such new products as transparent plastic bags for clothing and pantyhose, which found a market among the growing number of women entering the workplace. Other new products included the first Xerox photocopier, the first transistorized portable television, and the first nuclear merchant ship, the USS *Savannah*. Automobiles became both more luxurious and more pragmatic: On the one hand, Cadillac introduced cruise control to its cars, jeweled rear grills, electric door locks, air conditioning, and pointed fins; on the other, smaller cars such as the Ford Falcon gained in popularity. Computer applications for business were greatly enhanced with the development of COBOL, the first programming language designed especially for business needs.

SCIENCE AND TECHNOLOGY

Throughout the 1950s, physicians and the lay public alike regarded most forms of cancer as inevitably fatal, but in 1959, several important advances were made in understanding and treating cancer. DNA isolated from a cancer-inducing virus was shown to cause cancer on its own, the Vienna Cancer Institute opened the first bone-marrow bank after it was shown that bone-marrow cells could be used for treating radiation overdoses, and the American Cancer Society launched its first cancer prevention study. Other medical developments included the isolation of cephalosporin C, an antibiotic effective against bacteria resistant to penicillin, and the development of a method for making human chromosomes visible and sorting them into pairs. This enabled researches to demonstrate that congenital conditions, such as Down's syndrome, can be attributed to errors in chromosomal composition. Addressing a different kind of deep human structure—the unconscious—the American Medical Association sanctioned hypnosis as a medical aid.

Research in subatomic physics forged ahead, as L. W. Alvarez and his colleague built a bubble chamber for detecting subatomic particles created by the Cosmotron accelerator. Alvarez used the chamber to detect the neutrally charged xi particle. Other energy-related developments included the opening of the first geothermal power station in New Zealand, and the discovery of large reserves of natural gas offshore from the Netherlands. Twelve countries signed a treaty designating the Antarctic continent a region for scientific exploration and forbidding military activity there.

SPORTS, ENTERTAINMENT, AND THE ARTS

Sports

Although baseball remained the national pastime throughout the 1950s, by the end of the decade professional football was poised to challenge it. The exciting overtime championship game between the Baltimore Colts and New York Giants at the end of 1958 and expanded, coast-to-coast live television coverage of the sport stirred up enthusiasm for professional football, which hitherto had often been overshadowed by college rivalries. In 1959, the Colts, led by quarterback, John Unitas and his favorite receiver, Raymond Berry, repeated their domination of the Giants in a championship rematch. Other dominant players of the year included the Cleveland Browns's phenomenal running back Jim Brown and New York's quarterback Charles Conerly, the Most Valuable Player (MVP) of the NFL. Unitas and Brown, who opposed each other in the 1964 championship game won by Cleveland, are still regarded among the best players ever at their positions. Vince Lombardi, considered one of the best football coaches of all time, began his career as the head coach of the Green Bay Packers, which went on to dominate the league in the 1960s. The growing interest in the professional sport sparked the formation of a rival American Football League, which Lamar Hunt organized with eight teams that later merged with the NFL. Louisiana State and Syracuse Universities shared the college football title. Louisiana State's running back, Billy Cannon, won the Heisman Trophy.

Professional basketball, which had likewise been overshadowed by college play, was also coming into its own, as the Boston Celtics, led by Bill Russell and Bob Cousy, began their unparalleled string of eight consecutive championships. The NBA All-Pro First Team included Celtics Russell, Cousy, and Bill Sharman, Minneapolis's Elgin Baylor, and St. Louis's Bob Pettit, who was the league's MVP. Wilt "the Stilt" Chamberlain, who towered over the court at seven feet tall, debuted with Philadelphia after starring with the all-black Harlem Globetrotters in 1958. The rivalry that developed between the two young centers, Russell and Chamberlain, fueled interest in the sport for years to come. Founded in 1927, the Globetrotters attracted basketball fans throughout the decade with their showmanship, athletic skill, and comic aptitude in their many exhibition games against a hapless traveling team of college all-stars. In 1959, they stirred interest in the sport in the Soviet Union and Eastern Europe, where they traveled as part of a goodwill cultural exchange. Khrushchev greeted them, and they received an audience with Pope John XXIII. The University of California was the top college basketball team, and the University of Cincinnati's Oscar Robertson was named Player of the Year.

Baseball, of course, remained enormously popular. Organized Little League teams that sprang up in the suburbs during the decade encouraged boys to compete. And the newly developed transistor radios enabled students and workers to furtively keep tabs on the ongoing pennant races and World Series games, which were still played entirely during the daytime. Despite the offensive power displayed by Milwaukee's Henry "Hank" Aaron, who led the National League in batting, and Eddie Matthews, who led the major leagues with 46 home runs, the Los Angeles Dodgers capitalized on a strong pitching staff led by Don Drysdale and offensive support from players such as Duke Snyder, Gil Hodges, and Wally Moon to win the National League pennant and then to prevail in six games over the Chicago White Sox. Chicago's second baseman, Nelson "Nellie" Fox, was the American

Basketball star Wilt Chamberlain starred with the Harlem Globetrotters before joining the NBA's Philadelphia 76ers in 1959. *(Photofest)*

League's MVP; Chicago Cubs shortstop Ernie Banks was named MVP in the National League.

In other sports, Montreal won hockey's Stanley Cup for the fourth consecutive year. It won again in 1960 as well, before Chicago won the title in 1961. Neale Fraser and Maria Bueno prevailed in the men and women's singles tennis championships at the U.S. Open. Bill Casper, Jr., won golf's U.S. Open. Swedish fighter Ingemar Johansson knocked out title-holder Floyd Patterson, an American, to claim boxing's world heavyweight title.

Television

By 1959, television had become the most relied upon source of news in the country. In superseding papers, radio, and magazines as the public's major source of news, television changed the way viewers constructed their own individual views of reality, including their personal pictures of the political and social upheavals of their time. Through television Americans, Canadians, and Western Europeans experienced accounts of the outside world more visually and less verbally than at any other point in history, and this had a profound effect on how they perceived and related to events beyond their firsthand experience. Television's capacity for manipulation and its ability to pass off fiction as reality was highlighted in 1959 by the congressional investigations into the fixed, high-stakes quiz shows, but the nation's profound disillusionment at this deception did not generally extend to news reporting.

For the third year in a row, westerns were the most popular shows on television in 1959–60, and they continued to dominate through the 1961–62 season. In a time of increasing cold war tension and social upheaval associated with the lingering Red Scare, civil rights activism, the increasing entry of women into college and the workplace, fears of automation—which had been at the heart of the steel strike—and other changes in the social norms, westerns offered viewers a chance to retreat into a kind of mythical golden place and time in American history where life seemed less complicated, choices about right and wrong appeared obvious, traditional gender roles were clear cut, racial disharmony was seemingly nonexistent, and figures of authority were almost uniformly strong, honorable, morally upright, unwavering in their commitment to virtue, and capable of making life safe and fair for ordinary citizens. In addition, the wide-open spaces and general absence of legal restrictions on the frontier suggested a time of greater individual freedom and adventure, with fewer demands for conformity.

That the idealized depictions of life in the American West were routinely oversimplified and often historically inaccurate, or that they rarely acknowledged the presence, much less achievements of women and minority groups, was rarely a matter of concern to viewers, producers, or even educators. After all, the shows purported to be only entertainment, not history, and some care was taken to create authentic sets, costumes, and other visual aspects of the shows. But if westerns, like movies and other forms of narrative fiction, never claimed to be accurate in their representation of social, business, and political relations on the frontier, they nonetheless were the primary source of knowledge about the history of the American West for many, if not most, Americans. This, in turn, had significant implications for how citizens viewed their own times, which seemed in most ways less appealing than the golden age of the television West.

The three highest-rated shows were westerns: *Gunsmoke, Wagon Train,* and *Have Gun Will Travel. Wanted: Dead or Alive,* which starred Steve McQueen as a bounty hunter with a Winchester rifle, was also among the top 10 TV shows. New westerns included *Rawhide,* which featured Clint Eastwood as Rowdy Yates, the assistant trail boss on a cattle drive, and *Bonanza,* which starred Lorne Green as Ben Cartwright, the upright, widowed owner of the Ponderosa Ranch. Along with his grown sons, each by a different now-deceased wife, he helped keep the peace in Virginia City, Nevada. The sons were played by Dan Blocker, Michael Landon, and Pernell Roberts. *Bonanza* ran through 1973 and trailed only *Gunsmoke* as network television's longest-running western. As was the case in *Bachelor Father, My Little Margie,* and *My Three Sons, Bonanza* was one of several shows from the 1950s and early 1960s that presented a family headed by a single father, who succeeded in raising his child or children through the judicious application of wisdom, responsibility, and moral rectitude. (And like Ben Cartwright, the fathers on those other shows were single due to circumstances other than divorce, which was still regarded by many in the 1950s as a source of shame.) No single mother was so prominently featured on American television until *One Day at a Time* debuted in 1975. Other new westerns included *Bronco, The Deputy, Johnny Ringo, Laramie, Law of the Plainsman, The Rebel, Riverboat,* and *The Texan.*

Other top 10 shows included *The Danny Thomas Show* and *Father Knows Best,* situation comedies that also presented families led by strong fathers; *The Red Skelton Show,* which was a comedy revue; *77 Sunset Strip; Perry Mason;* and a low-stakes game show, *The Price Is Right.* Among the year's new programs was *The Untouchables,* which applied the western's preoccupation with asserting law and order to the 1920s era of Prohibition. Featuring Robert Stack as Elliot Ness, the head of a team of crime-fighting government agents, it capitalized on the federal government's ongoing efforts to thwart organized crime and on the popularity of the FBI during the 1950s, when the bureau was perceived as the nation's leading force in combating communism. (FBI director J. Edgar Hoover's 1958 book, *Masters of Deceit,* was still a best-seller in 1959.)

The Bell Telephone Hour was a new musical series that offered a wide range of music. The CBS network's growing recognition of the importance of teenagers as a television market was manifested in *The Many Loves of Dobie Gillis,* the first situation comedy to center fully on teenagers. It starred Dwayne Hickman as the love-prone Dobie and Bob Denver, who later starred as Gilligan in *Gilligan's Island,* as his would-be Beatnik pal, Maynard G. Krebs. Denver's portrayal of Maynard as wacky, irresponsible, fundamentally out-of-touch with reality, and averse to hard work reflected a common view among middle Americans of the Beats and their followers.

Another new show in the 1959–60 season was Rod Serling's *The Twilight Zone.* Still regarded as one of the best-written television series ever produced, it explored the challenge that science has posed to religion in America since the late 1950s. The show appealed to the possibility that there is more to existence than we commonly apprehend, but its sense of awe was attuned to the wonder produced by scientific advances, especially space exploration and the nascent field of parapsychology, rather than to divine intervention, which was presented as a more common source of unexpected possibility in 1950s American culture. Thus, *The Twilight Zone* offered a form of secular mysticism that suggested in nonreligious terms that everything occurs for a purpose, as part of a larger design. The grand design might be benevolent and moral or merely perverse or diabolical, but it is probably not random, and many of the episodes concluded with an ironic twist that provided poetic justice. Appearing just two years after the launch of the *Sputnik* satellites, when the U.S. government and educational leaders were actively promoting the sciences which were increasingly viewed as essential to national security, and when a rational, analytical point of view was increasingly regarded as the key to success in most human endeavors, *The Twilight Zone* was especially popular among people interested in science, perhaps because it speculated about otherworldly occurrences without providing definitive explanations or relying on stock religious interpretations.

Movies

Television typically avoided overtly religious or other subjects that might be divisive, as advertisers feared alienating viewers/consumers who held opposing beliefs and affiliations from those expressed on a show. This is why, until the 1970s, prime-time American television programming often seemed bland and unprovocative. Movies, on the other hand, did not depend on advertising revenues, and by 1959, the film industry was less fearful of controversy, which, it realized, could spark interest and thereby often increase attendance at the box office. Unlike television, which is broadcast over publicly owned airwaves and therefore subject to government regulation, movies enjoy greater freedom of expression and are free from pressures for equal time for other points of view.

Thus, movies more readily addressed religious themes that appealed to the largely Christian American public. Religious stories set before the 16th-century Protestant Reformation offered the additional virtue of not having to favor one denomination over another. William Wyler's *Ben-Hur* benefited from these considerations, as well as spectacular visual effects in its depiction of the conflict between Romans and Jews during the time of Christ. Like other cold war–era epics, the story decries political oppression and affirms Judeo-Christian values; moreover, its immense cast, vast sets, expensive props, and enormous scope put on display the seemingly endless repository of resources in capitalist America. *Ben-Hur,* which includes a memorable chariot race, received the Academy Award for best film, and Charlton Heston won for best actor, Hugh Griffith for supporting actor, Robert L. Surtees for cinematography, and Wyler for director. The film also won awards for editing, art direction, costume design, sound, score, and visual effects.

Audrey Hepburn was nominated for best actress for her role as Sister Luke in Fred Zinnemann's *The Nun's Story,* which was also nominated for best picture, director, and cinematography. It is based on the biography of a nun who faced a crisis of conscience during World War II. Her decision to leave the convent in order to work against the Nazi occupation of her native Belgium was more controversial than most 1950s religious-oriented movies, and the Warner Brothers studio omitted music from the final credits because they wanted to avoid making an editorial judgment by providing either an upbeat, hence approving, score or a downbeat, disapproving one.

Cold war anxieties are treated in both Alfred Hitchcock's *North by Northwest* and Stanley Kramer's *On the Beach*. *North by Northwest* stars Cary Grant as George Kaplan, an advertising executive who accidentally becomes entangled in a plan by a federal intelligence agency to infiltrate a cell of Soviet spies. Famous for the scenes in which Grant is chased by a crop duster in a cornfield outside Chicago and in which he and costar Eva Marie Saint flee across the faces of the presidents on Mt. Rushmore, the movie is also notable for portraying the U.S. master spies as being almost as cold hearted as their Soviet counterparts, willing, with minimal regret, to write off the life of an innocent, American citizen as a simple casualty of war. Its essentially sympathetic treatment of Saint as Eve Kendall, a female American spy who sleeps with men in the line of duty, is also unusual for its time. On the other hand, *North by Northwest* also reflects the view of overbearing mothers frequently depicted in 1950s literature and film and made popular as "momism" by Philip Wylie in his 1942 best-seller, *A Generation of Vipers*. Momism regarded middle-class American mothers as self-righteous, self-absorbed, hypercritical, and sexually repressed women who dominated and metaphorically emasculated their sons and husbands. In the 1950s, they were accused of making the nation vulnerable to its enemies by producing a generation of weak sons. At the outset of *North by Northwest*, George Kaplan is such a son; however, the act of clearing his name, fighting for his survival, and combating the communists produces a change in his character that enables him to assert his independence from his mother and emerge as a worthy mate for the beautiful Eve, whose life he saves. Thus Kaplan's accidental and unwilling immersion into the seamy underside of cold war politics builds character as it bolsters national security and frees the protagonist from the shackles of momism.

Based on the 1957 novel by Nevil Shute, *On the Beach* provides a view of the future that is unusually bleak for 1950s Hollywood. Starring Gregory Peck, Ava Gardner, Fred Astaire, and Anthony Perkins, it follows the lives of an American submarine captain, his crew, and their Australian companions as they await the inevitable arrival in Australia of a lethal radioactive cloud, the product of an all-out nuclear war that has killed everyone in the Northern Hemisphere. The story highlights the different kinds of denial the awaiting victims experience and questions how an impending doom should or should not alter traditional loyalties, values, and ethics. Although neither Shute nor Kramer seems to have intended this, the story questions whether cultural priorities that value men's love of country over their love of women might, in fact, be responsible for the Armageddon. More explicitly, the nuclear bomb, itself, appears as the culprit. The film ends slightly more optimistically than the book, as the final shot of Melbourne, now literally a ghost town, focuses on a religious banner stating, "There's still time." That message is just wishful

Cary Grant and Eva Marie Saint elude communist spies chasing them across Mt. Rushmore in Alfred Hitchcock's *North by Northwest*. *(Photofest)*

thinking for the characters in the story, and it provides a deeply ironic, even sarcastic conclusion to their plight, but the banner was also admonishing the viewing audience in 1959. *On the Beach* premiered in 18 cities located in all seven continents. Its featured Australian folk song "Waltzing Matilda" briefly enjoyed popularity in the United States after the film opened.

Another cold war film of note is the British-made satire *The Mouse That Roared,* directed by Jack Arnold and starring Jean Seberg and Peter Sellers, who plays three roles. Grand Fenwick, a tiny, fictional European country, declares war against the United States with the intention of losing quickly so it can then receive foreign aid that will resuscitate its failing economy, as Japan and Germany did after World War II. However, when its absurdly armed band of soldiers accidentally captures the prototype of the Q-bomb during an air-raid drill, Grand Fenwick suddenly becomes the most powerful country on Earth and must deal with the consequences.

The ongoing civil rights movement provided an especially provocative new context for Douglas Sirk's remake of John M. Stahl's *Imitation of Life* (1934). The story about a widowed mother who opens a business with her African-American maid addresses not only racism and materialism but also the breakdown of the nuclear family, the difficulties of being a single mother, and the problems faced by a white-looking black girl who tries unsuccessfully to live in both worlds.

Elizabeth Taylor, Katharine Hepburn, and Montgomery Clift star in Joseph L. Mankiewicz's *Suddenly, Last Summer,* which reflects the growing public interest in abnormal psychology, in its depiction of emotional trauma and electroshock therapy, which was then used to treat extreme cases of depression. (Sylvia Plath describes her experiences with shock therapy during the 1950s in her 1963 memoir, *The Bell Jar.*) John Wayne, Dean Martin, and Ricky Nelson (from television's *Ozzie and Harriet*) star in Howard Hawks's western *Rio Bravo.*

Simone Signoret won the Academy Award for best actress and Neil Paterson for best adapted screenplay in Jack Clayton's British-made *Room at the Top.* Laurence Harvey costarred in this sexually explosive exposé of the ruthlessness of the British class system. Otto Preminger's *Anatomy of a Murder,* which stars James Stewart, Lee Remick, and Ben Gazzara, also foreshadows the more sexually frank movies of the 1960s, as it speaks with unusual openness of rape, contraception, and even women's underwear. The film, which stars Stewart as a dedicated trial lawyer representing a reprehensible but innocent client, was nominated for several Academy Awards. The judge is played by Joseph Welch, the lawyer who represented the U.S. Army in the 1954 McCarthy hearings.

Billy Wilder's *Some Like It Hot* is one of the most enduring comedies of the 1950s. Tony Curtis and Jack Lemmon star as jazz musicians fleeing from mobsters after they inadvertently witness the St. Valentine's Day massacre in a Chicago garage. To escape, they dress as women and join an all-girl band headed to Florida. In the process, Lemmon is proposed to by a wealthy, elderly man and Curtis falls in love with one of the other musicians, played by Marilyn Monroe, who believes that he is a woman. He woos her by disguising himself as a yacht owner and imitating the voice of Cary Grant. Doris Day, Rock Hudson, and Tony Randall star in Michael Gordon's *Pillow Talk,* one of a series of vaguely risqué pairings between Day and Hudson, who was the top box office attraction of the year. Day was the fourth, preceded by Cary Grant and

James Stewart and followed by Debbie Reynolds, Glenn Ford, Frank Sinatra, John Wayne, Jerry Lewis, and Susan Hayward. The year is notable for the comparatively larger number of women among the top 10 most favorite stars and for the continued preference for older male actors associated with responsible and virtuous action.

Notable French films include Alain Resnais's *Hiroshima, mon amour,* which reminded audiences of the ramifications of nuclear holocaust as it cut between contemporary Hiroshima and Hiroshima just after the atomic bombing of 1945. Considered one of the most influential films ever made because of its cinematic technique and fragmented approach to storytelling, *Hiroshima, mon amour* presents a brief love affair between a Japanese architect and a French woman whose German lover was killed at the end of the war. Another influential, experimental film that suggested radically new ways of telling a story through the cinematic medium is Jean-Luc Godard's *Breathless.* It too employs nontraditional narrative structures as it interweaves elements from the detective, suspense, and comedy genres in its study of human behavior. In many ways as much about film itself as about the characters and their story, *Breathless* mirrors the literary achievements of experimental writers from the early part of the century, such as the Dadaists and James Joyce, whose fiction was often as much about language and the conventions of storytelling as about plot and character.

Tony Curtis (left) and Jack Lemmon hide from gangsters by joining an "all-girls band" in Billy Wilder's *Some Like It Hot. (Photofest)*

French critic François Truffaut, whose 1954 article articulated the notion of the director as author, or *auteur,* helped introduce the realistic French New Wave film tradition in his first full-length directorial effort, his semiautobiographical *The 400 Blows.* Like such 1950s American films as *The Blackboard Jungle* or *Rebel Without a Cause,* it is about a troubled and neglected adolescent who has difficulty conforming to adult authority. But its exploration of the subject goes far deeper, with greater nuance and offers less facile and less judgmental explanations for the boy's behavior.

Like Jean Cocteau's *Orpheus* (1949), Marcel Camus's *Black Orpheus* updates the Greek myth of the poet who follows his lover to the Underworld to restore her to life after death. This more sensual version, set in Rio de Janeiro during Carnival, depicts Orpheus as a local musician who becomes the star performer in the city's lavish festival. Italian director Federico Fellini's *La Dolce vita* stars Marcello Mastroianni as a jaded reporter who becomes caught up in the opulent but ultimately vacuous world of Rome's rich and famous. (Woody Allen's 1998 film, *Celebrity,* is significantly indebted to it.)

Literature

Although it was the dominant political event of the decade, the cold war received comparatively little direct treatment in the popular and critically acclaimed fiction of the decade, except in spy novels like those in the James Bond series. However, cold war tensions provoked by the ongoing Berlin crisis, the space race, and the ever-increasing capacities of nuclear missiles and bombs exerted a stronger presence in the literature of 1959. Nuclear war and its aftermath were the topic of Pat Frank's best-selling *Alas, Babylon,* which eventually sold more than 2 million copies and was required reading in many public schools for decades afterward. In the foreword, Frank, a military writer who had had assignments at the Strategic Air Command (SAC), claims he wrote the book after a businessman responded to his estimate that 50 or 60 million Americans might die in a nuclear war by exclaiming that such an outcome would create a terrible economic depression.

Alas, Babylon follows the survivors of a nuclear war living in a small town in central Florida. Cut off from the larger cities that typically furnish them with food, fuel, and other staples, the survivors find that provisions are increasingly hard to come by and money rapidly loses its value. High-priced luxury items like Cadillacs and fancy homes become virtually worthless in comparison to more practical necessities: bicycle tires, evaporated milk, and safety pins. Ultimately, the surviving society learns to live without electricity or anything but the most primitive technologies, and it adopts a barter system for its economy. In an apparent swipe at Frank's acquaintance who had inspired the book, a bank president commits suicide because he cannot accept a world without money. Nonetheless private property is still respected, and the novel's moral universe punishes the wicked when recipients of looted jewelry suffer burns on their wrists and neck from radioactive contamination. The dedicated local doctor helps most of the townspeople pull through, and the survivors begin to rebuild society and reassert basic American values, from which the prewar society had strayed. They form vigilante groups for their mutual protection, rediscover the Yankee wisdom of Ben Franklin, and return to church. At the same time, however, the book expresses liberal social sentiments, too. In the postnuclear society, women prove capable and assume more crucial roles (the female protagonist named Elizabeth is nicknamed Lib), and the races work together cooperatively for their mutual survival. Racists and McCarthyites fare badly.

Helen Clarkson's *The Last Day* is one of the few novels about nuclear war published by a woman in the 1950s. Unlike Judith Merril's comparatively optimistic pre–hydrogen bomb novel, *Shadow on the Hearth* (1950), *The Last Day* presents a vision as bleak as Shute's *On the Beach,* which in some ways inspired it. Written from a feminine, if not feminist, perspective, *The Last Day* presents a before-and-after view of a community struck by a nuclear attack. The well-being of the children is the foremost concern, and Clarkson explicitly rejects the notion that overnurturing mothers are responsible for the country's problems. She insists instead that Americans require more nurturing love, not less. The protagonist takes exception to a *Life* magazine editorial that maintains that the only people who wanted to end nuclear testing were scared mothers, fuzzy liberals, and weary taxpayers, because the editorial represents mothers as a minority group from the lunatic fringe. Unlike most apocalyptic novels, *The Last Day* provides a detailed political analysis of the events leading up to the war that ultimately eradicates all human life. Mordecai Roshwald's *Level 7* imagines the postnuclear fate of military personnel deep in an underground command bunker that controls the nuclear missiles.

Walter M. Miller, Jr.'s *A Canticle for Leibowitz* is frequently cited as one of the first and best novels that imagines humanity returning to an anti-intellectual, religion-dominated medieval era in the aftermath of a nuclear apocalypse, before eventually re-evolving into a scientifically based society. Miller sets the story in three 600-year postnuclear periods from about A.D. 2600 to 4300. It begins in a new Dark Age following the nuclear conflagration, in which the landscape is desolate and the few clusters of human society are isolated from one another. In the second section, a new Renaissance follows in which a limited amount of scientific inquiry is permitted, and a modern Newton takes the first steps to reintroduce science to human culture. In the last section, history again replays itself, as computers, space satellites, and nuclear bombs provide the backdrop for human life. Excessive pride remains a fundamental human characteristic even in the distant future, and it continues to condemn the human race to repeating its mistakes. Thus Miller presents a cyclical view of history that replays the historic tension between science and religion and between the forces of progress and restraint—a tension very much present in 1950s American society. The author finally suggests that religion requires scientific open-mindedness and inquiry, while science needs a greater sense of religious humility and responsibility.

In *Advise and Consent,* Allen Drury conveys the drama around the nomination for secretary of state of a candidate based loosely on Alger Hiss. The Pulitzer Prize–winning novel spent 102 weeks on the *New York Times* best-seller list, and in 1962 Otto Preminger directed the film adaptations, which stars Henry Fonda, Walter Pidgeon, Charles Laughton, and Gene Tierney. The story describes the various political machinations involved in the Senate confirmation hearings, including political blackmail over alleged homosexuality and allegations of the candidate's past affiliations with a communist cell when he was teaching at the University of Chicago. *Advise and Consent* is the first in Drury's six-part series of political novels dealing with the struggle between liberals and conservatives to lead the country through the cold war. Drury's values are emphatically conservative, and the book vilifies the liberal press, a persistent theme throughout his political novels.

In other fiction of note, Philip Roth published his first major work, *Goodbye Columbus and Five Short Stories.* The title story deals with the attraction of a young Jewish man to a Christian girl and to the lifestyle of her Protestant family. The other stories also address the Jewish-American experience within a primarily Christian culture. William Faulkner completed his perversely funny Snopes trilogy in *The Mansion,* about a poor, rural white family.

Kurt Vonnegut, Jr.'s *Sirens of Titan* reflects the existential pessimism that is characteristic of much post–World War II fiction. Like the French existentialists, Vonnegut posits an absurd, ironically perverse universe, and his book tells the story of a space traveler from another planet who is trapped aboard his ship because he needs to replace a malfunctioning part. We learn that the entire history of human civilization does indeed have a purpose—to evolve to a state of technology where humanity is capable of replacing that part so the traveler can continue on his trivial mission. Saul Bellow also addresses existential dilemmas in *Henderson, the Rain King,* an uncharacteristically optimistic comedy set in Africa. In "The Man Who Studied Yoga," a story in *Advertisements for Myself,* Norman Mailer cautions against excessive introspection. Like the Beat poets and such contemporary authors as Henry Miller, William Burroughs seeks meaning in life through visceral experience rather than intellectual illumination in *Naked Lunch*. He presents heroin addiction both literally and as a metaphor for all addictions, including governments' addiction to power and people's to cruel behavior. By successfully challenging the Obscene Publications Act of 1959 with the first U.S. publication of D. H. Lawrence's *Lady Chatterley's Lover* (1928), Penguin Press expanded the range of sexual expression permissible in publications distributed within the United States.

Nonfiction also addressed the cold war and attendant issues. Admiral Hyman Rickover, founder of America's nuclear submarine fleet, whom Frank praises in *Alas, Babylon* for his bold and innovative thinking, published *Education and Freedom*. Education in the aftermath of *Sputnik* was also the topic of James Bryant Conant's critically acclaimed *The American High School Today*. Conant proposed a widely adopted system of tracking students through public school according to their intellectual aptitude. William Laurence, the only journalist permitted to cover the entire atomic bomb project, released *Men and Atoms: The Discovery, the Uses, and the Future of Atomic Energy*. Norman O. Brown and Christopher Lasch published *Life against Death,* a Freudian-based interpretation of social history and mass culture that influenced both political and sexual liberation movements of the 1960s. The book introduces the term *polymorphously perverse* to describe a child's natural experience of sexuality, before it has been channeled into genital sex. Another highly regarded thinker, Jacques Barzun, published *The House of Intellect;* Shelby Foote issued his study of the American Civil War; Richard Ellmann published his acclaimed biography of James Joyce; and C. P. Snow released *The Two Cultures,* which addresses the problem of reconciling the culture of science with that of art and the humanities. Tamas Aczel, a Hungarian émigré who came to the United States after the 1956 revolution, published *Revolt of the Mind,* a classic work of intellectual history that describes prerevolutionary intellectual activity in Hungary and the attraction communism held for the intelligentsia there.

Among the collections of poetry issued in 1959 were Robert Lowell's *Life's Studies;* e.e. cummings's *100 Selected Poems;* James Wright's *Saint Judas;* Robert Duncan's *Selected Poems, 1942–1950;* Jack Kerouac's *Mexico City Blues;* David Wagoner's *A Place to Stand;* and William Snodgrass's Pulitzer Prize–winning *Heart's Needle.*

Theater, Music, and the Visual Arts

New plays on Broadway included William Gibson's Pulitzer Prize–winning *The Miracle Worker,* which starred Patty Duke and Anne Bancroft in the story of how Helen Keller overcame her isolation after her loss of sight and hearing in childhood; Hal Holbrook's celebrated one-man performance of the witty Mark Twain entitled *Mark Twain Tonight;* Saul Levitt's *The Andersonville Trail,* which starred George C. Scott, Herbert Berghof, and Albert Dekker in an adaptation of MacKinlay Kantor's book about the notorious Civil War prison camp; *Rashomon,* Fay and Michael Kanin's stage adaption of Akira Kurosawa's 1950 film by the same title about subjective reality, starring Rod Steiger and Claire Bloom; Tennessee Williams's character study *Sweet Bird of Youth,* starring Paul Newman and Geraldine Page; and *A Raisin in the Sun,* by Lorraine Hansberry.

Presented to critical acclaim as the nation was desegregating, *A Raisin in the Sun* depicts an urban black family aspiring to improve their lot in life but held back by the racism of whites; the condescension, envy, and duplicity of other blacks; and their own personal attitudes and limitations. In particular, the play deals with discrimination in housing and the problems faced by young black men living in a matriarchy and by talented black women whose aspirations are limited by the actions of men. It also addresses the taboo question of abortion in an era when it was illegal.

The Sound of Music by Richard Rogers and Oscar Hammerstein II won the Pulitzer Prize for best musical. Starring Mary Martin, Theodore Bikel, and Kurt Kazner, it tells the inspiring story of how a novitiate nun helped the Von Trapp family escape Nazi persecution in Austria. Robert Wise adapted it into an Academy Award–winning film in 1965, starring Julie Andrews. Other musicals included Mary Rodgers and Marshall Barer's *Once Upon a Mattress,* starring Carol Burnett; *Take Me Along,* Robert Merrill's comedy about businessmen and their wives, starring Jackie Gleason, Robert Morse, Eileen Herlie, and Walter Pidgeon; and Jule Styne and Stephen Sondheim's *Gypsy,* the story of stripper Gypsie Rose Lee, starring Ethel Merman, Jack Klugman, and Sandra Church. The off-Broadway Living Theater produced Jack Gelber's experimental play *The Connection,* which introduced jazz-inspired improvisation to theater and collapsed the traditional separation of the audience from the actors.

The New York City Ballet premiered *Episodes,* choreographed by Martha Graham and George Balanchine and performed by Graham and Sallie Wilson. Jerome Robbins's troupe Ballets U.S.A. toured Europe to great acclaim, and the Bolshoi Ballet Theatre of Moscow was enthusiastically received in the United States. As part of the cultural exchange between the superpowers, Leonard Bernstein conducted the New York Philharmonic to great acclaim in Russia.

Theater, television, and film were sources of many of the top songs of the year. Bobby Darin's rendition of "Mack the Knife," written by Kurt Weill for Bertolt Brecht's long-running *Threepenny Opera,* sold more than 10 million copies; it was surpassed only by Bing Crosby's "White Christmas." Nina Simone's "I Loves You Porgy," from George Gershwin's *Porgy and Bess* (1935) was another top hit, as were "Let Me Entertain You" from *Gypsy* and several songs from *The Sound of Music,* notably "The Sound of Music" and "Do-Re-Mi." The music from Rodgers and Hammerstein's *Flower Drum Song* (1958), featuring the original Broadway cast, was one of the top-selling albums. Henry Mancini's *Peter Gunn,* featuring the jazzy theme from the television show of the same title, and Mantovani's *Film Encores* were other top-selling albums.

Fans of rock 'n' roll were saddened by the death in a plane crash of stars Buddy Holly, J. P. "Big Bopper" Richardson, and Richie Valens. Among their hits were Holly's "Peggy Sue" and "That'll Be the Day,"

Playwright Lorraine Hansberry's *A Raisin in the Sun* was a Broadway hit. *(Photofest)*

Richardson's "Chantilly Lace," and Valens's "Donna" and "La Bamba." Canadian-born Paul Anka, who first came to fame in 1958 with "Diana" and "You Are My Destiny," topped the charts in 1959 with "Lonely Boy" and "Put Your Head on My Shoulder." The son of Lebanese immigrants to Ottawa, Anka became an instant teen idol, and he appeared in two movies before his popularity dimmed: *Girls Town* (1959) and *Look in Any Window* (1960). Philadelphian Frankie Avalon, who became a regular on Dick Clark's *American Bandstand,* also first came to prominence in 1958 and had several hits in 1959, including "Venus," in which a teenager asks the goddess to make him a girl to love, "Why?" "A Boy Without a Girl," and "Bobby Sox to Stockings."

The year 1959 was pivotal for jazz, as what is now known as modern jazz came into being. Ornette Coleman's *The Shape of Jazz to Come* suggested a new direction for the music, as did Miles Davis and John Coltrane's *Kind of Blue* joint album introducing "free jazz," which relies on scales rather than chords. Dave Brubeck's *Time Out* also offered significant innovations. Three of the most accomplished and influential jazz performers of the decade died: Lester Young, Billie Holiday, and Sidney Bechet.

Notable architectural achievements included the Time-Life Building in New York City, designed by the firm of Harrison, Abramovitz and Harris, and Philip Johnson's Asia House in New York. Frank Lloyd Wright, who was one of the great innovators of 20th-century architecture, died in April, about six months prior to the opening of his grand, spiraling Solomon R. Guggenheim Museum for modern art in Manhattan. The building was designed to realize Wright's belief that the exhibition space should interact with the art on display and play a significant role in how viewers regard the art they see. However, when the building opened in October, Wright was criticized posthumously for arrogantly competing with the art on display.

The so-called March Gallery Group, also known as the "doom artists," presented exhibits of visual art in New York centered on nuclear destruction. Prominent among them were Boris Lurie, Sam Goodman, and Stanley Fisher. Intended to shock audiences, their work featured destroyed artifacts from American society: bloody and dismembered dolls, sensational photographs from the *National Enquirer,* and erotic pictures from men's magazines. In general, however, although abstract and pop art continued to dominate what the established museums and galleries were promoting within the visual arts, many, if not most, Americans who were neither artists nor students of art failed to understand or appreciate why the doom artists or such abstract multimedia artists as Jasper Johns, Hans Hofmann, Stuart Davis, Robert Rauschenberg, and Willem de Kooning were trying redefine the purpose of art and even the very conception of what art is and what it can become. More realistic painters such as Andrew Wyeth were better received, and the general public took notice when a Gilbert Stuart portrait of Thomas Jefferson from around 1800 was discovered.

CHRONICLE OF EVENTS

1959

January 1: Fidel Castro's army enters Havana and takes control of the Cuban government.

January 3: Alaska becomes the nation's 49th state.

January 4: A Soviet rocket travels almost 350,000 miles and misses the Moon by just 5,000 miles.

January 6: A British jet travels twice the speed of sound.

January 7: Castro's government, headed by provisional president Manuel Urrutia, is recognized by the United States.

January 8: Charles de Gaulle is inaugurated as the first president of France's Fifth Republic, which gives expanded powers to the office of the president.

January 16: The Atomic Energy Commission (AEC) displays an atomic generator smaller than a man's hat.

January 21: Pioneering film director and producer Cecil B. DeMille dies.

January 25: American Airlines introduces coast-to-coast service from New York to Los Angeles, using Boeing 707 jets.

January 26: At a conference in Geneva, the United States and Britain offer guarantees to the Soviet Union for international control of a nuclear test ban, but the proposal is rejected.

January 27: NASA selects candidates for Project Mercury, the first series of American manned space flights.

January 27–28: The Soviet Communist Party denounces the revisionist movement led by Yugoslavia's Marshal Tito.

February 2: Arlington and Norfolk, Virginia, peacefully desegregate their public schools.

February 3: Rock 'n' roll stars Buddy Holly, J. P. "Big Bopper" Richardson, and Richie Valens are killed along with their pilot when their chartered plane crashes in bad weather outside of Mason City, Iowa. The musicians were en route to Fargo, North Dakota, as part of a concert tour.

February 16: Rejecting a Soviet proposal for a 28-nation conference on German unification, the United States asks instead for a meeting of the Big Four: Britain, France, the Soviet Union, and the United States.

Rock 'n' roll star Buddy Holly died in a February 1959 plane crash. Also killed were rock singers J. P. "Big Bopper" Richardson and Richie Valens. *(Photofest)*

February 16: Castro officially becomes premier of Cuba.

February 17: The United States launches the world's first weather satellite, *Vanguard 2.*

February 18: White students boycott classes in Front Royal, Virginia, after 22 black students enroll.

February 19: Britain, Greece, and Turkey agree on autonomy for Cyprus.

February 20: Meeting in Acapulco, Mexico, Eisenhower and Mexican president López Mateos agree to build the Diablo Dam on the Rio Grande to generate electricity for the region.

February 23: Britain and the Soviet Union expand their trade and cultural relations.

March 2: Iran renounces its 1921 treaty with the Soviet Union.

March 11: Lorraine Hansberry's play *A Raisin in the Sun* opens to favorable reviews on Broadway.

March 13–27: China crushes a rebellion in Tibet and forces the Dalai Lama, the spiritual leader of Tibetan Buddhists, to flee to India.

March 14: By refusing to put one-third of France's navy under NATO command, President de Gaulle begins the gradual French withdrawal from the NATO command. The United States transfers 200 aircraft from France to bases in West Germany and Great Britain.

March 18: Eisenhower signs a bill admitting Hawaii into the Union as the 50th state.

March 19: U.S. scientists establish the first radar contact with the planet Venus.

March 24: In the aftermath of the 1958 coup that deposed the pro-Western government of King Faisal, Iraq withdraws from the Baghdad Pact. On August 21, the Baghdad Pact changes its name to the Central Treaty Organization (CENTO) and expresses concern over communist activity in Iran.

April 3: The United States begins a new study of radioactive fallout from nuclear tests.

April 7: A referendum in Oklahoma ends a 51-year ban on the sale and consumption of alcohol.

April 7: The AEC announces the first conversion of atomic energy directly into electricity.

April 9: Innovative architect Frank Lloyd Wright dies.

April 12: The Soviet Union's famed Bolshoi Ballet arrives in New York to begin an eight-week tour of the United States and Canada.

April 13: Pope John XXIII forbids Catholics to vote for procommunists.

April 18: Eisenhower appoints Christian Herter as secretary of state, after the ailing John Foster Dulles resigns for health reasons.

April 25: The St. Lawrence Seaway opens.

May 1: The Texas Company changes its name to Texaco, Inc.

May 2: Jockey Willie Shoemaker rides Tommy Lee to his second Kentucky Derby victory.

May 7: The United States agrees to sell Britain components of nuclear weapons other than warheads.

May 11: Foreign ministers from the United States, Britain, France, and the Soviet Union meet to discuss the crisis in Berlin. Although these negotiations do not result in any final agreements, they provide Khrushchev with a face-saving reason for letting his May 27 deadline pass without taking further action.

May 14: Eisenhower breaks ground on Manhattan's new Lincoln Center for the Performing Arts.

Architect Frank Lloyd Wright died half a year before the opening of his spiraling Solomon R. Guggenheim Museum in New York City. *(Photofest)*

May 15: Scientists warn that the blue whale, one of the largest mammals on earth, faces extinction within five years unless restrictions are placed on the whaling industry.

May 20: Japanese Americans regain citizenship status lost during World War II.

May 22: The United States and Canada sign a pact to cooperate on development of nuclear resources.

May 27: Khrushchev's deadline for allied withdrawal from Berlin passes without comment by any of the governments involved.

May 27: John Foster Dulles dies.

May 28: The United States launches a rocket containing two monkeys 300 miles into outer space. The safe return of the capsule and its occupants demonstrates that human space travel is feasible.

May 31: NASA announces its plan to use satellites for transcontinental radio broadcasts.

June 2: An actors' strike, the first by Actors' Equity since 1919, closes Broadway theaters.

June 9: The United States launches the *George Washington,* the first nuclear submarine armed with ballistic missiles.

June 11: Eisenhower advises Congress that he will place nuclear weapons in Greece. The weapons remain under U.S. military control.

June 11: In England, the land-sea hovercraft is unveiled.

June 12: The Actors' Equity strike is settled.

June 15: The New York Stock Exchange reports that some 13 million Americans hold its stocks.

June 16: George Reeves, the actor who plays Superman on the popular television show, dies of a gunshot wound believed to be self-inflicted.

June 18: Famed actress Ethel Barrymore dies at age 79.

June 25: Mass murderer Charles Starkweather is electrocuted.

June 26: Swedish boxer Ingemar Johansson knocks out American Floyd Patterson to claim the world heavyweight title, the first time in 25 years that a non–American becomes the world heavyweight champion.

June 26: In Quebec, Eisenhower, Canadian prime minister John G. Diefenbaker, and Queen Elizabeth II of England formally dedicate the opening of the St. Lawrence Seaway.

July 17: Blues singer Billie Holiday dies at age 44, a few weeks after her arrest for narcotics possession.

July 18: Castro becomes president of Cuba.

July 21: The U.S. National Academy of Sciences and its Soviet counterpart agree to exchange information and organize joint forums for scientists of both nations.

July 21: The United States launches the first atomic-powered merchant ship, the USS *Savannah.*

July 23: Vice President Nixon brings the American National Exhibition to Moscow. On July 24, he and Khrushchev argue about the relative merits of communist and capitalist economies in their "kitchen debate," which takes place within the kitchen of a model American home. On August 1, Nixon appears on Soviet television and tells the Soviet people that the end of worldwide fear depends on Khruschev's actions. Nixon is later denied access to a Soviet missile factory.

August 4: Laos declares a state of emergency after the Pathet Lao, a communist guerilla movement backed by China and North Vietnam, launches a campaign to win back northern provinces it had lost two years earlier. Eisenhower approves economic aid but refuses to send military assistance, hoping instead that the United Nations will resolve the situation.

August 12: Despite protests in which 21 whites are arrested, Little Rock's Central High School, which was closed during 1958, reopens and admits black students.

August 13: In New York, construction begins on the $320 million Verrazano Narrows Bridge, which becomes the world's longest suspension span bridge when it opens in 1964.

August 21: Hawaii becomes the nation's 50th state.

August 22: Leonard Bernstein conducts the New York Philharmonic Orchestra before an appreciative audience in Moscow.

September 2: Eisenhower arrives in Paris, where he is welcomed by a million French supporters.

September 12: The Soviet satellite, *Lunik 2,* crashes onto the surface of the Moon.

September 15: Khrushchev begins his 13-day visit to the United States in New York.

September 28: The Los Angeles Dodgers and Milwaukee Braves tie for first place in baseball's National League, the third time for a tie in major league history. (The Dodgers, then located in Brooklyn, were also involved in the other two ties.) The Dodgers prevail in a best-of-three playoff for the pennant and on October 8 become the Major League champions by defeating the Chicago White Sox in six games in the World Series.

The White Sox's star infielder Nelson "Nellie" Fox is named the American League's MVP, and their pitcher, Early Wynn, wins the Cy Young Award. At 40 years old, Wynn becomes the oldest pitcher to win 20 games in a season. Detroit's Harvey Kuenn (.353) is the league's batting champion, and Chicago's Robert Shaw has a win-loss record of 18-6. Ernie Banks, who plays infield for the Chicago Cubs, wins the National League's MVP award. Milwaukee Brave Henry Aaron (.355) is the National League batting champion, and Eddie Matthews, also from the Braves, leads the major leagues with 46 home runs. Pittsburgh Pirate pitcher Elroy Face compiles a league-leading 18-1 record. Earlier in the season Pittsburgh's Harvey Haddix pitched 12 perfect innings against Milwaukee before surrendering a hit in the 13th, and Cleveland Indian Rocky Colavito hit four home runs in a single game.

October 10: Nixon dedicates the Dales Dam on the Columbia River between Oregon and Washington.

October 11: Pope John XXIII announces that Mother Elizabeth Anne Seton will be the first American-born Catholic to be beatified by the church.

October 18: The Soviet spacecraft *Lunik 3* sends back to Earth photographs of the dark side of the moon, which no human has ever before seen. The Soviets release the photos on October 27.

October 19: Television producer Dan Enright testifies before Congress that he rigged such game shows as *Tic Tac Dough, Dotto,* and *Name That Tune* in order to bolster ratings.

October 21: The Solomon R. Guggenheim Museum, designed by Frank Lloyd Wright, opens in New York City.

November: Twenty-One champion, Charles Van Doren, who had become a much admired celebrity on the TV show in 1958, testifies that he cheated and apologizes for deceiving his friends and millions of viewers, which he claims he did to advance the stature of learning and education. On December 7, the FCC opens hearings on TV crime and standards.

November 3: Anti-American riots break out in Panama in protest of U.S. control of the Panama Canal.

November 16: Mary Martin and Theodore Bikel star in the debut Broadway performance of Richard Rodgers and Oscar Hammerstein II's hit musical *The Sound of Music.*

November 24: The United States and the Soviet Union sign a pact agreeing to cooperate in the areas of science, culture, and sports.

November 29: U.S. troops suppress Panamanian protests over the canal.

December 1: Signed by 12 countries, the Antarctic Treaty bans military activities in Antarctica but permits scientific research.

December 12: The United Nations adopts a resolution drafted by the United States and Soviet Union promoting the peaceful use of outer space.

December 17: Stanley Kramer's film about nuclear apocalypse, *On the Beach,* becomes the first movie to premiere simultaneously on both sides of the Iron Curtain, as it opens in 18 cities around the world.

December 19: At a meeting in Paris, the Western leaders agree to invite Khrushchev to attend a summit conference in April 1960 in hopes of defusing the Berlin situation.

December 27: The Baltimore Colts defeat the New York Giants (31–16) for the second year in a row to win the NFL football title.

EYEWITNESS TESTIMONY

What I really remember is how hard we worked to be attractive to each other: peroxided hair, engineer boots, penny loafers, bobby sox, pops, turned-up collars, duck-tails, hoop skirts, hair wax, padded bras. Few thrills rivaled turning 16 and being allowed to drive.

We had slow dancing, the bop, the P.C., the bunny hop, the dirty bop, and last dance. Lights swirled around the gym, and we listened to Lee Willie Douglas, the Man with the Final Solution. We would double-date, and only boys called girls. Majorettes with hula hoops were the most provocative thing going. Boys wore blue jeans and t-shirts and sported flat-tops. Girls in ponytails wore skirts and blouses with little lace collars. Pierced ears were considered by some the work of the devil, and today's styles of body ornaments were then known only to people who lived in jungles. Sexual orientation was never ambiguous—or so it seemed to us. We would break up, make up, and experiment with butterfly kisses and french kisses. But sex was mostly an intellectual concept, and birth control was managed with terror, not pills.

Mike Jenkins recalling at the 40th reunion of the Class of 1960 life as a teenager in the late 1950s at Montgomery, Alabama's, Lanier High School, April 7, 2000.

It was like the emperor's clothes. You parade it down the street and you say, "This is great art," and the people along the parade route will agree with you. Who's going to stand up to Clem Greenberg and later to the Rockefellers who were buying it for their bank lobbies and say, "This stuff is terrible?"

Jason Epstein recalling the unassailable role of abstract expressionism in the late 1950s New York art scene in a 1994 interview with Frances Stonor Saunders, in Saunders, The Cultural Cold War: The CIA and the World of Arts and Letters (2000), p. 275.

[I was] thunderstruck, the entire art movement had become an enormous business venture.

Art patron Peggy Guggenheim on returning to the United States in 1959 after a year's absence, in Frances Stonor Saunders, The Cultural Cold War: The CIA and the World of Arts and Letters (2000), p. 274.

Abstract Expressionism was at the zenith of its popularity, to such an extent that [by 1959] an unknown artist trying to exhibit in New York couldn't find a gallery unless he was painting in a mode derived from one or another member of the New York School.

Critic John Canaday writing about abstract expressionism in 1959 in an August 8, 1976, New York Times article, in Francis Stonor Saunders, The Cultural Cold War: The CIA and the World of Arts and Letters (2000), p. 274.

I am sure that all of you have heard that old wives' tale .. that no hypnotized subject may be forced to do that which is repellent to his moral nature, whatever that is, or to his own best interests. That is nonsense, of course [Yen Lo cites several academic studies]. . . . For any of you who are interested in massive negative conditioning there is Frederic Wertham's *The Seduction of the Innocent,* which demonstrates how thousands have been brought to antisocial actions through children's cartoon books. . . . The conception of people acting against their own best interests should not startle us. We see it occasionally in sleepwalking and in politics, every day. . . .

Neurotics and psychotics . . . are too easily canted into unpredictable patterns." . . . Of course, he explained .. paranoiacs had always provided us with the great leaders of the world and always would. This was a clinical, historical fact. . . .

Although the paranoiacs make the great leaders, it is the resenters who make their best instruments because the resenters, those men with cancer of the psyche, make the great assassins. . . .

It has been said . . . that only the man who is capable of loving everything is capable of understanding everything. The resentful man is a human with the capacity for affection so poorly developed that his understanding for the motives of others very nearly does not exist. . . . Raymond is a man of melancholic and reserved psychology. He is afflicted with total resentment.

Fictional Chinese "brainwashing" expert Dr. Yen Lo, in the 1959 novel The Manchurian Candidate, explaining why American POW Raymond Shaw is his choice for a political assassin, in Richard Condon, The Manchurian Candidate (1988), pp. 38–41.

Marco said that there was not a healthy woman alive who would not gladly agree to rush into bed if that action displaced only the present and did not connect with the past nor had any possibility of any shape in the future. . . . It meant sex without sin. . . .

Sergeant Marco, a character in the 1959 book The Manchurian Candidate, *explaining the philosophy behind his seduction technique when he is in a new city, in Richard Condon,* The Manchurian Candidate *(1988), pp. 107–8.*

Deterrents might work if men were governed by reason, but we all know they are not.

From The Last Day, *Helen Clarkson's novel about nuclear war, in Clarkson,* The Last Day *(1959), p. 35.*

Is it communism to want peace in a nuclear age? You're sounding now like that editorial in *Life,* long ago, that said the only people who wanted to end nuclear testing were "scared mothers, fuzzy liberals and weary taxpayers." In other words: mothers are a lunatic fringe, a minority group, and if they don't like it here, let's send them back where they came from.

Lois, a middle-age wife and mother, contemplating contemporary politics, in Helen Clarkson's novel, The Last Day *(1959), p. 42.*

They had warned mothers of my generation not to be overprotective. They had written treatises and plays and novels to show the evils of possessive love. They had made love unfashionable, hardly respectable, for they implied that all love was possessive, a vice of the loving and a burden to the loved. For centuries Puritanism had poisoned sexual love, but it had remained for the Twentieth Century to attack parental love as well. How strange that those sophisticated thinkers had been able to spare so little of their ammunition for a far more common emotion, hatred. Every citizen of every nation-state had cultivated the hate that leads to war as if it were a rare flower, but the thinkers were too busy discussing the evils of love to pay much attention to that.

Lois, the protagonist of the novel The Last Day, *rejecting "momism," in Helen Clarkson,* The Last Day *(1959), p. 95.*

I have an acquaintance, a retired manufacturer . . . who has recently become worried about international tensions, intercontinental missiles, H-bombs, and such.

One day, knowing that I had done some writing on military subjects, he asked: "What do you think would happen if the Russkies hit us when we weren't looking—you know, like Pearl Harbor?" . . .

It was a big question. I gave him a horseback opinion, which proved conservative compared with some of the official forecasts published later. I said, "Oh, I think they'd kill fifty or sixty million Americans—but I think we'd win the war."

He thought this over and said, "Wow! Fifty or sixty million dead! What a depression that would make!"

I doubt if he realized the exact nature and extent of the depression—which is why I am writing this book.

Author Pat Frank's foreword to Alas, Babylon, *a novel about the aftermath of a nuclear war, in Frank,* Alas, Babylon *(1959), pp. v–vi.*

"Where did we slip [in the cold war competition with Russia]?"

"It wasn't lack of money. . . . It was a state of mind. Chevrolet mentalities shying away from a space-ship world. Nations are like people. When they grow old and rich and fat they get conservative. They exhaust their energy trying to keep things the way the are—and that's against nature. Oh, the services were to blame too. Maybe even SAC [Strategic Air Command]. We designed the most beautiful bombers in the world. . . . We improved and modified them each year, like new model cars. We couldn't bear the thought that jet bombers themselves might be out of style. . . . It's a state of mind that money alone won't cure."

"What will?" . . .

"Men. . . . Bold men, audacious men, tenacious men. Impatient, odd-ball men like [Admiral Hyman] Rickover pounding desks for his atomic sub. Ruthless men who will fire the deadheads and ass-kissers. Rude men who will tell the unimaginative . . . sons of bitches to go take a jump. . . . Young men because we've got to be a young country again."

Mark Bragg, a fictional air force officer, decrying American policies, in Pat Frank, Alas Babylon *(1959), p. 16.*

Long ago . . . certain proud thinkers had claimed that valid knowledge was indestructible, that ideas were deathless and truth immortal. But that was true only in the subtlest sense. . . . For Man was a culture-bearer as well as a soul-bearer, but his cultures were not immortal and they could die with a race or an age. . . .

Author Walter M. Miller, Jr., contemplating the end of civilization, in Miller, A Canticle for Leibowitz *(1959), p. 133.*

Lady Reporter: Are you in favor of Motherhood? . . .

Defense Minister: I am sternly opposed to it, Madam. It exerts a malign influence on youth, particularly on young recruits. The military services would have superior soldiers if our fighting men had not been corrupted by Motherhood.

Author Walter M. Miller, Jr., satirizing "momism," in Miller, A Canticle for Leibowitz *(1959), p. 228.*

The closer men came to perfecting for themselves a paradise, the more impatient they seemed to become with it, and with themselves as well. . . . When the world was in darkness and wretchedness, it could believe in perfection and yearn for it. But when the world became bright with reason and riches, it began to sense the narrowness of the needle's eye, and that rankled for a world no longer willing to believe or yearn. Well, they were going to destroy it again . . . this garden Earth, civilized and knowing, to be torn apart again that Man might hope again in wretched darkness.

Author Walter M. Miller, Jr., contemplating human self-destructiveness, in Miller, A Canticle for Leibowitz *(1959), p. 265.*

This [television] is a medium unlike any other which, of necessity, has to not only supply several thousand hours of entertainment each month, but has as its implicit aim the satisfaction of the vast majority of the viewing audience. Contrast this to the standards of success which apply to either a novel or a legitimate play, in which a minute fraction of the population can be pleased, with a corollary guarantee of success. A successful television venture has to please thirty million people. Consequently, television programming must be developed with an eye toward what is a mass taste. With this as its basic nature, I think it is altogether understandable that we find low level programming and a low level approach as a standard operational procedure. . . .

I think we are discussing legitimacy now. We are discussing taste and morality. We are concerning ourselves with ethics. [The front page from the *Los Angeles Examiner* highlighting a sensational sex scandal involving actor Errol Flynn and relegating to the bottom of the page a story about the death of former secretary of state and defense General George Marshall] is commentative [sic] on all of these areas. I heard not one whit of protest from the PTA, which uses a blunderbuss on us in television from week to week because of the violence we show. There was not one letter of protest from a religious organization who specifically decry our presentation of naked sex on television and accuse us almost hourly of presenting sensational, immoral sex relations or intimations of such relations on television. To the best of my knowledge, no member of the United States Government ever made a statement as to what has been the responsibility of the daily press in connection with a similar responsibility that we in television are asked to exert.

Television writer-producer Rod Serling testifying before the Federal Communications Commission in early January 1959, in Joel Engel, Rod Serling *(1989), pp. 194–95.*

I'm here to make a film about the end of the world, and this sure is the place for it.

Film star Ava Gardner at a press conference on January 5, 1959, upon arriving in Melbourne, Australia, to film On the Beach, *in Harry Haun,* The Cinematic Century *(2000).*

When I read the decision of the Oslo [Norway] Town Court [to ban the sale of Henry Miller's novel *Sexus*] . . . I did so with mingled feelings. If occasionally I was obliged to roll with laughter . . . I trust no one will take offense. . . .

I failed to be impressed . . . by the weighty, often pompous or hypocritical, opinions adduced by scholars, literary pundits, psychologists, medicos and such like. How could I be when it is precisely such single-minded individuals, so often devoid of humor, at whom I so frequently aim my shafts? . . .

If I were there, in the dock, my answer would probably be—"Guilty! Guilty! On all ninety-seven counts. To the gallows!" For when I take the short, myopic view, I realize that I was guilty even before I wrote the book. Guilty, in other words, because I am the way I am. The marvel is that I am walking about as a free man. I should have been condemned the moment I stepped out of my mother's womb.

Author Henry Miller's letter of February 27, 1959, to Trygve Hirsch in reaction to the designation in Norway of Sexus (1949) as obscene writing, in Barney Rosset, ed., Evergreen Review Reader: 1957–1961 *(1979), p. 259.*

Gary Cooper [in *High Noon*] ran around trying to get help and no one would give him any, and that's a rather silly thing for a man to do, so I said, we'll do just the opposite and take a real professional viewpoint.

Director Howard Hawks explains, on March 18, 1959, his rationale for making the film western Rio Bravo, *in Harry Haun,* The Cinematic Century *(2000).*

As most of you know, last year, Southwest was chosen as one of the top 38 high schools in the country. This is an honor of which everyone at Southwest is justly proud. Being proud, however, is not enough. *We must work to maintain, and even improve, the high standards we now have, to make Southwest an even better school.* Therefore, the two planks in my platform are concerned with bringing about further improvement of our school. The first is a plan which would give you, the individual student, more voice in your student council. . . . One day, every other week, you would be given some time during the home-room period to write out on paper any suggestion you may have for the student council. . . .

My other idea would be to improve our school spirit, which, although it is good, could be even better. To do this, I would propose to make it my duty, as sergeant-at-arms, to attempt, through correspondence with other schools, and personal interviews with principals, teachers, and educators, to form . . . a definite set of plans for long-term improvement of SCHOOL SPIRIT.

I have already . . . received one idea which, it was felt, greatly improved spirit at another local Kansas City high school. At this school, a certain week was declared to be school spirit week, and during this time, special emphasis was put on improving school spirit, both in and out of the classroom. This could be . . . made even more effective with the addition of a school spirit assembly to be held at the end of school spirit week. Films of our athletic teams in action, talks about all-school functions, and a leading citizen of the community could comprise a program which would give pride and inspiration to all loyal Indians.

Phil Marcus's campaign speech in spring 1959 for the position of sergeant-at-arms in the student government at Southwest High School in Kansas City, Missouri, in private correspondence with the author, November 5, 2001.

I was completely unaware that animals with white fur were considered blood relations to white human beings.

Garth Williams responding in May 1959 to complaints by the director of Alabama's library system that his children's book, The Rabbit's Wedding, *promoted interracial marriage because a black and a white rabbit wed, in Bettye Collier-Thomas and V. P. Franklin,* My Soul Is a Witness *(1999), p. 107.*

I do not contend that driving people crazy—even for a few hours—is a pleasant prospect. But warfare is never pleasant. And to those who feel that *any* kind of chemical weapon is more horrible than conventional weapons, I put this question: Would you rather be temporarily deranged, blinded, or paralyzed by a chemical agent, or burned alive by a conventional bomb?

Major General William Creasy, chief officer of the Army Chemical Corps, in an interview published in This Week *magazine, May 17, 1959, about use of psychochemicals for purposes of national security, in Martin A. Lee and Bruce Shlain,* Acid Dreams, The Complete History of LSD: The CIA, the Sixties, and Beyond *(1985), p. 37.*

Europeans, and especially the inhabitants of East Europe, are somewhat anxious about the positions of Negroes . . . in the U.S.A. They hear the Negro slaves were liberated in 1863 and later became citizens enjoying social and political equality. They also hear about widespread lynching, murder, and mob violence. . . .

The facts correspond with reality in both cases. Negro slavery has been abolished . . . by law. However, at least five million U.S. inhabitants of Negro origin are still outcast slaves living in poverty. The majority . . . can read and write, but millions of them are as yet illiterate. They are being pushed onto the path of crime and poverty by the system of private capitalism and by racial hatred of white workers competing with them. . . .

The matter concerns, first of all, the problems of labor and wages. The U.S. Negroes need socialism. They need something similar to what is possessed by the national minorities in the Soviet Union: the opportunity to develop their own national culture.

Black leader W. E. B. DuBois, "The Negro Problem in the U.S.A.," originally published in Pravda *and broadcast on "Moscow in Russian for Abroad," June 17, 1959, and reproduced in the FBI file on DuBois, in Kenneth O'Reilly,* Black Americans: The FBI Files *(1994), pp. 113–15.*

Why, then, don't some of the big corporations sponsor an occasional program dealing with "ideas and information," as Mr. Murrow suggested? Again, because they feel they can't afford to. It costs a sizable fortune to put on an evening program on a national network. The sponsor will get his money back only if he draws the largest possible audience. If horse opera sells more autos than Ed Murrow—as it does—then the advertiser has to go for horse opera. The fact that he, personally, may prefer Murrow makes no difference. If he should yield to such a whim, his harder-headed competitors will soon run him out of the market. . . .

The upshot is that we are all paying dearly for something we don't get. We are letting broadcasters use valuable public property for free—and they are not delivering in return the public service which they promised.

John Fischer, discussing the prevalence of inferior television programming, in Fischer, "The Editor's Easy Chair," Harper's Magazine *(July 1959), pp. 12–13.*

Where do guided missiles get their "brains"?

Bell System–designed guidance systems give pinpoint accuracy to many of the nation's missiles.

Guiding a surface-to-air missile to its quarry, or an intercontinental ballistic missile to its target area, calls for communications that rival the human brain and nervous system. . . .

We are proud that our experience in communications serves the nation's defense. That experience, plus continuing research and development, is also at work every day improving telephone service.

Advertisement for the Bell Telephone System in Harper's Magazine *(July 1959), p. 1.*

Nothing in the Constitution says people can't get together and make jackass rules for themselves.

Executive secretary of the National Association for the Advancement of Colored People (NAACP) Roy Wilkins commenting on a recent decision by New York's West Side Tennis Club to refuse membership to black United Nations officials, at a meeting on July 12, 1959, celebrating the end of lynching in America and other major achievements in civil rights, in Clifton Daniel, ed., 20th Century Day by Day *(2000), p. 828.*

There is a serious and genuine undercurrent running beneath the styles and anti-styles of our time, an undercurrent that honestly distrusts art as art, a conviction that whatever is organized must therefore be falsified. It has led—not only in experimental drama but in other media as well—to a notion that truth is never to be found in meditation, and certainly not in premeditation, but only in what pops out on the spur of the moment, only in what is wholly or at least partially improvised. A craftsman can lie, but a reflex cannot. . . .

I have a feeling that the distrust of art, because art may distort the truth, may in the end leave us with very little to hold in our hands.

Theater critic Walter Kerr reviewing the Living Theater's production of Jack Gelber's jazz play The Connection, *which opened on July 15, 1959, in Stuart W. Little,* Off-Broadway: The Prophetic Theater *(1972), pp. 206–7.*

What is it? Do you have rocket launching pads there? Is there an epidemic of cholera there or something? Or have gangsters taken hold of the place that can destroy me?

Soviet premier Nikita Khrushchev complaining on August 28, 1959, about being denied access to Disneyland, in Clifton Daniel, ed., 20th Century Day by Day *(2000), p. 831.*

The 1959–60 season began with the usual theatre shortage, and, at its end, a battle between the actors and the producers closed all Broadway's legitimate theatres from June 2 to June 12. It was the first such blackout since the Actors' Equity strike in 1919. It was an event to remember in an otherwise uneventful and rather drab season. New plays opened and closed faster than within memory, and a run of one or two performances was not unusual. In fact, fourteen new attractions played only five or less times before oblivion. . . .

Among the plays that deserved better box office treatment than they received were: the historical drama *The Andersonville Trial,* the political play *The Gang's All Here,* the elaborately produced *Caligula,* the psychological drama *The Deadly Game,* and the problem play *The Long Dream.* . . .

Off-Broadway continued to flourish as an important facet of the theatre with nearly one hundred attractions presented within the year . . . [including] Chekhov's first play, never before produced in America, *A Country Scandal, The Connection,* [Edward Albee's]

The Zoo Story, The Prodigal, Between Two Thieves, all by new promising playwrights; Dos Passos' *U.S.A.* . . . Indeed, Off-Broadway was far more rewarding than Broadway this season.

> *Daniel Blum reviewing the 1959–60 theater season, in*
> *Blum,* Theatre World: Season 1959–60 *(1960), p. 6.*

In the fall of 1959, when we first contemplated moving to a more distant suburb in Greater Miami, I remember thinking about the neighborhood I would be leaving. Like many other young families after World War II, my husband and I bought our first home outside the city center in the late 1940s, and we lived there throughout the 1950s. I remember the thrill of buying our very own home and knowing I was settling down to enjoy my life. There were additional perks in these post-Depression years: a regular paycheck and my first washing machine—I hung the clothes out to dry on a clothesline in the back yard. Later, we bought a self-defrosting refrigerator. Before that, the children and I would periodically attack the thick layers of ice that built up in the freezer with ice scrapers, and sometimes even hammers for the big chunks. In addition the new wrinkle-free, "wash and wear" fabrics eliminated time-consuming chores. I have always thought that these time-savers were what made women decide that they could run a household and also work outside the home.

Our little family quickly became an integral part of a neighborhood, which was situated on a single block on S.W. 25th Street in unincorporated Dade County. Such neighborhoods were commonplace; yet each was unique. We all felt we "belonged," especially the children, who were remarkably close in age—infants at the beginning of the decade to elementary school graduates by the end . . . 12 girls and 8 boys.

The gravitating place was the "watering hole," the Hart's swimming pool, the only one on the block at that time, where young and old, alike, followed the rules—or else! Before they built their pool, we gathered in the shade of Dottie and Bill's front yard. This was before air conditioning was common in private homes, and though the temperatures were not quite as high as today, Miami in the long summer months was uncomfortably hot and humid. These were still the days of stay-at-home moms and mostly one-car families. While the kids played in the sandbox, we mothers "kept an eye on them" and yakked. As time

passed, the street, which at that time was a dead end, became part of the children's playground.

It was truly remarkable how such a diverse group of families could so easily mesh together. Catholics, Southern Baptists, and other Protestant sects. Ours was the only Jewish family, but we never felt any less welcomed or less accepted on that account. It wasn't until 35 years later that we learned that one of our friends descended directly from German Jews. It was he and his wife who set the fine standards for the neighborhood.

Even though we moved away over 40 years ago, I still keep in touch with several of the families. About ten years ago, my son was the best man in the wedding of his best friend from across the street. Even the Cuban family who moved next door in 1959, after Castro came to power, shared our good will, if not much of a common language. They introduced us to Cuban coffee and Cuban crackers, and my son and their daughter used to play together and sell lemonade together at their own little, street-side stand. Coincidentally, 30 years later the girl and her mom attended my son's wedding, but as guests of his Cuban-American bride's family.

In retrospect, the period seems so much less hectic, and our neighborhood was a place where lasting friendships flourished. Looking back then, in 1959, as well as now, I remembered our neighborhood as a place of quiet contentment and bliss.

> *Evelyn Schwartz recalling fall 1959 and her neighborhood as she prepared to move to a more distant Miami suburb, in private correspondence with the author, August 24, 2001.*

The face of humanity is more beautiful than its backside.

> *Soviet premier Nikita Khrushchev reacting to the filming of* Can-Can *at the studios of 20th Century-Fox on September 19, 1959, in Harry Haun, The Cinematic Century (2000).*

Gentlemen, we're going to have a football team. We are going to win some games. Do you know why? Because you are going to have confidence in me and my system. By being alert you are going to make fewer mistakes than your opponents. By working harder you are going to out-execute, out-block, out-tackle every team that comes your way.

I've never been a losing coach, and I don't intend to start here. There is nobody big enough to think he's got the team made or can do what he wants. Trains and planes are coming in and going in and coming out of Green Bay, and he'll be on one of them. I won't. I'm going to find thirty-six men who have the pride to make any sacrifice to win. There are such men. If they're not here, I'll get them. If you are not one, if you don't want to play, you might as well leave right now. . . .

I know that in a small town you need definite rules and regulations. And anybody who breaks the rules will be taken care of in my own way . . . You may not be a tackle. You may not be a guard. You may not be a back. But you *will* be a professional.

> *Vince Lombardi addressing his football team on September 27, 1959, before his first game as head coach of the Green Bay Packers, against the Chicago Bears, in Robert Torricelli and Andrew Carroll, eds., In Our Own Words (1999), p. 215.*

Russia put into deep space a new device—labeled an "interplanetary station"—that left U.S. scientists impressed but puzzled.

Generally, American space experts were inclined to wait and see before judging Russian predictions that the new rocket would circle around the unseen side of the moon and then go into an elongated orbit around Earth.

What skimpy data is coming out of Moscow, however, is prompting this speculation. First, that the Russians have developed a new and fairly good system of radioing commands to the rocket from Earth, and, second, that the Reds might have indulged in a bit of Madison Avenue–type exaggeration by calling the rocket an "interplanetary space station" instead of a satellite or space probe. . . .

"We recognize the significance of this effort to send a probe around the moon and extend our congratulations," Mr. [T. Keith] Glennan [chief of the National Aeronautics and Space Administration] said. "With the rest of the world's scientific community we shall await the data from this new probe in its journey between Earth and the moon." . . .

U.S. experts were careful to stress that they were not attempting to belittle the Russian feat. Questions were raised, however, about calling the vehicle an "interplanetary space station." . . .

The time of the launching was notable from two standpoints. It came on the second anniversary of the first Russian *Sputnik*. It also came at about the same time U.S. space planners are understood to have wanted to send their own deep space probe aloft, probably to orbit the moon. U.S. plans for the moon shot apparently were called off when an Atlas missile of the type to be used blew up on the launching pad last month. The first few days in October were the most favorable time for launching a moon probe because of the moon's position in relation to the earth.

> *"Russia Fires Rocket to Circle Moon, Earth; Data on Device Is Meager,"* Wall Street Journal, *October 5, 1959, p. 1.*

Comrade Mao Tse-Tung [Zedong] . . . said that they fully approve of this foreign policy step of the CPSU [Communist Party of the Soviet Union], and that they have no differences in evaluation of the significance of this trip [by Soviet premier Khrushchev to the United States]. In a half-joking tone, I asked Mao Tse-Tung whether one could consider that on this question we are united on all ten fingers. Mao Tse-Tung said, that it is so, and added, that in general, whenever we have some sort of disagreements, they consist of just one finger out of ten, or more precisely, just half a finger. . . . In fact, on all important and fundamental matters there is always unity between us [China and the Soviet Union].

[Mao] agreed . . . that as a result of Comrade N. S. Khrushchev's visit to the USA there had been carried out a real relaxation of tensions in the international situation. Mao Tse-Tung expressed extreme approval of the Soviet government proposal for general and complete disarmament which N. S. Khrushchev made during his voyage to the USA, and which was submitted for review to the United Nations. The proposal of the Soviet government for full disarmament, said Mao Tse-Tung, really is the best means of resolving the entire problem of disarmament. Precisely general and complete disarmament is necessary, he underlined. . . . At the present time, he said further, the Peoples Liberation Army of China counts in its ranks approximately 2 million people. The internal needs of the Chinese People's Republic do not require an army of such size. Control over the internal situation in the country can be entirely realized by the people's militia, which consists not of military personnel but of people working in industry. In the event that the matter leads to the real achievement of general

Charlton Heston stars in the epic film *Ben-Hur. (Photofest)*

disarmament, the size of the army could definitely be reduced.

> *From S. F. Antonov's report of his meeting with China's party chairman Mao Zedong on October 14, 1959, following Soviet premier Nikita Khrushchev's visit to the United States, in Antonov, "A Conversation with Mao" (2001), available online.*

Charioteering is a hard-won and largely useless skill, but I can't help taking pride in it.

> *Actor Charlton Heston writing in his diary while filming* Ben-Hur, *which premiered in November 1959, in Harry Haun,* The Cinematic Century *(2000).*

All pupils in the elementary and high schools here except one little girl knew their way home today when an unrehearsed "go-home" air-raid drill was called while classes were in session.

Some parents had predicted that the younger children, usually picked up by adults at the end of the school day, would get lost and perhaps even trampled in the rush. The two schools occupy one campus on the busy Albany Post Road. . . . [E]very child was off the grounds in eight minutes and . . . only three mothers were waiting in cars at the curb.

The lost child was seen by . . . a school board member. He reported that other children had told her how to get home.

> *"Dobbs Ferry Pupils Sent Home in Drill,"* New York Times, *November 11, 1959, p. 26.*

Rehearsing *The Sound of Music* was not an easy chore. . . . The play was set in Austria just before and during the Anschluss, a time and place I was all too familiar with. I had witnessed perfectly nice and ordinary people turn into unfeeling brutes, sporting swastikas and threatening all who would not obey the party line. The second act of *The Sound of Music* is exactly about people and situations like that. One would have expected .. some adherence to accuracy, if not to history, then at least to the emotional wallop carried by those events. . . . But no. This was musical theatre, where the edges had to be softened and the world viewed through tinted glasses. Our Nazis wore .. swastika armbands only for the first dress rehearsal; they were ordered to take them off even before the first performance .. because their shock value was deemed too great. . . . Years later, during the era of *Cabaret* and thanks to Hal Prince, musicals got to be more biting about the portrayal of unpleasant historical memories. . . .

Ironically, almost all the actors who played Nazis or Nazi sympathizers were Jews.

Actor Theodore Bikel describing his experience with the musical The Sound of Music, *which debuted on Broadway on November 16, 1959, in Bikel,* Theo *(1994), pp. 207–8.*

When I heard "Edelweiss" for the first time, I thought, Ah, at last I have something that I can get my teeth into. It had that folk feeling, it used my guitar to the best advantage, and it integrated itself into the action very well. But frankly, the nostalgia was not heartfelt. I never had much nostalgic feeling toward Austria. It was not a country that behaved terribly well to the Jews.

Actor Theodore Bikel commenting on The Sound of Music, *which opened on Broadway on November 16, 1959, in Myrna Katz Frommer and Harvey Frommer,* It Happened on Broadway *(1998), p. 114.*

Perhaps more than any other book since Scott Fitzgerald's THE CRACK-UP, this book [*Advertisements for Myself*] reveals how exciting, yet tragic, America can be for a gifted writer. It is a remarkably full book; all of Mailer up to now is in it; and that is exactly what is wrong with it. . . . [Mailer] has put together an anthology of all his works, from undergraduate short stories to two sections of the novel in progress, that includes his columns from a Greenwich Village weekly, social and political comment, his now famous essay on "The White Negro" and other sociosexual themes. . . . By the time you get through what is often a very brilliant if screamingly self-conscious book, you feel that Mailer has worked so hard to display everything he has done and everything he knows that it has all collected on the surface. Mailer's performance here reminds me of the brilliant talker who impresses the hell out of you at a cocktail party but who, when he turns his back to go home, seems vaguely lost.

Yet ADVERTISEMENTS FOR MYSELF is a remarkable performance, and it is clearer to me than ever that Mailer is a powerful, courageous talent admirably provoked by our culture.

Literary critic Alfred Kazan reviewing Norman Mailer's Advertisements for Myself *in* The Reporter, *November 26, 1959, in Robert F. Lucid,* Norman Mailer, the Man and His Work *(1971), pp. 89–90.*

On New Year's Eve in 1959, I told a friend that I was sure of just two things about the year (and probably the decade) which lay ahead: hemlines would rise far and Richard Nixon would never be my president.

Writer Nora Sayre predicting the future on December 31, 1959, in Sayre, Previous Convictions: A Journey through the 1950s *(1995), p. 232.*

EPILOGUE

Final Thoughts on the Decade

"It was the best of times. It was the worst of times." Charles Dickens's famous opening to *A Tale of Two Cities,* his novel set during the French Revolution of the 1790s, doubtlessly applies to every era—no less to the 1950s. Despite its reputation as a placid period of conformity, stasis, and complacency, the decade was actually a time of great transformation at all levels of society. Like all change, these alterations in American life created opportunities and setbacks, winners and losers, and gains and losses. So, naturally, people's experiences of the decade varied depending on who they were and where they stood.

Change was evident in the political realm, as the 1950s ended 20 years of Democratic power and reintroduced Republican rule for most of the decade—although for most of his time in office, Eisenhower had to accommodate a Democratic Congress. Still, Eisenhower's pull back from the social activism of the New Deal and the Fair Deal was an important change in American government and society, as Eisenhower favored a more limited role for the federal government and believed that a strong economy was the best avenue for constructive social change, as well as for the national defense. Meanwhile, right-wing demagogues such as Senator McCarthy sought, with some success, to redefine as treason the New Deal liberalism that had been the cornerstone of Roosevelt's popularity and success in the 1930s and 1940s.

Supreme Court rulings that outlawed longstanding racial segregation of public schools and other public facilities triggered violent resistance, civil rights activism, and a constitutional crisis in which Eisenhower was compelled to order army troops to Little Rock, Arkansas. In so doing, he forcefully reasserted the primacy of the federal government over the individual states. Certainly, the 1954 Supreme Court ruling that struck down the Jim Crow laws that had legally condoned and codified a racially segregated society in the South was one of the most dramatic and far-reaching causes of cultural change in the period.

Internationally, change was even more pronounced, and to many Americans, as well as others, the world seemed increasingly unfamiliar and difficult to understand. The European colonial empires that had dominated the world since the 17th century crumbled, and the Soviet Union went from being a

World War II ally to a bitter enemy, while World War II foes Germany and Japan became allies. Meanwhile, little-known countries in the Middle East and Asia suddenly became focal points of U.S. foreign policy and military intervention. And more than at any time in its history, foreign policy dominated the political landscape, and economic, political, and military initiatives were made for reasons of power politics and ideology, as the nation somewhat reluctantly came to acknowledge and accept its role as international superpower.

The economy was strong for most of the decade, except during the Korean War and a brief recession in 1958. The healthy economy was nurtured by a decade-long housing boom, baby boom, and boom in auto sales and defense industries that yielded strong corporate profits, created comparatively well-paying jobs, and generated ample consumer spending. Out of these grew a culture of consumer capitalism, in which businesses used sophisticated advertising to create new needs for new products and thereby promote an unending stream of consumer expenditures. The new concept of planned obsolescence was further calculated to ensure future sales.

But if the robust economy was good for corporations, it also benefited the personal finances of individual Americans. The Diner's Club card (1950), the American Express Card (1958), and the BankAmericard (1959) facilitated spending and short-term borrowing, which both stimulated the economy and enabled Americans to purchase goods more often and with greater convenience—as well as run a greater risk of incurring heavy debt. More and more women entered the workforce, and expanded opportunities for higher education and home ownership that emanated largely from the G.I. Bill further enabled vast numbers of middle-class American men to achieve financial stability unavailable during the Great Depression or World War II, and to become "upwardly mobile." Therefore, unlike 10 or 20 years earlier, most middle-class Americans felt assured of financial stability and expected that they would be better off than their parents, at least in material terms.

Science and technology were also sources of great optimism for most Americans, as scientists and engineers continued to achieve things previously not imaginable in any other century. Powerful, fast cars became available to average citizens, who could now travel thousands of miles over smooth, reliable highways to visit faraway parts of the country in relatively short times. Likewise, passenger jets enabled ordinary citizens to experience other cultures firsthand. Television broadcasts offered the next best thing to being at the remote location, and transistors enabled people to carry music, sports, and news reports with them via pocket radios. Inoculations eradicated deadly diseases, and new machines kept alive people whose own hearts or kidneys failed. New methods were also developed for alleviating emotional problems. Immense dams converted the energy of powerful rivers into abundant, inexpensive electricity, and nuclear reactors similarly harnessed the power of the atom for peaceful uses. Powerful computers performed calculations that hitherto had been too complicated or numerous to attempt, subatomic particles and distant galaxies were discovered, and the origins of time and of the universe fell under scrutiny. Fabrics were invented that did not wrinkle, and plastics and other synthetic materials with exceptional properties of weight, durability, and strength were introduced. Pesticides controlled infestations of insects capable of destroying entire harvests, the deepest secrets of the DNA molecule were revealed, the St.

Lawrence Seaway joined the Great Lakes to the Atlantic Ocean, a nuclear sub-marine cruised beneath the North Pole, a long-imagined northwest passage was discovered across the North American continent, and greater exploration was made of the hitherto impenetrable cold and remote arctic regions. Finally, of course, the grandest dream of people throughout the ages was realized when the first human-made objects left Earth's atmosphere, and earthly life forms took their first steps into the heavens.

These and numerous other scientific and technological achievements all suggested that people would continue to exert more and more control over their environments—and thereby control their lives to an increasingly greater extent. The strides made by science thus pointed to an exciting future of easier, longer, safer but more exciting lives filled with a wide new range of human experiences.

At the same time, the down sides of consumerism, science, and technology became increasingly apparent in the ever-increasing traffic jams and air pollution, the problems of overcrowding among a longer-living population, the loss of personal identity that was sometimes the collateral damage from scientifical-ly run social and corporate systems, the economic threat to the workforce from automation, expanded possibilities of government and business intrusion into private lives through the use of advanced technology and even mind-control techniques, and, of course, the threat of nuclear annihilation.

In the 1950s, more Americans expressed greater religious affiliation than at any other time previously in the century, and the overwhelming majority of them were Christians, predominantly Protestants. No doubt their faith offered believers of all denominations a source of stability and hope during these changing and dangerous times. The dominating role that religion played in American society is evidenced by the fact that religious leaders were regarded as the most trustworthy figures of authority, and in the popularity of the 1952 Revised Standard Version of the Holy Bible, which topped the best-seller lists in each of the first three years of its release and by the popularity of such movies as Cecil B. DeMille's *The Ten Commandments* (1956) and William Wyler's *Ben-Hur* (1959), both of which starred Charlton Heston. The place of religion is also apparent in the growing enthusiasm for and influence of such evangelists as Billy Graham and television priests such as Bishop Sheen; it can also be seen in the addition of "under God" to the Pledge of Allegiance in 1954 and in the introduction of the national motto, "In God We Trust," in 1956.

Moreover, religion and capitalism frequently were singled out as the strongest bulwarks against communism, and the conflict between Christian-dominated capitalism and the international forces of atheistic communism was widely viewed in the United States as a moral struggle between good and evil, and by some, such as Graham and his followers, as a battle between God and Satan. However, one effect of this interconnection between capitalism and Christianity was that it obscured some very significant differences in the underlying values of the two systems of practice and belief. Although only rarely addressed during the decade, in such books as William H. Whyte's *The Organization Man* (1956) and in occasional debates about West Coast and East Coast values, the inherent clash in values between consumer capitalism and the Protestant ethic provoked tension and confusion, especially among young people who were more attuned to the disparities and unsure what to believe and how to behave. If, on the one hand, the Protestant ethic encouraged thrift, self-control, self-sacrifice, and self-improvement through hard work, consumer capitalism bombarded Americans with advertisements telling them to spend freely, indulge their passions and their impulses, and find the easy road to success.

The messages were especially mixed when the subject was sex. On the one hand, sex sells, and advertisers, publishers, entertainers, and film and TV producers made good money by giving the public what it clearly wanted, even if they did so within the restrictions of official and unofficial censorship. On the other hand, in Christian theology lasciviousness is a sin, and Christians were encouraged to be modest in their sex appeal, to remain virgins until marriage, and monogamous within their marriages. Thus, throughout the decade Americans were pulled in powerful but opposite directions in matters of basic values and primal impulses.

The popular culture of the time sometimes tried to reconcile these differences but did not typically treat them very deeply. In such movies as *Pillow Talk* (1959), Rock Hudson and Doris Day titillate viewers and each other with their sexuality but are able to act on their lust only after they marry. In most teenage-oriented films, "going all the way" is also shown to be a wrong choice, but few movies dealt with the mixed messages about sex that children in the culture had to decipher in everyday life. One exception is *Rebel Without a Cause* (1955), in which parents' refusal even to acknowledge, much less deal with, the nascent sexuality of their children compels the adolescents to negotiate their own way imperfectly through a confusing maze of right and wrong action. Mixed messages about sexuality appear more violently in the best-selling detective novels of Mickey Spillane, whose protagonist, Mike Hammer, physically gratifies numerous women in the course of his adventures, but they often meet unhappy, sometimes brutal ends.

For many sexy women, the movies defined success as marriage to a respected and wealthy, or potentially wealthy man—such as Marilyn Monroe does in *Gentlemen Prefer Blondes* (1953; although her friend, Jane Russell marries happily for love). Frequently in such films the man need not be attractive or youthful, so long as he is rich. Ideally, he should be morally upright too, but his attraction is his wealth and power; therefore, true fulfillment in these films is connected to the affluence and upward mobility promoted by consumer capitalism.[1] Of course, other stories project contrary messages. In *Guys and Dolls* (play, 1950; film, 1955), a female Salvation Army worker achieves fulfillment when she reforms and marries an attractive but wayward gambler, who surrenders his big-spending lifestyle and adopts her sober, devout, and humble ways. But such renunciations of material well-being and libidinal pleasure in favor of a more spiritually rewarding existence were rare in 1950s American films, despite the country's pronounced identification with Christian values. Beat poetry denounced the spiritual destructiveness of capitalism more vehemently, although its critique is rooted more in a Buddhist-inspired tradition than a Christian one, and it expresses a left-wing political position that condemns America's cold war efforts to contain communism as suicidal and dehumanizing.

Apart from the disparity between traditional Protestant values and those of 1950s consumer capitalism, other important divisions are evident in the arts and culture of the decade. Most striking is the contrast between an optimistic worldview typically broadcast on television and expressions of deep despair found in much of the enduring literature and theater, and in some films. Television shows were sponsored by advertisers who, by and large, wanted happy associations for their products, and associations of integrity and trustworthiness. Moreover, as a mass medium, television seeks to appeal to the broadest possible spectrum of viewers, and most people prefer to have their spirits lifted rather than brought down when seeking out entertainment. This may account for the large number of comedies and westerns on 1950s television and for television's tendency to avoid controversy and project domestic situations in which most families are loving, supportive, oblivious to troublesome current events, and financially secure—such as we see in *I Love Lucy, Leave It to Beaver, Father Knows Best, The Donna Reed Show, The Real McCoys,* and *The Adventures of Ozzie and Harriet,* for example. On such shows, children, if sometimes headstrong and inclined to challenge authority, inevitably respect the authority of their parents and learn the value of acting responsibly. These programs typically conclude with happy endings in which the family unit is strong, cohesive, and reassuring.

The continual presence in the living rooms of America of such fictional families no doubt created, and continues to create, a disjuncture between the ideal, nurturing, nuclear family and real-life Americans. The fact that most families did not achieve the levels of nurturing harmony, understanding, and support practiced by their television counterparts—and in fact were not always headed by both a father and a mother—may account in part for the sense of despair and the outbreak of dysfunctional families in the serious fiction and theater of the time. In these works, family members are hostile to one another, seek to dominate or humiliate, are motivated by pride, parental jealousy, sibling rivalry, greed, and licentiousness, and/or are simply themselves too emotionally damaged to satisfy the emotional needs of husbands, children, wives, and parents. These include J. D. Salinger's *Catcher in the Rye* (1951) and his long stories "Franny" (1955) and "Zooey" (1957), Carson McCullers's *The Ballad of the Sad Café* (1951), James Baldwin's *Go Tell It on the Mountain* (1953) and "Sonny's Blues" (1957), Tennessee Williams's *Cat on a Hot Tin Roof* (1955), Sloan Wilson's *The Man in the Gray Flannel Suit* (1955), Eugene O'Neill's *Long Day's Journey into Night* (1956), Tillie Olsen's "I Stand Here Ironing" (1956), Saul Bellow's *Seize the Day* (1956), John Barth's *The Floating Opera* (1956), John Cheever's *The Wapshot Chronicle* (1957), Lorraine Hansberry's *A Raisin in the Sun* (1959), and Philip Roth's *Goodbye, Columbus* (1959). Not infrequently in these and other exposés of American family life, alcohol abuse is present, although it is rarely labeled as such or even presented as something out of the ordinary. (Alcohol also features prominently in the movies of the period, and one of the 1950s film clichés shows the loving housewife greeting her husband at the door after a hard day of work with a kiss and a martini.)

Hence, the pictures of family life in American letters are much more tormented than those seen on television. Sometimes, literary families stifle the protagonists instead of supporting them, and sometimes, such as in Arthur Miller's *Death of a Salesman* (play, 1949; film, 1952), the American dream collapses when the head of the family too fully and unquestioningly adopts the values of consumer capitalism and confuses material success and popular acceptance with love.

In sum, the challenge of the 1950s was to deal constructively, within the framework of consumer capitalism and the cold war, with legitimate fears that ranged from national defense to greater isolation of individuals within families and spiritual enervation, while still moving forward toward the future with confidence and optimism. America's record in meeting that challenge was certainly mixed, but in the long run it emerged from the decade at peace, albeit locked in a nuclear stalemate, with its international alliances strong and its economy vibrant. By the end of 1959, it had cast off the worst aspects of the Red Scare, and despite simmering, and sometimes overboiling racial tensions, it was becoming a more tolerant society, as attested not only by the growing opportunities for black Americans and increased recognition of their achievements but also by the election in 1960 of John F. Kennedy, a liberal Democrat who was the first Catholic to become president. Moreover, in electing Kennedy the nation chose forward-looking youth over politicians and policies tied to the past. And like the new president, who vowed to put a man on the moon by the end of the 1960s, many Americans concluded the 1950s excited by the opening of new frontiers in outer space, the awe-inspiring advances in scientific knowledge and technological capability, and the vast, new opportunities to imagine and realize social and personal aspirations—if a hydrogen bomb did not kill them first.

APPENDIX A
Documents

1. President Harry S. Truman's announcement of the atomic bomb, August 6, 1945
2. Winston Churchill's warning of an "iron curtain" descending on Eastern Europe, March 5, 1946
3. The Truman Doctrine, March 12, 1947
4. Secretary of State George Marshall's European Recovery Plan (the Marshall Plan), June 5, 1947
5. Senator Joseph McCarthy's speech before a Republican women's group in Wheeling, West Virginia, February 9, 1950
6. Senator Margaret Chase Smith addressing the U.S. Senate, June 1, 1950
7. Listing for Arthur Miller in *Red Channels* (an entertainment industry blacklist), June 1950
8. President Truman announcing his decision to fire General MacArthur, April 11, 1951
9. President Dwight Eisenhower's first inauguration speech, January 20, 1953
10. President Eisenhower's "Atoms for Peace" address to the United Nations, December 8, 1953
11. President Eisenhower's second inauguration speech, January 21, 1957
12. President Eisenhower's address to the nation announcing his decision to have the U.S. Army enforce the court-ordered integration of Central High School in Little Rock, Arkansas, September 24, 1957

1. PRESIDENT HARRY S. TRUMAN'S ANNOUNCEMENT OF THE ATOMIC BOMB, AUGUST 6, 1945

Sixteen hours ago an American airplane dropped one bomb on Hiroshima, an important Japanese Army base. That bomb had more power than 20,000 tons of T.N.T. It had more than two thousand times the blast power of the British "Grand Slam," which is the largest bomb ever yet used in the history of warfare.

The Japanese began the war from the air at Pearl Harbor. They have been repaid many fold. And the end is not yet. With this bomb we have now added a new and revolutionary increase in destruction to supplement the growing power of our armed forces. In their present forms these bombs are now in production and even more powerful forms are in development.

It is an atomic bomb. It is a harnessing of the basic power of the universe. The force from which the sun draws its power has been loosed against those who brought war to the Far East.

Before 1939, it was the accepted belief of scientists that it was theoretically possible to release atomic energy. But no one knew any practical method of doing it. By 1942, however, we knew that the Germans were working feverishly to find a way to add atomic energy to the other engines of war with which they hoped to enslave the world. But they failed. We may be grateful to Providence that the Germans got the V-1's and the V-2's late and in limited quantities and even more grateful that they did not get the atomic bomb at all.

The battle of the laboratories held fateful risks for us as well as the battles of the air, land, and sea, and we have now won the battle of the laboratories as we have won the other battles. . . . We have spent two billion dollars on the greatest scientific gamble in history—and won.

But the greatest marvel is not the size of this enterprise, its secrecy, nor its cost, but the achievement of scientific brains in putting together infinitely complex pieces of knowledge held by many men in different fields of science into a workable plan. And hardly less marvelous has been the capacity of industry to design, and of labor to operate, the machines and methods to do things never done before so that the brain child of many minds came forth in physical shape and performed as it was supposed to do. . . . What has been done is the greatest achievement of organized science in history. It was done under high pressure and without failure.

We are now prepared to obliterate more rapidly and completely every productive enterprise the Japanese have above ground in any city. We shall destroy their docks, their factories, and their communications. Let there be no mistakes; we shall completely destroy Japan's power to make war.

It was to spare the Japanese people from utter destruction that the ultimatum of July 26 was issued at Potsdam. Their leaders promptly rejected that ultimatum. If they do not now accept our terms, they may expect a rain of ruin from the air, the like of which has never been seen on this earth. Behind this air attack will follow sea and land forces in such numbers and power as they have not yet seen and with the fighting skill of which they are already well aware. . . .

The fact that we can release atomic energy ushers in a new era in man's understanding of nature's forces. Atomic energy may in the future supplement the power that now comes from coal, oil, and falling water, but at present it cannot be produced on a basis to compete with them commercially. Before that comes, there must be a long period of intensive research.

It has never been the habit of the scientists of this country or the policy of this Government to withhold from the world scientific knowledge. Normally, therefore, everything about the work with atomic energy would be made public.

But under present circumstances it is not intended to divulge the technical processes of production or all the military applications, pending further examination of possible methods of protecting us and the rest of the world from the danger of sudden destruction.

I shall recommend that the Congress of the United States consider promptly the establishment of an appropriate commission to control the production and use of atomic power within the United States. I shall give further consideration and make further recommendations to the Congress as to how atomic power can become a powerful and forceful influence towards the maintenance of world peace.

2. WINSTON CHURCHILL'S WARNING OF AN "IRON CURTAIN" DESCENDING ON EASTERN EUROPE, MARCH 5, 1946

The United States stands at this time at the pinnacle of world power. It is a solemn moment for the American democracy. For with this primacy in power is also joined an awe-inspiring accountability to the future.... Opportunity is here now, clear and shining, for both our countries. To reject it or ignore it or fritter it away will bring upon us all the long reproaches of the after-time. It is necessary that constancy of mind, persistency of purpose, and the grand simplicity of decision shall guide and rule the conduct of the English-speaking peoples in peace as they did in war. We must and I believe we shall prove ourselves equal to this severe requirement....

A shadow has fallen upon the scenes so lately lighted by the Allied victory. Nobody knows what Soviet Russia and its Communist international organization intends to do in the immediate future, or what are the limits, if any, to their expansive and proselytizing tendencies....

We understand the Russian need to be secure on her western frontiers ... by the removal of all possibility of German aggression. We welcome Russia to her rightful place among the leading nations of the world. We welcome her flag upon the seas. Above all, we welcome or should welcome constant, frequent, and growing contacts between the Russian people and our own people on both sides of the Atlantic. It is my duty, however ... to place before you certain facts about the present position in Europe.

From Stettin in the Baltic to Trieste in the Adriatic, an iron curtain has descended across the Continent. Behind that line lie all the capitals of the ancient states of central and eastern Europe. Warsaw, Berlin, Prague, Vienna, Budapest, Belgrade, Bucharest, and Sofia, all these famous cities and the populations around them lie in what I might call the Soviet sphere, and all are subject, in one form or another, not only to Soviet influence but to a very high and increasing measure of control from Moscow. . . . Athens alone, with its immortal glories, is free to decide its future at an election under British, American, and French observation.

The Russian-dominated Polish Government has been encouraged to make enormous and wrongful inroads upon Germany, and mass expulsions of millions of Germans on a scale grievous and undreamed of are now taking place. The Communist parties, which were very small in all these eastern states of Europe, have been raised to preeminence and power far beyond their numbers and are seeking everywhere to obtain totalitarian control. Police governments are prevailing in nearly every case, and so far, except in Czechoslovakia, there is no true democracy....

Whatever conclusions may be drawn from these facts—and facts they are—this is certainly not the liberated Europe we fought to build up. Nor is it one which contains the essentials of permanent peace....

However, in a great number of countries, far from the Russian frontiers and throughout the world, Communist fifth columns are established and work in complete unity and absolute obedience to the directions they received from the Communist center. Except in the British Commonwealth, and in the United States, where communism is in its infancy, the Communist parties or fifth columns constitute a growing challenge and peril to Christian civilization. These are somber facts for anyone to have to recite on the morrow of a victory gained by so much splendid comradeship in arms and in the cause of freedom and democracy, and we should be most unwise not to face them squarely while time remains....

On the other hand ... I repulse the idea that a new war is inevitable; still more that it is imminent. It is because I am sure that our fortunes are still in our hands, in our own hands, and that we hold the power to save the future, that I feel the duty to speak out now that I have an occasion to do so.

I do not believe that Soviet Russia desires war. What they desire is the fruits of war and the indefinite expansion of their power and doctrines....

From what I have seen of our Russian friends and allies during the war, I am convinced that there is nothing they admire so much as strength, and there is nothing for which they have less respect than for military weakness. For that ... reason the old doctrine of a balance of power is unsound. We cannot afford, if we can help it, to work on narrow margins, offering temptations to a trial of strength. If the western democracies stand together in strict adherence to the principles of the United Nations Charter, their influence for furthering these principles will be immense and no one is likely to molest them. If, however, they become divided or falter in their duty, and if these all-important years are allowed to slip away, then indeed catastrophe may overwhelm us all.

Last time I saw it all coming, and cried aloud to my own fellow countrymen and to the world, but no one paid any attention. Up till the year 1933 or even 1935, Germany might have been saved from the awful fate which has overtaken her and we might all have been spared the miseries Hitler let loose upon mankind. . . .

We surely must not let that happen again. . . . If the population of the English-speaking Commonwealth be added to that of the United States, with all such cooperation implies in the air, on the seas all over the globe, and in science and in industry, and in moral force, there will be no quivering, precarious balance of power to offer its temptation to ambition or adventure. On the contrary there will be an overwhelming assurance of security. If we adhere faithfully to the Charter of the United Nations and walk forward in sedate and sober strength, seeking no one's land or treasure, seeking to lay no arbitrary control upon the thoughts of men, if all British moral and material forces and convictions are joined with your own in fraternal association, the high roads of the future will be clear, not only for us but for all, not only for our time but for a century to come.

3. THE TRUMAN DOCTRINE, MARCH 12, 1947

The gravity of the situation which confronts the world today necessitates my appearance before a joint session of the Congress. The foreign policy and the national security of this country are involved.

One aspect of the present situation, which I wish to present to you at this time for your consideration and decision, concerns Greece and Turkey.

The United States has received from the Greek Government an urgent appeal for financial and economic assistance. Preliminary reports from the American Economic Mission now in Greece and reports from the American Ambassador in Greece corroborate the statement of the Greek Government that assistance is imperative if Greece is to survive as a free nation.

I do not believe that the American people and the Congress wish to turn a deaf ear to the appeal of the Greek Government.

Greece is not a rich country. Lack of sufficient natural resources has always forced the Greek people to work hard to make both ends meet. Since 1940, this industrious and peace-loving country has suffered invasion, four years of cruel enemy occupation, and bitter internal strife.

When forces of liberation entered Greece they found that the retreating Germans had destroyed vir-

tually all the railways, roads, port facilities, communications and merchant marine. More than a thousand villages had been burned. Eighty-five per cent of the children were tubercular. Livestock, poultry and draft animals had almost disappeared. Inflation had wiped out practically all savings.

As a result of these tragic conditions, a military minority, exploiting human want and misery, was able to create political chaos which, until now, has made economic recovery impossible.

Greece is today without funds to finance the importation of those goods which are essential to bare subsistence. Under these circumstances the people of Greece cannot make progress in solving their problems of reconstruction. Greece is in desperate need of financial and economic assistance to enable it to resume purchases of food, clothing, fuel and seeds. These are indispensable for the subsistence of its people and are obtainable only from abroad. Greece must have help to import the goods necessary to restore internal order and security so essential for economic and political recovery.

The Greek Government has also asked for the assistance of experienced American administrators, economists and technicians to insure that the financial and other aid given to Greece shall be used effectively in creating a stable and self-sustaining economy and in improving its public administration.

The very existence of the Greek state is today threatened by the terrorist activities of several thousand armed men, led by Communists, who defy the Government's authority at a number of points, particularly along the northern boundaries. A commission appointed by the United Nations Security Council is at present investigating disturbed conditions in northern Greece and alleged border violations along the frontier between Greece on the one hand and Albania, Bulgaria and Yugoslavia on the other.

Meanwhile, the Greek Government is unable to cope with the situation. The Greek Army is small and poorly equipped. It needs supplies and equipment if it is to restore the authority of the Government throughout Greek territory.

Greece must have assistance if it is to become a self-supporting and self-respecting democracy.

The United States must supply that assistance. We have already extended to Greece certain types of relief and economic aid but these are inadequate.

There is no other country to which democratic Greece can turn.

No other nation is willing and able to provide the necessary support for a democratic Greek Government.

The British Government, which has been helping Greece, can give no further financial or economic aid after March. Great Britain finds itself under the necessity of reducing or liquidating its commitments in several parts of the world, including Greece.

We have considered how the United Nations might assist in this crisis. But the situation is an urgent one requiring immediate action, and the United Nations and its related organizations are not in a position to extend help of the kind that is required.

It is important to note that the Greek Government has asked for our aid in utilizing effectively the financial and other assistance we may give to Greece, and in improving public administration. It is of the utmost importance that we supervise the use of any funds made available to Greece, in such a manner that each dollar spent will count toward making Greece self-supporting, and will help to build an economy in which a healthy democracy can flourish.

No government is perfect. One of the chief virtues of a democracy, however, is that its defects are always visible and under democratic processes can be pointed out and corrected. The Government of Greece is not perfect. Nevertheless it represents 85 per cent of the members of the Greek parliament who were chosen in an election last year. Foreign observers, including 692 Americans, considered this election to be a fair expression of the views of the Greek people.

The Greek Government has been operating in an atmosphere of chaos and extremism. It has made mistakes. The extension of aid by this country does not mean that the United States condones everything that the Greek Government has done or will do. We have condemned in the past, and we condemn now, extremist measures of the Right or the Left. We have in the past advised tolerance, and we advise tolerance now.

Greece's neighbor, Turkey, also deserves our attention.

The future of Turkey as an independent and economically sound State is clearly no less important to the freedom-loving peoples of the world than the future of Greece. The circumstances in which Turkey finds itself today are considerably different from those of Greece. Turkey has been spared the disasters that have beset Greece. And during the war, the United States and Great Britain furnished Turkey with material aid.

Nevertheless, Turkey now needs our support.

Since the war Turkey has sought financial assistance from Great Britain and the United States for the purpose of effecting that modernization necessary for the maintenance of its national integrity.

That integrity is essential to the preservation of order in the Middle East.

The British Government has informed us that, owing to its own difficulties, it can no longer extend financial or economic aid to Turkey.

As in the case of Greece, if Turkey is to have the assistance it needs, the United States must supply it. We are the only country able to provide that help.

I am fully aware of the broad implications involved if the United States extends assistance to Greece and Turkey, and I shall discuss these implications with you at this time.

One of the primary objectives of the foreign policy of the United States is the creation of conditions in which we and other nations will be able to work out a way of life free from coercion. This was a fundamental issue in the war with Germany and Japan. Our victory was won over countries which sought to impose their will, and their way of life, upon other nations.

To ensure the peaceful development of nations, free from coercion, the United States has taken a leading part in establishing the United Nations. The United Nations is designed to make possible lasting freedom and independence for all its members. We shall not realize our objectives, however, unless we are willing to help free people to maintain their free institutions and their national integrity against aggressive movements that seek to impose upon them totalitarian regimes.

This is no more than a frank recognition that totalitarian regimes imposed on free peoples, by direct or indirect aggression, undermine the foundations of international peace and hence the security of the United States.

The peoples of a number of countries of the world have recently had totalitarian regimes forced upon them against their will. The Government of the United States has made frequent protests against coercion and intimidation in violation of the Yalta agreement, in Poland, Rumania, and Bulgaria. I must also state that in a number of other countries there have been similar developments.

At the present moment in world history nearly every nation must choose between alternative ways of life. The choice is too often not a free one.

One way of life is based upon the will of the majority, and is distinguished by free institutions, representative government, free elections, guaranties of individual liberty, freedom of speech and religion, and freedom from political oppression.

The second way of life is based upon the will of a minority forcibly imposed upon the majority. It relies upon terror and oppression, a controlled press and radio, fixed elections, and the suppression of personal freedoms.

I believe that it must be the policy of the United States to support free peoples who are resisting attempted subjugation by armed minorities or by outside pressures. I believe that we must assist free peoples to work out their own destinies in their own way. I believe that our help should be primarily through economic and financial aid which is essential to economic stability and orderly political processes.

The world is not static, and the status quo is not sacred. But we cannot allow changes in the status quo in violation of the Charter of the United Nations by such methods as coercion, or by such subterfuges as political infiltration. In helping free and independent nations to maintain their freedom, the United States will be giving effect to the principles of the Charter of the United Nations.

It is necessary only to glance at a map to realize that the survival and integrity of the Greek nation are of grave importance in a much wider situation. If Greece should fall under the control of an armed minority, the effect upon its neighbor, Turkey, would be immediate and serious. Confusion and disorder might well spread throughout the entire Middle East.

Moreover, the disappearance of Greece as an independent State would have a profound effect upon those countries in Europe whose peoples are struggling against great difficulties to maintain their freedoms and their independence while they repair the damages of war. It would be an unspeakable tragedy if these countries, which have struggled so long against overwhelming odds, should lose that victory for which they sacrificed so much. Collapse of free insti-tutions and loss of independence would be disastrous not only for them but for the world.

Discouragement and possibly failure would quickly be the lot of neighboring peoples striving to maintain their freedom and independence.

Should we fail to aid Greece and Turkey in this fateful hour, the effect will be far-reaching to the West as well as to the East. We must take immediate and resolute action.

I therefore ask the Congress to provide authority for assistance to Greece and Turkey in the amount of $400,000,000 for the period ending June 30, 1948. In requesting these funds, I have taken into consideration the maximum amount of relief assistance which would be furnished to Greece out of the $350,000,000 which I recently requested that the Congress authorize for the prevention of starvation and suffering in countries devastated by the war.

In addition to funds, I ask the Congress to authorize the detail of American civilian and military personnel to Greece and Turkey, at the request of those countries, to assist in the tasks of reconstruction, and for the purpose of supervising the use of such financial and material assistance as may be furnished. I recommend that authority also be provided for the instruction and training of selected Greek and Turkish personnel.

Finally, I ask that the Congress provide authority which will permit the speediest and most effective use, in terms of needed commodities, supplies and equipment, of such funds as may be authorized.

If further funds, or further authority, should be needed for purposes indicated in this message, I shall not hesitate to bring the situation before the Congress. On this subject the executive and legislative branches of the Government must work together.

This is a serious course upon which we embark. I would not recommend it except that the alternative is much more serious.

The United States contributed $341,000,000,000 toward winning World War II. This is an investment in world freedom and world peace. The assistance that I am recommending for Greece and Turkey amounts to little more than one-tenth of 1 per cent of this investment. It is only common sense that we should safeguard this investment and make sure that it was not in vain.

The seeds of totalitarian regimes are nurtured by misery and want. They spread and grow in the evil soil of poverty and strife. They reach their full growth when the hope of a people for a better life has died. We must keep that hope alive.

The free peoples of the world look to us for support in maintaining their freedoms. If we falter in our leadership, we may endanger the peace of the world and we shall surely endanger the welfare of our own nation.

Great responsibilities have been placed upon us by the swift movement of events. I am confident that the Congress will face these responsibilities squarely.

Available online. URL: http://www.tamu.edu/scom/ pres/speeches/hstaid.html.

4. SECRETARY OF STATE GEORGE MARSHALL'S EUROPEAN RECOVERY PLAN (THE MARSHALL PLAN), JUNE 5, 1947

I need not tell you gentlemen [at Harvard University] that the world situation is very serious. That must be apparent to all intelligent people. I think one difficulty is that the problem is one of such enormous complexity that the very mass of facts presented to the public by press and radio make it exceedingly difficult for the man in the street to reach a clear appraisement of the situation. Furthermore, the people of this country are distant from the troubled areas of the earth and it is hard for them to comprehend the plight and consequent reactions of the long-suffering peoples, and the effect of those reactions on their governments in connection with our efforts to promote peace in the world.

In considering the requirements for the rehabilitation of Europe, the physical loss of life, the visible destruction of cities, factories, mines, and railroads was correctly estimated, but it has become obvious during recent months that this visible destruction was probably less serious than the dislocation of the entire fabric of European economy. For the past ten years conditions have been highly abnormal. The feverish preparation for war and the more feverish maintenance of the war effort engulfed all aspects of national economies. Machinery has fallen into disrepair or is entirely obsolete. Under the arbitrary and destructive Nazi rule, virtually every possible enterprise was geared into the German War machine. Long-standing commercial ties, private institutions, banks, insurance companies, and shipping companies disappeared, through loss of capital, absorption through nationalization, or by simple destruction.

In many countries, confidence in the local currency has been severely shaken. The breakdown of the business structure of Europe during the war was complete. Recovery has been seriously retarded by the fact that two years after the close of hostilities a peace settlement with Germany and Austria has not been agreed upon. But even given a more prompt solution of these difficult problems, the rehabilitation of the economic structure of Europe quite evidently will require a much longer time and greater effort than had been foreseen. . . .

Aside from the demoralizing effect on the world at large and the possibilities of disturbances arising as a result of the desperation of the people concerned, the consequences to the economy of the United States should be apparent to all. It is logical that the United States should do whatever it is able to do to assist in the return of normal economic health in the world, without which there can be no political stability, and no assured peace.

Our policy is directed not against any country or doctrine but against hunger, poverty, desperation, and chaos. Its purpose should be the revival of a working economy in the world so as to permit the emergence of political and social conditions in which free institutions can exist. Such assistance, I am convinced, must not be on a piecemeal basis as various crises develop. Any assistance that this Government may render in the future should provide a cure rather than a mere palliative. Any government that is willing to assist in the task of recovery will find full cooperation, I am sure, on the part of the United States Government. Any government which maneuvers to block the recovery of other countries cannot expect help from us. Furthermore, governments, political parties, or groups which seek to perpetuate human misery in order to profit therefrom politically or otherwise will encounter the opposition of the United States.

It is already evident that, before the United States Government can proceed much further in its efforts to alleviate the situation and help start the European world on its way to recovery, there must be some agreement among the countries of Europe as to the requirements of the situation and the part those countries themselves will take in order to give proper effect to whatever action might be undertaken by this Government. It would be neither fitting nor efficacious for this Government to undertake to draw up unilaterally a program designed to place Europe on its feet economically. This is the business of the Europeans. The initiative, I think, must come from Europe.

The role of this country should consist of friendly aid in the drafting of a European program and of later support of such a program so far as it may be practical for us to do so. The program should be a joint one, agreed to by a number, if not all, of European nations.

An essential part of any successful action on the part of the United States is an understanding on the part of the people of America of the character of the problem and the remedies to be applied. Political passion and prejudice should have no part. With foresight, and a willingness on the part of our people to face up to the vast responsibility which history has clearly placed upon our country, the difficulties I have outlined can and will be overcome.

5. Senator Joseph McCarthy's Speech Before a Republican Women's Group in Wheeling, West Virginia, February 9, 1950

Today we are engaged in a final, all-out battle between communistic atheism and Christianity. The modern champions of communism have selected this as the time. And, ladies and gentlemen, the chips are down. They are truly down. . . .

Lest there be any doubt that the time has been chosen, let us go directly to the leader of communism today, Joseph Stalin. Here is what he said, not back in 1928, not before the war, not during the war, but two years after the last war was ended: "To think that the communist revolution can be carried out peacefully, within the framework of a Christian democracy, means one has either gone out of one's mind and lost all normal understanding, or has grossly and openly repudiated the communist revolution." Ladies and gentlemen, can there be anyone here tonight who is so blind as to say that the war is not on? Can there be anyone who fails to realize that the communist world has said, "The time is now," that this is the time for the showdown between the democratic Christian world and the communist atheistic world?

Unless we face this fact, we shall pay the price that must be paid by those who wait too long. . . .

The reason why we find ourselves in a position of impotency is not because our only powerful potential enemy has sent men to invade our shores, but rather because of the traitorous actions of those who have been treated so well by this nation. It has not been the less fortunate or members of minority groups who have been selling this nation out, but rather those who have had all the benefits that the wealthiest nation on earth has had to offer—the finest homes, the finest college education, and the finest jobs in government we can give.

This is glaringly true in the State Department. There the bright young men who are born with silver spoons in their mouths are the ones who have been worst. . . . In my opinion the State Department, which is one of the most important government departments, is thoroughly infested with communists.

I have here in my hand a list of 205—a list of names that were made known to the secretary of state as being members of the Communist Party and who nevertheless are still working and shaping policy in the State Department.

One thing to remember in discussing the communists in our government is that we are not dealing with spies who get thirty pieces of silver to steal the blueprints of a new weapon. We are dealing with a far more sinister type of activity because it permits the enemy to guide and shape our policy. . . .

6. Senator Margaret Chase Smith Addressing the U.S. Senate, June 1, 1950

Mr. President, I would like to speak briefly and simply about a serious national condition. It is a national feeling of fear and frustration that could result in national suicide and the end of everything that we Americans hold dear. It is a condition that comes from the lack of effective leadership either in the legislative branch or the executive branch of our government. . . .

Mr. President, I speak as a Republican. I speak as a woman. I speak as a United States senator. I speak as an American.

The United States Senate has long enjoyed worldwide respect as the greatest deliberative body in the world. But recently that deliberative character has too often been debased to the level of a forum of hate and character assassination sheltered by the shield of congressional immunity. . . .

Those of us who shout the loudest about Americanism in making character assassinations are all too frequently those who, by our own words and acts, ignore some of the basic principles of Americanism: the right to criticize, the right to hold unpopular beliefs, the right to protest, the right of independent thought. The exercise of these rights should not cost one single American citizen his reputation or his right to a livelihood. . . . Otherwise none of us could call our souls our own. Otherwise thought control would have set in. . . .

The nation sorely needs a Republican victory. But I do not want to see the Republican Party ride to political victory on the Four Horsemen of Calumny—Fear, Ignorance, Bigotry and Smear. . . . I do not want to see the Republican Party win that way. While it might be a fleeting victory for the Republican Party; it would be a more lasting defeat for the American people. . . .

As a woman, I wonder how the mothers, wives, sisters, and daughters feel about the way in which members of their families have been politically mangled in Senate debate—and I use the word debate advisedly. As a United States senator, I am not proud of the way in which the Senate has been made a publicity platform for irresponsible sensationalism. I am not proud of the reckless abandon in which unproved charges have been hurled from this side of the aisle. I am not proud of the obviously staged, undignified countercharges which have been attempted in retaliation from the other side of the aisle.

As an American, I am shocked at the way Republicans and Democrats alike are playing directly into the communist design of "confuse, divide, and conquer." As an American, I do not want a Democratic administration whitewash or cover-up any more than I want a Republican smear or witch hunt.

As an American, I condemn a Republican fascist just as much as I condemn a Democrat communist. I condemn a Democrat fascist just as much as I condemn a Republican communist. They are equally dangerous to you and me and to our country. As an American, I want to see our nation recapture the strength and unity it once had when we fought the enemy instead of ourselves.

7. LISTING FOR ARTHUR MILLER IN *RED CHANNELS* (AN ENTERTAINMENT INDUSTRY BLACKLIST), JUNE 1950

ARTHUR MILLER

Playwright—"Death of a Salesman," "All My Sons"
Reported as:

American Youth Congress	Signer of call. Official proceedings, 1/28, 30/38
Book Find Club	Writer. *Book Find News,* 5/46, p. 7; 1/46, p. 6. Author of Club selection. *Book Find News,* 1/48, p. 3.
Civil Rights Congress	Signer. Statement in defense of Eisler. *Daily Worker,* 2/28/47, p. 2. Signer. Statement defending Communist Party. *Daily Worker,* 4/16/47, p. 2. Speaker, "Abolish America's Thought Police." *Daily Worker,* 10/6/47, p. 8.
Committee of Welcome for the Very Rev Hewlett Johnson	Member, *Daily Worker,* 9/22/48, p. 5.
International Workers Order	Defender of tax exemption for IWO. *Fraternal Outlook,* 11/48, p. 6.
Jewish Life	Contributor. *Jewish Life,* publication of Morning Freiheit Association, 3/48, p. 7.
Mainstream and New Masses	Speaker at rally to defend Howard Fast, 10/16/47, p. 2.
National Council of the Arts, Sciences and Professions	Signer for [Progressive Party candidate and former vice-president Henry] Wallace. *Daily Worker,* 9/21/48, p. 7. Co-chairman. Performance, "The Journey of Simon McKeever," and "I've Got the Tune," Official Program. Sponsor. Committee to Abolish the House Un-American Activities Committee. *NY Journal-American,* 12/30/48.

New York Council of the Arts, Sciences and Professions	Speaker. Rally against the "Foley Square Convictions," 10/27/49. *Daily Worker,* 10/24/49, p. 5.
Progressive Citizens of America	*Sponsor. Program,* 10/25/47.
Council for Pan-American Democracy	Chairman, "Night of the Americas." Letterhead
Independent Citizens Committee of the Arts, Sciences, and Professions	Participant on 5/20/45 program. *Independent,* 6/45, p. 16.
Joint Anti-Fascist Refugee Committee	Participant. Spanish Refugee Appeal, "Salute to Spanish Republicans," Madison Square Garden, 9/24/45. *Daily Worker,* 9/25/45, p. 2; U.S. Senate Hearings on S1832, Part 2, p. 534.
Win the Peace	Sponsor. Program, 4/5/46.
Progressive Citizens of America	Candidate, Executive Board, 2/11/47. *Un-Am. Act in California,* 1947, p. 239.

8. President Truman Announcing His Decision to Fire General MacArthur, April 11, 1951

I want to talk to you tonight about what we are doing in Korea and about our policy in the Far East. In the simplest terms what we are doing in Korea is this: We are trying to prevent a third world war.

I think most people in this country recognized that fact last June. And they warmly supported the decision of the government to help the Republic of Korea against the communist aggressors. Now, many persons . . . have forgotten the basic reasons for our action. It is right for us to be in Korea now. It was right last June. . . . I want to remind you why this is true.

The communists in the Kremlin are engaged in a monstrous conspiracy to stamp out freedom all over the world. If they were to succeed, the United States would be numbered among their principal victims. It

must be clear to everyone that the United States cannot and will not sit idly by and await foreign conquest. The only question is: When is the best time to meet the threat and how?

The best time to meet the threat is in the beginning. . . . And the best way to meet the threat of aggression is for the peace-loving nations to act together. . . . [I]f the free countries had acted together to crush the aggression of the dictators, and if they had acted in the beginning, when the aggression was small—there probably would have been no World War II.

If history has taught us anything, it is that aggression anywhere in the world is a threat to the peace everywhere in the world. . . .

The aggression against Korea is the boldest and most dangerous move the communists have yet made. The attack on Korea was part of a greater plan for conquering all of Asia. . . .

The question we have had to face is whether the communist plan of conquest can be stopped without a general war. Our government and other countries associated with us in the United Nations believe that the best chance of stopping it without a general war is to meet the attack in Korea and defeat it there. That is what we have been doing. . . .

We do not want to see the conflict in Korea extended. We are trying to prevent a world war, not to start one. . . . But you may ask why can't we take other steps to punish the aggressor. Why don't we bomb Manchuria and China itself. Why don't we assist the Chinese nationalist troops to land on the mainland of China.

If we were to do those things, we would be running a very grave risk of starting a general war. If that were to happen, we would have brought about the exact situation we are trying to prevent. . . . What would suit the ambitions of the Kremlin better than for our military forces to be committed to a full-scale war with Red China? . . .

I have thought long and hard about this question of extending the war in Asia. I have discussed it many times with the ablest military advisers in the country. I believe that we must try to limit the war to Korea for these vital reasons: to make sure that the precious lives of our fighting men are not wasted; to see that the security of our country and the free world is not needlessly jeopardized; and to prevent a third world war.

A number of events have made it evident that General MacArthur did not agree with that policy. I have therefore considered it essential to relieve General MacArthur so there would be no doubt or confusion as to the real purpose and aim of our policy. It was with the deepest personal regret that I found myself compelled to take this action. General MacArthur is one of our greatest military commanders. But the cause of world peace is greater than any individual.

9. President Dwight Eisenhower's First Inauguration Speech, January 20, 1953

My friends, before I begin the expression of those thoughts that I deem appropriate to this moment, would you permit me the privilege of uttering a little private prayer of my own. And I ask that you bow your heads:

Almighty God, as we stand here at this moment my future associates in the executive branch of government join me in beseeching that Thou will make full and complete our dedication to the service of the people in this throng, and their fellow citizens everywhere.

Give us, we pray, the power to discern clearly right from wrong, and allow all our words and actions to be governed thereby, and by the laws of this land. Especially we pray that our concern shall be for all the people regardless of station, race, or calling. May cooperation be permitted and be the mutual aim of those who, under the concepts of our Constitution, hold to differing political faiths; so that all may work for the good of our beloved country and Thy glory. Amen.

My fellow citizens:

The world and we have passed the midway point of a century of continuing challenge. We sense with all our faculties that forces of good and evil are massed and armed and opposed as rarely before in history....

Since this century's beginning, a time of tempest has seemed to come upon the continents of the earth. Masses of Asia have awakened to strike off shackles of the past. Great nations of Europe have fought their bloodiest wars. Thrones have toppled and their vast empires have disappeared. New nations have been born....

This trial comes at a moment when man's power to achieve good or to inflict evil surpasses the brightest hopes and the sharpest fears of all ages. We can turn rivers in their courses, level mountains to the plains. Oceans and land and sky are avenues for our colossal commerce. Disease diminishes and life lengthens.

Yet promise of this life is imperiled by the very genius that has made it possible. Nations amass wealth. Labor sweats to create—and turns out devices to level not only mountains but also cities. Science seems ready to confer upon us, as its final gift, the power to erase human life from this planet.

At such a time in history, we who are free must proclaim anew our faith....

This faith rules our whole way of life.... It asserts that we have the right to choice of our own work and to the reward of our own toil. It inspires the initiative that makes our productivity the wonder of the world. And it warns that any man who seeks to deny equality among all his brothers betrays the spirit of the free and invites the mockery of the tyrant....

The enemies of this faith know no god but force, no devotion but its use. They tutor men in treason. They feed upon the hunger of others. Whatever defies them, they torture, especially the truth....

In pleading our just cause before the bar of history and in pressing our labor for world peace, we shall be guided by certain fixed principles. These principles are:

(1) Abhorring war as a chosen way to balk the purposes of those who threaten us, we hold it to be the first task of statesmanship to develop the strength that will deter the forces of aggression and promote the conditions of peace....

(2) Realizing that common sense and common decency alike dictate the futility of appeasement, we shall never try to placate an aggressor by the false and wicked bargain of trading honor for security. Americans, indeed all free men, remember that in the final choice a soldier's pack is not so heavy a burden as a prisoner's chains.

(3) Knowing that only a United States that is strong and immensely productive can help defend freedom in our world, we view our nation's strength and security as a trust upon which rests the hope of free men everywhere. It is the firm duty of each of our free citizens and of every free citizen everywhere to place the cause of his country before the comfort, the convenience of himself.

(4) Honoring the identity and the special heritage of each nation in the world, we shall never use our strength to try to impress upon another people our own cherished political and economic institutions.

(5) Assessing realistically the needs and capacities of proven friends of freedom, we shall strive to help them to achieve their own security and well-being. . . .

(6) Recognizing economic health as an indispensable basis of military strength and the free world's peace, we shall strive to foster everywhere, and to practice ourselves, policies that encourage productivity and profitable trade. For the impoverishment of any single people in the world means danger to the well-being of all other peoples.

(7) Appreciating that economic need, military security and political wisdom combine to suggest regional groupings of free peoples, we hope, within the framework of the United Nations, to help strengthen such special bonds the world over. The nature of these ties must vary with the different problems of different areas. . . .

(8) Conceiving the defense of freedom, like freedom itself, to be one and indivisible, we hold all continents and peoples in equal regard and honor. We reject any insinuation that one race or another, one people or another, is in any sense inferior or expendable.

(9) Respecting the United Nations as the living sign of all people's hope for peace, we shall strive to make it not merely an eloquent symbol but an effective force. . . .

The peace we seek, then, is nothing less than the practice and fulfillment of our whole faith among ourselves and in our dealings with others. . . . More than escape from death, it is a way of life. More than a haven for the weary, it is a hope for the brave.

This is the hope that beckons us onward in this century of trial. This is the work that awaits us all, to be done with bravery, with charity, and with prayer to Almighty God.

10. PRESIDENT EISENHOWER'S "ATOMS FOR PEACE" ADDRESS TO THE UNITED NATIONS, DECEMBER 8, 1953

I know that the American people share my deep belief that if a danger exists in the world, it is a danger shared by all—and equally, that if hope exists in the mind of one nation, that hope should be shared by all. . . .

My recital of atomic danger and power is necessarily stated in United States terms, for these are the only incontrovertible facts that I know. I need hardly point out to this assembly, however, that this subject is global, not merely national in character. On July 16, 1945, the United States set off the world's first atomic test explosion. Since that date in 1945, the United States has conducted forty-two test explosions. . . . Today the United States' stockpile of atomic weapons, which, of course, increase daily, exceeds by many times the explosive equivalent of the total of all bombs and all shells that came from every plane and every gun in every theater of war through all the years of World War II. A single air group, whether afloat or land based, can now deliver to any reachable target a destructive cargo exceeding in power all the bombs that fell on Britain in all of World War II. . . .

The Soviet Union has informed us that, over recent years, it has devoted extensive resources to atomic weapons. During this period, the Soviet Union has exploded a series of atomic devices, including at least one involving thermonuclear reactions.

If at one time the United States possessed what might have been called a monopoly of atomic power, that monopoly ceased to exist several years ago. Therefore, although our earlier start has permitted us to accumulate what is today a great quantitative advantage, the atomic realities of today comprehend two facts of even greater significance. First, the knowledge now possessed by several nations will eventually be shared by others, possibly all others. Second, even a vast superiority in numbers of weapons, and a consequent capability of devastating retaliation, is no preventive, of itself, against the fearful material damage and toll of human lives that would be inflicted by surprise aggression. . . .

My country wants to be constructive, not destructive. It wants agreements, not wars, among nations. It wants, itself, to live in freedom and in the confidence that the people of every other nation enjoy equally the right of choosing their own way of life. So my country's purpose is to help us move out of the dark chamber of horrors into the light, to find a way by which the minds of men, the hopes of men, the souls of men everywhere, can move forward toward peace and happiness and well-being. . . .

It is not enough to take this weapon out of the hands of the soldiers. It must be put into the hands of those who will know how to strip its military casing and adapt it to the arts of peace. . . .

I therefore make the following proposals:

The governments principally involved to the extent permitted by elementary prudence, to begin now and continue to make joint contributions from their stockpiles of normal uranium and fissionable materials to an international atomic energy agency. We would expect that such an agency would be set up under the aegis of the United Nations. . . .

Second, begin to diminish the potential destructive power of the world's atomic stockpiles.

Third, allow all peoples of all nations to see that, in this enlightened age, the great powers of the earth, both of the East and of the West, are interested in human aspirations first rather than in building up the armaments of war.

Fourth, open up a new channel for peaceful discussion and initiate at least a new approach to the many difficult problems that must be solved in both private and public conversations if the world is to shake off the inertia imposed by fear and is to make positive progress toward peace. . . .

To the making of these fateful decisions, the United States pledges before you—and therefore before the world—its determination to help solve the fearful atomic dilemma—to devote its entire heart and mind to find the way by which the miraculous inventiveness of man shall not be dedicated to his death, but consecrated to his life.

Available online. URL: http://www.tamu.edu/scom/pres/speeches/ikeatoms.html.

11. President Eisenhower's Second Inauguration Speech, January 21, 1957

Before all else, we seek, upon our common labor as a nation, the blessing of Almighty God. And the hopes in our hearts fashion the deepest prayers of our whole people.

May we pursue the right without self-righteousness.

May we know unity without conformity.

May we grow in strength without pride in self.

May we, in our dealings with all peoples of the earth, ever speak truth and serve justice.

And so shall America—in the sight of all men of good will—prove true to the honorable purposes that bind and rule us as a people in all this time of trial through which we pass.

We live in a land of plenty, but rarely has this earth known such peril as today. In our nation work and wealth abound. Our population grows. Commerce crowds our rivers and rails, our skies, harbors, and highways. Our soil is fertile, our agriculture productive. The air rings with the song of our industry-rolling mills and blast furnaces, dynamos, dams, and assembly lines—the chorus of America the bountiful. . . .

In too much of the earth there is want, discord, danger. New forces and new nations stir and strive across the earth, with power to bring, by their fate, great good or great evil to the free world's future. From the deserts of North Africa to the islands of the South Pacific one-third of all mankind has entered upon a historic struggle for a new freedom; freedom from grinding poverty. Across all continents, nearly a billion people seek, sometimes almost in desperation, for the skills and knowledge and assistance by which they may satisfy from their own resources, the material wants common to all mankind. . . .

Thus across all the globe there harshly blow the winds of change. And, we—though fortunate be our lot—know that we can never turn our backs to them. We look upon this shaken earth, and we declare our firm and fixed purpose—the building of a peace with justice in a world where moral law prevails. . . .

We are called to meet the price of this peace. To counter the threat of those who seek to rule by force, we must pay the costs of our own needed military strength, and help to build the security of others. We must use our skills and knowledge and, at times, our substance, to help others rise from misery, however far from the scene of suffering may be from our shores. For wherever in the world a people knows desperate want, there must appear at least the spark of hope, the hope of progress—or there will surely rise at last the flames of conflict.

We recognize and accept our own deep involvement in the destiny of men everywhere. We are accordingly pledged to honor, and to strive to fortify, the authority of the United Nations. For in that body rests the best hope of our age for the assertion of that law by which all nations may live in dignity. . . .

Only in respecting the hopes and cultures of others will we practice the equality of all nations. Only as we show willingness and wisdom in giving counsel, in receiving counsel, and in sharing burdens, will we wisely perform the work of peace. For one truth must rule all we think and all that we do. No people can live to itself alone. The unity of all who dwell in freedom is their only sure defense. The economic need of all nations—in mutual dependence—makes isolation an impossibility; not even America's prosperity could long survive if other nations did not prosper. . . .

And so we voice our hope and our belief that we can help to heal this divided world. Thus may the nations cease to live in trembling before the menace of force. Thus may the weight of fear and the weight of arms be taken from the burdened shoulders of mankind.

This, nothing less, is the labor to which we are called and our strength dedicated. And so the prayer of our people carries far beyond our own frontiers, to the wide world of our duty and our destiny. May the light of freedom, coming to all darkened lands, flame brightly—until at last the darkness is no more. May the turbulence of our age yield to a true time of peace, when men and nations shall share a life that honors the dignity of each, the brotherhood of all.

Available online. URL:http://www.tamu.edu/scom/pres/speeches/ikeinaug.html.

12. President Eisenhower's Address to the Nation Announcing His Decision to Have the U.S. Army Enforce the Court-Ordered Integration of Central High School in Little Rock, Arkansas, September 24, 1957

Good Evening, My Fellow Citizens:

For a few minutes this evening I want to speak to you about the serious situation that has arisen in Little Rock. To make this talk I have come to the President's office in the White House. I could have spoken from Rhode Island, where I have been staying recently, but I felt that, in speaking from the house of Lincoln, of Jackson and of Wilson, my words would better convey both the sadness I feel in the action I was compelled today to take and the firmness with which I intend to pursue this course until the orders of the Federal Court at Little Rock can be executed without unlawful interference.

In that city, under the leadership of demagogic extremists, disorderly mobs have deliberately prevented the carrying out of proper orders from a Federal Court. Local authorities have not eliminated that violent opposition and, under the law, I yesterday issued a Proclamation calling upon the mob to disperse.

This morning the mob again gathered in front of the Central High School of Little Rock, obviously for the purpose of again preventing the carrying out of the Court's order relating to the admission of Negro children to that school.

Whenever normal agencies prove inadequate to the task and it becomes necessary for the Executive Branch of the Federal Government to use its powers and authority to uphold Federal Courts, the President's responsibility is inescapable. In accordance with that responsibility, I have today issued an Executive Order directing the use of troops under Federal authority to aid in the execution of Federal law at Little Rock, Arkansas. This became necessary when my Proclamation of yesterday was not observed, and the obstruction of justice still continues.

It is important that the reasons for my action be understood by all our citizens. As you know, the Supreme Court of the United States has decided that separate public educational facilities for the races are inherently unequal and therefore compulsory school segregation laws are unconstitutional.

Our personal opinions about the decision have no bearing on the matter of enforcement; the responsibility and authority of the Supreme Court to interpret the Constitution are very clear. Local Federal Courts were instructed by the Supreme Court to issue such orders and decrees as might be necessary to achieve admission to public schools without regard to race—and with all deliberate speed.

During the past several years, many communities in our Southern States have instituted public school plans for gradual progress in the enrollment and attendance of school children of all races in order to bring themselves into compliance with the law of the land.

They thus demonstrated to the world that we are a nation in which laws, not men, are supreme.

I regret to say that this truth—the cornerstone of our liberties—was not observed in this instance.

It was my hope that this localized situation would be brought under control by city and State authorities. If the use of local police powers had been sufficient, our traditional method of leaving the problems in those hands would have been pursued. But when large gatherings of obstructionists made it impossible for the decrees of the Court to be carried out, both the law and the national interest demanded that the President take action.

Here is the sequence of events in the development of the Little Rock school case.

In May of 1955, the Little Rock School Board approved a moderate plan for the gradual desegregation of the public schools in that city. It provided that a start toward integration would be made at the present term in the high school, and that the plan would be in full operation by 1963. Here I might say that in a number of communities in Arkansas integration in the schools has already started and without violence of any kind. Now this Little Rock plan was challenged in the courts by some who believed that the period of time as proposed in the plan was too long.

The United States Court at Little Rock, which has supervisory responsibility under the law for the plan of desegregation in the public schools, dismissed the challenge, thus approving a gradual rather than an abrupt change from the existing system. The court found that the school board had acted in good faith in planning for a public school system free from racial discrimination.

Since that time, the court has on three separate occasions issued orders directing that the plan be carried out. All persons were instructed to refrain from interfering with the efforts of the school board to comply with the law.

Proper and sensible observance of the law then demanded the respectful obedience which the nation has a right to expect from all its people. This, unfortunately, has not been the case at Little Rock. Certain misguided persons, many of them imported into Little Rock by agitators, have insisted upon defying the law and have sought to bring it into disrepute. The orders of the court have thus been frustrated.

The very basis of our individual rights and freedoms rests upon the certainty that the President and the Executive Branch of Government will support and insure the carrying out of the decisions of the Federal Courts, even, when necessary with all the means at the President's command.

Unless the President did so, anarchy would result.

There would be no security for any except that which each one of us could provide for himself.

The interest of the nation in the proper fulfillment of the law's requirements cannot yield to opposition and demonstrations by some few persons.

Mob rule cannot be allowed to override the decisions of our courts.

Now, let me make it very clear that Federal troops are not being used to relieve local and state authorities of their primary duty to preserve the peace and order of the community. Nor are the troops there for the [purpose] of taking over the responsibility of the School Board and the other responsible local officials in running Central High School. The running of our school system and the maintenance of peace and order in each of our States are strictly local affairs and the Federal Government does not interfere except in a very few special cases and when requested by one of the several States. In the present case the troops are there, pursuant to law, solely for the purpose of preventing interference with the orders of the Court.

The proper use of the powers of the Executive Branch to enforce the orders of a Federal Court is limited to extraordinary and compelling circumstances. Manifestly, such an extreme situation has been created in Little Rock. This challenge must be met and with such measures as will preserve to the people as a whole their lawfully-protected rights in a climate permitting their free and fair exercise. The overwhelming majority of our people in every section of the country are united in their respect for observance of the law—even in those cases where they may disagree with that law.

They deplore the call of extremists to violence.

The decision of the Supreme Court concerning school integration, of course, affects the South more seriously than it does other sections of the country. In that region I have many warm friends, some of them in the city of Little Rock. I have deemed it a great personal privilege to spend [time there] in our Southland tours of duty while in the military service and enjoyable recreational periods since that time.

So from intimate personal knowledge, I know that the overwhelming majority of the people in the South including those of Arkansas and of Little Rock—are of good will, united in their efforts to preserve and respect the law even when they disagree with it.

They do not sympathize with mob rule. They, like the rest of our nation, have proved in two great wars their readiness to sacrifice for America.

A foundation of our American way of life is our national respect for law.

In the South, as elsewhere, citizens are keenly aware of the tremendous disservice that has been done to the people of Arkansas in the eyes of the nation, and that has been done to the nation in the eyes of the world.

At a time when we face grave situations abroad because of the hatred that Communism bears toward a system of government based on human rights, it would be difficult to exaggerate the harm that is being done to the prestige and influence, and indeed to the safety, of our nation and the world.

Our enemies are gloating over this incident and using it everywhere to misrepresent our whole nation. We are portrayed as a violator of those standards of conduct which the peoples of the world united to proclaim in the Charter of the United Nations. There they affirmed "faith in fundamental human rights" and "in dignity and worth of the human person" and they did so "without distinction as to race, sex, language or religion."

And so, with deep confidence, I call upon the citizens of the State of Arkansas to assist in bringing to an immediate end all interference with the law and its processes. If resistance to the Federal Court orders ceases at once, the further presence of Federal troops will be unnecessary and the City of Little Rock will return to its normal habits of peace and order and a blot upon the fair name and high honor of our nation in the world will be removed.

Thus will be restored the image of America and of all its parts as one nation, indivisible, with liberty and justice for all.

Good night, and thank you very much.

Available online. URL: http://www.tamu.edu/scom/ pres/speeches/ikefederal.html.

APPENDIX B
Biographies of Major Personalities

Acheson, Dean (1893–1971) *secretary of state (1949–1953)*

The son of an Episcopal bishop, Acheson grew up in New England where he attended the prestigious Groton Preparatory School and Yale University. He graduated from Yale in 1915, served in the navy during World War I, then returned to New England where he received a law degree in 1918. In 1933, President Franklin D. Roosevelt named him undersecretary of the treasury, but Acheson resigned after six months in protest to Roosevelt's reduction of the gold content in the U.S. dollar. However, during World War II he served as Roosevelt's assistant secretary of state for economic affairs and played an active role in the lend-lease program to the Soviet Union. Acheson also played an active role in preparing for the postwar era, helping organize the United Nations Relief and Rehabilitation Agency (UNRRA), the World Bank, the International Monetary Fund, and the Food and Agriculture Organization.

After Roosevelt's death in 1945, Harry S. Truman appointed James Byrnes secretary of state, and Byrnes appointed Acheson undersecretary of state. During Byrnes's frequent trips abroad, Acheson served as acting secretary. In that capacity he gave the president daily briefings on foreign affairs and thereby developed a close relationship with him.

In the years immediately following World War II Acheson also became deeply involved with atomic energy. He initially favored international control of the bomb and the international development of peaceful uses for atomic energy and called for the exchange of atomic information among the United States, Great Britain, and the Soviet Union and the eventual international control of atomic material.

In the immediate aftermath of World War II, Acheson favored a policy of conciliation with the Soviet Union; however, by spring 1946, Soviet actions in Turkey, Iran, and the eastern Mediterranean caused him to reverse his position and support George Kennan's recommendation that the United States contain communist expansion throughout the world. Much of his subsequent work as undersecretary and then as secretary of state was dedicated to pursuing this containment policy. In 1947, Acheson helped formulate the Truman Doctrine aimed at containing the Soviets within their existing sphere of influence.

Acheson became secretary of state at the beginning of 1949, after George Marshall stepped down due to poor health. He pictured the superpower confrontation as a matter of power politics and did not believe in formulating policies according to abstract principles of morality or internationalism. He felt such idealistic motivations would compel the United States to avoid its responsibilities as a superpower to exercise power in order to create and sustain world order. He also believed that negotiation with the Soviet Union was futile because that nation was unwilling to bargain in good faith. Thus Acheson increasingly came to view the world as divided into distinct Eastern and Western spheres of influence.

Acheson worked to establish the German Federal Republic (West Germany), which he helped bring into the Western anticommunist alliance and whose eventual rearmament he promoted. He also promoted a large U.S. military buildup to counter communism, and he advocated that the United States assume unilateral responsibility for the defense of the noncommunist world. During his first year as secretary, Acheson opposed sending aid to Chiang Kai-shek, who was in the process of losing the Chinese civil war to communist forces under Mao Zedong. In a 1949 White Paper on China, Acheson maintained that Chiang lacked the support of the Chinese people and that propping him up would simply squander U.S. resources. A month later the communists assumed complete control of the Chinese mainland, and Chiang's defeat allowed Acheson's right-wing critics to charge him and the State Department of "selling out" China. Then, in 1950, Senator Joseph McCarthy claimed to have names of highly placed Communists within the State Department. Acheson defended his aides in congressional hearings, but the fierce right-wing attack that persisted throughout his term in office compelled him to modify some of his policies.

Acheson advocated military intervention after North Korea invaded South Korea in June 1950. He believed the Soviets were behind the North Korean action, probing for weaknesses in the Western alliance. He assumed responsibility for coordinating the political efforts that brought about the UN "police action" in Korea, lobbying Congress and the United Nations and working with diplomats from nonaligned countries. Acheson, however, opposed Republican calls to extend the war to China. He adhered to a policy of containment elsewhere in Asia, too, and he supported France's efforts to suppress Vietnamese nationalists under the communist leadership of Ho Chi Minh.

Ball, Lucille (1911–1989) *television and film actress*
Born near Jamestown, New York, Ball dropped out of high school at age 15 to attend drama school in New York City and pursue her dream of being an actress. Initially unable to find work as a performer, she was compelled to take employment as a model. A poster on which she was featured caught the eye of a Hollywood studio executive and led to her receiving small roles in *Roman Scandals* (1933), *Moulin Rouge* (1933), and *The Three Musketeers* (1935). In the late 1930s, her parts became somewhat larger in such films as *Room Service* (1938), which stars the Marx Brothers. She was given a starring role in *Too Many Girls* (1940), which also featured Cuban bandleader Desi Arnaz, whom Ball married later in the year. During the 1940s, Ball earned more important roles and did well at the box office, although she was never a major star. In 1950, she and Arnaz founded Desilu Productions, and on October 15, 1951, they premiered and starred in their television comedy *I Love Lucy*. The domestic sitcom was an immediate hit, and *I Love Lucy* became the single most popular TV show of the 1950s. The episode in which Lucy gave birth to Little Ricky aired the same day that Ball gave birth to her real-life son, Desi, Jr. (January 19, 1953). Ninety-two percent of all viewers watched the episode, the largest prime-time audience for a single show in history. President-elect Dwight Eisenhower complained only half jokingly that the interest in Lucy's baby was diverting attention from his inauguration, which took place the following day.

Production of *I Love Lucy* stopped when Ball and Arnaz divorced, and the final episode aired on June 24, 1957. After the divorce, Ball became the head of Desilu Studios. In that capacity, she was the only female head of a major Hollywood studio, and under her leadership Desilu expanded considerably, producing a number of other television shows. In 1962, Ball bought out Arnaz's interest in the company, which she sold to Paramount in 1967. She then formed her own production company, Lucille Ball Productions and continued to perform in movies and theater and on television until just a few years before her death. She is still regarded as one of television's funniest and most accomplished comedians.

Baruch, Bernard M. (1870–1965) *presidential adviser, representative to the United Nations Atomic Energy Commission (1946–1947)*
Born in Camden, South Carolina, the son of a German-Jewish doctor and a Portuguese-Jewish mother from a prominent South Carolina family, Baruch graduated from City College in New York in 1889. He rose from office boy in a Wall Street brokerage house to broker and became a millionaire by the age of 30. Baruch was an active supporter of President Woodrow Wilson, who named him chairman of the War Industries Board during World War I. Baruch thus acquired vast powers for mobilizing the country and, indeed, became known as the second most powerful man in the United States. Baruch secretly advised Republican presidents during the 1920s. Franklin Roosevelt offered to appoint Baruch secretary of the treasury, but the financier declined. Instead he unofficially advised on politics and the economy until Roosevelt's death in 1945.

In 1946, Truman appointed Baruch the U.S. representative to the Atomic Energy Commission of the United Nations (UN), which was drawing up a plan for international control of atomic energy. Baruch, fearing that Soviet vetoes in the Security Council could impede the work of a UN atomic agency, insisted on amending the plan to prohibit Security Council vetoes on votes concerning atomic energy. He insisted on other alterations as well. These changes were unacceptable to the Soviets, who then vetoed the entire proposal. The subsequent intensification of the cold war in 1947 and 1948 made further top-level efforts for international control of atomic energy politically impossible.

Although Baruch supported Truman in the presidential election of 1948, he opposed Truman's deficit spending and instead promoted a balanced budget. Their falling out intensified just prior to the election, and Baruch's role in Truman's administration diminished thereafter. In 1952, Baruch finally broke with the Democratic Party and supported Dwight Eisenhower for president. He continued to advise U.S. presidents until his death in 1965.

Berle, Milton (Milton Berlinger) (1908–2002)
television comedian

Born in New York City as Milton Berlinger, Berle grew up in theater, first performing in vaudeville at the age of 10. He acted in numerous silent films and worked in night clubs as a comedian and a master of ceremonies during the Great Depression. Berle's breakthrough came when Texaco sponsored his first television show, *The Texaco Star Theater,* in fall 1948. The visual medium was well suited to his broad, slapstick style of comedy, and Berle soon became the most popular figure on early television. His was the top-rated show in the 1949–50 and 1950–51 seasons, the number-two-rated show in 1951–52, and number five in 1952–53. Berle's program was so successful in the early days of television that it was said to have sold more TV sets than any advertising campaign. Consequently, Berle became widely known as "Mr. Television," as well as "Uncle Milty."

Texaco dropped its sponsorship in 1953, but Buick then picked it up for the next two years. In 1955, Berle moved from New York to Hollywood, where he produced *The Milton Berle Show,* one of the first variety shows broadcast in color. Among the guests on the final program in 1956 was rising rock star Elvis Presley. In 1958–59, Berle hosted the *Kraft Music Hall,* a variety show, and he continued to appear on television in various capacities throughout the 1960s.

Buckley, William F., Jr. (1925–   ) *conservative journalist, novelist, founding publisher of the* National Review *magazine*

Buckley was born in New York to a devout Catholic family headed by William F. Buckley, Sr., a Texas lawyer who lost his fortune in Mexican oil when the revolutionary government there confiscated his holdings in 1922. Subsequently, Buckley, Sr., instilled in his 10 children a hatred of revolution and communism that greatly influenced his son.

In 1946, Buckley enrolled at Yale University, where he became editor of the student paper and an outspoken critic of the faculty's advocacy of left-wing causes. His first book, *God and Man at Yale: The Superstitions of Academic Freedom* (1951), which was released on the university's 250th anniversary, exposes the faculty's anticapitalist and antireligious positions, which Buckley believes were inappropriate for a university that had been founded as a religious institution and benefited from American capitalism. Although the book received many negative reviews, the controversy surrounding it made it an unexpected best-seller. In 1951, Buckley was accepted into the Central Intelligence Agency (CIA), and after completing his training, he was stationed in Mexico City. He coauthored his second book, *McCarthy and His Enemies: The Record and Its Meaning* (1954), with his brother-in-law, Brent Bozell. The defense of Senator Joseph McCarthy, issued the same year as the senator's fall from power, received only one review in the mainstream press—a negative one in the *New York Times.* In 1962, Buckley published a defense of the House Un-American Activities Committee (HUAC) entitled *The Committee and Its Critics.*

Following the failure of the McCarthy book to receive attention in the national press, Buckley founded the *National Review* to create a nationwide forum for conservative views. In addition, Buckley sought to redefine American conservatism by eliminating the anti-Semitic and isolationist tendencies that were characteristic of the right-wing during the late 1940s and early 1950s. The first issue appeared on November 14, 1955, with Buckley serving as editor-in-chief and publisher. He remained publisher until 1957 and stayed as editor-in-chief until 1990, when he stepped down to become editor-at-large.

In the early 1960s, Buckley expanded his efforts to promote the conservative cause. He began a syndicated newspaper column, "A Conservative Voice," and helped found such conservative organizations as Young Americans for Freedom and the Conservative Party of New York. At the same time, his politics moderated somewhat, and Buckley reversed his earlier defense of racial segregation in the South; moreover, he used his influence to have the ultra-right-wing John Birch Society disassociated with mainstream conservatism. His television show, *Firing Line,* which featured debates between Buckley and prominent liberals and other political advocates, established his reputation for a quick wit, expansive vocabulary, and erudition. In the 1970s and 1980s, he published several best-selling spy novels that center around a James Bond–like superhero, Blackford Oakes.

Cliburn, Van (1934–   ) *classical pianist*
Born in Shreveport, Louisiana, Cliburn first studied with his mother, a concert pianist, and then with Rosina Lhévinne at New York City's Juilliard School of Music. At age 23, he won first prize in the 1958 International Tchaikovsky Competition in Moscow. The competition took place at the beginning of the second Berlin Crisis, one of the most intense periods of the cold war, and it occasioned a hopeful front-page headline in the *New York Times,* proclaiming that "an artistic bridge" between the United States and Russia had been created. In 1962, Cliburn inaugurated the Van Cliburn International Piano competition in Fort Worth, Texas. He went on to become a personal friend of President Lyndon B. Johnson and performed at the latter's Texas ranch for visiting heads of state.

Dean, James (1931–1955) *film actor*
Born in Marion, Indiana, and raised on a farm by his aunt and uncle, Dean studied the Method acting technique at the Actors Studio, which Lee Strasberg and Elia Kazan founded in the late 1940s. After appearing in small roles in the films *Has Anybody Seen My Gal?* (1951), *Sailor Beware* (1951), *Fixed Bayonets* (1951), and *Trouble Along the Way* (1953), Dean gained some recognition for his performance as an Arab who blackmails people in the play *The Immoralist.* He subsequently starred in Kazan's *East of Eden* (1955), and became an immediate hit as a sensitive but troubled and misunderstood young man. He played characters with similar attributes in *Rebel Without a Cause* (1955) and *Giant* (1956) but died in 1955 in an automobile accident shortly after the filming of *Rebel* was completed. Nonetheless, Dean has remained an inspiration for young people who feel alienated and disaffected from middle-class society.

DeMille, Cecil B. (1881–1959) *film producer, director*
One of the pioneers of the film industry, DeMille played an important role in developing the classic Hollywood style of filmmaking and shaping the structure of the Hollywood system. He and Samuel Goldwyn made one of Hollywood's first feature-length movies, *The Squaw Man* (1914). DeMille went on to pioneer the epic film genre and become one of the most famous and accomplished directors in the first half of the 20th century. His early films include *The Ten Commandments* (1923) and *King of Kings* (1927), a retelling of the story of Jesus that was viewed by more than 800,000 people. Several of DeMille's other epics also celebrated Christian and democratic values, which, in the 1950s, he maintained were the first line of defense against communism. These values are most conspicuous in *Samson and Delilah* (1949) and *The Ten Commandments* (1956). His other films from the period are the Academy Award–winning circus extravaganza *The Greatest Show on Earth* (1952) and *The Buccaneer* (1959), a remake of his 1938 movie that he had produced but not directed.

DeMille opposed the unions in the film industry, and in the late 1940s and 1950s, he emerged as a leader among Hollywood's right-wing faction. His Cecil B. DeMille Foundation regularly provided information to the House Un-American Activities Committee (HUAC) and other bodies investigating communist influences in Hollywood, and in 1950, he led a successful, pivotal battle within the Screen Directors Guild to require a loyalty oath of all members.

Diefenbaker, John G. (1895–1979) *prime minister of Canada (1957–1963)*
Born in Gray County, Ontario, Diefenbaker attended the University of Saskatchewan, where he was awarded a bachelor's degree in 1915 and a master's degree in political science and economics in 1916.

Diefenbaker was elected to the House of Commons in 1940 as representative of Lake Centre, and he became leader of the Progressive Conservative Party in 1956. The Conservative victory in the elections of 1957 concluded 22 years of Liberal Party rule in Canada and made Diefenbaker prime minister. After the 1958 elections, his party enjoyed an overwhelming majority in the House of Commons.

But Diefenbaker often alienated members of his own party by promoting an active agenda of social legislation that included expanded rights for women and indigenous Canadians and support for farmers. He also created closer ties between Canada and some of the communist countries than the United States did. His Agricultural Rehabilitation and Development Act assisted many farmers across Canada, and he established new markets in China for their wheat. Diefenbaker also supported projects to revive the Maritime Provinces. In 1957, Diefenbaker appointed Canada's first female cabinet minister, Ellen Fairclough, and in 1958, he named James Gladstone Canada's first Native senator. He also supported the Canadian Bill of Rights in 1958. Diefenbaker's antiapartheid position in 1961 contributed to South Africa's decision to leave the British Commonwealth of Nations. His refusal to support U.S. policies against Fidel Castro's Cuba strained his relations with the United States in the early 1960s. The Conservatives lost power in 1962, and Diefenbaker was voted out of office in 1963. Lester B. Pearson, a Liberal, succeeded him.

Dior, Christian (1905–1957) *fashion designer*
Born in Granville, France, Dior opened his own fashion design house in 1946 and introduced his first collection in 1947, the "Corolle" line. Soon dubbed the "New Look," Dior's line reintroduced femininity into women's fashions after the more severe look of the war era. He remained a top fashion designer until his death, and among his contributions were such sophisticated designs as the three-piece outfit of cardigan, top, and skirt; box-shaped jackets with short skirts; coolie hats; three-quarter-length sleeves; and horseshoe collars.

Disney, Walt (1901–1966) *animator, film-studio owner, television producer*
The creator of the immensely popular Mickey Mouse cartoon character, Disney was the son of a carpenter and a teacher. He grew up on a farm in Marceline, Missouri, a small, midwestern town that is said to have inspired Mainstreet U.S.A. in the theme parks Disneyland and Disney World. After his family moved to Kansas City, he studied cartooning, first through a correspondence school and then at the Kansas City Art Institute and School of Design. He attended high school in Chicago and served as a truck driver for the American Red Cross during World War I. In 1919,

Disney met cartoonist Ub Iwerks, and the two soon founded their own small studio. In 1928, they introduced Mickey Mouse in *Steamboat Willie,* shortly after sound movies first appeared. *Snow White and the Seven Dwarfs* (1935) was Disney's first feature-length animated film, and it was the first of his successful series of movies based on fairy tales, legends, and other folk stories. These later also became the basis for portions of his theme parks. In the 1940s, Disney moved his studio to Burbank, California. Among the animated films he released immediately before and during World War II were *Pinocchio* (1940), *Fantasia* (1940), *Dumbo* (1941), *Bambi* (1942), and *The Three Caballeros* (1945), which combines animation and live action. After the war, Disney Studios released such popular animated hits as *Song of the South* (1946), *Cinderella* (1950), *Alice in Wonderland* (1951), *Peter Pan* (1953), *Lady and the Tramp* (1956), and *Sleeping Beauty* (1959).

In 1954, Disney sought to reach an even wider audience, and his *Disneyland* show became the first major investment in television production by a Hollywood movie studio. Early episodes featuring actor Fess Parker as Davy Crockett established the program as a popular favorite that went on to became the longest-running prime-time series in network history. Disney also featured the Crockett character in follow-up movies that created the Davy Crockett fad of 1955 and 1956. In 1955, Disney also introduced the popular children's television show *The Mickey Mouse Club,* which featured "Mouseketeers" who wore caps with mouse ears that Disney was able to merchandise along with Davy Crockett coonskin caps and other related products.

In 1955, Disney opened the first large-scale, modern theme park in Anaheim, California. An immediate success, Disneyland pioneered state-of-the-art forms of both entertainment and corporate marketing, as Disney used the theme park to promote his films and television show, *Disneyland,* and vice versa. Before his death, he began plans for an even larger amusement park, Walt Disney World, which opened outside Orlando, Florida, in 1971. The Walt Disney Company went on to become one of the largest and most thoroughly integrated corporations in the entertainment industry.

Dulles, Allen W. (1893–1969) *director of the Central Intelligence Agency (CIA) (1953–1961)*
Dulles was born in Watertown, New York. His younger brother, John Foster Dulles, served as President Dwight

Eisenhower's secretary of state, while Allen headed the Central Intelligence Agency (CIA) during the 1950s. After attending private schools in New York and Paris, Dulles graduated from Princeton University in 1916 and entered the diplomatic corps. During World War II, he served as chief of the Office of Strategic Services (OSS) in Berne, Switzerland, and in 1945, he helped negotiate the German surrender in Italy. After the fall of Germany, Dulles headed the OSS in Berlin. He played a major role in creating the CIA, which in 1948 was authorized to conduct covert operations, with the proviso that the operations remain secret and that the government be able to plausibly deny their existence. As deputy director of plans, Dulles oversaw the agency's covert activities. He also recommended organizational changes that defined the CIA's structure for the following two decades.

In November 1951, Dulles was appointed the CIA's deputy director. Believing that Eastern Europe could still be liberated and that the Soviet armies could be driven back to within Soviet borders, Dulles oversaw a number of covert operations behind the Iron Curtain. In 1952, the CIA initiated a program to intercept and read mail passing between the United States and certain foreign countries. Although it clearly violated the CIA's charter, the program continued for 21 years, presumably with the unspoken approval of three postmasters general. Upon Eisenhower's inauguration, Dulles became director of the CIA. As a public figure, the pipe-smoking Dulles projected a calm, urbane demeanor that became associated with the agency. He convinced the government and the public that the work of the CIA required strict secrecy and thereby managed to hide the agency from close congressional oversight and media inquiry. Dulles's CIA worked to overthrow several leftist governments and install regimes more friendly to U.S. interests. In 1953, it helped depose Iran's prime minister, Mohammad Mossadegh, and restore the shah. And in 1955, it played a critical role in deposing the leftist government of Guatemalan president Jacobo Arbenz Guzmán. It also helped South Vietnam's president, Ngo Dinh Diem, remain in power, despite strong opposition from his country's military and major religious sects. Dulles was forced out of his position by President John F. Kennedy following the failed attempt by Cuban expatriates to overthrow Fidel Castro at the Bay of Pigs in 1961—an operation planned and supported by the CIA. He returned to

private practice but in 1964 served as President Lyndon B. Johnson's special emissary to evaluate problems with law enforcement in Mississippi after three civil rights workers disappeared there.

Dulles, John Foster (1888–1959) *secretary of state (1953–1959)*

The older brother of CIA director Allen Dulles, with whom he worked closely, Dulles graduated from Princeton University in 1908, then attended the Sorbonne in Paris, and received his law degree from George Washington University in 1911. During World War I, he was legal counsel to the War Trade Board and advised President Woodrow Wilson during the Versailles treaty negotiations that ended that war. From 1946 to 1948 and in 1950, Dulles served as U.S. delegate to the United Nations. During that period he was also a special adviser to Secretaries of State George Marshall and Dean Acheson at the Councils of Foreign Ministers in London (1945), Moscow (1947), and Paris (1949). He briefly served as a U.S. senator in 1949, filling an open seat in New York, but he lost in the general election that fall. As ambassador, he helped negotiate the 1951 peace treaty with Japan, which formally ended World War II in the Pacific.

Upon his election, Eisenhower, who greatly admired Dulles's wisdom and dedication, appointed him secretary of state, and Dulles held the position until just before his death in May 1959. Dulles enjoyed considerable latitude in formulating U.S. foreign policy throughout the 1950s. He took a very hard line against international communism, which he believed was a unified, monolithic, and immoral force dedicated to world conquest, and Dulles advocated going beyond mere containment by enacting a "liberation policy" that would eventually free countries under communist rule, especially those in Eastern Europe. However, in practical terms such a policy was inapplicable within the nuclear stalemate.

Dulles believed the United States needed to be willing to go to "the brink of war" in order to halt the spread of communism around the world—a form of diplomacy that became known as "brinkmanship," which he credited ending the Korean War, forestalling a Chinese invasion of the islands in the Formosa Strait, Quemoy, and Matsu, and settling the Indochina war between the French and Vietnamese communists.

On January 11, 1954, Dulles announced a nuclear-based U.S. defense policy predicated on instant and massive retaliation against any aggressor at any target the United States deemed appropriate. Developed at a time when the United States had unquestioned nuclear superiority, massive retaliation asserted that the United States could respond with a nuclear attack against the Soviet Union if the USSR attacked a U.S. ally anywhere in the world. However as the Soviet Union developed its own nuclear arsenal and intercontinental ballistic missiles during the late 1950s, massive retaliation became an increasingly problematic strategy, as the Soviets could then employ a similar policy directed against the United States.

Dulles recognized the value of forming alliances with the underdeveloped African and Asian nations, and in his first year in office he not only visited European capitals but also toured Southeast Asia and the Middle East. He formulated a policy predicated on evenhandedness to both Israel and Arab nations, and in 1955, devised a plan to promote stability in the Middle East by developing water resources to provide arable land for 900,000 Arab refugees from Israel. In 1956, he successfully argued against U.S. support of the French-British-Israeli invasion of Egypt after that country seized the Suez Canal, because he feared U.S. approval would alienate anti-Israeli Arab countries and be poorly received by underdeveloped nations leery of military intervention by former colonial powers. In 1957, Dulles encouraged Eisenhower to intervene on behalf of black schoolchildren seeking to attend white schools in Little Rock, Arkansas, because he wanted to defuse communist charges of U.S. racism that the Soviets and their allies were using to turn underdeveloped countries against the United States. That year, Dulles also helped formulate the Eisenhower Doctrine, which stated that the United States would give military and economic aid to any Middle Eastern country requesting assistance against communism. In 1958, the president invoked that doctrine to send U.S. Marines to Lebanon in support of the presidency of Camille Chamoun, whose pro-West policies had sparked rebellion in Beirut.

Concerned that communists were trying to gain control of the world's "rice bowl" in Thailand, Indochina, Burma, and Malaya in order to gain power over India and Japan, Dulles promoted the formation of the Southeast Asia Treaty Organization (SEATO) among the United States, Great Britain, Australia, France, New Zealand, Pakistan, the Philippines, and Thailand. He also helped form the Baghdad Pact, which later evolved into the Central Treaty Organization (CENTO). Combined, these organizations surrounded the Soviet Union with hostile forces.

In 1955, West Germany gained recognition from both superpowers and joined the NATO alliance, but because Dulles hoped to achieve the eventual unification of Germany under terms agreeable to the United States, he argued against U.S. recognition of East Germany. He fell ill from cancer in 1958, as the three-year-long Berlin crisis was beginning, and he resigned in April 1959, while the crisis was still ongoing. Dulles died the following month; he was replaced by Christian A. Herter.

Eisenhower, Dwight D. (1890–1969)
U.S. president (1953–1961)

Born in Abilene, Kansas, to a working-class family of Swiss descent, Eisenhower graduated from the U.S. Military Academy at West Point in 1915. He served as a tank instructor in World War I and during the 1920s attended the U.S. Army Command and General Staff College and U.S. Army War College. During the 1930s, Eisenhower served as personal assistant to General Douglas MacArthur and assistant military adviser to the Philippines. When the United States entered World War II, General George Marshall made him his chief of operations. Impressed by Eisenhower's administrative capabilities and his diplomatic skills, President Franklin D. Roosevelt selected Eisenhower over many more senior generals to assume command first of U.S. forces in Europe and then of all Allied forces in Europe. Eisenhower commanded the Allied invasions of North Africa (1942) and Sicily and Italy (1943). In 1944, he commanded the Normandy invasion. After the war, he succeeded Marshall as army chief of staff, a position he held until becoming president of Columbia University in 1948. He declined offers from both political parties to run for president. In 1951, Truman appointed Eisenhower commander of the forces being assembled by the newly created North Atlantic Treaty Organization (NATO).

Concerned that the Republican Party would back Senator Robert Taft, whose isolationist foreign policies Eisenhower believed would undermine U.S. interests, Eisenhower ran for and received the Republican presidential nomination in 1952. He then easily defeated the Democratic nominee, Adlai E. Stevenson. However, throughout his presidency, Eisenhower needed to achieve consensus with a Democratic

Congress in order to govern, and he later established a good working relationship on foreign policy, at least, with Senate Majority Leader Lyndon B. Johnson and Speaker of the House Sam Rayburn, after the Democrats took control of both houses of Congress in November 1954.

In terms of domestic policy, Eisenhower favored a restricted role for the federal government and did not propose many social initiatives. He believed that a healthy, unrestricted economy offered the best basis for a socially, politically, and militarily strong United States; therefore, in his domestic agenda he promoted limited government and a sound economy. Most of his cabinet appointments came from the upper managerial positions in big business. However, having learned during World War II of the importance of a good road system for military defense, he promoted the 1956 Interstate Highway Act, which initiated the interstate highway system. This was one of the most far-reaching domestic developments from his presidency, as the interstate highways went on to radically change U.S. commerce, geography, and lifestyles. Eisenhower did not always take a forceful role in promoting civil rights, because he did not believe social change could or should be legislated, but he used the powers of the executive branch to order greater integration of federal facilities and in 1957 ordered army paratroopers to Little Rock, Arkansas, to enforce the 1954 Supreme Court decision calling for the racial integration of public schools.

In contrast to his domestic policy, Eisenhower promoted an activist foreign policy. In order to conclude the Korean War, shortly after taking office he threatened communist China and pressured South Korea. The war ended soon thereafter; however, many historians attribute this more to the death of Stalin in March 1953 than to Eisenhower's actions. Eisenhower worked closely with Secretary of State John Foster Dulles, whom he admired greatly, but Eisenhower was more reluctant to take strong military action than the more ideologically driven Dulles. Although he authorized covert CIA operations directed at driving the Soviets from Eastern Europe (and later the Bay of Pigs invasion intended to topple Castro in Cuba, carried out under John F. Kennedy), Eisenhower refused to risk a major military confrontation in 1953, when an anticommunist populist movement arose in East Berlin, or in Hungary in 1956, when anticommunist populists there briefly overthrew the Soviet-backed

government and appealed to the United States for protection. In each instance, the Soviets sent tanks into the key cities to crush the rebellions. In 1954, despite Dulles's warning that a French defeat in Indochina (Vietnam) could produce a "domino effect" in which other Southeast Asian countries would fall to communist insurgency, Eisenhower declined to send substantial military assistance to save the surrounded French army at Dien Bien Phu, because he feared becoming deeply involved in another land war in Asia. He also turned down requests to employ nuclear bombs on behalf of the French in Vietnam and restrained the Taiwan-based Nationalist Chinese government, which wanted to bomb the mainland in retaliation for its shelling of the islands of Jinmen (Quemoy) and Mazu (Matsu).

In September 1955, Eisenhower suffered a mild heart attack; however, he recovered quickly and easily won reelection in 1956. A firm believer that a strong economy was the greatest basis for American security, Eisenhower worked to restrict the defense budget, which he feared could undermine the economy if it became too large. He therefore promoted a policy of national security centered around the hydrogen bomb, which was developed in 1953, because the H-bomb promised to give, in popular terms, "a bigger bang for the buck." Consequently, in 1956 Eisenhower reduced the military by 25 percent, mostly in conventional forces. That year, he opposed the British-French-Israeli attack on Egypt and was outraged that he was not informed ahead of time about it. The Suez Canal crisis, which coincided with the Hungarian uprising and the final days of Eisenhower's reelection campaign, created a serious rift in the United States's relations with its closest traditional allies. However, when the Soviets threatened a missile attack against France and England, Eisenhower declared that such an attack would provoke a nuclear response from the United States.

Tensions in the Middle East continued throughout his presidency, and in 1957, he issued the Eisenhower Doctrine, announcing U.S. willingness to send military and economic aid to any Middle Eastern country requesting U.S. assistance against communism. In July 1958, he invoked that doctrine when he ordered marines to Lebanon to support the pro-Western government there against popular uprisings. At the end of that year, Eisenhower refused to accede to Soviet premier Nikita Khrushchev's demand that the Western allies evacuate the divided city of Berlin within six months. The situation evolved into the on-again, off-again Berlin crisis that climaxed after Eisenhower left office, in fall 1961.

In his farewell address in January 1961, Eisenhower warned of the growing "military-industrial complex," which had united "an immense military establishment and a large arms industry. . . . The total influence—economic, political, even spiritual—is felt in every city, every state house, every office of the federal government." He cautioned against "the disastrous rise of misplaced power," which could "endanger our liberties or our democratic processes." After leaving office, Eisenhower retired to a farm near Gettysburg, Pennsylvania, where he wrote his memoirs. He continued to oppose increases in defense spending and called for smaller troop commitments to NATO. He supported President Johnson's policies for Vietnam and frequently advised the Democratic president. He suffered a heart attack three weeks before Richard M. Nixon, his vice president, was elected president in November 1968, and he died in March 1969.

Ginsberg, Allen (1926–1997) *poet*
Born in Newark, New Jersey, to a Jewish family, Ginsberg received a bachelor's degree from Columbia University in 1948. Among his formative childhood experiences was his mother's paranoid fear of political persecution for her leftist beliefs. Naomi Ginsberg was institutionalized for three years during his adolescence and then permanently later in life, and Ginsberg's major poem "Kaddish," written after her death in 1956 and named after the Jewish prayer for the dead, describes the effect her mental illness had on him. Ginsberg's father was an English teacher and poet, but unlike Allen, the patriarch's personality and poetry celebrated order and personal restraint. Ginsberg attributed his homosexuality to the "usual oedipal entanglement."

Ginsberg befriended William Burroughs and Jack Kerouac in 1944 and with them became a major figure in the literary and social movement known as Beat. Finding conventional middle-class American society unimaginative, unduly repressive, and spiritually confining, the Beats pictured themselves as social outcasts and advocated the spontaneous and free expression of libidinal impulses. As a poet, Ginsberg sought to take poetry from the insulated university classrooms out into the streets, where it would be performed, not simply read, and where it could find a wider, more populist, less culturally elite audience. The Beat movement reflected despair over a world gone mad with nuclear weapons and other forms of mass destruction and with an apparently insatiable need to impose conformity and deny creativity. Ginsberg's most powerful expression of these sentiments appears in his famous poem "Howl" (1956). During the 1960s, Ginsberg, a vocal protestor of the Vietnam War, experimented with LSD and other drugs to heighten his consciousness and enable him to draw on unexplored aspects of his subconscious. He remained interested in spiritual and leftist political issues throughout his life.

Graham, Billy (1918–) *Christian evangelical minister*
Born in Charlotte, North Carolina, the son of a prosperous dairy farmer, Graham attended rural schools. At age 16, he accepted Jesus Christ as his personal savior at a revival meeting and went on to study at the fundamentalist Christian schools Bob Jones College in Cleveland, Tennessee, and the Florida Bible Institute outside Tampa. After graduation, Graham enrolled at Wheaton College in Wheaton, Illinois, where he received a bachelor's degree in anthropology. During and immediately after World War II, Graham held numerous tent revival meetings and made radio broadcasts that earned him a limited following.

His rise to national prominence occurred during a Protestant revival he held in Los Angeles in fall 1949. The revival coincided with the Soviet Union's first successful test of an atomic bomb, and Graham played upon the attendant anxieties by merging old-fashioned fire and brimstone with cold war anticommunism. He insisted that the communists, whose basic doctrine is inherently atheistic, had declared war on God; that communism was masterminded by Satan; and that Americans had to choose between God and Satan in the cold war struggle. In the fourth week of the revival, publisher William Randolph Hearst, another anticommunist, ordered his editors to promote Graham, and bolstered by the attendant publicity from Hearst publications, Graham began to emerge as a major figure in 1950s American culture. Graham's next revival was held in Columbia, South Carolina, where Governor Strom Thurmond and former secretary of state James Byrnes endorsed him, and Henry Luce, the publisher of *Time* and *Life* magazines, flew down to meet him. Over the next five years, Graham's picture appeared on the cover of *Life* four times. He was also featured on the cover of Luce's rival, *Newsweek,* six times. By 1958, the Billy Graham Evangelistic Association was receiving and answering more than 10,000 letters a week and collecting and distributing more than $2 million each year. Throughout the 1950s, Graham repeatedly appeared in magazine lists of the 10 most admired men in America.

In addition to writing a nationally syndicated newspaper column, Graham was among the first ministers to employ the new medium of the postwar era, television. Between 1951 and 1954, his Billy Graham Evangelical Association sponsored *Hour of Decision,* a series of regular Sunday night talks on ABC, and between 1957 and 1959, Graham held four widely viewed television "crusades," during which he held services every Saturday night for a two- to three-month period. He often employed a formula of combining fundamentalist Christianity with anticommunism. Graham was antiunion. Although he condemned America's growing materialism, he favored a strong economy and spoke as though capitalism and Christianity were inextricably fused. In sum, he anticipated the "religious Right" of the 1980s by representing right-wing political views as the true Christian position and by projecting fundamental Christianity as the essence of American patriotism. A spiritual adviser to several presidents during the second half of the 20th century, most notably Richard M. Nixon, Graham remains an active Christian evangelist as of 2002.

Hiss, Alger (1904–1996) *State Department official under President Franklin D. Roosevelt, president of the Carnegie Endowment for International Peace (1946–1949)*

Born in Baltimore, Hiss was raised by his mother after his father committed suicide when he was two. He had a distinguished undergraduate career at Johns Hopkins University, where he was elected president of the student government, and he received his law degree from Harvard Law School in 1929. Professor Felix Frankfurter, later a Supreme Court justice, recommended Hiss to Justice Oliver Wendell Holmes as his law secretary, and Hiss served in that prestigious position for a year. He joined President Franklin D. Roosevelt's New Deal administration in 1933, in the legal division of the Agricultural Adjustment Admin-

istration (AAA), where he unsuccessfully tried to add protection for sharecroppers and tenant farmers to the standard contract the government used with farmers. Hiss became identified with a group of reformers within the AAA that was later "purged" after he had left to become legal assistant to the Nye Committee, which was investigating the weapons industry. Between 1936 and 1945, Hiss held a number of government jobs before becoming director of the Office of Special Political Affairs. In that capacity he played a major role in creating the United Nations. He also served as a senior adviser to Roosevelt at the Yalta Conference in February 1945 and as executive secretary to the Dumbarton Oaks conference that established the framework for the United Nations. He was later elected temporary secretary general. He resigned from the State Department in 1945 to become president of the Carnegie Endowment for International Peace, whose mission was to foster efforts to eliminate war. During his two-and-a-half-year tenure in that office, Hiss's policy objectives coincided with those of the United Nations.

In August 1948, Whittaker Chambers, a former Communist Party member working as a senior editor for *Time* magazine, testified before the House Un-American Activities Committee (HUAC) that he, Hiss, and other members of Roosevelt's liberal administration had belonged to the same underground communist cell in Washington. Hiss was the most senior and most prominent of those Chambers named. Two days later Hiss appeared before the committee and denied ever belonging to the Communist Party or any of its front organizations.

On August 25, Hiss and Chambers delivered their conflicting stories before HUAC in a televised session. Hiss challenged Chambers to repeat his accusations outside of the committee hearing so Hiss could sue him for slander. Two days later Chambers complied, asserting on *Meet the Press* that "Alger Hiss was a communist and may still be one." After being criticized for his delay, Hiss filed a $75,000 legal suit for slander.

Until this point in the proceedings Chambers had only accused Hiss of Communist Party membership and willingness to promote a communist agenda within Roosevelt's administration; however, after Hiss filed for slander, Chambers escalated his charges, claiming that Hiss had also been guilty of passing classified State Department documents to the Soviet

Union. Chambers maintained that he had previously withheld the espionage charges in order to protect Hiss, but that he now needed to convince the world that he was being truthful about his earlier charges.

In December 1948, Chambers responded to a HUAC subpoena by submitting five roles of microfilm, which he had concealed the day before inside a carved-out pumpkin at his farm in Maryland. Republican congressman Richard Nixon, a member of HUAC, arranged for extensive press coverage of the theatrical retrieval of the microfilm from its bizarre hiding place, and the Hiss case became an even greater public drama and spectacle. Two roles of the microfilm contained classified State Department material that Hiss had initialed.

Shortly after the HUAC revelations, a New York grand jury heard extensive testimony from both Chambers and Hiss and concluded that Hiss had lied. Hiss was immune from charges of espionage, as the statute of limitations had expired; however, on December 15, the grand jury indicted Hiss for perjury. The first trial, begun in May 1949, ended in a hung jury, but Hiss was convicted in January 1950 in a retrial. The Hiss case remained controversial throughout the cold war, as right-wing anticommunists pointed to Hiss as proof that communists had infiltrated the Democratic administrations and were influencing policy decisions in the late 1940s and early 1950s. They also used Hiss's role in the formation of the United Nations to substantiate their claims that the United Nations was largely a tool of the communists. Liberals, on the other hand, maintained that Hiss was the victim of a right-wing conspiracy to discredit the New Deal and the liberal Democrats. Although Hiss went to his death denying that he had ever spied for the Soviet Union, the Venona files—secret messages from the Soviet Union that U.S. intelligence officers decoded in the 1940s—demonstrated his guilt when they were released in the 1990s.

Hoover, J. Edgar (1895–1972) *director of the Federal Bureau of Investigation (FBI) (1924–1972)*
Born and raised in Washington, D.C., the son of a government bureaucrat, Hoover worked his way through George Washington University Law School. He graduated in 1916 and joined the Justice Department as a clerk. In 1919, he became assistant to Attorney General A. Mitchell Palmer and assumed responsibility for coordinating the so-called Palmer raids, in which thousands of immigrants who were alleged anarchists and communists were rounded up, interrogated, and deported during the Red Scare of 1919–20. In 1921, Hoover became assistant director of the Justice Department's Bureau of Investigation, which was then only a small, investigatory agency plagued by scandals and staffed by political appointees. In 1924, Hoover consented to become director but only if he could hire agents via the merit system, and he began transforming the bureau into a highly professional organization.

In 1936, President Franklin D. Roosevelt authorized the renamed Federal Bureau of Investigation (FBI) to investigate espionage and sabotage, and Hoover used that authority to maintain a watch on both political extremes. Throughout his long tenure as director, Hoover had his agents perform similar political favors for other U.S. presidents from both parties.

During the 1940s and early 1950s, the FBI arrested some prominent members of and people associated with the Truman administration, among them Alger Hiss, William Remington, and John S. Service. The FBI also cracked a spy ring that during World War II had passed secrets about the atomic bomb project to the Soviets. Klaus Fuchs and Julius and Ethel Rosenberg were among those convicted. In 1957, the FBI arrested Soviet colonel Rudolf Abel as the head of a large spy ring, and in 1958, it uncovered another major Soviet spy operation.

In 1952, Truman expanded the FBI's wiretapping powers; however, Hoover exceeded his new authority by ordering that the mail of U.S. citizens be opened and by authorizing burglaries to secure evidence against perceived enemies of the state. In 1954, Hoover maintained that the FBI had investigated 5 million federal employees. Throughout the 1950s, Hoover remained one of the most respected, as well as most ardent and visible anticommunists, and in 1958, he published *Masters of Deceit: The Story of Communism in America and How to Fight It,* a widely read book about the practices of domestic communists and how ordinary Americans can work with the FBI against them.

Kazan, Elia (1909–   ) *film and theater director*
The son of Anatolian Greeks, Kazan was born in Turkey but immigrated with his family to the United States when he was four years old. He worked his way through Williams College and Yale Drama School as a

waiter, an experience that, in his words, provoked an antagonism to privilege, good looks, and WASPs. That attitude ultimately led him to the Communist Party, which he joined in 1934. Kazan left in 1936, after the party wanted to use him to take over the Group Theater. According to Kazan, the experience gave him a taste of what a police state is like, and he wanted nothing to do with it. Along with Lee Strasberg, he helped found the Actors Studio, which introduced Stanislavski-based Method acting in the late 1940s. The Actors Studio trained such important 1950s performers as Lee J. Cobb, Marlon Brando, Julie Harris, and James Dean.

Considered the premier director of the late 1940s and early 1950s, Kazan directed numerous films and plays known for their social content and liberal values. In 1947, he directed Brando in the widely acclaimed theatrical performance of Tennessee Williams's *A Streetcar Named Desire,* and in 1949 he directed the successful Broadway debut of Arthur Miller's *Death of a Salesman,* for which Cobb received glorious reviews in his role as Willy Loman. During that period, Kazan also directed several important films, including *Gentleman's Agreement* (1947), about anti-Semitism; *Pinky* (1949), about racial discrimination; and *Viva Zapata!* (1952), about revolution and land reform in Mexico. He received Academy Award nominations for directing the film adaptation of *A Streetcar Named Desire* (1951) and for *East of Eden* (1955), in which Dean made his first major cinematic appearance. Kazan also won acclaim for *Baby Doll* (1956), which, based on Tennessee Williams's play *27 Wagonloads of Cotton,* stirred controversy for its sexual content. Other films from the period include *Man on a Tightrope* (1953), *Face in the Crowd,* and *On the Waterfront* (1954), which celebrates an act of informing (on a murder).

In 1952, Kazan was subpoenaed to testify before the House Un-American Activities Committee (HUAC). Despite pressure from friends, including Arthur Miller, not to cooperate with the committee, Kazan identified several communists. He also listed the 25 productions he had by then directed and defended the political content of each. The day after his testimony was released, he took out a large ad in the *New York Times* explaining that he had informed because communism represented a grave danger to democracy and urging others to recognize their patriotic duty to cooperate with HUAC. Kazan's testi-

mony provoked a break with Miller, who, in 1953, went on to write *The Crucible,* a play that condemns informing and witch hunts. In 1963, Kazan and Miller reconciled when they were named resident director and resident playwright for the premier season of New York's Lincoln Center, and Kazan directed Miller's autobiographical *After the Fall.* In 1988, Kazan published his autobiography, *Elia Kazan, A Life.* He later received a Lifetime Achievement Award from the Motion Picture Academy, but even then, almost 50 years later, his testimony before HUAC provoked passionate reactions by supporters and critics.

Kerouac Jack (Jean Louis Kerouac)
(1922–1969) *novelist*

Born Jean Louis Kerouac to working-class, French-Canadian parents in Lowell, Massachusetts, Kerouac spoke a French-Canadian dialect as his first language until he attended a parochial school run by Jesuits. He studied at Columbia University on a football scholarship in 1939, but broke his leg and dropped out. He subsequently joined first the Merchant Marines and then the U.S. Navy, but he was discharged for reasons of personal character. In 1944, Kerouac met William Burroughs and Allen Ginsberg while passing time on the Columbia University campus, and he soon adopted their Bohemian lifestyle. In the late 1940s, he and Neal Cassady, another member of the group, took a number of car trips around the country. These later became the basis for Kerouac's most famous novel, *On the Road* (1957), which he wrote in a frenetic three-week writing session. He composed the manuscript by typing on a continuous, 120-foot roll of paper that he fed into his typewriter. The book was an instant hit, and Kerouac suddenly found himself a leader of an antiauthoritarian literary movement known as Beat—a term Kerouac coined in 1952 to describe the down-and-out members of his generation. The Beats rejected not only middle-class American values and modes of behavior, they also repudiated the modernist literary tradition of highly cerebral, highly structured literary forms and sought to open up poetry and other forms of literature to a broader, less culturally elite readership—to take poetry and fiction out of the universities and into the streets. Moreover, unlike the literary modernists of the 1920s and 1930s, who tended to be politically conservative and desirous of sustaining social order, the Beats expressed leftist values, concerned themselves with the experiences of the underclass, and embraced the concept of perpetual change. In addition, Kerouac's writing shows the influence of jazz, bebop, and Buddhism, which also expresses a philosophy predicated on change and impermanence. His interest in Eastern philosophy is apparent in his fiction, which includes several additional works from the 1950s: *The Dharma Bums* (1958), *The Subterraneans* (1958), *Doctor Sax* (1959), *Excerpts from Visions of Cody* (1959), *Maggie Cassidy* (1959), and *Mexico City Blues* (1959).

King, Martin Luther, Jr. (1929–1968) *Baptist minister, civil rights leader*

Born in Atlanta to a Baptist minister and his wife, King enrolled in Morehouse College at age 15, in a special program for gifted children. He received his bachelor's degree in 1948, the same year that he entered the ministry, at the behest of his father. He then attended the Crozer Theological Seminary in Chester, Pennsylvania, where he was elected president of the student body and where he became familiar with Mohandas Gandhi's philosophy of nonviolent social protest. King received a Bachelor of Divinity in 1951, then attended Boston University, where he was influenced by theologian Paul Tillich, who became the subject of King's doctoral dissertation. He was awarded his Ph.D. in 1955.

While he was studying in Boston, he met Coretta Scott, whom he married in 1953 and with whom he had four children. They moved to Montgomery, Alabama, where King became pastor of the Dexter Avenue Baptist Church. On December 5, 1955, four days after Rosa Parks was arrested for refusing to surrender her seat on a public bus to a white person, King delivered a powerful speech in support of a bus boycott in Montgomery, which, a year later, proved successful after the Supreme Court declared segregation of public transportation unconstitutional. In the interim, King, who began putting into practice his version of Gandhi's nonviolent activism, was arrested for violating a city ordinance against boycotts, and his house was bombed.

King, whose activism was informed by his Christianity, subsequently organized the Southern Christian Leadership Conference to promote a larger civil rights agenda throughout the country. He remained active in civil rights causes throughout the 1960s. The apex of his career came in August 1963, when he organized a massive march on Washington, D.C., in opposition to racial discrimination and delivered his famous "I Have a Dream" speech before thousands of supporters. These efforts played a large role in the passage of the 1964 Civil Rights Act, which outlawed racial discrimination in public housing and in employment. That year, he was awarded the Nobel Peace Prize. King was assassinated in Memphis on April 4, 1968.

LeMay, Curtis (1906–1990) *U.S. Air Force vice chief of staff (1957–1961)*

Educated at Ohio State University's School of Engineering, LeMay was commissioned as a second lieutenant in the U.S. Army Air Corps in 1930. He rose steadily through the ranks, becoming a major general in 1937. During World War II, he helped formulate tactics in the European theater and planned the B-29 fire bombings of Tokyo in the final months of the war. Afterward, he headed the U.S. Air Force in Europe and helped direct the Berlin airlift of 1948–49. In fall 1948, he returned to the United States to head the Strategic Air Command (SAC), a position he retained even after his promotion to U.S. Air Force vice chief of staff in 1957. Throughout the 1950s, LeMay warned of a "bomber gap" between the United States and Soviet Union and predicted that the United States would become increasingly vulnerable to a Soviet attack unless it invested further in air power. He also sought the development of reliable intercontinental ballistic missiles (ICBMs), and some of his statements gave credence to the loudly proclaimed but erroneous assertion in the late 1950s that the Soviet Union had acquired missile superiority.

MacArthur, Douglas (1880–1964) *commander of UN forces in Korea (1950–1951)*

Born in Little Rock, Arkansas, the son of a Union army general, MacArthur attended the U.S. Military Academy at West Point, where he graduated first in the class of 1903. During World War I, he was highly decorated for his bravery, and in 1918, he was promoted to brigadier general. In 1930, he became a four-star general and the youngest U.S. Army chief of staff in history. Four months prior to the Japanese attack on Pearl Harbor, he was promoted to commander of army forces in the Far East. After the U.S. entry into the war in December 1941, MacArthur led the fight against the Japanese on the Philippines; however, in March President Franklin D. Roosevelt ordered him to evacuate to Australia, where he became commander of the Allied forces in the southwest Pacific and was subsequently promoted to five-star general. As supreme commander of the Allied powers in the Pacific, MacArthur accepted the Japanese surrender aboard the U.S. battleship *Missouri*. After the war, he was appointed to administer the U.S. military occupation of Japan.

After the Korean War began, MacArthur charged that the Truman administration had ignored his warnings of an impending North Korean invasion; nonetheless, Truman appointed him commander-in-chief of United Nations armies in Korea. Initially, the outnumbered UN troops were driven back and pinned within the Pusan perimeter; however, MacArthur implemented a daring and successful landing behind enemy lines at Inchon on September 15, 1950, and then took the offensive. Confident that communist China would not enter the war, MacArthur predicted final victory by the new year, but in late November, with the UN armies deep into North Korea, Chinese armies invaded and quickly drove the outnumbered UN troops back to the 38th parallel that divided the two Koreas. Arguing that "there is no substitute for victory," MacArthur urged Truman to authorize the bombing of Chinese supply depots in Manchuria and destruction of bridges over the Yalu River, which separates China from North Korea. Truman preferred to fight a limited war rather than risk provoking an all-out war that might eventually involve the Soviets and evolve into World War III, and MacArthur's public criticisms of administration policy angered Truman. On April 5, 1951, Representative Joseph Martin read on the floor of Congress a letter MacArthur had written him objecting to the administration's pursuit of a limited war. Truman regarded the letter as an act of insubordination and fired MacArthur on April 11.

Despite MacArthur's immense popularity on his return from Korea and his dramatic farewell appearance before Congress soon after, he was unable to remain a major political figure after his retirement. In 1952, he gave the keynote address at the Republican National Convention, but his bid for the Republican nomination that year was squelched by another World War II military hero, Dwight Eisenhower.

McCarran, Patrick A. (1876–1954) *Democratic senator from Nevada (1933–1947, 1949–1953)*
Born in Reno, Nevada, McCarran graduated from the University of Nevada in 1901, after which he began ranching and studying law in his spare time. Between 1903 and 1932, he established a law practice and subsequently was elected to the Nevada Supreme Court; in 1932, he was elected to the U.S. Senate, where he soon joined the conservative anti–New Deal contingent. During the late 1940s and early 1950s, McCarran led a bipartisan coalition of conservatives who passed a number of anticommunist bills. McCarran was also an outspoken critic of Truman's China policy, which gave only token support to Chiang Kai-shek's Chinese Nationalists. Like Senator Joseph McCarthy, McCarran criticized the State Department, and McCarran was one of McCarthy's few Democratic supporters. He unsuccessfully fought the Senate's attempts to condemn McCarthy in late 1954. McCarran died shortly thereafter from a heart attack he suffered while addressing a political rally in Nevada.

McCarthy, Joseph R. (1909–1957) *Republican senator from Wisconsin (1947–1957)*
McCarthy was one of the most powerful and most feared politicians during the early 1950s, and his aggressive, often reckless pursuit of alleged communists and communist sympathizers gave rise to the term *McCarthyism*. He grew up on his father's farm in northwestern Wisconsin and quit school after the eighth grade to become a chicken farmer; however, he returned at age 19 and completed four years of high school work in a single year. He then attended Marquette University and he received his law degree in 1935. When World War II broke out McCarthy waived his deferment and enlisted in the marines. In 1946, McCarthy ran for the U.S. Senate, defeating incumbent Robert La Follette, Jr., to win the Republican nomination, and then beating the Democratic nominee in the general election.

He first rose to national prominence on February 9, 1950, about a month after the perjury conviction of Alger Hiss, when he maintained in a speech in Wheeling, West Virginia, that the State Department's failures in China stemmed from treason and that ranking members of the department were Soviet agents. Holding up a copy of a 1946 letter, McCarthy declared, "I have here in my hand a list of 205" members of the

Communist Party who, although known to the State Department, "nevertheless are still working and shaping the [department's] policy." The accusation created an immediate furor, and the Senate appointed a Foreign Relations Subcommittee to investigate. Chaired by Democrat Millard Tydings, the committee tried unsuccessfully to discredit McCarthy. Testifying before the committee, McCarthy named 10 people from his list including Ambassador at Large Philip Jessup and China scholar Owen Lattimore, who was then a professor at Johns Hopkins University. All of the accused protested their innocence, and the committee ultimately exonerated them. None was ever found guilty of treason. Although Tydings's committee labeled McCarthy "a fraud and a hoax," McCarthy repeated his charges on radio and television. When called upon to produce his evidence, he refused, adding new accusations instead. McCarthy emerged from the controversy as a chief spokesman for the growing anticommunist contingent, and from that national base of support, he became a powerful and prominent member of the Republican Party.

Between February 1950, when he gave the speech in Wheeling, West Virginia, and spring 1954, when the Senate held hearings to investigate charges against him by the U.S. Army, McCarthy remained virtually impervious to attacks by his critics. He savagely attacked the State Department and General George Marshall, the World War II hero who was Truman's secretary of state during the late 1940s and secretary of defense during the Korean War. McCarthy won reelection in 1952 and became chairman of the Government Operations Committee, the Senate's permanent subcommittee for investigations. He used this position to conduct hearings into allegations of communist subversion in numerous areas. Despite the fact that a Republican administration was now in power, he continued his attacks on the State Department, and in 1953, he first accused the army of concealing communist activity, charging it was protecting communists at the Fort Monmouth Army Signal Corps Center. In early 1954, he accused World War II hero General Ralph Zwicker of "coddling" communists after Zwicker refused to discipline the commander of Camp Kilmer who approved a routine promotion to a leftist dentist. During the investigation of Camp Kilmer, McCarthy also criticized U.S. Army secretary Robert Stevens so savagely that Stevens offered to resign.

In April 1954, with Eisenhower's approval, the army fought back, and the resulting U.S. Army–McCarthy hearings led to the senator's political downfall. The army charged that McCarthy tried to blackmail the army by threatening to conduct further investigations unless the senator's recently drafted aide, David Schine, was commissioned as an officer. In response to these accusations, the Senate opened new televised hearings. Even though the Republican-controlled committee ultimately exonerated McCarthy, the widely viewed hearings led to his political downfall. The American public saw McCarthy's intimidating style, his threats, his incessant use of points of order and points of personal privilege to confuse his opponents, and his incoherent ranting. McCarthy's conduct during the army hearings, along with questionable financial dealings and other improprieties, provoked the Senate to condemn him on December 2, 1954. (The language of the motion uses the term *condemn,* not *censure,* which led McCarthy to claim that he had not been censured, even after William Fulbright read on the Senate floor a dictionary definition of *censure* as meaning "to condemn.") Although McCarthy remained in the Senate until his death in 1957, after the condemnation, he was no longer a significant force in American politics.

McCarthy, Mary (1912–1989) *writer*
McCarthy was born in Seattle to an affluent Irish-Catholic father and a half-Jewish mother. Her parents died in the influenza epidemic of 1918, and McCarthy was raised by a severe great-aunt on her father's side. At age 11, she was sent away to be educated at a convent. McCarthy recounts her childhood experiences in her nonfiction book *Memories of a Catholic Girlhood* (1957). She graduated from Vassar College in 1933 and soon began writing for such liberal political magazines as the *Nation* and the *New Republic.* During the Great Depression, McCarthy associated with left-wing intellectuals but remained aloof from the Communist Party, which she denounced after World War II. In 1938, she married writer-critic Edmund Wilson but divorced him in 1946 and married Bowden Broadwater, who worked for the leftist *Partisan Review.* Based on her personal experiences and acquaintances, her award-winning novel *The Oasis* (1949) satirizes a group of liberals who try to create an ideal society atop a mountain. *The Groves of Academe* (1952) was written and set

during the Red Scare, and it, too, satirizes liberals. In 1959, the State Department sponsored a tour of Poland, Yugoslavia, and Britain in which McCarthy developed lectures on "The Fact in Fiction" and "Characters in Fiction." She later collected these essays in *On the Contrary* (1961). During this period, her marriage to Broadwater dissolved, and in 1961, McCarthy married James West, a State Department officer whom she had met during the tour. Other works from the 1950s include the novel *A Charmed Life* (1955) and *The Stones of Florence* (1959), a well-respected travel guide to the city.

Mailer, Norman (1923–) *writer*
Born in Long Branch, New Jersey, to a Jewish family, Mailer grew up in New York City and graduated from Harvard in 1943 with a degree in engineering. He served in the U.S. Army during World War II, and his experiences formed the basis of his first novel, *The Naked and the Dead* (1948), which explores the differences in background, personal styles, and philosophies of a conservative general and his liberal aide. For both men, historical events prove to be less subject to individual control than they had assumed. In Mailer's second novel, *The Barbary Shore* (1951), the rational universe breaks down even further, as the amnesiac narrator cannot distinguish fact from fiction or memory from imagination. Communism proves bankrupt in the book, as does American culture, and the protagonist must find meaning beyond the failed institutions of politics and religion. Mailer, who claimed to be attempting to bridge Marx and Freud, insists on the connections between sex and other psychological and political issues and on the importance of representing history in personal terms. He addresses similar themes in his next novel, *The Deer Park* (1955). In 1955, Mailer also helped found the *Village Voice* to provide an outlet for nontraditional voices. Mailer remained a major literary figure throughout the remainder of the 20th century, as he consciously interweaved his own life with his fiction, virtually insisting that his readers and the public at large respond to him personally, as well as to his work.

Miller, Arthur (1915–) *playwright*
Miller was born in Harlem to a family of Jewish immigrants of Austro-Hungarian descent. He graduated from high school with a poor academic record but after reading Fyodor Dostoyevsky's *Brothers Kara-*

mazov, decided to become a writer. He entered the University of Michigan in 1934, where he studied drama and won awards for his plays. In 1937, he and Tennessee Williams were each awarded the Theater Guild Bureau of New Plays Prize. The pair went on to become the dominant American playwrights of the late 1940s and 1950s, and arguably of the 20th century.

Miller's first play to be produced professionally, *The Man Who Had All the Luck,* closed after just four performances in 1944. But he explored father-son dynamics more successfully in his next two plays, *All My Sons,* a 1947 tragedy about a corrupt wartime defense contractor, and *Death of a Salesman* (1949), which is widely regarded as one of America's outstanding dramas from any period. Elia Kazan directed and Lee J. Cobb starred in the Broadway production, which opened to rave reviews. The tragedy revolves around a good but flawed, hard-working salesman whose family is destroyed because of his sexual infidelity and misplaced values that emphasize outer appearances over inner virtue.

In 1951, Miller and Kazan tried to interest Columbia Pictures in his screenplay *The Hook,* but the studio turned it down when Miller refused to change the corrupt union officials to communists. Eventually *The Hook* became the basis for Kazan's film *On the Waterfront.* Miller's collaboration with Kazan temporarily ended in 1952, when Kazan identified Communist Party members before the House Un-American Activities Committee (HUAC). Miller had tried to dissuade Kazan from testifying, and shortly thereafter he began writing *The Crucible* (1953), a story about the 17th-century Salem witch hunts that is widely read as an allegory about the Red Scare and the practice of informing on one's fellow citizens—although Miller has always resisted such a narrow reading of the play. Miller later wrote the screenplay for Nicholas Hytner's outstanding film adaptation of *The Crucible* (1996), which stars Daniel Day-Lewis and Winona Ryder. *A View from the Bridge* (1955), a tragedy about an immigrant who informs on an illegal alien and consequently dies because of it, also condemns the practice of informing. Other plays from the 1950s include *Enemy of the People* (1950), an adaptation of Henrik Ibsen's drama, and *A Memory of Two Mondays* (1955).

Already blacklisted for his political beliefs, Miller, who had never been a communist, was subpoenaed to testify before HUAC in 1956. Although willing to tell the committee about his own activities and beliefs, he refused to discuss anyone else or identify anyone he believed to be a communist. Because he did not invoke the Fifth Amendment, he was guilty of contempt of Congress and faced a jail sentence; however, he was only fined $500 and given a 30-day suspended sentence. About a week after his testimony, Miller married actress Marilyn Monroe, but they divorced some five years later. Miller wrote the screenplay for John Huston's *The Misfits* (1961), in which Monroe starred; it was her last movie before her death in 1962. In 1963, Miller and Kazan reconciled, and Kazan directed Miller's play *After the Fall,* which centers on a former communist who breaks with a friend who is about to inform before a congressional committee. One of the characters is based on Monroe. Miller remained an active playwright throughout the rest of the 20th century, but his later work never achieved the stature of *Death of a Salesman* or *The Crucible.*

Monroe, Marilyn (Norma Jean Mortenson, Norma Jean Baker) (1926–1962) *film actress*

Born in Los Angeles as Norma Jean Mortenson (also known as Norma Jean Baker), Monroe went on to become the predominate female sex symbol of the 1950s and remains a major cultural icon. She was raised in 12 different foster homes and an orphanage and was first married in 1942, at age 16. She divorced shortly after World War II and supported herself as a popular photographers' model. In 1946, she assumed the name Marilyn Monroe after signing a short-term contract with Twentieth Century Fox, but her film career failed to develop at that time. Consequently, she returned to modeling but was rediscovered by Howard Hughes and Darryl Zanuck after she posed nude for a men's calendar. Zanuck felt that she was especially photogenic and that her flesh, in particular, projected effectively on screen. After her hair was dyed platinum and her chin was surgically reconstructed, Monroe landed her first role, a minor part in *Scudda Hoo, Scudda Hay* (1948). She had additional small roles in several other films from the late 1940s and early 1950s, including *The Asphalt Jungle* (1950) and *All About Eve* (1950). Monroe's film career took off after she was given a starring role as a neurotic wife in Henry Hathaway's *Niagara* (1952). She won praise for that performance

and appeared on the cover of *Life* magazine in April 1952. But she truly became a star after her role as Lorelei Lee in Howard Hawk's delightful musical comedy *Gentlemen Prefer Blondes* (1953), in which she costarred with Jane Russell and performed the hit song and dance routine "Diamonds Are a Girl's Best Friend." The same year, she costarred with Lauren Bacall and Betty Grable in another comedy, *How to Marry a Millionaire,* which plays off a similar theme of the lovable female gold digger.

When Hugh Hefner used an earlier photo from her modeling days for the nude centerfold in the premiere issue of *Playboy* magazine, in December 1953, many observers believed Monroe's career would be destroyed; instead, the exposure enhanced her reputation as a sex idol. She went on to star in *River of No Return,* a dramatic role costarring Robert Mitchum, and *There's No Business Like Show Business* (1954). In 1954, Monroe married and divorced her second husband, baseball star Joe DiMaggio, and their short-lived union attracted intense public attention.

Wanting to transcend the image of a sex goddess with limited talent, Monroe took time off in 1955 to become a more accomplished actress. She studied with Lee Strasberg at the renowned Actors Theater, where she met her third husband, playwright Arthur Miller, to whom she was married from 1956 to 1961. Her subsequent films were mostly comedies, which was her strongest acting talent. These include Billy Wilder's *The Seven-Year Itch* (1955); *The Prince and the Showgirl* (1957), a British-made film comedy directed by and costarring Laurence Olivier; *Some Like It Hot* (1959), Wilder's movie about cross-dressing jazz musicians fleeing from gangsters in the 1920s, costarring Tony Curtis and Jack Lemmon; and George Cukor's *Let's Make Love* (1960). In addition, she starred in Joshua's Logan's adaptation of William Inge's play *Bus Stop* (1956) and John Huston's *The Misfits* (1961), for which Miller wrote the screenplay.

In addition to being a world-famous movie star and the quintessential female sex idol of the 1950s, Monroe attracted public interest through the rumors of her affairs with John F. Kennedy and other powerful and influential men of the late 1950s and early 1960s. In spite of, or because of, her fame, she suffered from severe bouts of unhappiness and depression, and in 1962, in what is widely assumed to be a suicide, she died in her home from an overdose of sleeping pills.

Murrow, Edward R. (1908–1965) *television journalist*

Born in Greensboro, North Carolina, Murrow attended Washington State College (now University) at Pullman. In 1935, he joined the Columbia Broadcasting System (CBS) as a radio correspondent and in 1937 moved to London to head its European bureau. In that capacity, he won respect from the public and professionals alike for his radio coverage of events leading up to and during World War II. His on-the-scene reports of the German bombings of London during the Battle of Britain were especially memorable. After the war, Murrow returned to the United States, where CBS made him vice president in charge of news, education, and discussion programming.

On November 18, 1951, Murrow and producer Fred Friendly introduced the half-hour news program *See It Now,* in which Murrow interviewed world leaders and provided in-depth reporting on important issues. On the opening broadcast, as he showed a split screen featuring real-time shots of the Brooklyn Bridge and the Golden Gate Bridge, Murrow described to his audience the power of the new medium, which he described as a powerful "weapon for truth." At a time when American television was reluctant to engage in political controversy or challenge the power of Senator Joseph McCarthy, Murrow did so. His most significant broadcast, "A Report on Senator Joseph R. McCarthy" (March 9, 1954), was the first time that network television directly addressed McCarthy's reckless demagoguery. Murrow's documentary exposé of McCarthy has since come to be regarded as one of the high points in television journalism.

After the demise of *See It Now* in July 1958, Murrow remained another year at CBS hosting *Person to Person,* a show he inaugurated in 1953, in which he would interview various celebrities who were sitting in their homes while Murrow was in his studio. Interviewees included Fidel Castro, Speaker of the House Sam Rayburn, Senator John F. Kennedy, and such movie stars as Marilyn Monroe and Zsa Zsa Gabor. On CBS's *Small World* (1958–60), Murrow held four-way telephone conversations with political and cultural figures throughout the world.

Murrow left CBS in 1961, when he became head of the U.S. Information Agency from 1961 to 1964. A notorious chain smoker, Murrow died from cancer in 1965 at the age of 57.

Nixon, Richard M. (1913–1994) *Republican congressman, senator, vice president (1953–1961), U.S. president (1969–1974)*

Born in Yorba Linda, California, to a middle-class Quaker family, Nixon received his bachelor's degree from Whittier College in 1934 and a law degree from Duke University in 1937. At the beginning of World War II, he worked for eight months at the Office of Price Administration, an experience that forever disillusioned him about government bureaucracy. He served in the South Pacific as a noncombat naval officer from 1942 to 1945. In 1946, Nixon was elected to Congress, where he served on the House Un-American Activities Committee (HUAC) and earned a reputation for his probes into alleged communist infiltration of the federal government. His role in the investigation of Alger Hiss brought him national prominence.

In 1950, Nixon defeated incumbent senator Helen G. Douglas, a Democrat who, he claimed, "follows the Communist Party line" and was "pink right down to her underwear." Dwight Eisenhower selected him for his vice presidential running mate in 1952, in an effort to appeal to the Republican Party's right wing. He was almost dropped from the ticket following allegations of financial improprieties, but Nixon generated overwhelming public support when he defended himself on national television in a speech now known as the "Checkers speech"—so named for his children's gift cocker spaniel, which he maintained he would never give back. Eisenhower and Nixon went on to defeat the Democrats in a landslide.

As vice president, Nixon contributed little to policy formulation, although he made several trips overseas and worked closely with the Republican Party. He resisted attempts by the party to replace him on the ticket when Eisenhower ran for reelection in 1956. In May 1958, he and his wife, Pat, were attacked by anti-American demonstrators in Peru and Venezuela while on a goodwill tour of Latin America. In response, Eisenhower placed soldiers in the Caribbean on a standby alert to protect them. In July 1959, during a lull in the ongoing Berlin crisis, Nixon opened the American National Exhibition in Moscow, and he and Soviet premier Nikita Khrushchev toured an American-style ranch house together. In what became known as the "kitchen debate," Nixon and Khrushchev argued before a large following of reporters and television cameras about the relative merits of each country's economic system.

Nixon received the 1960 Republican nomination for president but lost a close election to John F. Kennedy. In 1962, he ran unsuccessfully for governor of California and after his defeat declared that the press would not "have Nixon to kick around anymore." However, he remained active in the Republican Party and in 1968 beat out California's governor, Ronald Reagan, for the Republican presidential nomination. Claiming to possess a "secret plan" to end the increasingly unpopular Vietnam War, Nixon won a narrow victory over Vice President Hubert Humphrey. He won reelection overwhelmingly in 1972 but was forced to resign from office in 1974, following revelations of his involvement in the cover-up of the Watergate scandal. His successor, Gerald Ford, immediately granted Nixon an unconditional blanket pardon that forestalled any further criminal investigations. The only president to resign before completing his term, Nixon rehabilitated his reputation in the 1980s and 1990s, as he tried with some success to assume the role of elder statesman.

Parker, Charlie (1920–1955) *jazz musician*

Affectionately known to his friends and admirers as Yardbird, or just Bird, because of his penchant for fried chicken, Parker was born in Kansas City. He turned to music as a way of life at a young age and in 1939 moved to New York to join the jazz scene there. A saxophonist, Parker was engaged by a new form of improvisation that stressed dissonance, and he developed a style he called formulaic improvisation that keeps the listener wondering how the melody and rhythms will develop. Between 1942 and 1945, Parker played with trumpeter Dizzy Gillespie, with whom he made several recordings and developed the energetic jazz style called bop. Another collaborator, Thelonious Monk, also contributed to the development of bop. Trumpetist Miles Davis also worked with Parker during the late 1940s and early 1950s and, although Davis went on to develop his own "cool jazz," he remained influenced by Parker, as was almost every major saxophonist to follow. A passionate innovator, Parker is still regarded as one of the greatest jazz musicians of the 20th century. He introduced elements of African-American folk music to his compositions, but he was also aware of other developments in modern music, and he often based his numbers on

a 12-bar blues formula that used a limited range of harmonies.

Parker suffered from alcohol and drug abuse, and his career deteriorated in the early 1950s as he fell deeper under their influence. He attempted suicide in 1954, after the death of his daughter, and in 1955, he died of pneumonia and cirrhosis of the liver, afflictions that probably emanated from his excessive use of heroin and alcohol.

Pollock, Jackson (1912–1956) *artist*

Born in Cody, Wyoming, Pollock studied art at Manual Arts High School in Los Angeles, where initially he planned to become a sculptor, before he turned to painting. Before graduating from high school, he moved to New York in 1929 to study with Thomas Benton at the Art Student's League. His first New York show took place in 1940, at the McMillan Gallery, where his work appeared with that of Willem de Kooning and Leonore (Lee) Krasner, who went on to become both his artistic confidant and adviser, and, in 1944, his wife. Pollock had his first one-man show in 1943 at the gallery of Peggy Guggenheim and Howard Putzel and continued to exhibit there every year until 1947, when the gallery closed. Through 1953, he continued to have one-man shows at other galleries and museums. A major inspiration in the development of American abstract expressionism, Pollock was known for his "action paintings" in which he would express pure emotion by pouring, or violently hurling, paint onto the canvas. He died in a car crash on August 11, 1956.

Presley, Elvis (1935–1977) *rock 'n' roll star*

Born to a poor family in Tupelo, Mississippi, Presley became the dominant rock 'n' roll star of the 1950s, and since his death in 1977, he remains a major cultural icon. Presley's family moved to Memphis, when he was a teenager. He soon began performing and recording blues and country songs and gospel hymns. Because he sometimes attended a biracial Pentecostal church with his parents and frequented Memphis blues clubs, he soon became familiar with African-American music, which he later incorporated into his own sound.

His first significant recording was of Arthur Crudup's song "That's All Right (Mama)" in July 1954. In 1955, Colonel Tom Parker became Presley's manager and promoter, and his rise to stardom soon followed. In 1956, Presley had his first hit songs—"Heartbreak Hotel," "I Want You, I Need You, I Love You," "Don't Be Cruel," "Hound Dog," and "Love Me Tender"—and he went on to dominate the popular charts between 1956 and 1958, when he was dubbed "the King" of rock 'n' roll. His stature was further enhanced by his appearances on television and in the movies. He first appeared on television in January 1956, on Jimmy Dorsey's *Stage Show,* but he is best remembered for his appearances on the popular *Ed Sullivan Show* in fall and winter 1956 and January 1957. At the last appearance, Sullivan introduced Presley as a fine, wholesome young man but appeased critics of the singer's "lascivious" hip-grinding motion by filming him only from the waist up. This reinforced another popular nickname, "Elvis the Pelvis."

In 1956, Presley began his film career when he starred in Robert D. Webb's *Love Me Tender.* He made his second and third movies the following year, Hal Kanter's *Loving You* and Richard Thorpe's *Jailhouse Rock,* for which Presley received praise for his spirited choreography of the title song, which became a top hit. *Jailhouse Rock* established Presley's image as a rebel with a guitar, but in March 1958, he willingly complied with his draft notice and elected to serve as a private in the army in Germany, rather than join the entertainment division of the Special Services. He was stationed in Germany when the second Berlin crisis began, and he served there until 1960, during some of its tensest moments.

Upon his return to civilian life in 1960, Presley's career picked up pretty much where it had left off before his induction. He had several more hit songs and starred in numerous movies. He also acquired a flashier image and made frequent appearances at Las Vegas clubs. Presley did not connect well with the 1960s counterculture, whose lack of patriotism disturbed him and whose hard rock and psychedelic orientation were foreign to him. In the last years of his life, Presley abused prescription drugs, which were believed to be the cause of the heart attack that killed him on August 16, 1977.

Reagan, Ronald W. (1911–   )
president of the Screen Actors Guild (1947–1951, 1959), governor of California (1967–1975), U.S. president (1981–1989)
Born in Tampico, Illinois, to a working-class family, Reagan graduated from Eureka College in 1932. He worked as a radio sports announcer before beginning a career as a movie actor in 1937. As a liberal Democrat in the 1930s and 1940s, he supported Franklin D. Roosevelt. He served as an officer during World War II, making army training films and attaining the rank of captain. By the 1950s, Reagan's political orientation had turned to the right, and he endorsed the Dwight Eisenhower–Richard Nixon ticket in 1952. He served as president of the Screen Actors Guild from 1947 to 1951 and again in 1959. In that capacity, he contributed to the conservative effort to eliminate communists and communist sympathizers from the Hollywood film industry. In addition to his national exposure as a movie star, he gained further public recognition in 1954, when he began hosting the popular television dramatic anthology *General Electric Theater,* a position he occupied through 1962.

In 1962, Reagan became a Republican and in 1964 campaigned for Barry Goldwater. In 1966 he was elected governor of California, promising to crack down on campus radicals protesting the Vietnam War, eliminate welfare fraud, and reduce taxes. He easily won reelection in 1970 and in 1980, was elected president, despite concerns that at age 69 he was too old for the job. He was reelected in 1984, and he left office as one of the most revered and most vilified presidents in the 20th century.

Robeson, Paul (1898–1976) *singer, film actor*
Born in Princeton, New Jersey, Robeson was the son of an ex-slave who had escaped and later joined the Union army in the Civil War before becoming a Protestant minister. His mother was a teacher of African, Indian, and English descent. Robeson won a competitive scholarship to Rutgers College (later Rutgers University) in 1915 and became only the third black student in that institution's history. Robeson was popular at the school, where he won prizes for his oratory and earned 12 varsity letters in four sports: football, baseball, basketball, and track. He entered Columbia University Law School in 1920, paying his way by playing professional football. He also began his acting career while in law school, first appearing in amateur college performances and then on the professional stage. He graduated in 1923, but after practicing law for a short time, Robeson turned instead to singing and theater. Prior to World War II, he toured the United States, England, and Europe singing Negro spirituals and folk songs, and he

released more than 300 recordings. Although he had substantial roles in 10 movies between 1924 and 1942, Robeson largely abandoned the medium because the Hollywood film industry was not interested in depicting the people and issues that were important to him. In 1934, he visited the Soviet Union for the first time and was impressed by the social experimentation and examples of racial equality he witnessed there.

In the late 1940s and 1950s, Robeson, who was active in left-wing causes, fell victim to the Red Scare. He was blacklisted on television and in film, his records were removed from stores, and newspaper editorials frequently denounced him. In response, Robeson reaffirmed his support for the Soviet Union and declared at the 1949 World Peace Congress in Paris that black Americans would not fight against the Soviet Union. In 1950, the State Department ordered him to surrender his passport and refused to issue him a new one unless he swore that he was not a communist and promised not to give political speeches abroad. Robeson refused on principle and challenged the State Department's action in court. He eventually prevailed in 1958, when the Supreme Court ruled in a similar case that the government's actions were unconstitutional. However, during the eight-year period of his appeal Robeson was unable to work abroad, where he could still attract enthusiastic audiences, and he was blacklisted at home.

Robeson was an outspoken opponent of anti-Semitism in the Soviet Union, and he shocked a Moscow audience in 1949 when he ended a concert with a song celebrating the Jewish Warsaw uprising against the Nazis during World War II. When he regained his passport in 1958, the Red Scare had subsided somewhat, and he was able to give a farewell performance at New York's Carnegie Hall and make a short tour of the West Coast before leaving the United States. While visiting the Soviet Union in 1959, he fell ill from exhaustion and a circulatory ailment and was hospitalized off and on in Moscow, Eastern Europe, and London until his return to the United States in 1963.

Rosenberg, Ethel (1915–1953) and
Julius Rosenberg (1918–1953) *American spies for the Soviet Union*
Born in New York City, both Ethel and Julius Rosenberg grew up on the Lower East Side, the children of Jewish workers in the garment industry. Ethel graduated high school in 1931, attended a stenography course, and then secured a low-paying office job. After becoming active in her union she was fired for organizing a strike. Julius attended the City College of New York (CCNY) and received a degree in electrical engineering in 1939. As a teen, he had become interested in radical politics and became a member of the Communist Party while at CCNY. In 1939, he married Ethel, also a Communist Party member, and took a job as civilian junior engineer in the U.S. Army Signal Corps. Ethel became a housewife and mother. Julius remained in the Signal Corps until 1945, when he was fired for his communist views. Afterward, he operated a small machine shop with David Greenglass, Ethel's brother.

On June 16, 1950, nine days before the outbreak of the Korean War, FBI agents arrested the Rosenbergs and charged them with leading a Soviet spy ring that included British physicist Klaus Fuchs, who had already been arrested and had admitted his guilt. Also charged were Harry Gold, Morton Sobell, and David Greenglass. They were charged with stealing technical information about the atomic bomb between 1944 and 1945, while it was under development in Los Alamos, New Mexico. Gold and Greenglass confessed their guilt, but Sobell and the Rosenbergs steadfastly proclaimed their innocence; nonetheless, on March 29, 1951, a federal jury convicted them. Judge Irving Kaufman sentenced Sobell to 30 years in prison and Greenglass to 15. Believing the Rosenbergs to have headed the spy ring, he sentenced the couple to death, declaring that they had facilitated the Soviet development of the bomb, which in turn had emboldened the Soviets to authorize the Korean War, in which thousands of Americans had died.

The Rosenbergs appealed the conviction, arguing that the espionage statute was vague and that Kaufman had been prejudiced in favor of the prosecution. In 1952, the Federal Court of Appeals rejected the Rosenbergs' appeal. Later that year, the Supreme Court unanimously turned down a further appeal. After the Supreme Court overturned a last-minute stay of execution that Justice William O. Douglas had granted, the Rosenbergs were executed in New York state's Sing Sing prison on June 19, 1953. Although they went to their deaths steadfastly maintaining their innocence, in July 1995 the Central Intelligence

Agency (CIA) released documents from the Venona Project that decoded secret cables to the Soviet Union from suspected spies in the 1940s. These documents clearly indicate the Rosenbergs' complicity, although Ethel's role was limited. Many historians believe that her actions, which largely involved typing notes, did not merit the death penalty but that she was charged with a capital crime in order to pressure Julius into confessing.

St. Laurent, Louis (1882–1973) *prime minister of Canada (1948–1957)*

While the United States was under conservative leadership through most of the 1950s, Canada was led by a Liberal government headed by St. Laurent, who was also the nation's first French-speaking prime minister. Born in Compton, Quebec, St. Laurent studied at St. Charles College and Laval University, and in the early part of the 20th century, he was one of Canada's leading lawyers. He was first elected to the House of Commons in 1942 and was continually reelected as representative from East Quebec until his retirement in 1950. St. Laurent was elected leader of the Liberal Party in 1948 and became prime minister that year. During his time in office, he supported Canada's involvement in the Korean War, brought Newfoundland into the Dominion, and expanded the government's commitment to social security, university education, and the arts and letters. He also enhanced pensions and health insurance. In conjunction with U.S. president Dwight Eisenhower's administration, he initiated construction of the St. Lawrence Seaway in 1954 and cooperated in the mutual defense of North America. In 1956, he overcame political opposition to establish equalization payments to the provinces, and that year his administration played an important role in resolving the Suez Canal crisis.

While St. Laurent was prime minister, Canada paid off its wartime debts and prospered economically. His government won election by large margins in 1949 and 1953, but in 1957, although St. Laurent was personally reelected, the Liberals lost to the Conservatives, and he was succeeded as prime minister by Progressive Conservative Party leader John G. Diefenbaker, who held office from 1957 to 1963. St. Laurent remained leader of the opposition until 1958, when he stepped down in favor of Lester B. Pearson. He retired from public office in 1960.

Saint Laurent, Yves (1936–   ) *fashion designer*

Saint Laurent was born in Algiers of French parents. In 1954, he won first prize for his design of a cocktail dress in an international competition. The following year, he went to work for Christian Dior, who was then the most famous designer in the Western world. He took over Dior's fashion house in 1957, after Dior died. Saint Laurent's "Trapeze" dress of 1958 and other popular, youth-oriented styles stirred controversy among Dior's more conservative clients, and in 1961, Saint Laurent was replaced by Marc Bohan. In 1962, he founded his own successful house, which introduced the smoking jacket, see-through blouses, thigh-length boots for women, and safari jackets for men.

Sheen, Fulton J. (1895–1979) *Catholic bishop, author, television figure*

Born in El Paso, Illinois, Sheen received bachelor's degrees from St. Viator College and Catholic University, a Ph.D. from the University of Louvain in Belgium, and a Doctorate of Divinity from the University of Rome. He became a Catholic priest in 1919 and joined the faculty of Catholic University in 1926. He was made titular bishop of Caesariana, New York, in 1951 and bishop of Rochester, New York in 1966. Sheen's anticommunist credentials date back to the 1930s, when he equated communism with Nazism during his appearances on the radio show *The Catholic Hour*. He supported Francisco Franco against the communist-supported Loyalists during the Spanish Civil War and wrote a vast number of anticommunist sermons, articles, and speeches, as well as 50 books. One of the themes that unify his work is his argument that communism is the antithesis of Roman Catholicism. *Communism and the Conscience of the West* (1948) maintains that communism is a kind of secular religion that evokes great dedication from its adherents, a fact that makes it especially difficult to combat. He argues that the communist has passion but no ideals; while Americans have ideals but no passion.

After presenting *The Catholic Hour* on NBC radio for 22 years, Sheen moved to television in 1952. His highly rated show *Life Is Worth Living* began on the DuMont network but later moved to ABC. By 1954, he had an audience of some 25 million Americans each week. At its peak, 170 American stations and 17 Canadian stations carried the show. Sheen's spinoff book, *Life Is Worth Living* (1953), attained fifth place on the best-seller list. After a falling out with his superior, Francis Cardinal Spellman, Sheen left the air in 1957 but returned in 1961 on *The Bishop Sheen Program,* which ran through 1968.

Spillane, Mickey (Frank Morrison Spillane)
(1918–) *novelist*

Born in Brooklyn as Frank Morrison Spillane, "Mickey" began writing for comic books and pulp magazines in order to pay his education. In the late 1940s and 1950s, he became popular for his detective novels that exuded sex, violence, licentiousness, and elements of sadism. His recurring character, private investigator Mike Hammer, debuted in Spillane's first novel, *I, the Jury* (1947), an immediate best-seller. A tough, virile, individualistic ex-marine who detests criminals, policemen, bureaucrats, intellectuals, communists, and fellow travelers and savagely metes out justice against malefactors, Hammer apparently gave voice to sentiments that were shared by millions of Americans, either overtly or in silence. Spillane went on to write six of the top 10 fictional best-sellers of the 1950s: *My Gun Is Quick* (1950), *Vengeance Is Mine* (1950), *The Big Kill* (1951), *One Lonely Night* (1951), *The Long Wait* (1951) and *Kiss Me Deadly* (1952). By 1953, Spillane had sold more than 17 million books.

Sullivan, Ed (1901–1974) *television variety show host, newspaper columnist*

Born in New York City to a custom's inspector and his wife, Sullivan began his career in journalism as a sports writer. In 1932, he began a column about Broadway in the *New York Daily News* and soon earned a reputation for discovering and promoting good talent. In 1948, Sullivan was writing a nationally syndicated newspaper column, entitled "Little Old New York," when CBS asked him to become master of ceremonies for a new television show, *The Toast of the Town.* One of the pioneering television variety shows, it was renamed *The Ed Sullivan Show* in 1955, aired continuously from 1948 to 1971, and held the Sunday 8:00–9:00 P.M. time-slot at CBS for 22 years. Although as a TV persona Sullivan was bland, he was successful at providing mainstream American audiences with entertainment that appealed to them, and his show came to embody, and to some extent define, the tastes and values of mainstream America throughout the 1950s. Although he would not tolerate communists or explicit sexuality—his decision to black

out Elvis Presley's swaying hips in 1957 is notorious—overall Sullivan's tastes were remarkably tolerant and diverse, ranging from such highbrow offerings as concert pianists, opera performers, and the Bolshoi Ballet, to Broadway show tunes, Las Vegas entertainers, the June Taylor Dancers, rock 'n' rollers, and lesser known and sometimes eccentric acts.

Truman, Harry S. (1884–1972) *U.S. president (1945–1953)*

Born in Lamar, Missouri, the son of an agricultural businessman, Truman grew up in Independence, Missouri. His mother was a devout Baptist who valued education, and both parents were committed Democrats. After graduating high school, Truman wanted to pursue a military career, but the U.S. Military Academy at West Point rejected him because of his poor vision. He served as an artillery officer during the war, and afterward he and a friend opened a haberdashery in Kansas City. However, the joint venture failed during the economic slump in 1921–22, and subsequently Truman turned to politics. Supported by Missouri's powerful Democratic Party machine, he was elected county judge in 1922 and to the U.S. Senate in 1934. Although more moderate than Franklin D. Roosevelt, Truman consistently supported the president and generally voted along Democratic Party lines.

Roosevelt selected Truman in 1944 as a compromise vice presidential candidate over the incumbent vice president, Henry Wallace, whom the party's left wing favored, and the director of war mobilization, James F. Byrnes, whom the party's conservatives endorsed. When Roosevelt died suddenly on April 12, 1945, Truman became president.

Truman assumed office at a dynamic moment in world history. Within two weeks of his inauguration, he signed the United Nations charter; within a month, Germany surrendered and World War II concluded in Europe; and within two months, the cold war was under way, as the Allies partitioned Germany into four sectors to be controlled individually by the United States, Great Britain, France, and the Soviet Union.

Disregarding the Soviet insistence on secure borders with Eastern Europe, Truman and Byrnes, whom Truman appointed as secretary of state, promoted the revitalization of Germany, the founding of democratic governments in Germany and Eastern Europe, and the eventual evacuation of Soviet troops from occupied European territories. Truman represented the United States at the Potsdam Conference, where the so-called Big Three—the United States, Great Britain, and the Soviet Union—set policies for controlling Germany during the occupation and warned Japan to surrender unconditionally or risk total destruction.

While attending the conference, Truman, who had not even known about the atomic bomb project before he became president three months earlier, learned that the bomb had been successfully tested. In early August, four days after the conference concluded, Truman authorized the atomic bombing of Hiroshima and Nagasaki; shortly thereafter Japan surrendered.

As communist influence spread after the end of the war, Truman accepted as the conceptual basis of his foreign policy George Kennan's recommendation that the United States contain Soviet expansion. In January 1947, Truman appointed George Marshall as secretary of state, a move that signaled a harder line toward the Soviet Union. The policies that Marshall and Truman implemented in the late 1940s ultimately created and defined the cold war—at least on the American side—and together they formulated the Truman Doctrine that included the Marshall Plan for the economic recovery of Europe; the Four Point Program to provide technical aid to underdeveloped countries in Asia, Africa, and Latin America; and in 1949, the formation of the North Atlantic Treaty Organization (NATO), a military alliance to oppose Soviet expansion.

Initially, Truman favored an economic approach over military-based policies. He declined to intervene in the communist takeover of Czechoslovakia in February 1948, and when the Soviets blockaded the surface access routes to West Berlin, he rejected a more confrontational course of action recommended by General Lucius Clay in favor of Marshall's proposal for airlifting supplies into the city. The success of the Berlin airlift enabled Truman to avert an unpopular, election-year military expedition. Efforts by southern Democrats notwithstanding, Truman won the Democratic Party nomination in 1948. Despite possible defections to Wallace, who was running as the Progressive Party candidate, Truman sought to retain Roosevelt's New Deal coalition of poor, urban, and agricultural voters. Moreover, his decision in May to recognize the newly formed state of Israel helped attract Jewish voters. With support from blacks and the emerging class of blue-collar, middle-class industrial workers, Truman achieved one of the greatest political upsets in U.S. history. He defeated the greatly favored Republican candidate, Thomas E. Dewey, by 2 million popular votes and 114 electoral votes.

Elected in his own right, Truman felt freer to pursue his own policies. Maintaining that every citizen had a right to expect a "fair deal" from his or her government, he submitted to Congress extensive social legislation. The comprehensive housing bill for aiding veterans and people from low-income groups became the basis for most government housing programs during the 1950s. Truman also led the effort to extend Social Security benefits, increase the minimum wage, expand rural electrification and flood control programs, and tighten farm price supports. He tried unsuccessfully to enact universal health insurance. Truman also advanced civil rights legislation and used his executive power to enact rights for black Americans when Congress resisted. He ordered the desegregation of the armed services and appointed an African-American judge to the federal judiciary. His administration also supported efforts to end segregation of the public schools.

Even before his election, Truman responded to right-wing demands for tighter security against internal subversion by domestic communists. In 1947, he ordered an investigation of communist activities and subsequently mandated loyalty checks for all government workers. The attorney general's list of subversive organizations also expanded during the Truman years and figured more prominently in congressional and executive-branch investigations; nonetheless, Truman tried to moderate the more excessive restrictions called for by the Right.

Truman had to forge his cold war policy while under constant attack from the Right, which was claiming not only that his State Department was riddled with subversive, pro-Soviet agents but also that his administration was "soft" on communism, especially in Asia where by refusing to aid Chiang Kaishek and the Chinese Nationalists, his critics argued, the Truman administration had "lost China" to Mao Zedong's communists.

After communist North Korea attacked South Korea in June 1950, Truman committed the United States to South Korea's defense. Commanded by General Douglas MacArthur, who engineered a successful surprise attack behind enemy lines at Inchon, the mostly American UN forces soon reversed their initial losses, assumed the offensive, and appeared headed for a quick victory. MacArthur advocated liberating North Korea after the military situation in South Korea stabilized, but he seriously underestimated the Chinese resolve to attack if the UN forces crossed the 38th parallel into North Korea and was caught off guard when communist China entered the war in November 1950. Unable to negotiate a suitable peace treaty, Truman resisted calls from leading Republicans to extend the war to China. When MacArthur publically challenged Truman's policy of prosecuting a limited war, Truman fired the popular general for insubordination. The controversial action provoked a congressional inquiry, but no wrongdoing was found. Nonetheless, opposition from a conservative Congress continued to undermine Truman's social agenda and pushed him to take strong anticommunist measures both at home and in foreign policy.

Truman declined to run for reelection in 1952. In his final State of the Union message in January 1953, he warned Soviet leader Joseph Stalin against provoking a war with the United States and urged the West to continue resisting worldwide communist expansion, but to avoid a nuclear war at the same time. He also denounced the domestic Red Scare and warned against legislation directed against American communists that would promote "enforced conformity."

Wayne, John (Marion Michael Morrison)
(1907–1979) *film actor*

Wayne, a popular icon of American strength, determination, and masculinity, appeared in more films than any other major star of his time. Born in Winterset, Iowa, as Marion Michael Morrison, Wayne attended the University of Southern California, where he played football. During the summers, he worked as a prop man at Twentieth-Century Fox, where he befriended

director John Ford. This led to small roles in movies; Wayne's first credited appearance was in *The Drop Kick* (1927), and his first leading role was in Raoul Walsh's *Big Trail* (1930). Between 1930 and 1939, Wayne appeared in more than 80 low-budget movies. Ford's *Stagecoach* (1939) finally established him as a star.

Wayne was a large and physically powerful person, and "Duke," as he became known, typically chose roles that reinforced his view of rugged American individualism—characters who are strong, emotionally restrained, straightforward, loyal, tough but fair minded, fully resolved to do what is right, and not afraid to use force to protect their own interests and those of people too weak to protect themselves from unfair abuse. In these respects, Wayne embodied much of the view the United States had of itself throughout the 1940s and 1950s and beyond. For these reasons, in 1971, the Marine Corps League named Wayne "the man who best exemplifies the word *American*."

Among his movies from the 1950s are *Big Jim McClain* (1952), which celebrates the work of a House Un-American Activities Committee (HUAC) investigator; *The High and the Mighty* (1954), about a passenger plane in distress; *The Searchers* (1956), about a man searching for his dead brother's daughter who has been abducted and raised by Indians; *Jet Pilot,* about communist spies; and *Rio Bravo* (1959), about a western sheriff committed to seeing that justice is done. In 1960, Wayne produced, directed, and starred as Davy Crockett in *The Alamo,* a popular movie that appeared during the second Berlin crisis and celebrated the gallantry, determination, and self-sacrifice of American fighters who are surrounded and outnumbered by their foe, as were the U.S. soldiers in Berlin. During the 1960s, he actively supported U.S. participation in the Vietnam War, and in 1968, at the height of the war, he directed and starred in *The Green Berets* to celebrate and promote the efforts of American soldiers in that conflict.

APPENDIX C
Maps

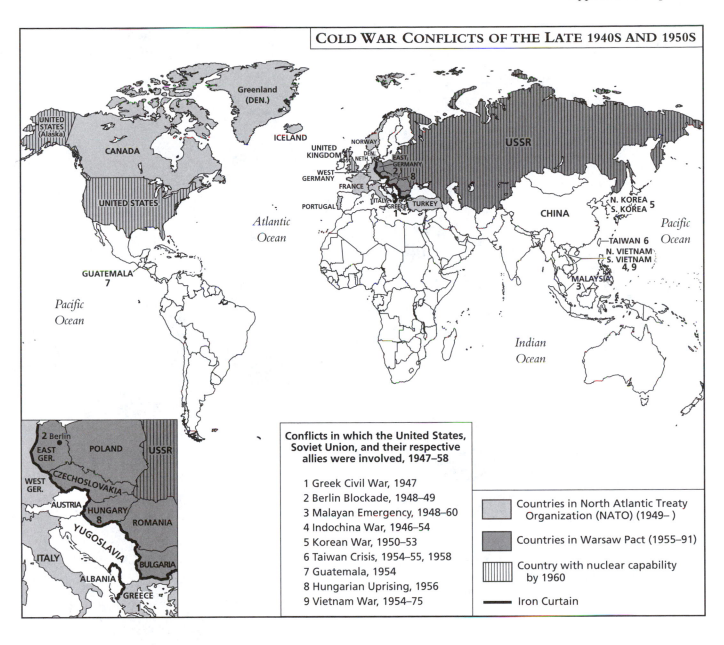

COLD WAR CONFLICTS OF THE LATE 1940S AND 1950S

Conflicts in which the United States, Soviet Union, and their respective allies were involved, 1947–58

1 Greek Civil War, 1947
2 Berlin Blockade, 1948–49
3 Malayan Emergency, 1948–60
4 Indochina War, 1946–54
5 Korean War, 1950–53
6 Taiwan Crisis, 1954–55, 1958
7 Guatemala, 1954
8 Hungarian Uprising, 1956
9 Vietnam War, 1954–75

Countries in North Atlantic Treaty Organization (NATO) (1949–)

Countries in Warsaw Pact (1955–91)

Country with nuclear capability by 1960

Iron Curtain

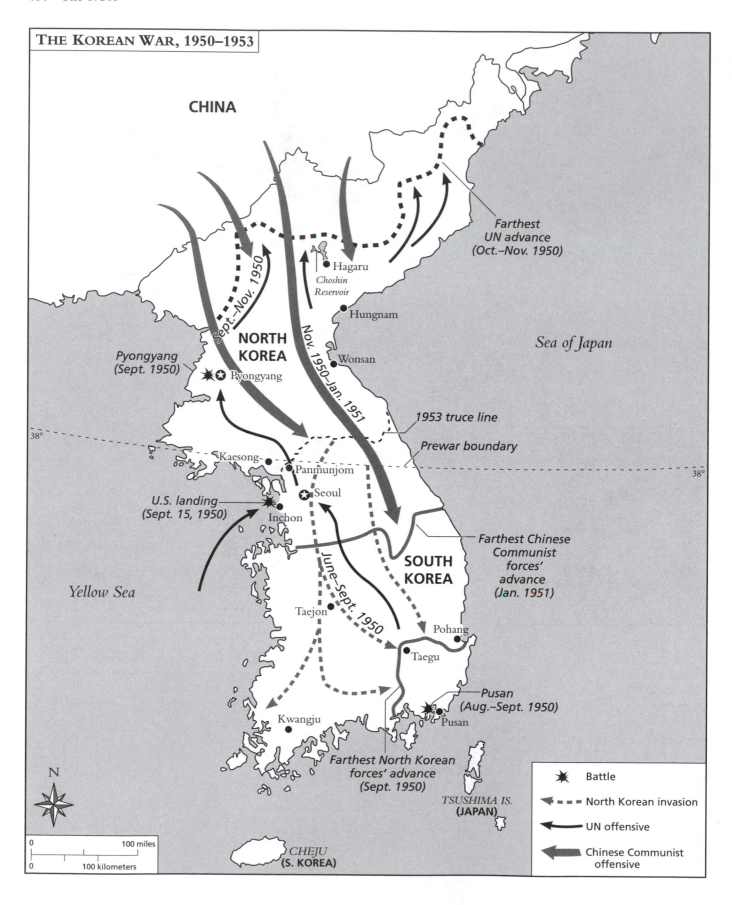

THE KOREAN WAR, 1950–1953

CHINA

Farthest
UN advance
(Oct.–Nov. 1950)

Hagaru
Choshin
Reservoir

Hungnam

Sea of Japan

NORTH
KOREA

Wonsan

Pyongyang
(Sept. 1950)

Pyongyang

1953 truce line

Prewar boundary

38°

Kaesong

Panmunjom

Seoul

U.S. landing
(Sept. 15, 1950)

Inchon

Farthest Chinese
Communist
forces'
advance
(Jan. 1951)

SOUTH
KOREA

Yellow Sea

Taejon

Pohang

Taegu

Pusan
(Aug.–Sept. 1950)

Kwangju

Pusan

Farthest North Korean
forces' advance
(Sept. 1950)

TSUSHIMA IS.
(JAPAN)

N

CHEJU
(S. KOREA)

0   100 miles
0   100 kilometers

Battle

North Korean invasion

UN offensive

Chinese Communist
offensive

NATO AND WARSAW PACT COUNTRIES, 1955

NATO countries
Warsaw Pact countries
Neutral countries

0   300 miles
0   300 kilometers

ICELAND

N

FAEROE IS.

SHETLAND IS.

NORWAY

SWEDEN

FINLAND

USSR

North
Sea

UNITED

IRELAND

KINGDOM

DENMARK

Baltic Sea

Atlantic
Ocean

NETHER-
LANDS

BELGIUM

WEST

GERMANY

EAST
GERMANY

POLAND

LUXEMBOURG

GERMANY

CZECHOSLOVAKIA

FRANCE

SWITZ.

LIECHTENSTEIN

AUSTRIA

HUNGARY

ROMANIA

Black Sea

SAN
MARINO

YUGOSLAVIA

BULGARIA

PORTUGAL

ANDORRA

MONACO

ITALY

SPAIN

CORSICA
(FR.)

ALBANIA

TURKEY

SARDINIA
(IT.)

Mediterranean Sea

GREECE

SICILY
(IT.)

MOROCCO
(FR.)

ALGERIA
(FR.)

TUNISIA
(FR.)

CRETE (GR.)

CYPRUS (BR.)

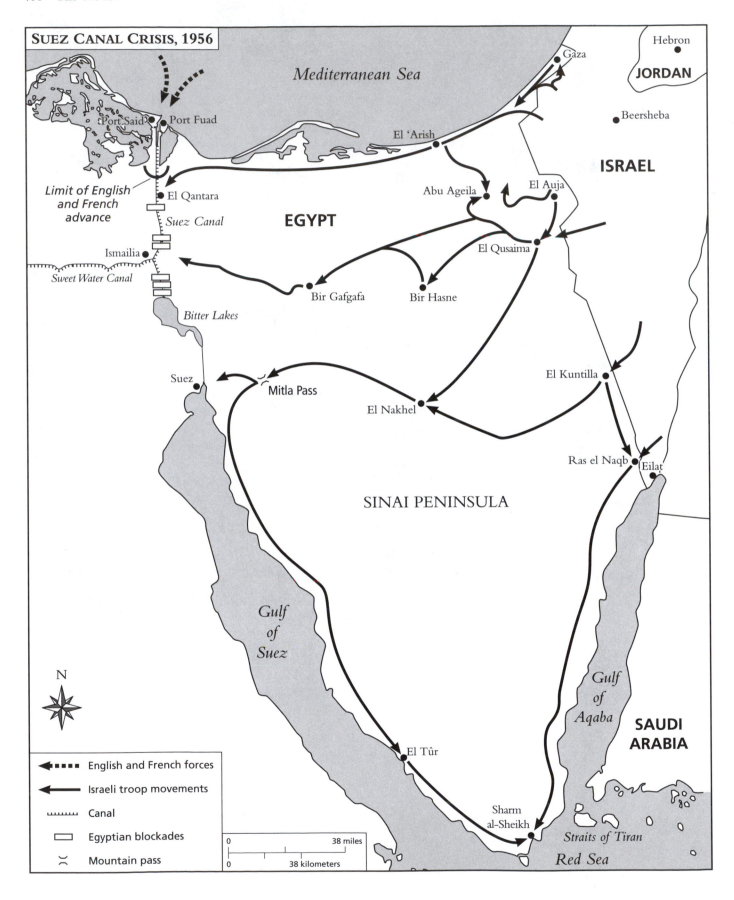

SUEZ CANAL CRISIS, 1956

Mediterranean Sea

Hebron

Gaza

JORDAN

Port Said   Port Fuad

El 'Arish

Beersheba

*Limit of English
and French
advance*

El Qantara

Abu Ageila   El Auja

ISRAEL

Suez Canal

EGYPT

Ismailia

El Qusaima

Sweet Water Canal

Bir Gafgafa   Bir Hasne

Bitter Lakes

Suez

Mitla Pass

El Kuntilla

El Nakhel

Ras el Naqb   Eilat

SINAI PENINSULA

N

*Gulf
of
Suez*

*Gulf
of
Aqaba*

SAUDI
ARABIA

El Tûr

Sharm
al-Sheikh   *Straits of Tiran*

Red Sea

➤▪▪▪▪ English and French forces

➤━━━ Israeli troop movements

⌇⌇⌇⌇ Canal

▭ Egyptian blockades

⌣ Mountain pass

0		38 miles

0		38 kilometers

NOTES

INTRODUCTION

1. Brett Harvey, *The Fifties: A Women's Oral History* (New York: HarperCollins, 1993), p. 128.
2. Stephen J. Whitfield, *The Culture of the Cold War* (Baltimore, Md.: Johns Hopkins University Press, 1996), p. 153.
3. Ibid., p. 83.
4. Ibid., pp. 83–84.
5. Ibid., p. 83.

CHAPTER 1—POSTWAR PRELUDE: 1945–1949

1. David McCullough, *Truman* (New York: Simon & Schuster, 1992), p. 587.
2. Stephen J. Whitfield, *The Culture of the Cold War* (Baltimore, Md.: Johns Hopkins University Press, 1996), p. 75.
3. Robert Torricelli and Andrew Carroll, eds., *In Our Own Words* (New York: Washington Square Press, 1999), p. 220.
4. Lois Gordon and Alan Gordon, *American Chronicle* (New Haven, Conn.: Yale University Press, 1999), pp. 436, 445, 454, 463.
5. Ibid., pp. 445, 454, 463.

CHAPTER 2—AMERICA BECOMES THE WORLD'S POLICEMAN: 1950

1. John Earl Haynes and Harvey Klehr, *Venona: Decoding Soviet Espionage in America* (New Haven, Conn.: Yale University Press, 1999), pp. 167–73.
2. Ibid., 307–11.
3. Stephen J. Whitfield, *The Culture of the Cold War* (Baltimore, Md.: Johns Hopkins University Press, 1996), p. 49.
4. John Cogley, *Report on Blacklisting*, vol. 2 (New York: Arno Press, 1971), p. 34.

5. David Halberstam, *The Fifties* (New York: Fawcett Columbine, 1993), p. 501.
6. Glenn Garvin, "'Mr. Television' Boosted Growth of a New Medium," *Miami Herald* (March 28, 2002), pp. 1A, 11A.
7. James Olson, *Historical Dictionary of the 1950s* (Westport, Ct.: Greenwood Press, 2000), p. 85. See also Clifton Daniel, ed., *20th Century Day by Day* (London: Dorling-Kindersley, 2000), p. 690.
8. David McCullough, *Truman* (New York: Simon & Schuster, 1992), p. 829.

CHAPTER 3—THE COLD WAR SETTLES IN: 1951

1. John Hersey, *Aspects of the Presidency* (New Haven, Conn.: Ticknor Fields, 1980), pp. 137–38.
2. Victor Navasky, *Naming Names* (New York: Penguin, 1980), p. 371.
3. For a more detailed discussion, see Richard Schwartz, "How the Film and Television Blacklists Worked," *Film & History Annual for 1999* (Film & History, 1999, CD-ROM).
4. McCullough, p. 871.
5. McCullough, p. 870.
6. Eric F. Goldman, *The Crucial Decade—And After: America, 1945–1960* (New York: Random House, 1960), p. 190.
7. Lois Gordon and Alan Gordon, *American Chronicle: Year by Year through the Twentieth Century* (New Haven, Conn.: Yale University Press, 1999), pp. 485, 493.
8. U.S. Department of Commerce, *Statistical Abstract of the United States: 1953* (Washington, D.C.: U.S. Government Printing Office, 1953), pp. 296–97.
9. Clifton Daniel, ed. *20th Century Day by Day* (London: Dorling-Kindersley Publishing, 2000), p. 705.

10. See Peter Biskind, *Seeing Is Believing* (New York: Pantheon, 1983), pp. 101–60. See also Nora Sayre, *Running Time* (New York: Dial, 1982).

CHAPTER 4—"I LIKE IKE": 1952

1. Eric Bentley, ed., *Thirty Years of Treason* (New York: Viking Press, 1971), p. 537.

2. Adlai E. Stevenson, *Major Campaign Speeches of Adlai E. Stevenson, 1952* (New York: Random House, 1953), pp. 25–26.

3. David McCullough, *Truman* (New York: Simon & Schuster, 1992), pp. 887–88.

4. Ibid., p. 889.

5. Ibid., pp. 889–92.

6. Geoffrey Perret, *Eisenhower* (New York: Random House, 1999), p. 417.

7. Stevenson, p. 129.

8. Ibid., p. 137.

9. Clifton Daniel, ed., *20th Century Day by Day* (London: Dorling-Kindersley Publishing, 2000), p. 727.

10. McCullough, p. 886.

11. Ibid., p. 886.

12. Ibid., pp. 901–2.

13. Lois Gordon and Alan Gordon, *American Chronicle* (New Haven, Conn.: Yale University Press, 1999), p. 494.

14. Martin Gilbert, *A History of the Twentieth Century*, vol. 3 (New York: Perennial Press, 2000), p. 51.

15. Daniel, p. 732.

16. Daniel, p. 724.

17. Stephen J. Whitfield, *The Culture of the Cold War* (Baltimore, Md.: Johns Hopkins University Press, 1996), p. 171.

18. Victor Navasky, *Naming Names* (New York: Viking, 1980), pp. 156–64.

19. Whitfield, pp. 148–49.

20. Bentley, p. 494.

21. Frances Stonor Saunders, *The Cultural Cold War: The CIA and the World of Arts and Letters* (New York: New Press, 2000), p. 195.

22. *This Fabulous Century*, vol. 6, ed. Time-Life Books (New York: Time-Life Books, 1970), pp. 182–83.

CHAPTER 5—NEW LEADERSHIP IN WASHINGTON AND MOSCOW: 1953

1. Martin Gilbert, *A History of the Twentieth Century*, vol. 3 (New York: Perennial Press, 2000), p. 34.

2. Ibid., p. 43.

3. Clifton Daniel, ed., *20th Century Day by Day* (London: Dorling-Kindersley Publishing, 2000), p. 745.

4. Dwight D. Eisenhower, *The White House Years,* vol. 1 (Garden City, N.Y.: Doubleday, 1963), p. 254.

5. Daniel, p. 743.

6. Frances Stonor Saunders, *The Cultural Cold War: The CIA and the World of Arts and Letters* (New York: New Press, 2000), p. 193.

7. Eric Bentley, ed., *Thirty Years of Treason* (New York: Viking Press, 1971), p. 671.

8. Lois Gordon and Alan Gordon, *American Chronicle* (New Haven, Conn.: Yale University Press, 1999), p. 511.

9. Gilbert, p. 51.

10. Gordon and Gordon, pp. 503, 511.

11. Daniel, p. 746.

12. James S. Olson, *Historical Dictionary of the 1950s* (Westport, Conn.: Greenwood Press, 2000), pp. 224–25. See also Jane Stern and Michael Stern, *Encyclopedia of Pop Culture* (New York: HarperPerennial, 1992), pp. 388–94.

13. Brett Harvey, *The Fifties: A Women's Oral History* (New York: HarperCollins, 1993), p. 2.

14. Gordon and Gordon, p. 511.

15. Olson, p. 288.

16. Harry Haun, *The Cinematic Century* (New York: Applause, 2000).

CHAPTER 6—SEPARATE IS NOT EQUAL: 1954

1. Martin Gilbert, *A History of the Twentieth Century*, vol. 3 (New York: Perennial Press, 2000), p. 56.

2. Ibid., p. 58.

3. Ibid., p. 326.

4. Quoted in *This Fabulous Century*, vol. 6 (New York: Time-Life Books, 1970), p. 130.

5. Clifton Daniel, ed., *20th Century Day by Day* (London: Dorling-Kindersley Publishing, 2000), p. 759.

6. Edward Moran, *America in the 1950s,* cassette 2 (New Rochelle, N.Y.: GAA Corp., 1999).

7. Stephen J. Whitfield, *The Culture of the Cold War* (Baltimore, Md.: Johns Hopkins University Press, 1996), p. 83.

8. Fred McGunagle, "A Suspect Emerges" (available online: September 1, 2001).

9. Lois Gordon and Alan Gordon, *American Chronicle* (New Haven, Conn.: Yale University Press, 1999), pp. 512, 520.

10. David Halberstam, *The Fifties* (New York: Fawcett Columbine, 1993), p. 495.

11. William L. Lawrence, "Salk Polio Vaccine Proves Success," *New York Times* (April 13, 1955), p. 1.

12. Gilbert, p. 79.

13. Gordon and Gordon, p. 520.

14. Ibid., p. 520.

15. Whitfield, p. 16.

16. Gordon and Gordon, p. 520.

17. "Children's Bones Were Secretly Tested," *Miami Herald* (October 1, 2001), p. 6A.

18. Whitfield, p. 49.

CHAPTER 7—DISNEYLAND AND COLD WAR ANGST: 1955

1. Matin Gilbert, *A History of the Twentieth Century,* vol. 3 (New York: Perennial Press, 2000), p. 95.

2. Quoted in Gilbert, p. 91.

3. Victor Navasky, *Naming Names* (New York: Viking, 1980), pp. 85, 178.

4. Quoted in Sanford Wexler, *An Eyewitness History of the Civil Rights Movement* (New York: Checkmark Books, 1999), p. 67.

5. Lois Gordon and Alan Gordon, *American Chronicle* (New Haven, Conn.: Yale University Press, 1999), p. 529.

6. Lary May, ed., *Recasting America: Culture and Politics in the Age of the Cold War* (Chicago: University of Chicago Press, 1989), p. 27.

7. Gordon and Gordon, p. 521.

8. Brett Harvey, *The Fifties: A Women's Oral History* (1993), p. 128.

9. James S. Olson, *Historical Dictionary of the 1950s* (Westport, Conn.: Greenwood Press, 2000), pp. 72, 79–80.

10 Gordon and Gordon, p. 529.

11. Edward Moran, *America in the 1950s,* cassette 2 (New Rochelle, N.Y.: GAA Corp., 1999).

12. John Hersey, *Hiroshima* (New York: Vintage Books, 1989), pp. 144–46.

13. Henry Hampton, Steve Fayer, and Sarah Flynn, eds., *Voices of Freedom: An Oral History of the Civil Rights Movement from the 1950s through the 1980s* (New York: Bantam Books, 1990), p. 6.

CHAPTER 8—IKE AND ELVIS, BUDAPEST AND SUEZ: 1956

1. Martin Gilbert, *A History of the Twentieth Century,* vol. 3 (New York: Perennial Press, 2000), p. 143.

2. Eric Bentley, ed., *Thirty Years of Treason* (New York: Viking Press, 1971), p. 727.

3. Frances Stonor Saunders, *The Cultural Cold War: The CIA and the World of Arts and Letters* (New York: New Press, 2000), p. 191.

4. Alex McNeil, *Total Television* (New York: Penguin Books, 1991), p. 538.

5. Dwight D. Eisenhower, *The White House Years,* vol. 2 (Garden City, N.Y.: Doubleday, 1965), p. 17.

6. Lois Gordon and Alan Gordon, *American Chronicle* (New Haven, Conn.: Yale University Press, 1999), pp. 530, 538.

7. Ibid., p. 531.

8. Clifton Daniel, ed., *20th Century Day by Day* (London: Dorling-Kindersley Publishing, 2000), p. 786.

9. Gordon and Gordon, p. 538.

10. *The Movie Guide* (New York: Perigee Books, 1998), p. 28.

11. Stephen J. Whitfield, *The Culture of the Cold War* (Baltimore, Md.: Johns Hopkins University Press, 1996), p. 99.

12. Ibid., p. 99.

13. Woody Allen, *Woody Allen on Woody Allen: In Conversation with Stig Björkman* (New York: Grove Press, 1995), p. 210.

14. Gordon and Gordon, p. 538.

CHAPTER 9—*SPUTNIK* AND LITTLE ROCK: 1957

1. Clifton Daniel, ed., *20th Century Day by Day* (London: Dorling-Kindersley Publishing, 2000), p. 802.

2. Dwight D. Eisenhower, *The White House Years,* vol. 2 (Garden City, N.Y.: Doubleday, 1965), pp. 193–95.

3. Daniel, p. 802.

4. Martin Gilbert, *A History of the Twentieth Century,* vol. 3 (New York: Perennial Press, 2000), p. 151.

5. Victor Navasky, *Naming Names* (New York: Viking, 1980), p. 26. Stephen J. Whitfield estimates party membership in 1957 to have been 5,000.

6. Stephen J. Whitfield, *The Culture of the Cold War* (Baltimore, Md.: Johns Hopkins University Press, 1996), p. 50.

7. Gilbert, p. 168.

8. Brett Harvey, *The Fifties: A Women's Oral History* (New York: HarperCollins, 1993), p. 25.

9. Lois Gordon and Alan Gordon, *American Chronicle* (New Haven, Conn.: Yale University Press, 1999), pp. 539, 547.

10. Whitfield, p. 162.

11. *The Movie Guide,* eds. CineBooks (New York: Perigee Books, 1998), p. 737.

12. Gordon and Gordon, p. 547.

13. Daniel, p. 796.

CHAPTER 10—AMERICA ENTERS OUTER SPACE: 1958

1. Dwight D. Eisenhower, *The White House Years,* vol. 2 (Garden City, N.Y.: Doubleday, 1965), p. 521.

2. Clifton Daniel, ed., *20th Century Day by Day* (London: Dorling-Kindersley Publishing, 2000), p. 809.

3. Ibid., p. 815.

4. Martin Gilbert, *A History of the Twentieth Century,* vol. 3 (New York: Perennial Press, 2000), p. 177.

5. Lois Gordon and Alan Gordon, *American Chronicle* (New Haven, Conn.: Yale University Press, 1999), p. 548.

6. James S. Olson, *Historical Dictionary of the 1950s* (Westport, Conn.: Greenwood Press, 2000), p. 50.

CHAPTER 11—AMERICA EXPANDS INTO THE PACIFIC: 1959

1. Dwight D. Eisenhower, *The White House Years,* vol. 2 (Garden City, N.Y.: Doubleday, 1965), p. 448.

2. Lois Gordon and Alan Gordon, *American Chronicle* (New Haven, Conn.: Yale University Press, 1999), pp. 557, 565.

EPILOGUE: FINAL THOUGHTS ON THE DECADE

1. Of course, the theme of women trading sex for upward mobility can be traced back at least to the 18th century, during the rise of capitalism and the beginning of the Industrial Revolution. It is evident, for example, in Samuel Richardson's *Pamela: Or Virtue Rewarded* (1740), which is regarded as the first English novel—a literary form that emanated from capitalist culture. Henry Fielding later spoofs it in *Shamela* (1741), whose heroine realizes that although she can earn a good sum with her body, she can make a fortune from her virginity—her *virtue*—and so the maid holds out for marriage with her aristocratic employer, whom she has driven mad with lust.

BIBLIOGRAPHY

Acheson, Dean. *Present at the Creation: My Years in the State Department.* New York: W. W. Norton, 1969.

Adams, Robert Martin. "Fiction Chronicle." *Hudson Review* (Summer 1958): 283–90.

Adams, Val. "Davy Crockett Returning to TV." *New York Times,* November 2, 1955, L70.

Allen, Woody. *Woody Allen on Woody Allen: In Conversation with Stig Björkman.* New York: Grove Press, 1995.

Allport, Gordon W. *The Individual and His Religion.* New York: Macmillan, 1950.

Alsop, Joseph, and Stewart Alsop. "Why Has Washington Gone Crazy?" *Saturday Evening Post* (July 29, 1950): 20.

Ambrose, Stephen, and Douglas Brinkley, eds. *Witness to America: An Illustrated Documentary History of the United States from the Revolution to Today.* New York: HarperCollins, 1999.

Andreadoria.org. "Bellomo Recollection." Available online. URL: http://www.andreadoria.org/Recollections/Bellomo. Downloaded September 6, 2001.

Antonov, S. F. "A Conversation with Mao." Cold War International History Project, Woodrow Wilson International Center for Scholars. Available online. URL: http://cwihp.si.edu/cwihplib.nsf. Downloaded September 10, 2001.

Arendt, Hannah. *Totalitarianism.* New York: Harcourt, Brace, 1968.

Atkinson, Brooks. "Darkness at Noon." *New York Times,* January 15, 1951, 3.

———. "'Death of a Salesman.'" *New York Times,* February 11, 1949, 27.

———. "Mr. Inge in Top Form." *New York Times,* March 13, 1955, II: 1.

———. "'A Streetcar Named Desire.'" *New York Times,* December 4, 1947, 42.

———. "Williams' 'Tin Roof.'" *New York Times,* April 3, 1955, 11.

"The Atom." *Time* (Fsebruary 6, 1950): 1.

Baldwin, Hanson. "'Nautilus' Skipper Helps to Mitigate a Snub to Rickover." *New York Times,* August 9, 1958, 1.

Barson, Michael. *"Better Dead Than Red!": A Nostalgic Look at the Golden Years of Russiaphobia, Red-Baiting, and Other Commie Madness.* New York: Hyperion, 1992.

Barth, John. *The End of the Road.* 1958. Reprint, New York: Doubleday, 1989.

———. *The Floating Opera.* 1956. Reprint, New York: Doubleday, 1989.

Bartley, Numan V. *The Rise of Massive Resistance: Race and Politics in the South during the 1950's.* Baton Rouge: Louisiana State University Press, 1999.

"Baruch Says Inflation's Effects, Not Stock Prices, Pose Whatever Danger Is Ahead." *Wall Street Journal,* March 24, 1955, 3–4.

Baxter, James, and Annette Baxter. "The Man in the Blue Suede Shoes." *Harper's Magazine* (January 1958): 45–48.

Bell, James. "Battle of No Name Ridge." *Time* (August 28, 1950): 22.

Bellow, Saul. *Seize the Day.* 1956. Reprint, New York: Penguin, 1996.

Benny, Jack, and Joan Benny. *Sunday Nights at Seven.* New York: Warner Books, 1990.

Bentley, Eric, ed. *Thirty Years of Treason: Excerpts from Hearings before the House Committee on Un-American Activities, 1938–1968.* New York: Viking Press, 1971.

Bertsch, Leonard M. "The Problems of Victory in Korea." *America: National Catholic Weekly Review* (November 4, 1950): 129.

Bess, Demaree. "How Long Will This War Last?" *Saturday Evening Post* (September 9, 1950): 22–23.

Bigart, Homer. "Faubus Compares His Stand to Lee's." *New York Times,* October 5, 1957, 1.

Bikel, Theodore. *Theo.* New York: HarperCollins, 1994.

Biskind, Peter. *Seeing Is Believing: How Hollywood Taught Us to Stop Worrying and Love the Fifties.* New York: Pantheon, 1983.

Blum, Daniel. *Theatre World: Season 1959–60.* Philadelphia: Chilton, 1960.

Bogdanovich, Peter. *Pieces of Time: Peter Bogdanovich on the Movies.* New York: Arbor House, 1973.

Bradley, David, and Shelley Fisher Fishkin, eds. *The Encyclopedia of Civil Rights in America.* New York: M. E. Sharpe, 1998.

Brandon, Henry. "Flat on Our Faces: A Conversation with Frank Lloyd Wright." *New Republic* (September 8, 1958): 14–15.

Brynner, Rock. *Yul: The Man Who Would Be King.* New York: Simon & Schuster, 1989.

Buber, Martin. *Good and Evil.* New York: Charles Scribner's Sons, 1952.

Buckley, William F., Jr. *The Committee and Its Critics.* New York: Putnam, 1962.

———. *McCarthy and His Enemies: The Record and Its Meaning.* 1954. Reprint, New Rochelle, N.Y.: Arlington House, 1970.

Caesar, Sid. *Where Have I Been?* New York: Crown, 1982.

Canby, Edward Tatnall. "The New Recordings: 3-D Sounds." *Harper's Magazine* (August 1953): 104.

Carson, Rachel. *Lost Woods: The Discovered Writing of Rachel Carson.* Ed. Linda Lear. Boston: Beacon Press, 1998.

Chai Chengwen. *Banmendian Tanpan.* Beijing: People's Liberation Army Press, 1989. Woodrow Wilson International Center for Scholars, Cold War International History Project. Available online. URL: http://cwihp.si.edu/ cwihplib.nsf/16c6b2fc83775317852564a400054b28/fac3a402f6ca00ea85 256928006f80c9?OpenDocument. Downloaded October 25, 2001.

Chamberlain, Betty. "How to Get and Spend a Million Dollars for Art." *ARTnews* (April 1956): 37.

"Charlie Parker, Jazz Master, Dies." *New York Times,* March 15, 1955, 17.

"Chicago Health Board Bans Re-Use of Glasses for Viewing 3-D Films." *Wall Street Journal,* August 5, 1953, 10.

"Children's Bones Were Secretly Tested." *Miami Herald,* October 1, 2001, 6A.

Clarke, Alison J. *Tupperware: The Promise of Plastic in 1950s America.* Washington, D.C.: Smithsonian Institution Press, 1999.

Clarke, Charles Walker. "Social Hygiene and Civil Defense." *Journal of Social Hygiene* (January 1951): 3–7.

Clarke, W. Norris. "The End of the Modern World?" *America: National Catholic Weekly Review* (April 19, 1958): 106–7.

Clarkson, Helen. *The Last Day: A Novel of the Day after Tomorrow.* New York: Dodd, Mead, 1959.

Cogley, John. *Report on Blacklisting.* 2 vols. 1956. Reprint, New York: Arno Press, 1971.

Cohn, Roy. *McCarthy.* New York: New American Library, 1968.

Collier-Thomas, Bettye, and V. P. Franklin. *My Soul Is a Witness: A Chronology of the Civil Rights Era, 1954–1965.* New York: Henry Holt, 1999.

Condon, Richard. *The Manchurian Candidate.* 1959. Reprint, New York: Jove Books, 1988.

Conquest, Robert. *Stalin: Breaker of Nations.* New York: Penguin, 1992.

Cooke, Mervyn. *The Chronicle of Jazz.* New York: Abbeville Press, 1997.

Cooper, Lee E. "Vast GI Housing to Rise Near Site of World's Fair." *New York Times,* November 30, 1947, 1.

Crossman, Richard, ed. *The God That Failed.* 1949. Reprint, Freeport, N.Y.: Books for Libraries Press, 1972.

Crowdus, Gary, ed. *The Political Companion to American Film.* Chicago: Lakeview Press, 1994.

Crowther, Bosley. "'An American in Paris' Arrives at Music Hall." *New York Times,* October 5, 1951, 24.

———. "'The Asphalt Jungle.'" *New York Times,* June 9, 1950, 29.

———. "'Big Jim McClain.'" *New York Times,* September 18, 1952, 35.

———. "'Communist for F.B.I.,' New Picture at Strand Theatre." *New York Times,* May 3, 1951, 34.

———. "'Death of a Salesman,' with Fredrick March and Mildred Dunnock, at Victoria." *New York Times,* December 21, 1951, 21.

———. "'Don't Bother to Knock.'" *New York Times,* July 19, 1952, 8.

———. "'The King and I.'" *New York Times,* June 29, 1956, 15.

———. "'Paths of Glory.'" *New York Times,* December 26, 1957, 23.

———. "'Pickup on South Street.'" *New York Times,* June 18, 1953, 38.

———. "'Salome.'" *New York Times,* March 25, 1953, 37.

———. "'The Spirit of St. Louis.'" *New York Times,* February 22, 1957, 25.

———. "'The Young Lions.'" *New York Times,* April 3, 1958, 23.

Curran, Charles. "The Bang and the Whimper." *New Republic* (February 3, 1958): 19.

Cvetic, Matt. "I Posed as a Communist for the FBI." *Saturday Evening Post* (July 15–July 29, 1950).

Daley, Arthur. "Gazing at the Stars." *New York Times,* July 13, 1955, 29.

———. "Just a Singles Hitter." *New York Times,* May 20, 1954, 42.

Daniel, Clifton, ed. *20th Century Day by Day.* London: Dorling-Kindersley, 2000.

Daniel, Pete. *Lost Revolutions: The South in the 1950s.* Chapel Hill: University of North Carolina Press for Smithsonian National Museum of American History, 2000.

Darby, William. *Necessary American Fictions: Popular Literature of the 1950s.* Bowling Green, Ohio: Bowling Green State University Popular Press, 1987.

Department of Commerce, U.S. *Statistical Abstract of the United States: 1950.* Washington, D.C.: U.S. Government Printing Office, 1950.

Department of Commerce, U.S. *Statistical Abstract of the United States: 1953.* Washington, D.C.: U.S. Government Printing Office, 1953.

Department of Commerce, U.S. *Statistical Abstract of the United States: 1957.* Washington, D.C.: U.S. Government Printing Office, 1957.

Department of Commerce, U.S. *Statistical Abstract of the United States: 1959.* Washington, D.C.: U.S. Government Printing Office, 1959.

Devree, Charlotte. "The U.S. Government Vetoes Living Art." *ARTnews* (September 1956): 34.

"Dobb's Ferry Pupil Sent Home in Drill." *New York Times,* November 11, 1959, 26.

Doherty, Thomas Patrick. *Teenagers and Teenpics: The Juvenilization of American Movies in the 1950s.* Boston: Unwin Hyman, 1988.

Doty, Paul, Carl Kaysen, and Jack Ruina, eds. *The Nuclear Age Reader.* New York: Knopf, 1989.

Downing, David. *Marlon Brando.* New York: Stein & Day, 1984.

Dreishpoon, Douglas. *Between Transcendence and Brutality: American Sculptural Drawings from the 1940s and 1950s: Louise Bourgeois, Dorothy Dehner, Herbert Ferber, Seymour Lipton, Isamu Noguchi, Theodore Roszak, David Smith.* Tampa, Fla.: Tampa Museum of Art, 1994.

Du Ping. *My Experience at the Headquarters of the Chinese People's Volunteers.* Beijing: People's Liberation Army Press, 1989. Woodrow Wilson International Center for Scholars, Cold War International History Project. Available online. URL: http://cwihp.si.edu/cwihplib.nsf/16c6b2fc83775317852564a400054b28/fac3a402f6ca00ea85 256928006f80c9?OpenDocument. Downloaded October 25, 2001.

Eisenhower, Dwight D. "Atoms for Peace." Speech Archive, the Program in Presidential Rhetoric. URL: http://www.tamu.edu/scom/pres/speeches/ikeatoms.html. Downloaded August 24, 2001.

———. "The Chance for Peace." Speech Archive, the Program in Presidential Rhetoric. URL: http://www.tamu.edu/scom/pres/speeches/ikechance.html. Downloaded August 24, 2001.

———. "Federal Court Orders Must Be Upheld." Speech Archive, the Program in Presidential Rhetoric. URL: http://www.tamu.edu/scom/pres/speeches/ikefederal.html. Downloaded August 24, 2001.

———. "First Inaugural Address." Inaugural Addresses of the Presidents of the United States. Available online. URL: http://www.bartleby.com/124/pres54/.html. Downloaded August 24, 2001.

———. "Second Inaugural Address." Inaugural Addresses of the Presidents of the United States. Available online. URL: http://www.bartleby.com/124/pres55/.html. Downloaded August 24, 2001.

———. *The White House Years.* Vol. 1, *Mandate for Change: 1953–1956.* Garden City, N.Y.: Doubleday, 1963.

———. *The White House Years.* Vol. 2, *Waging Peace: 1956–1961.* Garden City, N.Y.: Doubleday, 1965.

Ellison, Jerome. "Is Traffic Strangling Our Cities?" *Saturday Evening Post* (August 5, 1950): 34–35.

Ellison, Ralph. *Invisible Man.* 1952. Reprint, New York: Random House, 1995.

Ellmann, Richard. "Wallace Stevens' Ice-Cream." *Kenyon Review* (Winter 1957): 89.

Engel, Joel. *Rod Serling.* Chicago: Contemporary Books, 1989.

Farrow, Mia. *What Falls Away: A Memoir.* New York: Bantam Books, 1998.

Ferrell, Robert H. *Off the Record: The Private Papers of Harry S. Truman.* New York: Penguin, 1980.

Fischer, John. "The Editor's Easy Chair." *Harper's Magazine* (July 1959): 12–13.

Foreman, Joel, ed. *The Other Fifties: Interrogating Midcentury American Icons.* Urbana: University of Illinois Press, 1997.

Foster, Edward H. *Understanding the Beats.* Columbia: University of South Carolina Press, 1992.

"Franco Has a Job for NATO." *Nation* (January 4, 1958): 1.

Frank, Pat. *Alas, Babylon.* New York: Bantam, 1959.

Fried, Richard M. *The Russians Are Coming! The Russians Are Coming! Pageantry and Patriotism in Cold-War America.* New York: Oxford University Press, 1998.

Friedlander, Paul. *Rock and Roll: A Social History.* New York: Westview Press, 1996.

Friedman, Leon. *The Civil Rights Reader.* New York: Walker, 1968.

Frommer, Myrna Katz, and Harvey Frommer. *It Happened on Broadway: An Oral History of the Great White Way.* New York: Harcourt Brace, 1998.

Funke, Lewis. "'Damn Yankees' Tells of Witchery." *New York Times,* May 6, 1955, 17.

Garvin, Glenn. "'Mr. Television' Boosted Growth of a New Medium." *Miami Herald,* March 28, 2002, 1A, 11A.

Gilbert, Martin. *A History of the Twentieth Century.* Vol. 2, 1933–1951, and Vol. 3, 1952–1999. New York: Perennial Press, 2000.

Goldman, Eric F. *The Crucial Decade—And After: America, 1945–1960.* New York: Random House, 1960.

Goodman, Walter. *The Committee: The Extraordinary Career of the House Committee on Un-American Activities.* New York: Farrar, Straus & Giroux, 1968.

Gordon, Lois, and Alan Gordon. *American Chronicle: Year by Year through the Twentieth Century.* New Haven, Conn.: Yale University Press, 1999.

Gould, Jack. "TV: Heading for the Fall Round-Up." *New York Times,* September 27, 1959, II:17.

Greenberg, Cara. *Mid-Century Modern: Furniture of the 1950s.* New York: Harmony Books, 1984.

Grose, Peter. *Gentleman Spy: The Life of Allen Dulles.* New York: Houghton Mifflin, 1994.

Halberstam, David. *The Fifties.* New York: Fawcett Columbine, 1993.

Halberstam, David J. "Thomson's 'Shot' Heard 50 Years Ago." *Miami Herald,* October 3, 2001, 2D.

Hamilton, Thomas J. "Chief of U.N. Gives a Plan for Mideast." *New York Times,* August 9, 1958, 1.

Hampton, Henry, Steve Fayer, and Sarah Flynn, eds. *Voices of Freedom: An Oral History of the Civil Rights Movement from the 1950s through the 1980s.* New York: Bantam Books, 1990.

Hangen, Welles. "'Porgy' Is Hailed in Moscow Debut." *New York Times,* January 11, 1956, 36.

Harper, Mr. "Elvis the Indigenous." *Harper's Magazine* (April 1957): 86.

Hartnett, Robert C., S.J. "Mr. Lee 'Examines' Catholic School Policy." *America: National Catholic Weekly Review* (February 17, 1951): 581.

Harvey, Brett. *The Fifties: A Women's Oral History.* New York: HarperCollins, 1993.

Haun, Harry. *The Cinematic Century.* New York: Applause, 2000.

Haynes, John Earl, and Harvey Klehr. *Venona: Decoding Soviet Espionage in America.* New Haven, Conn.: Yale University Press, 1999.

"The Heat's On." *Time* (September 4, 1950): 13.

Hellman, Lillian. *Scoundrel Time.* Boston: Little, Brown, 1976.

Henriksen, Margot A. *Dr. Strangelove's America: Society and Culture in the Atomic Age.* Berkeley: University of California Press, 1997.

Hersey, John. *Aspects of the Presidency.* New Haven, Conn.: Ticknor & Fields, 1980.

———. *Hiroshima.* 1946. Reprint, New York: Vintage Books, 1989.

Hess, Jerry N. "Oral History Interview with Karl L. Bendetsen (November 21, 1972)." Truman Presidential Museum & Library. Available online. URL: http://trumanlibrary.org/oralhist/bendet3.htm. Downloaded August 24, 2001.

Holmes, Clellon. "This Is the Beat Generation." *New York Times Magazine* (November 16, 1952): 10.

Hong Xuezhi. *Kangmei Yuanchao Zhanzheng Huiyi.* Beijing: People's Liberation Army Press, 1990. Woodrow Wilson International Center for Scholars, Cold War International History Project. Available online. URL: http://cwihp.si.edu/cwihplib.nsf/16c6b2fc83775317852564a400054b28/fac3a402f6ca00ea85256928006f80c9?OpenDocument. Downloaded October 25, 2001.

Huston, Luther A. "High Court Hears South Will Defy Quick End to Bias." *New York Times,* April 13, 1955, 1.

Huxley, Aldous. *Brave New World Revisited.* New York: Harper & Brothers, 1958.

Hyde, Douglas. "How Red China Takes Over." *America: National Catholic Weekly Review* (January 21, 1956): 450.

Hyman, William C. *The Cold War.* New York: Random House, 1991.

Jackson, Lesley. *Contemporary: Architecture and Interiors of the 1950s.* London: Phaidon Press, 1994.

"Jackson Pollock: 1912–56." *ARTnews* (September 1956): 44, 57.

Judge, Edward H., and John W. Langdon. *The Cold War: A History through Documents.* Upper Saddle River, N.J.: Prentice Hall, 1999.

———. *A Hard and Bitter Peace: A Global History of the Cold War.* Upper Saddle River, N.J.: Prentice Hall, 1996.

Kaledin, Eugenia. *Mothers and More: American Women in the 1950s.* Boston: Twayne, 1984.

Karnow, Stanley. *Vietnam: A History.* New York: Viking, 1983.

Kasher, Steven. *The Civil Rights Movement: A Photographic History, 1954–68.* New York: Abbeville Press, 1996.

Kazan, Elia. *A Life.* New York: Knopf, 1988.

Kendall, Alan. *The Chronicle of Classical Music.* London: Thames & Hudson, 2000.

Kenedy, Dermod. "Night Shift." *The Dude* (August 1956): 65.

Kennan, George. *Memoirs: 1925–1950.* Boston: Little, Brown, 1967.

Kerman, Joseph. "Roger Sessions." *Hudson Review* (Spring 1951): 126–32.

Kleinberg, Howard. *Miami Beach: A History.* Miami: Centennial, 1994.

Knox, Donald. *The Korean War. Pusan to Chosin, An Oral History.* Orlando, Fla.: Harcourt Brace Jovanovich, 1985.

Laurence, William L. "Salk Polio Vaccine Proves Success." *New York Times,* April 13, 1955, 1.

Lawrence, William E. "Atomic Bombing of Nagasaki Told by Flight Member." *New York Times,* September 9, 1945, 1, 35.

Lederer, William J., and Eugene Burdick. *The Ugly American*. 1958. Reprint, New York: W. W. Norton, 1965.

Lee, Martin A., and Bruce Shlain. *Acid Dreams, the Complete Social History of LSD: The CIA, the Sixties, and Beyond*. New York: Grove Weidenfeld, 1985.

Leviero, Anthony. "Censorship Move Denied by Wilson." *New York Times*, April 13, 1955, 1.

———. "Rogue Nike Missile 'Runs Away,' Explodes in Flight." *New York Times*, April 15, 1955, 1, 11.

Levy, Peter B. *The Civil Rights Movement*. Westport, Conn.: Greenwood Press, 1988.

Lhamon, W. T. *Deliberate Speed: The Origins of a Cultural Style in the American 1950s*. Washington, D.C.: Smithsonian Institution Press, 1990.

Lindey, Christine. *Art in the Cold War: From Vladivostok to Kalamazoo, 1945–1962*. London: Herbert Press, 1990.

Little, Stuart W. *Off-Broadway: The Prophetic Theater*. New York: Coward, McCann & Geoghegan, 1972.

Lucid, Robert F. *Norman Mailer, the Man and His Work*. Boston: Little, Brown, 1971.

McCarthy, John G. "Letter to the Editor." *America: National Catholic Weekly Review* (January 13, 1951): 432.

McCarthy, Mary. *The Groves of Academe*. 1952. Reprint, New York: Harcourt Brace, 1992.

McCullough, David. *Truman*. New York: Simon & Schuster, 1992.

McGilligan, Pat, ed. *Backstory 2: Interviews with Screenwriters of the 1940s and 1950s*. Berkeley: University of California Press, 1991.

McGunagle, Fred. "A Suspect Emerges." Sam Sheppard, Dark Horse Multimedia. Available online: URL: http://va.crimelibrary.com/sheppard/shepsuspect.htm. Downloaded September 1, 2001.

McKeever, Porter. *Adlai Stevenson: His Life and Legacy*. New York: William Morrow, 1989.

McNeil, Alex. *Total Television*. New York: Penguin Books, 1991.

Mailer, Norman. *The Naked and the Dead*. New York: New American Library, 1948.

Mao Zedong. "Mao's Telegrams during the Korean War, October–December 1950." Trans. Li Xiaobing and Glenn Tracy. Woodrow Wilson International Center for Scholars, Cold War International History Project. Available online. URL: http://cwihp.si.edu/cwihplib.nsf/16c6b2fc83775317852564a400054b28/355ddfb8b5441aae85 2569280072b0d4?OpenDocument. Downloaded October 25, 2001.

Marling, Karal Ann. *As Seen on TV: The Visual Culture of Everyday Life in the 1950s.* Cambridge, Mass.: Harvard University Press, 1994.

Martin, Kingsley. "The American Witch-Hunt." *New Statesman and Nation* (July 5, 1952): 5–6.

Mason, Francis, Jr. "Ballet Chronicle." *Hudson Review* (Autumn 1951): 462–66.

Mast, Gerald, and Bruce F. Kawain. *A Short History of the Movies.* 7th ed. Boston: Allyn & Bacon, 2000.

May, Lary, ed. *Recasting America: Culture and Politics in the Age of the Cold War.* Chicago: University of Chicago Press, 1989.

Mencken, H. L. "The Marriage Game." *The Dude* (July 1957): 51, 61.

Merril, Judith. *Shadow on the Hearth.* Garden City, N.Y.: Doubleday, 1950.

Michener, James A. *The Bridge at Andau.* New York: Fawcett Crest, 1957.

———. *The Bridges at Toko-Ri.* New York: Fawcett Crest, 1953.

Mickelson, Sig. *The Decade That Shaped Television News: CBS in the 1950s.* Westport, Conn.: Praeger, 1998.

Miles, Barry. *Ginsberg: A Biography.* New York: Simon & Schuster, 1989.

Miller, Arthur. *Collected Plays.* New York: Viking Press, 1957.

Miller, James E., Jr., ed. *Heritage of American Literature.* Vol. 2, *Civil War to the Present.* New York: Harcourt Brace Jovanovich, 1991.

Miller, Merle. *The Judges and the Judged.* 1952. Reprint, New York: Arno Press, 1971.

———. *Plain Speaking: An Oral Biography of Harry S. Truman.* New York: Berkley, 1974.

Miller, Walter M., Jr. *A Canticle for Leibowitz.* New York: Bantam, 1959.

Millet, Martha, ed. *The Rosenbergs: Poems of the United States.* New York: Sierra Books, 1957.

Millstein, Gilbert. "Books of the Times." *New York Times,* September 5, 1957, 27.

Mingo, Jack, ed. *The Whole Pop Catalogue.* New York: Avon, 1991.

Mississippi Writers Page. "William Faulkner." Available online. URL: http://www.olemiss.edu/depts/english/ms-writers/dir/faulkner. Downloaded August 24, 2001.

Moffi, Larry. *This Side of Cooperstown: An Oral History of Major League Baseball in the 1950s.* Iowa City: University of Iowa Press, 1996.

Moran, Edward. *America in the 1950s.* New Rochelle, N.Y.: GAA, 1999. Audio-cassettes.

Mordden, Ethan, *Coming Up Roses: The Broadway Musical in the 1950s.* New York: Oxford University Press, 1998.

Morrison, Craig. *Go Cat Go!: Rockabilly Music and Its Makers.* Urbana: University of Illinois Press, 1996.

Morton, James. "I Was King of the Thieves." *Saturday Evening Post* (August 19, 1950): 30–33.

Mosley, Leonard. *Dulles: A Biography of Eleanor, Allen, and John Foster Dulles and Their Family Network.* New York: Dial Press, 1978.

The Movie Guide. Eds. CineBooks. New York: Perigee Books, 1998.

Murrow, Edward R. *In Search of Light: The Broadcasts of Edward R. Murrow.* New York: Knopf, 1967. Videocassettes.

Nadel, Alan. *Containment Culture: American Narratives, Postmodernism, and the Atomic Age.* Durham, N.C.: Duke University Press, 1995.

Navasky, Victor S. *Naming Names.* New York: Viking, 1980.

"Negotiate on What?" *Nation* (January 4, 1958): 1.

"9 Pacifists Seized in Defying Alert." *New York Times,* May 7, 1958, 30.

Nixon, Richard M. "'The Fund Crisis' Speech." Richard Nixon Library & Birthplace, Selected Speeches and Quotes. Available online. URL: http://www.nixonlibrary.org/Research_Center/Nixons/Speeches_and_Quotes.shtml. Downloaded November 9, 2001.

Oates, Guy. *The Imaginary War: Civil Defense and American Cold War Culture.* New York: Oxford University Press, 1994.

O'Connell, Robert J. "Modern Art Isn't All Crazy." *America: National Catholic Weekly Review* (March 24, 1956): 693.

O'Connor, Flannery. "The Church and the Fiction Writer." *America: National Catholic Weekly Review* (March 30, 1957): 733–35.

———. *Mystery and Manners.* Eds. Sally Fitzgerald and Robert Fitzgerald. New York: Farrar, Straus & Giroux, 1969.

"Of What Is Past, Passing, and to Come." *The Dude* (August 1957): 37.

Okun, Rob A. *The Rosenbergs: Collected Visions of Artists and Writers.* New York: Universe Books, 1988.

Olsen, Tillie. *Tell Me a Riddle.* 1961. Reprint, New York: Dell, 1976.

Olson, James S. *Historical Dictionary of the 1950s.* Westport, Conn.: Greenwood Press, 2000.

O'Reilly, Kenneth. *Black Americans: The FBI Files.* New York: Carroll & Graf, 1994.

Orwell, George. *Nineteen Eighty-Four.* 1949. Reprint, New York: Plume, 1983.

Owens, Thomas. *Bebop: The Music and Its Players.* New York: Oxford University Press, 1995.

Parks, John G., ed. *American Short Stories since 1945.* New York: Oxford University Press, 2002.

Parks, Rosa, with Jim Haskins. *Rosa Parks: My Story.* New York: Dial Books, 1992.

Peacock, John. *The 1950s.* London: Thames & Hudson, 1997.

Pells, Richard H. *The Liberal Mind in a Conservative Age: American Intellectuals in the 1940s and 1950s.* New York: Harper & Row, 1985.

Perkins, George, and Barbara Perkins. *Contemporary American Literature.* New York: Random House, 1988.

Perkins, George, et al., eds. *The American Tradition in Literature.* Vol. 2, 6th ed. New York: Random House, 1985.

Perret, Geoffrey. *Eisenhower.* New York: Random House, 1999.

Plath, Sylvia. *The Bell Jar.* New York: Harper & Row, 1971.

Popkin, Henry. "Theatre Letter." *Kenyon Review* (Summer 1952): 493.

Porter, Katherine Anne. *Letters of Katherine Anne Porter.* Ed. Isabel Bayley. New York: Atlantic Monthly Press, 1990.

Prados, John. *Presidents' Secret Wars: CIA and Pentagon Covert Operations from World War II through the Persian Gulf.* Chicago: Ivan R. Dee, 1996.

"Profit Sharers in Los Angeles." *America: National Catholic Weekly Review* (December 3, 1952): 262.

Pynchon, Thomas. *Slow Learner: Early Stories.* Boston: Little, Brown, 1984.

Pyron, Darden Asbury. *Liberace: An American Boy.* Chicago: University of Chicago Press, 2000.

Quain, Kevin, ed. *The Elvis Reader: Texts and Sources of the King of Rock 'n' Roll.* New York: St. Martin's Press, 1992.

Rawnsley, Gary D., ed. *Cold-War Propaganda in the 1950s.* New York: St. Martin's Press, 1999.

Reisner, Robert George. *Bird: The Legend of Charlie Parker.* New York: Da Capo Press, 1975.

"Reuther's Proposal for Profit-Sharing." *New Republic* (February 17, 1958): 6–7.

Rieff, Philip. "George Orwell and the Post-Liberal Imagination." *Kenyon Review* (Winter 1954): 49.

Riesman, David, with Nathan Glazer and Reuel Denney. *The Lonely Crowd.* New Haven, Conn.: Yale University Press, 1950.

Rosset, Barney, ed. *Evergreen Review Reader: 1957–1961.* New York: Grove Press, 1979.

Rosteck, Thomas. *"See It Now" Confronts McCarthyism: Television Documentary and the Politics of Representation.* Tuscaloosa: University of Alabama Press, 1994.

"Russia Fires Rocket to Circle Moon, Earth; Data on Device Is Meager." *Wall Street Journal,* October 5, 1959, 1.

Sahl, Mort. *The Next President.* New York: Verve Records, 1960. Record album.

Salinger, J. D. *The Catcher in the Rye.* 1951. Reprint, New York: Bantam, 1964.

Sandeen, Eric J. *Picturing an Exhibition: The Family of Man and 1950s America.* Albuquerque: University of New Mexico Press, 1995.

Satin, Joseph Henry, ed. *The 1950s: America's Placid Decade.* Boston: Houghton Mifflin, 1960.

Saunders, Frances Stonor. *The Cultural Cold War: The CIA and the World of Arts and Letters.* New York: New Press, 2000.

Savage, William J., and Daniel Simon, eds. *The Man with the Golden Arm / Nelson Algren: 50th Anniversary Critical Edition.* New York: Seven Stories Press, 1999.

Sayre, Nora. *Previous Convictions: A Journey through the 1950s.* New Brunswick, N.J.: Rutgers University Press, 1995.

———. *Running Time: Films of the Cold War.* New York: Dial Press, 1982.

Schaub, Thomas Hill. *American Fiction in the Cold War.* Madison: University of Wisconsin Press, 1991.

Schulberg, Budd. *The Disenchanted.* New York: Random House, 1950.

———. *Waterfront.* New York: Donald I. Fine, 1955.

Schwartz, Richard A. "The Best Minds of My Generation." *Journal of Evolutionary Psychology* 18, nos. 3, 4 (August 1997): 177–83.

———. *Cold War Culture.* New York: Facts On File, 1998.

——— *The Cold War Reference Guide.* Jefferson, N.C.: McFarland, 1997.

———. "Dr. Einstein and the War Department." *Isis* 80, no. 302 (June 1989): 281–84.

———. "The F.B.I. and Dr. Einstein." *Nation* 237, no. 6 (September 3–10, 1983): 168–73.

———. "How the Film and Television Blacklists Worked." *Film & History Annual 1999.* Film & History, 1999. CD-Rom.

Senzel, Howard. *Baseball and the Cold War.* New York: Harcourt Brace Jovanovich, 1977.

Shute, Nevil. *On the Beach.* 1957. Reprint. New York: Ballantine Books, 1974.

Sikov, Ed. *Laughing Hysterically: American Screen Comedy of the 1950s.* New York: Columbia University Press, 1994.

Simon, Rita James, ed. *A Look Backward and Forward at American Professional Women and Their Families.* Lanham, Md.: University Press of America, 2000.

"Specialists in Jazz Team for Concert." *New York Times,* November 15, 1952, 14.

Spigel, Lynn. *Make Room for TV.* Chicago: University of Chicago Press, 1992.

Stark, Bonnie. *McCarthyism in Florida: Charley Johns and the Florida Legislative Investigation Committee July 1956 to July 1965.* 1985. Florida Heritage Collection. Available online. URL: http://susdl.fcla.edu/fh/. Downloaded August 24, 2001.

Steele, Valerie. *Fifty Years of Fashion: New Look to Now.* New Haven, Conn.: Yale University Press, 1997.

Stern, Jane, and Michael Stern. *Encyclopedia of Pop Culture.* New York: Harper-Perennial, 1992.

Stevenson, Adlai E. *Major Campaign Speeches of Adlai E. Stevenson, 1952.* New York: Random House, 1953.

Stone, I. F. *The Truman Era.* New York: Vintage Books, 1953.

Stone, Joseph, and Tim Yohn. *Prime Time and Misdemeanors: Investigating the 1950s TV Quiz Scandal, a D.A.'s Account.* New Brunswick, N.J.: Rutgers University Press, 1992.

Szatmary, David P. *Rockin' in Time: A Social History of Rock and Roll.* Englewood Cliffs, N.J.: Prentice Hall, 1987.

Tate, Allen. "To Whom Is the Poet Responsible?" *Hudson Review* (Autumn 1951): 326–34.

Theoharis, Anthony, ed. *From the Secret Files of J. Edgar Hoover.* Chicago: Ivan R. Dee, 1993.

This Fabulous Century. Vol. 6, *1950–1960.* Eds. Time-Life Books. New York: Time-Life Books, 1970.

Thompson, Dorothy. "Race Suicide of the Intelligent," *Ladies Home Journal* (May 1949): 11.

Thurber, James. *The Seal in the Bedroom & Other Predicaments.* New York: Harper & Brothers, 1950.

————. *Selected Letters of James Thurber.* Eds. Helen Thurber and Edward Weeks. Boston: Little, Brown, 1981.

Tillich, Paul. *Dynamics of Faith.* New York: Harper & Row, 1957.

Torricelli, Senator Robert, and Andrew Carroll, eds. *In Our Own Words: Extraordinary Speeches of the American Century.* New York: Washington Square Press, 1999.

"Truman Statement on Atom." *New York Times,* September 24, 1949, 1.

Trussell, C. P. "Witness Describes Shooting, Capture." *New York Times,* March 2, 1954, 1, 16.

Tyler, Parker. "Movie Note: The 3-D's." *Kenyon Review* (Summer 1954): 468–72.

Van Minnen, Cornelis A., Jaap van der Bent, and Mel van Elteren, eds. *Beat Culture: The 1950s and Beyond.* Amsterdam: VU University Press, 1999.

Vatter, Harold G. *The U.S. Economy in the 1950s: An Economic History.* New York: W. W. Norton, 1963.

Vaughn, Robert. *Only Victims.* New York: G. P. Putnam's Sons, 1972.

"Visitors from Venus." *Time* (January 9, 1950): 49.

Von Hallberg, Robert. *American Poetry and Culture, 1945–1980.* Cambridge, Mass.: Harvard University Press, 1985.

Wagner, C. Ronald. "The Moral Perspective of Humanism." *Hudson Review* (Spring 1958): 140–41.

Wakefield, Dan. *New York in the Fifties.* New York: Houghton Mifflin, 1992.

Walker, Martin. *The Cold War: A History.* New York: Henry Holt, 1993.

Ward, Ed, Geoffrey Stokes, and Ken Tucker. *Rock of Ages: The* Rolling Stone *History of Rock & Roll.* New York: Rolling Stone Press, 1986.

Warren, Earl. "Opinion of the Supreme Court of the United States." *Brown v. Board of Education* National Historic Site. Available online. URL: http://www.nps.gov.brvb/pages/decision54.htm. Dowloaded October 4, 2001.

Watson, James D. *The Double Helix.* New York: Atheneum, 1968.

Weathersby, Kathryn. "New Findings on the Korean War: Translation and Commentary." Woodrow Wilson International Center for Scholars, Cold War International History Project. Available online. URL: http://cwihp.si.edu/cwihplib.nsf/16c6b2fc83775317852564a400054b28/beafeba11560992c85 2564bf00669691?OpenDocument. Dowloaded October 25, 2001.

Weiler, A. H. "It Came from Outer Space." *New York Times,* June 18, 1953, 38.

———. "Richard Wright Plays Hero in Movie Adaptation of His Novel, 'Native Son.'" *New York Times,* June 18, 1951, 19.

Weinstein, Allen. *Perjury: The Hiss-Chambers Case.* New York: Random House, 1978.

Wexler, Sanford. *An Eyewitness History of the Civil Rights Movement.* New York: Checkmark Books, 1999.

Whitfield, Stephen J. *The Culture of the Cold War.* 2d ed. Baltimore, Md.: Johns Hopkins University Press, 1996.

Whyte, William H., Jr. *The Organization Man.* New York: Simon & Schuster, 1956.

Wilson, Earl. *Sinatra: An Unauthorized Biography.* New York: Macmillan 1976.

Wilson, Sloan. *The Man in the Gray Flannel Suit.* New York: Arbor House, 1955.

Winn, Janet. "A Star Is Borne." *New Republic* (December 24, 1956): 22.

Woods, Randall Bennett, and Howard Jones. *Dawning of the Cold War: The United States' Quest for Order.* Athens: University of Georgia Press, 1991.

Wylie, Philip. *Tomorrow!* 1954. Reprint, New York: Popular Library, 1956.

Yang Dezhi. *Yang Dezhi Huiyliu.* Beijing: People's Liberation Army Press, 1993. Woodrow Wilson International Center for Scholars, Cold War International History Project. Available online. URL: http://cwihp.si.edu/cwihplib.nsf/16c6b2fc83775317852564a400054b28/fac3a402f6ca00ea85256928006f80c9?OpenDocument. Downloaded October 25, 2001.

Yoder, Edwin. *Joe Alsop's Cold War: A Study of Journalistic Influence and Intrigue.* Chapel Hill: University of North Carolina Press, 1995.

Zamora, Lois P. *The Apocalyptic Vision in America.* Bowling Green, Ohio: Bowling Green University Popular Press, 1982.

Zubok, Vladislav. "Working Paper #6: Krushchev and the Berlin Crisis (1958–62)." Wilson International Center for Scholars, Cold War International History Project. Available online. URL: http://cwihp.si.edu/cwihplib.nsf. Downloaded October 22, 2001.

INDEX

Page locators in **boldface** indicate main entries.
Page locators in *italic* indicate illustrations. Page locators followed by an *m* indicate maps.